Mastering ESL/ EFL Methods

Differentiated Instruction for Culturally and Linguistically Diverse (CLD) Students

Third Edition

Socorro G. Herrera
Kansas State University

Kevin G. Murry
Kansas State University

PEARSON

Boston ▪ Columbus ▪ Hoboken ▪ Indianapolis ▪ New York ▪ San Francisco ▪
Amsterdam ▪ Cape Town ▪ Dubai ▪ London ▪ Madrid ▪ Milan ▪ Munich ▪
Paris ▪ Montreal ▪ Toronto ▪ Delhi ▪ Mexico City ▪ São Paulo ▪
Sydney ▪ Hong Kong ▪ Seoul ▪ Singapore ▪ Taipei ▪ Tokyo

VP and Editorial Director:
Jeffery W. Johnston
Senior Acquisitions Editor: Julie Peters
Program Manager: Megan Moffo
Editorial Assistant: Andrea Hall
Executive Product Marketing Manager:
Christopher Barry
Executive Field Marketing Manager:
Krista Clark
Team Lead Project Management:
JoEllen Gohr
Team Lead Program Management:
Laura Weaver

Project Manager: Janet Portisch
Procurement Specialist: Deidra Skahill
Art Director: Diane Lorenzo
Art Director Cover: Diane Ernsberger
Cover Design: Cenveo® Publisher Services
Cover Art: Jennifer Brunenn
Media Producer: Allison Longley
Editorial Production and Composition
Service: Cenveo® Publishing Services
Printer/Binder: RR Donnelley/Crawfordsville
Cover Printer: Phoenix Color/Hagerstown
Text Font: Sabon

Credits and acknowledgments borrowed from other sources and reproduced, with permission, in this textbook appear on the appropriate page within text.

Many of the designations by manufacturers and sellers to distinguish their products are claimed as trademarks. Where those designations appear in this book, and the publisher was aware of a trademark claim, the designations have been printed in initial caps or all caps.

Library of Congress Cataloging-in-Publication Data

Herrera, Socorro Guadalupe, author.
  [Mastering ESL and bilingual methods]
  Mastering ESL/EFL methods : differentiated instruction for culturally and linguistically diverse (CLD) students / Socorro G. Herrera, Kansas State University ; Kevin G. Murry, Kansas State University. -- Third Edition.
      p. cm
  Includes bibliographical references and index.
  ISBN 978-0-13-359497-3
  ISBN 0-13-359497-1
  1. English language—Study and teaching—Foreign speakers. 2. English language—Study and teaching—United States. 3. Multicultural education—United States.
4. Language and culture— United States. I. Murry, Kevin G., editor. II. Title.
  PE1128.A2H4675 2014
  428.0071—dc23
                                                                              2014034510

10 9 8 7 6 5 4 3 2 1

ISBN-10: 0-13-359497-1
ISBN-13: 978-0-13-359497-3

*Este libro está dedicado a la memoria de nuestras madres,
cuyos sacrificios y dedicación han abierto tantas puertas
que sin ellas se hubieran quedado cerradas,
sueños que hubieran sido sólo posibilidades.*

*To the memory of our mothers, Esther Jaquez de Herrera
and Sammie Arline Ellis Murry, without whose sacrifice
and perseverance so many doors might have remained closed,
so many dreams remained just possibilities.*

Dr. Socorro Herrera is a professor in the Department of Curriculum and Instruction in the College of Education at Kansas State University and directs the Center for Intercultural and Multilingual Advocacy (CIMA). Her K–12 teaching experience includes an emphasis on literacy development, and her research focuses on literacy opportunities with culturally and linguistically diverse (CLD) students, reading strategies, and teacher preparation for diversity in the classroom. Dr. Herrera has authored six textbooks and numerous articles for publication in journals such as the *Bilingual Research Journal, Journal of Hispanic Higher Education, Journal of Research in Education, Journal of Curriculum and Instruction,* and *Journal of Latinos and Education.* In addition to her writing, Dr. Herrera conducts multistate and international professional development on issues related to teacher preparation for preservice teachers, biography-driven instruction, and classroom accommodations for CLD students.

Dr. Kevin Murry is an associate professor in the Department of Curriculum and Instruction in the College of Education at Kansas State University and Director of Research and Development for the Center for Intercultural and Multilingual Advocacy (CIMA). His scholarship has emphasized the professional development of general education teachers for the assets/needs of culturally and linguistically diverse (CLD) students. Dr. Murry's recent research and publications have emphasized teacher readiness for best practice with CLD students, culturally responsive teaching, and the cross-cultural dynamics of critically reflective teaching. In addition to his textbook and chapter publications, he has contributed articles to journals such as *Cultural Studies in Science Education, Journal of Curriculum and Instruction,* and *Journal of Teaching and Learning.*

■ contents

■ **c h a p t e r 3**

Linguistic Dimension of Methods for Culturally and Linguistically Diverse Students   61

■ **p a r t t w o**

Accommodation Readiness   101

■ **c h a p t e r 4**

Changing Perspectives in Platform Development for Instructional Methods   102

chapter 5

A Framework of Accommodation Readiness   **131**

■ part three

Professionalism in Practice   179

■ chapter 6

Planning and Grounding Instructional Methodology   180

■ chapter 7

The Integrated Content-Based Method of Instruction   219

chapter 8

The Sheltered Method of Instruction   260

chapter 9

The CALLA Method of Instruction   314

chapter 10

Achieving Standards-Driven Professional Practice   352

When David Livingstone's work in Africa became known, a missionary society wrote to him and asked, "Have you found a good road where you are?" If he had, the letter indicated that the society was prepared to send some men to help with his work. Livingstone's answer was clear and to the point: "If you have men who will come only over a good road, I don't need your help. I want men who will come if there is no road." Increasing cultural and linguistic diversity in the grade-level classroom is, for many educators, as unfamiliar and intimidating as the wilds of Africa were to Livingstone's contemporaries over 150 years ago. As a consequence of this trepidation, many educators are searching for the *good road*, the recipe, for successful teaching amid diversity. As Livingstone understood, however, changing times and a changing world demand a different sort of pioneer, a new brand of vigilance and empathy, a willingness among those who seek to educate to pursue the road less traveled.

∎ New to This Edition

- *Illustrated Concepts* for each chapter provide educators examples of practical ways to implement the theoretical concepts found in the book.
- *Global Connections* feature English language teaching from a global perspective by connecting what is learned to EFL settings.
- *Tips for Practice* for EFL classrooms include advice for teachers to implement strategies and techniques for EFL/global settings.
- *Video Links* offer teachers a multimedia approach to see our theoretical concepts in actions via short video clips, available only through the Pearson eText (other eText formats do not support video).
- A revised framework for conceptual definitions of approach, method, strategy, and technique in Chapter 6 allows educators to be able to articulate how their instruction is grounded in current theory and research.
- An expanded glossary includes accessible definitions of key terms to support readers' understanding of context.
- New and updated figures and tables assist teachers to visualize the theories and scholarship discussed within each chapter.
- New and updated sources and resources and an updated reference list familiarize readers with the latest being written and talked about in the education of CLD students.

∎ Purpose

This text offers in-service teachers, district or building administrators, school specialists, preservice teachers, and paraprofessionals the opportunity to rediscover the value, potential, richness, and adventure of diversity as they develop the capacity to professionally address the differential learning and transition needs of culturally and linguistically diverse learners. Although we recognize each student as a unique individual, throughout this text we use the term *culturally and linguistically diverse (CLD)* to refer to those learners whose cultures or languages are different from that of a dominant culture or language. Our journey pursues the road less traveled, and along the way we gain new insights into and reflective perspectives on ourselves and the rich cultural and linguistic assets CLD learners bring to the classroom. Among the highlights of the adventure are innovative approaches, the latest tools, contemporary procedures, exceptional strategies, and new ways of knowing, all of which enhance our effectiveness with English learners. By taking a few turns that others may have missed, our route explores novel ways to reach and maximize relationships with the parents, caregivers, and extended family members of these students, as partners in appropriate pedagogical practices. By traveling the extra mile to achieve effectiveness amid diversity, we stretch ourselves to develop new capacities for cross-cultural sensitivity, critical thinking, reflective student accommodation, and best practice with CLD students in both domestic and international settings. Ultimately, we each reach our destination, our goal, having rediscovered our own abilities, our own sensitivities, and our own professionalism, as well as having discovered our own potential, which we have perhaps never explored.

As the title implies, this text is about methods. Yet it is also about differentiating instruction and professional practice to accommodate the distinct learning and transition needs of CLD students in both English as a second language and English as a foreign language settings. Yes, the world of the classroom is changing. Nevertheless, each of us is capable of effecting the changes necessary to accommodate that shift and demonstrate our effectiveness amid diversity. We begin our journey by discussing the changes occurring in the classroom and by developing a better understanding of English learners. Other facets of our expedition examine the work of practitioners and researchers and the contributions they offer us in differentiating our own practices for cultural and, especially, linguistic diversity. At about the midpoint of our journey, we begin to investigate our readiness for the destination. That is, we assess our emergent capacities to provide appropriate classroom accommodations for the CLD student.

During the last leg of our quest for effectiveness amid diversity, we acquire the tools for success, understand their historical foundations, practice their use, listen to the voices of other teachers who have used them successfully, and apply them to various dilemmas of practice. Benchmarks along the way designate where and when various tools are appropriate and when they are not. Other hallmarks of the adventure distinguish between tools and perspectives and critically assess their utility in particular situations by examining differences among an *approach,* a *method,* a *strategy,* and a *technique.* This is first accomplished by revisiting the nature, history, and applications of three major approaches to instruction for CLD students: the grammatical, the communicative, and the cognitive. Subsequently, we consider which instructional methods are products of each approach and which offer the best history of success with these students. Later, our discussions detail the contemporary and effective methods of instruction for English learners, including the integrated content-based method, the sheltered instruction method, and the cognitive academic language learning approach (CALLA) method. Among the details considered in these discussions are the components, sequences, strategies, and techniques associated with each method and their applications in professional practice.

Ultimately, we arrive at our destination having reached the goal of *instructional preparedness for cultural and linguistic diversity in the classroom.* Our adventure closes with key facets of a platform for best practice with CLD students. With these key facets, we can self-assess our ongoing effectiveness with English learners and refine our capacities and skills so that we are increasingly successful in our professional and reflective practice amid diversity.

■ Content Coverage

This third edition of *Mastering ESL/EFL Methods: Differentiated Instruction for Culturally and Linguistically Diverse (CLD) Students* is contemporary, comprehensive, theory and research based, and aligned with the Teachers of English to Speakers of Other Languages (TESOL)/National Council for the Accreditation of Teacher Education (NCATE) standards (TESOL, 2010). Each chapter in this text represents a concerted effort to enhance the professional development and preparation that educators need for today's diverse and changing classrooms.

■ Organization

Part One of this text, "Hallmarks of Accommodative Instruction," examines the hallmarks of mutually accommodative instructional methods for CLD students. This mindful instruction intentionally accounts for and incorporates findings from the sociocultural, cognitive, academic, and linguistic dimensions of the CLD student biography and schooling experience. Chapters 1 through 3 specify and discuss the sociocultural realities, cognitive growth potentials, academic challenges and processes, and linguistic development of English learners.

Part Two, "Accommodation Readiness," encourages school educators, based on their understanding of the four dimensions of the CLD student biography, to preassess their readiness for the accommodative instruction of the CLD student. Chapter 4 first describes the ways in which programming decisions (at the district or school level) can frame or restrict a teacher's instructional options for accommodation. On the other hand, in those districts and schools where language programming is not already prescribed, programming decisions provide new opportunities for the appropriate instructional accommodation of English language learners. In either case, research on program models is summarized as a basis for teacher advocacy. Chapter 5 introduces the accommodation readiness spiral as a framework for teachers' preassessments of their readiness to deliver mutually accommodative instruction given a specified programming decision. The spiral serves as a preassessment tool for readiness in the following areas: critical reflection, CLD students and families, environment, curriculum, programming, instruction, application, and advocacy.

Part Three, "Professionalism in Practice," recommends a professional approach to the instructional accommodation of the CLD student. This professionalism is conceptualized as involving three sequential components: planning, implementation, and evaluation. Chapter 6 provides and rationalizes recommendations for planning appropriate practices for CLD students. Chapters 7 through 9 discuss and detail three contemporary and robust methods of effective implementation. Finally, Chapter 10 discusses ways to appropriately engage in the evaluation of prior instructional planning and implementation. These processes of evaluation use nationally and internationally recognized standards of best practice with English learners as touchstones of comparison.

More specifically, the text is divided into ten chapters. Chapters 1 through 3 detail not only the assets that CLD students bring to the school but also the singular sociocultural, cognitive, academic, and linguistic challenges they face as well as the processes they must accomplish in the classroom. Chapter 1 is particularly concerned with those sociocultural factors that may influence the academic and transitional success of English learners, including impacts on the affective filter, the influences exerted by the culture of the school, and the dynamics of the acculturation process. Chapter 2 explores both the cognitive and academic dimensions of the CLD student biography and details factors in each dimension that may prove especially challenging for these students. Also described are the characteristics of instruction designed to promote cognitive development and academic success, especially classroom practice that is contextualized, relevant, cognitively demanding, elaborative, differentiated for multiple learning styles and strategies, constructivist, and metacognitive. Chapter 3 examines the challenges and processes of the linguistic dimension of learning for CLD students. Of particular interest to teachers and other educators are the processes of first and second language acquisition, each of which is detailed, compared, contrasted, and discussed. Also described are the characteristics that English learners tend to exhibit at each of the various stages of second language acquisition—from the silent period (preproduction stage) to the stage of advanced fluency.

Chapter 4 offers guidance regarding the range of programming models available for CLD students. Included is a discussion of the foundations, characteristics, and concerns associated with each program model. Research on the effectiveness of dominant models with varying populations of English learners is highlighted. The chapter closes with a brief overview of judicial and legislative foundations of programming, including the results of groundbreaking court precedents that have influenced programming and decision making in schools.

Chapter 5 encourages the reader to self-assess both understanding of the foundations offered in Chapters 1 through 4 and his or her readiness for the appropriate accommodation of CLD students. This accommodation readiness spiral offers a rubric for self-assessment in the following progressive domains of readiness:

critical reflection on practice, students and families, internal and external environment, curriculum, programming, instruction, application, and advocacy.

Chapters 6 through 9 detail appropriate instructional practices for English learners, with particular emphases on contemporary, theory and research-driven, culturally sensitive, developmentally appropriate, and content-based instructional methods. Chapter 6 first differentiates among approach, method, strategy, and technique as a basis for communication, collaboration, and effectiveness. Subsequently, one historical (the grammatical) and two contemporary (the communicative and the cognitive) approaches to instruction for CLD students are described, explained, and discussed. Each chapter that follows is devoted to contemporary and effective methods of instruction for English learners. Chapter 7 focuses on the integrated content-based method, Chapter 8 explores the sheltered instruction method, and Chapter 9 discusses the CALLA method and introduces briefly biography-driven instruction, an emerging method in the field. Each of these chapters also illustrates the implementation of these methods in classroom practice.

Chapter 10 brings closure by highlighting recent efforts in the development of standards of best practice for the instruction of English learners. Following an exploration of the key facets of a platform for best practice with CLD students, self-assessment rubrics are provided to facilitate (1) self-assessment comparisons of practice with national standards and benchmarks, (2) critical reflection on practice, and (3) suggestions for the refinement of professional practice with CLD students.

■ Special Features

To motivate reader interest, accommodate different learning styles, and offer additional insights on topics covered, this text offers the following special features:

Chapter Outline: Each chapter begins with a chapter outline, which provides readers with both an advance organizer and a fundamental understanding of the content of each chapter.

Learning Outcomes: Every educator should have access to the purpose and the ideas behind a particular lesson or chapter. Therefore, each chapter briefly specifies the learning outcomes that guided the development of content associated with that chapter.

Key Theories and Concepts: In each chapter, a list of key theories and concepts is provided to remind the reader of the critical content discussed in that particular chapter.

Figures, Tables, and Photographs: Each chapter of the text offers explanatory or illustrative figures, tables, and/or photographs that have been specifically designed to enhance or bolster the content of the chapter. Educators can capitalize on these features to understand the scope and breadth of various research-based practices identified in this text.

Text Boxes: Content enhancements in the form of text boxes are included in each chapter. Some of these features provide explanatory or illustrative information on topics covered in that chapter. Others introduce new but related information. Three types of text boxes are used throughout the text to illustrate (*Illustrated Concepts*), offer additional perspectives (*Voices from the Field*), and adapt for EFL classrooms (*Global Connections*). Three additional types of text boxes recur in all chapters:

- *Theory into Practice:* These text boxes briefly summarize a theory or theoretical concept before encouraging the reader to consider the implications of the theory or applications of it in professional practice with CLD students. Some also prompt thought and reflection on the content of the text box through guiding questions.
- *Dilemmas of Practice:* These content enrichments (some of which are framed in the form of a critical incident) first pose a dilemma of practice with English learners. Each then offers information and suggestions regarding an appropriate resolution of such a dilemma in practice. The resolutions typically use theories, methods, strategies, and information discussed in the various chapters.
- *Snapshots of Classroom Practice:* These teaching and learning enhancements provide a greater level of detail surrounding theory-into-practice applications of key theories or concepts discussed.

Connect, Engage, and Challenge Activities: The purpose of these end-of-chapter exercises is to offer teachers a structure for their theory-into-practice applications of chapter content. These three-part activities encourage teachers to: (1) connect with the material discussed in the chapter, (2) engage in dialogue with peers about content and learning, and (3) challenge themselves to apply what they have learned to differentiated practices for CLD students and families.

Tips for Practice: This is a differentiating feature that provides elementary, secondary, and EFL educators with highly specific extensions of chapter content. Chapters 1 through 7 offer elementary tips, secondary tips, and EFL tips for educators. The "Tips for Practice" section of Chapter 8 is organized according to the eight components of the sheltered instruction observation protocol, the primary subject of that chapter. The tips included for Chapter 9 have been structured according to three main categories of learning strategies emphasized in the CALLA instructional sequence, which is detailed in that chapter. Finally, the tips for Chapter 10 have been organized according to the four key facets of a platform for best practice with CLD students, which provide an organizational framework for that chapter.

Assessment Tips and Strategies: This feature appears at the end of Chapter 3 and summarizes the preassessment issues addressed in Chapters 1 through 3. It also appears at the end of Chapter 6 to summarize the assessment issues discussed in Chapters 4 through 6. Because Chapters 7, 8, and 9 address specific instructional methods, this feature also appears at the end of each of these chapters.

Glossary: This feature is an auxiliary resource for current readers and for future applications of content in practice. Attention has been given to those terms that are likely to be unfamiliar to practicing educators and future educators who have had limited professional experiences with CLD learners.

Appendix A: Critical Standards Guiding Chapter Content: As a model for professionalism in practice with diversity, this special addition aligns the content of all chapters of the text with the nationally recognized TESOL/NCATE Standards (2010). The TESOL/NCATE teacher standards reflect professional consensus on standards for the quality teaching of P–12 CLD students. (For a more in-depth rationale of our decision to use these particular sets of standards, see Chapter 10.)

Appendix B: Examples of Activities Specific to Mexican American Students: Because the overwhelming majority of English learners in the United States are Spanish-language-dominant and because many of these students are Mexican American, this distinctive section provides examples of classroom activities specific to the background experiences and growth needs of these students. These activities are organized according to those applicable to elementary, middle, and high school. Within each of these categories, the activities are further subdivided according to those that apply to mathematics, language arts, and social studies.

References: Assembled in American Psychological Association (APA) style, this feature documents the theory, research, and analyses that support our discussions, content, conclusions, recommendations, and advocacy. The list is a resource for preservice and in-service educators of English learners.

◾acknowledgments

Many classroom teachers, teaching faculty members, and other colleagues have contributed to the preparation of this text. We especially wish to recognize Melissa Holmes and Shabina Kavimandan for their insightfulness, conscientiousness, and persistence. Melissa brought many valuable qualities to the development of this third edition. Special thanks are also in order to Cristina Fanning, Miki Loschky, and Melissa Prescott, teacher-educators who, despite many other pressing obligations, took time to provide insightful perspectives, thoughtful contributions, pragmatic refinements, and critical reviews. Their willingness to brainstorm, discuss, and deliberate issues and concepts was extremely valuable. We would also like to thank the reviewers of this third edition: Nancy Mae Antrim, Sul Ross State University; Nancy L. Hadaway, University of Texas at Arlington; and Maria Simeonova, University of Cincinnati.

At the same time, we fully recognize that this text would not have been possible without the tactical and technical expertise of others, especially Sheri Meredith, Jennifer Brunenn, and Gisela Nash. Sheri's contributions as master organizer were inestimable. Among these have been file management, text formatting, graphical refinement, syntax reviews, archive management, motivation, and encouragement. Her collaboration and agenda setting were both greatly appreciated. Jennifer, who offered her technological expertise to our project, contributed valuable knowledge, skill, and insights to the product of all our efforts. Gisela, who cheerfully motivated and inspired us, was instrumental in reminding us daily of our deadlines.

Finally, we thank the classroom teachers who serve the differential learning and transition needs of CLD students and who have provided insights from their professional practice. Their input is much appreciated and has been included primarily in the *Voices from the Field* and the *Snapshots of Classroom Practice* features of the text. Their experiences and adaptations illustrate the ways in which instructional methods and other aspects of professional practice can effectively and mutually accommodate the needs and assets of CLD students.

Socorro Herrera

PART one

Hallmarks of Accommodative Instruction

In Part One of this text, we examine the hallmarks of mutually accommodative instructional methods for culturally and linguistically diverse (CLD) students. This accommodative instruction accounts for, and incorporates findings from, the sociocultural, cognitive, academic, and linguistic dimensions of the CLD student biography and schooling experience. In Chapters 1 through 3, we specify and discuss the sociocultural realities, cognitive growth potentials, academic challenges and processes, and linguistic development of CLD students.

Multidimensional Foundations of Methods for Culturally and Linguistically Diverse Students

our mission

Our mission for this chapter will be to:

· Explore social and cultural aspects of what CLD students bring to the classroom.

We will accomplish this mission by helping you to meet the following learning outcomes:

· Explain how preparation for cultural and linguistic diversity in the classroom benefits those in the teaching field.

· Describe what teachers need to know about cultural and linguistic diversity in the classroom and how to differentiate between an asset perspective and deficit perspective of CLD students.

· Analyze the sociocultural dimension of the CLD student biography and ways in which it influences the realities of teaching in diverse classrooms.

Socorro Herrera

key theories and concepts

acculturation

affective filter hypothesis

asset perspective

culture of the school

deficit perspective

enculturation

equity vs. equality

input hypothesis

prism model

psychosocial processes

sociocultural dimension

sociocultural processes

U-curve hypothesis

Rapidly Changing Demographic Patterns and Student Diversity

Across the United States, student populations and the rise of new education standards continue to rapidly and radically change the dynamics of education. No less changed is the increasingly global workplace for which students, especially high school graduates, must be prepared. Fundamentally, today's educators teach in a transnationally competitive age in which communication, technology, research, and human potential make incredible advances in every field possible—on a daily basis! We call attention to the complexity that teachers may expect in the classrooms of today and tomorrow. As we walk through the doors of today's classrooms, we notice that learning is no less important to success than it has been in the past. However, we are more likely to observe that the nature of expected learning has changed.

    In this new era, information is pervasive, connections to it abound, and the speed at which each connection is shared grows exponentially. Not surprisingly, learning in this age focuses less on content knowledge than artfully developing and refining processes and perspectives that maximize data, information, connections, and collaborations. The capacity for such learning will prove essential to the success of individuals and the productivity of nations.

    Effective teaching for this new age will, in many ways, contrast sharply with the trends of the past century. Outcome-based attainment of relevant goals will replace an emphasis on time on tasks. What students know and can accomplish will prove far more integral to success than memorization of content-based facts. Successful students will interact purposefully as a community of inquiry. Literacy development will be a distinct curricular focus across content areas and will emphasize not just the three Rs (i.e., reading, writing, and arithmetic) but also task- and problem-relevant dimensions such as viewing and representing as well as cross-disciplinary vocabulary development (NGA & CCSSO, 2010; Herrera, Perez, Kavimandan, & Wessels, 2013). Students who learn effectively will be goal-driven, active, engaged, collaborative, thoughtful, and intent on reasoning. Strategies will be used to focus students on personalized capacity building for cognition, metacognition, problem solving, and reflection (Herrera, 2010). Recurrent, formative assessment will monitor capacity building among students and provide ongoing data for contingency-based instruction.

Global Connections 1.1
Emphasis on the sociocultural dimension is essential in EFL classrooms. Often the classroom is the only English-speaking environment to which students are exposed. The daunting task of learning English as a new language is made more manageable when teachers consider, understand, and incorporate the elements of students' biographies that bring them life, laughter, and love. Such actions help educators promote student motivation, lower affective filters, increase engagement, and thus strengthen learning.

Teaching and learning will target distinctly youthful student populations, especially in the United States. The fertility rate in the United States has reached its highest level in 45 years (Kotkin, 2010) and the nation is on the verge of a baby boomlet, in which the children of the largest generation in U.S. history will have school-age children of their own. Another emergent characteristic of this new age will be growing levels of cultural and linguistic diversity. The U.S. population of CLD students and families, currently 30 percent of the total, is expected to exceed 50 percent before 2050. In fact, the largest share of the U.S. population growth will occur among diverse families. Asian and Latino populations, for example, are expected to triple. Perhaps one of the least predictable developments of this emergent population will be a resurgence of growth in the school-age population of rural communities.

Clearly, what the nation does to best prepare this diverse youth to be productive and creative will prove pivotal to its capacity for economic competitiveness and a high-quality standard of living in this increasingly global era. Note how these multicultural education scholars explain the importance of valuing and celebrating the rapidly changing demographics in the classroom by watching this video.

■ Describing Cultural and Linguistic Diversity in the Classroom

Discussion of changing demographics and demands in public school classrooms invariably includes use of an array of terms and acronyms. Such terminology facilitates national and international conversations about trends, issues, and practices that involve the CLD student. For this reason, we now explore the definitions and nuances of some of the most frequently used terms and acronyms (see Table 1.1). We also discuss our rationale for our preferred choices among those that are used to describe students. Some are more exacting, more descriptive, and more cross-culturally sensitive than others.

■ **table 1.1**   Common Acronyms from ESL/EFL Education

Acronym/Explanation	Definition
BDI—biography-driven instruction	A research-based instructional method that emphasizes reciprocal facilitation and navigation of the official classroom space and the unofficial space of students' lives outside the classroom, which draws on assets of both spaces to promote culturally responsive teaching and learning.
BICS—basic interpersonal communication skills	The language ability needed for casual conversation, which usually applies to the interpersonal conversation skills of CLD students (i.e., playground language).
CALLA—cognitive academic language learning approach	A method of instruction that is grounded in the cognitive approach and focuses on the explicit instruction of learning strategies and the development of critical thinking as a means of acquiring deep levels of language proficiency.
CALP—cognitive academic language proficiency	The language ability needed for learning academic skills and concepts in situations in which contextual clues are not present and an abstract use of language is required.
CLD—culturally and linguistically diverse	A preferred term for an individual or group of individuals whose culture or language differs from that of the dominant group.
CREDE—Center for Research on Education, Diversity & Excellence	Now based out of the University of Hawai'i at Mānoa; a diverse team of experts who provide educators with a variety of tools to implement best practices for CLD students, including the standards for effective pedagogy: 1. Joint Productive Activity 2. Language and Literacy Development 3. Contextualization 4. Challenging Activities 5. Instructional Conversation
CUP—common underlying proficiency	The conceptual knowledge that acts as the foundation on which new skills are built. Both languages, L1 and L2, facilitate the development of such fundamental cognitive patterns within individuals. The language biographies serve as a bridge, connecting new information with previously acquired knowledge.
EFL—English as a foreign language	The use or study of the English language by non-native speakers in communities and/or countries where English is not the dominant language of communication.
ELD—English language development	A term used in some states for the programming model most commonly referred to as English as a second language (ESL).

(continued)

■ **table 1.1**   Continued

Acronym/Explanation	Definition
ELL—English language learner	A term for individuals who are in the process of transitioning from a home or native language to English. However, *CLD* is the preferred term because CLD emphasizes both the cultural and linguistic assets that a student brings to the classroom.
ESL—English as a second language	A programming model in which linguistically diverse students are instructed in the use of English as a means of communication and learning. This model is often used when native speakers of multiple first languages are present within the same classroom.
ESOL—English for speakers of other languages	Instruction that focuses primarily on the development of vocabulary and grammar as a means of learning English.
i + 1—comprehensible input	New information that an individual receives and understands that is one step beyond his or her current stage of competence. Accordingly, if the learner is competent at stage *i*, then understandable input at *i* + 1 is most useful for language progression.
ICB—integrated content-based	A communicative method that involves the concurrent teaching of academic subject matter and second language acquisition skills. This method often employs thematic units as well as content and language objectives across subject areas.
L1—first language	The first or native language acquired by an individual.
L2—second language	The second language acquired by an individual.
NCLB—No Child Left Behind	The No Child Left Behind Act of 2001 was signed into law by President George W. Bush on January 8, 2002. Designed to close the achievement gap between disadvantaged students and their peers, this U.S. education reform calls for greater accountability for assessment results in K–12 education.
OCR—Office for Civil Rights	The entity of the U.S. Department of Justice responsible for exacting compliance with Title VI of the Civil Rights Act of 1964.
SDAIE—specially designed academic instruction on English	A variation of sheltered instruction that emphasizes a cognitively demanding, grade-level appropriate core curriculum for CLD students. This variation primarily applies to students who have attained an intermediate or advanced level of proficiency in L2 (English).
SIOP—sheltered instruction observation protocol	A vehicle for delivering scaffolded instruction of the existing curriculum so that instruction is more comprehensible for students who are acquiring English.
SUP—separate underlying proficiency	The separate conceptual knowledge bases in L1 and L2, assuming that the two languages operate independently. According to this perspective, no transfer of skills occurs between the two languages.

■ **table 1.1**   Continued

Acronym/Explanation	Definition
WIDA—World-Class Instructional Design and Assessment	Per the 2012 Amplification of the ELD standards, there are five levels of language proficiency ascribed to CLD students.

> Level 1: Entering
>
> Level 2: Emerging
>
> Level 3: Developing
>
> Level 4: Expanding
>
> Level 5: Bridging

The sixth level, Reaching, ends the continuum, rather than establishing another level of language proficiency. In other words, the CLD student has met all the requirements determined in Level 5. Model performance indicators (MPIs) provide malleable guidelines for pre-K–12 students' processing or production of English in specific contexts.

Key Terms and Acronyms: It's All in the Context

Educators and researchers use many terms to describe students whose languages and cultures differ from the "typical" grade-level student. The term *limited English proficient (LEP)*, popularized by the federal government in the 1960s and 1970s, is one example. However, it is especially problematic because LEP does not emphasize the *assets* of multilingualism that the student may demonstrate in school. Rather, the term implies an assumed level of *deficit* in English proficiency that may not necessarily be accurate.

The long-standing use of the term *language minority student (LM or LMS)* is equally troublesome. This term, often derived from what is assumed to be typical classroom or school demographics, characteristically presupposes that students who speak a language other than English are in the demographic minority for a given school or district. Today, however, one in four children in the United States is from an immigrant family and resides in a household where a language other than English is spoken (Samson & Collins, 2012). As a result, these students are, in a variety of schools across the nation today, language *majority* students, thus rendering the acronyms LM and LMS not only inappropriate, but inaccurate as well.

Similarly, use of the term *mainstream* when referring to "typical" students implies that any students whose cultures, languages, or learning abilities differ from the norm are somehow *less than,* or not a part of, the students for whom our school systems were supposedly designed. However, diversity in the classroom is increasingly the reality of U.S. schools in the twenty-first century. It has been argued that such diversity is now the fabric, the mainstream, of new-millennial

> **Illustrated Concept 1.1**
>
> Prevent misunderstandings and misinterpretations of behavior such as eye contact, space issues, or physical contact by learning as much as possible about the cultures of your CLD students and by holding informal conversations with students when needed.

Illustrated Concept 1.2

Reinforce the value of your students' languages and cultures by familiarizing yourself with the original or native names of your students (and how to pronounce and use them correctly); have CLD students teach you basic greetings and commonly used phrases in their native languages; encourage CLD students to wear their native clothing or to bring objects representative of their heritage; and select curriculum materials that reflect the cultures of your students, as well as circumstances specific to second language learners.

classrooms (Lynch, 2012; Nieto & Bode, 2012; Samson & Collins, 2012). Therefore, we favor the use of the term *grade-level students* when referring to this segment of the student population.

In a more exacting and cross-culturally respectful vein, we advocate the use of the term *culturally and linguistically diverse (CLD) student* when referring to a student whose culture or language is different from other grade-level students. This term is the most inclusive and, in our view, the most holistically descriptive of students whose culture or language is different from that of the dominant culture or language in U.S. society. The use of this term and its associated acronym are increasingly prevalent in educational literature (California Department of Education, 2013; Gonzalez, Pagan, Wendell, & Love, 2011; Perez, Holmes, Miller, & Fanning, 2012). It is CLD students who bring diverse cultural and linguistic biographies, heritages, and assets to the learning environment. We believe that educators must be fully aware of the influence that a CLD student's biography, especially his or her culture, has on his or her preferred learning processes, language use, and performance potential in the classroom. Each of these represents powerful assets, which, if appropriately maximized, can powerfully impact achievement among CLD students.

These terms and acronyms from the field demonstrate the importance of using appropriately descriptive, cross-culturally respectful terminology when referring to the complex environment of and instructional programming for CLD students. While in no way an exhaustive list, Table 1.1 details other acronyms that are commonly used in language education, each of which has been reviewed for descriptive accuracy, professional utility, and cross-cultural implications.

The CLD Student: Asset or Liability?

As evident in the continued use of terms such as *limited English proficient* and *mainstream* in our world of public school education (e.g., LEP.gov), questions regarding the most appropriate ways of serving the differential learning and affective needs of this rapidly growing population of CLD students often stem from perceptions about assets and liabilities. You might well ask, Why assets and liabilities? The sad fact is that some of our schools continue to perceive the CLD student as a liability—a student who is liable to fail because he or she cannot understand or speak the language of instruction, a student who is more likely to migrate and move away than to benefit from teacher instruction, a student who is likely to experience academic failure because of inadequate schooling or time on task, a student who is likely to bring down a school's test scores because he or she cannot keep up with other students, and more. Remarkably persistent in the educational literature, this view of the CLD student appears as the deficit orientation to the linguistically or culturally different student. Basically, this perspective stresses not the assets that the CLD student brings to the school and the classroom but the liabilities or deficits that, according to this view, characterize the hopelessness of appropriate educational accommodations for the student.

This perspective holds that CLD students are language (presumably English) deficient and culture and home deficient and, as a result, at risk of academic failure. In one sense, the prevalence of this liability or **deficit perspective** is not surprising given the fact that the United States is one of the few countries in the world that does not value either bilingualism or multilingualism (Crawford, 2000; Olson, 2013). This deficit point of view is evident in common statements such as, "If they would only learn English . . ." and "They can't learn science until they speak English."

An alternative **asset perspective** on the CLD student more affirmatively recognizes and celebrates the advantages, talents, and experiences this student brings to the classroom and the school. Assets that this perspective acknowledges include:

- Multilingualism
- Experiences and schooling in another country
- Familiarity with multiple cultures and ethnicities

Just as management specialists recognize and use diversity in the workforce as one of the most powerful influences on an organization's capacity for creativity in the world of business (Florida, Cushing, & Gates, 2002; Terrisse, 2001), educators should recognize and use cultural and linguistic diversity as a powerful enrichment of a school's learning community. In fact, when CLD student differences are appropriately accommodated and classroom instruction is purposefully differentiated for diversity, these students not only match the academic performance of their native-English-speaking peers, but their academic gains may actually exceed those of their grade-level contemporaries (Goldenberg, 2008; Thomas & Collier, 1997, 2002).

■ Recognizing the Realities of Cultural and Linguistic Diversity in the Classroom

As previously discussed, the demographic realities of today's schools demonstrate that the composition of the average classroom in the United States is rapidly changing and will continue to do so in the foreseeable future. Because schoolteachers, administrators, and specialists are responsible for educating *all* students, we seek to understand what increasing cultural and linguistic diversity will mean for curriculum, instruction, pedagogy, standards, and the teaching profession. Understanding the difference between equality and equity is fundamental to this discussion. The notion of **equality** suggests that all students have appropriate access to a high-quality education when the *same* resources, instructional methods, curricular opportunities, and so forth are provided. **Equity**, on the other hand, reflects the recognition that each student is unique and that his or her access to a high-quality education is dependent on resources, instructional methods, curricular opportunities, and more that are responsive to his or her differential assets and needs.

This section of the chapter explores the realities of CLD students as a foundation for discussion of appropriate instructional methods that can be used to accommodate cultural and linguistic diversity in a professional, responsible, empathetic, and purposeful manner. We first explore a framework from which we can begin to examine the many factors that must be accounted for in creating educational conditions that both accelerate English language acquisition and promote the CLD students' academic achievement.

The Prism Model and Beyond: Understanding Students from a Holistic Perspective

The **prism model** (see Figure 1.1) is the product of long-term, multiage, and multisite research and analyses (Collier, 1987, 1989, 1992; Collier & Thomas, 1989, 2007, 2009; Gonzalez et al., 2011; Thomas & Collier, 1997, 2012) in public school districts across the United States. This model represents a uniquely holistic way to frame the differential learning and transition needs and diverse assets that CLD students bring to the school.

Many school educators who are first confronted by the complexities of accommodating CLD students naturally assume that the students' greatest needs and most formidable challenges are language-related. In fact, a common phrase heard in schools across the country is "If they [CLD students] would just learn English, everything else [in their school performance] would just fall right into place." However, the research behind the prism model demonstrates that not one but four different dimensions of the CLD student must be addressed if they are to be successful academically. Figure 1.1 illustrates each of these four dimensions

■ **figure 1.1**

Language Acquisition for School: The Prism Model

Source: C. Ovando, M. Combs, and V. Collier (2006), *Bilingual and ESL Classrooms: Teaching in Multicultural Contexts,* 4th ed. (Boston: McGraw-Hill). Page 124. Reprinted by permission of the McGraw-Hill Companies.

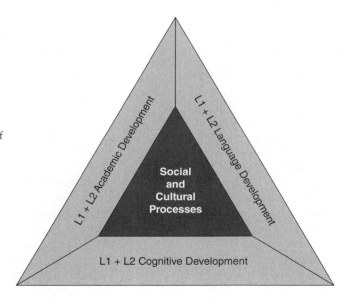

of the model: linguistic, academic, cognitive, and sociocultural. Consistent with the findings of Thomas and Collier (1997), no single dimension of CLD student success should be addressed in isolation. Instead, each of the four dimensions of the prism model is interrelated and involves developmental processes that occur simultaneously for the CLD student.

In this and subsequent chapters, we move beyond the defining characteristics of the prism dimensions. We examine and discuss the challenges and processes of each dimension that we have witnessed in our work with CLD students and their teachers in states across the nation, as well as in the work of others in the fields of English as a second language (ESL), English as a foreign language (EFL), and bilingual education. These analyses have informed our conceptualization of the CLD student biography, which provides a more in-depth view of the factors and dynamics associated with each of the four dimensions that influence the degree of success students experience in their linguistic and academic endeavors.

Illustrated Concept 1.3
Provide a welcoming and safe classroom environment. Take the time to praise students genuinely with positive remarks for participation and involvement in classroom activities; make it a point to have daily contact and show interest in the personal lives of your CLD students (e.g., ask about family); and implement consistent and predictable daily routines to clarify classroom expectations.

As we will see in chapters to follow, biography-driven instruction (BDI) is a highly effective product of this expanded emphasis on the four dimensions of the CLD student biography (Herrera, 2010). Biography-driven classroom practices are uniquely suited to the challenges of the increasingly diverse classroom because they bridge the gap between high-quality instruction for grade-level students and differentiated instruction for CLD students. They support the teacher in meeting the needs of all learners because they begin with the assets that each individual student already brings to learning. Finally, although BDI constitutes good teaching for all learners, it builds new learning skills and provides instructional supports that are essential for CLD students' engagement, motivation, comprehension, and retention.

Although beyond the scope of this text, Herrera has detailed the rationales, development, and range of strategies for biography-driven instructional and assessment practices (Herrera, 2010; Herrera, Kavimandan, & Holmes, 2011; Herrera et al., 2013). Biography-driven strategies are a product of long-standing development, field testing, refinement, and evaluation. They each encourage the teacher's holistic perspectives on the sociocultural dimension, the linguistic dimension, the cognitive dimension, and the academic dimension of the student's biography. One hallmark of these strategies is that they guide teachers to use insights about these dimensions to support student learning at the opening of the lesson, during the work time of the lesson, and at the closing of the lesson. As BDI strategies reflect, the sociocultural dimension of the biography is often pivotal to CLD students' success in the classroom.

The **sociocultural dimension** encompasses the student's heritage, culture, family interactions, and more. Highly effective teachers of CLD students take time to understand and build on student experiences associated with this dimension. Therefore, this critical aspect of CLD student potential will be the subject of remaining sections of this chapter of the text. Chapter 2 will examine the cognitive and academic dimensions of the biography—dimensions that are often perceived as pivotal to CLD student performance on assessments. Ultimately, Chapter 3 will explore the linguistic dimension and its importance to student literacy—an emergent focus of standards for grade-level classrooms, especially those of the Common Core (NGA & CCSSO, 2010).

The Sociocultural Dimension of the CLD Student Biography

At the heart of the CLD student biography is the sociocultural dimension. This dimension encompasses the complex social and cultural factors and variables that are critical to the transitional adjustments and the academic success of CLD students. Insightful teachers realize the significance of this dimension in the lives of CLD students and families and are careful to account for it as they plan their differentiated instruction. A significant number of CLD students have either recently immigrated to the United States or recently migrated to the school. These students face a surprising number of sociocultural (especially acculturational) challenges, many of which are anxiety provoking and some of which may promote culture shock.

Sociocultural Challenges

Among such sociocultural challenges are those highlighted in Table 1.2. From a cultural standpoint, such challenges include but are not limited to the following:

- *The CLD student must adjust to a new country, city, or neighborhood.*
  Implications: The student faces difficult, survival-based challenges outside the school, many of which may influence her or his punctuality, alertness, attentiveness, ability to concentrate, and more.

- *The CLD student must adapt to a new education system.*
  Implications: Significant differences may exist between the current and former education systems. Such differences include public versus private, hours of school day, length of school day, type of instruction, level of interaction in the classroom, rule systems, **culture of the school**, and so forth. Such differences may confuse the student, puzzle the parents or caregivers, prompt the student to act inappropriately, slow the learner's progress, and more.

- *The student must cope with the nuances of the school's culture.*
  Implications: Regrettably, the culture of the school does not always welcome diversity, affirm languages other than English, accommodate differential learning needs, or seek out parents or caregivers as partners. The messages that this culture conveys are often subtle and incomprehensible. As a result, CLD students cope with ambiguity, anxiety, and frustration, each of which interferes with their capacity to learn effectively. Their parents or caregivers may also have to cope with misgivings, uncertainty, and alienation from the educational process.

■ **t a b l e 1 . 2**   Sociocultural Dimension of the CLD Student Biography

Challenges	Processes
Cultural	**Cultural**
Adjustment to new country, town, city, or school	Acculturation
Recency of immigration	Developing conflict resolution skills
Adaptation to a new education system	Learning to view situations from multiple points of view
Culture of the school • Disrespect for L1 and/or diversity • Minority/majority cultures • Emphasis on equality and meritocracy versus equity • School/class environment • Distance/space perspectives • Time/punctuality perspectives	
Psychosocial	**Psychosocial**
Affective • Ambiguity/anxiety • Homesickness • Anger and/or depression • Instructional input and environmental demands on the affective filter	Self-esteem Cultural identity formation Motivation building Social identity formation Establishing positive interpersonal relationships Creating a psychosocial support network
Intragroup challenges • Language brokering • Separation from support network/family	
Intergroup • Prejudices and discrimination	
Socioeconomic • SES/income stability • Family employment • Access to health care • Residency status demands	
Sociopolitical environment • Community and/or school • National debate over bilingual education and immigration policy • Increased terrorism and subsequent rise in xenophobia	

Equally formidable for the CLD student are psychosocial challenges of the sociocultural dimension, including (1) ambiguity; (2) anxiety; (3) prejudice; and (4) discrimination on the basis of skin color, nationality, language, and more. As we will discuss, any one of these multifaceted challenges can significantly inhibit the performance of a CLD student in the classroom.

Cultural Challenges of the Sociocultural Dimension. As illustrated in Table 1.2, the sociocultural dimension encompasses various cultural challenges to the success of CLD students. For example, a review of educational research and literature strongly supports the argument that the culture of the school influences student outcomes, particularly for CLD students (MacNeil, Prater, & Busch, 2009; Nieto & Bode, 2012). The culture of the school can profoundly influence a CLD student's educational experience, including her or his perspective on schooling, attitude toward learning, behavior in the school, and performance in the classroom. In this sense, a school's culture encompasses at least three salient elements:

- The attitudes and beliefs of members (in this case, teachers, administrators, and staff)
- The norms and rules to which members adhere
- The relationships that exist among its members

School culture affects not only students but also educators. Specifically, school culture is often pivotal in shaping teachers' attitudes toward and beliefs about change, including (1) their perspectives on increasing cultural and linguistic diversity in the school and (2) the necessity of adapting curricula and student services that accommodate such diversity (Carroll, 2006; Cushner, McClelland, & Safford, 2011; Glassett & Schrum, 2009). Entrenched educator beliefs (Haberman, 2013; MacNeil, Prater, & Busch, 2009; Sewell, 2009) include but are not limited to:

- Real change in schools is not feasible.
- Discipline problems are an overwhelming barrier to school success.
- Educational bureaucracy precludes progressive educational practices (i.e., accommodations in school and classroom practices for a changing student population).

Findings by Murry (1996) suggest that such beliefs are often the product of at least four counterproductive influences associated with rigid, entrenched school cultures:

- A strict focus on norms and rule systems
- A strong emphasis on conformity
- A distinct self-consciousness about the image of the school (among staff members of the dominant culture)
- Pervasive scapegoating

Such influences can create a school culture characterized by negativity, barriers to collegiality, competition, resistance to change, and the subversion of individual efforts to accommodate change, especially changing student populations.

Ultimately, these characteristics associated with rigid and entrenched school cultures tend to stimulate a variety of myths and misconceptions regarding cultural and linguistic diversity. The persistence of many of the myths has been demonstrated in recent research, as have the findings that these myths tend to pose formidable, sociocultural challenges for the CLD student (Comber & Kamler, 2004; Fránquiz, 2012; Herrera & Rodriguez Morales, 2009; Murry, 1996). For example, one such myth holds that learning is due to innate abilities. Presumably, CLD students, regardless of their culture or language, are less capable of educational excellence than grade-level students of the dominant culture. Because the school culture considers both the cultures and native languages of CLD students to be inferior, neither the educators nor the curricula place value on the celebration or affirmation of other cultures or native language support. Such myth-based cultural norms can deny many CLD students any sense of motivational pride in and affirmation of their heritage or any benefit from ongoing native language support as a means to second language acquisition.

> **Illustrated Concept 1.4**
>
> Create positive, productive relationships between home and school through home visits of your CLD students; share successful school experiences with parents and caregivers (with the help of an interpreter if needed); maintain consistent contact with parents or caregivers of CLD students to involve them in their students' learning and language acquisition processes; and encourage familial visits and contributions to the school, classroom, and curricular topics.

This myth of learning abilities is but one among many that can arise from a rigid and entrenched school culture. When such myths are shared among school educators, the consequences for CLD students are both numerous and worrisome. Many of these consequences relate to schooling, others to behavior, and still others to learning and performance. To illustrate, the following are often instilled in CLD students:

- A growing conviction that schools are not places that respect or value the presence and contribution of CLD students or their families
- A conception that CLD students are intellectually inferior to the dominant (White) culture
- A perceived sense of hopelessness about new learning in an unfamiliar language and in unaffirming learning environments
- A belief that efforts in school will not be rewarded
- An increasing reluctance to participate or produce in class for fear of ridicule
- A generalized disengagement from learning and withdrawal from active participation in the learning process
- A growing resentment toward the educational system that often results in resistant, if not rebellious, behavior

In rigid and entrenched schools, the curriculum (and often the instruction that CLD students receive) does not recognize, build on, or value the student's cultural heritage or his or her prior socialization in a different culture. School programming neither affirms nor supports the student's native language as a means to second language acquisition. Classroom instruction does not account for the **acculturation** (discussed in the subsequent section) or the language, academic, or cognitive transitions through which the CLD student must pass in order to compete with his or her grade-level peers.

Instead, the dominant school culture tends to argue that it treats all kids the same and that each student, regardless of cultural or linguistic background, should be able to learn the content as it is presented if she or he makes sufficient effort to participate in the classroom, study the material, and complete assigned homework. The consequences of this myth for CLD students, as fostered and supported by a rigid and entrenched school culture, include the following:

- Few instructional accommodations for CLD students (a situation that arises from the belief that such accommodations would be unfair to other students)
- A conviction that CLD students and their families, not educators, are responsible for addressing the linguistic challenges that students confront
- A pervasive certainty that CLD students choose to fail in school because neither they nor their parents value education
- A distrust of the native language when used for instructional purposes
- A view of ESL and paraprofessional support as unfair, special treatment
- The placement of CLD students in remedial or lower-track classes

Although the sentiment that "we treat all students the same" does not, on the surface, appear to suggest prejudice, this viewpoint in effect denies the accommodations that would provide CLD students with meaningful instruction. As a consequence, CLD students do not have the same educational opportunities that would allow them to be as academically successful as their native-English-speaking peers. Thus, the equity-based affirmation "We recognize and value the different experiences, cultures, and languages that all our students bring to the classroom" can serve as a more inclusive alternative to the equality-based statement "We treat all students the same." Reflective school educators who target schoolwide success use their CLD students' sociocultural backgrounds as an entry point to active student engagement for developing cognitive, academic, and linguistic abilities. Professional educators counter the unproductive influences of a rigid and negative school culture by doing the following:

Illustrated Concept 1.5
Group or pair CLD students of various proficiency levels to challenge them academically and cognitively. By doing this, students at lower levels of language proficiency can gain a better understanding of complex concepts through the help of their peers. Students with higher levels of language proficiency have opportunities to practice the language as they explain or clarify concepts with peers.

- Affirming and celebrating CLD students as school assets
- Modeling appropriate accommodations for CLD students in the classroom
- Dispelling culture-bound myths about CLD students through research, experience, collaboration, and professional practice

Psychosocial Challenges of the Sociocultural Dimension. The notion of the affective filter helps us understand how certain psychosocial challenges of the sociocultural dimension (especially anxiety) might inhibit (or occasionally bolster) the classroom performance of the CLD student. The concept of the affective filter is most notably associated with the work of Krashen (1981, 1982) and his attempts to explain certain processes, especially second language acquisition, through which CLD students progress. The outcomes of this work include five hypotheses, at least two of which are relevant to this discussion.

To understand Krashen's concept of the affective filter, we must first explore his **input hypothesis**. According to this hypothesis, the CLD student is able to best incorporate new information (i.e., progress in language acquisition) when the input the student receives is *one step beyond* his or her current stage of competence. Krashen labels this type of ideal input with the designation $i + 1$. Accordingly, if the learner is competent at stage i, then input at $i + 1$ is most useful for producing new understandings. One might wonder how it is possible for a student to understand information that is beyond his or her current stage of competence. According to Krashen (2002), this type of language input is *comprehensible input* for students when they are able to capitalize on context (e.g., visual aids), extra-linguistic information (e.g., nonverbal or body language), and their prior knowledge of the world.

Krashen (1982) also developed the **affective filter hypothesis**, which incorporates the work of Dulay and Burt (1977) and argues that the amount of input reaching the CLD student is influenced by a number of affective variables, including anxiety, self-confidence, and motivation. For Krashen, second language learners with a low level of anxiety, high motivation, strong self-confidence, and a good self-image are better equipped for classroom performance and second language acquisition. On the other hand, high levels of anxiety, low motivation, low self-esteem, and other affective factors can combine to raise the affective filter, reduce academic achievement, and slow language acquisition. The hypothesis argues that once the affective filter is raised, the teacher's instructional input, no matter how well planned or well delivered, is unlikely to aid language acquisition or improve academic performance in the classroom.

As we have illustrated, the culture of the school and several associated myths concerning diversity constitute a significant challenge to the success of CLD students in school. However, the sociocultural dimension also encompasses psychosocial challenges through which the school culture must support CLD students if the goal is to promote success in the classroom. As CLD students confront this variety of cultural and psychosocial challenges, they will also develop through a series of **sociocultural processes**. The outcomes of these processes will profoundly influence a student's level of performance in the classroom, collaboration with peers, and achievement in school.

Sociocultural Processes

Table 1.2 summarizes many of the sociocultural processes that influence the performance, behaviors, and resiliency of CLD students inside and outside the classroom. These processes are as central to the dynamics of the sociocultural dimension as this dimension is to the CLD student biography and our understanding of the complex and differential needs of CLD students. Unfortunately, many educators have not been prepared to understand the importance of the intercultural dynamics that occur within schools and between the school and its community (Bradford Smith, 2009; Fránquiz, 2012; Lewis, 2001; Li, 2013; Milner, 2003; Sleeter, 2001). As a result, educators may fail to take students' sociocultural processes into consideration when developing curricula and delivering instruction.

As illustrated in Table 1.2, probably the most significant of sociocultural processes, especially for the newly or recently arrived CLD student, is the process of acculturation. Before discussing acculturation, however, the **enculturation** process demands attention. Through the subtle process of enculturation, we are gradually initiated into our home or native culture, and almost without even knowing it, we develop a sense of group identity that forms our set of values, guides our beliefs, patterns our actions, and channels our expectations. Enculturation gives us an ethnocentric view of the validity of our own social and cultural ways, leading us to believe our ways to be better than those of others. Although each of us tends to progress through a more or less lifelong process of enculturation, not all will brave the trials and tribulations of an acculturation process, which can result from geographical relocation or significant and frequent cross-cultural encounters.

On the other hand, CLD students must not only come to understand the powerful yet subtle influences of their own enculturation but they must also excel in a distinctly difficult and complex additional process of adjustment to another culture and its dominant language. This additional process of acculturation has been described as a series of stages that have been characterized as often impossible "without severe psychological costs" (García-Castañón, 1994, p. 200; Li, 2013). Whether these costs are debilitating and without purpose, or developmental and transforming, tends to be a function of the acculturation environment.

dilemmas *of Practice* 1.1

Ms. James is a recent graduate of her teacher education program and is about three months into her first year of teaching. Based on her preservice education, she is seeking to adapt and modify her instruction to accommodate the differential learning needs of her predominantly Vietnamese students. On this day she has asked the advice of a fellow teacher, Mrs. Davis, about appropriate instructional accommodations. Mrs. Davis responds as follows:

Every student has individual issues and wants the rules bent in one way or another. Making changes to instruction for each student is simply unrealistic. When I was growing up, you had to make the most of whatever you were given. Why should anything different be expected of students today? Part of learning how to succeed in society means following the rules and working within defined parameters. Making exceptions to accommodate students only sets them up for failure in the real world.

Ms. James has just experienced her first encounter with the *culture of the school*. Regrettably, the culture of the school does not always welcome diversity, tolerate languages other than English, accommodate differential learning needs, or seek out parents and caregivers as partners. The messages it conveys are often subtle and incomprehensible. As a result, CLD students cope with ambiguity, anxiety, and frustration, each of which interferes with their capacity to learn effectively. Their parents and caregivers struggle with misgivings, uncertainty, and alienation from the educational process.

■ *What advice would you offer Ms. James as she responds to the comments of Mrs. Davis? In what ways can a teacher appropriately accommodate CLD students in such an environment? How would you go about influencing the culture of the school in more positive ways?*

- The environment should account for the stages of acculturation through which the student will progress.

  Teacher Implications: Teachers who are aware of these stages or phases of acculturation better understand not only the painful adjustments their students must endure but also the process through which they, as teachers, will progress in accommodating cultural and linguistic diversity as a classroom reality.

- The environment should support the individual's long-standing ethnic identity.

  Teacher Implications: Ethnocentrism, or the tendency to judge others based on one's own standards (Cushner, McClelland, & Safford, 2011), is an inevitable outcome of long-standing enculturation in a particular culture. It is a product of pride, buy-in, and investment. Effective teachers know that students are best motivated in ways that support (rather than demean) their ethnic or cultural heritage. For such teachers, the affirmation of the student's home culture is a daily goal, not a once-a-year celebration.

- The environment should reflect and respond to the ways in which the acculturation process can affect students' academic, linguistic, and cognitive growth.

  Teacher Implications: The influences that the acculturation process can exert on the students' development are a product of the challenges that CLD students endure at each phase of acculturation. Reflective teachers empathize with students at each phase of the acculturation process and strive to better understand the influences it may have on the students' language development, cognitive growth, and academic achievement. These teachers understand the students' struggles, even in cases of misbehavior arising from the hostility phase of the **U-curve hypothesis.**

Acculturation—the process of adjusting to a new or non-native culture—is perhaps best illustrated by the four phases of the U-curve hypothesis (Cushner, McClelland, & Safford, 2011; Trifonovitch, 1977). The U-curve hypothesis, shown in Figure 1.2, specifies that the process of acculturation may be understood as a sequential series of four phases that occur over time. During the first, or *honeymoon,* phase of the acculturation process, the individual often experiences a certain sense of exhilaration or euphoria as he or she enjoys the novelty of life in a new culture. For instance, among CLD students and families, coming to the United States may represent a lifelong dream, a new opportunity, or a chance to reunite with family. Each of these situations tends to foster a sense of exhilaration.

However, as time passes in the new culture, the many subtle and hidden differences that exist across cultures begin to surface. Often the actions of others in the new culture seem difficult to understand, if not incomprehensible. At other times, one's own actions do not yield expected results. Ultimately, long-standing, culture-bound responses and solutions to typical questions and problems do not produce the same results. As an outcome of this cultural mismatch, CLD students commonly experience impatience, anxiety, frustration, and even anger. During this so-called *hostility* phase of the acculturation process, CLD students

■ figure 1.2
U-Curve Hypothesis

Source: K. Cushner, A. McClelland,
and P. Safford (2009), *Human
Diversity in Education: An
Integrative Approach,* 6th ed.
(Boston: McGraw-Hill). Page 113.
Reprinted by permission of the
McGraw-Hill Companies.

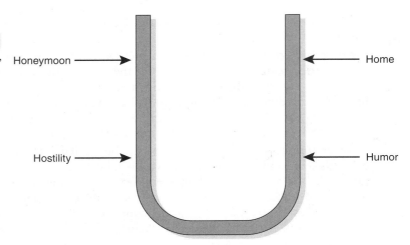

may begin to disengage from school. They may frequently complain of being tired or sick. They may feel so overwhelmed that they start to daydream in class, and some students may exhibit signs of rebellion against the new culture or new school setting.

Rebellious behavior is often a sign of culture shock, a worst-case scenario of the acculturation process that occurs as more and more cultural differences surface in increasingly intense, cross-cultural encounters. As CLD students experience the increasing conflict between the cultures they know and the cultures they are learning, they may feel threatened. Students sometimes rebel against the new culture as a way of negotiating personal identity and meaning. Among the reactions that CLD students typically experience during this phase are:

- A sense of alienation
- Actions that are interpreted as hostile
- Patterns of indecision
- Feelings of frustration and sadness
- An intense desire to withdraw from situations
- Symptoms of physical illness
- Exhibitions of anger grounded in resentment

Some students, especially secondary-level CLD students, never quite recover from this phase of the acculturation process (Clayton, Barnhardt, & Brisk, 2008; Collier, 2010; Suarez-Orozco & Suarez-Orozco, 2001). The frustration that CLD students encounter during the hostility phase can lead to an increased rate of school absenteeism, maladaptive behavior, suspensions from class and school, or dropping out. School educators can significantly reduce the possibility of these negative results by providing a supportive, respectful, and caring school environment. Students who are experiencing the hostility phase of the U-curve also benefit from discussions with their teachers that help them better understand their own acculturation processes.

If CLD students transcend the hostility phase of the U-curve, a newfound awareness of cross-cultural differences and their significance in a diverse world typically emerges from the acculturation process. The CLD students learn to confront the new cultural environment in more reflective and proactive ways. In the process, they manage feelings of embarrassment, disappointment, and frustration as they begin to reshape their cultural identity in this *humor* phase of the U-curve hypothesis. Although this phase remains stressful, the trials of this step in the acculturation process are, perhaps after a time for reflection, met with humor on the part of the students. They are able to laugh at mistakes in word use and pronunciation and find humor in miscommunication that might result from cross-cultural interactions. Confronting challenges in this phase yields an enhanced cross-cultural understanding of differences, norms, values, beliefs, and behaviors. Some CLD students learn to cope through a higher level of engagement with either the language learning community or their own academic endeavors. In fact, Brown (1986, 1992) has characterized this aspect of the acculturation process as a period during which the individual must learn to synchronize his or her linguistic and cultural development.

Having reached the final leg of the acculturation journey, the CLD student enters the decisive pinnacle of the U-curve, appropriately characterized as the phase called *home*. Cross-culturally sensitive perspectives that enable culturally adept performance and productive social interactions in a second culture characterize the student's thinking and actions in this phase of the acculturation process. At this stage, CLD students not only respect but also affirm cross-cultural differences. They value and celebrate their own bicultural and bilingual identity. The CLD student delves into and understands those nuances of culture and language that allow her or him access to the full repertoire of connotative meanings of social interaction and language. Most CLD students who reach this acculturation threshold (Acton & de Félix, 1986) have attained near-native literacy development and second culture understanding. Unfortunately, such individuals tend to be the exception rather than the norm. Figure 1.3 illustrates one student's acculturation journey in relation to the U-curve.

In like manner, the CLD student's sense of self, as well as his or her understanding of self in relation to social groups, is often shaped by the **psychosocial processes** of the sociocultural dimension. These psychosocial processes include the following:

- Self-esteem development
- Self-concept formation
- Social identity development
- Ethnic identity formation

In particular, the dynamics of ethnic identity formation illustrate one reason why sociocultural processes can so powerfully influence CLD students' perceptions of the school or community environment, as well as their appraisals of success probabilities in those environments.

■ **figure 1.3**   Gisela's Journey

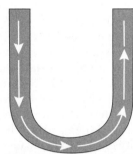

HONEYMOON

I was so excited to go to the United States! I could hardly wait to start school there. Some of my uncles were already living there. I couldn't wait to be together with more of our family. They assured me that anything was possible in the United States.

HOME

I have been in the U.S. for two years now. I have many friends at school and in my neighborhood. Although I still have to work very hard in school to learn everything in English, I know I can do it. I am beginning to love school just as much as I used to.

HOSTILITY

I hated it in the United States. No one understood me at school, and I couldn't understand them! Most of the time I felt frustrated, dumb, and lonely. The teachers either ignored me or acted like I was a problem. What I wanted more than anything else was to go back to my country. At least there I had friends, I could talk to people, and I understood what was expected.

HUMOR

After about four months, I started to feel better about school. I still felt like I would never learn English, but I realized that my teachers cared about me. Some of my teachers even tried to learn words in my language! It was so funny to hear them try to pronounce things correctly. Still, it meant so much to me that they tried, and that the rest of the class tried to learn the words, too. We all laughed at our mistakes as we learned a new language, and it made us feel closer—more like a family.

Illustrated Concept 1.6

Collaborate with other teachers to share observations and information regarding the assets that CLD students bring to the classroom. Capitalize on this knowledge within your own classroom. SMILE ☺. It's a universal language!

Ethnic identity formation is a complicated process that is influenced by various factors (e.g., home, school, community, geographical space), and it is important to note that this formation process is different for each individual. For some, ethnic identity formation is greatly influenced by the social climate in their community. More specifically, some individuals have been raised to feel that their ethnic identity is somehow "less than" the dominant ethnic identity within the community, which causes individuals to internalize a sense of inferiority. Because of this internalization, individuals will unfortunately cast aside parts of their ethnic identity in order to assimilate into the dominant ethnic group (Alba & Nee, 2005) in order to move up economically, politically, and socially within their communities.

On the other hand, individuals who are not part of the dominant ethnic group experience discrimination and racism much differently than those who are part of the dominant group. Those individuals who strongly identify with their ethnicity can experience discrimination more strongly than those who want to attain the same privileges as the dominant group. For example, a study of ethnic identity dynamics (Félix-Ortiz, Newcomb, & Myers, 1994) found that perceptions of discrimination were proportional to the degree of ethnic identification and inversely proportional to levels of acculturation. Because perceptions of discrimination are often pivotal in the self-concept development and motivation levels of CLD students (Clayton, Barnhardt, & Brisk, 2008), these findings indicate that the sociocultural process of ethnic identity formation is sometimes central to the students' sense of self-worth and their motivation to succeed in life and in school.

Teachers, however, need to view the ethnic identity formation process as a continuum. The aforementioned ways students form their ethnic identity are merely two examples; however, students may find themselves both strongly identifying with their ethnicity while simultaneously casting some cultural aspects aside. Furthermore, the same student might react differently to discrimination one day than the next. This can be difficult for teachers to assess, but understanding the ethnic identity formation process is paramount to meeting the needs of CLD students.

One way for teachers to understand better the degree of a student's identification with her or his own culture and her or his level of acculturation is to have teacher–student conversations prior to instructional planning. Although these conversations are more extensively explored in Chapter 5, teachers who purposefully converse with their CLD students prior to instructional planning (through an interpreter, if necessary) often find that teaching effectiveness is improved, reteaching is reduced, and students are more motivated.

Sociocultural Dimension: Implications for Classroom and School Practice

The success of any CLD student in any classroom depends on educators' understandings of and responses to the teaching and learning implications of the four interrelated dimensions of the CLD student biography (sociocultural, cognitive, academic, and linguistic). Because the sociocultural dimension lies at the core of CLD student success or failure in school, the implications of this dimension should form the foundation of any discussion of appropriate teaching practices for CLD students. Therefore, as increasing cultural and linguistic diversity transforms the average classroom, the implications of this dimension for teaching practice become increasingly relevant. The following list summarizes two of these sociocultural implications:

- Reflective teachers understand that increasing diversity in the school need not be perceived as a liability. Frustration and negativity toward increasing school diversity are not uncommon responses among teachers, staff members, and school administrators who are unprepared for the changes. Yet changing student and

■ Snapshot of Classroom Practice 1.1   Cultural Quilt

(Courtesy of Josiah Wilson)

Teachers often ask their students to free-think aspects of their culture they would like to share with the rest of the class. By using a cultural mind map, the class is able to learn about the countries of origin of their peers; for the teacher, it is a window into their background.

(Courtesy of Jesse Davila)

For students, it is exciting to see themselves in relation to the whole. It provides a springboard for conversations that begin with the self and have the potential for moving students toward academic talk. In classrooms where the cultures and languages of students are visible and valued, a sense of community develops among their members.

(Courtesy of Kendra Herrera)

Information from students becomes a source for planning and teaching. This information can be used to modify instruction, decide grouping configurations, tie content to prior knowledge, and much more. Knowing the biography of the student is essential for success in the classroom!

■ Voices from the Field 1.1

Schools have become much more focused on the use of data to drive decisions around student needs. Indeed, there is much we can learn by monitoring a student (or group's) response to instruction. As we grow capacities in this regard, it is important to consider sources of data that inform equally important considerations about whether the climate in these settings is conducive to developing language.

The first thing I tend to notice when entering a class is how it feels. That's hard to quantify but I always note whether students' faces appear relaxed, intent, or engaged as opposed to unfocused, unhappy, or disengaged. If everyone is facing forward in rows, I won't be able to see them, but that's telling as well.

There need to be times when seating purposefully shifts to small group configurations or pairs. What happens in those spaces is critical for deep learning but there are also immediate benefits. Not only can students hear each other much better, they're also better able to watch others' faces and monitor or repair communication in real time. This is how we develop and improve language naturally and there is no curriculum or technology that comes close to our brain's sociolinguistic wiring, so let's use it for learning!

■ *From Dr. Robin Morales Cabral, Director, Student Support Services, Wichita, Kansas, United States of America. Copyright © by Dr. Robin Morales Cabral. Reprinted by permission.*

community demographics are not a trend but an emergent reality of schools. At the same time, the support of CLD family members is often critical to the accommodations and modifications that school systems must make to this changing reality. Their families are a source of cultural identity, self-esteem, and social grounding for students. Family members are also a sociolinguistic resource for ongoing literacy development in the student's first language. To allow frustration and negativity within the school culture to alienate and isolate CLD students and their families is to further complicate the sociocultural challenges of reaching the new students, adapting and modifying for their needs, and ensuring their grade-level academic performance from the time they begin school until high school graduation. If the numbers of CLD students are increasing in the schools, and if we continue to alienate and push them out, what then is the purpose and productivity of our schools? What has been achieved? What has the school accomplished in our society? The heritage of U.S. education has developed from the preparation of the common student for the uncommon challenges of each new age, of each new frontier. In a rarely cited ruling of the United States Supreme Court, the case of *Lau v. Nichols* (1974), Justice Douglas affirms this underlying belief in the following majority opinion:

> There is no equality of treatment merely by providing students with the same facilities, textbooks, teachers, and curriculum; for students who do not understand English are effectively foreclosed from any meaningful education. Basic English skills are at the very core of what these public schools teach. Imposition

of a requirement that, before a child can effectively participate in the educational program, he must already have acquired those basic skills is to make a mockery of public education. We know that those who do not understand English are certain to find their classroom experiences wholly incomprehensible and in no way meaningful. (414 U.S. 56)

Reflective teachers value the cultural and linguistic diversity that their students bring to the classroom, and they use this diversity to enrich the learning of all students.

- Effective teachers know that instructional decision making should include time for the preassessment of CLD students in order to determine the potential impact of the affective filter on the comprehensibility of that instruction. As this chapter explores, Krashen's (1982) affective filter hypothesis tells us that instruction for CLD students, no matter how well planned or well delivered, will not affect the student if it or the surrounding circumstances of instruction raise the affective filter. Therefore, insightful teachers preassess. The professional practice of preassessment helps educators avoid instructional decisions that may prove counterproductive. Variables to preassess include:
  - Recency of immigration
  - Cultural background
  - Prior schooling in the home country
  - First language (L1) and second language (L2) proficiency
  - Family dynamics
  - Prior knowledge in the content areas

Because guardians, parents, family, and extended family members critically influence instructional success, home visits are an extremely effective strategy for preassessing students' sociocultural realities.

theory *into* Practice 1.1

The affective filter hypothesis (Krashen, 1982) asserts that the amount of language or instructional input that reaches the CLD student is influenced by a number of affective variables, including anxiety, self-confidence, and motivation. Thus, CLD students with a low level of anxiety, high motivation, self-confidence, and a good self-image are better equipped for classroom performance and second language acquisition. On the other hand, high anxiety, low self-esteem, low motivation, and other affective factors can combine to raise the affective filter, reduce academic achievement, and slow language acquisition. The hypothesis argues that once the filter is raised, the teacher's instructional input, no matter how comprehensible, is unlikely to aid language acquisition or improve academic performance in the classroom.

- *What are the implications of this hypothesis for your professional practice (or your future practice) as an educator?*

- *In what ways will you adapt or modify instruction to reduce the likelihood that your instruction will raise the affective filter?*

Connect, Engage, Challenge

CONNECT
Review and Reflect on the Reading

1. What are the four dimensions of the prism model? Which dimension is central to the model, and why?
2. What type of input is central to Krashen's input hypothesis? Why is this type of input considered important? What are the characteristics of this type of input?
3. What is the affective filter? What sorts of conditions raise the affective filter? What are typical consequences of instruction that raises the affective filter?
4. What are the phases of the U-curve hypothesis? Which of these phases is typically most problematic for CLD students, and why? What does the U-curve hypothesis explain?
5. What sociocultural challenges for CLD students are associated with schooling in the United States? Name and explore at least three.
6. What characteristics are associated with a supportive classroom environment for acculturation among CLD students?
7. What reactions do CLD students typically experience during the hostility phase of the U-curve? Why should teachers be aware of these potential reactions? What can teachers do to support CLD students during this phase of acculturation?

ENGAGE
Share What You Learned

1. Given the ways in which enculturation takes place, discuss what aspects of socialization might prompt teachers to hold a deficit perspective of CLD students.
2. This chapter explores the many challenges that the culture of the school can pose for CLD students. Discuss ways in which an informed teacher might reduce the counterproductive influences of such a culture.
3. The differences between a perspective that emphasizes equality and one that stresses equity were summarized in this chapter. Discuss the following questions:
   a. Which of the perspectives did you identify with before you read this chapter?
   b. According to which perspective were you socialized?
   c. Which perspective is most likely to prove effective with CLD students? Why?

CHALLENGE
It's Not Real until You Practice

Preservice Teachers
1. Based on information learned from this chapter, create a protocol and interview a CLD student. Based on the findings of your interview, identify two sociocultural challenges that the student confronts in all-English classroom settings. Finally, discuss the planning implications of these challenges for classroom instruction.
2. Read the following case study of Raja, a student from Saudi Arabia. Identify student strengths and needs in terms of sociocultural processes. List activities or accommodations to maximize teaching and learning for this student.

Raja

Raja grew up in Saudi Arabia, where he attended school regularly, was a very good student, and enjoyed his childhood and preteen years. Recently, he turned 13 years old and his family moved to Kansas City. Raja had studied some English in school, but like the rest of his family, he knew only a few phrases. His father was a teacher in Saudi Arabia, but with such limited English, he could find a job only as a janitor at a major shopping mall. Following the events of 9/11, Raja experienced alienation from classmates who had once spoken to him. Even some of his teachers treated him differently. Consequently, Raja began conversing more in English outside his household, even with those he used to hold conversations with in his first language. He also felt reluctant about speaking with his family members in his native language. Raja started to feel lonely, cut classes on a regular basis, and look for work outside school to occupy his time. He did not feel that he fit in.

3. Interview a local ESL or dual-language teacher to determine how he or she assesses CLD students for placement. In what ways does the teacher collect information about a CLD student's sociocultural background? Discuss recommendations that you would offer, based on what you have learned.

In-Service Teachers

1. Think about your school and CLD students in relation to the material presented in this chapter. Discuss with a colleague the demographics of your student population as well as actions being taken to address arising needs within your school. Think about two sociocultural challenges you have observed among your CLD students and explain strategies that you have implemented (or will implement) for addressing these needs.

2. Consider what you have learned from this chapter and create a student and family intake questionnaire that asks, in a nonthreatening manner, key questions about the sociocultural backgrounds of CLD students. List multiple ways to obtain this information. Try the questionnaire on students in your classroom. Discuss what you learned and the implications that this new knowledge has for teaching.

3. The sociocultural adjustment challenges of CLD students differ in elementary, middle, and high school. Think about observations you have made during your teaching career and list 10 ways to address and accommodate these sociocultural age differences. What implications do these differences have for teaching and learning?

tips for practice

In elementary classrooms, consider:

- Helping CLD students find an appreciation and validation of their own heritage within the lessons, through storytelling themes, songs, rhymes, or poems that incorporate their cultures; having bilingual parents or caregivers of CLD students come read with the class; and providing a buddy system between CLD students who share the same cultural background.

- Observing the progress that your CLD students have made in their development of first and second language literacy skills through informal assessment. This might involve having them draw or write about activities they have engaged in with their families, and making anecdotal notes as they subsequently share their drawings or read their writing projects with classroom partners.

- Setting challenging yet attainable goals regarding literacy or academic development with your CLD students. Individually meet with them on a frequent basis to discuss their progress in reaching these goals.

- Working to increase the understanding and respect that your students have for one another by asking CLD students to share their insightful perspectives on lessons as related to their own cultural heritage.

In secondary classrooms, consider:

- Organizing a mentoring program (with an organization, an institute of higher education, or a business) for CLD students in order to provide professional role models from the community.

- Assisting CLD students in making connections to new content vocabulary and concepts by previewing in their first languages before presenting the lesson in English.

- Using interactive journals between CLD students and yourself in order to encourage the development of literacy skills, a positive student–teacher relationship, and meaningful communication through writing.

- Enhancing the self-esteem of CLD students by continually reinforcing their potential to succeed and making it a point to praise their efforts rather than overcorrecting their errors.

- Helping newcomer CLD students feel welcome and comfortable in their new classroom environment by pairing them with classmate mentors who have progressed farther through the acculturation process and can provide support and encouragement.

In EFL classrooms, consider:

- Planning lessons that directly relate to your students' ethnic heritages by using bilingual versions of songs, poems, and stories.

- Inviting bilingual speakers to the classroom, so they may share their own English language acquisition process through stories and pictures. These visits can be in-person, or if technology is available, visitors may be seen via video conferencing.

- Focusing on praising students' accomplishments in language production rather than overly correcting grammar, punctuation, or pronunciation errors. By celebrating the successful communication of messages, students become more engaged in the classroom and more invested in learning the second language. Student progress is more likely in positive learning environments where targeted feedback is provided in strategic ways.

Cognitive and Academic Dimensions of Methods for Culturally and Linguistically Diverse Students

our mission

Our mission for this chapter will be to:

- Explore cognition and schooling issues associated with CLD student backgrounds and their academic success.

We will accomplish this mission by helping you to meet the following learning outcomes:

- Explain the cognitive dimension of the CLD student biography.
- Summarize key cognitive challenges and processes for CLD students and discuss teaching implications.
- Explain the academic dimension of the CLD student biography.
- Summarize academic challenges and processes for CLD students and discuss their implications for teaching.

Socorro Herrera

key theories and concepts

academic dimension

academic language development

affective involvement

cognitive dimension

cognitive learning strategies

cognitively demanding

cognitively undemanding

constructivist learning environments

context-embedded

context-reduced

contextualization

elaboration

learning styles

metacognitive learning strategies

reductionist curricula

relevance

social/affective learning strategies

Classroom performance is significantly based on learning, and at the heart of learning is understanding. That is, to learn something new, students must derive the meaning of new information. Among conscious or subconscious questions the learner may ask are the following:

- How is the new information similar to or different from what I already know? Where does it fit?
- Is it consistent with patterns or schemata of knowledge I have already developed? If not, how will I resolve the difference?
- Does it seem to make sense? If not, how can I make sense of it?
- Is a new perspective on this information or my schema needed? If so, does this change what I know or what I thought I knew?

Each of these questions involves *cognition*—the act or process of coming to know or understand something. If an individual uses such questions to purposefully examine what he or she knows or is seeking to understand, then these questions involve *metacognition*, or thinking about one's thinking processes.

Therefore, if we can describe learning in terms of understanding and cognition, then it ought to concern us a great deal when research and analysis (e.g., Burns, 1993; Shepard, 1997; Sousa, 2011) suggest that the understandings that many children come to achieve as a result of instruction can be characterized as *fragile.* If the goal of instructional methodology is to achieve learning, then what has been accomplished when the result is a fragile understanding? More fundamentally, what is a fragile understanding?

Basically, a fragile understanding exists when the student appears to know a concept in one context but does not appear to know that same concept in another way or in another setting (Burns, 1993). Although such a situation might arise as a result of incomplete learning processes, it is not uncommon for a student to master the learning of a concept but prove unable to transfer that learning. Shepard (1997) has argued that this inability to transfer learning—that is, a fragile understanding— often occurs because the student has mastered not the concept but certain classroom routines. For Shepard, instructional methods that emphasize robust understandings are the supports that students need to ensure the transfer of understandings. Current instructional agendas move toward students taking ownership of their learning through cognitively challenging activities. An example in the United States is Common Core, which has been adopted by 45 states, the District of Columbia, and four U.S. territories: Guam, the American Samoan Islands, the U.S. Virgin Islands, and the Northern Mariana Islands (CCSSI, 2012). Teachers who use instructional methods that target these robust understandings do the following:

- Frequently check students' prior knowledge.
- Regularly prompt students to think about existing understandings in novel ways.
- Encourage students to derive new connections between existing schemata and new contexts.

The notion of *transfer* is a particularly critical one for culturally and linguistically diverse (CLD) students. If these students are to prove successful in the content areas, they must exhibit the ability to transfer knowledge, skills, and capacities learned in the first language to learning and understandings in content-area domains taught in a second language. Ultimately, it becomes apparent that the instructional methods necessary to prevent fragile understandings and to ensure transfer must focus on the **cognitive dimension** of student learning, especially the student's capacity for the metacognition necessary to achieve deep and robust understandings. The next section explores this cognitive dimension of the CLD student biography and the many implications for understanding, transfer, and learning.

Illustrated Concept 2.1

Provide CLD students with opportunities to use their native language as a means to develop cognitive academic language proviciency. Teach key concepts and vocabulary in L1 with assistance from a community volunteer or bilingual peer. Provide students with translated key concepts to preview prior to the lesson.

■ The Cognitive Dimension of the CLD Student Biography

Chapter 1 summarizes the four interrelated dimensions of the prism model: the sociocultural, the cognitive, the academic, and the linguistic. The prism model (Collier & Thomas, 2007, 2009; Thomas & Collier, 1997, 2012) represents a uniquely holistic way to frame and better understand the differential learning needs of CLD students, as well as the many adjustment and process difficulties faced by this population.

A deep understanding of the cognitive dimension requires us to transcend this dimension's defining characteristics. To this end, we explore and specify the challenges and processes of this dimension that we have witnessed in our work with CLD students and in the work of others. Such explorations of the cognitive and academic dimensions of the CLD student biography are the subjects of this chapter. These analyses begin with the many challenges and processes we have associated with the cognitive dimension.

Perhaps the most neglected challenges and processes that influence CLD students' success in school settings are those of the cognitive dimension. One reason for this neglect may be the complexities of this dimension and the recency of research that genuinely integrates our understanding of how this dimension interrelates with other dimensions of the CLD student biography. In fact, August and Hakuta (1997), in conjunction with the meta-analyses of the National Research Council, have argued that serious research questions remain in at least seven major domains of the cognitive dimension, including:

- The nature of the relationship between language proficiency and literacy skills
- The consequences of acquiring nominal content knowledge in a first language and then switching languages for the learning of higher levels of content material
- The identification of which features of second language knowledge and acquisition are additive for cognition

Exploring questions related to these areas of research remains a priority in second language acquisition scholarship. For example, Robinson and Ellis (2008) present the most current research on cognitive linguistics and second language acquisition, in which scholars emphasize that language acquisition cannot happen in a vacuum. Rather, this acquisition process is dependent on an individual's cognition processes, as well as his or her knowledge of the world, environment, length of use, and even motivation. Given the many factors that create a very complex picture of the relationship between cognition and second language acquisition, we will begin with an overview of some of the pivotal cognitive challenges that CLD students encounter in academic settings.

Cognitive Challenges

Personal experiences with CLD students, as well as recent research and analysis in education, provide some insights into certain key challenges that students face within the cognitive dimension of the CLD biography (Chamberlain, 2005; Chamot, Dale, O'Malley, & Spanos, 1992; Chi, de Leeuw, Chiu, & LaVancher, 1994; Cobb, 1994; Fitzgerald, 1995; Herrera, 2010; Purcell-Gates, 1996; Rosebery, Warren, & Conant, 1992; Sousa, 2011; Young & Leinhardt, 1996). Among these cognitive challenges for CLD students are those summarized later in Table 2.1.

■ **t a b l e   2 . 1**   Cognitive Dimension of the CLD Student Biography

Challenges	Processes
Cognitive development in the first language (L1) is interrupted.	Development of the declarative knowledge base
Second language learners devote cognitive effort to interpreting and hypothesis testing of the system of rules that organizes the second language (L2).	Development of the procedural knowledge base
Curricula and programming for the culturally and linguistically diverse students are reductionist and skills-based, which limits opportunities for higher-order thinking.	Capacity building for short-term, working, and long-term memory
Learning tasks and environments are cognitively demanding and decontextualized.	Ongoing cognitive academic language proficiency (CALP) development in L1 (a process of at least three dimensions of the CLD student biography)
Instruction fails to target a variety of preferred learning styles.	CALP development in L2 (a process of at least three dimensions of the CLD student biography)
U.S. classroom instruction often fails to tap the deep, prior knowledge structures that CLD students bring to complex problem solving.	Learning strategy development • Cognitive • Social/affective • Metacognitive
Alphabetic writing systems represent words at a deep level of abstraction.	Capacity building for concept formation in L2
In English, vocabulary knowledge and comprehension are primary determinants of reading comprehension ability.	
Successful second language learners often focus on word meaning, whereas mainstream reading instruction often emphasizes word phonetics.	
The core structures or epistemologies of some subject areas (e.g., history, science) are exceptionally difficult for CLD students.	
Some content areas (e.g., history) require a high level of declarative and procedural knowledge integration.	

A number of these cognitive challenges highlight the interrelationships between the cognitive and the sociocultural dimensions. For example, interrupted cognitive development in a student's first language is a frustrating challenge for CLD students, some of whom have emigrated from war-torn countries where long periods of irregular schooling are commonplace. Demographic evidence suggests that the number of CLD students emigrating from such environments may be increasing (Roxas, 2011).

In like manner, strong cognitive–sociocultural connections exist with respect to **learning styles**. Learning styles can be understood as the emotional needs and the environmental and interaction preferences that students have for processing new information and relating to others in the classroom (Putintseva, 2006). Students' preferred learning styles are influenced largely by socialization and cognitive development in the primary or home culture. When a persistent discrepancy exists between the modes of educational interaction in the classroom (instruction, inquiry, problem solving, dialogue, etc.) and the modes of learning to which students have been primarily socialized, challenges to student learning and success are heightened (Bennett, 2010; Garcia, 1996, 2010). Therefore, effective teachers will preassess the kind of prior teaching the CLD student has received and the types of learning environments to which she or he has been exposed.

Students from the African American, American Indian, Asian American, and Mexican American cultural groups often employ styles of inquiry and response that differ from predominant styles in classrooms. Students from these groups who exhibit strong cultural affiliations may favor oral and communal interactions (Appiah & Gates, 1997; Nieto, 1999), divergent (exploratory) lines of inquiry (Valdes, 1996), and inductive (whole-to-part) lines of reasoning (Freeman & Freeman, 2011). On the other hand, teachers socialized in the dominant culture tend to emphasize convergent (prompt-answer) questions and model deductive problem solving (Bennett, 2010; Gay, 2000, 2010). These teachers are likely to structure classroom interactions that focus on the particular, build from part to whole, reason from the specific to the general, and emphasize a didactic dialogue. Given these discrepancies, schools often recognize and wish to act on the differences in socialization between teachers and CLD students. Nonetheless, in attempts to defend their practice, many teachers tend to argue the impossibility of targeting the preferred learning styles of all students in the classroom. These educators fail to realize that the intent of the learning styles research was not to argue the necessity of planning instruction that targets all the preferred learning styles represented in a given classroom. Instead, this research informs us that an awareness of the major groups of learning styles present within a classroom can assist the teacher in targeted, instructional planning that anticipates different student needs. Such awareness also facilitates teaching modifications that are:

- Cross-culturally sensitive
- Effective in reducing the need for reteaching
- Designed to reduce the slope of the learning curve for all students

Interrelationships between the cognitive and sociocultural dimensions become alarmingly evident when curriculum programming in the school or instruction in the classroom evolves from untested assumptions. This is especially the case when school educators make assumptions about the prior knowledge that a CLD student does or does not bring to the learning environment. Because a CLD student, by definition, generally exhibits some level of limited English proficiency, schools often mistakenly assume that the student's prior knowledge in the content areas is limited as well. Additionally, some educators assume that because a CLD student does not speak English well, she or he cannot learn in an English-speaking environment.

Not surprisingly, then, educators who make these sociocultural attribution errors seldom set aside appropriate time or secure support (e.g., translators or native language collaborative groups) to assess students' prior knowledge in the content areas before planning instruction. As a result, many CLD students are not cognitively

■ **Snapshot of Classroom Practice 2.1**   Academic Mind Map

(Courtesy of Jessica Barrand, Lawrence, Kansas)

Mind maps are great for tapping into students' experiences and academic knowledge. They also serve as a point of departure for making connections to vocabulary and concepts to be taught.

(Courtesy of Kendra Metz, Lawrence, Kansas)

Transformative learning begins when students can use linguistic and nonlinguistic representations to share what they know and what they are learning. Time used to allow for this type of learning benefits both the teacher and the learner.

(Courtesy of Denise Johnson, Lawrence, Kansas)

The ultimate goal is to take student words and representations and turn them into text. Learners begin to see themselves as contributors in the learning process when opportunities are provided for them to be actively involved, regardless of linguistic proficiency.

stretched toward new and grade-level learning in the content areas. Regarding the cognitive dynamics of this challenge for CLD students, August and Hakuta (1997) have noted:

> The depth, interconnectedness, and accessibility of prior knowledge all dramatically influence the processing of new information. . . . Knowledge is a complex integrated network of information of various types: ideas, facts, principles, actions, and scenes. Prior knowledge is thus more than another chunk of information. It might facilitate, inhibit, or transform a new learning task. Students must connect their own prior knowledge with new information continuously, while teachers must understand how well students are making these connections. (pp. 69–70)

As this passage explains, the **elaboration** of a student's prior knowledge is critical to cognitive development and transformative learning. When classroom instruction does not explicitly teach and encourage CLD students to make connections between their prior knowledge and the key content concepts they are learning, these students face formidable challenges to their academic success and to their ongoing cognitive development.

Other cognitive challenges for CLD students (see Table 2.1) underscore the interrelationship between the cognitive and the linguistic dimensions of the prism model. For example, the ongoing debate over phonics versus whole language has significantly influenced classroom literacy development instruction in schools throughout the nation (Routman, 1996; Freeman & Freeman, 2011). Many English as a foreign language (EFL) and English as a second language (ESL) programs are still grounded in the grammatical approach; however, there has been a recent move, globally speaking, to approach language learning from a constructivist/communicative approach. Focusing on phonics learning rather than whole language is especially problematic for CLD students because long-standing research and analysis regularly indicate that successful second language learners benefit from literacy instruction that emphasizes word meaning rather than the phoneme structure of the word (Adams, 1990; Escamilla, 2004; Herrera, Perez, & Escamilla, 2010; Jimenez, García, & Pearson, 1996; Krashen, 2000, 2002). For instance, the research of Jimenez and colleagues (1996) indicates that CLD students benefit most from a *constructivist* literacy development environment, in which students focus on the construction of meaning as central to learning. According to these and other authors (e.g., Au & Carroll, 1997; Moore, 2012; Morrow, Pressley, Smith, & Smith, 1997), a constructivist, cognitively demanding learning environment encourages students to make cognitive connections between their prior knowledge and current content context. Because CLD students have access to two or more languages, linguistic connections such as cognates and reading strategies can facilitate meaning construction between languages and enhance their growth in the cognitive dimension.

Constructivist learning environments make possible the cognitive–linguistic and cognitive–sociocultural connections at the contextual, intracultural, and affective levels. First, the rich use of context in these environments encourages pattern recognition, especially in literature-based instruction (Au, 2000). This pattern recognition in turn fosters the derivation of meaning through integration with what the learner already knows (Freeman, 1995; García, 2000). For example, a constructivist learning environment at the elementary level might emphasize a lesson on colors in connection with a literature-based story on colors, such as *Mouse Paint* (Walsh, 1989). Students might begin with a hands-on activity involving the primary colors red, blue, and yellow. The teacher would then encourage mixed groups of students to discover what other colors they might create by mixing the primaries. As students discover new colors, they would be named in Spanish, in other languages represented in the classroom, and in English, and the names would be placed on separate language word walls, along with the primary colors combined to achieve them. Then students might be prompted to discuss how each color makes them feel. Names of these feelings would be added to the word walls. Later, students would be encouraged to use prior experiences to make a list of things they know are associated with each color created, and these would be added to the word walls in Spanish, in other languages represented, and in English. Having established the context of the story, the book would then be previewed in the native language for the CLD students. Finally, the story would be read and learned in English with an emphasis on the fact that the mice in the story mix paint to create new colors according to the same patterns the students used in their hands-on activity.

Global Connections 2.1
Regardless of context, educators who believe in creating constructivist environments will plan lessons for English language development and academic success. Lessons that have relevance to the learner are as important in the EFL classroom as they are in an ESL classroom. All learning, regardless of context, must be both cognitively challenging and relevant for the learner.

Constructivist environments also tend to emphasize the **relevance** of new information to the learner. Relevance is connected to the learner's cultural lens, which filters incoming information according to schemata established by long-standing socialization in that culture. When teachers present information or instructional input that relates to what the CLD student already knows and understands, the student is more likely to recognize the information as relevant and worthy of integration into existing schemata. On the other hand, students will most likely treat learning input that markedly differs from prior knowledge and experiences as irrelevant. Research on how the brain learns confirms the importance of relevancy to students' retention of learning (Sousa, 2011). Thus, constructivist learning environments highlight the need for teachers to preassess what prior knowledge and experiences the CLD student brings to the ESL/EFL classroom as a basis for enhancing cognitive development.

Finally, constructivist learning environments often encourage the active and **affective involvement** of the learner in the construction of meaning. Research on this emphasis indicates that a strong affective (emotional) response to what is being learned helps students remember what they learn (Cahill, Prins, Weber, & McGaugh, 1994; Jensen, 2008; Sousa, 2011). Therefore, effective teachers foster a learning environment that emphasizes prior knowledge, creates a context for understanding, makes new concepts relevant, and helps students connect emotionally to what they are learning. In such an environment, CLD students have the greatest potential for cognitive growth.

■ **Snapshot of Classroom Practice 2.2**   Students Sharing Empanadas

Within-group differences related to language and culture must be explored in order to understand the individual student. Although these students are Latino, their backgrounds vary and empanadas have a different meaning for each within their family units.

(Courtesy of Isa Davila, Zayra Espinoza, Jesse Davila, and Adaly Espinoza)

Students in ESL/EFL classrooms often encounter cognitive challenges when they need to communicate in a second language and perform in cognitively demanding academic settings. Cummins (1991) has described a theoretical framework he developed for understanding some of the situational environments and demands that CLD students encounter as they go through the process of developing a cognitive, academic level of second language proficiency. In his model of situational environments, Cummins considered three critical processes influencing second language acquisition:

- The development of communicative competence in the target language
- Different cognitive and contextual demands on language competence
- The correlations between first and second language development

Cummins created the framework by using two intersecting continua. One continuum considers communicative situations to the extent that they are **context-embedded** versus **context-reduced**. In a *context-embedded* situation, CLD students use readily available, paralingual cues—such as the context in which the discourse occurs, body language, and prior knowledge—to actively construct meaning. A routine interpersonal conversation is an example of a context-embedded situation. If a CLD student does not understand, he or she might ask for clarification or derive the meaning of a communication from the context of the conversation. Another example of a context-embedded situation would be a conversation concerning the weather.

In a *context-reduced* situation, the CLD student has few if any paralinguistic cues to facilitate meaning construction. Therefore, meaning must come from the language itself. One such situation is a classroom lecture on valence theory in a high school chemistry course. These context-reduced situations are extremely valid when it comes to assessment and evaluation; however, during the instructional cycle, a teacher must make attempts to provide situations where there is a relevant context available to students that can facilitate comprehension and, in turn, output.

The second continuum in Cummins's model considers communicative situations to the extent that they are **cognitively undemanding** versus **cognitively demanding**. In a *cognitively undemanding* situation, CLD students process small amounts of information requiring little cognitive engagement. An academic example of such a situation in language arts would be a classroom discussion of a story that is illustrated by a Big Book, which is shared among class members. In a *cognitively demanding* situation, CLD students deal with significant amounts of complex information that they are asked to process and assimilate. Such a situation typically demands tremendous cognitive engagement. An example of such a situation might be one in which a teacher asks students to identify, analyze, and discuss at least five major themes of the novel *Moby Dick*.

In describing the development of communicative competence or proficiency, Cummins (1991) integrated the two continua in an intersecting manner in order to create four quadrants describing situational language demands (see Figure 2.1). Quadrant A distinguishes a context-embedded, cognitively undemanding communicative situation. Quadrant B defines a context-embedded, cognitively demanding communicative situation. Quadrant C characterizes a context-reduced, cognitively undemanding communicative situation. Finally, quadrant D describes a context-reduced, cognitively demanding communicative situation.

As a language learner develops greater communicative competence or proficiency, tasks that were once cognitively demanding become less demanding, and the understanding that once required heavy contextual support becomes more easily comprehensible with fewer paralinguistic cues. As the learner acquires a second language, the before-and-after charting of the language demands of a particular situation will reveal a shift from the bottom right quadrant (quadrant D) to the top left quadrant (quadrant A). For example, when a CLD student first moves to the United States and begins to learn English, writing a paragraph that lists three factors that led to the U.S. Civil War would most likely be an extremely context-reduced, cognitively demanding situation. However, if that student is schooled in the United States for several years through various academic environments that directly or indirectly address U.S. history, writing the same paragraph could prove a less context-dependent and more cognitively undemanding situation.

The most important understanding that teachers can gain from this theoretical framework is that what may appear to a teacher as a relatively simple task may actually be quite demanding in a cognitive sense for the CLD student. This is often the case for a student who does not have the prior knowledge and the second language capacities necessary to successfully complete the task. To develop cognitive,

■ figure 2.1   Range of Contextual Support and Degree of Cognitive Involvement in Communicative Activities

Source: Adapted from Cummins (1981), p. 12. Used with permission.

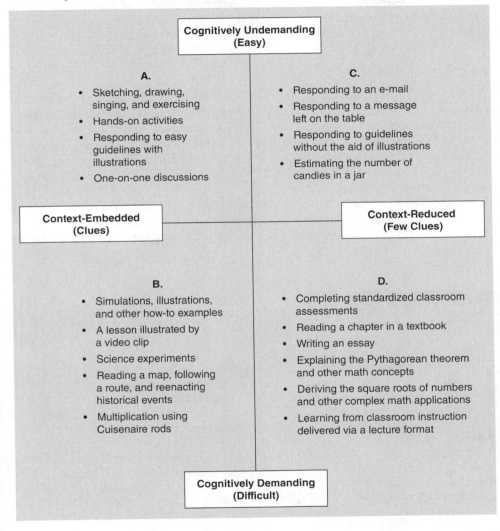

academic language competence or proficiency in a second language (L2), CLD students need to participate in a highly contextualized, language-rich instructional environment generated by a curriculum that focuses on meaning construction and cognitive, **academic language development.** Subsequent chapters of this text provide an in-depth exploration of ways to foster such an environment for content and language learning.

As these examples illustrate, the cognitive dimension encompasses a variety of challenges for students acquiring a new language. Many of these challenges involve not just the cognitive dimension but also the sociocultural and linguistic dimensions. These challenges must be addressed during all phases of lesson delivery for teachers to meet the unique and individual needs of the learner.

Cognitive Processes

No less important to the success of the CLD student are the key processes of the cognitive dimension. Many of these cognitive processes are summarized in Table 2.1. Interest in cognitive processes has caused researchers to explore the potential value of learning strategy development for CLD students (e.g., August, Calderón, & Carlo, 2002; Calderón, 2007; Chamot & El-Dinary, 1999; Chamot, 2009; Chamot & O'Malley, 1994; Cohen, 2011; García, 1998; Herrera, Perez, & Escamilla, 2010; Jimenez, 1997).

Learning strategies are the patterns of thinking or goal-driven activities that help the learner attain targeted learning outcomes. The notion of a cognitive approach to learning strategies is grounded in a constructivist perspective on

---

dilemmas *of Practice* 2.1

Mrs. Bailey, a tenth-grade history teacher at Carver High, frequently encourages her CLD students to watch one hour of television in English daily. She also shows movies in English to her CLD students. Are television and movies in the second language a good source of comprehensible input for second language acquisition?

Television and movies can be useful for promoting second language acquisition *if* they are connected to grade-level content. **Contextualization** is essential when using television and movies in the classroom, and these types of media should be connected to content objectives. Although some teachers feel that simply submerging students in the second language is an effective way of enhancing their linguistic capabilities, Mrs. Bailey *may* be doing a disservice to her adolescent CLD students. Snow and colleagues (1976) argue that, without support and guidance, adolescents are neither emotionally receptive nor able to interact productively with others in order to achieve the *i* + 1 level of comprehensible input that Krashen (1982) proposes for L2 acquisition. Television and movies in a second language may cause anxiety if they are not contextualized or are not viewed at intervals with time for group discussion.

Better yet, Mrs. Bailey might use video segments for meaningful development of an integrated or thematic unit. Pally (1994) argues that the potential for learning is much higher when the medium is maximized in this fashion. Mrs. Bailey might also have the students videotape special moments from lessons, such as presentations, performances, or discussion circles, and then share them with their family members.

■ *What other strategies involving media or technology might Mrs. Bailey use to help her CLD students learn English? What does it mean to contextualize media and technology appropriately within your classroom practice or your future practice?*

learning as a proactive and dynamic process. According to this view, learning involves selecting information, organizing it, relating it to prior knowledge, using it in appropriate contexts, and reflecting on the process (Chamot, 2007; Chamot, 2009; Chamot & O'Malley, 1994; Gagné, 1985).

Research and analysis suggest that a focus on learning strategies with CLD students holds much promise for supporting their development of English literacy skills as well as high-order thinking skills. Key research findings include:

- More proficient CLD students use more strategies more frequently than less proficient second language learners (Chamot & El-Dinary, 1999; Cohen, 2011; García, 1998; Jimenez, Garcia, & Pearson, 1996).
- More proficient CLD students better monitor their comprehension than less proficient students (Chamot & El-Dinary, 1999; Jimenez et al., 1996).
- More proficient CLD students use more effective strategies (or the same strategies more effectively) than less proficient learners (Chamot & El-Dinary, 1999; Cohen, 2011).
- Through explicit instruction and modeling, CLD students can learn to use new learning strategies (Chamot & O'Malley, 1996; Cobb, 2004; Gersten, 1996; Jimenez, 1997).
- Transfer of learning strategies can occur between languages (García, 1998; Goldenberg, 2008; Jimenez et al., 1996; Wolfersberger, 2001).
- When CLD students make strategic use of both languages to construct meaning from text, they have greater comprehension (Cummins, 2000; Fox, 2003; García, 1998; Jimenez, 1997; Jimenez et al., 1996; Walqui, 2012).

Chamot and O'Malley (1994) have summarized three broad categories of learning strategies: cognitive, metacognitive, and social/affective. Although the classification scheme for learning strategies has been modified more recently to address instructional purposes (see Chapter 9 of this text and Chamot, 2009, for additional details), these three categories illustrate the cognitive processes that CLD students use to construct meaning. **Cognitive learning strategies** are among the first described. These strategies typically involve the mental or physical manipulation of the material to be learned. For example, a student might physically separate items to be learned into groups (words, grammar rules, etc.), or he or she might mentally categorize information using a graphic organizer in order to create a more relevant organization for long-term memory. Among specific cognitive strategies highlighted by Chamot and O'Malley are resourcing, grouping, note taking, and elaboration. *Elaboration* of prior knowledge involves the mental manipulation of new information. In this process, a language learner compares new information with known information and draws analogies from her or his existing background knowledge. Accordingly, the cognitive strategy of elaboration applies to all four literacy domains: listening, speaking, reading, and writing. By first assessing the prior experiences and knowledge that CLD students bring to the classroom and then guiding them to make curricular connections to those experiences and understandings, teachers encourage students to elaborate on their prior knowledge. Cognitive learning strategies set classroom conditions for the students to take ownership of their learning. Students who are taught to capitalize on using cognitive learning strategies that are effective for their personal learning often are much more successful in acquiring a new language regardless of context. It is important that both EFL and ESL teachers understand the significance of modeling, rehearsing, and supporting the use of learning strategies in their classroom.

> **Illustrated Concept 2.2**
>
> To enhance academic and cognitive growth, ask the students to describe their thought processes in solving a problem or addressing a particular academic challenge.

Social/affective learning strategies highlight the interconnectedness of the cognitive and the sociocultural dimensions of the CLD student biography and may involve the learner as an individual or the learner in interaction with another or others. At the individual level, one such strategy is using self-talk as a means to increase self-confidence. Chamot and O'Malley (1994) argue that self-talk benefits students because it tends to reassure students and lower their anxiety levels, thereby lowering the affective filter. At the interactive level, social/affective learning strategies include cooperation and questioning for clarification. According to Chamot and O'Malley, "*Asking questions for clarification* is particularly critical for ESL students because they will so often need to exercise this skill in their grade-level classrooms" (1994, p. 63). This strategy enables students to obtain additional explanations for clarification or verification of their understanding from peers or the teacher. Teachers may promote these social/affective strategies by fostering a communicative learning environment in which CLD students are encouraged to voice their concerns and interact with others in content learning, regardless of their L2 abilities. From our own work both in U.S. schools and abroad, we have learned that social/affective strategies are the most underutilized tools for increasing student engagement, communication, and application of the English language.

> **Illustrated Concept 2.3**
>
> Challenge CLD students academically and cognitively by fostering collaboration of heterogeneous cooperative groups that guide students to collectively discuss and practice new concepts and skills as well as share with each other how concepts relate to their cultures, home environments, and past experiences.

Metacognitive learning strategies relate solely to the student and his or her own cognitive processes. Planning, monitoring, and evaluating the learning process represent further subdivisions of metacognitive strategies. Culturally and linguistically diverse students use metacognitive strategies to understand and enhance their learning processes. At the level of planning, metacognitive strategies include advance organization, organizational planning, selective attention, and self-management (Chamot & O'Malley, 1994). The selective attention strategy emphasizes metacognitive planning for specific words, phrases, images, or types of information that contribute to learning.

The metacognitive strategies involving literacy development include monitoring comprehension and monitoring production (Chamot & O'Malley, 1994). As CLD students monitor comprehension, their metacognition focuses on whether they understand what they are listening to or reading. If the students do not understand, they apply corrective strategies to construct meaning. As CLD students are speaking or writing, they monitor production to ensure that the language being produced is understandable to others. Students can then evaluate the extent to which they met their goals by reflecting on and self-assessing their learning at the end of the task.

■ **Snapshot of Classroom Practice 2.3**   Learning Strategies

Cognitive Learning Strategy
This student uses a word wall with words and images to assist him with his daily journaling. All students are allowed to take these words back to their seats to aid them in their writing.

(Courtesy of Amanda Ryan, Ft. Riley, Kansas)

Social/Affective Strategy
Through cooperation, these students are able to gain multiple perspectives on the key vocabulary words of the lesson.

(Courtesy of Heather Lofflin, Lawrence, Kansas)

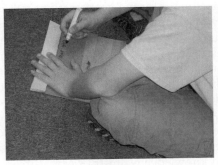

Metacognitive Learning Strategy
A student uses a vocabulary foldable to organize his learning of new terms.

(Courtesy of Jenny Wilk, Lawrence, Kansas)

Cognitive Dimension: Implications for Classroom and School Practice across All Contexts

The teacher's thorough understanding of the CLD student's prior schooling, language experiences, or knowledge base enables informed instructional planning. Students' prior schooling experiences may vary by country of origin and type of school (e.g., private versus public school). Proactive teachers explore the environment of prior schooling, language use and exposure to the target language outside the classroom, and the teaching styles used. Since these experiences greatly influence preferred learning styles, effective teachers use this information to gauge CLD student responses to the new environment and make decisions based on the information they have gathered about the learner and classroom community.

> **Illustrated Concept 2.4**
>
> Make instruction more meaningful through the incorporation of manipulatives and games. The Internet can be a great resource! Ensure that activities involve students in the learning process in relevant and authentic ways.

Assumptions about the knowledge base that CLD students bring to the classroom are common. A student's limited English proficiency does not imply a limited knowledge base. Conversely, even though CLD students come to school with rich knowledge and experiences, educators cannot assume that all students come with the same knowledge and experiential backgrounds. In a culturally rich classroom, insightful teachers pay particular attention to the extensive prior learning and experiences of each student. For example, although a student who has just arrived in the United States from Bosnia or Cambodia may know little about the U.S. Civil War, she or he may have an extensive understanding of the realities of civil war as well as its socioeconomic impact on a country.

Global Connections 2.2
Music, media, technology, and the movement of English-speaking people across continents may provide students in EFL classrooms with opportunities they may not have had in the past. Providing time and setting conditions for the learner to share her or his experiences, language, and knowledge base during the English lesson may set the stage for using student knowledge and experience to make connections to new concepts and vocabulary.

Such a student may possess a much richer understanding than students who have spent their entire lives in the United States. Similarly, a student from Costa Rica may have extensive personal knowledge of the rain forest. Teachers might capitalize on such knowledge in a lesson on climate. Think about the student in the Voices from the Field 2.1 and reflect on your own past experiences.

Reflective teachers use informal conversations (translated as necessary) with the CLD student (or family caregiver) to avoid assumptions regarding prior learning and cognitive development. These teachers maximize such conversations to understand the extensive and rich experiences that their students bring to the classroom. Such practices facilitate accommodative instructional planning and eliminate redundancy. As meaning has a great impact on

whether information and skills will be learned and stored, teachers strive to make curricular connections to *students'* past experiences, not just their own (Sousa, 2011). Acknowledging students' background knowledge is illustrated by watching this video.

■ Voices from the Field 2.1

The Reward of Student

"One of the students that made incredible gain last year in academic knowledge was a newly arrived female senior from Mexico. When she arrived, she was definitely in the silent period. Not only was she vocally silent, but she was silent, so to speak, in the other areas of reading and writing, too. A veteran district ESL instructor tested her by using the IPT test. Her results showed that she was a non-English reader, writer, and speaker.

Partway through the first quarter, I began questioning her diagnosed level according to the IPT tests. She was making gains that seemed way too fast. I went downstairs to the counselor's office and we pulled her academic transcript from Mexico. She had been very successful in Mexico and she had even taken English classes for three years there! So next, I set up a meeting and invited her and her father. She was still fairly silent and her father started by translating for her. He then challenged her to try to use some of the language skills she had already learned from school in Mexico and speak. She did hesitantly at first, but as the meeting went on she grew in courage and began communicating more and more.

Once we discovered where she was at in her content knowledge through the use of more authentic assessments than the IPT test, I was able to help her achieve in a greater way. She completed all of her credits and graduated with a 4.0 her senior year. She is now enrolled in a community college.

This situation showed me many things. One is that I should never underestimate what a student is capable of, despite his or her score on a standardized test, because given the right support, that student can really excel. Another is that it is so important to authentically assess my students and not rely heavily at all on standardized test scores. This student accomplished much more than any other student in that graduating class who may have scored higher than her on a standardized test. She went from underachieving, without much motivation, to being very successful and even helping the other CLD students in the class."

■ *James Callahan, high school teacher*

theory *into* Practice 2.1

Three broad categories of learning strategies emphasized in the literature on methods for CLD students are cognitive, metacognitive, and social/affective (Chamot & O'Malley, 1994). These strategies are a product of cognitive theory (Gagné, 1985; Shuell, 1986) and research on learning strategies (O'Malley & Chamot, 1990). In regard to learning strategies, Chamot and O'Malley (1994) have argued that (1) active learners are better learners, (2) academic language learning is more effective when it is supported by learning strategies, and (3) learning strategies transfer to new tasks. Metacognitive learning strategies primarily relate to the student and his or her own planning, monitoring, and evaluating of cognitive processes. The metacognitive learning strategy of selective attention encourages students to listen or read selectively, scan, and find specific information such as key words, phrases, ideas, linguistic markers, and more.

■ *What are the implications of this metacognitive learning strategy for literacy development among CLD students? In what ways might you teach CLD students to maximize this learning strategy in their literacy development? What do you anticipate would be the most difficult aspect of the strategy to teach? How might you overcome this difficulty?*

Reflective teachers find an appropriate balance through instruction that is cognitively demanding yet comprehensible. They take into consideration the cognitive–developmental level of the student while making necessary accommodations for his or her level of L2 proficiency. Such a balance will enhance student success in the classroom. Just as an assessment of prior knowledge or cognitive skills should guide planning for cognitively demanding instruction, teacher monitoring for L2 proficiency and stage of second language acquisition (SLA) should guide the comprehensibility of instructional input. Empathetic teachers recognize that comprehensible input should flow from the student's current language abilities, as suggested by his or her stage of SLA (these stages of SLA are detailed in the next chapter). Incomprehensible instructional input increases the need for reteaching and slows the student's progress toward language and academic growth. Instruction that targets comprehensible input involves frequent checks for understanding. Figure 2.1 provides a useful tool for assessing the balance to be targeted between cognitively demanding and comprehensible instruction.

■ The Academic Dimension of the CLD Student Biography

The **academic dimension** of the CLD student biography involves those readily apparent aspects of the curriculum and instruction that students receive in their matriculation from prekindergarten classrooms to high school graduation and beyond. Less apparent but equally critical to this dimension is an understanding of the differential academic challenges that CLD students encounter, especially those that relate not only to curriculum and instruction but also to academic policy.

This dimension also accounts for those processes that are crucial to successful academic performance in the public schools. Culturally and linguistically diverse students must not only master a second language but also develop the academic language necessary to perform well in the subject-area domains.

Global Connections 2.3
In EFL contexts, curriculum often reduces language learning to a set of phrases for conventional use. Current trends in EFL are beginning to move to a more literacy-based teaching in order to prepare students to more fully participate in additional academic activities. This focus necessitates a holistic approach to understand the challenges students will face as they transition from programs where language is taught for social purposes to those where learners are moving toward global citizenship.

Academic Challenges

The range of multifaceted academic difficulties that CLD students frequently encounter in schools is formidable and is exemplified by those challenges summarized in Table 2.2. Many of these challenges intensify with each succeeding grade level and increasingly test students' academic language abilities. These academic challenges (see Table 2.2) can be categorized according to those that primarily relate to issues of curriculum and instruction or those

■ **t a b l e   2 . 2**   Academic Dimension of the CLD Student Biography

Challenges	Processes
Curriculum and Instruction	Transfer of academic knowledge and skills from L1 to L2
Reductionist curriculum often driven by a strict focus on high-stakes assessments	Integration of concepts learned and to be learned across academic disciplines
Inadequate opportunities for classroom interactions involving academic, especially domain-specific, language	The resolution of knowledge gaps based on current and prior curriculum and academic experiences
Content-area assessments	Academic language development in L2 (a process of at least three dimensions of the CLD student biography)
• Inordinately product- versus process-centered	• BICS/CALP distinction
• Decontextualized, often standardized	Domain-specific capacity building for academic performance
• Sometimes norm- rather than criterion-referenced	• To address domain-specific:
• Frequently focused on declarative versus procedural knowledge	• Discourse organization
• Typically lack opportunities to demonstrate critical thinking	• Grammatical forms and structures
Lack of readiness among subject-area and grade-level teachers for the differential academic learning needs of CLD students	• Vocabulary
Disproportionate number of CLD students placed in special education and remedial classrooms and the curricular difference between those settings and grade-level classrooms	• Academic language skills
Academic presentation formats of content-area textbooks	
• Technical vocabulary	
• Vocabulary with domain-specific meanings	
• Unfamiliar grammatical structures	
• Complex discourse organization	
• Assumptions about prior knowledge and experiences grounded in the dominant culture	
Academic Policy	
Language learning as a remedial focus versus language acquisition as a subcomponent of content-area academic learning	
Lack of recognition or reward structures for process gains as well as incremental gains in academic performance and product-measured improvement	
Criterion- and assessment-based exclusion from gifted and talented programs	

that relate mostly to academic policies (especially those formulated at the district level). Among the academic challenges involving curriculum and instruction are product- versus process-centered assessments in the content areas, the presentation formats of content-area textbooks, and inadequate opportunities to practice domain-specific academic language. Academic policy challenges for CLD students include a compensatory focus on language learning, a lack of recognition or reward structures for process gains, and virtual exclusion from gifted and talented programs.

From the standpoint of curriculum and instruction, one of the most contemporary and harmful academic challenges for language learners is the trend toward increasingly reductionistic curricula driven by a strict focus on high-stakes assessments at the national, state, and local levels. National reform agendas in the United States, which came to the forefront with the No Child Left Behind Act of 2001 (NCLB, 2002), continue to drive current educational agendas. Although these initiatives are implemented to increase accountability, as measured by high-stakes assessments, it is often at the expense of low socioeconomic status (SES) and CLD students. Such efforts have been the trend for a number of years, not only at the national level but also in states across the country.

Several researchers have tracked, studied, and analyzed the outcomes of many such reform initiatives (Abedi & Dietel, 2004; Bastian, Fruchter, Gittell, Greer, & Hoskins, 1986; Berlak, 1999; Darling-Hammond, 1992, 2007; Earl & LeMahieu, 1997; Lieberman & Grolnick, 1997; McLaren, 2007; McNeil, 2000a, 2000b). In general, these outcomes indicate that school and practitioner accountability systems that are directly linked to high-stakes assessments yield a number of problematic consequences, especially for students in schools with high percentages of low SES and CLD students. First among these consequences is a predictable tendency among educators, whose performance evaluations and employment may depend on student standardized test scores, to *teach to the test* (Berlak, 1999; McCarthey, 2008; McNeil, 2000b). This focus on facts and decontextualized processes, in turn, leads to teacher- and district-initiated efforts to substitute commercial test-preparation materials for the regular curriculum (Earl & LeMahieu, 1997; Jones, Jones, & Hargrove, 2003; McNeil, 2000b). Such substitutes for the regular curriculum prevent many educators from using their professional knowledge of the subject and of the students to provide cognitively, academically, and linguistically rich instruction that speaks to the sociocultural realities of our society.

Indeed, this setting aside of teachers' professional knowledge and capacities yields a reductionist curriculum that is inordinately focused on basic skills, redundant workbooks, drill-and-practice approaches to instruction, rote memorization of decontextualized facts and declarative knowledge, isolated practice of computations, and repetitive routines that target the retention of basic test-taking strategies.

In turn, this "dumbing down" of the curriculum yields notable consequences for students, especially low SES students and CLD students, whose likelihood of academic success is profoundly threatened and challenged (Ketter & Pool, 2001; McNeil, 2000a, 2000b; Menken, 2009). According to McNeil (2000b), who researched the outcomes of high-stakes testing and **reductionist curricula**, the major content areas (especially reading, writing, and mathematics) show evidence of such consequences. In the area of reading, the teachers she studied reported that curriculum reductionism and concentrated test-preparation actually hampered students' ability to "read for meaning outside the test setting"

(McNeil, 2000b, p. 3). Teachers who participated in her research reported that students:

- Were undermined in their ability to read sustained passages
- Exhibited a reduced capacity to read longer works
- Had so internalized the format for reading test skills that many had not formed the habits necessary to read for meaning and comprehension

In the area of writing, the teachers whom McNeil studied reported that students, especially low SES students, had become so programmed to basic skills of the test format for the persuasive essay that what they wrote was "of virtually no importance; conforming to the form was the requirement, and the students practiced every day" (2000b, p. 4). In this situation, teaching to the test ingrained in students the necessity of form and structure to the detriment of communication.

Of perhaps greatest concern are McNeil's (2000b) findings regarding the impact of a reductionist, test-focused curriculum on the mathematics skills and capacities of low SES and CLD students. Her findings indicate that instruction driven by this curriculum did not focus on critical capacities such as problem conceptualization, selection among possible approaches, or metacognition about the procedural knowledge used to solve the problem. Instead, teachers were prompted (consistent with the notion of teaching to the test) to emphasize reductive mathematics, computational accuracy, familiarity with basic operations, and test-taking strategies.

As these examples illustrate, a reductionist curriculum driven by the anticipated performance of students, their teachers, and their schools in high-stakes assessments poses a formidable obstacle to the school success of CLD students. Academic challenges, whether most directly related to curriculum and instruction issues or to policy issues, demonstrate that the success of language learners in the content areas involves much more than the question of whether the student is willing to learn English.

In addition, a misunderstanding of the role of native language in a student's academic development can limit a CLD student's academic growth potential. In fact, the findings of Saville-Troike (1984) strongly suggest that for many complex challenges and tasks in the academic areas, CLD students may actually be delayed in their development by the insistence that such challenges be addressed in the target language (i.e., English). Her findings indicate that CLD students are more successful in addressing such complex cognitive tasks in their own native language. Among such challenges are the context-reduced tasks of reading, writing, drawing inferences, and forming schemata. When these challenges are targeted in the native language, the skills attained and the processes learned will then transfer

> **Illustrated Concept 2.5**
>
> To target the differential needs and diverse learning styles of students, use a variety of strategies, such as visuals, graphic organizers, hands-on activities, and guarded vocabulary (adjusting the pace and complexity of vocabulary used).

Global Connections 2.4
Academic strengths and challenges tend to differ between students in ESL and EFL classrooms. According to Hinkel and Fotos (2002), students in ESL classrooms gain a high L2 oral ability but struggle to acquire fundamental grammatical distinctions in that same language. However, students in EFL classrooms have a high-functioning knowledge of grammar rules through drills and repetition, but this does not result in true comprehension of the language.

Global Connections 2.5
Using strategies such as preview-view-review (Freeman & Freeman, 1998) for introducing and reviewing vocabulary may increase engagement, motivation, and learning. It is important to use the native language in purposeful, strategic, and structured ways when in the EFL classroom. Ultimately, the native language—as a bridge to new English vocabulary—is relevant and useful in all contexts.

to a target or second language, such as English (Saville-Troike, 1984).

Likewise, Kersaint, Thompson, and Petkova (2009) argue that CLD students should be allowed to use their native language as a resource for learning mathematics. When teachers encourage students to first process information in the language in which they are most familiar, students are able to utilize their existing mathematical knowledge to enhance their concept development. Then students can focus on communicating their new understandings in English. Regardless of the content area, an academic environment that maximizes social interaction among students to build both native and target language proficiency among CLD students facilitates the transfer of content, processes, and strategies from L1 to L2.

Academic Processes

No discussion of the academic dimension of methods for CLD students would be complete without an exploration of the processes involved for the students. The right-hand column of Table 2.2 provides an overview of these processes. Some of these processes, like others associated with dimensions already explored, continue to demonstrate the interrelatedness of the four dimensions of the CLD student biography. For example, the processes of academic language development and the transfer of academic knowledge and skills from L1 to L2 emphasize relationships among the cognitive, linguistic, and academic dimensions. Similarly, the processes that seek to integrate concepts from prior knowledge with those to be learned in the content areas again stress both the academic and cognitive dimensions of the CLD student biography.

The process of academic language development in L2 is particularly difficult for language learners. It is also a process that often generates confusion within the learning community. Much of this confusion arises from a lack of understanding about the distinction between basic interpersonal communication skills (BICS) and cognitive academic language proficiency (CALP). That is, the confusion is grounded in the difference between conversational and academic language use. This distinction evolved during the 1970s and 1980s when second language educators and researchers became concerned that CLD students who exhibited second language proficiency in primarily oral and interpersonal communications did not perform well when using their second language in academic contexts (Chamot, 2009; Chamot & O'Malley, 1994). In response to this ambiguity, Cummins (1981) developed a theory describing second language proficiency in terms of BICS and CALP. Cummins (1994) began to refer to these different constructs of language proficiency simply as *conversational language* and *academic language*.

Students who have achieved a conversational level of language proficiency have the ability to communicate interactively in familiar situations in which the context of communication tends to support the meaning of the discourse (Cummins, 1989). Most students in a second language environment can acquire conversational proficiency in two to three years (Diaz-Rico, 2014; Genesee, Lindholm-Leary, Saunders, & Christian, 2006; Ovando, Combs, & Collier, 2011). These language learners *appear* to be fluent speakers of the second language. However, according to Cummins (1989), students who have acquired only a conversational and not an academic level of proficiency have difficulty when trying to understand and communicate about cognitively complex concepts in the target language, especially in academic contexts.

Competitive performance in the content areas involves more than interpersonal communication skills. Because CLD students must typically communicate in English in the school environment, the content classes such as science, social studies, mathematics, and language arts become their communicative environment (Mohan, 1986). Collier (1995) has argued that such academic contexts demand a deep level of academic language proficiency in L2.

Constructing meaning using unfamiliar academic concepts and new cognitive processes can be difficult for any student. Learning in a second language multiplies the difficulty of the task because students must construct meaning from a less familiar language, unfamiliar academic concepts, and new cognitive processes all at the same time. In routine conversational language uses, a CLD student can focus on meaning construction alone. For academic language uses, a student in an ESL/EFL classroom must negotiate meaning while juggling multiple processes.

Accordingly, instructional support must encompass the development of cognitive and academic language skills in the second language (Cummins, 1989). Informed teachers plan instruction that targets academic language development using the content-area curriculum. As needed, key curriculum concepts are previewed or contextualized. Teachers may also choose to scaffold their instruction. Such scaffolding involves the incorporation of instructional aids, student interaction, and other lesson modifications to ensure that content concepts are comprehensible to language learners.

Academic language proficiency in L2 involves the capacity to understand and produce language that is both abstract and complex. Second language learners who have acquired academic language proficiency have reached an advanced level of language development. The advanced language competencies associated with this development include the ability to understand language in a decontextualized, unfamiliar situation with limited interaction (Cummins, 1989). The CLD students who have acquired academic language in L2 do not require nonverbal cues to construct meaning from a given situation (Chamot, 2009; Chamot & O'Malley, 1994).

Another set of academic processes involves capacity building that is particular to subject-area domains with the goal of enhanced academic performance. This domain-specific capacity building is particularly difficult for CLD students because it typically demands a number of adjustments, each of which varies by subject area and involves increasing academic language proficiency in the second language. These demands require the student to excel in domain-specific adjustments to the following:

- Discourse organization of the domain
- Grammatical forms and structures particular to that domain
- Specialized vocabulary of the domain
- Particular academic language skills necessitated by the nature of the domain

Each of these difficult adjustments for CLD students depends on the content area in question. Some examples from the key content areas illustrate the complexities involved.

In mathematics, adjustments to the vocabulary of the subject domain are often difficult for language learners for at least three reasons. First, the mathematics classroom tends to abound in assumptions concerning students' prior knowledge of specialized terms such as *denominator, subtraction, divisor,* and *multiplication*. Second, terms that have one meaning in one subject domain can assume an entirely different meaning in the vocabulary of mathematics; such terms include *quarter, column, product, rational, even,* and *table* (Chamot, 2009; Chamot & O'Malley, 1994). Finally, the vocabulary of mathematics tends to encompass a variety of homophones (words that sound like other common words) and can be especially troublesome for CLD students who are unaccustomed to the new language. Examples of such domain-specific homophonic pairs include *angle* and *ankle, addition* and *audition,* and *factor* and *factory* (Garbe, 1985). Accordingly, reflective teachers review the academic curriculum for vocabulary that may be problematic for CLD students. These teachers are then in a proactive instructional position to preview, scaffold, or contextualize this vocabulary as needed to enhance the academic development of CLD students.

> **Illustrated Concept 2.6**
>
> Provide grade-level instruction that is content-based and uses age-appropriate material. Note that modifications such as scaffolding may be necessary for the clarification of content being taught.

The domain of science is exceptionally demanding on the academic language skills and capacities of CLD students. Scientific inquiry requires students to propose and defend hypotheses, or arguments, and to use complex linguistic structures and advanced reasoning. These linguistic structures often prove exceedingly complex for second language learners (Anstrom, 1998; Chamot, 2009; Chamot & O'Malley, 1994; Rosebery, Warren, & Conant, 1992). Teachers can assist language learners in this domain by teaching metacognitive strategies that focus the students' attention not only on the products of academic thinking but also on the processes.

In the language arts domain, the variety of texts and materials used often demands extraordinary capacity building for academic performance among CLD

dilemmas of *Practice* 2.2

Huy, a 16-year-old adolescent, recently enrolled in a rural midwestern school district after only two weeks in the United States. After taking a language proficiency test, he scored as a non-English speaker. He has had formal and continuous schooling since the age of 4. However, no formal school records have been provided to the school. Therefore, he has been placed in ninth-grade, remedial content-area courses. Huy excels in his art, mathematics, and science classes. He is even asked to assist his peers with their math assignments. He is quiet and well-mannered with both students and staff. After several weeks, his math teacher notices that Huy has become distracted and inconsistent in completing his classwork. His math teacher also notices that Huy becomes frustrated when asked to assist his peers with assignments.

Individualized Instruction

Academic Needs: Huy has had continuous and formal schooling. His teachers should assess his level of literacy development and capacities for math, science, and social studies using his native language. It is also important to assess what his strongest subjects have been.

Instructional Modifications: Assess Huy's existing content-area knowledge through conversations (translated as necessary) with him, his parents or caregivers, or a paraprofessional who speaks his first language. Build on Huy's existing skills to capitalize on prior knowledge. (It may be that he does not need to be placed in remedial classes, especially if he is provided accommodative instruction.)

Linguistic Needs: Huy has scored as a non-English speaker in language proficiency. He may need time to discuss content with peers who speak the same native language. He will need extensive instructional adaptations in the content areas and in grade-level vocabulary.

Instructional Modifications: Provide extensive wait time; use enunciated and slightly slower speech. Review and illustrate key terms for lessons. Create opportunities for Huy to use his native language in class with other peers. Heterogeneous grouping may alleviate his recent problem of working with peers.

Cognitive Needs: Huy enjoys working alone. He excels in art, math, and science, especially when given the freedom to express himself. When not challenged, Huy becomes bored, even angry.

Instructional Modifications: At times, give Huy the choice to work alone. Do not impose the task of tutoring other students unless he has offered to do so. Find ways for Huy to extend his learning by asking him to do his own research on topics of interest related to your class; such modifications are more likely to keep him challenged.

Sociocultural Needs: Huy is concerned with pleasing his teachers. He is the youngest of five sisters and brothers. His siblings often supervise him.

Instructional Modifications: Find out about Huy's interests and hobbies. Integrate his interests into your daily instruction. Teach the class about Huy's native country and make connections to your grade-level content. Such accommodations will prove to be a validating experience for Huy and will provide an opportunity for other students to learn about different cultures.

■ *If you were Huy's math teacher, what would be your first "next step" toward ensuring that Huy's academic, linguistic, cognitive, and sociocultural needs were met appropriately?*

students. Earlier discussion in this chapter highlights the many ways in which students can maximize past experiences and prior knowledge to make sense out of texts and draw meaning from learning materials. Yet, CLD students in the language arts classroom often are asked to read and comprehend (at a high level of complexity) texts and materials that are culturally unfamiliar, use complex vocabulary, involve

Global Connections 2.6
When learners in EFL classrooms pay special attention to strategies such as planning and self-monitoring, the interactive reading processes pave the way for reading development and comprehension. Learning how to read with ease promotes students' motivation to read more English materials, which, in turn, increases their English proficiency.

convoluted themes and propositions, rely on antiquated syntax, or are grounded in culturally different writing genres (Anstrom, 1998; August & Hakuta, 1997; Escamilla, 2000; Coyne, Kameenui, & Carnine, 2010; Sasser, 1992). Effective teachers help CLD students with these difficulties by using differentiated instructional strategies such as:

- Preteaching culturally different concepts
- Previewing key vocabulary
- Webbing or otherwise illustrating major themes
- Discussing the ways in which writing genres can differ

As these examples demonstrate, there are a number of content areas in which domain-specific capacity building for academic performance involves difficult processes for the CLD student. Such processes dramatically illustrate the interconnectedness of the four dimensions of the CLD student biography: the academic, the cognitive, the linguistic, and the sociocultural. Think about the strategy depicted in Figure 2.2; in what ways does it support the four dimensions?

Academic Dimension: Implications for Classroom and School Practice

Reflective teachers avoid a reductionist approach to lesson planning. Often, educators associate a limited ability to speak the language of instruction with an inability to perform academic tasks at grade level. Teachers both in EFL and ESL classrooms sometimes use materials that are reductionist and unmotivating, such as drill-and-practice methods for language learning or content-area teaching. However, CLD students often are able to learn grade-level academic language and concepts when the curriculum (or instruction) is appropriately adapted to accommodate CLD learners. Effective teachers provide all learners with culturally, academically, cognitively, and linguistically rich instruction. High expectations for the academic performance of all students are realistic when this instruction is appropriately adapted and modified for CLD students.

Insightful teachers know that the BICS/CALP distinction is crucial to the academic success of language learners. If CLD students are to build academic language proficiency, then the academic curriculum must serve as the content for language instruction. Effective teachers maximize accommodative strategies to adapt the curriculum and classroom instruction for students' CALP development in L2. For example, teachers can examine the curriculum to identify the key academic vocabulary to teach in lessons. This vocabulary can then be previewed before each lesson. Teachers should isolate critical concepts to teach from the content-area curriculum. They can then modify and scaffold instruction to teach these concepts in a comprehensible manner. Such modifications might include photo illustrations of concepts, hands-on activities with manipulatives, heterogeneous peer group learning, and more.

■ **f i g u r e   2 . 2**

From Pictures to Words

What I See . . .	What I Think . . .
Picture #1	Picture #1
Picture #2	Picture #2

Classroom Directions:

- Select appropriate pictures to support the inductive acquisition of key vocabulary terms.
    - You can copy pictures from the text or pull images from other sources (e.g., the Internet, magazines, newspapers, books, picture cards).
- Show students the preselected images one at a time (allow a few minutes for students to complete the "What I See . . ." and "What I Think . . ." handout).
    - Encourage students to reach into their permanent memory folder to get to all the words that they can think of.
    - Make sure to utilize the question prompts as students work on the handout by asking them to describe all the things they see in the picture as well as what they think of when they look at the picture.
- After students have completed the handout, read a passage from the text that defines the meaning of the words in context and have students match the picture to the appropriate part of the text.
    - Have students discuss in pairs or small teams how they are matching the pictures before discussing them as a whole group.
- Next, show students the actual dictionary definitions for the words and have them again match the pictures to the appropriate definition.
    - Be sure to have students discuss in pairs or small teams how they are matching the definitions before discussing them as a whole group.
- Finally, show students the actual words and ask students which pictures they think match the words, based on what they have written.
    - To make sure all students have a chance to provide a rationale, have them individually or in pairs or small teams create a group statement that explains how and why they matched the pictures to the words.

The ongoing use of peers or small teams supports CLD students' language and academic development throughout this activity.

Source: From Socorro Herrera; Kevin Murry; Robin M Cabral (2007) *Assessment Accommodations for Classroom Teachers of Culturally and Linguistically Diverse Students* published by Kansas State University. Copyright © 2007 by Kansas State University. Reprinted by permission.

Connect, Engage, Challenge

CONNECT
Review and Reflect on the Reading

1. What does it mean to *contextualize* a learning environment, and what does it involve? Reflect on and discuss the ways in which your socialization has or has not prepared you to contextualize learning.

2. What is the primary origin of students' preferred learning styles? Should all instruction target the preferred learning style of the CLD student? Why or why not?

3. List at least three characteristics of a constructivist learning environment. In what ways is such an environment beneficial for CLD students?

4. Explain the concept of *elaboration*. What are the connections that teachers should be aware of between elaboration and the prior knowledge, skills, and capacities that a CLD student brings to the classroom?

5. What sorts of factors external to the school, especially sociopolitical factors, often lead to reductionist curricula in schools? Reflect on and discuss the teacher's potential role in countering such influences.

6. What types of learning strategies help CLD students cope with the complex demands of content-area lessons or classes? Describe instructional strategies that a teacher can implement to also aid CLD learners in the subject-area domains.

7. Describe the importance of the relevance of new information to the CLD learner. In what ways do constructivist learning environments emphasize instructional relevance?

8. In what ways might a teacher encourage CLD students to maximize the social/affective learning strategy of asking questions for clarification? Reflect on and explain why the CLD student might not already be comfortable with the use of such a strategy.

ENGAGE
Share What You Learned

1. Explore various learning tasks for students. Then discuss whether each task is context-embedded or context-reduced and whether each task is cognitively undemanding or cognitively demanding. Chart your findings for each task according to the quadrant described in this chapter.

2. This chapter details three types of learning strategies that CLD students can use to enhance their cognitive development and improve their academic performance. Discuss ways in which an educator might teach each of these three types of learning strategies: cognitive, metacognitive, and social/affective.

3. Among the four dimensions of the CLD student biography, one dimension is frequently neglected. Discuss some of the challenges and processes of this dimension that CLD students must transcend in order to be successful in school.

CHALLENGE
It's Not Real until You Practice

Preservice Teachers

1. Observe a grade-level class in which CLD students are instructed. What modifications or accommodations is the teacher making to deliver more comprehensible classroom instruction?

2. By observing her or his instructional methods, identify the specific strategies the teacher incorporates to ensure that the content is cognitively challenging for CLD students.

3. Interview a CLD student regarding the learning strategies the teacher incorporates that seem to help the student acquire the language and content more easily.

In-Service Teachers

1. Imagine that you are a middle school science teacher who instructs a grade-level class that is composed of native-English-speaking and CLD students who are at varying levels of English proficiency. You are about to begin a unit on volcanoes. What instructional accommodations can you add that will help *all* students in your class meet the academic standards embedded in the topic?

2. Keeping in mind the various backgrounds of your students, list some of the varied types of learning styles your students bring to the classroom and how you can capitalize on each one with instructional accommodations.

3. Give students a list of challenging or new vocabulary words they will be encountering in a lesson. Once they are in heterogeneous cooperative groups, instruct them to group related words and then create their own categories under which to place these grouped words. They may need to use a thesaurus or dictionary to get some sense of the meaning of the words during this process. Before beginning the lesson, have groups discuss and compare their categories and their rationale for placing specific words in these categories. The purpose of this activity is to activate prior knowledge and stimulate students' thought processes as they manipulate these words in the context of their own experiences and prior knowledge. This strategy makes vocabulary words more personally relevant and provides a foundation for encountering them in the lesson, which may present a less familiar context.

tips for practice

In elementary classrooms, consider:

- Prompting CLD students to think of different ways to solve problems by asking questions such as "In what other ways could Carina figure that out? Are there other possible solutions?"

- Providing opportunities for students to practice content-area vocabulary through choral reading or paired writing activities.

- Identifying the prior knowledge your students bring to the classroom in order to make connections to the ideas and concepts that you are teaching through KWL charts, freewriting, observation, and journals.

- Establishing learning centers so that your CLD students can explicitly practice the learning strategies on which you are focusing.
- Using visuals such as timelines, maps, and diagrams to clarify complex concepts as much as possible, specifically in social studies units.

In secondary classrooms, consider:

- Modeling or demonstrating the steps of a science experiment as CLD students observe. Then, in cooperative groups, students can discuss and create an outline that includes the main steps that you modeled.
- Identifying where the students in your classroom are from and then using graphic Venn diagrams or T-charts to compare/contrast languages and cultures of your students' native countries or regions, which can then connect to your social studies/history lesson.
- Having CLD students create a story problem that applies to the new math concepts learned. Students will then trade story problems with another group that will solve the problem.
- Providing closure to your content-area lesson with learning logs for language arts lessons. Learning logs consist of journal entries written by the students, which provide them with an opportunity to reflect on the concepts and processes they have learned. This allows students to solidify their thoughts through writing.
- Helping students monitor their language use. For example, learners need to construct

meaning simultaneously as they read for new information. Model expectations of how to complete an academic literacy task by providing questions about the task, how to "fix" comprehension breakdown, how to connect the task to prior knowledge about the topic, and how one might organize the information in the text.

- Emphasize to the students that once a learning strategy has been mastered, they can apply that strategy to other subjects.

In EFL classrooms, consider:

- Providing constructivist learning environments where language development is approached in a holistic manner without an overemphasis on grammar and rules, allowing students the opportunities to develop processes, skills, and positive attitudes toward language learning.
- Integrating opportunities for students to practice the target language within the community (local or global) to ensure their engagement in authentic communication experiences.
- Emphasizing reading strategies in the initial stages of language learning. Such efforts increase the value for students of written materials as important sources of language input.
- Focusing on learning strategies as an avenue for language construction, not just reproduction. A strategic and purposeful approach to learning strategies can especially help students identify the nuances of language in order to communicate more effectively.

Linguistic Dimension of Methods for Culturally and Linguistically Diverse Students

our mission

Our mission for this chapter will be to:

- Explore the language assets and language acquisition needs that CLD students may exhibit in education settings.

We will accomplish this mission by helping you to meet the following learning outcomes:

- Compare and contrast first and second language acquisition processes.
- Summarize key challenges of the linguistic dimension, including the time required for SLA and the dynamics of teaching for authentic literacy development.
- Identify key processes of the linguistic dimension and gain an understanding of concepts about print.
- Summarize instructional planning for CALP development in L1 and L2 that fosters constructivist language acquisition.

Socorro Herrera

**The Linguistic Dimension of the CLD
Student Biography**
> Dynamics of First Language Acquisition (FLA)
> Differences between First and Second Language
>   Acquisition
> Demands of Second Language Acquisition (SLA)

Challenges of the Linguistic Dimension
> Time Required for Second Language Acquisition
> Exposure to Authentic Literacy Instruction and
>   Activities

Processes of the Linguistic Dimension
> Linguistic Process of Second Language Acquisition
> Linguistic Process of Understanding Concepts
>   about Print

**Linguistic Dimension: Implications for Classroom
and School Practice**
> Instructional Planning for CALP Development in
>   L1 and L2
> Anticipating and Preassessing for the Array of
>   Student Biographies
> Fostering Communicative, Constructivist Language
>   Acquisition Environments

key theories and concepts

behaviorist
communicative competence
communicative language learning environment
discourse competence
first language acquisition
grammatical competence
innatist
interactionist

linguistic dimension
natural order hypothesis
scaffolding
silent period
sociolinguistic competence
stages of second language acquisition
strategic competence

Discussions about education for the English learner tend to focus on issues that pertain to the **linguistic dimension** of the culturally and linguistically diverse (CLD) student biography. Chapter 1 summarizes the four dimensions of this biography: the sociocultural, the cognitive, the academic, and the linguistic. As discussed, this more inclusive perspective of a student biography represents a more holistic way to frame the differential learning needs and transition adjustments of CLD students. In this chapter, we focus our attention on the challenges and processes of the linguistic dimension of the student biography, and we discuss relevant issues that have surfaced during our work with students and their teachers.

The Linguistic Dimension of the CLD Student Biography

Not only is a focus on the linguistic dimension predictable in discussions of the student, but it is also a dimension about which a great deal of confusion frequently exists. The following are examples of questions that tend to arise:

- "She speaks English, yet I can't get her to write well in English!"
- "He's been in my class for weeks and has scarcely said one word in English. Do you think we ought to refer him for special education testing?"
- "I've heard her. She speaks English just fine when she's in a game on the playground. Why can't she understand in the classroom?
- "Why do these students always speak in their native language to each other when they have already learned English?"
- "They will never learn English since there are so few opportunities for them outside my classroom to practice. What can I do?"

Dynamics of First Language Acquisition (FLA)

Language and literacy development, whether in the first or the second language, involve difficult challenges and complex processes. For native English speakers, it is often easy to forget the difficulties and transitions that every individual progresses through in learning his or her first language. None of us was born fluent in our native language. However, we sometimes expect students acquiring a new language to respond as if they simply acquired a new language by sitting in our classroom and listening. Each of us, in acquiring our own first language, completed a complex series of processes and transitions, beginning with the development of our oral language capabilities.

> **Illustrated Concept 3.1**
>
> Encourage students' creativity and participation by initiating drama, art, music, and other forms of creative expression.

First language acquisition is the process through which children learn their first language. There are three main theories that explain how children learn their first language: the behaviorist, the innatist, and the interactionist. The **behaviorist** theory states that children are born without any linguistic knowledge, so all language learning is a result of the environment. Children react to language stimuli with responses; if their responses are correct, their language is reinforced and those patterns become habitual. The **innatist** theory states that learning is natural for human beings, meaning that babies enter the world with a biological propensity, an inborn device to learn language (Reutzel & Cooter, 2004). This built-in mechanism for learning language has been coined the *language acquisition device (LAD)*. The **interactionist** theory states that language develops through interaction. Essentially, language acquisition is similar to acquisition of other skills and knowledge. All of these theories help to describe some aspects of first and second language acquisition. Fortunately, many of us experienced nurturing environments for this oral language acquisition. We were bathed in the language through so-called motherese, and our language acquisition trials were praised, scaffolded, supported, and reinforced by family, extended family, friends, and caregivers. By age 5, most of us had subconsciously developed rudimentary understandings of our first language phonology (sound patterns), morphology (word formation), syntax (sentence structure), semantics (word meanings), and pragmatics (understandings of language use in context). Yet our first language development saga was not yet half completed.

A significant number of us experienced our introduction to written language through our transition to formal schooling. Our progression through the various grade levels of this formal education in our first language enhanced our mastery of the language domains (phonology, morphology, syntax, semantics, and pragmatics). As we developed, more complex aspects of oral language acquisition were occurring, including enhanced understandings of the following: the structure of language; discrete distinctions among phonemes (the basic sound units of the language); and differences in meaning, vocabulary, and uses of the language (Lightbrown & Spada, 2013; Ninio & Bruner, 1978; Ochs & Schieffelin, 1984). Indeed, by the time we reached adolescence, successive, incremental exposure to the core subject areas (including science, mathematics, and language arts) had progressively increased our capacity to comprehend the cognitively complex language of instruction, textbooks, and media. Nonetheless, our process of first language development was not yet complete. In fact, many researchers argue that only 50 percent of our first language acquisition processes are complete by age 6, and most individuals require the remainder of their lifetime to complete these processes (Akmajian, Demers, Farmer, & Harnish, 2010; Schieffelin & Eisenberg, 1984).

Differences between First and Second Language Acquisition

No less complex, and in many ways much more intimidating, is the task of second language acquisition. Table 3.1 explores the similarities and differences between first and second language acquisition. As any student proceeds through second language acquisition, he or she is seldom afforded the luxury of an extended period of oral language development as a foundation for other aspects of literacy development. Additionally, the CLD student is rarely able to rely on a home environment that bathes her or him in the second language and scaffolds the trials of second language acquisition. Many parents and caregivers of CLD students are also learning a second language themselves and cannot provide an environment that is conducive to practicing the new language. This is not to say that their capacity to continue the CLD student's development in L1 at home is not also valuable. On the contrary, ongoing development in the native language is indispensable to the student's continuing development in English (Grabe, 2009). Nonetheless, parents and the community environment are not always able to immerse the student in the language that the school culture tends to expect.

The student learning English as a second language struggles with balancing literacy learning skills across different subject areas. On the other hand, the student learning English as a foreign language, depending on the program, is not often provided a classroom context that moves beyond students simply being "bathed"

■ **table 3.1**   Ways in Which First and Second Language Acquisition Compare and Contrast

L1 Acquisition	L1 and L2 Acquisition	L2 Acquisition
Parents or caregivers are the primary language models for first language learners.	Through a process called overgeneralization, a language learner may indiscriminately apply a language rule to many different situations (e.g., *He goed to the store yesterday*).	Second language learners already have a language for communication and thought.
First language learners have innumerable opportunities to interact with language models.	Learners acquire language by interacting with others.	Second language learners can transfer knowledge about language (metalinguistic awareness) and thought processes from the first to the second language.
Most first language learners acquire a high level of first language proficiency.	Learners go through a silent period.	Peers and teachers are the primary language models for second language learners.
First language acquisition is arguably internally motivated by an innate cognitive process, although environmental factors shape development.	Learners need comprehensible input.	Second language learners have a greater repertoire of language learning strategies.
Most people develop a first language.	A highly contextualized, language-rich environment will facilitate language acquisition.	The second language learner may make language mistakes in the second language because he or she is applying rules from the first language to the second language.
Language acquisition is cognitively demanding.	During the initial stages of language acquisition, learners may need more time to process information.	Second language learners can code-switch, which involves using both languages to create greater meaning than could be achieved by relying on only one language.
Language acquisition involves conceptualizing information in new ways and developing new ways of processing information.	Many people do not acquire a high level of second language proficiency.	Second language learners can use cognates to comprehend new words in the second language.
Language acquisition occurs in predictable stages.		Second language learners who reach high levels of bilingual proficiency tend to have greater cognitive abilities than monolingual language learners.
Language acquisition is a dynamic process during which learners actively construct meaning using prior knowledge, experience, and context.		

in a new language. Opportunities for cognitively demanding and age-appropriate EFL language-learning contexts that prepare students for academic participation in the English language frequently are limited.

Seldom is the language learner able to maximize an incrementally successive transition to the cognitively complex forms of the second language used in subject areas such as the sciences and mathematics. Instead, most CLD students, especially secondary-level students, must spend their school days catching up with their peers not only in the language of instruction but also in the prior linguistic knowledge expectations of their subject-area instructors. Elementary school-age, native-English-speaking children begin kindergarten or first grade with at least five years of conversational English development. Older native-English-speaking children begin middle or high school with several years of both conversational and academic English development. Often, CLD students begin schooling in English with little or no conversational or academic development in English. Yet, some schooling systems expect such students to understand and function *without accommodations* at grade level, even while their native-English-speaking peers have spent several years developing the necessary English language skills for grade-level academic achievement.

Of particular concern is the fact that schools rarely afford the CLD student the sort of educational environment that research has suggested is critical to second language acquisition. Specifically, Wong Fillmore (1991) found that at least three environmental components are crucial to second language learning. The first component involves learners who recognize the need to learn the second or target language and who are motivated to do so. Second, the processes involved require speakers of the target language. These speakers must be fluent enough in the target language to provide learners with access to the language and assistance in language transitions. Third, a social setting is necessary to second language learning. This setting must bring together the learners and the fluent speakers of the target language in contact that is frequent enough to enable language learning. Furthermore, the findings of Wong Fillmore indicate that all three environmental components are necessary to successfully target language learning. Wong Fillmore argues that an environment that is missing any one of these components renders language learning difficult, if not impossible.

Current brain research (Jensen, 2008; Marzano, 2004; Sousa, 2011) has concluded that an environment must also consider the setting conditions within the classroom that:

- Allow for making connections to the student's linguistic and academic background
- Make time for practice and application of new academic vocabulary
- Ensure the environment is conducive to lowering the anxiety level of the student

The learning environment sets the stage for both social and academic language to develop. Teachers must design their EFL/ESL classroom environments in ways that support students' progression on the journey of acquiring the English language.

Global Connections 3.1

In EFL contexts, the teacher becomes the facilitator for setting conditions that allow for use of the target language in authentic ways. Using technology to provide students with opportunities to listen to the target language must be systematically implemented for successful results. When possible, students should be grouped heterogeneously to provide them with a setting where more proficient language models are available.

Illustrated Concept 3.2

To help reduce anxiety and encourage students with their reading development, provide students with sticky notes as they read and ask them to chunk the text. As students read in chunks, have them summarize the portion they read on the sticky note. Tell them to follow the sequence until they have read the entire selection. Further provide opportunities for students to share and discuss their summaries in pairs and small groups before sharing with the entire group.

Demands of Second Language Acquisition (SLA)

Additional research and analysis has also indicated that the complex processes involved in second language acquisition not only demand certain crucial environmental conditions but also require the targeting of a certain type of language competence. Since Hymes (1972) introduced the term **communicative competence,** our understanding of the complexities involved in knowing a language has greatly expanded. Communicative competence is that level of language expertise that enables users to depict and decode messages and to personally navigate the meanings within particular contexts (Brown, 2006). This notion of language knowledge suggests that understanding grammatical structures is insufficient as a goal for second language acquisition. Rather, the curriculum and instruction required for communicative competence in a second language must target at least four areas of language knowledge: grammatical competence, sociolinguistic competence, discourse competence, and strategic competence (Canale, 1983). As each of these is discussed, think about ways in which teachers can target these four areas of language knowledge as they plan their curriculum and instruction for students acquiring a new language.

Grammatical competence calls for curriculum and instruction that prepares the CLD student to incorporate and apply the language code. This competence requires at least some knowledge of pronunciation, vocabulary, word formation and meaning, sentence formulation, and spelling. Grammatical competence gains in importance as the student advances through the various stages of language proficiency.

Sociolinguistic competence is a goal of curriculum planning and language instruction that is intentionally focused on appropriate use of the target language in social and cultural contexts. Educators must consider several factors related to this competence, including the norms of interaction, the status of communicators, and the purposes of interaction. Often development of this competence necessitates a curriculum that emphasizes paralinguistic cues such as language registers. One such register is the use of formal versus informal language. Language programming that emphasizes the rules and basic skills of the target language seldom addresses sociolinguistic competence.

Discourse competence requires reflective curriculum planning and interactive language instruction. Such competence reflects the CLD student's capacity to combine, recombine, and connect language utterances into a meaningful product. The notion of discourse competence accounts for the fact that a grammatically correct language utterance may, nonetheless, prove incomprehensible to the recipient of that language message.

Strategic competence refers to the language user's ability to overcome linguistic problems or challenges during interaction. According to Canale (1983), speakers of the target language may employ strategic competence to:

- Compensate for breakdowns in communication (as when a speaker does not know the precise term he or she wishes to use and is forced to use an imprecise, sometimes confusing one as a substitute).

- Enhance the efficacy of the message communicated (as is the case when a speaker adds body language to her or his message to reinforce communication).

The process of second language acquisition, therefore, requires development of a variety of skills and understandings necessary for the effective use of the second language. The linguistic dimension of the CLD student biography involves a number of complex challenges, some of which directly relate to this and other linguistic processes.

■ Challenges of the Linguistic Dimension

Although the range of linguistic challenges described is by no means exhaustive, Table 3.2 summarizes those challenges that directly or indirectly relate to issues of

■ **table 3.2** Linguistic Dimension of the CLD Student Biography

Challenges	Processes

Language Transition
• Lack of authentic, constructivist, and interactive environments for language transition in schools and classrooms
• Lack of understanding about the time required for language development and language transition
• Inappropriate levels of educators trained to teach bilingual education or provide native language support to CLD students
 	
Curriculum and Instruction
• Limited efforts toward either curricular or instructional accommodations and modifications for the CLD student
• Widespread reliance on ineffective program models for language transition
• Shortage of supplementary materials with which to provide instructional native language support
• Limited exposure to authentic literacy activities
• An instructional focus on isolated basic skills of the target language
• Fragmented literacy instruction and postponed exposure to writing in L2
• A phonics focus in language arts instruction
• An inordinate focus on decoding skills in reading classes
• Lack of understanding about the invalidity of the interference hypothesis
	Ongoing CALP development in L1
	Second language acquisition
	CALP development in L2
	Literacy development processes
	• Vital literacy processes
	  • Comprehension
	  • Composition
	• Necessary but not sufficient literacy processes
	  • Word recognition
	    • Contextual clues
	    • Word families
	    • High-frequency words
	    • Alphabetic principle
	  • Spelling
	    • Provincial
	    • Invented
	• Intermediate literacy processes
	  • Concepts about print
	  • Phonemic awareness
	  • Letter identification

language transition as well as curriculum and instruction. Among the challenges associated with language transition are the following:

- A lack of authentic, constructivist, and interactive environments for language transition in schools and classrooms
- A lack of understanding about the time required for language development and language transition
- A shortage of educators trained to teach bilingual education or to provide native language support to CLD students

These challenges suggest that a number of variables—including environment, teacher expectations, and staffing—may contribute to the language transition challenges of the linguistic dimension that CLD students must transcend to be successful in school. Among the challenges for students acquiring a new language associated with curriculum and instruction are the following:

- Weaknesses in curricular accommodations for the CLD student
- Widespread reliance on ineffective programming models for language transition and acquisition
- A shortage of resource materials that enable native language support
- Limited exposure to authentic literacy development activities
- An instructional focus limited to the basic skills of the target language
- Postponed exposure to the literacy domain of writing
- A phonics focus in language arts instruction
- An inordinate focus on decoding skills in reading instruction

Time Required for Second Language Acquisition

> **Illustrated Concept 3.3**
>
> Provide language-learning environments that foster the construction of meaning from context and from communication. Focus learning objectives on areas in which students are able to use hands-on applications to contextualize language.

If one closely examines the language transition challenges of the linguistic dimension, perhaps the most pervasive is a general lack of understanding about the time required for a CLD student to acquire cognitive academic language proficiency (CALP) skills in the second or target language. As prior discussion has detailed, the CLD student must attain CALP proficiency in the target language if he or she is to be successful in content-area learning and achievement throughout schooling and to reach high school graduation, college, and career readiness. Students acquiring a second language, many of whom have no prior experience with the target language (i.e., English), must build both social and academic language proficiency in English in order to be successful academically.

Multifaceted and longitudinal research has consistently demonstrated that when the CLD student is schooled only in L2, meeting this linguistic challenge of attaining grade-level norms will require a minimum of 5 to 10 years and will require even more time when the student does not already have an established literacy base in L1 (Collier, 1987, 1989, 1992; Collier & Thomas, 1989, 2009; Cummins, 1981, 1991, 1992; Cummins & Swain, 1986; Dolson & Mayer, 1992; Genesee, 1987; Ramírez, 1992; Thomas & Collier, 2012). On the other hand, when the CLD student has been schooled in L1 and L2 at least through the fifth or sixth grade, she or he is often able to maintain grade-level norms in L1 and attain grade-level norms in L2 in four to seven years (Collier, 1992; Collier & Thomas, 2009; Genesee, 1987; Hakuta, 2011; Ramírez, 1992; Thomas & Collier, 2012).

To effectively address curricular and instructional challenges, it is especially important for educators to understand the ways in which these findings of field research with CLD students stand in direct contrast to:

- A history of dual language programs that fund simultaneous L1 and L2 education only through third grade
- A long-standing history in some school districts of ESL pull-out programs that provide no support in L1 and transition CLD students to all-English classrooms as early as the second or third grade
- A national trend toward programs that exit students from language support services after one year
- A national trend to focus on prescriptive curriculum for meeting the linguistic and academic needs of a very diverse population

Just as first language acquisition is a complex, long-term endeavor, so, too, is the challenge of acquiring grade-level academic language proficiency in a second language. Therefore, effective ESL/EFL educators consider the complex relationships among the linguistic, sociocultural, cognitive, and academic dimensions of the CLD student biography as their students work to address the multifaceted challenges that the linguistic processes present.

Exposure to Authentic Literacy Instruction and Activities

As illustrated in Table 3.2, a complex set of curricular and instructional challenges are associated with the linguistic dimension of the CLD student biography. Therefore, instruction and classroom activities that provide limited exposure to authentic literacy pose considerable difficulties for students learning the English language. Nonetheless, it is not uncommon among teachers in grade-level, ESL, and EFL classrooms to approach literacy development for students as a series of sequential hurdles through which the student must progress, beginning with oral literacy activities focused on basic concepts and skills. At

---

Illustrated Concept 3.4

Provide cooperative learning experiences to encourage student discussion. Allowing CLD students to interact with a more capable peer who speaks the same native language will also support the use of the first language for clarification.

Global Connections 3.2

Regardless of context, exposure to authentic literature, use of technology, and other experiences that provide students with the opportunity to use language for different purposes, with different audiences, accelerates English language development. Educators often have difficulty letting go of the prescribed curriculum for fear that they will miss important content or lose valuable class time. In EFL classrooms, this fear can lead to lower levels of student participation and English language acquisition.

theory *into* Practice 3.1

Canale (1983) found that successful second language development must target at least four critical forms of language knowledge in order for the language learner to acquire communicative competence. These forms of knowledge are discourse competence, grammatical competence, sociolinguistic competence, and strategic competence. *Strategic competence* enables speakers of the target language to (1) compensate for breakdowns in communication (as when a speaker does not know the precise terms he or she wishes to use and is forced to use an imprecise, sometimes

confusing one as a substitute) and (2) enhance the efficacy of the message communicated (as is the case when a communicator adds paralinguistic cues such as body language to her or his message to reinforce communication).

■ *What types of paralinguistic cues do you typically use when someone does not understand your message? What are the implications of strategic competence for teaching methods used with CLD students?*

the heart of these practices is often the belief that students learning the English language need to have specific (especially basic) skills in place before engaging in authentic literacy experiences.

However, research on literacy development indicates that CLD students should be bathed in rich and authentic literacy activities from the early stages of literacy development (Anderson, 1999; Clay, 1991; Kole, 2003; National Reading Panel, 2000; Perez, 2002). This research stresses the value of allowing students learning the English language to maximize their own prior

Illustrated Concept 3.5

Support and elaborate on the language acquisition processes of students by teaching key vocabulary and concepts using pictures and real objects that the students label and manipulate; using visuals, physical movements, gestures, and verbal cues; and providing reading materials with a pattern.

experiences, culture, background knowledge, and reasoning to actively and interactively contribute to instruction and activities designed to promote literacy development.

It is important to recall that before entering school, CLD students have often been exposed to a variety of activities that have contributed to their own literacy development. For example, many students have prior experiences with reading and writing in their native language. The notion of common underlying proficiency (CUP) (Cummins, 1981) informs us that most reading and writing skills learned in the native language will transfer to a second language and therefore need not be redeveloped in English (the concept of CUP is detailed in Chapter 4). Likewise, many students have experiences with environmental print in both the native language and English. As these experiences illustrate, CLD students may bring a variety of literacy assets to the classroom. These experiences may be overlooked unless they are explored by the classroom teacher. Effective teachers preassess these prior experiences and skill bases before they assume that classroom instruction and literacy activities should begin with basic skills and concepts.

Authentic literacy instruction maximizes not only the prior literacy experiences of the CLD student but also her or his background knowledge and cultural heritage. This brand of literacy development emphasizes relevancy, elaboration on prior socialization and experiences, the actual daily instruction and activities of the classroom, and the daily out-of-school experiences of learners. To ensure that literacy instruction is authentic, Coyne, Kameenui, and Carnine (2010) suggest that school educators do the following:

- Focus on the most critical concepts within the content areas.
- Emphasize explicit strategies for learning words and concepts from context.
- Scaffold student instruction through the gradual deepening of vocabulary knowledge.
- Build a connection between new knowledge and existing knowledge.
- Review the most important conceptual knowledge in a way that deepens the CLD learner's understanding as efficiently as possible.

These recommendations, which are echoed by numerous researchers (e.g., Calderón, 2007; Farstrup & Samuels, 2008; Herrera, Perez, & Escamilla, 2010; Sousa, 2011), have a number of implications for literacy development among CLD students. For example, a focus on the most critical concepts within the content areas suggests that authentic literacy instruction and activities should be content-based rather than grounded in basic concepts such as colors and letters that often are not aligned with grade-level curriculum.

Global Connections 3.3
Technology has made it possible for many more students to hear the English language in their communities. Music, movies, and other media now connect the world in ways that were not previously possible. Never assume or underestimate what experiences your students have had with the English language. Regardless of context, set conditions to learn what students already know before introducing new content.

In addition, instructional scaffolding enables the CLD student, with support, to engage in literacy activities that build on a prior skill or knowledge base while stretching toward the development of new literacy skills. **Scaffolding** involves extensive instructional and contextual support in the early stages of learning, followed by a gradual withdrawal of such support as the student's performance suggests independence. Scaffolding can also be used to deepen the meaning of literacy activities. For example, instead of asking CLD students to learn about the seasons of the year by memorizing their names and illustrating them, students might be engaged in a series of authentic activities designed to teach various weather phenomena associated with a season change. Thus, to learn about the rains often associated with the change from winter to spring, students might be scaffolded in authentic activities such as (1) observing clouds and noting their types, (2) placing a rain gauge and collecting data on rainfall over time, (3) observing the impact of rain on the environment, and (4) comparing spring rainfall in the United States to rainfall typical in the students' home countries.

Related literacy activities might then involve reading about the cloud types that were observed, discussing and comparing data on rainfall, and writing about comparisons of spring rainfall across countries. Students also might write about the impact of rainfall on the environment of the various countries. Because these activities involve phenomena that are part of students' personal experiences, they are *relevant* to the learners. In addition, because these literacy development activities encourage comparisons across countries, they can be designed to emphasize multiculturalism or the affirmation of a CLD student's prior knowledge and socialization in a particular culture. Activities designed in this manner tend to prompt a sense of pride in one's heritage as well as the motivation to learn about other cultures and languages.

■ Processes of the Linguistic Dimension

Table 3.2 also summarizes many of the processes that are most associated with the linguistic dimension of the CLD student biography. Many of these processes are interrelated. For instance, the linguistic process of ongoing CALP development in the first language is essential to the process of second language acquisition. The literacy development processes, also summarized in Table 3.2, illustrate the complexities of attaining literacy in either one's first language or a second language.

Linguistic Process of Second Language Acquisition

The linguistic process of second language acquisition is perhaps most relevant to the appropriate education of CLD students. Although competing theories abound as to the nature of this process (Bialystok, 1990; Dulay & Burt, 1974; Krashen, 1982; McLaughlin, 1990), the literature exhibits a generalizable consistency as to the fundamental stages of the second language acquisition process.

Krashen's Natural Order Hypothesis

The notion of **stages of second language acquisition** is consistent with Krashen's (1982) **natural order hypothesis**. This hypothesis asserts that language is acquired in a more or less natural order—a predictable sequence of progression. Although individual variations will exist among students, certain grammatical features of the language tend to be acquired earlier, whereas others are acquired later in development. For example, morphemes that serve as verb endings (as in the bound morpheme *-ing*, found in the word *studying*) tend to be acquired early in development. On the other hand, morphemes that enable possession (as in the possessive *-s* in the sentence *We rode Irma's horse*) tend to be acquired late in the developmental process. In a larger sense, this natural order accounts for the fact that language learners tend to progress from listening to speaking and then develop capacities for reading and writing.

Stages of Second Language Acquisition

Table 3.3 describes the various stages of the linguistic process of second language acquisition (Krashen & Terrell, 1983), beginning with the stage of preproduction and culminating in the stage of advanced fluency. Although the stages are discussed from the perspective of secondary education, they are applicable to CLD students of every age. The first stage of the process of second language acquisition, the preproduction stage, is often called the **silent period** because the student may not communicate during this period except in nonverbal ways. During this period, the student is primarily listening to the new or target language and trying to understand its patterns and rules before attempting production in that language. Students who are nonverbal during this stage of acquisition, which may last for several months (Ovando & Combs, 2011), nonetheless have been found to progress in L2 acquisition as well as, or better than, their more verbal peers (Saville-Troike, 1984; Wong Fillmore & Valadez, 1986). Generally, the silent period is a nonproblematic stage of the second language acquisition process, except in those cases in which educators or staff members erroneously conclude that the student's silence is somehow indicative of other, nonlinguistic problems such as a learning disability. After the preproduction stage, language learners generally proceed through the stages of early production, speech emergence, intermediate fluency, and advanced fluency (see Table 3.3). In this way, the capabilities of CLD students advance from the early production stage of phonetic reading in the new language to the advanced fluency stage of abstract thinking in the new or target language. Think about the following: In what ways is this teacher supporting Sonia's learning?

> With the arrival of the new student, Sonia, who does not speak English, I have implemented 15 minutes each day for the English-speaking students to learn Spanish words, which is inclusion for Sonia. Sonia feels very proud to correct me and all the other English-speaking students when we mispronounce a Spanish word. Within the classroom, I have Spanish posters helping all the English-speaking students, which also makes Sonia feel included. We, as a class, have focused on the similarities between Sonia's native language, Spanish, and English. As an example, the word *excelente* in Spanish is very close to *excellent* in English.

Like other linguistic processes, second language acquisition involves certain challenges that are also part of the linguistic dimension of the CLD student biography. Such challenges include the many misunderstandings that surround the silent period of the process. Therefore, effective teachers not only understand the dynamics of each stage of SLA but also realize the implications of each stage for curriculum and instruction.

Often teachers mistake test scores as synonymous with the stages of SLA. However, these two designations provide information for different purposes. Whereas language assessments provide a point-in-time score of a CLD student's literacy performance, the stages of SLA provide a lens for monitoring the student's language growth in the classroom. Krashen and Terrell's (1983) stages serve as a tool to help educators know what to expect in the learning progress of students. For more information on the importance of linguistics in relation to the CLD student, watch this video.

■ **t a b l e 3 . 3**   Stages of Second Language Acquisition, with Emphasis on the Adolescent CLD Student

Please note: This chart represents the stages of second language acquisition. Many students may fall between stages and/or remain in one stage for a temporary period of time. Students' levels are not always consistent across the reading, writing, speaking, and listening domains. For example, students who are at the intermediate or advanced fluency levels in speaking may be at the early production or speech emergence levels in reading and writing.

Stage of SLA	Student Descriptors	Student Performance Outcomes	Tips for Teachers
Preproduction	Students tend to be in a nonverbal (silent) period in which the second language may be mostly, if not completely, incomprehensible. Adolescent CLD students may exhibit high levels of anxiety, frustration, and withdrawal due to a variety of stressors such as cultural differences; self-concept; peer acceptance; and developmental, physical changes. Adolescent CLD students often demonstrate faster academic language growth than younger students based on superior L1 in reading, writing, speaking, and listening, as well as superior cognitive development in L1. Adolescent CLD students may demonstrate nonverbal communication for understanding such as pointing, nodding, and smiling.	The adolescent CLD student will typically be able to: • Readily gain familiarity with sounds, rhythms, and patterns of English based on his or her prior foundational knowledge and experiences with the first language. • Depend more heavily on visuals related to academic content such as labeled pictures, diagrams, charts, graphic organizers, maps, and word walls for understanding. • Focus on listening to and internalizing the language. She or he may not participate orally but may demonstrate understanding nonverbally through pointing, gesturing, and drawing. • Use reference points for guidance, clarification, and clues as to what is being taught and addressed (such as procedures posted; written directions; posted homework assignments, dictionaries, or word walls in the room). The CLD adolescent may also need clarification of directions and content in the first language with the help of a bilingual peer.	Provide adolescent CLD students with comprehensible classroom experiences by using more English-proficient peers as models. Pair CLD students who are less proficient in English with more English-proficient bilingual students who can preview the lesson in the native language. Use a variety of visuals, physical movements, gestures, and verbal cues to support and expand the non-English-proficient (NEP) student's language acquisition process. Avoid forcing any CLD student to speak prematurely by appropriately allowing for the silent period. Allow the student to speak when he or she is ready and comfortable to take risks in English. Tap into the NEP adolescent's prior knowledge by having a bilingual peer assist the NEP student in filling out KWL charts. Tie students' personal experiences into lessons as much as possible. Using students' experiences validates the knowledge and culture the CLD student brings to the classroom. Provide models for the students to use as a guide with assignment checklists on the chalkboard.

(continued)

■ **table 3.3** Continued

Stage of SLA	Student Descriptors	Student Performance Outcomes	Tips for Teachers
Preproduction (*continued*)	Students may display periods of inattentiveness. Learning in a second language can be exhausting because students must construct meaning in a new culture for cognitive and academic purposes.	• Speak and understand high-frequency, contextualized words and simple phrases.	Look for NEP student understanding through observation of student demonstrations, nodding, pointing, and answering yes or no questions. Recognizing and accepting NEP students' nonverbal communication will lower the affective filter so that he or she may feel more comfortable taking risks in English.
			Provide a print-rich classroom with labels and word walls for students to use as a reference throughout units on which you may be working.
			Provide additional wait time to students.
			Guard vocabulary through slowed rate of speech, clear enunciation, idiom avoidance, repetition, and key vocabulary emphasis.
			Write language and content objectives on the board for CLD students and refer to them throughout the lesson. Try to include a variety of listening, speaking, reading, and writing activities to achieve your language objectives.
			Provide an outline of notes (in the student's first language, if possible) to CLD students during a lecture presentation.
			Provide a predictable daily routine so that the adolescent CLD student understands teacher expectations. Frequently, an apparent problematic behavior is a symptom of the NEP student's inability to understand.

■ **t a b l e   3 . 3**   Continued

Stage of SLA	Student Descriptors	Student Performance Outcomes	Tips for Teachers
Preproduction (*continued*)			Provide choral reading experiences and chants to lessen the anxiety level (lower the affective filter) for taking risks in English.
Early Production	The adolescent CLD student tends to read phonetically according to his or her native language pronunciation and literacy skills. The adolescent CLD student listens with greater understanding to contextualized, basic information and social conversation. The adolescent CLD student repeats memorable language commonly used in social conversation with peers. Students recognize connections between the native language and second language and use these connections as tools in acquiring the second language. The adolescent CLD student will use contextual cues such as pictures, graphs, and prior knowledge to facilitate reading comprehension.	The adolescent CLD student may be able to: • Speak using isolated words and phrases. • Verbally identify people, places, and objects. • Manipulate objects and ideas mentally using foundational knowledge from his or her L1. • Use routine expressions independently. • Participate in guided, highly contextualized discussions.	Provide a classroom library of scaffolded reading material that has age-appropriate content for the adolescent at this stage. Inappropriate age-level reading material may be insulting or embarrassing to adolescents who are accustomed to a much higher level of literature in the first language. Use age-appropriate, relevant, and rich literature in classroom instruction. Preteach key vocabulary and concepts in order to increase student comprehension. Have students label or manipulate pictures and real objects to promote comprehension. Provide students with learning strategies to discover connections between the native language and English. For example, teach Spanish speakers to look for cognates (e.g., *animales* = *animals*). Provide cooperative learning experiences to encourage student discussion. Support the use of the first language for clarification of content-area concepts.

(*continued*)

■ **table 3.3**   Continued

Stage of SLA	Student Descriptors	Student Performance Outcomes	Tips for Teachers
Early Production (*continued*)			Provide students with opportunities for problem solving to promote higher-order thinking skills. A common misconception is that CLD students' limited English language proficiency also limits their reasoning skills. Students should be challenged regardless of their language proficiency levels.
			Provide as many visual aids as possible to support meaning construction.
Speech Emergence	The adolescent CLD student may exhibit increased proficiency in decoding and comprehending English text.	The adolescent CLD student may be able to:	Guard vocabulary and introduce concepts through the use of KWL charts, webs, story maps, and picture prompts.
	As the student becomes more comfortable with the school culture, she or he may take more risks with oral language and speak in short sentences with syntax errors.	• Understand grade-level concepts more clearly and be able to increase the transfer from prior knowledge concepts learned in his or her native language.	Model responses to literature for students by explaining, describing, comparing, and retelling.
	The CLD student may demonstrate increased understanding of extended conversation and dialogue, simple stories with some details, and simple idiomatic expressions.	• Engage in much more independent reading as a result of increased oral language proficiency. • Write using a more extensive vocabulary and varied writing style. • Begin self-evaluation of writing through editing.	Provide a variety of content-area texts, trade books, and newspapers related to the subject or topic.
			Focus on communication in meaningful contexts in which students express themselves in speech and print.
			Respond genuinely to student writing, hold conferences that highlight student strengths and progress, and have students set their own realistic language goals.
			Provide students with opportunities to read, write, listen, and speak in their native languages.

■ **table 3.3** Continued

Stage of SLA	Student Descriptors	Student Performance Outcomes	Tips for Teachers
Speech Emergence (*continued*)			Post tips for writing and editing as an easy reference and reminder to students. Model reading comprehension strategies.
Intermediate Fluency	The adolescent CLD student has increased understanding and application of word-attack and comprehension skills. The adolescent CLD student exhibits growth in accuracy and correctness regarding listening, speaking, reading, and writing. The adolescent CLD student uses his or her native language as a resource and may also be eager to help peers and teachers with translations and brokering. The adolescent CLD student uses richer and fuller sentences with a varied vocabulary. In reading comprehension, the adolescent CLD student can extract more meaning from the actual text and relies less on contextual cues.	The adolescent CLD student may be able to: • Explore and use extensive vocabulary and concepts in the content areas and make more language connections to L1. • Read a wider range of narrative genre and content texts with increased comprehension. • Summarize and make inferences in reading more readily. • Use language to express and defend opinions. • Experiment with more sophisticated vocabulary and complex sentence structure.	Structure and guide group discussions to facilitate more advanced literature studies. Provide for a variety of realistic writing experiences that are relevant to students. Encourage creativity and an increased sense of aesthetics by initiating drama, art, music, and other forms of creative expressions. Publish student-authored stories, newsletters, poems, and more. Continue to shelter instruction and check for CLD adolescent understanding. Encourage students to continue growth in the native language by providing them with materials to read in the native language, allowing them to assist less proficient peers, and encouraging them to help new CLD students with their transitions to a new school and culture. Be aware of the common misconception regarding the CLD student's level of social language (BICS) with her or his level of understanding of the academic content language (CALP). Continue to provide scaffolding in instruction such as cooperative learning, visuals relating to the content area, experiences using manipulatives, previewing of key terms and concepts, etc.

(continued)

■ **t a b l e 3 . 3**   Continued

Stage of SLA	Student Descriptors	Student Performance Outcomes	Tips for Teachers
Advanced Fluency	This adolescent CLD student is characterized as an abstract thinker. His or her reading interests become individualized and more varied. The adolescent CLD student develops highly accurate language and grammatical structures that approximate those of native-English-speaking peers. This student may (and ideally should) view her or his native language as an asset on which to draw for the enhancement of her or his acquisition of English. At this level, the adolescent CLD student uses multiple strategies to facilitate reading comprehension.	The adolescent CLD student may be able to: • Produce language with varied grammatical structures and more complex vocabulary, including idiomatic expressions. • Capitalize on the native language as a constant resource for understanding the second language. • Demonstrate writing skills that approximate that of a native-English-speaking peer. • Read frequently for information and pleasure.	Promote ongoing development through integrated language arts and content-area activities. Encourage adolescents to continue growth in their native language at home, at school, and in the community. For lesson closure, have students review daily content and language objectives to assess their progress. Encourage students to interact and support other English learners who are transitioning into a new school and culture. Provide opportunities for more proficient students to work as peer tutors, not only to reinforce their own learning, but also to assist others with comprehension. Arrange collaborative groups so that advanced English-proficient CLD adolescents are partnered with CLD students who are not as proficient. Encourage students to engage in metacognitive regulation concerning their own learning processes and strategies.

Linguistic Process of Understanding Concepts about Print

Concepts about print relate to the various aspects of how the written word is structured. According to Herrera (2001), critical concepts about print that CLD students should acquire include (1) understanding that print carries a message; (2) realizing that print corresponds to speech, word for word; (3) perceiving the directionality of print; and (4) recognizing the parts of texts. Therefore, when

dilemmas *of Practice* 3.1

Mr. Hauschild, third-grade teacher at Stover Elementary in Sunshine, California, teaches Emilio Vasquez, who arrived from Monterrey, Mexico, in January. Six weeks after arriving, Emilio still rarely speaks in class and is generally unresponsive to questions. Mr. Hauschild has concluded that Emilio may have a learning disability and should be tested for special education. He has made a referral for testing next week.

The first stage of the process of second language acquisition, the preproduction stage, is often called the silent period because the student may not communicate during this period except in nonverbal ways. During this period, the student is primarily listening to the new or target language and trying to understand its patterns and rules before attempting production in that language. Students who are nonverbal during this stage of acquisition, which may last for several months (Ovando & Combs,

2011), nonetheless have been found to progress in L2 acquisition as well as, or better than, their more verbal peers (Saville-Troike, 1984; Wong Fillmore & Valadez, 1986). Generally, the silent period is a nonproblematic and temporary stage of the second language acquisition process, except in those cases in which educators or staff members erroneously conclude that the student's silence is somehow indicative of other nonlinguistic problems such as a learning disability. Although teachers should always check to ensure that instruction is not raising the student's affective filter, a period during which the CLD student does not produce significant language is often a natural stage of second language acquisitions.

■ *Should Mr. Hauschild refer Emilio? If not, what teaching actions should Mr. Hauschild take? In what ways might he involve Emilio's parents?*

---

instructing students, it is important for teachers to consider each of these concepts about print and the implications they may have on the literacy development of CLD students.

Print Carries a Message

Of pivotal importance to literacy development is the critical concept that print carries a message. Messages are incorporated into various forms of text through the written word. For example, storybooks, magazines, letters, e-mail, texts, and notes are all vehicles of communication. Grade-level students are typically engaged in a variety of daily literacy activities that incorporate these venues of communication. From such activities, they gradually develop the understanding that all print carries meaning. In the classroom setting, some of the ways that teachers demonstrate the communicative power of print are by reading aloud, posting daily calendars, and engaging students in rich literacy activities throughout the day. In this manner, teachers build on students' communicative abilities and constructs to provide contextual foundations for literacy development.

Culturally and linguistically diverse students sometimes have difficulty with associations between print and meaning. This is especially the case when classroom instruction does not recognize the communicative capacities and constructs that CLD students already bring to the literacy process.

Global Connections 3.4
In order to help learners create meaning from print effectively, we must look at reading as a communicative act of discourse. One way to support students' focus on communication is to have them generate questions while looking at the title and then, as a prereading strategy, have them skim the content based on questions generated. By implementing such prereading strategies, we pave the way for students to monitor their own reading throughout the text.

Although students may not yet be able to convey this capacity in their L2 (second language, i.e., English), some of them have already developed an emergent understanding that print carries meaning because they have been exposed to the various uses of print for multiple purposes in their L1. Unfortunately, classroom instruction that does not build and elaborate on these emergent understandings is not only redundant but also tends to negate the potential value of the student's assets in ongoing literacy development.

Effective teachers, therefore, preassess and maximize what the student already knows about connections between print and meaning. Among the strategies that can be used to elaborate on students' emergent understandings of print concepts are hands-on activities. For example, CLD students might gain hands-on experience with bouncing balls as a way to associate meaning with the text of a story about basketball.

Print Corresponds to Speech

The recognition that print corresponds to speech word for word is also crucial to literacy development. This concept about print first draws attention to the organization of the individual letters that are used to make up words and ultimately the body of a text. Later, individuals become familiar with the sounds that correlate to these symbols. Then students learn to manipulate and join smaller, isolated sounds to form syllables that compose words, which ultimately extend into phrases and sentences. These processes of increasing familiarity with sound–symbol correspondences later facilitate the capacity to decode words. This capacity serves as the precursor to an understanding that print corresponds to speech.

Regrettably, instruction for CLD students too often emphasizes the organization of the individual letters used to make up words and the sounds that are associated with each letter. Such phonics-based instruction tends to over-engage students in drill and practice focused on individual letters and sounds taught in isolation. Although phonics instruction has its place in teaching students about sound–symbol correlations, its strict emphasis on letters and sound patterns does little to encourage balanced literacy development or reading comprehension. As demonstrated by Table 3.2 and research on literacy development (Anderson, 1999; Clay, 1991; Delgado-Gaitán, 1989; Freeman & Freeman, 2004; Hudelson & Serna, 1994; National Reading Panel, 2000; Perez, 2002), reading comprehension and balanced literacy development involve much more than proficiency in decoding skills.

Many CLD students have already developed extensive decoding skills in their first language. They use their native language to make sound–symbol correspondences to the written word. This capacity need not be learned twice. Instead, given an appropriate instructional environment that emphasizes elaboration of prior knowledge, this capacity will transfer to the second language.

Second language learners benefit also from literacy development that highlights cognates. A *cognate* is a word in a particular language whose form and definition resemble that of a word in a different language (e.g., *animals* [English] and *animales* [Spanish]). An emphasis on cognates is especially effective with students whose first language is Spanish because a significant number of cognates exist between English and Spanish. Such cognates can facilitate the rapid transfer of capacities in L1 to L2 with regard to the recognition of sound–symbol correspondences.

Directionality

The recognition of the directionality of print is equally crucial to literacy development. For instance, a child learning to read in English may not understand immediately that text is to be read from the top of the page to the bottom, or that each line of a text is to be read from left to right. Students who are unfamiliar with directionality might begin reading on the right side of the page instead of the left as they use visual cues to decipher meaning.

Issues of directionality may be of particular concern with certain CLD students, depending on the script typically used in their native language. Those students whose languages do not follow the written directionality patterns of the English language may struggle with this concept about print. Prime examples of directionality differences can be found in script languages such as Arabic, Hebrew, Chinese, and Hmong.

Insightful teachers are aware of these cross-linguistic differences and provide additional instructional scaffolding designed to ease students through transitions to unfamiliar patterns of directionality. These teachers typically begin with comparisons across languages to establish context. Subsequent instruction often stresses short segments of text and progresses to longer segments as students build the capacity to manage changes in directionality. Special attention is given throughout to the pace of instruction; a rapid pace used at any juncture in the learning process has a tendency to raise the student's affective filter.

Parts of Texts

Of crucial importance to reading comprehension is the recognition of the various parts of a text (front cover, back cover, title page, table of contents, etc.). Culturally and linguistically diverse students, however, may arrive in the classroom having little experience with texts or the organization of texts. For students who arrive from war-torn countries, their prior experiences with schooling and literacy development are often interrupted and inconsistent. Other CLD students may be children of poverty who have only limited familiarity with the written word. Still others may have been socialized to cultural traditions emphasizing stories passed down orally from generation to generation. The early literacy experiences of such students typically do not stress texts or the organization of texts. Therefore, the potential for instructional assumptions related to this concept about print is high.

When providing literacy instruction, teachers can engage students in rich explorations of text. Development activities typically associated with such explorations

■ **f i g u r e   3 . 1**

Reading Proficiency

The majority of skills that a student learns as he or she builds the capacity to read in the native language will transfer to a second language. These skills do not need to be retaught or relearned (Escamilla, 1987; Krashen, 1987; Lesher-Madrid & García, 1985; Modiano, 1968; Skutnabb-Kangas, 1975).

Reading Skills That Transfer from L1 to L2

- Knowledge:
  - Once a CLD student has learned a concept, it does not need to be relearned.
- Literacy is symbolic:
  - Regardless of the language spoken or written, words in any language symbolize underlying concepts, ideas, or concrete objects.
- Literacy is communicative:
  - The purpose of text is for the reader to understand the message being sent by the author.
- Phonological awareness:
  - Each CLD student develops phonological awareness based on the sound system of his or her native language.
- Alphabetic and orthographic awareness:
  - All text is made up of a series of letters or symbols that are put together in a specific written format.
- Concepts about print:
  - Each text has specific features that are learned by CLD students through exposure to print.
- Habits and attitudes:
  - Study skills, task completion, persistence, and motivation are all factors that aid CLD students in literacy development.
- Self-esteem:
  - The more CLD students believe that they are competent readers and writers, the more likely they are to become successful readers and writers.

Reading Skills That Do Not Transfer from L1 to L2

- Orthographic awareness (spelling, decoding):
  - Explicit differences need to be explained.
- Syntax (order and relationship of parts of a sentence):
  - Sentences are put together in different ways.
- Cultural concepts:
  - What makes a good story in one language does not necessarily make a good story in another.
- Rhetorical structure:
  - Writing styles, including the order of events, amount of emphasis on personal/social relationships, and extent of the detail included, may vary.
  - Different languages encourage people to think in different ways.

Sources: Escamilla (1987), Krashen (1987), Lesher-Madrid & García (1985), Modiano (1968), Skutnabb-Kangas 1975.

include (1) surveying texts; (2) explicitly teaching students how to identify the title page; (3) demonstrating the use of the table of contents; and (4) manipulating back matter sections, such as the index and appendixes. Students in EFL/ESL classrooms also gain from additional and explicit strategy instruction that stresses both the manner in which texts may be organized and the ways in which that organization can be maximized to improve comprehension. For example, when the student recognizes that the chapters of certain texts might close with a summary of events or concepts discussed, she or he may use those summaries to better comprehend the text. Similarly, when the student recognizes that the illustrations of a text can depict certain key events or messages, she or he may occasionally refer to these to establish the context of a story. Figure 3.1 provides an overview of literacy and the CLD student.

Linguistic Dimension: Implications for Classroom and School Practice

This chapter summarizes many of the challenges and processes associated with the linguistic dimension of the CLD student biography and schooling experience. Through the remaining chapters of the text, we elaborate, analyze and discuss many of these processes and challenges in relation to instructional approaches, methods, and strategies for EFL/ESL classrooms. Nevertheless, at this juncture, it is useful to explore briefly some of the immediate implications of these linguistic challenges and processes for classroom practice.

Instructional Planning for CALP Development in L1 and L2

Reflective teachers know that effective practice for CLD students requires an understanding of the dynamics involved in first and second language acquisition. Table 3.4 illustrates the ways in which first and second language acquisition are similar and different. Because ongoing CALP development in L1 accelerates L2 acquisition, educators should give special consideration to learning environments and forms of classroom instruction that provide whatever levels of ongoing native language support are feasible. Insightful teachers also recognize that errors are inevitable as one learns a second language. The student may not always be able to articulate successfully what he or she knows. However, through such errors, students build their cognitive and academic levels of proficiency in L2 as they explore the nuances of the target language. Teachers might provide opportunities for CLD students to demonstrate what they understand in a variety of ways. Figure 3.2 shares some of the language-specific dynamics that affect language and literacy development for CLD students.

Global Connections 3.5
In EFL settings, authentic texts and materials play a significant role in language acquisition, as they can increase students' motivation for learning and expose learners to authentic language use. Teachers can target international language materials that cover knowledge from different cultures all over the world. When introducing authentic materials, educators can scaffold the learning process by adding audiovisual materials.

■ Voices from the Field 3.1

"In my second-grade class, I have a student from India. He has been in Iowa for four years. His English is quite good, but he is still developing some sounds such as the *th* and *sh* sounds. This student is very bright and social. However, I was noticing that his reading scores on tests and probes were very low, below the passing level. These scores were not indicative of this student's demonstrated ability in class. I decided that his BICS are well developed; however, his CALP is still in the developing stages (which is normal for an ELL [CLD] student). Because his CALP is still developing, his comprehension of a story from his brain to pencil and paper is a weak area. This student does much better when retelling a story or when he is allowed to read tests out loud with assistance with words he does not know.

As I thought about these language issues, I wondered how the teachers who had him in class the previous two years did not see this problem. I was told that he is a little above average in reading, and he will "do just fine" in the English language–based classroom. I was completely under the impression that he would be like any other student in my class; he had a very solid English base and would progress as all my other students would. I also found out that his parents speak little or no English at home, so he speaks a different language at home (which is good, as this enables him to develop L1).

I am also wondering how and why he has been passed on from grade to grade with little ESL support. To my knowledge, the first time that this boy was assessed using an ELL test (our district uses the IDEA) was this year. I fully realize that we have only two ELL [CLD] students in our district, but do those two children not matter enough to our administration to try to make some changes? I am glad I have taken ESL/Dual Language Methods and am currently in ESL Assessment. I hope that the information that I learn will only help me teach *all* of my students better.

At the same time, I feel challenged to learn more and to do better for this student. I have realized that he is still acquiring his CALP, and I need to be supportive as a teacher to enable him to learn the best that he can. But how can I continue to assess him properly when the support of our district isn't necessarily there? I want to be able to serve as a resource for this child's teacher next year, who probably has had little or no training in educating ELL students, but am I really that much more educated?

I am constantly thinking, How can I be a resource for other teachers and our administration, when I really have so little knowledge of ESL instruction *and* assessment myself? I also wonder if my district should be justified in hiring a trained ESL teacher, even though we have only two ELL students. At what point do they hire an outside professional?

As I completed the first class, I understood that I had made some invalid assumptions concerning my ELL student. First, I had assumed that because he has been in a full-English educational program since preschool, his language would be well developed and I would treat him as I would any other student in my class when it came to language skills. I also had assumed that because his oral comprehension was good, he could automatically transfer that knowledge to paper. Neither of my assumptions held any validity. Based on what he has shown me academically in this area, I now know that he is still learning language skills and vocabulary. He continues to struggle with unfamiliar words, therefore impeding his comprehension. I also realized during this revelation that I need to continue to learn about ELL students because my ELL student this year will *not* be my last."

■ *Reprinted by permission from Sara Van Manen. Copyright © Sara Van Manen.*

■ **table 3.4** Similarities and Differences between a Student Engaged in First Language (L1) Acquisition and a Student Engaged in Second Language (L2) Acquisition

	L1	L2
Reads more slowly		X
Needs more processing time		X
Silent period	X	X
More likely to need to monitor comprehension		X
Has more than one language to draw on to construct meaning (cognates, root words, and more)		X
Tends to have more metalinguistic awareness		X
More likely to experience anxiety over language production		X
Needs comprehensible input	X	X
Uses prior knowledge to construct meaning	X	X
More likely to have 5 years of exposure to dominant language of school before beginning school	X	
Tends to overestimate L1 language ability	X	
Tends to underestimate the potential role of L1 proficiency in L2 acquisition		X
Usually has experience with multiple cultures		X
Goes through stages of language acquisition	X	X

Anticipating and Preassessing for the Array of Student Biographies

Effective teachers anticipate that CLD students may bring to the classroom a vast array of student biographies. Therefore, as professionals, they preassess these student biographies as a basis for instructional planning. At *minimum*, such educators preassess the following for each student:

- Sociocultural/acculturation biography
- First language biography
- Second language biography
- Schooling/academic knowledge biography

Figure 3.3 illustrates two student biography cards that educators can use to preassess and summarize CLD student biographies as they work to effectively differentiate classroom instruction. These are provided as examples; however, teachers can modify the student biography cards in ways that will best support their instructional planning.

Table 3.5 provides a summary of the biography characteristics typically associated with CLD students who (1) have newly arrived in the United States and are below grade level, (2) have newly arrived in the United States and are at grade

■**figure 3.2**

Language Detective

The information in this figure highlights some of the language-specific dynamics that can affect English language acquisition among CLD students. Consider the ways these dynamics might affect the students in your classroom. How might you become a "language detective" so that you can identify the various language elements that may affect English language acquisition rates among your students?

Language Element	Considerations
Phonology	• Phonology refers to the sound system of a particular language. • CLD students need to have an awareness of the sounds of a language in order to read.
Pragmatics	• Pragmatics is the use of language in particular contexts. For example, the context of how language is used is different in: ■ Home ■ Work ■ School
Semantics	• Semantics is the meaning of language used in a given context. • Semantic illustration: ■ Coco lives on top of the _____ in the house with the purple _____.
Morphology	• Morphology refers to the study of the forms of words, including the structure of words themselves. • A morpheme can be a root word, prefix, or suffix. like <u>un</u>like like<u>ly</u>

Syntax	• Syntax refers to the rules that govern how sentences are formed in a language. This includes both the grammar and structure of a language.
	• English follows a sentence construction that consists of subject + verb + object.
	  ■ Example: I bought a book.
	  In this sentence, *I* is the subject, *bought* is the verb, and *book* is the object.
	• The sentence structure of another language may differ from that of English.
	  ■ In Spanish, for example, sentence structure sometimes follows a verb + object construction, in which the subject is only implied.
	  ■ The example sentence would be *Compré un libro,* or literally, "bought a book."
	  ■ The sentence only contains verb + object and no subject; however, the verb implies the subject *I*.

■**figure 3.3**

Elementary CLD Student Biography Card

*Note: This is a teacher strategy to inform you of key aspects associated with the CLD student biography as they relate to assessment issues (information can also be used to support multiple grouping configurations).

Name:

Age:

Grade:

Born:

L1:
R:
W:

L2 Proficiency (LAS/IPT/Other):

O:
R:
W:
SLA:

Prior Academic Experiences:

Preferred Grouping:

Student Processing:

Other Assessment Consideration:

Insert a photograph of the student (this is a helpful visual reminder for you as a teacher).

Sociocultural:
Complete the **demographic information** on each student by interviewing the student, his or her family, or a past teacher.

Language:
Step One: Determine (informally or fomally):
L1: First language proficiency (speaking/listening)
R: First language reading proficiency
W: First language writing proficiency
Step Two: Determine the CLD student's English language proficiency (scores can be obtained from the district/school ESL teacher as needed).
O: English oral proficiency (speaking/listening)
R: English reading proficiency
W: English writing proficiency
SLA (stage of second language acquistion):
  This will be discussed in depth in Session 4.

Academic:
What **prior academic experiences**/exposure does the student have to promote academic knowledge and transfer?
In what **grouping** configurations is the student most comfirtable (**T**PSI—**T**otal Group, **P**artner, **S**mall Group, or **I**ndependent)?

Cognitive:
How does the *student process* information (e.g., solve a math problem, complete a science experiment, summarize a story)?
What *other assessment considerations* should be taken into account for this student?

(continued)

■figure 3.3 Continued

Secondary CLD Student Biography Card

*Note: This is a teacher strategy to inform you of key aspects associated with the CLD student biography as they relate to assessment issues (information can also be used to support multiple grouping configurations).

Student Information	L1 Proficiency	L2 Proficiency	Prior Schooling/ Academic Experiences	Student Processing
Name:	Oral (O):	Oral (O):		
Age:	Writing (W):	Writing (W):		
Grade:	Reading (R):	Reading (R):	**Preferred Grouping:**	**Other Assessment Considerations**
Born:	Based on: ___ Observation	Based on: ___ Observation		
Time in United States:	___ Test ___ Both	___ Test ___ Both		♡

Sociocultural:	Language:		Academic:	Cognitive:
Complete the **demographic information** on each student by interviewing the student, his or her family, or a past teacher.	Determine the **first language (L1) proficiency** of the CLD student (this can be done formally or informally). **O:** First language oral proficiency (speaking/listening) **W:** First language writing proficiency **R:** First language reading proficiency	Determine **English language (L2) proficiency** (test scores can be obtained from the district English language proficiency test/ESL teacher). **O:** First oral proficiency (speaking/listening) **W:** English writing proficiency **R:** English reading proficiency	What **prior schooling/academic experiences** does the student have to promote academic knowledge and transfer? In what **grouping** configurations is the student most comfortable (**TPSI:** **T**otal Group, **P**artner, **S**mall Group, or **I**ndependent)?	How does the **student process** information (e.g., solve a math problem, complete a science experiment, summarize a story)? What **other assessment considerations** should be taken into account for this student?

Source: From Herrera, S. (2007) in *By teachers, with teachers, for teachers: ESL Methods* course module
Published by Kansas State University. Copyright © 2007 by Kansas State University.

level, (3) have had some education in the United States but are two or more years below grade level, and (4) have had variable levels of education in the United States and are at grade level. Patterns of classroom and school behaviors and actions that are characteristic of CLD students within each of the previously mentioned groups are also explored in Table 3.5.

After preassessing the biographies of their CLD students, effective teachers reflect on the ways in which they can modify their instruction to better accommodate the needs and assets these students bring to the classroom. Although by no means exhaustive, Table 3.5 provides ideas for teacher actions that would be professionally appropriate given the individual backgrounds of the CLD students present in the classroom. For example, to best accommodate a student who has newly arrived and is below grade level, a teacher would recognize that the child may not be speaking much because he or she is still in the preproduction stage (silent period). Therefore, the teacher emphasizes language comprehension rather than speech production. The teacher also scaffolds instruction and support. In

■ **Snapshot of Classroom Practice 3.1**   CLD Student Biography Cards

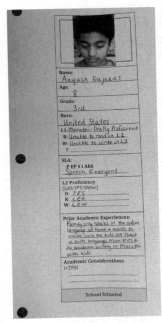

Name:
  Aayush Gajakas
Age:
  8
Grade:
  3rd
Born:
  United States
L1: Marathi- Orally Proficient
R: Unable to read in L2
W: Unable to write in L2
?: _____

SLA:
  P EP S I Ahh
  Speech Emergent

L2 Proficiency
(LAS/IPT/Other)
O: FES
R: LER
W: LEW

Prior Academic Experiences:
  Family only speaks in the native
  language at home + wants to
  make sure the kids are fluent
  in both languages. Mom tries to
  do academic writing in Marathi
  with kids.

Academic Considerations:
  i+TPSI

School Situated

Use of CLD student biography cards provides classroom teachers with insights into each learner's unique background. Given this student's pattern of language use at home, his teacher can encourage the family's continued emphasis on CALP development in the native language.

(Courtesy of Aayush Gajakas)

contrast, if a CLD student has been in the United States for four years and is at grade level, a teacher might best accommodate the student by emphasizing literacy development, especially reading and writing. The teacher also provides (1) content-based sheltered instruction; (2) learning strategy instruction; and (3) scaffolded auxiliary support from paraprofessionals, peers, or parents.

Fostering Communicative, Constructivist Language Acquisition Environments

Insightful teachers understand that second language acquisition takes place most effectively in a **communicative language learning environment**. In such classroom contexts, teachers provide multiple opportunities for academic language interaction among students. Successful teachers foster students' construction of meaning from context and from communication. For example, thematic units grounded in interactive learning encourage hands-on applications that contextualize language. These units also encourage language interactions that are cognitively demanding and academically relevant. Similarly, heterogeneous peer groupings for thematic activities provide the assistance of the more language-capable peer in academic and social interactions focused on learning. Figure 3.4 highlights considerations for utilizing each of the four dimensions of the CLD student biography in practice.

table 3.5 Array of CLD Student Biographies

CLD Student Description	Typical Characteristics of Sociocultural/Acculturation Biography	Typical Characteristics of First Language Biography	Typical Characteristics of Second Language Biography	Typical Characteristics of Schooling/Academic Knowledge Biography	Typical Characteristics of Classroom/School Behaviors/Actions	Professionally Appropriate Teacher Actions
Newly arrived and below grade level (NABG)	In U.S. 2 yrs or less; Ltd. socialization outside home or work Env.; May have lived in a war-torn country; LA may range from culture shock to a transition stage; Score of 8–16 on AQS	Strong BICS, but ltd. CALP dev. in L1; Sometimes illiterate in L1; Will require high levels of ongoing NLS	Ltd. BICS or CALP dev. in L2; Is quite likely to be in silent period of SLA; Will require considerable time to acquire L2 literacy; Is likely to experience difficulty in acquiring CALP skills in L2	Ltd., interrupted, or inconsistent schooling in HC; Will require in-depth, translated preassessment of prior academic knowledge and high-level aux. instructional support; Unlikely to use learning strategies	May exhibit: • Fear of or confusion in the school/classroom env. • Lack of eye contact with the teacher and/or understanding of classroom protocol • Anxiety, withdrawal, hyperactivity; ltd. interaction with peers or unexpected levels of touch	Home visit-based welcome, preassessment, and planning; Heavy emphasis on acclimatization to school/class; Ongoing CALP dev. in L1 via paraprofessionals, parents, resources, media; SLA emphasis on comprehension v. production; Scaffolded instruction/support
Newly arrived and at grade level (NAGL)	In U.S. 2 yrs or less; Some socialization outside home or work env.; LA may range from culture shock to more acculturated; Score of 16–20 on AQS	Strong BICS, and moderate-high level of CALP dev. in L1; Will require moderate-high levels of ongoing NLS	Ltd. BICS or CALP dev. in L2; May be in the preproduction or early production stage of SLA; Will require considerable time to acquire L2 literacy	Expected levels of schooling in HC; Will require appropriate levels of translated preassessment of prior academic knowledge and moderate levels of aux. instructional support	May exhibit: • Frustration with inability to perform at expected levels in school • Desire to seek ways to demonstrate to teacher what he or she knows	Home visit-based welcome, preassessment, and monitoring; Heavy emphasis on acclimatization to school/class; Ongoing CALP dev. in L1 via paraprofessionals, parents, resources, media

Newly arrived and at grade level (NAGL) (*Continued*)			May be likely to experience difficulty in acquiring CALP skills in L2	May use learning strategies	• Rapid drop in level of self-esteem; may display frustration, acting out, boredom, attention-getting actions	SLA emphasizes L2 literacy dev. Content-based and scaffolded instruction, aux. support
Some education in the U.S., but 2 years or more below grade level (USBG)	In U.S. 3 or more years At least moderate socialization outside the home LA may range from transitional to more acculturated Score of 20–24 on AQS	Strong BICS, and medium-moderate level of CALP dev. in L1 Will require moderate levels of ongoing NLS	High-level BICS, and moderate CALP dev. in L2 May be in the early production or speech emergence stages of SLA	Low-variable levels of ed. in HC May have experienced inconsistent ed. in U.S. Appropriate levels of preassessment and instructional support essential Ltd. learning strategy use	May exhibit: • Increasing understanding of school/classroom protocol • Responsiveness to teacher, but ltd. class participation, ltd. response to homework/other assignments • Lack of confidence in academic tasks, reliance on oral responses and participation, ltd. independence	Stress homogeneous and heterogeneous, cooperative learning groups Ongoing CALP dev. in L1 via paraprofessionals, parents, resources, media SLA emphasizes L2 literacy dev. Content-based, sheltered instruction with scaffolded aux. support from teacher, paraprofessionals, peers, parents

(continued)

■ t a b l e 3.5 Continued

CLD Student Description	Typical Characteristics of Sociocultural/Acculturation Biography	Typical Characteristics of First Language Biography	Typical Characteristics of Second Language Biography	Typical Characteristics of Schooling/Academic Knowledge Biography	Typical Characteristics of Classroom/School Behaviors/Actions	Professionally Appropriate Teacher Actions
Variable levels of education in the U.S. and at grade level (USGL)	In U.S. 3 or more years Significant socialization outside the home LA may range from transitional to more acculturated Score of 24+ on AQS is not uncommon	Strong BICS and CALP dev. in L1 are typical Will require maintenance levels of ongoing NLS	High-level BICS, and variable-high levels of CALP dev. in L2 Is often in the speech emergence or intermediate fluency stages of SLA	Expected levels of ed. in HC Typically consistent patterns of ed. in U.S. Appropriate levels of preassessment and instructional support needed Learning strategy use is likely	May exhibit: • Participation and some volunteerism in school protocol and activities • Increasingly appropriate understanding and interaction with teacher/peers • Moderate to medium levels of self-esteem and confidence	Stress independent and cooperative learning Ongoing CALP dev. in L1 via paraprofessionals, parents, resources, media SLA emphasizes production, reading, and writing Content-based, sheltered, and learning strategy instruction with scaffolded aux. support

Legend
AQS—acculturation quick screen
Aux.—auxiliary
BICS—basic interpersonal communication skills
CALP—cognitive academic language proficiency
Dev.—development
Ed.—formal education
Env.—environment
HC—home country
LA—level of acculturation
Ltd.—limited
Literacy—listening, speaking, reading, and writing
NLS—native language support
SLA—second language acquisition

■figure 3.4

Highlights of the Four Dimensions

Sociocultural Processes (core of the prism and the CLD student biography)

- Teachers consider student adjustments to school, community, and home environments.
  - Community Environment—The community environment affects a student's attitude in attending school. Issues of prejudice and discrimination can influence a student's achievement as well as her or his acculturation or assimilation.
  - School Environment—Teachers consider the stressors that may inhibit or enhance a student's learning and act accordingly to reduce his or her affective filter.
  - Classroom Environment—The classroom environment is greatly affected by the climate the teacher creates (i.e., classroom as a community of learners).
  - Home Environment—Native language support from parents is essential. Without it, a student may struggle to successfully transfer CALP in the native language (L1) to CALP in English (L2).
- Other notes: Teachers consider students' self-esteem, anxiety, and other affective factors. This dimension involves all aspects of a student's daily life.

Language Development

- The internal classroom environment fosters the development of the four literacy domains: listening, speaking, reading, and writing.
- External environments promote the status of students' L1 to increase parent, family, and community involvement.
- Students' L1 is viewed as an asset and is used to promote the transfer of skills to L2.
- Opportunities are fostered for social, student–student interaction regardless of linguistic ability.
- L1 and L2 development are supported through the use of culturally responsive materials such as bulletin boards, books, and so on, that represent students' L1 and cultural backgrounds.

Academic Development

- Teachers act as ethnographers, community builders, and facilitators of learning.
- Subject matter is contextually bound and related to the real world to increase CLD students' engagement, connection, and motivation.
- The physical layout of the classroom is conducive to peer collaboration and support of CLD students within content-area lessons.
- High and achievable expectations are placed on CLD students.
- Inclusion of *all* students is the key philosophy within the classroom and school.
- Families' funds of knowledge are valued and incorporated within the classroom and school environments.

Cognitive Development (most overlooked with ELL students)

- Contextual classroom conditions support CLD students to become problem solvers and self-regulators.
- Stretch students cognitively by providing opportunities for the development of higher-order thinking skills ($i + 1$).
- Explicit learning strategy instruction is provided to support CLD students' learning; from this, students can develop pride and ownership of their work and achievements.
- Students' transfer of metacognitive strategies is fostered by purposefully stimulating and igniting connections within the brain to increase brain activity and cellular regeneration.
- Student questioning, dialogue, and funds of knowledge are central components of student learning.

Source: From Herrera, S. (2007) in *By teachers, with teachers, for teachers: ESL Methods* course module Published by Kansas State University. Copyright © 2007 by Kansas State University.

Connect, Engage, Challenge

CONNECT
Review and Reflect on the Reading

1. Reflect on the process of first language acquisition. What percentage of first language acquisition is typically complete by age 6? How long does it typically take an individual to acquire the remainder of her or his first language?

2. Define communicative competence. What is the crucial role of context in communicative competence?

3. Reflect on your own experiences in first language acquisition. At what age and in what ways did you acquire the phonology of your primary language? At what age and in what ways did you acquire the syntax of your primary language?

4. What are the stages of second language acquisition? Explain which stage you would consider the most difficult.

5. Reflect on the stages of SLA. Which stage(s) is (are) associated with limited language production in L2? At what stage does the CLD student possess CALP capacities in L2, and how did you arrive at that conclusion?

6. What is involved in understanding the semantics (i.e., word meaning) of a language? Why is the notion of language semantics so important to a constructivist language-learning environment?

7. When the CLD student is schooled only in L2, what period of time is typically required for him or her to attain grade-level norms?

8. When the CLD student has been schooled in L1 and L2, at least through the fifth or sixth grade, what period of time is typically required for him or her to attain grade-level norms?

ENGAGE
Share What You Learned

1. Discuss why school educators who are charged with the responsibility of educating CLD students often focus almost exclusively on the linguistic dimension of the student biography. Discuss how this dimension is interrelated with the other three dimensions of the CLD student biography (refer to Chapters 1–2 for detailed descriptions).

2. Discuss the ways in which first and second language acquisition compare and contrast. Discuss how the comparisons can be used as a foundation for teaching students in ESL, EFL, and grade-level classrooms.

3. Discuss which three environmental components are crucial to second language acquisition (SLA), according to Wong Fillmore (1991). Discuss in detail the implications of the third component for the teacher's organization of the classroom environment.

CHALLENGE
It's Not Real until You Practice

Preservice Teachers

1. Negotiate with a teacher of CLD students in order to target three separate observations of one CLD student. Through observation, identify what level of second language

acquisition the student demonstrates. Based on your observations, provide a rationale about why this student is at this specific level of second language acquisition. What characteristics are apparent? What successful modifications does the teacher provide for this specific level of second language acquisition? Discuss what further modifications you would add.

2. Sergio, a sixth-grader of Cuban descent, demonstrates understanding of questions asked by the teacher but still cannot respond in English. At baseball practice, Sergio can be overheard occasionally discussing baseball figures with some of his native-English-speaking peers in the dugout. At what level of second language acquisition would you identify Sergio? What characteristics support your finding? Discuss three strategies an educator serving Sergio could use in his or her classroom to foster Sergio's English language acquisition.

3. Imagine your future practice as an educator of CLD students. List and describe three ways you will adapt and modify instruction or practice for CLD students at the various stages of second language acquisition represented in your classroom (choose at least three stages to highlight). How will this affect your instructional planning? What type of literacy environment will be helpful for promoting literacy in the second language for your students?

In-Service Teachers

1. Digitally record a lesson that you teach to your class. Watch it at a later time and identify ways you provide modifications for the various stages of English language acquisition represented in your classroom. Discuss the different ways you address the needs of your CLD students at the initial stages of English language acquisition and the needs of those who are more experienced or proficient with the English language. Are your current modifications successful? What challenges exist? List two ways to address the challenges and then describe at least two additional modifications you would make for students who are at varying language proficiency levels in English (L2).

2. Alba is a tenth-grade student from Bolivia who recently arrived in the United States. She has no language proficiency in English but has been schooled in Bolivia up to grade level in Spanish. Your colleagues are struggling with how to educate her appropriately within their own content areas. What role can native language support provide for Alba's academic success? List and explain five ways your colleagues can help lower the affective filter and meet Alba's academic language proficiency needs within their content areas.

3. Select a content area of focus. What linguistic challenges do you encounter within this content area? Are language expectations unrealistic for the levels of language proficiency represented by students? Is there a real or perceived shortage of materials to enable L1 support? Collaborate with colleagues to brainstorm ways you can address these challenges for students with various language proficiency levels represented in your classroom.

tips for practice

In elementary classrooms, consider:

- Tapping into the prior knowledge and experiences of CLD students and the varying levels of language proficiencies they have in order to make connections between content and students' previous experiences. This will help motivate them as well as engage them in relevant discussions.

- Providing CLD students with a wide variety of authentic grade-level reading material that is linguistically simplified for varying proficiency levels, is relevant to students' lives, supports content taught within the classroom, and includes text in the students' native language.

- Helping to overcome CLD student frustration when beginning to write in English by writing interactively with students (through journals, letters, etc.), freewriting in English or their native language for different periods of time (begin with two-minute sessions and progress to longer periods), or writing a language experience story together (draft a version with the entire class and then have students rewrite their own to make it more personal).

- Increasing student comprehension and helping support the language acquisition process by teaching content vocabulary and concepts using visual cues and simple language, and focusing on communication in meaningful contexts that allow students to express themselves in speech and print.

- Keeping the affective filter low for CLD students by encouraging them to use the second language in various ways, such as labeling pictorial charts with key vocabulary and concepts, accepting inventive or creative spelling, modeling correct speech instead of correcting errors directly, providing opportunities for students to collaborate on projects, and continuing development of content knowledge and skills

through integrated language arts and content-area activities.

In secondary classrooms, consider:

- Posting a guide with a structured checklist for the activities each student needs to complete. Keep these on display for everyone to refer to throughout the lesson in order to check for progress.

- Providing an outline of lessons (in the native language, if possible) for CLD students. Students can use these outlines for note taking and for following along during presentations.

- Promoting higher-order thinking for students of all language proficiency levels through opportunities to problem solve. *Be aware that CLD students' limited English proficiency does not limit their cognitive skills.*

- Scaffolding a lesson for student understanding by asking students to write down one question on a strip of paper about the content or topic. Ask students to share that question with a partner, discuss their answers, and then have pairs share their discussions with the class, on a voluntary basis.

- Encouraging writing for a purpose and creating meaningful connections between content and writing by providing students the opportunity to write in different ways (narrative, comparative, informative essays, etc.).

- Providing a low-risk way to orally practice the second language, review content, and promote oral skills by allowing students to open and close lessons by orally reading or reviewing the day's posted language and content objectives.

In EFL classrooms, consider:

- Having students write the connections they make from their first language in their journal. For example, as the students see cognates or hear a word while listening to music, have them jot it down to help them draw associations and remember these connections to prior knowledge.

- Placing students in heterogeneous groups so that students with different levels of language proficiency can model and scaffold language learning for students with lower proficiency levels.

- Setting conditions where students can practice vocabulary and grammar in low-risk environments with support from the teacher.

- Reminding students of the many opportunities that are available through the use of technology for listening to and practicing their English skills.

assessment tips and strategies

The following preassessment tips and strategies are drawn from the content of Chapters 1 through 3

PREASSESSMENT

Prior to instructional planning, educators should preassess the degree to which CLD students identify with their own cultures as well as the students' levels of acculturation. Preassessment determines the potential impact of the affective filter on the comprehensibility of instruction, and helps educators avoid instructional decisions that may be counterproductive. Constructivist learning environments highlight the need for teachers to preassess the prior knowledge and experiences CLD students bring to the classroom. Rather than assuming that classroom instruction and literacy activities should begin with basic skills and concepts, effective teachers of CLD students use the information gathered from preassessments to guide their instruction. Educators should preassess the following areas of the CLD student biography:

- Sociocultural/acculturation biography
- First language biography
- Second language biography
- Schooling/academic knowledge biography

Preassessment Tips

- Explore the student's cultural background and prior schooling experiences.
- Preassess levels of capacities and development in math, science, and social studies that the student has achieved. Some of these will have been achieved mostly in L1 and in the native country.

Others may have been achieved in the United States through instruction in L2.

- Identify what the CLD student's strongest subject has been.
- Preassess L1 and L2 proficiency.
- Preassess the CLD student's family dynamics and extended family resources.
- Preassess the CLD student's sociocultural realities, including recency of immigration.
- Provide opportunities for the CLD student to demonstrate what he or she understands in a variety of ways and through different media of discourse.
- Preassess the student's levels of literacy development in order to maximize what the CLD student already knows about the connections between print and meaning.

Preassessment Strategies

- Use informal conversations to improve teaching effectiveness, reduce reteaching, motivate students, and avoid making assumptions regarding the learning and cognitive development of CLD students.
- Identify the prior knowledge your students bring to the classroom in order to make connections to the ideas and concepts you are teaching:
  - Use KWL charts.
  - Use freewriting and journal activities.
  - Ask questions and talk with the student about the topic.
  - Preassess the sociocultural realities of CLD students by conducting home visits.

(Courtesy of Jenny Wilk, elementary teacher, Lawrence, Kansas)

PART two

Accommodation Readiness

In Part Two, we encourage educators to preassess their readiness for the accommodative instruction of their language learning students based on their understanding of the four dimensions of the CLD student biography. In Chapter 4, we describe the ways in which programming decisions can serve to frame or restrict a teacher's instructional options for accommodation. On the other hand, in those districts and schools where CLD student programming is not already set, programming decisions provide new opportunities for the appropriate instructional accommodation of CLD students. We also summarize research on program models as a basis for teacher advocacy. In Chapter 5, we introduce the accommodation readiness spiral as a framework for teachers' preassessments of their readiness to deliver mutually accommodative instruction given a specified programming decision. The accommodation readiness spiral is a preassessment tool for readiness in the following areas: critical reflection, CLD students and families, environment, curriculum, instruction, application, and advocacy.

CHAPTER 4

Changing Perspectives in Platform Development for Instructional Methods

our mission

Our mission for this chapter will be to:

· Explore the sorts of programs that have been effective for CLD students whose first language is not English.

We will accomplish this mission by helping you to meet the following learning outcomes:

· Summarize theory and research on effective programming for CLD students.

· Identify variables that may challenge schools' capacities to implement the most effective programming for CLD students.

· Explain the range of program models for CLD students, including English as a second language, transitional bilingual education, developmental bilingual education, two-way immersion, and others that experience limited use.

· Describe sociopolitical foundations of programming for CLD students.

Socorro Herrera

key theories and concepts

additive (or proficient) bilingualism

common underlying proficiency (CUP)

developmental bilingual education

English as a second language (ESL) programs

English-only movement

iceberg metaphor

interference hypothesis

"less equals more" rationale

multilingualism

separate underlying proficiency (SUP)

subtractive (or limited) bilingualism

transfer hypothesis

transitional bilingual education

two-way immersion

When considering the generally unfavorable attitudes many Americans have toward non-English languages spoken in the United States, it is ironic that one of the distinguishing characteristics of the original 13 colonies was **multilingualism** (Kloss, 1997). By 1800, Dutch, French, German, Russian, Spanish, and Swedish communities existed in the United States, many of which had established schools where students were either taught bilingually or exclusively in languages other than English (Brisk, 1981). In fact, not until the passage of the Nationality Act of 1906 did the United States begin to require male immigrants to pass an English proficiency test as a means of limiting immigration, primarily from China and southern Europe (Leibowitz, 1971). In light of our world's increasing use of technology, the ways in which we think about multilingualism are ever changing. These rapid technological advancements allow us to network with others—teachers, family, friends, and scholars—while simultaneously disregarding national borders. Globalization—the use of the Internet, Facebook, Twitter, and other social media outlets that advance learning—leads us to ask the question: Should new program models emerge that are more aligned with current advancements in technology and our move toward globalization? The way in which we answer this question is pivotal, and time is of the essence. In the past, most programs have been a result of parents wanting an equitable education for their children. Although many positive programs have emerged from parents' advocacy for their children, the enacted laws and policies have been reactionary. It is time for us, as educators, to be forward thinking in our policies and classroom practice, instead of merely reacting to the crisis of the moment.

The wave of bilingual education programs across the United States that occurred as a result of Supreme Court cases such as *Lau v. Nichols* (1974), as well as the passage of the Bilingual Education Act (1968), marked a rebirth of some appreciation for multilingualism in this country. Bilingual education encompasses both a philosophical and theoretical orientation to understanding linguistic and academic development. Bilingual education programs for culturally and linguistically diverse (CLD) students have emerged as a result of not only sociopolitical influences but also sociocultural influences. For example, Chicano/a and other Latino/a activists who were interested in school curricula that more actively reflected the contributions of Mexicans and Mexican Americans to U.S. society played a significant role in the reemergence of bilingual education during the 1960s and 1970s (Crawford, 1992; Donato, 1997; Valdez & Steiner, 1972).

This chapter explores a variety of widely used program models for students learning the English language, including bilingual (e.g., dual language) and ESL education, and it summarizes some of the recent research on the effectiveness of various program models for CLD students. The chapter also explores various sociopolitical influences on programming for CLD students. As we discuss these sociopolitical influences on programming, we emphasize the role of court precedent in shaping the range of program models available to school districts and their educators as well as the current characteristics of those models.

■ Effective Program Models for CLD Students: Research and Analysis

Among the most robust and purposeful studies on program effectiveness has been the multifaceted, multisite, longitudinal research of Virginia Collier and Wayne Thomas (Collier, 1987, 1988, 1989a, 1989b, 1992; Collier & Thomas, 1988, 1989; Thomas, 1992, 1994). This research primarily examined the following:

- Length of time needed for students to reach grade-level academic proficiency in L2
- Program and instructional variables influencing language learning and students' academic achievement

From a similar study, Collier and Thomas also acquired, analyzed, and compared findings to the Ramírez data set (Ramírez, Yuen, Ramey, & Pasta, 1991). The school systems that were studied operated established, strongly supported programs with experienced staff. The sample consisted of approximately 42,000 students a year. The types of data analyzed included student background variables; program types; academic achievement, as measured by standardized tests; performance assessment measures; courses in which students were enrolled; and grade-point average. The findings of these studies have greatly contributed to the debate on programming in the United States.

Predictors of Academic Success among CLD Students

Among all possible variables studied, the researchers found that three key predictors of academic success were more influential than any other factors analyzed. More predictive of CLD student success than poverty or socioeconomic status (SES), school location, status of the student's language group, or the student's background were these three variables:

1. Cognitively complex academic instruction primarily delivered through the student's first language and maintained for as long as possible, but secondarily delivered through the second language for a portion of the school day.
2. The intentional use of current approaches in the teaching of the academic curriculum through both L1 and L2, including active, discovery, and cognitively complex learning.
3. Purposeful changes in the sociocultural context of schooling, such as the integration of CLD students with English speakers in a context that is supporting and affirming for all; the development of an additive bilingual context, in which bilingual education is perceived and respected as a gifted and talented program for all students; and the transformation of majority and minority relations in school to a positive, safe environment for all students.

> **Global Connections 4.1**
> Foreign language program types are not yet clearly defined in current research literature. Current language agendas are exploring how implementation of bilingual and dual language programs will look, given the resources and goals of programs. Regardless, many of the variables discussed have generalizability across contexts. Use of L1 and cognitively demanding tasks are critical to L2 development and academic literacy development.

Not only were these three variables found critical to student success, but it was also found that schools incorporating all three of these variables into their pedagogical structure were more likely to graduate CLD students who were academically successful in high school and in higher education.

Findings of Research: The Case for Bilingual Education

Among other analyses arising from this research were conclusions regarding program effectiveness, as summarized by Thomas and Collier (Collier & Thomas, 2009; Thomas & Collier, 1997, 2002, 2012). In general, these conclusions are consistent with those of long-standing research on program models that target second language acquisition (SLA) and academic achievement among English learners (General Accounting Office [GAO], 1987; Ramírez, 1992; Willig, 1981, 1985). These analyses examined the effectiveness of a number of program models for SLA among CLD students, including ESL and bilingual education programs.

Among the conclusions Thomas and Collier (Collier & Thomas, 2009; Thomas & Collier, 1997, 2002, 2012) arrived at, after analyzing over 6.2 million student records, is the following take-away message, which is paramount for CLD student programming.

> All linguistically diverse groups benefit enormously in the long-term from on-grade-level academic work in their first language, for as many years as possible. The more children develop their first language academically and cognitively at an age-appropriate level, the more successful they will be in academic achievement in English by the end of their school years. If learning English is an important instructional goal (and of course it is), full proficiency in academic English (as opposed to only social English or partial English proficiency) is enhanced by long-term bilingual programs. (Collier & Thomas, 2009, p. 48)

Among characteristics found to enhance the effectiveness of long-term bilingual programs (e.g., dual language programs) were the following: (1) the promotion of equal status for each language; (2) the fostering of parental involvement; and (3) the use of instructional approaches that stressed whole language, natural language acquisition in the content areas, and cooperative learning environments. These researchers also concluded that bilingual programs that remained in place at least through the sixth grade yielded substantial academic and cognitive development in L1 and L2 among CLD students. These students were generally able to reach the 50th percentile of the normal curve equivalent (NCE) within four to seven years. The students also maintained their academic gains at the secondary level in content-area classes taught in English. For more on how dual language programs work, watch this video.

Finally, Thomas and Collier (Collier & Thomas, 2009; Thomas & Collier, 1997, 2002, 2012) have summarized their findings regarding the length of time required for CLD students to reach the 50th percentile on standardized tests in the second (English) language. Briefly, their findings are as follows: When CLD students are schooled all in L2 (English) in the United States and tested in L2, (1) students who have completed at least four to five years of on-grade-level schooling in their home country (that is, in L1) require five to seven years to reach the 50th percentile, and (2) students who do not have such a solid educational foundation in their home country (the majority of young immigrant students) rarely reach this goal by the end of high school; those who do require at least seven to ten years, with some support for academic and cognitive development in L1 at home.

On the other hand, when CLD students are on grade level in their L1 and are schooled bilingually in L1 and L2 in the United States, shorter periods of time are typically needed to reach the 50th percentile. For example, when CLD students are tested in L1, they tend to be at or above grade level. When they are tested in L2 (English), even students who would, by inference, otherwise require seven to ten years to reach the 50th percentile, generally need only four to seven years to reach the benchmark.

Accordingly, the conclusions of this longitudinal research, as reported in Thomas and Collier (Collier & Thomas, 2009; Thomas & Collier, 1997, 2002, 2012), strongly indicate that the most effective programming for CLD students is bilingual education. Specifically, two-way immersion (also known as two-way dual language education) programs were most effective in maintaining grade-level skills in the first language and in reducing the time needed to achieve at least the 50th percentile of NCE in the second language.

Bilingual Education and the SUP–CUP Distinction

Another strong rationale for bilingual education was provided by Cummins (1981) as the SUP–CUP distinction (separate underlying proficiency–common underlying proficiency). According to Cummins, individuals who view the assimilation of immigrant students as a critical function of schools typically argue that the school must maximize experiences and practice with English if second language learners are to be successful in school. This view, according to Cummins (1981), is grounded in a perspective on language dynamics that he calls **separate underlying proficiency (SUP)**.

As illustrated in Figure 4.1, the SUP perspective assumes that the two languages operate independently. Therefore, no transfer occurs between them. From this perspective, providing CLD students with resources, instruction, or literacy development in their native language would be a futile effort; increasing English language exposure is the path to English language development and, therefore, school success. This **interference hypothesis** holds that ongoing development in the first language so interferes with second language learning that effort should not

Relationships between First and Second Language Proficiency

When we build on the native language, we build on the potential for English language proficiency.

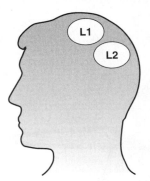

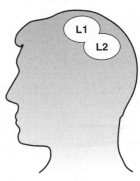

Separate Underlying
Proficiency (SUP)

Common Underlying
Proficiency (CUP)

■ f i g u r e 4 . 1
Separate Underlying
Proficiency (SUP)/
Common Underlying
Proficiency (CUP)

Source: Reprinted by permission from Cummins, J. (1981). The role of primary language development in promoting educational success for language minority students. In C. F. Leyba (Ed.), *Schooling and language minority students: A theoretical framework* (pp. 3–49). Copyright 1981 by Legal Books Distributing, Los Angeles CA.

be wasted in either native language support or ongoing development in the first language.

On the other hand, Cummins (1981) argues that, although the two languages may seem separate on the surface, they are actually quite interdependent at the deeper level of cognitive functions. For example, it is a well-established finding that students who learn to read and write in their first language are able to readily transfer those abilities to a second language (Edelsky, 1982; Faltis, 1986; Hudelson & Serna, 1994; Krashen, 1996). This **transfer hypothesis** is equally valid in other subject domains, including math and science (Henderson & Landesman, 1992; Minicucci, 1996). Regarding the transfer of literacy skills, Brown (1994) notes that our natural tendency to notice the language errors that are inevitable for students often obscures our capacity to also notice the facilitating effects of the first language. Brown emphasizes the benefits a language learner receives when this transfer occurs. Cummins (1981) maintains that these facilitating effects arise from a **common underlying proficiency** (**CUP**) that, like an operating system, connects the two languages of a bilingual individual so that prior knowledge and academic skills in one language are transferable to learning and performance in another (see Figure 4.1).

A more graphic representation of these underlying and facilitating effects associated with CUP is provided by the **iceberg metaphor** (Cummins, 1981) of Figure 4.2. These subsurface facilitating effects that may be associated with the notion of CUP also provide a strong rationale for bilingual education (Faltis & Hudelson, 1998) because what is learned well in one language need not be relearned in a second (Krashen, 1996).

Cummins (1981) has discussed this argument as a **"less equals more" rationale** for bilingual education. That is, CLD students will learn more English when they are first permitted to meaningfully participate in school activities that are provided in the language with which they are comfortable, the language that already equips them for oral and written communication. Thus, an environment that provides less English early on eventually leads to more

> **Global Connections 4.2**
> Teachers of EFL often wonder about the use of the L1 during instruction. It is important to understand the SUP–CUP distinction and plan instruction accordingly. Instruction should be planned strategically and for systematic use of the native language. Learning the English language can be more meaningful and engaging when students' native language is used as a bridge for second language learning.

■ **figure 4.2**

Iceberg Metaphor of Second Language Comprehension and Production

Source: Reprinted by permission from Cummins, J. (1981). The role of primary language development in promoting educational success for language minority students. In C. F. Leyba (Ed.), *Schooling and language minority students: A theoretical framework* (pp. 3–49). Copyright 1981 by Legal Books Distributing, Los Angeles CA.

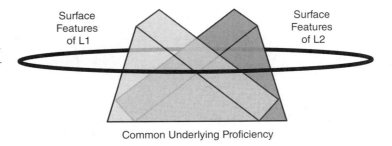

Surface Features of L1   Surface Features of L2

Common Underlying Proficiency

theory *into* Practice 4.1

The *transfer hypothesis* (Cummins, 1981) holds that the CLD student who develops literacy in the first language is able to transfer those abilities to a second language. This transfer hypothesis is equally valid in other subject domains, including math and science (Henderson & Landesman, 1992; Minicucci, 1996). The transfer hypothesis is particularly important to the developing reading skills of CLD students. For example, research by Nagy, Garcia, Durgunoglu, and Hancin-Bhatt (1993) demonstrated a strong relationship between phonological awareness in Spanish and word recognition in English. Specifically, CLD students who could perform well on tests of phonological awareness in Spanish were more likely to demonstrate the ability to read English words and English-like pseudowords than were students who performed poorly on tests of phonological awareness in Spanish. The researchers have argued that this cross-language transfer pattern suggests that phonological awareness in L1 facilitates word recognition, schooling, and learning to read in L2.

■ *What classroom environment would you structure to foster cross-language transfer? What sorts of instructional strategies might build on the CLD student's literacy skills in L1 as a means to literacy development in L2?*

English later because students are able to first elaborate on shared language understandings, knowledge bases, and repertoires of literacy skills.

Nonetheless, there are at least two ways in which bilingualism, as a means to English acquisition (SLA), may occur. **Subtractive (or limited) bilingualism** may occur when the student's first language is gradually replaced by the more dominant language (Cummins, 1979). In the case of subtractive bilingualism, students may develop relatively low levels of academic proficiency in both languages. Conversely, **additive (or proficient) bilingualism** is associated with positive cognitive effects that enable the CLD student to attain high levels of proficiency in both languages. Research has demonstrated that CLD students who are the product of additive bilingualism outperform monolinguals on a variety of cognitive tasks (Bialystok, 2001; Carlson & Meltzoff, 2008; Emmorey, Luk, Pyers, & Bialystok, 2008; Mezzacappa, 2004).

■ **Snapshot of Classroom Practice 4.1**   Bilingual Vocabulary Book

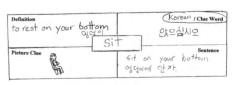

A teacher uses a bilingual vocabulary book in her classroom to assist a Korean student with transferring words from L1 to L2.

(Courtesy of Geraldine Bukaty, elementary school teacher, Lawrence, Kansas)

When the Ideal Is Not Ideal

As the number of CLD students in the United States continues to grow at a phenomenal rate and the families of the students increasingly migrate to previously unaffected regions of the country (as is increasingly the case with many midwestern and southern states), there are times, places, and situations in which the ideal is not always ideal. That is, circumstances sometimes preclude the maximization of what research and analysis has demonstrated to be the most effective programming for CLD students. Certainly, this scenario is often frustrating and demoralizing, especially for advocates of students and families. It is a reality that must be reflectively and proactively addressed if existing school-specific circumstances are to be confronted in a manner that maximizes the possibilities for CLD students.

> **Illustrated Concept 4.1**
>
> Involve CLD students in extracurricular activities and lower their affective filters by showcasing the talents of various cultural groups, publishing bilingual student newspapers, or organizing international clubs or festivals.

Complicating Variables

As these dynamics manifest themselves each day in school systems throughout the nation, a variety of variables complicate the implementation of ideal programming for English learners. These variables include the following examples.

Complicating Geographic Variables

Implementing the most effective programming for CLD students is difficult in rural school systems in which the following issues exist:

- The population of CLD students is increasing, but the population size remains insufficient to enable bilingual programming or program models.
- The increasing numbers of CLD students who speak a common first language (e.g., Spanish) would enable bilingual programming, but qualified bilingual teachers either do not reside in the region or community or cannot be successfully recruited to that rural region.
- The number of CLD students justifies bilingual programming, but the school system is geographically isolated from four-year degree-granting institutions to which bilingual and other paraprofessionals who are interested in teacher education careers can be persuaded to matriculate after their community college experiences.

Implementing the most effective programming for CLD students is difficult in urban school systems in which the following issues exist:

- The number of languages represented among CLD students is too varied to enable bilingual programming.
- The student distribution patterns across schools (court-ordered attendance patterns) preclude bilingual programming.

dilemmas of *Practice* 4.1

Mr. Jensen, a teacher at Great Plains High School, offers his opinion about English language learners while eating lunch in the teachers' lounge. He believes that students should be immersed in English-only classes in order to learn English as quickly as possible. He argues that his ancestors from Europe did not have special services and they "did just fine."

■ *If you were a colleague of Mr. Jensen's with the knowledge you have now of additive and subtractive bilingualism, how would you respond?*

Complicating Sociopolitical Variables

National Level. Sociopolitical initiatives at the national level, including the **English-only movement** (U.S. English, 1990), have argued that the nation confuses immigrants by offering them any language option except English—in schools, voting, documentation materials, and so forth. Such groups (despite the studies highlighted in this chapter) have argued that "no research" exists that supports bilingual education (Stevens, 2002). A more recent example of the English-only movement was during the 2012 presidential campaign, in which presidential candidate, Rick Santorum, advocated for Puerto Rico to become English-only if the territory opted to be a state (Seelye & Parker, 2012). With this political move, Santorum essentially isolated much of the Puerto Rican population, most of whom speak Spanish, by suggesting that, if opting into statehood, the territory would have to make English its primary language.

State Level. In states such as California, Arizona, Colorado, Massachusetts, and Oregon, initiatives have sought to limit or eliminate bilingual education (Mora, 2009). Most recently, voters in Nashville, Tennessee, were faced with a decision to make the capital city English-only, which would have halted many bilingual programs, including education and civic translation services. Nashville residents did not vote for the English-only bill, but if it had passed, Nashville would have been the largest city to move toward an English-only culture (Harris, 2009). In some states (e.g., California), such initiatives have limited, at least by title, the range of program models that can be implemented for CLD students (Crawford, 2000). Some states either do not offer a bilingual education endorsement or certification for school educators or have eliminated it from the endorsements or certificates that school educators can acquire. These circumstances limit the pool of qualified educators available to implement bilingual education.

Global Connections 4.3
All educators must strive to create a community of learners who are ready for the challenges of this global world. In language classrooms with international students, practitioners can help students explore topics through each other's cultural and linguistic lenses. For example, the teacher can pose a simple question such as "How is it done/viewed in your native country or home?" By allowing learners to share their unique perspectives, we open doors for innumerable linguistic and cross-cultural connections.

Local Level. In certain regions and localities of the country, the lack of advocacy for the rights of CLD students to an appropriate education has fostered district-programming policies that have effectively limited the availability of appropriate program models for English learners. An example of these district-programming policy changes is the ban of the Mexican American Studies program in Tucson, Arizona. In 2010, the Tucson Unified School District voted to ban their Mexican American Studies program, arguing that the books and curriculum offered to the students incited racial division and suggested an overthrow of the U.S. government (Robbins, 2013; Planas, 2013). In light of this ban, teachers were forced out of their jobs and Mexican American students had no access to their histories.

Many times, parents who encounter this type of situation do not have the appropriate resources to advocate for their students' needs in the classroom. However, in the Tucson, Arizona, Mexican American Studies case, teachers, parents, and former and current students were outraged that the school district had taken away the opportunity for ethnic histories to be told in the classroom. Due to their protests, the federal government called the bill unconstitutional and required the school district to reinstate the program, but not without some obstacles. Although the school district reinstated the program, the state still views the district's new curriculum as inappropriate, thus leaving teachers, parents, and students caught in the middle of a messy sociopolitical battle (Planas, 2013).

For a variety of reasons, many parents of CLD students unfortunately are unable to successfully advocate for appropriate and effective programming for their children (de Lopez & Montalvo-Cisneros, 1986; Escamilla, 1999; Kang, Kuehn, & Herrell, 1996; Ovando, Combs, & Collier, 2011). Reasons for this situation include:

Illustrated Concept 4.2

Create a positive environment in your school and classroom by learning about the demographic groups represented in your school and validating each, promoting cross-cultural appreciation among staff members by informing them of what you have learned or know about the cultures represented, developing a guiding mission statement that reflects the diversity of your school and your classroom, and advocating for a schoolwide environment that ensures equitable distribution of materials, facilities, and resources for all cultures and nationalities represented.

- Language differences
- Parental or caregiver work schedules
- Parent–teacher conference schedules and limited home visits by school educators and counselors
- Prior negative experiences with schools or teachers
- Culture-based deference to teachers in matters of schooling, instruction, and assessment
- Perceptions of cultural or language deficiency
- Shortage of school educators of that cultural or ethnic group, especially school counselors or outreach staff
- Perceptions that school is not a welcoming environment

As these examples demonstrate, although research has informed our understanding of effective and ideal programming for CLD students, other variables of environment, circumstance, and situation sometimes limit our capacity to implement the ideal. Therefore, it is important for us as educators to become acquainted with the more inclusive range of program models available for English learners. Educators who serve as advocates for the best programming possible need to understand the range of possibilities and make their voices heard in doing what is best for CLD students and their families.

■ Range of Program Models for CLD Students

Although the range of program models available to English learners across the United States is broad, it is perhaps not as diverse as the many titles by which similar programs are often labeled. Accordingly, the subject of programming for CLD students may at times seem complex and confusing. Yet a foundational understanding of program models is essential to the selection of appropriate instructional methods for students.

This description of program models is intended to simplify the seeming complexities of program labels while focusing on four basic aspects of each program model described: (1) the foundations of the program model, (2) key program characteristics, (3) essentials of program implementation, and (4) concerns regarding that program model. Consistent with the findings on program effectiveness described by Thomas and Collier (Collier & Thomas, 2009; Thomas & Collier, 1997, 2002, 2004, 2012), these descriptions of general-use program models proceed from least effective to most effective. Four general-use program models are discussed in detail, followed by an overview of two additional, limited-use program models. When reviewing these models, readers are encouraged to think about the programs with which they are familiar and consider the characteristics they share with the following descriptions.

English as a Second Language (ESL)

In the literature of the field, **English as a second language (ESL) programs**, also referred to as ESOL (English to speakers of other languages) models, are variously considered:

- Crucial components of any bilingual program (Ovando, Combs, & Collier, 2011)
- Programs of a transitional perspective, grounded in a philosophy suggesting that the use of native language retards English development (Faltis & Hudelson, 1998)
- Models of immersion (that is, immersion in L2) education (Linquanti, 1999)

Various types of ESL programming exist. First, ESL content models are typically (but not necessarily) implemented in self-contained classrooms (e.g., structured immersion), usually for the full school day. Next, ESL pull-out models require auxiliary classrooms and teachers for varying periods of time during the school day and are therefore the most expensive (but least effective program models

■ Voices from the Field 4.1

"Our school uses the ESL pull-out method when working with CLD students. I had assumed this approach was the best method and that the students were receiving adequate instruction. However, I had not taken into account the curriculum the students were missing out on within my classroom. I had presumed the ESL teacher was teaching the same material and curriculum as I was in the regular education classroom. Yet, as a classroom teacher, I did not meet with the ESL teacher to see what she was teaching, nor did I receive reports about what the students did while they were pulled out. After learning about the downfalls of ESL pull-out, I decided to schedule weekly meetings with the ESL teacher. During these meetings, I shared my lesson plans for the upcoming week with her. Before our meetings, I had taught certain letters during the week and she had taught completely different letters. Instead of receiving multiple exposures to the same material, the students had been introduced to more material, which had caused confusion. When we began to teach the same material, we saw an improvement within our students. They experienced more success inputting the information into their permanent memory."

■ *Reprinted by permission from Lorle Bolt. Copyright © by Lorle Bolt, elementary school teacher, Fort Riley, Kansas.*

[Collier & Thomas, 2009; Crawford, 1997; Thomas & Collier, 1997, 2002, 2004, 2012]). Last, ESL subject models are less frequently implemented and require from one to two periods of classroom instruction a day.

English as a second language program models, although less effective with CLD students than certain bilingual education programs (e.g., dual language programs), often arise as a result of complicating variables, including geographic and sociopolitical variables. For example, at the geographic level, bilingual program models are often not possible in rural school districts that have moderately high numbers of English learners but are unable to recruit qualified bilingual educators. Sociopolitical variables may also complicate the use of bilingual program models. For example, some states do not offer school educators an endorsement in bilingual education. Therefore, even when districts have a sufficient number of interested local and bilingual educators (e.g., paraprofessionals) for the development of a self-generated certification program, these states preclude the endorsement of educators in bilingual education. In such districts, an ESL program model is sometimes the only adequate alternative.

Foundations

English as a second language programming tends to be grounded in the philosophy that through appropriate instructional support (including scaffolding, guarded vocabulary, conceptualization, hands-on cooperative learning, etc.), CLD students can be transitioned to an instructional and learning environment that offers no significant first language support (Faltis & Hudelson, 1998; Linquanti, 1999). Therefore, the model is grounded on the premise that the teacher need not be fluent in the student's first language and that comprehensible input in L2 will carry the day. Although stronger types of ESL programming emphasize second language learning through content-area instruction, other types treat language learning in isolation from content-area learning. Although ESL pull-out programs are the most implemented type of ESL, they are also the least effective (Collier & Thomas, 2009; Thomas & Collier, 1997, 2002, 2004, 2012).

Characteristics

Program models for ESL vary significantly in the extent to which they emphasize clearly delineated language and content objectives. Certain types, including integrated content-based ESL and sheltered instruction, strongly emphasize both categories of objectives. Others, most notably ESL pull-out programs, typically treat language learning in isolation and as a compensatory issue, paying little or no attention to content objectives (Chambers & Parrish, 1992; Faltis & Hudelson, 1998; Ovando, Combs, & Collier, 2011).

In contrast to "sink or swim" or extremely limited ESL programming, more effective models of ESL programming (e.g., CALLA instruction [Chamot, 2009; Chamot & O'Malley, 1994], sheltered content instruction [Echevarria & Graves, 2010]) typically emphasize frequent opportunities for language interaction, the scaffolding of instruction, and constructivist activities focused on the derivation of meaning from context, language, and support structures (Echevarria & Graves, 2010; Linquanti, 1999; Ovando, Combs, & Collier, 2011). A focus on language interactions typically involves frequent and sometimes extended opportunities for teacher–student and student–student communication that integrates use of listening, speaking, reading, and writing skills. A language interaction environment that reduces the affective filter and emphasizes literacy development and the construction of meaning from these experiences is most favorable.

Through scaffolding, teachers restructure instruction to a level that encourages student success until the learner is ready for increasingly higher levels of understanding. Scaffolding might involve contextualization of the lesson, peer-to-peer interactions, elaboration of prior knowledge or student responses, outlines of the material to be covered in a lesson, and more. Constructivist student activities in an ESL environment are made meaningful through the use of hands-on or application activities that directly relate to the grade-level or content-area curriculum. For example, a lesson on estimation can be rendered more meaningful when it is enriched by a hands-on activity involving estimates about the number of items in a jar, followed by the actual counting of those items.

Essentials and Concerns

Effective ESL program models demand a number of prerequisites to ensure the likelihood that CLD students are able to comprehend the instruction and prove successful in both content-area and language learning. To achieve this level of effectiveness, it is first essential that ESL instruction be intentionally grounded in the grade-level or content-area curriculum. Second, school educators must receive adequate professional development to deliver appropriately restructured instruction that scaffolds or shelters the curriculum to ensure comprehension, learning, and application (Herrera, Murry, & Perez, 2008). Finally, authentic alternative assessments are crucial to the measurement of both process and product gains in language, acculturation, and content-area learning among CLD students. At minimum, such assessments should encompass criterion-referenced, incremental, and informal measures, including rubrics, self-assessments, and portfolios (Herrera, Cabral, & Murry, 2013). Whenever possible, alternative assessments in L1 should also be incorporated, including journals, one-on-one (translated) discussions, interviews, and so forth.

Administrative buy-in and support of the program model is essential to the effectiveness of ESL programs. Site-based administrators must be at least as well informed and trained as the school and classroom educators who are serving CLD students. Informed administrators are capable of creating a vision for the program, monitoring its appropriate implementation, and evaluating both classroom assessments and program effectiveness (Herrera & Fanning, 1999; Short, Vogt, & Echevarria, 2008).

The following represent some of the concerns regarding ESL program models. Such programs, especially ESL pull-out programs, can prove costly because resource teachers must be recruited, trained, supported, and evaluated. Although a few ESL programs make provision for some level of auxiliary native language support, typically these programs do not support or further students' ongoing CALP development in L1. The consequences of this omission are one reason why ESL pull-out programs are the least effective of all program models. The pull-out programs also tend to stigmatize CLD students while isolating them from critical content-area instruction. Finally, some ESL programs may not be focused on both literacy development and language development in L2, and ESL educators may inadvertently engage in assumptions about the student's level of BICS versus CALP proficiency in L2.

Transitional Bilingual Education

Largely due to long-standing patterns of federal funding for bilingual education, transitional programs (also referred to as *early-exit programs* [Ramírez, 1992] due to the short-term nature of bilingual support typically provided) are the most common form of bilingual programming. In the United States, **transitional bilingual education** provides students with instruction in their native language for all subject areas, as well as instruction in L2 (English) as a second language. Nonacademic classes such as music, art, and physical education might also be delivered in L2 (Medina, 1995). However, this program of transitional instruction is sustained for only a limited number of years (typically two to three years in the United States). Students are then gradually transitioned into L2-only instruction. Although the native language of CLD students is transitionally supported by this program model, most transitional bilingual programs favor a goal of instruction in L2 (English) as soon as it is feasible (Genesee, 1999; Ovando, Combs, & Collier, 2011).

Foundations

Transitional bilingual education emphasizes the mastery of grade-appropriate academic skills and knowledge that are initially attained through the student's first language. At the same time, the model seeks to accelerate English (L2) language development so that students can be transitioned to English-only grade-level classrooms more rapidly. As with other bilingual programs, one key rationale for the transitional model rests with the SUP–CUP distinction and the transfer hypothesis (Cummins, 1981, 1991). That is, many literacy skills and a great deal of knowledge acquired in the first language will transfer to the second. In particular, students learn to read and write with the least degree of difficulty when they learn to do so in the language they already know. Too often the reading and writing aspects of literacy development are postponed until the student can comprehend and speak English (Anderson, 1999; Cooper, 1986; Cummins, 2001b; Cunningham, Moore, Cunningham, & Moore, 2003; National Reading Panel, 2000; Pearson, 1984; Peregoy & Boyle, 2012; Snow, Burns, & Griffin, 1998). In a transitional program, students can begin to read and write immediately in their first language as part of content-area learning. The literacy skills attained by this approach will transfer to English (Cummins, 1981), according to the dynamics of the transfer hypothesis.

The content-area instruction of CLD students through their first language as they are gradually learning English allows the students to perform on par with their grade-level peers in the content areas because they are learning in the language with which they are already comfortable. This transitional support in the early years of schooling not only lowers the affective filter but also increases motivation and confidence in academic learning. Genesee (1999) has noted that early instruction in the student's first language increases the likelihood that the student's parents, who often speak no English, will be involved in the educational process. The native language support provided in the content areas by the transitional model allows the student to maintain ongoing CALP development in L1 as he or she transitions into literacy development in the second language (Collier & Thomas, 2009; Cummins, 1981, 1991; Thomas & Collier, 1997, 2002, 2004, 2012).

Characteristics

Transitional bilingual programming provides students with native language support in the content areas as they are learning English. Along with this provision of the model, content-area instruction is also typically sheltered during the transition period (Genesee, 1999). The subsequent transition is often initiated with mathematics instruction in L2 (especially computations), followed by reading, then writing and science, and then social studies. Most transitional programs begin in kindergarten or first grade and target oral proficiency in L2 within two years.

These programs also typically target all-English instruction by the third grade for those who began in kindergarten, and the fourth grade for those who began transitional bilingual education in the first grade.

Essentials and Concerns

Transitional bilingual education is built on the premise that CLD students can learn to read and write in their first language and master grade-level skills, content, and concepts from subject-area instruction in that language. Accordingly, skillful and effective instruction in the first language is a programming prerequisite of paramount importance. This model relies on effective transitional instruction that (1) is gradual, (2) capitalizes on the transfer of reading and writing skills, and (3) minimizes the risk of raising students' affective filters. Ultimately, instruction must also be scaffolded or sheltered so that the academic content is made comprehensible to the students while the skills to be developed are introduced in an incremental, process-oriented manner. For these reasons, highly qualified instructors are essential to the effective implementation of transitional bilingual education.

Successful transitional programming also requires a challenging curriculum, demanding standards, and accurate assessment. Because students are receiving content-area instruction in their native language, and because this structure is provided for a limited period, the curriculum that grounds the instruction should stretch the learner toward new levels of performance (Ramírez, 1992; Linquanti, 1999). Rigorous standards and expectations are one way to better ensure that students attain such performance. Nonetheless, student assessments, particularly in the area of second language development, must be carefully implemented and accurately interpreted in order to ensure that students are progressing and to gauge what additional support will be needed when the students exit from the program.

Perhaps the most worrisome problem with transitional bilingual education is the limited time the students are allowed to transition to L2 (English). The premises on which this aspect of the model rests are not consistent with the research regarding the time required for English learners to attain grade-level proficiency and skills in the second language (Collier & Thomas, 2009; Thomas & Collier, 1997, 2002, 2012). Although some *late-exit* transitional programs exist that provide bilingual programming for four to six years, these still do not provide CLD students with the full benefits of more additive forms of bilingual education (Collier & Thomas, 2009; Thomas & Collier, 2012). Also of concern is the fact that transitional bilingual programs are often perceived, by both students and staff, as segregated, compensatory education (Faltis & Hudelson, 1998; Ovando, Combs, & Collier, 2011). Such programming may be viewed as stigmatizing, maintaining the status quo, or perpetuating a perception of a lower-class status among CLD students.

Global Connections 4.4
It is important to remember that students already have tools for developing new skills and acquiring new knowledge. When teachers acknowledge and capitalize on learners' *existing* skills and knowledge, students thrive. By using students' L1 strategically, we are able to engage them in higher levels of thinking and English language production.

Developmental Bilingual Education

Developmental bilingual education, unlike the transitional program model, is more consistent with what we know about how long it takes CLD students to reach high levels of CALP development in L2 (Collier & Thomas, 2009; Ramírez, 1992; Thomas & Collier, 1997, 2002, 2012). Despite the fact that developmental bilingual programming is far less prevalent than either the transitional bilingual or ESL program models, it is more effective (Thomas & Collier, 2012) and less likely to foster a perception of compensatory education (Genesee, 1999; Linquanti, 1999). Also referred to as *maintenance bilingual education* or *one-way dual language education* (Thomas & Collier, 2012), developmental programming enriches the education of CLD students by using both L1 and L2 for academic instruction. First introduced in the 1960s, the title was changed from "maintenance" to "developmental" (approximately 1984) in order to avoid negative political interpretations of the model as a perpetuator of first language maintenance (Genesee, 1999). In a developmental program, CLD students receive content-area instruction in their first and second languages through all grade levels provided by their school system. Most studies of the model indicate that a minimum of five to six years in such a program are required for participating students to demonstrate high academic achievement in L2 (Collier & Thomas, 2009; Collier, 1992; Cummins, 2001c; Thomas & Collier, 1997, 2002, 2012). Some developmental program models are implemented in grades K–12, and a smaller number also enrich the curriculum with lessons from the study of cross-cultural dynamics.

Foundations

At the foundational level, **developmental bilingual education** is well grounded in each of the dimensions of the prism model, a holistic model for CLD student education developed by Thomas and Collier (1997) and detailed in Chapter 1. From a sociocultural perspective, developmental programming clearly communicates to CLD students the value of both the cultural and the linguistic resources they bring to the classroom (Cummins, 1998). The model also better facilitates the involvement of parents (who may not speak English) in the student's socialization and education. At the cognitive and academic levels of the prism model, developmental bilingual education acknowledges and builds on research (Ramírez, 1992; Thomas & Collier, 1997, 2002, 2012) that stresses the importance of using L1 to develop cognitive capacities and academic knowledge and skills, which may then be transferred to the second language. From a linguistic viewpoint, developmental programming is consistent with what we know about CALP development in L1, language transfer, and second language acquisition.

Characteristics

Typically, developmental programming begins with kindergarten or first grade, and the program expands to include one additional grade each year thereafter. The critical subject areas are taught through both English (L2) and the student's first language (L1) for as many grades as the structure of the school system can support. Although most developmental models emphasize Spanish and English, other first languages can also be supported, including Chinese, Korean, Navajo, and Vietnamese. Whatever the primary language of programming, students at almost any level of proficiency in L2 can be served in the same developmental classroom. Full academic language proficiency in both languages is the goal of developmental programming. The exploration of information and knowledge across academic domains is targeted in both languages, as sheltered instructional techniques are often used to scaffold academic instruction in L2. As with two-way programs discussed in subsequent sections, program-specific decisions are made about the proportion of instruction provided in each language.

Developmental bilingual education also seeks to minimize perceptions of subtractive, compensatory education by emphasizing content-area learning in two languages, with proficiency in each valued as an additive objective. The first language is no longer treated merely as a bridge to the second; it is valued as an asset with various unique advantages (Cummins, 1998; Padilla & Gonzalez, 2001). The developmental model can also prove especially beneficial to students in those regions of the country where multilingualism reaps certain economic rewards.

Essentials and Concerns

First and foremost, school educators who are critical to developmental programming must receive adequate professional development in effective methods, strategies, and techniques of language and content-area instruction. Teachers who instruct in effective developmental programs use content-area curriculum, content-based instruction, hands-on and scaffolding materials, presentations that target a variety of learning strategies, peer and mixed groupings, extensive collaboration with paraprofessionals, multimodal presentations, computer resources, interactive and discovery learning techniques, multicultural resource tools, and more (Genesee, 1999; Moll, Amanti, & Gonzalez, 1992). Therefore, ongoing professional development for all staff, including qualified bilingual educators, is essential to classroom effectiveness in developmental bilingual education.

Successful implementation of developmental programming also requires both integration and separation. On the one hand, students must be integrated, regardless of their language proficiency in the language of instruction, in order to maximize learning from more capable peers. Heterogeneous student groupings are often essential in the content areas. On the other hand, the languages of instruction must be clearly separated in developmental programming. Language mixing and concurrent translation should be avoided in order to maximize the development of proficiency in each language of the program model. Most important, these two seemingly disparate goals of integration and separation must remain the target for the duration of the program. Research has consistently demonstrated that CLD students need four to seven years in such a program to acquire full proficiency in all aspects of both languages and to attain full parity with language majority students in the content areas (Collier, 1992, 1995; Hakuta, 2011; Ramírez, 1992; Thomas & Collier, 1997).

Among general concerns associated with developmental bilingual education are those regarding the following groups of students: (1) students who enter the program late, (2) students who are highly transient, and (3) students who exit the program early. It is often difficult to maintain the continuity of the program model across grade levels and schools. Certainly, a district-level coordinator is critical. A developmental program coordinator who collaborates closely with program teachers, program support staff, building-level administrators, and resource agents for the district is even more beneficial.

Two-Way Immersion

Two-way immersion programs, also known as *two-way dual language programs,* are an increasingly popular way to attract public support for multilingualism. The two-way model offers integrated language and academic instruction for both CLD students and native English speakers. Among the objectives of two-way programming are first and second language proficiency, strong academic performance in the content areas, cross-cultural celebration, and cross-lingual understandings (Christian, 1994; Cummins, 2001b).

Cummins (2001b) has argued that two-way programs may offer advocates the best hope of transforming the rhetoric of what he calls the "Us versus Them" discourse, which characterizes the bilingual debate. In making this argument, Cummins cites the work of Porter (1996) and Glenn and LaLyre (1991) in noting the mutually beneficial advantages of two-way programming, including a language-rich environment, a climate of cross-cultural respect, high expectations for every child, genuine bilingualism for the majority population, mutual learning and enrichment, and comparatively manageable implementation costs.

Two-way programming integrates language learning with content-based instruction. Subject-area instruction is delivered to all students through both English and the language of CLD students. Most two-way programs begin in kindergarten or first grade and extend through the completion of elementary school. Ideally, two-way programs extend at least through middle school, and through high school, if possible (Thomas & Collier, 2012). All students enrolled benefit from an additive bilingual environment because each language is engaged in the development of content knowledge.

Foundations

In general, two-way immersion programs are grounded in research and analysis pertinent to both first and second language acquisition (Bley-Vroman, 1988; Chomsky, 1966; Ney & Pearson, 1990; Ramírez, 1992; Thomas & Collier, 1997, 2002) and the dynamics of cross-cultural and multilingual interactions (Gleason, 1961; Lindholm, 1992; Veeder & Tramutt, 2000; Whorf, 1956). From the linguistic perspective, research has indicated that instruction in the second language, which is balanced with first language support, tends to yield higher levels of achievement among CLD students than instruction delivered only in the second language (Collier & Thomas, 2009; Genesee, 1999; Thomas & Collier, 1997, 2002, 2004, 2012). Additionally, academic knowledge and skills acquired in the first language facilitate the acquisition of new knowledge and skills in the second language (Collier, 1989b; Collier & Thomas, 2009). Research also indicates that a second language (i.e., English) is best acquired by CLD students, especially non-English-speaking (NES) students, only after their first language is firmly established (Edelsky, 1982; Lanauze & Snow, 1989; Saunders & Goldenberg, 1999). Quality immersion programming for native English speakers enables students to develop advanced levels of L2 proficiency without compromising academic performance or their first language development (Genesee, 1983, 1987; Swain & Lapkin, 1982).

From the sociocultural perspective, two-way immersion programming builds on the notion of mutually more capable peers (Vygotsky, 1978). That is, CLD students who are acquiring English will benefit from social and academic interaction with native-English-speaking students who are more capable in English. In like manner, native-English-speaking students who participate in a two-way program benefit from their CLD peers, who are more capable in their first language and more knowledgeable about their native culture and life outside the United States. At the same time, CLD students serving in this capacity for native-English-speaking students gain self-esteem, motivation, and an enhanced level of pride in their own culture (Lindholm, 1992).

Characteristics

Two basic versions of the two-way model have gained popularity in the United States: the 90–10 model and the 50–50 model. Both versions target bilingualism as the ultimate goal, and both focus on the core academic curriculum. The 90–10 version of two-way programming first targets development in the language of the CLD student. For example, in a Spanish–English program, grade 1 students would receive 90 percent of their instruction in Spanish from their classroom teachers. The remaining 10 percent of instruction, delivered in English, would emphasize oral language development in English. Grade 2 instruction in English would increase to 20 percent, with the addition of special courses such as music or art taught in English. Nominal literacy development activities in English would also be initiated and might stress choral reading or chants. By the end of the school year for grade 2, English instruction time would increase to 30 percent with the addition to the curriculum of formal English instruction. Over the course of grades 4, 5, and 6, the instructional time devoted to English would increase to 50 percent. Initially, math, language arts, and special courses would receive English instruction, while science and social studies would be taught in Spanish. Gradually, each of the subject-area domains would be taught in English. Ultimately, the program would attain a 50:50 ratio of language instruction and maintain that level for the duration of the program. The 50–50 version of two-way programming is similar in all respects to the 90–10, except that initial instruction begins at a 50:50 ratio.

Essentials and Concerns

Critical to either version of two-way immersion programming are carefully planned lessons to maintain the ratio of instruction in each language, as well as the separation of languages. Concurrent translation should not be employed and lessons should never be repeated. Nonetheless, concepts taught in one language may be reinforced in another through a spiraling curriculum and thematic units. The time of day or subject areas might be used to alternate the language of instruction (Ovando, Combs, & Collier, 2011; see also Thomas & Collier, 2012, for additional strategies to provide the appropriate balance of separate-language instruction).

Among other criteria integral to the success of two-way programming are the following: instruction that is grounded in the core academic curriculum, a minimum of five to six years of bilingual instruction, language arts instruction in both languages that targets all four aspects of literacy development, the instructional separation of the two languages, instruction in the non-English language for at least 50 percent of the time (up to a maximum of 90 percent in the early elementary grades), administrative understanding of and support for the program model, an additive bilingual learning environment, high levels of parental involvement, and highly qualified instructional personnel (Christian, 1994; Lindholm, 1990; Genesee, 1999; Thomas & Collier, 2012). Also important to the success of this program model is a balanced ratio of students who speak each language. Although local dynamics may make it difficult to comply with this criterion, a 50:50 ratio of students is ideal, and a 70:30 ratio should not be exceeded.

Although this is the most effective of the program models discussed in this chapter (Collier & Thomas, 2009; Thomas & Collier, 1997, 2012), certain concerns related to two-way immersion programming are worth noting. First, some programs experience great difficulty with the recruitment of native-English-speaking students and greater difficulties with retention. Likewise, the parents of these students may prove enthusiastic at program conception and belligerent or apathetic as the program progresses. Second, native-English-speaking students may acquire a privileged status as the program progresses, to the detriment of the CLD students involved (Valdes, 1997). Finally, the instructional language used in the early grades of the two-way program may be inappropriately or inadvertently modified by classroom instructors in order to accommodate native-English-speaking students (Valdes, 1997). Such a situation is detrimental to participating CLD students, who may be shortchanged in their L1 literacy development.

Limited-Use Program Models

This section discusses two limited-use program models that are often the subject of literature and discussion in the arena of second language learning. Newcomer programs are frequently a response to unexpected demographic trends in the United States, especially in rural school systems. Second or foreign language immersion programs are most prevalent in Canada, but they have also been established in the United States, particularly in Hawaii.

Newcomer Programs

Newcomer programs are often a response to increasing numbers of CLD students, especially secondary students, in school systems that have previously experienced little or no cultural or linguistic diversity in classrooms. Some newcomer programs serve CLD students for as long as four years, while others serve them for as little as 45 days. Although there are some programs at the elementary school level, many more are a response to increasing numbers of middle and high school immigrant students who have varying degrees of literacy skills in their primary language (Boyson & Short, 2003). Some newcomer programs are housed in the student's home school (by designated attendance area), and students in these schools also participate in special classes outside the program (e.g., art and music). Others are housed in separate locations; in these situations, CLD students are not transitioned to the home school until the newcomer program is considered complete. Most employ a set of courses distinct from those of traditional language transition programs. Many of these courses are designed to facilitate students' social and cultural integrations into U.S. life; others are formulated to instruct students with limited literacy skills (Genesee, 1999; Linquanti, 1999).

A variety of concerns are associated with newcomer programs (Feinberg, 2000; Linquanti, 1999; Trueba, 1994). Some programs approach complex content-area subject matter in a diluted manner. Other newcomer models target rapid mainstreaming without sufficient time for the development of English language proficiency. Some programs are largely a variation of the sink-or-swim method. Several variations of this program model focus on a social skills–school rules orientation to English language learning but neglect literacy development. Finally, some newcomer programs offer insufficient access to academic content while segregating students from their grade-level peers.

Ovando, Combs, and Collier (2011) report that, because some newcomer programs purport to implement a Canadian model but omit native language support for CLD students, they are in effect mislabeled as structured immersion programs. Such programs might substitute materials designed for students with learning disabilities for materials specifically designed to introduce students to the English language in a structured, step-by-step manner. Programs such as these have not proven effective with CLD students in the United States (Ovando, Combs, & Collier, 2011).

Second or Foreign Language Immersion

Second or foreign language immersion is similar to two-way immersion because native-English-speaking students are immersed in a second language as the medium of academic instruction and social interaction. It differs from two-way immersion because CLD students are not involved in the program. In second or foreign immersion programs, the second language is used for at least 50 percent and up to 100 percent of the academic instruction, and the program may be implemented in the elementary or secondary grades (Genesee, 1999). Such programs promote second language literacy, cultural enrichment, and grade-level achievement in the academic content areas. The research findings on the model indicate that long-term program participation does not interfere with first language development or academic achievement for native-English-speaking students (Genesee, 1987; Swain & Lapkin, 1991).

Nonetheless, it should be noted that, unlike CLD students, grade-level students who typically participate in such immersion programs (many of which have been implemented in Canada) frequently exhibit the following characteristics: (1) they have been socialized in the dominant (not the subordinate) culture, (2) their first language is the dominant language, and (3) many have already experienced significant levels of literacy acquisition in their first language before undertaking the immersion program. Indeed, although second language immersion programs were not specifically designed for CLD students, such programs have on occasion been inappropriately implemented with CLD students whose first language is not the dominant language.

Early immersion programs are initiated in kindergarten and typically extend through the end of elementary school. Late or secondary immersion programs offer intensive academic instruction through the second language for one to two years and usually begin in the seventh grade. Among concerns associated with second or foreign language immersion programs are the following: teachers must demonstrate native-like proficiency in the target language, inaccurate translations may cause problems in creating challenging instructional materials, such programming is sometimes inappropriately applied to CLD students, and support from the home and community is critical to program success.

◼ Sociopolitical Foundations of Quality Programming

Several pieces of federal legislation have laid a foundation in law and policy for high-quality programming in the service of CLD students. Among these is the Bilingual Education Act of 1968. It authorized federal funding to develop instructional materials for use in bilingual education; provide professional development for teachers, aides, and counselors; and establish, implement, and maintain special programs for second language learners. The 1984 reauthorization of this act added several new categories of funding, including monies for family literacy, special populations (e.g., bilingual special education), academic excellence (to replicate exemplary models), developmental bilingual education, and special alternative programs (e.g., for low-incidence language groups).

Title VII of the Improving America's Schools Act (IASA, formerly ESEA, the Elementary and Secondary Education Act) moved programming away from remedial, compensatory models of bilingual education toward enrichment and innovation, comprehensive school reform, and the systemwide integration of ESL/bilingual programs into the core of the schooling system. With No Child Left Behind (2001), Title VII (the Bilingual Education Act) became Title III (the English Language Acquisition, Language Enhancement, and Academic Achievement Act). Rather than cultivating bilingualism, Title III emphasizes CLD students' acquisition of English and achievement in English (Ovando, Combs, & Collier, 2011).

Many significant court cases have had an impact on the way programming and ESL-specific issues are dealt with in schools and classrooms on a daily basis. Although many decisions are still being made regarding program policies for English learners out of knee-jerk reactions to the situations that often arise due to lack of "enough" language or academic skills being exhibited by newly arrived students, the court cases that are discussed here have also provided a great impetus to many policy makers, school administrators, and educators across the nation in doing what's equitable for the needs of CLD learners. These court cases have often played a pivotal role in furthering the districts' and schools' recognition of the civil rights of English learners. As you become familiar with the court cases shown in Table 4.1, we challenge you to think both locally and globally. What's needed for the twenty-first

■ **table 4.1**   Significant Court Cases that have Laid Foundational Law and Policy for Quality Programming in the Service of CLD Students

Court Case Name	Date	The Dilemma	The Resolution
Méndez v. Westminster	1947	Orange County, California, school districts were challenged for their segregation practices due to the placement of children with Mexican ancestry in separate schools from White children.	Set the precedent for demanding social equality in U.S. public education regardless of a student's lineage.
Brown v. Board of Education	1954	*Plessy v. Ferguson* (1896) allowed state-sponsored segregation, in which separate public schools were created for Black and White students.	Rejected the doctrine that segregation was legitimate on a "separate but equal" basis.
Lau v. Nichols	1974	This class action lawsuit was filed on behalf of Chinese-speaking children attending San Francisco schools who were placed in mainstream classes despite their level of English language proficiency.	Provided a powerful impetus for the passage of the Equal Educational Opportunity Act (1974), which prompted the U.S. Office for Civil Rights (OCR) to enhance the oversight of programming designed for CLD students and funded with federal support.
Castañeda v. Picard	1981	The Raymondville, Texas, school district was charged with the violation of CLD student rights under the Equal Educational Opportunity Act.	Established criteria for high-quality programming and determining a school district's degree of compliance with the Equal Educational Opportunity Act.
Plyler v. Doe	1982	Texas public schools attempted to force $1,000 tuition payments for each student identified as having illegal immigrant status, which ultimately violated the Fourteenth Amendment.	Guaranteed the rights of undocumented immigrants to a free public education and, by implication, to high-quality programming that meets the Castañeda Test as the benchmark standard. Ultimately, U.S. public schools are prohibited from denying students admission on the basis of their undocumented status or that of their parents.

century is critical refection on our part regarding the multidimensional needs of our learners as we prepare them for a global society through linguistic, academic, cognitive, and sociocultural support embedded within the daily curricular activities of the classroom.

Taking a Stand for CLD Students

As we come to a conclusion of this chapter and of a discussion on multiple program models, we must reflect on some of the theories and research associated with these topics. It is important to remember that everything we read and discuss with our colleagues ultimately must be considered alongside the unique needs of our specific learning community. We must continually gauge our students' academic and language learning needs and be cognizant of the diverse biographies that our students present. No language program can be implemented or executed without a constant element of critical reflection on our pedagogy and practices. What might hold true today for our school/classroom community may not be real or meaningful in a few weeks or months. Many factors are at play, including the demographic composition of our schools/classrooms. Moreover, assessments and screeners used at the beginning of the school year to gauge the learning needs of students have a shelf life and so do students' specific placements in language development programs. Yes, our students need language support through many ESL and bilingual programs that we attempted to share via this chapter; however, the support is meaningless if learners' evolving language needs and skills are not continually discussed and acted on. Regardless of the decisions being taken due to the policies of federal and/or state agencies, we have to remember that successful program models that help facilitate CLD students' attainment of content standards and development of language and literacy are those that foster lifelong learning skills. To make the best use of district and community resources, we need to find ways to look beyond the scripted and the mandated in order to set our learners on a path that is full of access, engagement, and hope.

Connect, Engage, Challenge

CONNECT
Review and Reflect on the Reading

1. Reflect on key predictors of academic success among CLD students. In what ways would you plan instruction to address these predictors?
2. According to recent research, what factors enhance the effectiveness of bilingual education programs? What role would home visits play in bolstering the role of these factors?

3. What are the sociopolitical implications of the interference hypothesis?

4. What is the SUP–CUP distinction, and what should teachers know about it?

5. Reflect on the transfer hypothesis. What is the role of this hypothesis in reading instruction for CLD students?

6. According to Cummins (1981), in what way does less English early in a student's education lead to more English later?

7. List at least five complicating geographic variables and explain the ways in which each may operate to preclude a school district's use of bilingual education. What other types of native language support for CLD students might the district provide through whatever program model it selects?

8. List at least five complicating sociopolitical variables and explain the ways in which each may operate to preclude a school district's use of bilingual education.

9. First, explain some of the foundations of ESL program models. Second, describe some of the characteristics associated with these models.

10. Discuss the most effective model of programming for CLD students. Identify a few of the reasons that make it the most effective.

11. Why might the use of ESL pull-out programs be so widespread when research has found them to be the least effective program model for CLD students? Explain your answer.

12. Discuss the pros and cons of newcomer programs. What would you say to a school district that is contemplating the use of such a program?

13. What three court cases have significantly influenced programming for CLD students? Briefly discuss the highlights of the court's decision in each of these three cases.

ENGAGE
Share What You Learned

1. Discuss recent research on program and instructional variables that influence the academic achievement of CLD students. What variables are predictors of academic success among these students? What program models were found most effective?

2. Discuss the BICS–CALP distinction and the way it provides a rationale for bilingual programming with CLD students.

3. Compare and contrast the interference hypothesis and the transfer hypothesis. Discuss the role of each of these in the SUP–CUP distinction.

4. Discuss the pros and cons of widespread program models for CLD students. What role do complicating variables play in a school district's selection among available program models?

5. Discuss the key court cases that have influenced programming for CLD students. In what ways has the Castañeda Test been used to ensure appropriate education for CLD students?

CHALLENGE
It's Not Real until You Practice

Preservice Teachers

1. Investigate the types of programs for CLD students within a nearby school district. Determine the effectiveness of these models within an elementary, a middle, or a high school by dialoguing with CLD students, their teachers, and their parents.

2. Interview a non-native-born, non-native speaker of English who has attended school in the United States. Discuss with this person the kind of school experiences he or she has had in the United States. Focus particularly on what type of programming was available to him or her for developing the second language. In collaboration with this person, try to identify the societal and classroom implications of the various English-only movements in states such as California and Arizona.

3. Survey district and community members about their attitudes toward and perceptions about what services should be provided for CLD students. Write a mock proposal to the district's school board and city council to advocate for the most effective and realistic program model for CLD students. This proposal should be supported by current research and theory.

In-Service Teachers

1. It has been one week since Kim Dao, a recent immigrant from Vietnam, arrived in your classroom. She is schooled in her native language up to the fifth grade and has had a disrupted education because of the political turmoil and unrest in her home country. She has come to the United States with her parents and two younger siblings. With these factors in mind, what types of modifications and cross-cultural adaptations would you provide for Kim Dao in teaching a social studies lesson on climate and its relation to geographical regions?

2. Soultana has lived in the United States for almost one year. She has moderate oral language skills in Greek (her native language) and can understand the language perfectly. Her father is bilingual and well versed in the linguistic patterns of both Greek and English. Soultana's mother is literate only in Greek and has no English language skills. Soultana loves to socialize and does well in cooperative learning situations. She is currently in the speech emergence stage of second language acquisition. Her teachers are pleased with her work, given the limited amount of time she has been in this country. How would you capitalize on the strengths of the parents in order to assist Soultana in the ongoing development of her native language as she becomes more proficient in English?

3. Survey fellow colleagues about their attitudes toward and perceptions of CLD students. Do they believe that current programming is effectively serving this population? If they believe current services could be improved, ask them what suggestions they might have. With this information and the current research on best programming for CLD students in mind, provide a short in-service within a staff meeting as a means toward voicing recommendations for improvements in current practices.

tips for practice

In elementary classrooms, consider:

- Providing CLD students with graphic representations of the concepts they are learning (e.g., a diagram or graphic organizer) to help them make connections between the content and language.
- Creating word walls in your students' first and second languages in different locations around the classroom. Keep in mind that placing them side-by-side could promote confusion among students because of different vowel sounds and the temptation for students to rely heavily on literal translation between the two languages.
- Selecting curriculum materials that emphasize multicultural perspectives and that validate the importance of diversity in the classroom and affirm the cultural heritages of your students.
- Creating learning centers in your classroom that emphasize available technology, activities connecting reading and writing in both languages, and volunteers from the community who provide support to the students in their first or second languages.

In secondary classrooms, consider:

- Making classroom and schoolwide activities structured and predictable to provide CLD students with a clear sense of their daily schedules and giving them advance notice when a change of schedule is needed. Do not rely on simply telling students.
- Pairing less English-proficient CLD students to work with other, more language-proficient students.

- Providing extensive opportunities for CLD students to use oral and written language as they define, summarize, and report on activities through both their native and English language capacities. Students will enhance their literacy skills by including illustrations and descriptions when they report their observations.
- Helping students relate to terms and concepts in the new language by incorporating hands-on activities such as class projects. Have students identify outside resources available in the community, experts who can visit the classroom, and organizations that can be visited.
- Teaching CLD students how to recognize cognates (e.g., *animals–animales, exploration–exploración*) common to their L1 and L2 so that cross-language connections can be made within the content area.

In EFL classrooms, consider:

- Using the native language as a bridge to link grammar and vocabulary.
- Extending lessons beyond a scripted curriculum that focuses on grammar rules. Instead, purposely make connections to what students already understand about reading and writing from their first language.
- Providing opportunities for students to work in small groups to make sense and bring meaning to new concepts by making connections to their own experiences in and out of school.
- Selecting strategies and using techniques that advance oral language development during the lesson. For example, use choral readings or pair readings to practice pronunciation.

CHAPTER 5

A Framework of Accommodation Readiness

our mission

Our mission for this chapter will be to:

- Address the teacher's readiness for the mutual accommodation of CLD students using the accommodation readiness spiral.

We will accomplish this mission by helping you to meet the following learning outcomes:

- Summarize the meaning of accommodation for CLD students and families as well as the six levels of the accommodation readiness spiral (ARS).
- Define readiness for critical reflection on practice and explain the difference between reflection and critical reflection.
- Explain readiness for CLD students and families, as well as strategies for it, such as semi-structured conversations with CLD students and their families.
- Explain environmental readiness and ways to analyze the external and internal environment of the classroom.
- Define curricular readiness and summarize curricular trends and essentials for CLD students.
- Explain programming and instructional readiness with and without a current program model.
- Define readiness for application and advocacy with attention to currency, defensibility, and futurity.

Socorro Herrera

Chapters 1, 2, and 3 provide an examination of each of the dimensions of the culturally and linguistically diverse (CLD) student biography—the sociocultural, cognitive, academic, and linguistic dimensions. Each dimension has many complex challenges and processes through which CLD students must navigate to be successful in school and in life. These multifaceted complexities point to the need for school educators to possess professional readiness to appropriately accommodate students whose culture and language may be different from that of the school.

In this sense, we are targeting not one-way but **mutual accommodation** (Díaz, Moll, & Mehan, 1986; Nieto, 1992; Nieto & Bode, 2012). The notion of **one-way accommodation** explains the tendency among some educators to assume that unsuccessful students are either lesser, genetically speaking, than their classmates or are "culturally deprived" (Nieto, 1992). That is, when certain students, especially CLD learners, do not automatically acclimate to the culture of the school, the result is often questions about their intelligence, assumptions about their abilities, or suspicion concerning the capabilities of family members. Think about the following scenario; what may have been assumed in this situation?

We have had a lot of immigrant students move into our district over the past few years, and they seem to need a lot of special programs. The teachers and staff at the school are doing more for nothing extra, yet it seems to go unnoticed by these students and their parents. The parents are constantly pulling their children out of school for family trips or other things without realizing how important regular attendance is at school. The parents also never seem to be able to attend conferences or school functions. So, it becomes very frustrating as a teacher to have these high expectations placed on us for student achievement, without others realizing that the students and their parents don't seem to make education a high priority.

This teacher's perspective places the blame on the immigrant parents (and to some degree on the students themselves) for any obstacles to their children's learning, noting, among other things, that if they want their children to learn, then it is their responsibility to get their children to school. This teacher may be correct in stating that parents need to ensure that students get to school, yet the needs of the family in other areas, such as needing someone to serve as a language broker or someone to provide child care, may be more pressing for the immediate survival of the family. A move beyond one-way accommodation by the family becomes necessary to increase the chances of success for the CLD student.

The perspective of *mutual accommodation,* on the other hand, expects complete accommodation from neither the student nor the educator. Instead, both collaborate to maximize the resources each brings to the educational process and to select from among the best strategies for all personalities present (Nieto, 1992; Nieto & Bode, 2012). Thus, in mutual accommodation:

- The educator elaborates on the funds of knowledge that the student brings to the classroom and that the family brings to the school.
- The life circumstances of the student are considered in practice.
- The student's home language is affirmed and supported.
- The methods and strategies of instruction are adapted and closely monitored for effectiveness with the CLD student.

Mutual accommodation thus defines a process in which both teacher and student are enriched. As the CLD student biography is maximized, the teacher's professional responses to that biography typically include intentional use of preassessment, differentiated instruction, authentic assessment, and **critical reflection** on the needs of the student and their implications for practice. Such responses enable the teacher to mutually accommodate the needs of CLD students, despite the many challenges related to programming and sociopolitical contexts (see Chapter 4 for discussion of these challenges). This chapter examines the levels of readiness that school educators demonstrate as they appropriately (and mutually) accommodate language learners and deliver effective instructional methods for these students. Throughout the remainder of this text, we use the terms *mutual accommodation* and *accommodation* synonymously.

The Accommodation Readiness Spiral

Preparedness to accommodate the CLD student is demonstrated by the six levels of the **accommodation readiness spiral**, which are summarized in Figure 5.1. The accommodation readiness spiral is an emergent framework for readiness that has been developed by the authors and is based on over 30 years of field experience and evolving research with CLD students and their educators. The spiral ranges from the initial readiness level, readiness for critical reflection on practice, to readiness level 6, readiness for application and advocacy. Each of the six levels illustrated is sequential and increasingly indicative of an educator's capacity for effective praxis with CLD students.

Levels of Readiness

The process of capacity building for each subsequent level of the spiral is progressive. For example, the attainment of level 1 readiness, **readiness for critical reflection on practice**, serves as essential preparation for level 2 readiness, that is, readiness for language learners and families. This is the case because effective and productive interactions with CLD students and families require teachers to reflect on the assumptions they may make as they interact with individuals of a culture different from their own. Such interactions require a capacity for critical reflection because, as the chapter discussion to follow explores, it is one's prior **socialization** in a particular culture (a culture different from that of the CLD student) that is typically at the core of misconceptions and incorrect assumptions about CLD students and their family members.

Capacity building is also in a constant state of change dependent on teacher disposition, knowledge, skill set, and unique challenges in classroom practice. Therefore, movement up and down the spiral is always a possibility. For example, many of the high school teachers in our courses have written about students' limited participation in class. In fact, one particular teacher explained to us that it was rather frustrating to have ELL students fall asleep during the 8:00 A.M. class. Additionally, some of the ELL students were also late or had heavy absences. Although many of the students would listen in a respectful manner, their actions, to this teacher, seemed disrespectful. This educator believed that this type of behavior represented a lack of interest in school, which made him feel unmotivated to put forth a lot of effort in the class.

The reality of what was happening with many of the CLD high school students became evident for this teacher when he began exploring their biographies. After making several home visits, he discovered that the students were leaving school and working the night shift at a local meat-packing plant. In the morning,

■ figure 5.1   Accommodation Readiness Spiral

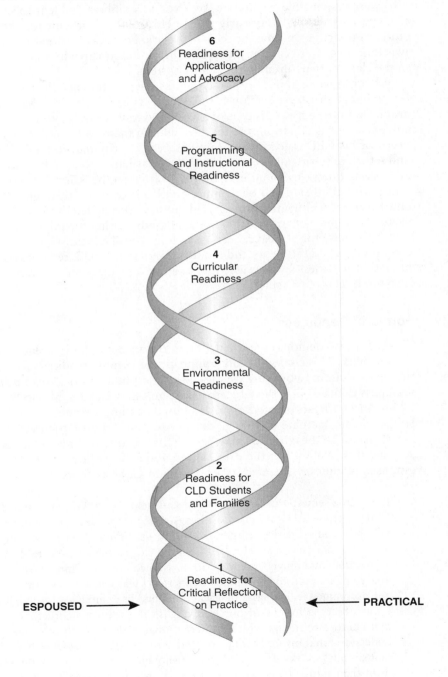

before driving to the high school to attend their own classes, some of the students also were responsible for making sure younger siblings made it to school because their parents worked very early shifts. This made it difficult for the high school students to arrive on time for their first class. For most of the students, the reality was that there were circumstances that limited their capacity for full participation in the class as structured by the school system.

After learning about the home situation of the students, the teacher advocated for a change in course section for the students to a later time, based on this biographical knowledge. This type of accommodation served both the teacher and the students. In this situation, the teacher, who in many ways was ready to meet the needs of his CLD students and families, temporarily had to regress on the spiral and return to posing questions about what was happening in this specific situation and asking questions about his own perspective on the issue. None of us was born a reflective thinker. Each of us must build this capacity through focus, practice, and experience. Critical reflection and question posing led this teacher to the home visits and a new way of understanding and advocating for the students.

A capacity for critical reflection among school educators, then, is essential to readiness for CLD students and families. Similarly, level 2 readiness of the accommodation readiness spiral is essential to a capacity for level 3 readiness, and so on, through level 6 of the spiral.

Forms of Readiness

Figure 5.1 also demonstrates the fact that the accommodation readiness spiral is a double helix. This configuration is appropriate because readiness for accommodation may occur in two forms: espoused readiness and practical readiness. **Espoused readiness** defines what the educator says, and may believe, about her or his level of readiness for accommodation. Espoused readiness operates at the conscious level and can fluctuate or change rather easily in response to new information or ideas. Although the educator may believe that espoused readiness guides his or her actions, this is often not the case. Think about the following scenario and what espoused readiness is, related to practice with CLD students:

> In my first semester of teaching a college-level English writing course, I had several Chinese students in my class. I always thought that learning another language—whether reading, writing, listening, and/or speaking—required a complete immersion into that language. This had been my experience when learning French at the high school and university levels. So, I assumed that my Chinese students should be able to pick up on the writing concepts that I was teaching the entire class without any accommodations, since that was what had been modeled for me. It wasn't until I was observed by one of our lead English department instructors that I realized that I needed to engage with my international students on a deeper level. I started to understand that my CLD students needed to be grouped differently in the class and that simply "speaking at them" wasn't enough for them to make those connections from their native language to English. With this experience, I began seeking out

ways—through conferences, journal articles, and collaboration sessions with other writing instructors—to incorporate and validate my international students' experiences in order to make the writing process more meaningful.

Regardless of context, what educators articulate (espouse) to believe should happen in the classroom is often absent in practice. Teachers often espouse to support students and plan instruction based on their language proficiencies, yet, when observed, mutual accommodation is absent; students are all doing the same things, at the same time. Few educators truly are aware of who sits in their classrooms, their families, and their individual needs. Often, teachers cite time as the key factor for not "knowing" their students and families. Readiness for mutually accommodating students cannot happen without critical reflection on what we say we do (espoused) and auditing our practice (practical).

Practical readiness, on the other hand, is so deeply ingrained in the educator's consciousness that she or he may not be able to fully articulate the nature of that readiness. Unfortunately, practical readiness is often indicative of frequently unchecked assumptions and beliefs that tend to shape and guide actions in practice. Unlike espoused readiness, an individual's level of practical readiness is formulated over years of socialization before and during professional practice. Therefore, one's level of practical readiness is not so easily recognized or changed. Keeping in mind the preceding teacher's espoused beliefs, consider her level of practical readiness, as reflected in the ways she puts her beliefs into practice in the classroom with CLD students.

Although I don't speak the native language of many of my students who I encounter, I whole-heartedly believe in language support. I provide texts in native languages, allow my students to bring in examples that are in their native language and/or have some personal meaning to them, and encourage them to write about lived experiences that tie into the concepts taught. These accommodations are important for those students who feel like the campus doesn't provide the necessary language support, especially considering I cannot speak their native language(s). In the end, I want my students to succeed. I've learned to provide many opportunities for them to use their native language within the classroom, even having them teach our domestic students about experiences that are important in other cultures.

Frequently, the decisions the educator makes, the actions that he or she takes, and the accommodation performance that he or she demonstrates in practice are governed by these two forms of readiness. At times, despite the level of espoused readiness, the assumptions (beliefs or attitudes) the educator holds tend to be reflected in the practical readiness demonstrated in practice. In these instances, the educator's practical level of readiness may not match the level espoused. When such discrepancies exist, the new intentions of espoused readiness are prevented from appropriately guiding the educator's professional actions. If the discrepancy between espoused and practical readiness grows sufficiently large, the double helix of the accommodation readiness spiral soon becomes so distorted that the spiral collapses. This situation is indicative of the educator's need to personally and professionally reconstruct her or his readiness for accommodation.

■ Voices from the Field 5.1

"As an educator, I have to be able to look at my current practices and identify what needs to be changed. To do that, I need to reflect on my own socialization and recognize how my experiences have molded me into the person I am today. How have my past experiences influenced my perceptions of CLD students and my teaching methods? The first step in the spiral encourages you to look within yourself and understand who you are as a person while examining your beliefs. Before change can occur, this is the first and most important step! Once you start to understand who you are as a person and an educator, you can begin to reflect on the remaining steps and make changes to your classroom environment, curriculum, and teaching style."

■ *Reprinted by permission from Lorle Bolt. Copyright © by Lorle Bolt, elementary school teacher, Fort Riley, Kansas.*

In the following discussion, we explore each of the six levels of the accommodation readiness spiral, as illustrated in Figure 5.1. As each is explored, you are encouraged to periodically review the spiral as a framework for self-examination of accommodation readiness. At the same time, you should recall that espoused readiness may significantly differ from practical readiness. Critical reflection is central to the alignment of these two forms of readiness in practice with CLD students and families.

■ Readiness for Critical Reflection on Practice

An educator's prior experiences and prior socialization concerning cultural and linguistic diversity can and will influence school and classroom practice with students (Banks et al., 2005; Lucas & Grinberg, 2008; Milner, 2003; Tutwiler, 2005). Beginning teachers typically bring at least 23 years of prior socialization and experiences in a particular culture to the classroom. More experienced educators may bring 40 or more years of their own socialization to their practice with CLD students. If this socialization did not significantly involve prior experience with cultural and linguistic diversity, especially with those cultures and languages of the English learners in the school, cross-cultural and cross-linguistic ambiguity, assumptions, miscommunications, attributions, and tensions are inevitable (Herrera, 1996; Milner, 2003; Murry, 1996; Tutwiler, 2005). Effective school educators learn to reflect as well as *critically reflect* on their perspectives about, their planning for, and their practice with CLD students and families.

Readiness for critical reflection in this sense involves validity testing, preceded by assumption checking (Murry, 1996), and this reflection lies at the heart of self-readiness for the accommodation of diversity. It should also be mentioned at this point that reflection defined as validity testing is a uniquely adult phenomenon (Mezirow, 1991; Murry, 1996). Most texts, especially texts of the cognitive approach that suggest that K–12 students should reflect (as in metacognitive learning strategies), are referring to a different notion of reflection. This different notion is one that we would define as *introspection*. One might further define this K–12 notion of reflection as thinking about one's thinking or actions.

Adult or teacher reflection, on the other hand, involves developing a capacity for confronting assumptions and testing the validity of those assumptions. The subsequent act of critical reflection emphasizes validity testing (i.e., reflection) that is specifically focused on one's prior socialization. The educator considers how those things she or he has experienced throughout life may influence action in classroom practice. The value of both reflection and critical reflection in preparing school educators for appropriate accommodative practice with CLD students is well documented (e.g., Hoffman-Kipp, Artiles, & López-Torres, 2003; Howard, 2003; Jacobs, 2006; Milner, 2003; Murry & Herrera, 1999). As illustrated in Figure 5.2, a teacher's readiness for critical reflection on practice with CLD students is demonstrated by a capacity for the confronting/checking of assumptions

■**figure 5.2**   Readiness for Critical Reflection on Practice

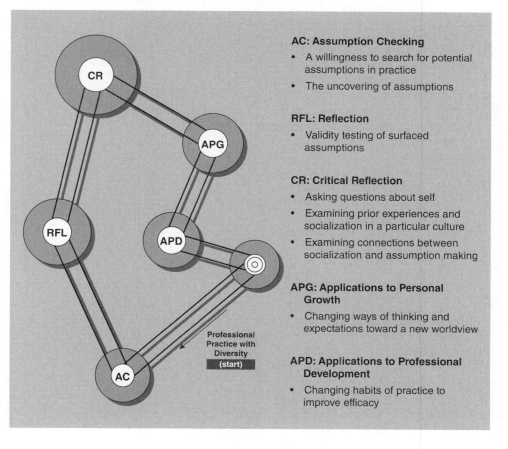

AC: Assumption Checking
- A willingness to search for potential assumptions in practice
- The uncovering of assumptions

RFL: Reflection
- Validity testing of surfaced assumptions

CR: Critical Reflection
- Asking questions about self
- Examining prior experiences and socialization in a particular culture
- Examining connections between socialization and assumption making

APG: Applications to Personal Growth
- Changing ways of thinking and expectations toward a new worldview

APD: Applications to Professional Development
- Changing habits of practice to improve efficacy

in practice, validity testing on those assumptions (reflection), and reflection on the influence of prior socialization on the origin of any assumptions made.

Critical reflection serves as the catalyst to prepare and deliver instruction. How often do we, as educators, metacognitively rehearse what the delivery of a lesson will look like and feel like before we ever actually deliver it? How often do we shy away from activities or strategies that may lead to chaos in our classroom or may take valuable time from something that is in the textbook and must be covered before the end of the lesson? Too often we predict the future without all the facts, before critically reflecting on the reality of our classroom community or the essential content for the lesson—no matter the context, grade level, or whether we're in an EFL, ESL, or dual-language classroom. When we really consider our assumptions and the power they hold, critical reflection will ensure that we are delivering instruction that is relevant to the learner and is standards-driven and student-centered.

As an example of these processes, let us examine the case of Soledad as a basis for understanding **readiness for critical reflection in practice** with diversity (see Figure 5.3). Soledad's case is complex but not unusual among educators of CLD students. Take a moment to review the case and let us begin with an examination of whether Soledad's teacher, Ms. Mooring, was accurate in her conclusions about the case. Specifically, Soledad's teacher has concluded that the parents are not interested in their daughter's education and that a social worker should be contacted to motivate the parents. To reflect on the case, Soledad's teacher must first ask: "Based on the facts of the case, did I make an *assumption* that the parents don't care about Soledad's education and must be motivated to do so?" This is assumption checking, in the sense that the teacher has surfaced a potential assumption in her practice. She can then test the validity of that sociocultural assumption by examining whether she was correct in making that assumption.

Reflection

Ms. Mooring can reflect on (validity-test) her assumptions by asking herself questions such as: "What other reasons might account for the problems I have recorded in the Soledad case summary? Could it be that Soledad's parents work very long hours for many days of the week just to survive as a family? Could it be that they read my letter but are afraid to contact or visit the school because of their prior negative experiences with schools and school educators? What about the parents' literacy levels? Could it be that Soledad's parents neither understand English nor are able to read written Spanish?" As a teacher who is willing to reflect on her professional practices, Ms. Mooring might explore any one or more of these alternative explanations. If she finds any one or more of these correct, she has made an invalid assumption.

That is *not* to say that Ms. Mooring was wrong or is a poor teacher. Instead, her reflection simply suggests that she made a cross-cultural assumption that may have limited the effectiveness of her practice. Such assumptions are common in cross-cultural encounters, especially those in which educators have limited experience

■ **figure 5.3**　The Case of Soledad

Biography:
- Fifth-grade, female, Hispanic
- Family emigrated from the state of Zacatecas, Mexico, two years ago
- Three years prior schooling in Mexico
- One year of schooling in Texas
- Early production stage of SLA
  —Reads phonetically, listens with understanding to contextualized communication, repeats memorable and some nonmemorable language, recognizes language connections, uses contextual clues to aid understanding and facilitate reading
- Parents work at local beef-packing plant; father was a ranch supervisor in Mexico

Classroom Behaviors:
- Attentive and generally on task
- Works extremely well in groups
- Generally participates well in classroom activities
- Stretches her communicative abilities in English
- Completes most classroom assignments when extra help is provided

Problems:
- Does not complete homework assignments; has no valid explanation
- Parents do not attend parent–teacher conferences despite extended hours

Actions to Date:
- Unable to reach parents or any other family members by telephone
- Two letters sent to home and translated into Spanish by classroom paraprofessional; no response

Conclusions:
- Parents don't seem interested in child's education
- Social worker should be contacted to visit the home and motivate parents

Questions:
1. *Are the teacher's conclusions accurate?*
2. *If so, what should be done?*
3. *If not, what is happening here?*

with cultures other than the one in which they were socialized. The more appropriate measure of professional effectiveness for Ms. Mooring is her willingness to validity-test (reflect on) any assumptions she surfaces by assumption checking. Through reflection, she will eventually improve the effectiveness of her practice with CLD students (Herrera, 1996; Murry, 1996, 1998).

In this case, professionalism on the part of Soledad's teacher yields positive implications. That is, through reflection on the case and a home visit, Ms. Mooring finds that her assumptions were invalid. Soledad's parents do indeed care very much about Soledad's education and wish to be involved as much as possible in her academic success. However, both parents work very long hours, seven days a week, and neither is sufficiently literate to read written Spanish. Therefore, as a result of reflection, Ms. Mooring is better able to understand the actions of both Soledad and her parents. She is now in a better position to structure appropriate teaching accommodations to improve her instructional effectiveness with Soledad.

Critical Reflection

After reflecting on assumptions in practice, Ms. Mooring's next professional step is to engage in critical reflection. Critical reflection begins with the self and one's socialization. That is, what in her prior experiences or prior socialization in a particular culture might have prompted Ms. Mooring to make an invalid cross-cultural assumption? Could it be that in her culture most parents have more time for their children—time to help the student with homework, time to attend parent–teacher conferences, and time to visit the school at the teacher's request? Could it be that, because of her socialization to that perspective, Ms. Mooring expected a more immediate and visibly concerned response from Soledad's parents on their receipt of the teacher's letter? From such efforts during critical reflection, teachers can learn the many ways that primary socialization acts as a cultural filter on perspectives, expectations, and actions in practice with diversity. Eventually, the teacher builds the capacity and the self-readiness to recognize such influences in cross-cultural encounters *before* making assumptions or engaging in actions in practice that are counterproductive.

Figure 5.2 summarizes the various steps of readiness for critical reflection in accommodative practice with diversity. As depicted in this figure, the cyclic nature of the processes involved illustrates that critical reflection must be an ongoing aspect of readiness for accommodation. Building a capacity for consistent critical reflection on practice often requires a resocialization in thinking as well as a great deal of reflective practice with CLD students in the school or in the classroom. Following are a few ways educators can build capacity in reframing the way they think:

Illustrated Concept 5.1
Enhance your readiness for critical reflection on practice by selecting one of your CLD students to profile. Briefly note what you know about the background knowledge and experiences of this student regarding his or her language development, academic development, and acculturation process. Then enlist the support of a translator, if needed, to either (1) conduct a home visit or (2) interview the student. Compare your notes on the background knowledge and experiences of this student with what you learned from either a home visit or an interview. Critically reflect on the process.

- Participate in professional development that prompts the posing of critical questions about beliefs and attitudes.
- Take courses that increase understanding of the dynamics of educating CLD students.
- Have critical conversations with colleagues.
- Practice critical reflection in relation to current research.
- Experience transformative events such as teaching in another country.

To learn more about critical reflection, watch this video that explains how our personal and students' biases can affect the classroom environment.

■ Readiness for CLD Students and Families

There never seems to be enough time. Time for planning, time for instruction, time for assessment, time for paperwork, time for grading, time to breathe—it always seems to be in short supply. Yet a little time invested in employing strategies such as semi-structured conversations with CLD students and their families will yield surprisingly useful, and sometimes unexpected, rewards. These rewards often result in a different type of **readiness for CLD students and families**, as depicted in Figure 5.1, and include, but are by no means limited to, enhanced teaching efficiency, improved student performance, and a reduction in the time required for instructional planning.

Students bring a variety of schooling, cultural, and language experiences to the classroom. Teachers can effectively maximize these experiences to focus instruction for cognitive and academic growth, reduce or eliminate reteaching, increase the perceived relevancy of instruction, keep students interested and motivated to learn, and more. Too often the tendency is to assume that limited English proficiency also implies limited schooling or an inadequate knowledge base. As a result, secondary-level CLD students who have taken calculus in Mexico have actually been placed in beginning mathematics classes in U.S. high schools. Such invalid assumptions are commonplace when time is not taken to explore the student's background. Designing and using strategies that create avenues for conversations with the student and his or her family members can be a pivotal step in enhancing professional practices and providing appropriate learning opportunities for the student.

Within the EFL setting, much discussion has surrounded the applicability and the readability of the materials provided to students. As practitioners, we pave a path for higher levels of reading comprehension to occur when we consider fully the relationship between students' background experiences and academic knowledge and the concepts, ideas, and language addressed in curricular materials. When we see our students comprehend at a certain level using their background knowledge, this process informs our selection of subsequent reading materials for students. According to Grabe (1991) and Jiang (2000), English learners' prior linguistic knowledge of L1 tends to encourage their treatment of L2 words as an additional illustration for a well-known concept. Capitalizing on this

Global Connections 5.1
What can be learned in EFL contexts from conducting semi-structured interviews with families? First, you'll learn that every family has unique ways of thinking and doing, related to their own family dynamics. When we worked as researchers in China, the response to discussions related to understanding CLD students and families often was, "We don't have diversity here; we are all Chinese." However, even countries such as Korea, China, Ecuador, Guatemala, and many others have diversity within their classroom community. Every family unit has, within it, unique dynamics that greatly influence how children learn. As educators learn about the family and the student, they become better prepared to engage in meaningful conversations with students and build relationships that lead to greater academic achievement.

idea in EFL contexts necessitates that we take advantage of, and build upon, students' prior linguistic, cognitive, academic, and sociocultural knowledge and skills.

Teachers who enhance their readiness for CLD student accommodation through the use of semi-structured conversations and other strategies increase both their effectiveness as teachers and their available time in the classroom. These strategies and conversations can occur both in and out of school settings; insightful teachers collaborate with bilingual paraprofessionals or parent and community volunteers as needed to visit with families who may not speak English. Time is further maximized when such conversations are undertaken as part of a home visit. Through home visits, the teacher learns about the student, the parent(s) or caregiver(s), the community, and sometimes extended family members who are key stakeholders in the CLD student's educational aspirations. In turn, parents and family members learn that the teacher values their participation in the educational process, is interested in the academic success of their child, and is willing to seek them out as valuable resources in accommodation. Table 5.1 further illustrates the many advantages of home visits compared to parent–teacher conferences. These proactive visits provide educators with an outstanding venue for teacher–student conversations.

Semi-Structured Conversations and More

Because these teacher–student or teacher–parent conversations are only **semi-structured conversations**, the affective filter is kept low, and the teacher remains free to further explore any information that surfaces as a means of enhancing teaching effectiveness with the CLD student. For the school educator, such conversations begin to establish an inclusive understanding of the students who will be accommodated in the school or the classroom. Following are some of the questions that will be answered through these conversations:

- What cultures are represented by students in the school and in the classroom?
- What native languages do students bring to the learning community?
- How many students will need accommodation and at what levels?

Although the conversations are semi-structured rather than structured (i.e., they do not follow a strict protocol), questions asked at various points of the conversation should generally address at least three domains related to the prior experiences, knowledge, and capacities of CLD students. Perhaps the most central of these domains arises from the *sociocultural dimension of the CLD student biography* and emphasizes the student's acculturation experiences and level of acculturation. Strategies and questions that may be incorporated into teacher–student or teacher–parent conversations that address this domain include the following:

1. Get to know the family by setting the stage for family members to share their stories.
2. Validate the ethic of care by sharing about your classroom and the student's participation from a positive perspective.

■ table 5.1   Parent–Teacher Conferences versus Home Visits: Comparisons and Contrasts

	In-School Parent–Teacher Conference	In-Community Home Visit
Typically accommodates CLD parents' work schedules		✓
Typically accommodates CLD parents' prior experiences with schooling		✓
Typically accommodates CLD parents' transportation issues		✓
Typically encourages involvement of extended family members (e.g., *abuelos* [grandparents], *padrinos* [godparents])		✓
Provides contextual information on the student's socialization in a particular culture		✓
Provides contextual information on family language biographies, literacy levels, and literacy access		✓
Provides contextual information on the community and culture(s) surrounding the school		✓
Provides contextual information on the CLD student's level of acculturation		✓
Provides contextual information about economic and acculturation stressors on the CLD student and family		✓
Typically lowers the affective filter for CLD parents		✓
Provides a contextualized opportunity to test assumptions about student and family		✓
Sends a message that the educator truly values the participation of parents, families, and community members		✓
Sends a message that the educator is truly concerned with the academic and transitional successes of the CLD student		✓
Sends a message that the educator is willing to seek out parents and family members as valuable resources		✓
Is typically student- and family-centered		✓
Is typically teacher-centered	✓	
Typically accommodates the educator's schedule and preferences	✓	
Typically follows the educator's agenda as a conversational focus	✓	

3. Get to know information such as:
   - From what country did the student emigrate?
   - How long ago did the student immigrate? To what extent has the student's family migrated within the United States?
   - Where do the parents work and according to what typical schedules?
   - What cultural transition stresses have been difficult for the CLD student and his or her family?
   - How has the student coped with these stresses?
4. Learn about culturally appropriate ways of communicating and think about your questions from a culturally responsive perspective.

Such strategies and questions, when incorporated into a nonthreatening conversation (or home visit discussion), begin to paint an informative picture of the student's current level of acculturation. As previously discussed, the student's level of acculturation, especially acculturation stressors, may profoundly influence concerns such as interest levels, motivation levels, attention span, language transitions, classroom behavior, and more. Table 5.2 suggests additional sources of information relevant to the student's level of acculturation. Nevertheless, there is no comparable substitute for the teacher–student conversation. Not only does it yield valuable information but it also demonstrates the teacher's interest in what the CLD student brings to the classroom.

> **Illustrated Concept 5.2**
>
> Provide CLD students with opportunities to converse with native English speakers and record these conversations. Allow students to watch the videos together to discuss the kinds of strategies they used to keep the conversation going and to comprehend the language and its use.

The second domain of guiding questions for semi-structured conversations or interviews is directly related to the *academic dimension of the CLD student biography* and addresses the CLD student's experiences, knowledge, and skills in the content areas. The academic performance of CLD students is significantly affected by the extent to which content-area instruction is perceived as relevant; builds on prior knowledge, skills, or capacities; and accommodates the construction of new meanings derived from connections to prior knowledge and concepts (especially connections fostered by hands-on, interactive learning experiences). Among guiding questions of the content-area or academic domain that may initiate purposeful conversations with students and families are the following:

- Was the CLD student schooled in the home country and to what extent?
- What content areas were emphasized and at what level?
- What are the beliefs of family members about schooling and the role of school educators?
- What are the student's preferred subject areas?
- With what subject area(s) does he or she have difficulties?

Table 5.2 provides a checklist that teachers can use as a primer in developing appropriate, site-specific questions for the semi-structured conversations of this domain.

■ **t a b l e 5 . 2** Checklist: Readiness for CLD Students and Families

Has the teacher or school educator, through teacher–student or teacher–parent conversations or other sources of information, explored the following concerns to enhance readiness for the accommodation of CLD students and their families?

Readiness Concern	Sources of Information
Student's Level of Acculturation	
Informal assessment of level of acculturation (selected aspects)	Primarily teacher–student (T/S) and teacher–parent/family (T/P) conversations
• Circumstances/culture in home country prior to immigration	CLD student, parent(s)/caregiver(s), extended family members
• Recency of immigration	CLD student, parent(s)/caregiver(s), extended family members
• Current home dynamics	CLD student, parent(s)/caregiver(s), extended family members
• Parents' work obligations	Parent(s)/caregiver(s), extended family members
• Acculturation stressors	CLD student, parent(s)/caregiver(s), extended family members
• Coping strategies	CLD student, parent(s)/caregiver(s), extended family members
• Student's involvement in language brokering dynamics	CLD student, parent(s)/caregiver(s), extended family members
• Proximity/transportation issues	Parent(s), social worker, school records
Formal assessment of level of acculturation	Acculturation Quick Screen (AQS) (C. Collier, 1987)
Student's Content-Area Knowledge/Capacities	
Informal assessment of content-area knowledge/ capacities:	Primarily T/S and T/P conversations
• Prior schooling in home country	CLD student, parent(s)/caregiver(s)
• Prior schooling in the United States	School records, CLD student, parent(s)/ caregiver(s)
• Content-area experiences/levels	CLD student, parent(s)/caregiver(s)
• Parent/family beliefs about schooling and educators	CLD student, parent(s)/caregiver(s), extended family members
• Student's preferred and most difficult subject areas	CLD student, parent(s)/caregiver(s)
Formal assessment of content-area knowledge/ capacities	Modified district tools or pretests; previous criterion-referenced and norm-referenced assessments of content-area knowledge

(continued)

■ **t a b l e   5 . 2**   Continued

Readiness Concern	Sources of Information
Student's Language Biography	
Informal assessment of language biography:	Primarily T/S and T/P conversations
• Dominant language of first schooling in home country	CLD student, parent(s)/caregiver(s), extended family members
• Dominant language spoken at home	CLD student, parent(s)/caregiver(s), extended family members
• Extent of L2 schooling in the United States	School records/CLD student
• Apparent CALP versus BICS development in L1 and L2	CLD student, parent(s)/caregiver(s), extended family members, paraprofessionals
Formal assessment of:	
• L1	Translated Language Assessment Scale (LAS), Bilingual Verbal Ability Tests (BVAT), etc.
• L2	Idea Proficiency Test (IPT), LAS, etc.

Teacher–student and teacher–family conversations should discuss also the *linguistic dimension of the CLD student biography* by inquiring about the student's prior language biography. The student's language exposures, experiences, and development in L1 and L2 should be explored. When interest in the linguistic dimension extends to a home visit by the school educator, the conversation also provides the opportunity to reinforce for the family the finding that the CLD student can benefit from conversations and learning in the home that are grounded in the native language (Diaz-Rico, 2014; Hancock, 2002; Roberts, 2009). Among pertinent and guiding questions that may establish this language biography are the following:

- What was the dominant language(s) of communication and education in the home country?
- Was the student schooled in the dominant language and to what level?
- What is currently the dominant language in the home and is it supported for the student by the parent(s) or caregiver(s)?
- To what extent has the student been schooled in L2 in the United States?
- If the student demonstrates some proficiency in L2, to what extent does she or he exhibit cognitive academic language proficiency (CALP) versus basic interpersonal communications skills (BICS) proficiency?
- What family literacy levels are suggested by the conversation, and is future follow-up (to gain more thorough information) needed?
- What literacy resources exist in the home and in the community?

Again, Table 5.2 provides a checklist that school educators can use as a tentative guide in developing questions for their semi-structured conversations related to this language domain. Nonetheless, effective teachers will pursue and elaborate their conversations with the recognition that all of the domains are interrelated.

theory *into* Practice 5.1

Accommodative school educators develop their readiness for CLD students and families in order to enhance the academic success of these students in the classroom. Yet for Ladson-Billings (1995), such efforts are not accommodative unless CLD students are permitted to target academic success while simultaneously maintaining their cultural identities. This *culturally relevant pedagogy*, as defined by Ladson-Billings, exhibits at least three notable characteristics. First, teachers, as members of the school community, develop fluid, reciprocal, and equitable relationships with their students and their communities. Second, these teachers tend to view knowledge as dynamic, shared, constructed, and recycled. Third, culturally sensitive teachers foster an academic community that promotes students' individual self-concepts, fosters a sense of belonging, honors human dignity, and values cultural competence alongside academic success.

■ *What are the potential consequences of asking CLD students to sacrifice their cultural identities in order to be academically successful in school? What do you know of the cultural backgrounds of the CLD students you teach or plan to teach? What aspects of their cultural identity tend to support their academic achievement? In what ways can teachers increase their capacities for student and family readiness and culturally relevant pedagogy?*

In summary, teacher–student (and teacher–family) conversations, especially those during a home visit, are powerful paths to teacher readiness for CLD student accommodation. The information obtained from these conversations enhances teaching effectiveness. The messages transmitted by these interactions tend to encourage parental or caregiver involvement and to motivate CLD students.

■ Environmental Readiness

Environmental readiness for best practice in the accommodation of CLD students, illustrated in Figure 5.1, demands an analysis of the external and internal environments that may affect professional effectiveness. Both of these environments constitute the context in which instruction takes place. In a classroom where students appropriately draw from their experiences, learning, and interactions to construct meaning, context is a powerful aid to academic achievement.

The External Environment

Most of us would like to believe that the environment that seems external to our practice is generally inconsequential. After all, we are typically taught to focus on internal factors such as the curriculum, instructional planning and delivery, monitoring, and evaluation. Yet research and analysis in education has repeatedly highlighted the powerful impact that the external environment can have on professional practice for an educator (e.g., Hargreaves & Fullan, 1998; Martinez, 2002; McCarthey, 2008; Routman, 1996; Valli & Buese, 2007). *External environment* refers to the sociopolitical context of the community, state, and country in which the school is located. No program, no classroom, and no instruction is an island unto itself. Rather, each is surrounded by an external context that can powerfully influence the success of the educator in practice.

Of particular importance in the external environment is the sociopolitical context of schooling and teaching in the service of CLD students. As discussed in Chapter 4, English as a second language (ESL) and bilingual education have often been wedged between sociopolitical agendas, leaving state standards, high-stakes testing, and curricular mandates to be ill-defined for the group of students who are in most need of the clearest path for achieving in school. In the last decade, No Child Left Behind (NCLB) left behind a legacy of unfinished business with English language learners. Ultimately, NCLB made its mark, dictating what practice should look like for language learners. Today, the new Common Core Standards, now being implemented in 45 states and four U.S. territories, raise many of the same questions that were often asked during the early years of NCLB (Pompa & Hakuta, 2012; Van Lier & Walqui, 2012; Walqui & Heritage, 2012). These externally driven agendas that impact curriculum choice, testing, and student placement are not limited to the United States. Educators in other countries must also learn about, navigate, and negotiate the external demands often driven by sociopolitical agendas.

This external political agenda has often resulted in scripted programs that limit the professionalism of teachers in classrooms across the globe. From this agenda comes the belief for many teachers that they cannot "color outside the lines" for fear they will be reprimanded by individuals charged with monitoring adherence to the program. So you can see how external politics can influence funding for ESL/EFL education, programming possibilities for students, public reaction to classroom instruction, and so on.

Equally influential on appropriate practice for CLD students is the status of students' native languages in the learning community. Escamilla (1994) demonstrated that the English language can exert such a force (hegemony) within the community (or the school itself) that bilingual education or, in some cases, native language support for CLD students is effectively precluded. Even among children in a bilingual school, Escamilla found notable discrepancies between the status afforded Spanish and English. Essentially, students in the school tended to interpret these discrepancies as a message that Spanish was useful, but solely as a transition to English. It is critical that educators strive to gain a deeper understanding of the societal pressures that can affect students' willingness to speak their native language in the classroom or school setting.

Often, external readiness addresses the preparedness of the teacher to respond to state and district mandates that support curricular trends that focus less on accommodation and, instead, move toward a one-size-fits-all approach to teaching certain content areas. These external forces promote rigid protocols for delivering instruction and assessing student learning. Such external factors affect the ability of teachers to do what is right in classroom practice.

Ultimately, external environmental readiness is concerned with the knowledge and understanding the educator has regarding ways in which what is happening outside the classroom can positively or negatively influence the success of CLD students. Following are some suggestions for examining the external environment in preparation for readiness to address issues or threats in professional practice.

- Keep current on threats at the local, state, and national levels that may have an impact on your practice.
- Critically reflect on current sociopolitical agendas and the impact they may have on CLD student and family involvement.
- Become involved in neighborhood meetings to gain a greater understanding of the questions and concerns facing CLD students and families.

Table 5.3 provides a checklist for school educators of potential external variables and professional actions in practice that could affect students' performance in the school setting. Although this checklist is by no means exhaustive, it does provide a sample range of the external environmental factors that may influence a teacher's effectiveness or schoolwide effectiveness with CLD students.

■ **table 5.3**   Checklist: Environmental Readiness

To enhance environmental readiness, consider the following variables and actions that may affect either CLD student productivity or professional practice with CLD students.

Readiness Concern	Appropriate Readiness Actions
External Environment	
Sociocultural mores/patterns of the community surrounding the school	Shop in the community; attend community functions; conduct schoolwide celebrations of other cultures; invite community members to present on their cultures
Socioeconomic characteristics of the community	Seek out demographic information about the community; remember that every family is unique
Families' views toward school	Conduct home visits to better understand families' perspectives on feeling welcome in the school, participating in school events, preferred language of communication, etc.
Media	Research how the media portrays new immigrants and the impact it has on students, families, and the community; create new media events to counter negative stereotypes
Relationship to school board	Invite members to the classroom; attend meetings; talk to members
Relationship to district/committees	Talk to administrators/members; participate, present, dialogue, and persuade

(continued)

■ **t a b l e 5.3** Continued

Readiness Concern	Appropriate Readiness Actions
Relationship to democratic process	Voice informed opinions; invite lawmakers to school events; vote; advocate for creating external environments that nurture both the social and academic growth of students and their families
Internal Environment	
Perceptions of school staff toward CLD students and families	Reflect on your school culture. Is it inviting to families from diverse cultures? Does it view diversity as an asset?
Multicultural and multilingual classroom library	Collaborate with the school librarian to check out books or write proposals to buy books; use books from home
Environmental print in students' native languages	Translate and post labels; create separate word walls in L1 and L2; create content-based boards in L1 and L2
Classroom arrangement	Structure to enable cooperative learning, heterogeneous and homogeneous grouping, centers, etc.
Learning centers	Structure around need, including literacy, science, math, technology, native language, etc.
Literacy support materials	Use picture dictionaries, realia, magazines, newspapers, how-to books, etc.
Examples of (all) student productivity	Designate areas; post in any language; include motivating feedback; incorporate process and product; invite parents/community

The Internal Environment

Informed educators of CLD students are also concerned with the internal environment of the school and classroom. *Internal environment* refers to the atmosphere of the school and classroom. Again, research and analysis in the field has repeatedly emphasized the potential influence of the internal context on CLD student success, especially literacy development in L2 (Baker & Freebody, 1988; Brisk, 2005; Hamayan, 1994; Perez & Torres-Guzman, 2002).

Within the realm of internal environment, the ecology of a classroom and the ways in which CLD students' background knowledge relates to our classroom ecology is of particular importance. *Ecology* is defined as the conditions educators set within the boundaries of their classroom community and how those conditions promote access and equity for all learners (Herrera, 2010). Classroom environment has long been limited in the scope of what can be managed by the teacher. Ecology, on the other hand, requires the educator to move beyond the superficial and stay tuned to the building of relationships by creating an environment (physical space and participants within that space) where every student sees himself or herself as equal contributors in the classroom. A classroom ecology that respects learners is more than posters on the wall. Ecology is important regardless of program, context, or curriculum. To maintain a shift from considering just the surface features of our physical environment, we must concern ourselves with questions at multiple levels. At a practical level, we should consider the following:

- Is the classroom a welcoming environment?
- Does the classroom affirm or celebrate the cultures and languages represented?
- Are bulletin boards and word walls thoughtfully designed to promote literacy in the content areas and to affirm the cultures and languages of CLD students?
- Does the classroom arrangement promote discovery, cooperative, thematic, and center-based learning?
- Do grouping configurations create conditions for all learners to become part of the community?

At a more humanistic level (ecology) of the classroom, we should consider the following:

- In what ways does my classroom encourage and promote social, cognitive, academic, and linguistic interactions as a means to learning?
- In what ways do I promote a community of learners and focus on grouping configurations that are biography bound?
- In what ways do I tap into the background knowledge of my students and utilize this information to promote effective student groupings, appropriate levels of questioning, and higher-order thinking among students?
- In what ways do my questions set the stage for higher-order thinking, provide opportunities for all students to articulate their views, and reflect validation of thinking?

Where CLD students are to be accommodated, teachers must be concerned with the capacity of the internal environment to promote content-based literacy development in both L1 and L2. Table 5.3 provides a summary of internal environmental factors that may affect students' success or teachers' effectiveness in practice, especially effectiveness in literacy development. Ways that teachers can foster a supportive literacy environment include establishing a multicultural and multilingual classroom library, providing environmental print in students' native languages, and using literacy support materials.

■ **Snapshot of Classroom Practice 5.1**   Internal Environment

---

In this kindergarten classroom, the calendar area is at eye level for the students to view. They can easily manipulate the materials as needed. In addition, many calendar items, such as the seasons, months, and shapes, are in Spanish and English.

(Courtesy of Amanda Ryan, elementary school teacher, Fort Riley, Kansas)

Literacy support materials, especially those applicable to the elementary classroom, sustain reading and/or writing as a focus of literacy development. For example, developmentally appropriate literature promotes a reading focus and is suitable for read-alouds. Dialogue journals can be used to enhance a writing focus. Other literacy support materials such as posters, ads, and brochures can be maximized in choral or buddy reading activities or the development of a classroom newspaper. Pattern books can also be used to promote reading and writing skills, and they are very effective when used for shared reading activities.

A sustained focus on the classroom ecology accounts for the effects of both the internal and the external environment of the classroom. How the educator chooses to orchestrate the conditions in the classroom is determined, in large part, by the ways students respond to the instruction, curriculum, teacher, and one another. Readiness in this area moves teachers beyond a superficial approach to representing students' languages and cultures within the environment. Instead, teachers use materials that represent students' languages and cultures and use students' experiences and knowledge for community building, planning, and instruction.

■ Curricular Readiness

Traditionally, **curricular readiness** for school educators has involved a basic understanding of curricular issues such as planning, scope, sequence, and consistency. Nonetheless, more recent curriculum trends have made it necessary to have a grasp of other, more complex dynamics such as the degree of alignment between the curriculum and selected standards for concept or context coverage and quality, the degree to which the curriculum encourages parental or caregiver involvement, how the curriculum addresses the unique needs of the student population being taught, and the cross-cultural sensitivity of the curriculum.

Diaz-Rico (2014) cautions that teachers who lack a solid foundation in multiculturalism are sometimes guilty of lessening the cultural context or content of the curriculum. That is, cultural references or affirmations might be limited to ethnic months, bulletin boards, holidays, or meals. Often, cultural and linguistic integration is superficial in nature and is represented without regard to within-ethnic-group differences.

One way to avoid the trivializing of the curriculum is through building a capacity for critical reflection. Readiness for critical reflection serves as the foundation for the accommodation readiness spiral depicted in Figure 5.1. Previously, we discussed critical reflection as validity testing (or reflection) on the influences of one's prior socialization on assumptions in practice. School educators who critically reflect on their curriculum are less likely to engage in assumptions that might lead to selection and use of the curriculum that may not be aligned with the cultural and linguistic needs of their CLD students. When engaging in critical reflection on the curriculum, school educators should begin with reflection or validity testing that focuses on questions such as the following:

> **Illustrated Concept 5.3**
>
> Reflect high expectations for all students through the alignment of ESL/EFL lessons and curriculum with local, state, or national standards. Such efforts on curricular readiness greatly enhance the teacher's capacity to argue best practice in the classroom.

- Do my texts, bulletin boards, and classroom discussions appropriately include and represent visuals and text that represent the makeup of my learning community?
- Are lessons planned and delivered in such a way that the curriculum is adapted and modified to address the challenges faced by CLD students in the classroom?
- Are avenues for dialogue created for all students to mediate their understanding of the curriculum from their cultural perspective?
- Are multiculturalism and multilingualism presented as assets or liabilities?
- Does the curriculum reflect higher-order thinking and challenging content regardless of the language proficiency of my students?
- Do the activities and strategies in the curriculum move instruction to a more culturally responsive level?

Teachers should question and/or validity-test the presentations, treatment, and discussion of persons and groups throughout the curriculum. If this reflection uncovers shortcomings, then curricular accommodations should be appropriately adapted and modified. At the level of critical reflection, teachers are often concerned with reflecting on the extent to which their own prior socialization and experiences may not prompt them to immediately locate shortcomings in the curriculum. This is especially true when curriculum is mandated without consideration of the population with whom it is going to be used.

In EFL settings, reflective educators shape and align curriculum by exploring first their own perceived notions about linguistic skills and knowledge that individual learners have

> **Illustrated Concept 5.4**
>
> Focus on communication strategies that help bridge the gap between the linguistic knowledge of the language learner and what is being presented in the classroom by using real-world communication such as newspaper articles, online journals, and so on.

not mastered. They plan ways to teach or reteach through relevant and appropriate language, specific curriculum, and instructional strategies. To bolster the effectiveness of these practices, they develop an understanding of students within the context of their own backgrounds rather than simplistically ranking them or comparing them on an assessment scale. Such teachers then use resulting biography-based insights to promote meaningful connections between the target skills and knowledge and students' lives.

Curriculum Trends

Emergent trends in curricular readiness have also brought about new competencies among school educators. For example, many school educators are now more aware of the needs of CLD students and consider these needs when asked to review, analyze, and vote on certain curriculum initiatives at the district or school levels. Such initiatives may or may not be normed on schools with high levels of cultural or linguistic diversity. Some curricular initiatives stress particular philosophies such as a back-to-basics perspective, a phonics orientation to literacy development, or a promise of enhanced efficacy with at-risk students. Reflective decision making amid such initiatives (e.g., direct instruction, No Child Left Behind) demands new capacities and skills in curricular readiness, including critical review skills, a capacity to surface assumptions inherent in the initiative (e.g., assumptions about the needs of CLD students), and a capacity to reflect on the potential impact of an initiative on CLD students.

Inevitably, then, curricular readiness as illustrated in Figure 5.1 must encompass an understanding of and reflection on the current curriculum, recent curricular trends, and the potential impact(s) of emergent curricular initiatives. The many complex and differential learning, language, and adjustment needs that CLD students bring to the school necessitate that teachers develop this curricular readiness. Such readiness should be highly and intentionally focused on the essentials of whatever curriculum is currently adopted.

Curriculum Essentials

Curricular readiness is suggested by critical reflection on each of the following questions concerning **curriculum essentials**:

- Have I identified and refocused instructional planning and methods on the core of the currently adopted curriculum?
- Have I identified content standards that must be targeted and appropriately modified the curriculum for CLD students in order to target those standards?
- Have I assessed the extent to which English learners are provided access to an appropriate curriculum?

At minimum, curricular readiness that effectively answers these fundamental questions involves certain specific understandings and proactive actions, each focused on the differential learning needs of CLD students. These understandings and subsequent actions then form a foundation for curricular accommodations specific to the English learner.

Curriculum Essential 1: Identify and Focus on the Core Curriculum

Effective teachers of CLD students are proactive in identifying and focusing on the core curriculum. Gonzalez (2002) suggests that lessons, most texts, and curricula can be examined and refocused to those critical concepts or premises that are essential to understanding and learning. These critical concepts or premises carry the essence of what a student would need to learn in order to know that material. When the curriculum and instruction for CLD students are focused on these critical concepts or premises, the teacher has established the core, content-based curriculum that may then also serve as the context for appropriate second language acquisition in the classroom. The teacher can then analyze the core curriculum to determine the critical vocabulary that students will need to learn and the discourse, genre patterns, and schemata associated with the content that may prove difficult for English learners.

Emphasizing and targeting curriculum essentials yields several positive results. First, the curriculum is not watered down for CLD students; rather, it is appropriately modified to refocus instruction on the critical concepts and premises that students should learn. Second, classroom instruction that also targets second language acquisition among CLD students is centered not on basic skills or concepts but on the core curriculum that they must learn in order to be academically successful. Third, the teacher remains free to elaborate on the core curriculum as students gain L2 proficiency. Similarly, the grade-level teacher—with the collaboration of a paraprofessional, parent volunteers, or more capable peers—is free to elaborate on the critical concepts and premises of the curriculum by maximizing the CLD student's proficiencies and understandings in her or his native language.

Curriculum Essential 2: Concentrate on Standards of Academic Achievement

Having focused their curriculum modification efforts on an appropriate response to Curriculum Essential 1, most teachers have little difficulty in addressing the second curriculum essential because most content standards are aligned with the content area or grade level and are usually mandated by the state. Therefore, if appropriate curriculum modifications for CLD students focus on the core curriculum, then by inference these modifications also target critical content standards for academic achievement. Effective teachers of CLD students also monitor their teaching practices to ensure that their curriculum and their instruction are consistent with national standards of best practice with English learners. Among such standards are the English as a New Language Standards (National Board for Professional Teaching Standards, 1998), the P–12 English Language Proficiency Standards (Teachers of English to Speakers of Other Languages, 2010), and the WIDA English Language Proficiency Standards (see Chapter 1, Table 1.1, for additional information; World-Class Instructional Design and Assessment Consortium, 2007, 2012).

Curriculum Essential 3: Ensure That CLD Students Are Provided Access to an Appropriate Curriculum

As we reiterate throughout this text, CLD students do not compete with their native-English-speaking peers from a level playing field. Each second language learner faces sociocultural, cognitive, academic, and linguistic challenges that grade-level students do not typically confront. Yet, most school systems and their curricula are based on the notion of meritocracy, which is grounded in the assumption that the playing field is level. In turn, these structures and assumptions lead to other assumptions that tend to deny CLD students access to an appropriate curriculum. For example, because a CLD student may demonstrate a limited ability to read and write in L2 (English), school officials and educators often tend to assume that the student is not capable of adequate academic performance in a grade-level classroom where instruction uses the grade-level curriculum. Accordingly, English learners are sometimes placed in a separate ESL or immersion classroom where the content-area curriculum is watered down to basic skills and concepts, most instruction is focused on language learning, and the texts and materials used bear little or no relationship to the grade-level curriculum.

> **Illustrated Concept 5.5**
>
> Use strategies such as peer reading, peer editing, and group-based dialogues that support development of reading and writing skills to encourage consistent and structured vocal communication among learners.

Recognizing the dangers of such assumptions and situations, the national organization of Teachers of English to Speakers of Other Languages (TESOL) has, based on extensive research (e.g., August & Shanahan, 2006; Bailey, 2007; Capps et al., 2005; Genesee, 2004; Gibbons, 2003; Gonzalez, Moll, & Amati, 2005; Kaufman, 2004; Lyster, 2007; Norris & Ortega, 2000; Riches & Genesee, 2006; Short & Fitzsimons, 2007) developed a set of ESL standards for Pre-K–12 students (TESOL, 2010). Along with these standards for professional practice with CLD students, TESOL has developed certain access guidelines in the form of questions, which are designed to ensure high-quality educational experiences for CLD students (TESOL, n.d.). These access guidelines include access to a positive learning environment, an appropriate curriculum, full delivery of services, and equitable assessment. Those access guidelines applicable to curriculum essentials suggest that educators of CLD students must be concerned with the extent to which CLD students are offered access to:

- Special instructional programs specifically designed to promote the CALP development in L2 necessary for participation in the full range of grade-level instruction.
- A core curriculum intentionally adapted to encourage the exchange, affirmation, and development of first and second languages and cultures among *all* students, and the development of those higher-order thinking skills necessary for grade-level performance across the curriculum.
- Instructional programs and associated services that seek to identify differential student needs, provide curricular and instructional support, and monitor

the effectiveness of those services. Such programs encompass, but are not limited to:

- Early childhood education
- Special education (only as determined to be appropriate by means of formal assessments, informal assessments, and a placement team)
- Gifted and talented education (especially programs that use linguistically and culturally adapted acceptance or referral criteria)
- Diverse education (e.g., migrant, recent immigrant, or newcomer, Title I)

These access guidelines, as developed by TESOL, suggest that curriculum access is a complex yet significant component of what teachers should consider curriculum essentials. The differential learning and adjustment needs of CLD students are complex, and therefore diverse programming, curriculum modifications, and instructional adaptations are essential to best practice for these students. Before educators can truly move forward with meeting the needs of CLD students, they must first ask if they have the knowledge and skill to look at their curriculum and ask questions that are relevant for adapting it to meet the needs of *all* students in their classrooms. The curriculum must be adapted to meet students' needs rather than requiring students to fit the curriculum.

> **Global Connections 5.2**
> Enhance your readiness for professional practice by investigating possible ways to adapt and modify your current EFL curriculum so that you can bolster your students' achievement. Ask yourself what key concepts, ideas, and relationships all students should learn from your curriculum, and how you might modify it so that students are challenged yet appropriately supported and motivated in their ongoing second language development.

Programming and Instructional Readiness

Although research has long documented the impact of **programming and instructional readiness** for linguistic growth and academic achievement of second language learners, implementation of high-quality programs continues to lag behind. In some school districts, increasing cultural and especially linguistic diversity in the schools has yet to be addressed. Educators who are prepared have unique opportunities. For example, these educators are more or less free to serve on committees and help with the selection of a program model that will best meet the needs of their district's dynamics. Other school districts have already implemented program models, which vary in their effectiveness to address the needs of English learners. Although teachers may initially feel limited by the constraints of a given model, they soon find ways to accommodate students' biographies despite the existing programmatic challenges.

Decision Making without a Current Program Model

In schools or school districts where a programming model has not yet been adopted, educators are more at liberty to examine the research on effective models before

dilemmas *of Practice* 5.1

Ms. Nuveau has just joined the faculty at Huron Elementary in August of this school year. She had been an educator of CLD students in her previous seven years of practice as a third-grade teacher in another state. This will be her first year as a second-grade teacher. The student body of the school is approximately 7 percent Mexican American, 1 percent African American, and 92 percent European American. Of the Mexican American children in Ms. Nuveau's class, about 35 percent speak no English and none is performing at grade level. During her first week of teaching, Ms. Nuveau learns that all Mexican American children in her class, as well as the English learners in all classes at her grade level, will be pulled out of the classroom for 30 minutes total each week for ESL instruction. Otherwise, grade-level teachers are responsible for meeting the needs of these students. Although her school has already adopted a very limited form of the ESL pull-out program model, Ms. Nuveau is certain that this level of ESL instruction will be insufficient to accommodate the language transition needs of her CLD students.

■ *In what ways might this program model be problematic for CLD students at this school? In what ways can Ms. Nuveau advocate for a change in program model at the school? What theory, research, or best practice arguments can she use to rationalize her advocacy?*

making their programming decisions. They are also at greater liberty to study the current demographics of their schools in order to better maximize programming decisions. Ideally, programming decisions should account for a variety of significant factors, including:

- Latest research on programming
- Culturally linguistic and diverse student numbers
- Languages represented in the school
- Recency of immigration among CLD students
- Teacher capacities to implement program models under consideration
- Recruiting potentials
- Available facilities
- Collaboration potentials across classrooms

In making programming decisions, it is important that educators are reflective about site-specific needs, particularly those of the students and families the site is intended to serve. Reflective decision making will ensure that potential assumptions about student dynamics, staff readiness, and district infrastructure are identified and challenged.

In school districts where educators have options in programming decisions, the program selection process should maximize the range of instructional methods available to classroom teachers. That is, the program model chosen should not limit the ability of teachers to use a variety of methods that are consistent with that model in order to address the particular needs of CLD students at their site. When appropriate models of ESL programming are selected, for example, educators can pursue a variety of classroom instructional methods, including content-based ESL, sheltered instruction, and CALLA.

Decision Making with a Current Program Model

In other schools or school districts, overarching programming models for CLD students have already been selected, usually at the administrative or central office level. These selection decisions tend to frame and sometimes limit the range of classroom instructional methods from which teachers may choose in serving their CLD students. For example, many school districts have mandated ESL pull-out programming in all schools that serve English learners. The decision by school districts to use pull-out programs is often based on:

- Low incidence of second language learners in their schools
- Limited resources
- Lack of understanding of types of programs and their implication on CLD student success
- Lack of trained personnel who understand the needs of second language learners

Decisions of this nature not only limit the range of instructional models available to teachers, but they also tend not to involve grade-level teachers with the education of CLD students. Teachers in such districts who are unaware of the significant limitations on their instructional choice should be informed. These teachers should also endeavor to vary and augment instruction (e.g., with auxiliary native language support) so that it better reflects research and targets maximum effectiveness within the bounds of such programming constraints. As teachers become more knowledgeable about the needs of CLD students, they may begin to explore how the ESL pull-out program teacher can align instruction with content and grade-level standards. Often, schools begin to redesign programming, moving toward more researched-based programs that can accelerate academic achievement for their English learners.

> **Illustrated Concept 5.6**
>
> As a means to programming and instructional readiness, visit with the ESL coordinator to become more informed about programming options for the CLD students you currently serve. Next, visit the homes of your CLD students. Later, compare the information provided by the parent(s) or caregiver(s) with that of the ESL coordinator. See if additional insights provided by the parent(s) or caregiver(s) can enrich programming decisions or inform instructional modifications and accommodations necessary to foster student success.

Programming and Instructional Readiness through Advocacy

Educators in school districts where programming has already been determined may advocate for programming changes toward models that are more consistent with the latest research on programming and more enabling of a variety of appropriate instructional methods in classrooms where CLD students are served. For example, the research of Thomas and Collier (Collier & Thomas, 2009; Thomas & Collier, 1997, 2002, 2012) demonstrates the limited effectiveness of ESL pull-out programming with CLD students compared to other program models (see Chapter 4 for in-depth discussions of program models). Such research can be used as a foundation for collaborative advocacy among schools and educators in order to encourage changes in district- or school-level programming.

Similarly, in districts with rapidly increasing numbers of CLD students, the pursuit of ESL pull-out programming quickly becomes unrealistic because the number of students pulled out would soon exceed the number of students remaining in the classroom. These sorts of changing demographics may provide a basis for teacher and administrator advocacy that encourages conversions in CLD programming. The best ESL conversions move programming toward models that emphasize the instruction of English learners in grade-level classrooms through research-driven approaches, methods, and strategies.

Thus, classroom teachers benefit from an awareness of programming dynamics at the school or district level. Such readiness among classroom teachers enables more informed decision making about appropriate instructional models for the particular CLD population served. Through readiness, informed teachers are able to maximize site-specific effectiveness with CLD students in the classroom. As illustrated in Figure 5.1, programming and instructional readiness encompasses but is not limited to:

- An understanding of which program models would be effective with and feasible for CLD students in a given school
- An awareness of programming dynamics at the district and school levels
- An understanding of the manner in which district and school programming dynamics can frame or limit decisions about instructional approaches or methods for CLD students in the classroom
- A grasp of which instructional methods would be effective with and realistic for students in a given ESL/EFL classroom
- An examination of opportunities for teacher-based, administrative, or collaborative advocacy to improve programming and classroom instruction for CLD students

■ Readiness for Application and Advocacy

Ultimately, personal and professional development, as well as capacity building for the accommodation of CLD students, must involve the application of what a teacher has learned about self, professional readiness, and CLD students in the school or classroom. As Figure 5.1 has shown, the processes involved in this transition to application requires a **readiness for application and advocacy**.

Readiness for Theory-into-Practice Applications

First and foremost, this readiness level of the accommodation spiral must encompass a realization that not all models and programs that have been proven effective in classrooms will also prove effective with CLD students. Many highly publicized popular models and programs of education fail to account for either cultural or linguistic diversity in the classroom (Cummins, 2001; Vavrus, 2002). Therefore, effective teachers of CLD students are critical readers of research on and theories of teaching (Kowal, 2001; Mettetal & Cowen, 2000).

Second, effective teachers of CLD students realize that *flexibility* in **theory-into-practice applications** for CLD students must be a goal of readiness. Although teachers maintain essential consistency with the theory, they also allow for flexibility in site-specific adaptations. Classroom practice with English learners must be grounded in, and remain true to, the particular needs and dynamics of the site-specific population being served.

Third, readiness for effective theory-into-practice applications highlights the teacher's understanding of sociocultural dynamics. No application of theory, no matter how robust the framework for effectiveness, will be successful with CLD students if that application is not cross-culturally and cross-linguistically sensitive. Culture and language are not only linked in an integral manner but are also central to what the CLD student brings to the classroom. Just as the teacher's cultural and language socialization filter her or his perceptions and actions in practice, the CLD student's socialization will filter her or his response to classroom practice. Culturally or linguistically insensitive accommodations with CLD students can result in a number of unintended negative consequences, including affective filter-based interferences with learning and students' withdrawal, anxiety, lack of motivation, anger, resentment, and so forth.

Readiness for Differentiated Instruction

Application readiness is also a function of the teacher's preparedness to deliver *differentiated instruction,* which is central to the accommodation of the CLD student. This readiness first demands an understanding that appropriately differentiated instruction for CLD students must be student-centered and grounded in a foundation of student or family preassessment. A teacher's awareness and understanding of the unique needs of CLD students and families is essential to his or her readiness for differentiated instructional applications.

Teachers who appropriately differentiate instruction for the English learner are also aware of the need to incrementally implement that instruction, not by template, but by student response. Differentiated instruction, by definition, does not imply recipes, disconnected sets of strategies and activities, or quick fixes. Therefore, reflective teachers realize that differentiated instruction, when appropriately and incrementally implemented, must be process and product focused, reflectively monitored for student response, and intentionally refined (based on the findings of evaluation).

Above all, insightful teachers know that appropriately differentiated instruction for CLD students is atypical. The classroom may be loud as students maximize their social and linguistic interactions for academic and linguistic development. The environment for learning may look different if seating arrangements are modified to accommodate various peer groupings and cooperative learning. The room may be bustling with activity as students construct new knowledge from hands-on or thematic applications of learning.

In EFL settings in many countries there is considerable investment in the English language; however, satisfactory English proficiency in students is generally not

---

■ **Snapshot of Classroom Practice 5.2**   Differentiated Instruction

---

(Courtesy of Chelsey Hiltibrandt, elementary school teacher, Ft. Riley, Kansas)

In this classroom, Ms. Hiltibrandt practices differentiated instruction with her students. During her literacy lesson, three different groups run simultaneously, each group focusing on a different task relevant to the story. By the end of the reading period, all students have taken part in each center.

Group One: The students in this group read and review the story with the teacher.

(Courtesy of Chelsey Hiltibrandt, elementary school teacher, Ft. Riley, Kansas)

Group Two: These students work in a small group to review the vocabulary terms in the literature.

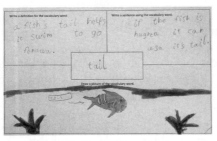

(Courtesy of Chelsey Hiltibrandt, elementary school teacher, Ft. Riley, Kansas)

Group Three: The students complete a graphic organizer using a vocabulary term from the story.

observed (Nunan, 2003). Therefore, it is necessary to recognize that when we differentiate for the language needs of students, we proactively support the affective climate of the classroom (Tomlinson & Edison, 2003). The need of the hour is to provide tasks that are differentiated among different groups of students while ensuring that the standards, concepts, or content of each assignment is the same. When planning and delivering instruction to promote language development within EFL settings, insightful teachers take into account the fact that students' language abilities tend to grow most effectively in humanistic- and learner-centered environments.

Readiness for Advocacy

Because administrators, fellow teachers, and parents may not fully understand why certain accommodative practices for CLD students are being implemented in the classroom, educators who are determined to promote CLD student success must develop a readiness for advocacy (see Figure 5.1). Elsewhere, we detail the consequences that may arise when educators fail to advocate for their CLD students, and we provide a framework for student advocacy both inside and outside the school (Herrera & Murry, 1999; Holmes & Herrera, 2009). Essentially, this framework suggests that teachers who demonstrate a readiness for advocacy share three common and critical characteristics: currency, defensibility, and futurity.

Advocacy as Currency

Currency, as a component of advocacy in practice, is concerned with the extent to which the teacher is current about best practice for CLD students and is aware of potential threats to appropriate services and accommodations for students and families. A teacher's best efforts to differentiate instruction for English learners in the grade-level classroom may be short-circuited by a community initiative that results in a school board decision to adopt an ESL pull-out model of language programming. Therefore, effective teachers of CLD students maintain currency regarding best practices and the internal and external environments of the school, especially the sociopolitical climate. These proactive teachers establish and maintain their currency through efforts such as:

- Periodically reviewing appropriate educational literature
- Attending local, state, and national conferences
- Paying attention to local and state issues in the media
- Inviting the media to document effective student accommodation in practice
- Attending local school board meetings
- Discussing their practices with school administrators, board members, and others

One powerful path to teacher readiness for currency is participation in a collaborative learning community of teachers and other educators who meet to discuss issues, literature, research, and best practice in the accommodation of CLD students. Hargreaves and Fullan (1998) claim:

> In complex, rapidly changing times, if you don't get better as a teacher over time, you don't merely stay the same. You get worse. . . . Professional learning and collegiality can therefore no longer be an optional luxury for course-going individuals, or a set of add-on workshops to implement government priorities. Professional learning must be made integral to the task of teaching as a basic professional obligation of teachers themselves. Only then will teachers be able to deal effectively with the numerous new challenges they face. (p. 48)

Hoffman-Kipp and colleagues (2003) similarly emphasize teacher inquiry groups that afford educators a space to envision together more equitable educational practices with CLD students. In such groups, teachers can use that time to reflect and learn about their own teaching practices with the intent to transform not only their own practices with their CLD students but also those of the school as a whole. Hoffman-Kipp and colleagues (2003) maintain that it is important for teachers to reflect on the political and historical contexts of their work while they collaborate to devise ways to thoughtfully enact their reflections on more effective educational practices. These ideas support the critical role of ongoing professional learning in the complex accommodation of diverse student populations.

Advocacy as Defensibility

Defensibility, as a component of a framework for advocacy, is concerned with the extent to which the teacher is capable of:

- Self-examination and self-reflection on practice
- Articulating research- and theory-based rationales for accommodations in practice
- The reflective development of a personal platform for best practice

Routman (1996) has argued that teachers must be able to articulate what they know and the rationale behind what they have implemented as best practice in the classroom. When the school administrator arrives to act on the complaints of fellow teachers that the accommodative classroom is too loud and disorganized, in what ways will the teacher be prepared to defend her or his classroom accommodations as best practice for CLD students? Will she or he be able to articulate the theory or research that supports hands-on, cooperative, and highly interactive learning for CLD students? Such questions illustrate why teachers must prove capable of *defending* their practices and demonstrate a readiness for advocacy in the accommodation of CLD student needs.

One of the best ways for teachers to ensure their capacity for advocacy is to challenge whether they are able to articulate their professional learning into a defensible position for what they are doing in the classroom. An effective way to document such learning and to synthesize it into an articulate defense for practice is the teacher's development of a best practice platform. Such a platform expresses one's philosophy of practice with regard to appropriate accommodations for CLD students. However, the platform also includes a defensibility component because it provides a theory- or research-based rationale for the educator's philosophy and defines what this philosophy means for critical aspects of effective practice with CLD students. A high-quality platform for best practice with CLD students should include sections that address the following questions (Murry & Herrera, 1999):

1. In what ways does the teacher use preinstructional assessment to inform practice?
2. What methodology does the teacher use for instruction?
3. In what ways does the teacher's postinstructional assessment document both the linguistic and academic growth of students?
4. How has the teacher used reflection on effectiveness and cross-cultural sensitivity in practice to guide decisions made during the lesson?

Interacting with other teachers within a collaborative learning community is also a critical way in which educators can enhance their capacity for defensibility of professional practice. As teachers dialogue with one another regarding the ways in which they successfully accommodate CLD students, they have opportunities to practice articulating rationales for their classroom practices. Therefore, effective educators maximize professional learning and collaboration with others in at least two ways. First, they use these opportunities to enhance their knowledge of best practice and potential threats to best practice. That is, they maximize professional learning and collaboration with others toward enhanced currency. Second, proactive educators synthesize professional learning, collaboration with others, and knowledge of their own practice environment and circumstances to both adapt practice in accommodative ways and articulate sound rationales for the defensibility of that practice.

Advocacy as Futurity

Futurity, as a component of advocacy in practice, reflects the extent to which teachers are able to demonstrate a readiness to step out of the box with regard to professional actions for CLD students and families (Herrera & Murry, 1999).

> In action for advocacy, educators engage in futurity in order to better serve student/family needs, and to [e]nsure the long-term viability of appropriate efforts to deliver needs-appropriate, culturally-relevant, and student-centered practices and programs within the school. . . . This notion of teacher leadership redefines the teacher's role in the learning community as one which influences and engages people to take individual and collaborative actions to prompt appropriate change and improvements in professional practice. p. 127)

Thus, in at least one sense, futurity involves teacher leadership in appropriate accommodations for CLD students. Indeed, teachers who step out of the box on a regular basis are often the teachers who are the most effective with, and the most motivating to, their CLD students. The teachers who risk the misunderstandings of their colleagues in order to provide hands-on instructional accommodations for their English learners are often the ones who sufficiently shelter the curriculum so that instruction is at last made comprehensible to their CLD students.

Futurity in the form of teacher leadership is increasingly an expectation of best practice with and advocacy for CLD students. Among examples of such futurity in practice are the following:

Ms. Quintanilla frequently collaborates with parent and community volunteers to enhance the level of native language support she is able to offer her sixth-grade CLD students. Yet she knows that many of her fellow teachers within the school believe there is little they can do to provide such support to their language-learning students. Many of these teachers hold inaccurate assumptions regarding the willingness of CLD parents to support the education of their children. Therefore, at a recent grade-level meeting, Ms. Quintanilla offered to accompany those of her colleagues who are willing to make home visits to meet with the parents of their CLD students and to learn about the home lives and cultures of these students. She and a bilingual paraprofessional volunteered to translate as needed during such visits. As key aspects of these visits, parents will be encouraged to articulate their beliefs about education for their children, and they will also be encouraged to volunteer in the classroom.

Mrs. Claymore, a fifth-grade teacher who recently completed her ESL endorsement, strongly believes that changing demographics in the classroom indicate that her school should move from an ESL pull-out programming model to the delivery of sheltered instruction in grade-level classrooms. She knows that most teachers in her grade level are now ESL-endorsed and capable of serving the needs of CLD students in the classroom. Therefore, she meets with her building-level administrator and proposes that she and two other teachers attend an upcoming institute, where they will receive in-depth professional development regarding the sheltered instruction observation protocol (SIOP). Mrs. Claymore also argues that she and her colleagues are willing to, and will be capable of, serving as trainers of trainers to other teachers within her grade level regarding the SIOP model of instruction for CLD students. Thus, she encourages her principal to consider a fifth-grade-level pilot of SIOP instruction for CLD students in grade-level classrooms.

Mr. Erichsen, a tenth-grade history teacher, has noted a recent and significant increase in the number of Mexican American CLD students in his classes. He knows little about the culture and language of these students, but he knows that most of them live in a small inner-city community near his high school. He decides that he will begin to shop in that community at least once a week and attend some of the community functions in order to learn more about these students, their parents, and their community. Based on these experiences, Mr. Erichsen has decided to propose at the next faculty meeting that the school begin to serve as a host for some of these community functions. He will argue that this hosting will provide teachers and administrators valuable opportunities to meet and collaborate with parents, extended family members, and community leaders.

In professional actions that involve "stepping out of the box," futurity often prompts teachers to reflect on the implications of inequitable opportunities for CLD students and families. Ultimately, advocating for these constituents may move educators to view their efforts not merely as demonstrations of professionalism but as moral decisions that have implications for school and society.

■ Voices from the Field 5.2

The following voice from the field was provided by an in-service teacher as part of her professional development sequence at Kansas State University. The format of the journal was developed by Murry (1996) and is designed to promote critical reflection on practice with CLD students.

Event

"I read about the 'Prism Model' in the books *Biography-Driven Culturally Responsive Teaching*, written by S. Herrera, and *Mastering ESL and Bilingual Methods: Differentiated Instruction for Culturally and Linguistically Diverse (CLD) Students*, written by S. Herrera and K. G. Murry. The books explain that the Prism Model reflects a unique theory that encompasses students' four dimensions which need to be taken into consideration by educators to understand what it is that greatly influences students' success in school. These four dimensions are the sociocultural, linguistic, cognitive, and academic dimensions. The authors remark that these four dimensions are at the center of decision making that supports students to develop optimally their skills for success in educational environments. The authors state that by learning about our students' backgrounds comprehensively (through the four dimensions), as educators we will be able to set the stage for them to make connections between the content and their real-life contexts by using adequate strategies that meet their needs. Those strategies and different tools are to be culturally

relevant, and in that way very effective for helping them to succeed. Additionally, the authors stress the importance of embracing this concept, and starting to put into practice little by little what we learn throughout the chapters. They say that it is not about perfectly incorporating all the new concepts into our daily work at once. Instead, it would be great to begin to be willing to shift our insight of how we have been doing our job as educators, and to start step by step, strategy by strategy, one technique at a time, to do our best, and to live the experience of stepping out of the box that will enhance our classroom practice and that will ultimately influence our students' achievements and academic success.

Feelings

- Curious
- Interested
- Responsible
- Challenged

Thoughts

After reading the chapter, I thought about the students in all the different educational institutions in my country that would benefit from the application of the Prism Model in their classrooms. I think that putting into practice this knowledge would yield lots of benefits for our students. The learning process of our students would be a lot more enjoyable and meaningful for them as well as for the educators themselves. Working on learning about our students' biographies and their sociocultural, linguistic, cognitive, and academic dimensions would enable the teachers to be effective educators.

I also thought that the Prism Model is essential for both teachers' and students' success. It benefits educators because they are able to identify students' needs, place them in a suitable instructional environment, and monitor their language learning progress. On the other hand, it is good for students because they are involved in their own learning process since they can make connections with their own realities and be motivated because they find what they understand and learn in the classroom meaningful. They find learning useful not only for their academic success but also for their life.

Learnings
Step 1
I had a couple of assumptions about the Prism Model. First, I assumed that it is not possible to apply this concept in Ecuadorian classrooms since the majority of the students in Ecuador are all Ecuadorians, and not foreigners or internationals. So, their backgrounds do not vary much and it is not worth the time spent on learning about them; diversity is not the case with Ecuadorian students, so studying in depth about their backgrounds will not be useful.

I also believed that what the students bring to school from their life, what they have learned from birth, was not important. Rather, I believed the only important thing was their academic knowledge about my subject, which is English. If they knew grammatical patterns and I could help them to develop the four skills of a second language learner—reading, writing, listening, and speaking—that would make everything fit or fall right into place for me as a teacher.

Step 2
My assumption that it is not possible to apply the Prism Model concept in Ecuadorian classrooms since the majority of the students in Ecuador are all Ecuadorians, and not foreigners or internationals,

came from my teaching experiences from the past. I have never had any student from another country in my classrooms. So, the first thing that came to my mind was that the Prism Model and its implications cannot be put into practice, because there are not big differences or diversity in Ecuadorian students' backgrounds. So, it is not worth spending the time on learning about them or studying in depth about their sociocultural, linguistic, cognitive, and academic dimensions. It was not useful. However, after reading and reflecting on the matter, I learned about how important it is to get to know your students' biographies.

I read the examples provided in the books and I realized that it actually takes place within Ecuadorian classrooms because of the cultural diversity that we do have in Ecuador. Even though we all are from the same country, we have many different cultures and diversity in there. In fact, nowadays families from other regions are moving from their native communities, seeking a better future for their families. So, we can easily find in one classroom students of different races, regions, and beliefs. Many of them even speak another language different from Spanish. In conclusion, this evidence proves that application of the Prism Model in our classroom practice would be very useful in Ecuador. As a matter of fact, it would be effective and would contribute directly to the students' success at school. Certainly, I found that my first assumption was not valid.

In regard to my second assumption, which states that what the students bring to school from their life, what they have learned from birth, was not important, and that I instead considered the only important thing to be their academic knowledge about my subject, which is English, I found it invalid. The reason why it is false is because exploration through the sociocultural dimension, students' assets and life treasures, moves educators beyond simple and boring classes and toward a real commitment due to the understanding and utilization of the students' background knowledge. This will enhance students' learning process when they make connections between the content and their own life experiences. The reading confirms it by stating that 'when students' language, culture and experience are ignored or excluded in classroom interactions, students are immediately starting from a disadvantage' (Cummins, 1996, as cited in Herrera, 2010, p. 29). That is why teachers must consider and build on their students' background knowledge, which is an important fundamental of the Prism Model.

Step 3

As I have mentioned before, I based my first assumption on my experiences from the past. Because I have never had foreigner students, I first thought that the Prism Model concept was not useful for me. I have had culturally and linguistically diverse students, though. Fully understanding the definition of the Prism Model and CLD students made me realize the importance and usefulness of this concept in my teaching practice.

I believe my second assumption came from memories of my personal experience as a second language learner. I recalled my second language acquisition/learning process and thought about all the information provided in the chapters. Most of my teachers were not interested in asking questions about matters not related to the content, and I still got to learn the language. So, I had the same idea that it was not bad to just teach English as a subject from a grammatical approach. The truth is that if the students feel motivated because they find the content useful and important for them, not just within the classroom, then they will take an active part in their learning process, their outcomes at school will be satisfactory, and teachers will succeed, too. Learning about our students' backgrounds and sociocultural life makes students go forward in their learning process, absolutely.

Application
Step 1

From my personal standpoint, I believe this reading has been helpful because I have realized that application of the Prism Model in my classroom practice is actually doable and very useful for my success as a teacher in Ecuador—which is based on my students succeeding. I am now aware of cultural and linguistic diversity in my classrooms and that it is part of the Prism Model. I know application of the Prism Model can enhance my effectiveness as a teacher of English as a second language.

Step 2

There are some changes that I will apply in my professional practice as a result of this reflection journal. The first is to acknowledge the fact that I have to learn about my students' four dimensions. It will make a direct impact on their academic success. It will also yield great benefits for their lives. I will be able to give effective instruction to them utilizing techniques relevant to the content and related to their own environments and backgrounds. Additionally, I have learned creative strategies to get to learn my students' backgrounds (four dimensions) and valuable information about their assets. Some of these are Cultural Quilt, Sociocultural Mind Maps, Picture This, Vocabulary Foldable, etc."

■ *Jenniffer Alexandra Velásquez Menoscal, Guayaquil, Guayas, Ecuador*

■ The Readiness Spiral: Implications for Teaching and Learning

The accommodation readiness spiral serves as a tool for educators to begin the reflection process. From classroom observations of over 3,000 teachers who possess the knowledge and skill, we have found there often exists a discrepancy between

■**figure 5.4**   Accommodation Readiness Spiral and One Teacher's Perspective

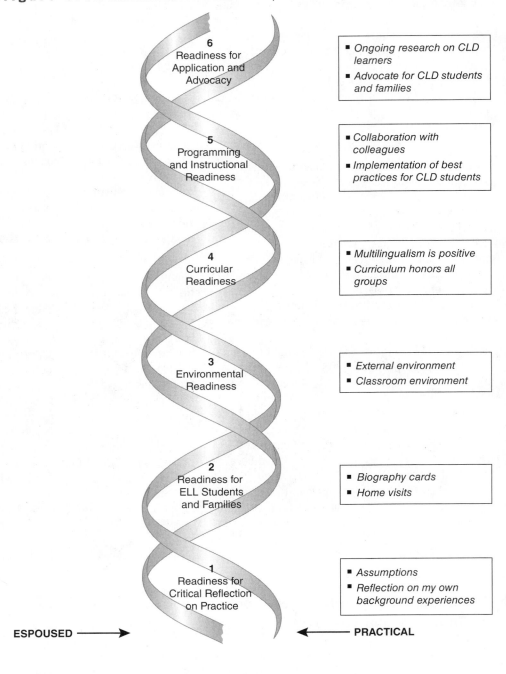

6
Readiness for
Application and
Advocacy

- *Ongoing research on CLD learners*
- *Advocate for CLD students and families*

5
Programming
and Instructional
Readiness

- *Collaboration with colleagues*
- *Implementation of best practices for CLD students*

4
Curricular
Readiness

- *Multilingualism is positive*
- *Curriculum honors all groups*

3
Environmental
Readiness

- *External environment*
- *Classroom environment*

2
Readiness for
ELL Students
and Families

- *Biography cards*
- *Home visits*

1
Readiness for
Critical Reflection
on Practice

- *Assumptions*
- *Reflection on my own background experiences*

ESPOUSED ⟶   ⟵ **PRACTICAL**

what teachers believe or espouse is best practice for their CLD students and what is observed in practice. Often, the educators we have worked with face challenges that are external in nature, and this occasionally keeps them from putting into practice what they have learned to best support CLD students' academic achievement. Educators who reach the highest level of the spiral often explore with other colleagues and their administrators ways to keep making the necessary changes regardless of challenges they may be facing to their practice. Figure 5.4 presents one teacher's use of the accommodation readiness spiral as a tool for reflection and advocacy in professional practice.

Connect, Engage, Challenge

CONNECT
Review and Reflect on the Reading

1. Explain the notion of critical reflection. In what ways does critical reflection differ from reflection?
2. In what ways must readiness for critical reflection on practice serve as a foundation for all other levels of the accommodation readiness spiral?
3. In what ways would you prepare for a home visit to the family of a CLD student whose culture and language are different from your own? In what ways would you avoid inappropriate cross-cultural and cross-linguistic assumptions about the student, his or her parents or caregivers, and his or her extended family members?
4. List at least five advantages of using a home visit versus a parent–teacher conference as a means to readiness for CLD students and families.
5. Reflect on the environments internal and external to the school. What factors should be assessed in the external and internal environments as a means to environmental readiness? (List and discuss at least four each.)
6. What are curriculum essentials? Discuss the significance of these curriculum essentials to curricular readiness.
7. What are two significant factors in programming for CLD students that should be considered? In what ways can teachers contribute to the attainment of these ideals?
8. What are at least two crucial factors to consider in ensuring that theory-into-practice applications for CLD students contribute to readiness for application and advocacy? Discuss why each is crucial.
9. Reflect on accommodations for CLD students. What are at least two critical factors to consider in ensuring that differentiated instruction contributes to readiness for application and advocacy? Discuss why each is critical.
10. What are the three essential components of effective advocacy for CLD students and families? Discuss why each is essential to effectiveness.

ENGAGE
Share What You Learned

1. Discuss one-way and mutual accommodation, with an emphasis on reasons why the mutual accommodation of CLD students is not more widespread in schools.

2. Discuss reflection and critical reflection, with an emphasis on the ways in which each contributes to a practitioner's readiness for critical reflection on practice.

3. Discuss the six readiness levels of the accommodation readiness spiral and your reflections on your preparedness for each.

4. Discuss the advantages of a home visit over a parent–teacher conference in promoting both parental or caregiver involvement and readiness for CLD students and families.

5. Discuss the components of advocacy and the ways in which each contributes to the educator's readiness for application and advocacy.

CHALLENGE
It's Not Real until You Practice

Preservice Teachers

1. An important aspect of serving the needs of CLD students is understanding and acknowledging how your personal values influence the way you teach. Figure 5.5 is a chart that you can use to gain insights into the ways in which your personal beliefs might affect your interactions with students and parents of different cultures. Please complete this chart and reflect on its various sections.

2. Obtain a copy of a school's handbook of policies and procedures that is given to parents. Put yourself in the shoes of parents of CLD students. How well would you be able to understand this handbook? Identify the gaps and barriers they may encounter when attempting to understand the school's expectations. How can these be addressed?

3. During a practicum experience, you walk into the teachers' lounge and overhear a teacher discussing how a particular student never completes his work and is always talking in Hindi to his best friend in class. According to her, it is not in her job description to teach a student who cannot speak or understand the English language. How would this comment make you feel? Would you address this situation? If so, how?

In-Service Teachers

1. When preassessing CLD students, it is important to make modifications that support their native languages and consider their sociocultural backgrounds. Figure 5.6 is a chart that can help you understand whether educators in your school are making such culturally responsive modifications.

2. Judy is a ninth-grade Hmong student who is doing very well in her courses. However, her parents have not participated in school activities, nor have they responded to any of the teacher's letters or phone calls home. Make a list of possible reasons you think may be contributing to this "lack of involvement." Discuss this list with a colleague and identify any possible assumptions you may have made.

3. Ask your students to journal about the value they and their family members place on education. Compare their responses to your own upbringing, values, and views about the importance of education. What sociocultural factors may play a part in any differences you see between the viewpoints you and your CLD students hold?

figure 5.5 Personal Perspectives Self-Reflection Tool

EFFECTIVENESS INDICATORS	ACTUAL SITUATION			EVALUATION			NEEDS				FUTURE GOAL
	In Progress	In Place	I Do This Well	I Do This Somewhat	I Need Improvement	Technical Assistance	More Time	Resources			
1. I am aware of my culture's dominant traditions, attitudes, interaction styles, and educational viewpoints.											
2. I am aware of situations in which my values, interaction styles, beliefs, and attitudes may positively affect my interactions with cultures different from mine.											
3. I am also aware of situations in which my values, interaction styles, beliefs, and attitudes may negatively affect these interactions.											
4. One of my primary goals when interacting with people of different cultures is to convey empathy and acceptance of their world as they define it.											
5. Another primary goal to further developing cross-cultural competence is: _____ _____ _____											

figure 5.6 Culturally Responsive Preassessment Tool

EFFECTIVENESS INDICATORS	ACTUAL SITUATION		EVALUATION			NEEDS				FUTURE GOAL
	In Progress	In Place	We Do This Well	We Do This Somewhat	We Need Improvement	Technical Assistance	More Time	Resources		
1. Our team regularly conducts preevaluation conferences to inform the family members about the assessment process and to learn their concerns, goals, and observations about their child.										
2. ESL, EFL, and/or bilingual educators are an inherent part of the preevaluation process.										
3. Our team uses various strategies to prepare the family for the actual evaluation (e.g., home visits).										
4. At the end of the preevaluation, our team provides the family with both a verbal and written summary of any information obtained in both English and the native language.										
5. Questionnaires for parents regarding information about their child's academic and linguistic background are provided in both English and the native language.										

tips for practice

In elementary classrooms, consider:

- Creating a "Welcome to School" video in the native language of your CLD population, perhaps even narrated by students who are bilingual and of the same background. This will help acquaint new students and their families with the school environment, procedures, and special events.
- Developing multiple ways to provide ongoing native language support for your CLD students as a means to CALP development in L1 and L2, thus enhancing your readiness for CLD students as well as their families. Some ways to accomplish this are maximizing the capacities of a bilingual paraprofessional; encouraging parents, guardians, or caregivers to volunteer in the classroom and to build on classroom instruction in the home; and utilizing students' bilingual peers as resources for native language support.
- Visiting the home of your CLD students before school begins to lower the affective filter of the student and of the parents or caregivers. Provide them with a welcome letter, a list of expectations, and possible ways the parent(s) or caregiver(s) can be helpful within the classroom—all in the family's native language. Remember that children's first teachers are their parents or caregivers, and these individuals are certainly the most influential.

In secondary classrooms, consider:

- Having bilingual personnel available during enrollment and registration of CLD students to explain the policies and expectations of the school to parents or caregivers in the native language and in English.
- Organizing a family night in the classroom or school, such as a family writing night, a family career fair, or even a family physical fitness fair. To validate the native cultures and languages of CLD students and their families, include activities in the first languages. Flexible, high-quality activities also function to lower the affective filter for risk taking among CLD parents or caregivers and extended family members.
- Collaborating with a paraprofessional to help CLD students gain the most from their educational experiences. Get to know each other and discuss your perspectives on ESL or bilingual education, learn about each other's background experiences with CLD students, attend community functions together, learn about the home environment of students together, plan instruction together in order to capitalize on the potential contribution each of you can bring to appropriate and accommodative instruction for CLD students, determine how to extend your ability to conduct ongoing informal assessment and monitoring of student progress, and work to encourage, promote, and enhance CLD parental or caregiver involvement in the instructional goals of the class.

In an EFL classroom, consider:

- Collaborating with parents and students to assess curriculum effectiveness.
- Organizing curriculum committees to create checklists for making decisions that are responsive to the needs of the students and which consider resources and communication processes to keep the students and their families at the center of effective educational practices.
- Identifying proactive ways to involve families in school or community activities that support the documentation of student needs and assets for use in planning and delivering instruction.

Socorro Herrera

PART three

Professionalism in Practice

In Part Three, we conceptualize and ground the preparation and professionalism of educators in three sequential components: planning, implementation, and evaluation. In Chapter 6, we provide a framework for reflection on planning instruction that is guided by a philosophical, theoretical, and practical orientation for planning appropriate practices for CLD students. In Chapters 7 through 9, we discuss and detail three methods of effective instruction and provide examples of what each has to offer educators in addressing the biographical and academic needs of their CLD students. Finally, in Chapter 10, we discuss ways to appropriately engage in the evaluation of instructional planning.

CHAPTER 6

Planning and Grounding Instructional Methodology

our mission

Our mission for this chapter will be to:

· Better understand ways to plan and ground our instruction for CLD students in effective approaches, methods, strategies, and techniques.

We will accomplish this mission by helping you to meet the following learning outcomes:

· Discuss ways to share a common language with our colleagues about how we thoughtfully and effectively plan and deliver instruction for CLD students.

· Compare and contrast the following terms: *approach, method, strategy,* and *technique*.

· Discuss the history and evolution of three approaches—the grammatical, the communicative, and the cognitive—to differentiated instruction for CLD students.

Socorro Herrera

key theories and concepts

acquisition-learning hypothesis

approach

behaviorism

cognition

cognitive approach

communication as the purpose of language

communicative approach

constructivism

grammatical approach

language acquisition device (LAD)

metacognition

method

monitor hypothesis

strategy

student-centered

technique

thematic units

working memory

zone of proximal development (ZPD)

Across the world, educators often struggle with fully understanding lesson planning and curriculum adaptation that is not already prescribed as they strive to meet the needs of their English language learners. At times, educators are unable to articulate their own framework when adapting curriculum that best addresses the population they are serving, which allows for a gap to exist between what is planned and taught and what the learner needs to be academically successful in the classroom. Teachers who have a clear understanding of the theories and scholarship that drive their teaching practice decisions are often more successful in advocating for their students. These knowledgeable educators are also proponents of planning and delivering instruction that serves the sociocultural, linguistic, cognitive, and academic needs of their students. Most often, with the best of intentions, educators deploy multiple tactics in their attempt to make the curriculum accessible for culturally and linguistically diverse (CLD) students. Practitioners try new activities that they have heard about from colleagues. Some practitioners read articles concerning wonder-working methods that promise miracles overnight. What *is* the first step on the path to creating long-lasting, systematic change in practice?

We believe that educators must have the desire to teach and accommodate students' needs, which means moving beyond merely implementing new activities in the classroom. Essential to the successful implementation of any program is a logical plan of action. Effective educators first critically think about and reflect on their personal beliefs about the overall goals of educating CLD students before determining the actual changes they plan to implement in the classroom. They ask themselves questions such as the following:

- What are the linguistic and academic needs of my students?
- What program is currently in place?
- What kinds of opportunities for student interaction would best support my differentiating instruction, given my curriculum?
- What are the challenges to implementing various activities?
- What are the rewards of community building to enhance student achievement?

Randomly incorporating new activities into instruction most often does not lead to eagerly anticipated positive results with students. Rather, the effective educator demonstrates logic-, theory-, and research-based reasons for the selection and sequence of actions that he or she chooses to incorporate in classroom instruction. Such practitioners choose a sound approach around which they can structure their teaching. They then choose an appropriate method and consider specific strategies and techniques. But what is meant by an *approach*, and aren't *methods, strategies,* and *techniques* basically the same thing? Although these terms are often used interchangeably in everyday speech, such inconsistency in terminology leads to confusion in the field of education. In this chapter, we discuss the need for consistent use of language and terminology among educational terms, and we provide an organizing framework for the conceptual definitions of *approach, method, strategy,* and *technique*. Because choosing an approach is the first step in developing a plan for accommodative and differentiated instruction, we also explore various approaches to second language acquisition.

■ A Common Use of Terms Enables Communication

The educational field continues to evolve due to constant technological advances. Educators communicate with one another across state and national boundaries with ease. Information resources that were once available only to those with funds for numerous literary subscriptions, or those who had the benefit of a nearby university library, are now available to educators through the Internet. For this reason, practitioners have greater access to the growing body of research and theory regarding the most effective instruction for students. Consequently, many ESL/EFL educators begin to implement changes in their curriculum and instruction in order to better accommodate students and prepare them to meet the evolving challenges of society. With increasing frequency, educators discuss, compare, contrast, and evaluate instructional ideas that were used in the past; those that are used in classrooms today; and those that represent the cutting edge of theory-based and scientifically based classroom practice.

Along with these emergent conversations about systemic change in education is a growing need for consistent terminology. Educators are often caught in a confusing mess of competing terms and left wondering how everything fits together. For example, the cognitive academic language-learning approach (CALLA) is one of the methods of instruction used for CLD students. Yet it is variously referred to in the literature and in classroom practice as a *model,* a *method,* and an *approach.* A similar problem arises with the integrated skills approach, which we would tend to characterize as a method of instruction. It is difficult for educators to effectively communicate with one another about ideas for instructional practice when each person is relying on a different conceptual understanding of a name for the same term.

As Oller (1993) relates, the quest to find a suitable form of organization for educational nomenclature began with the efforts of Ed Anthony (1963), who suggested that a distinction among an approach, a method, and a technique was necessary. As such, he described an *approach* as something similar to a theory; a *method* as the type of curriculum, program, or procedure that a school or educator chooses to adopt; and a *technique* as the specific actions taken in the classroom setting that put the method into practice (Oller, 1993). Further attempts to clarify educational concepts are numerous. Indeed, multiple definitions and relationships among *methods, techniques, procedures, designs, activities, tactics, strategies, curricula,* and other such terms have been variously proposed (Anthony & Norris, 1969; Richards, 1983; Richards & Rodgers, 1982, 2001; Strain, 1986; Strevens, 1980).

Assuredly, there is a need to provide educators with consistent terminology that affords clear direction for conceptualizing the pedagogical terms educators will use when referring to their practices. Accordingly, based on our review of the literature and our experiences with instructional methods in practice, we have developed operational definitions for the instructional terms outlined in Figure 6.1. These terms are used throughout the remainder of this text and ground our discussions of appropriate instructional methods for CLD students. By sharing identical concept definitions as seen in Figure 6.1, practitioners in different classrooms, schools, districts, states, and nations can effectively communicate and collaborate with one another to share information, as well as plan, implement, and evaluate ideas that lead to improved classroom instruction and enhanced student achievement.

To accommodate the assets and differential learning needs of *all* students, effective educators provide instruction that is grounded in theory and practice. Such educators first examine their beliefs concerning human and mental development, learning, and language acquisition. They review literature and research to acquire an understanding of the theories that guide current understandings regarding essential aspects of successful instruction. With the best interests of their students in mind, effective educators then choose an approach on which they will base their instruction.

Approach

An **approach** is the philosophical orientation to instruction that serves as a guide for choosing among methods that are consistent with the tenets of the theory and research that ground the philosophy. The educator ultimately makes classroom practice and

■**figure 6.1**   Comparisons in Nomenclature among *Approach, Method, Strategy,* and *Technique*

Approach *(Broadest Category)*

An approach *is the philosophical orientation to instruction that serves as a guide for choosing among methods that are considered to be consistent with the tenets of the theory and research that ground the philosophy.*

- Approaches are grounded in a research-based or theoretical framework for practice.
- Approaches to instruction reflect philosophies of human and mental development, learning, and language acquisition.
- Approaches guide the choice of related methods that are consistent with the theory and research that ground the philosophy.

Method

A method *is a body of philosophically grounded and purposively integrated strategies and techniques that constitutes one translation of an approach into professional practice.*

- Methods are consistent with a practitioner's approach to instruction.
- Methods represent the practical or applied aspect of an instructional approach.
- Methods are the umbrella for the strategies that one selects and uses because of their consistency with one's philosophy of instruction.

Strategy

A strategy *is a collection of philosophically grounded and functionally related techniques that serves as an implementation component of an instructional method.*

- Strategies are consistent with the practitioner's method, just as the method must prove consistent with the approach to instruction.
- Strategies represent an implementation component of a method, as applied to field practice.
- Strategies are the umbrella for techniques that are selected and used in practice.

Technique *(Most Specific Category)*

A technique *constitutes specific actions or action sequences that have been designed to achieve a defined, strategic objective.*

- Techniques must be consistent with the strategies that are chosen for their applicability to particular student populations.
- Techniques represent action subcomponents of strategies.
- Individual techniques may be combined with other related techniques to achieve effective implementation of a particular strategy.

---

instructional decisions based on rationales supported by her or his chosen approach. Accordingly, the choice of an approach should not be a rash decision. An educator's approach should be theory- and research-based and should simultaneously reflect his or her personal philosophy of education. Often, a teacher's philosophical orientation is derived from his or her previous postsecondary education. As the field of second language acquisition continues to change based on new research, it is important to revisit and reorient oneself to what is possible pedagogically.

Later in this chapter, we detail three instructional approaches. Although the grammatical approach is discussed primarily for historical purposes, the communicative and cognitive approaches reflect the most current thought in research-based approaches guiding instructional methods for CLD students.

Method

After deciding on the approach that will guide classroom practice, effective teachers choose a method. A **method** is a framework that has specific strategies and techniques associated with it; a method constitutes one translation of an approach into professional practice. In other words, appropriate methods fit under the umbrella of a particular approach. Figure 6.2 illustrates this and other relationships among the practice-based definitions explored in this chapter. A method represents the practical or applied aspect of the instructional approach and therefore must be consistent with the chosen approach.

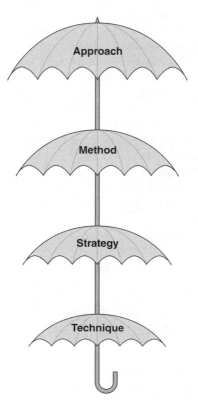

■ **figure 6.2**   Illustration of the Relationships among *Approach, Method, Strategy,* and *Technique*

For example, some educators decide to adopt the **communicative approach,** which emphasizes that language is acquired through meaningful student interaction. If this is the case, a method consisting of various strategies and techniques that promote meaningful student dialogue is needed. The sheltered instruction method, which is discussed extensively in Chapter 8, is an example of a research- and theory-based method grounded in the communicative approach. This particular method emphasizes authentic uses of language in both teacher–student and student–student interactions. On the other hand, if the same educators implement a method that lacks interaction strategies and techniques, the result will be instruction that is not consistent with the teachers' philosophy and chosen approach. Teachers whose instruction lacks consistent grounding in a research basis may have difficulty in understanding why some strategies may not result in student academic success. Teachers often select strategies based on school mandates or the strategy of the day. When instruction is guided by a method, strategy selection becomes more purposeful.

Strategy

In implementing their chosen method, which is purposefully aligned with their adopted approach, effective teachers choose appropriate strategies. A **strategy** is a collection of philosophically grounded and functionally related techniques that serve as an implementation component of an instructional method. Consequently, strategies fall under the umbrella of a specific method, as depicted in Figure 6.2. The strategies selected by an effective teacher are philosophically consistent with the method of classroom instruction. For example, the sheltered instruction method highlights the incorporation of hands-on activities. The use of hands-on activities constitutes a type of strategy that educators may employ when using the sheltered instruction method with their students. Another strategy of this method is the use of cooperative learning. Within each of these strategies there exist multiple techniques for implementing the strategy in classroom practice.

Strategies represent the "big ideas" that support the students' listening, speaking, reading, and writing. Selected strategies set the stage for the learner to be able to monitor his or her own learning, while providing the teacher with opportunities to formatively assess how the student is processing information presented during the lesson. Often, strategies are selected and used randomly at different points in the lesson, but they achieve no specific academic purpose beyond having students involved in structured talk or completing a Venn diagram to compare and contrast information. Such tasks yield more powerful results when they are purposefully integrated as part of a cohesive plan for learning. Strategies should set the stage for the techniques teachers use, as well as how and when they use them. The outcomes that result may then be used to scaffold student learning and inform the teacher for making ongoing decisions about the lesson.

Figure 6.3 highlights Linking Language, a biography-driven instructional strategy (see Chapter 9 for more information about the emerging biography-driven instruction [BDI] method). Strategies of this type support the teacher in orchestrating

■**figure 6.3**   Linking Language

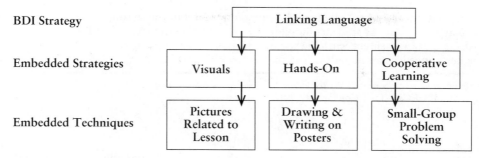

BDI Strategy	Linking Language		
Embedded Strategies	Visuals	Hands-On	Cooperative Learning
Embedded Techniques	Pictures Related to Lesson	Drawing & Writing on Posters	Small-Group Problem Solving

Classroom Directions:

- Select 3 or 4 pictures that illustrate key concepts from the lesson (pictures can be taken from the Internet, clipart, magazines, or the textbook).
- Tape each picture to the center of a large piece of chart paper (if using the textbook, place the textbook in the center of the chart paper).
- Give each student a different color marker or crayon (this way you can track that every student contributed something) and place the students in groups of 3 to 5, with one chart per group.
- Instruct the students to write down everything they think of or feel when they look at the picture (be sure to allow CLD students to draw or write in the native language as well).
- Allow only 1 to 2 minutes for students to write.
- Then have the whole group rotate to the next chart.
- Continue until all groups have been to each picture.
- When all groups have returned to their original charts, have the groups review all the information that was placed on the chart and identify common ideas/vocabulary by circling them.
- Have each group share with the class the circled information from the chart as well as other information the group believes is important.
- Share the key vocabulary words with students and ask them to work in their small groups to make connections between the words on their posters and the vocabulary related to the topic.
- Have groups share their ideas with the whole group.
- Next, have students work in their small groups to record predictions on what the reading/lesson will be about, based on the posters and the key vocabulary.
- Throughout the lesson, refer to the posters to support students' understanding of the ideas, concepts, and vocabulary discussed.
- Allow students to add to the posters to represent their new learning.

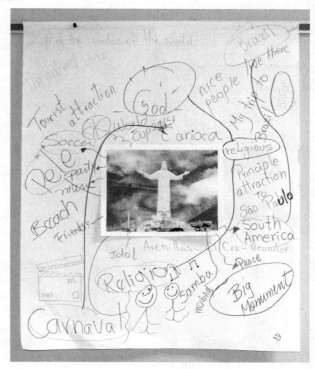

■**figure 6.3**   Continued

- Have students confirm/disconfirm their predictions about the lesson.
- Display the posters as students individually or in pairs complete end-of-lesson writing tasks (e.g., write sentences using the key vocabulary, write paragraphs summarizing the key concepts that include use of the key vocabulary).

Source: From Herrera. S. (2007). *By teachers, with teachers, for teachers: ESL Methods* course module. Manhattan, KS: KCAT/TLC. Copyright © 2007 by Kansas State University. Reprinted by permission.

the learning process by creating a unifying through-line for smaller strategies and techniques used throughout the lesson. When implementing the Linking Language strategy, students' background knowledge, which is documented at the beginning of the lesson, plays a role in connections made during the lesson. Moreover, the tool that students use during the lesson functions as a scaffold for their individual writing tasks at the end of the lesson.

Technique

Finally, alignment of strategies and techniques with content and language objectives set the stage for the effective practice. Educators determine the specific ways in which the chosen strategies will manifest themselves in the classroom, that is, they choose appropriate techniques. A **technique** is a specific action or an action sequence that has been designed to achieve a defined, strategic objective. As such, techniques fall under the umbrella of a chosen strategy or strategies, as illustrated in Figures 6.2 and 6.3, and represent action subcomponents of strategies. For example, if educators implement the strategy of Linking Language (see Figure 6.3), they may decide in the course of the lesson to have students collaborate by doing a think-pair-share in order to brainstorm ways the words on the posters connect to the key vocabulary. Actions such as these constitute the techniques that educators use to put the Linking Language strategy into practice with their students.

Individual techniques can also be combined effectively with other related techniques to achieve successful implementation of a particular strategy. For instance, adding a think-pair-share technique in the Linking Language strategy means that the practitioner has combined think-pair-share with the group problem-solving technique to effectively implement the cooperative learning strategy. In such a case, the teacher might group CLD students heterogeneously according to high and low levels of English proficiency. At this juncture, the more English-proficient CLD students may serve as more capable peers for students who are less proficient in English. As a whole group, the students then problem-solve together. Finally, each group shares its ideas with the rest of the class.

Illustrated Concept 6.1

Educators are often so focused on the curriculum that they fail to assess what theory has guided the curriculum developer. Curriculum often provides the educator with the skills, knowledge, and strategies to be used for teaching; however, the curriculum developer and curriculum do not always provide the teacher with the necessary adaptations that are crucial to meet the needs of the community of learners being served.

■ Consistency in Practice

In creating a plan for student instruction that best accommodates the needs and assets of every student, effective teachers use theory and research to make informed decisions regarding their instructional approach, method, strategies, and techniques. As Figure 6.1 illustrates, the effective teacher begins with the broadest category, which involves choosing an approach that reflects her or his personal philosophy of instruction. The educator then chooses a method that is consistent with the chosen approach and determines particular strategies that are aligned with her or his method. Ultimately, the teacher focuses on the choice of specific techniques that support the strategies chosen. Technique is the most specific category of instructional actions. Because the first step in planning for language instruction involves the choice of an instructional approach, the subsequent sections of this chapter present an overview of the three dominant approaches to second language instruction.

■ Three Dominant Approaches to Second Language Instruction

For more than 2,000 years, language teachers have been debating what the nature of second language instruction should be: deductive or inductive (Howatt & Widdowson, 1984; Kelly, 1976). In *deductive language instruction,* students learn the rules and patterns of the second language as a means of learning the language. Deductive instruction is structure-based. Conversely, *inductive language instruction* emphasizes authentic uses of the second language as a means of naturally acquiring the rules and patterns of the language. Inductive instruction is meaning-based.

Dominant language instruction methodology falls into one of three approaches: the grammatical approach, the communicative approach, or the cognitive approach. Of these approaches to language instruction, the grammatical approach fits into the structure-based deductive category of language instruction. The communicative and cognitive approaches, on the other hand, correspond to the meaning-based inductive language instruction category. These differing approaches to language instruction evolved from different philosophies of human development, learning, and language learning. These philosophies are comparatively distinct and inform the methodology of each approach. Table 6.1 further elaborates on each of the three approaches. In choosing appropriate second language approaches for students in ESL/EFL classrooms, educators must understand the philosophies and research that support and challenge the usefulness and educational value of each approach.

Grammatical Approach

The **grammatical approach** is a teacher-centered means of providing second language instruction. The underlying philosophy of the approach assumes that learners acquire language most efficiently by memorizing language rules and sentence patterns in a methodical, sequenced curriculum. Learners study these rules and patterns in ways that are often isolated from a meaningful context. For example, the sequenced

theory *into* Practice 6.1

Krashen (1982) summarizes the distinction between inductive and deductive second language learning environments with his **acquisition-learning hypothesis**. According to this hypothesis, when language learners have opportunities to interact with native speakers for purposes of authentic communication in inductive language learning environments, they are able to develop functional proficiency in the target language, or truly *acquire* the language. In contrast, when students receive deductive instruction, they develop only knowledge about a language (e.g., linguistic rules), or *learn* about a language. If CLD students are to use the target language to listen, speak, read, and write in social, academic, and professional settings, then language acquisition must be the goal.

Krashen clarifies his view on the role of conscious learning in the process of second language acquisition through his **monitor hypothesis**. This hypothesis explains that language learners consciously apply the rules of the target language to self-correct or to self-repair during language production. These efforts are needed in the context of authentic communication in order to enhance the comprehensibility of the intended message for the receiver.

■ *Krashen's* acquisition-learning hypothesis *lends support to which approach(es) to second language instruction (grammatical, communicative, or cognitive)? What are the implications of the* monitor hypothesis *on the language behaviors of students during communication and on the level of emphasis language teachers place on linguistic rules during instruction?*

curriculum of the grammatical approach typically begins with nouns, then verb conjugations, adjective use, possessives, and pronouns. Subsequent instruction, as well as drill and practice, tends to emphasize sentence structure, agreement rules, and idiomatic usage. Amid this sequential learning, a learner's first language is viewed as interfering with second language acquisition because differences in structure and syntax rules are considered points of confusion. According to the tenets of the grammatical approach, these points of confusion become the emphasis of instruction. At a superficial level, these propositions might seem logical. As this chapter explains, however, the nature of language contradicts this recipe approach to language acquisition.

Grammatical Approach: History and Evolution

The grammatical approach has been the predominant means of teaching a second language for several thousand years:

- Originally used in early Greek and Latin instruction
- Focuses on language learning as a mental discipline
- Dates back to 2500 B.C. in Mesopotamia (Kelly, 1976)
- Prevailed during the Middle Ages, the eighteenth century, the nineteenth century, and the first half of the twentieth century
- Now considered more of a historical artifact (Canale, 1983; Cummins, 2001; Krashen, 1981; Ovando, Combs, & Collier, 2011; Wong Fillmore & Valdez, 1986)
- Has been largely replaced in U.S. public schools by communicative and cognitive approaches as philosophical foundations for language instruction
- Still prevalent in EFL contexts

■ **t a b l e   6 . 1**   Dominant Philosophical Approaches to Language Instruction

	APPROACHES		
	Grammatical/ Grammar-Based	**Communicative**	**Cognitive**
When and what?	Approach has origins in nineteenth-century classical Greek and Latin instruction and maintains a teacher-centered emphasis on the rules and structure of the target language.	Approach primarily originates in 1960s–70s research on language learning through communication, constructivism, and social interaction. Maintains a student-centered emphasis on communication and meaningful acquisition of knowledge.	Origins in 1980s–90s research on learning functions, memory, and cognition. Maintains a learner-centered focus on explicit teaching of learning strategies (LS) in communicative ways.
Methods	**Grammar-Translation (Historical)** • More emphasis on development of reading, writing, and grammar • Less emphasis on oral language development • Rules of grammar are taught holistically **Direct (Historical)** • Focus on total immersion in L2 • No use of L1 in the classroom • Involves an open-ended response to materials the teacher brings into the classroom **Audiolingual (Historical)** • Grammar structures are carefully sequenced and taught • Minimal use of L1 • Emphasizes error correction, drills, and repetitive practice	**Silent Way (Historical)** • Teacher modeling/talk • Reinforcement through repetition/signals • Seldom content-based **Natural Way (Historical)** • Stresses comprehensible input • Minimal error correction/ production • Acceptance of students' L1 • Not necessarily content-based **Suggestopedia (Historical)** • Emphasis on relaxed physical setting • Minimal error correction • Use of L1 for explanations • Not necessarily content-based **Integrated Content-Based** • Emphasizes L2 development • Focus on content and language integration • Subject area integrated into thematic units **Sheltered Instruction** • Grade-level modified curriculum • Scaffolded instruction • Visuals, cooperative learning, and guarded vocabulary	**CALLA** • Developmentally appropriate language instruction • Intentional focus on CALP development in L1 and L2 as related to content areas • Focus on prior knowledge • Explicit instruction in the following learning strategies: — Metacognitive — Cognitive — Social/affective

(continued)

■ **table 6.1** Continued

	APPROACHES		
	Grammatical/ Grammar-Based	**Communicative**	**Cognitive**
Strategies	Examples from the direct method: • Drill and practice • Rote memorization	Examples from the sheltered instruction method: • Visuals • Guarded vocabulary • Cooperative learning • Hands-on activities	Examples from the CALLA method: • Cooperative learning • Explicit LS instruction • Maximizing content and language objectives
Techniques	General examples: • Dialogue memorization • Repetition • Mnemonics • Kinetics	General examples: • Reduced use of idioms • Use of manipulatives/realia • Use of simulations/big books • Heterogeneous grouping	General examples: • KWL chart • Questioning • Word walls • Outlines

Grammatical Approach: Philosophical Foundations

In the past, some theorists, such as John Locke and David Hume, believed that all human knowledge was the product of interaction with the world outside the individual—that is, the environment. Such knowledge, it was believed, was gained through the senses. These and other philosophers maintained that individuals acquired knowledge through what they tasted, touched, saw, heard, and felt. Later, John Watson and B. F. Skinner further developed this idea that the environment shapes human behavior through a series of environmental stimuli and responses that shape, or condition, human behavior. They believed that the environment shapes behavior by rewarding desirable behavior and punishing undesirable behavior. Watson and Skinner proposed that behaviors that are rewarded increase in frequency and behaviors that are punished decrease in frequency (Moshman, Glover, & Bruning, 1987). This theory of human behavior is called **behaviorism**, or *behavioral psychology*. Table 6.2 illustrates the influences of these and other theorists on the grammatical approach.

Educators who subscribed to the beliefs of behavioral psychology contended that language-learning experiences must emphasize the explicit teaching of grammar. Consistent error correction was considered essential to shape *correct* language acquisition among second language learners. Because the assumption of this perspective was that a person's language learning is shaped exclusively through explicit grammar—or rule-based instruction and correction and not by any instinctive language ability—language instruction occurred in a fixed scope and sequence. From this deductive view of language instruction, students first learned grammatical and syntactical rules. They then used these rules as a guide for producing language. Students began learning a second language by memorizing and practicing basic rules for common language uses. As the students progressed through each step in the language-learning process, they memorized and increasingly practiced

■ **table 6.2**   Philosophical Approaches to Language Instruction and Their Foundations

Philosophical Approach	Grammatical (Historical)	Cognitive (Contemporary)	Communicative (Contemporary)
Perspectives on human development	Fixed/staged/predictable	Typically staged but environmentally variable	Interactively variable
	Locke; Hume; Watson	Piaget	Vygotsky; Bakhtin
Perspectives on learning	Behaviorist	Cognitivist	Social constructivist
	Stimulus-response (S-R)	Guided or independent construction of meaning	Guided or independent construction of meaning
	Skinner	Gazzaniga; Edelman	Bruner; Ansubel; Papert
Perspectives on language learning	Deductive (general rule applied to a specific use of language in a particular context)	Inductive (language experiences in specific contexts used to derive a general rule)	Inductive (language experiences in specific contexts used to derive a general rule)
	Rule/structure driven	Interaction/guidance driven	Interaction driven
	Memorizing language rules and/or sentence patterns with drill-and-practice emphasis	Explicit teaching/modeling of learning strategies and language for communication	Language learning through and for authentic communication
	Palmer; Fries; Oller; Obrecht	Oxford; Chamot; O'Malley; Hakuta; Bialystok	Krashen; Terrell; Echevarria; Vogt; Short

the complex language structures. Educators following this grammatical behavioral philosophy believed that language does not develop from exposure alone. Instead, they believed that the student learns best through sequenced patterns of instruction, the reinforcement of correct language use, and the correction of erroneous language production.

Grammatical Approach: Methods

The grammatical approach to second language instruction has taken many forms over the past 2,000 years. Until the eighteenth century, the disputation method of the approach, which emphasized the memorization and application of language rules and structures, was the most prevalent venue for language instruction. The instructors would first read language treatises to the students, explaining each point in simple language. Next, the instructor would present a series of questions and then subsequently answer the questions through instruction. Finally, the instructor would pose questions to the students, and the students would respond with memorized answers to demonstrate their mastery of language rules (Kelly, 1976). The disputation method diminished in popularity and eventually disappeared completely with the development of the grammar-translation method. This and other methods of the grammatical approach are summarized in Table 6.1 and are discussed in the following sections.

Grammar-Translation Method. The grammar-translation method of language instruction developed during the eighteenth century and became popular during the nineteenth century (Kelly, 1976). In this method, the teacher first presented language rules to students. Then the students memorized a vocabulary list. Finally, the students applied the language rules and exceptions, as well as the vocabulary terms, to the translation of written text. At beginning levels of instruction, language learners often translated isolated sentences. As students became more proficient, they would translate increasingly complex classical texts (Howatt & Widdowson, 1984; Kelly, 1976). Translation was not for meaning. Instead, the grammar-translation method focused on grammatical accuracy (Kelly, 1976). The direct method replaced the grammar-translation method by the 1940s.

Direct Method. Among the grammatical approaches of the twentieth century, the direct method and the audiolingual method focused less on explicit instruction of grammar rules and structures and more on the repetition and memorization of language patterns. The direct method originated in the late nineteenth century and experienced popularity during the first half of the twentieth century (Kelly, 1976). The developers of the direct method—Harold Palmer, for example—sought to create a scientifically based teaching method for second language instruction (Palmer & Palmer, 1925). Behaviorist psychology and *ergonics,* the association of words with the specific contexts in which they were learned, formed the basis of the direct method (Kelly, 1976), which was most closely associated with the Berlitz language schools (Richard-Amato, 1996). In the direct method, students inferred grammar through exposure to carefully sequenced guided instruction in the target language. According to this method, teachers would model and students would practice language patterns, with the goal of internalizing grammatical patterns. Vocabulary was taught in context through dialogues and choral responses (Brooks, 1960). Because direct methodologists viewed a learner's first language as interfering with his or her ability to learn the target language, they heavily discouraged translation. However, the direct method did place some emphasis on context through the use of objects, photographs, diagrams, and drawings (Kelly, 1976).

Audiolingual Method. World War II brought a new emphasis on language learning. Military troops from the United States who were bound for destinations overseas needed a rapid means of learning foreign languages. The audiolingual method was developed in response to this need. The audiolingual method presented pattern drills and dialogue designed to develop grammatical structures and vocabulary in a highly sequential manner. Teachers reinforced accurate production and error correction through consistent feedback (Terrell, Egasse, & Voge, 1982). Developers of the audiolingual method believed that when language learners practiced pattern drills and dialogue designed to develop particular language structures, the new language structures would become a habit. They viewed language acquisition as the memorization and recall of language patterns.

Grammatical Approach: Synopsis

Given that the grammatical approach has since been superseded by other approaches more thoroughly grounded in research and U.S. public school practice, this text emphasizes more current approaches to language instruction for CLD students. The evolution of the grammatical approach is presented for historical purposes.

Several reasons account for the conclusion that the grammatical approach fails to offer the best available language instruction for CLD students:

1. The grammatical approach focuses on knowing about a language instead of emphasizing how to use the language for communication.
   - Most students study the target language for the express purpose of being able to use the language for social and academic purposes, not to learn the structure of the language (Krashen, 1981, 1982).
   - Students must learn to discuss, understand, read, write, and think for academic, social, and work-related purposes in the target language if the goal is to truly acquire a second (or third) language.
   - Conjugating verbs, practicing contrived sentence patterns, and memorizing lists of decontextualized vocabulary words does little to promote authentic language use for critical purposes.
2. The grammatical approach does not provide students with comprehensible input.
   - Drills are too far removed from a communicative context.
   - Drills provide no real motivation for students to communicate.
3. Educational research on second language acquisition programs reveals that CLD students who receive grammar-based ESL instruction do much worse on standardized tests that assess reading capacities in English than do their peers who participate in bilingual (e.g., dual language) and content-based ESL programs (Collier & Thomas, 2009; Thomas & Collier, 2002, 2012).

Communicative Approach

A more research- and theory-based approach to second language instruction is the communicative approach. As detailed in Table 6.1, the communicative approach emerged in the 1960s. The change in language teaching philosophy came from international concerns over the ineffectiveness of the grammar-based approaches in developing language learners who could actually use the target language in real-life situations (Blair, 1982). As the name implies, the communicative approach focuses on learning language through and for communication. The communicative approach assumes that language production contains an infinite number of possible language combinations, so memorizing patterns and rules does little to prepare language learners for authentic language use. In other words, language learners use language to communicate for a purpose. The role of the teacher (and the classroom) is to provide a context for authentic communication. From a communicative point

■ Voices from the Field 6.1

In order to significantly improve EFL teaching and learning in Ecuador, some changes need to take place. These changes must start with how teachers perceive their role inside and outside the classroom and must include breaking away from paradigms of traditional instruction in order to provide authentic EFL instruction. The skilled application of differentiated instruction in EFL classrooms can positively influence the teaching-learning process in Ecuador. Applying the principals of constructivism and involving students in cooperative learning are key practices. Teachers must facilitate students' construction of new knowledge by being creative and using authentic and meaningful activities that demand students naturally produce in the target language. Teachers must be able to identify students' strengths and weaknesses and use this important information when planning in order for students to produce and develop the second language at their maximum capacity. In addition, teachers can make the learning environment more effective by using real and authentic material, including that which involves content from other disciplines, as well as student-created material. Great advances come with great changes. In order to truly improve EFL instruction in Ecuador, educators, principals, parents, students, and all the members of the educational community must work together as a single team to support learners in reaching high academic standards.

■ *Yolanda Cecilia Molineros Cardenas, high school EFL teacher, Guayaquil, Ecuador*

of view, language acquisition is not a linear, sequential progression. Instead, language development occurs as a language learner (1) receives comprehensible input that is one step beyond her or his current stage of competence and (2) creates or tests hypotheses regarding language use as she or he interacts in authentic, language-rich, low-anxiety language acquisition environments (Blair, 1982; Krashen, 1982; Terrell, 1991). For more on comprehensible input, please watch this video.

Communicative Approach: History and Evolution

The communicative approach, one of the predominant inductive approaches to second language instruction:

- Has roots in the fourth century, during the height of Greek and Roman world influences, the Renaissance, and the last half of the nineteenth century
- Not widely adopted until the latter half of the twentieth century (Kelly, 1976)
- Initially used as a basis for modern language teaching with an emphasis on using target languages for authentic purposes
- In the 1960s and 1970s, emerged as the foundation for a more natural way to learn language, fostering second language acquisition in ways that more closely emulated how children learn their first language
- In the 1980s and 1990s, evolved to encompass constructivist language instruction in the context of the content-area curriculum

Communicative Approach: Philosophical Foundations

The communicative approach differs from the grammatical approach in that it does not subscribe to the behaviorist perspective (see Table 6.2). According to Blair (1982), much of the inefficiency in language training should be attributed to inappropriately applying a certain brand of psychology, coupled with sophisticated linguistics, to the instruction of second language learners.

> Part of the blame for current [1980s] inefficiency in language training must be laid at the door of a misguided faith that stimulus-response psychology, linked with sophisticated linguistic analysis, provides a scientific basis for language pedagogy. Conventional methods of language learning [grammar-based approaches], based on what must now be regarded as outmoded and unacceptable views of learning, may actually place formidable barriers in the path of learners. (p. viii)

theory *into* Practice 6.2

In addition to constructivism, the idea that people are born with a genetically predetermined capacity to learn language also contributed to the foundation of the communicative approach. This belief in a person's inherent capacity to develop language was the product of the work of Noam Chomsky (1986) and his theories of first language acquisition. Chomsky proposed that all people are born with a **language acquisition device (LAD)** that serves as an inherent mental system specifically devoted to language development and use (Akmajian, Demers, Farmer, & Harnish, 2010). According to Chomsky, the structure of the LAD provides the learner with an innate understanding of what Chomsky has referred to as *universal grammar*. This universal grammar consists of the rules and structures common to all languages (Akmajian et al., 2010). Another way to conceptualize universal grammar is as the logic of language.

Chomsky has argued that language acquisition is a natural process in which the LAD interacts with context to collect the linguistic information necessary to develop a particular language of thought and communication. He maintains that second language acquisition follows a developmental path similar to first language acquisition (Chomsky, 1986). In a speech to the Northeast Language Teachers' Association in 1965, Chomsky explained:

> A good deal of the foreign language instruction that is going on now . . . is based on a concept of language . . . [which assumes] that language is a system of skills and ought to be taught through drill and by the formation of S-R [stimulus-response] associations. I think the evidence is very convincing that that view of language is entirely erroneous, and that it's a very bad way— certainly an unprincipled way—to teach languages. If it happens to work, it would be an accident for some other reason. Certainly it is not a method that is based on any understanding of the nature of language. Our understanding of the nature of language seems to me to show quite convincingly that language is not a habit structure, but that it has a kind of a creative property and is based on abstract formal principles and operations of a complex kind. (Blair, 1982, p. 5)

Chomsky asserts that explicit instruction in the structure of language is pointless because all people are born with an innate understanding of grammar— a universal grammar. Like the constructivists, Chomsky maintains that languages develop as the brain gathers and uses linguistic information. He argues that the LAD, through communicative interaction, gathers the linguistic evidence necessary to derive the structure of a specific language (Chomsky, 1986).

■ *What are the implications of Chomsky's theories for teachers in ESL/EFL classrooms? What kinds of communicative interactions would provide the LAD with linguistic information ideal for promoting second language acquisition?*

The communicative approach represents a revolution in thought regarding language teaching. Instead of the more traditional viewpoint of behaviorism, constructivism serves as the theoretical foundation of the communicative approach.

Constructivism represents a theoretical body of literature that views the human brain as having certain fundamental structures of understanding that enable it to draw meaning from experience (Kukla, 2000; Searle, 1995). According to this developmental view of learning, people are born with the capacity to acquire specific abilities such as language comprehension and production. Although the behaviorists believed that learning occurs through environmental stimuli and a learner's responses to those stimuli, the social constructivists believe that learning occurs as a result of interactions between the environment and the learner's mind. In describing this interaction, Vygotsky (1978) stated: "The mastering of nature and the mastering of behavior are mutually linked, just as man's alteration of nature alters man's own nature" (p. 55). He claimed that the interaction between thought and language leads to higher-order thinking. In other words, rather than the mind being a passive recipient of input (a behaviorist perspective), the mind actively gathers information and constructs meaning (a constructivist perspective) (Moshman et al., 1987). Although the brain contains structures for language learning, the environment or context shapes the course of language and cognitive development (Vygotsky, 1978). The context provides a wide range of information, but the learner selects information and synthesizes that information with what he or she already knows to create a new understanding.

Social constructivists believe that interpersonal interaction leads to language and cognitive development and that all learning is socially constructed (Derry, 1999; Hacking, 2000; Kukla, 2000; Vygotsky, 1978). Vygotsky proposed that optimal learning occurs in a **zone of proximal development (ZPD)**—the gap between what a learner already knows and the upper limit of what a learner can accomplish with expert assistance (Vygotsky, 1978). The optimal level of instruction is a level just beyond what a learner can accomplish independently.

For example, Long and Porter (1985) claim that negotiated interaction based on modified input is necessary because receiving comprehensible input (Krashen, 1982) alone is not enough to improve English language learners' interlanguage. During interaction with native speakers, non-native speakers negotiate meaning through devices such as clarification requests, confirmation checks, and repetitions with redundancy. Observe the following interaction:

Native Speaker (NS):	Like part of a triangle?
Non-Native Speaker (NNS):	What is triangle?
NS:	A triangle is a shape—um, it has three sides.
NNS:	A peak?
NS:	Three straight sides.
NNS:	A peak?
NS:	Yes, it does look like a mountain peak, yes.

(Adapted from Yule, 2010)

Through this interaction with the native speaker, the non-native speaker is negotiating the meaning of a triangle, which allows the language input to become modified.

theory *into* Practice 6.3

Vygotsky's theories of learning and development have helped shape constructivist perspectives as well as methods of the communicative approach. Vygotsky (1978) maintained that learning is more than mirroring. He subscribed to the idea that children actively construct knowledge by collecting information from the environment of the learning situation in order to build meaning and understanding.

Vygotsky proposed that learning can actually lead development. In discussing the processes of learning and development, he differentiated between the external and the internal interactions in which the learner participates. To explain, the "expert" in the learning situation shares his or her own ways of knowing by externally modeling his or her thought processes for the learner. Then the learner externally manipulates the information the expert provided. The external learning interactions between the learner and the information may require the learner to question the expert or ask the expert to rephrase or repeat ideas for clarification. When the learner is able to take possession of the information, the new knowledge becomes internalized. This internalization of external learning is referred to as *development* (Vygotsky, 1978).

Vygotsky also developed his theory of the *zone of proximal development (ZPD)*. He defined this zone as the area between the level of independent performance and the level of assisted performance. He argued that learning occurs when new information and skills fall within the zone, or the space between what the learner already knows and what he or she can do with the help of an expert. The ZPD shifts as the individual learns more complex concepts and skills and becomes capable of independently achieving the tasks that once required the assistance of another (Vygotsky, 1978).

Finally, Vygotsky viewed language as a mechanism for thinking. Language is the means by which we express what is learned and understood. When children face a cognitively difficult task, they often talk out loud as a means of gaining control over the cognitive processes that are necessary to accomplish the task. Although adults may not verbally express this type of self-talk, they continue to use inward, private speech (Lantolf & Appel, 1996).

Within your own classroom practice:

- *In what ways do your CLD students construct knowledge?*
- *How do you target the ZPD with your CLD students?*
- *How do you use more capable or language-proficient peers to encourage learning in the ZPD?*
- *What role does cooperative learning offer for the support of potential development?*
- *How are parents or caregivers of CLD students welcomed and maximized in ways that increase the CLD students' potential development?*

The constructivist point of view led many educational theorists and researchers to conclude that environmental exposure to the target language and social interaction in that language is sufficient to prompt a learner's innate ability to develop the capacity to comprehend and produce that language. Nonetheless, this point of view does not negate the fact that educators may play a significant role in language acquisition. Instead, this perspective argues that the appropriate role of the educator shifts from purveyor of all knowledge (a behaviorist perspective) to enabler or facilitator of meaning construction (a constructivist perspective). Therefore, the communicative-constructivist perspective asserts that a language-rich instructional environment is necessary to activate a learner's genetic predisposition for language development. Figure 6.4 provides a graphic illustration of additional suggestions for the creation of a language-rich environment for language acquisition.

■**figure 6.4**   Suggestions for the Creation of a Language-Rich Environment for Language Acquisition

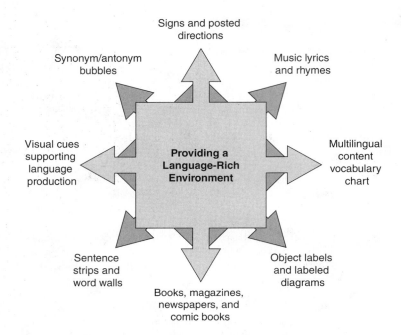

Accordingly, learners do not need explicit instruction in the structure and vocabulary of the language in order for the language to develop. Instead, they need meaningful social and communicative interaction in the target language. Furthermore, learners do not need explicit error correction because errors are recognized as developmental in nature and part of language learners' efforts to create and test hypotheses about how the target language works. Therefore, the role of the effective educator is to foster a communicative environment conducive to social interaction and the construction of meaning in context. That is, language, thought, meaning, and use should not be isolated as separate, disconnected components. Instead, they should be integrated in ways that emulate the natural progression of communication.

Communicative Approach: Methods

Perhaps the most common theme shared among methods derived from the communicative approach is their emphasis on **communication as the purpose of language**. Diaz-Rico (2014) concludes that these methods, most of which have evolved as a response to changing theory and research, reflect fundamental changes in perspectives on the appropriate nature of second language teaching. These methods increasingly acknowledge and elaborate on (1) language as embedded in social contexts; (2) the multiplicity of language functions; (3) the need for **student-centered**, teacher-facilitated language instruction; and (4) the need to stress communication versus rules in language teaching. The early methods derived from the communicative approach—the silent way, the natural way, and suggestopedia—targeted social language development as a goal of instruction. Contemporary methods, including integrated content-based (ICB) instruction and the sheltered method, strongly emphasize interactive, communicative, and contextual language acquisition through adaptations and modifications of the grade-level curriculum. The following overviews first summarize early communicative methods and follow with those methods that are considered contemporary. Table 6.1 provides an illustration of these relationships among communicative methods.

Early Methods of the Communicative Approach. Early methods of the communicative approach are primarily presented for historical purposes. Each of these early communicative methods was part of the evolution of the communicative approach toward a more inclusive, content-based, and interactive philosophy of instruction for language instruction. Accordingly, each of these early methods is briefly summarized in order to provide the reader with a sense of the foundation on which more contemporary communicative methods were designed (see Table 6.1). This and forthcoming chapters emphasize the more contemporary methods of the communicative approach, many of which are in widespread use in public school classrooms.

Silent Way. The silent way presented learners with simple linguistic situations that they were to observe and then describe in the target language, focusing especially on the actions they witnessed. The first language of learners was not used, and the teacher emphasized the pronunciation and word flow of the learner's descriptions while encouraging target language production. Unlike the protocol of grammatical methods, learners who learned according to the silent way developed their own criteria for the quality of language acquisition functions (listening, speaking, and correction) in which they engaged. In fact, the teacher's silence was intentionally designed to encourage student initiative, language production, and linguistic interactions (Gattegno, 1982).

Natural Way. The natural way, another method of the communicative approach, is sometimes referred to as the natural approach. Nonetheless, as Richard-Amato (1996) reminds us, Krashen and Terrell (1983) cultivated the natural approach, or the natural way, as a *method*. Accordingly, Richard-Amato refers to this method as the *natural way*. This early communicative method was based on four general premises:

1. Comprehension precedes production.
2. If allowed to proceed naturally, language production emerges in stages.
3. Communicative goals should guide instruction.
4. Interactive communicative activities should be designed to lower the affective filter.

Although the method did not include the content-based emphasis of its successors, it did much nonetheless to refine and extend the philosophy of the communicative approach to second language instruction.

Language instruction in the natural way followed a specific order. First, the teacher created a situation in which communication was made meaningful. Then the teacher communicated information in the target language. The teacher simultaneously modified the language to a level at which the learners could understand the messages of instruction. One way the teacher accomplished this was to ensure that instruction was adapted in such a way that language input was comprehensible (see Figure 6.5). Instruction through the natural way ensured that the silent period was recognized and respected. Accordingly, language-learning students spent much of their time building comprehension skills before they were prompted to produce language. Consequently, language instruction usually began with student understanding of oral language and then speaking, reading, and writing (Terrell, 1991). Although the natural way is still used in some foreign language classrooms, its incidence in U.S. public school classrooms is not widespread. To a considerable extent, the natural way created the foundation for the sheltered method of instruction.

Suggestopedia. The communicative method of suggestopedia was designed to place as much language teaching emphasis on learner personality and motivation as that typically placed on intellect. In particular, Georgi Lozanov (1982) was

■**figure 6.5**   Providing Comprehensible Input

Providing Comprehensible Input

Speak Slower
- Avoid an exaggerated slow pace.
- Use longer natural pauses between sentences and ideas.

Speak Clearly
- Use fewer reduced vowels.
- Use fewer deleted consonants.
- Use fewer contractions.
- Use fewer fused forms (*want to,* not *wanna*).
- Use key words stressed to support meaning.

Select Vocabulary Carefully
- Use high-frequency words.
- Use cognates.
- Use fewer idioms.
- Use less slang.
- Use fewer pronouns and more referents.

Use Visuals to Support Meaning
- Objects
- Pictures
- Gestures
- Labeled diagrams
- Body language and movement
- Videos
- Role-playing
- Demonstrations

Simplify Syntax
- Use shorter sentences.
- Use fewer clauses.

interested in what could be learned intuitively and spontaneously. He believed that fear of language learning often inhibited the rapid acquisition of the language. Consequently, he advocated the creation of a relaxing, stress-free environment that would, in his view, enhance language acquisition.

A suggestopedia lesson typically involved music playing in the background. First, students would read a translation of text in their first language. Then the instructor would remove the translation and present the same text in the target language. Visual aids would support the meaning of the text. Students would work with the text through conversation, retelling, and role-playing. By working with the target language text through multiple modalities and in a relaxing environment, language learners would acquire the target language rapidly (Lozanov, 1982).

Although suggestopedia never experienced widespread use, the idea of a relaxing, low-anxiety environment for language acquisition is a component of most contemporary methods of the communicative approach (see Figure 6.6). However, other researchers have criticized the method. Brown (2007) describes suggestopedia as more of a vocabulary memorization technique directed by a teacher than as a method of promoting second language acquisition.

Contemporary Methods of the Communicative Approach. Contemporary communicative methods involve content-based language instruction. The communicative environment in which students must excel is most often that found

> **Global Connections 6.1**
> According to recent studies, computer-assisted language learning (CALL) has emerged as a promising avenue in second language acquisition, specifically in EFL contexts. Al-Hashash (2007) urges EFL teachers to increase and develop their technology skills in order to provide students with digital opportunities to increase their English literacy. Likewise, Barani (2011) conducted a study that demonstrated that Iranian English learners who had more CALL opportunities had higher English listening skills than those students who had little to no technological component in their EFL classes. Although some classrooms around the world do not yet have the technology necessary to provide CALL as part of their program, the goal for many countries is to increase access to technology for all teachers and students.

■ **figure 6.6**   Suggestions for Providing a Low-Anxiety Language Acquisition Environment

- Develop choral reading experiences and chants to lessen CLD students' apprehensions about taking risks in L2 (English).
- Seek out and structure opportunities for the use of the target language in interpersonal communications.
- Attend to the needs, desires, and individual aspirations of students.
- Accept and do not constantly correct all attempts at target language production.
- Accept the use of the students' native languages in the classroom and encourage parents to support ongoing CALP development in L1 at home.
- Exhibit an interest in the home culture and languages of CLD students.
- Allow CLD students with very limited English proficiency to communicate through gestures, including nodding, pointing, gesturing, or drawing.
- Allow more capable or bilingual peers to assist in the completion of outlines, KWL charts, Venn diagrams, and so on.
- Write language and content objectives on the board and refer to them throughout lessons.
- Develop a predictable daily routine to enhance students' understandings of expectations, instructional protocol, and means of evaluation.

in content-area classrooms. Consequently, second language researchers and educators developed content-based communicative methods to help students acquire the language they need to be academically successful. The most common methods for teaching English learners academic language are the integrated content-based (ICB) method and the sheltered instruction method. Because these methods are detailed in Chapters 7 and 8, the following discussions provide only overviews of each of these contemporary communicative methods.

The Integrated Content-Based (ICB) Method. The ICB method involves the concurrent teaching of academic subject matter and second language acquisition skills. The language curriculum is based directly on students' academic and linguistic needs. At the secondary level, grade-level teams of educators are often formed to collaborate in the development of **thematic units** and the planning of instruction that emphasizes content and language objectives across subject areas. This communicative and cross-curricular method of instruction is new to many secondary teachers and requires a commitment from school faculty as well as administrators.

The Sheltered Instruction Method. The sheltered instruction method can be implemented in either a grade-level or a second language classroom. Sheltered lessons integrate language and content objectives into the same lesson. Content objectives are typically derived from the curriculum, as aligned with state or national standards. Language objectives are best derived from practice standards for CLD students, such as those put forth by the Teachers of English to Speakers of Other Languages (TESOL) and World-Class Instructional Design and Assessment (WIDA). For more information on these standards, refer to our longer discussion in Chapter 5. Essentially, language objectives are functionally linked to the CLD student's level of L2 (English) proficiency. Students receive grade-level content, but teachers scaffold their instruction in order to provide comprehensible language input and a modified grade-level curriculum.

Although there are several variations of sheltered instruction, each of these tends to share certain common themes, which are also strategies of the method. Among these common strategies are hands-on applications and social interactions, cooperative learning, guarded vocabulary, and visual support. The dominant model of sheltered instruction is the sheltered instruction observation protocol (SIOP) (Echevarria, Vogt, & Short, 2000, 2002, 2013), which uses 30 indicators of best practice with CLD students. Although the sheltered instruction method of the communicative approach is a widely implemented method of language instruction in U.S. public school classrooms, new understandings of the learning process have also fostered the development of a third approach to language instruction: the cognitive approach.

Ms. Espinoza recently has been assigned to teach evening EFL classes to learners ranging in age from 24 to 41 years. Most of her students have extensive family and work obligations outside of class. For the first two weeks of class, Ms. Espinoza has been using the standard curriculum that was provided. This curriculum frequently is used with young adolescent learners who are at the same level of English language proficiency as her current students. The curriculum places a heavy emphasis on students reading text controlled for language level and writing sentences that follow modeled patterns. Although the students in Ms. Espinoza's class are attentive and respectful in class, they do not seem especially enthusiastic about what they are learning.

■ *What advice would you offer Ms. Espinoza? In what ways might a teacher in this type of scenario promote motivation among students to learn English?*

Cognitive Approach

The **cognitive approach** (see Table 6.1) is a product of efforts to examine and analyze the cognitive psychological side of learning, language learning, and instruction to promote language learning (Awh & Jonides, 1998; Banich, 1997; Elman et al., 1997; Gilhooly, Logie, Wetherick, & Wynn, 1993; Johnson, 1996; Just & Carpenter, 1992; Kim & Hirsch, 1997; Newell, 1990; O'Malley & Chamot, 1990; O'Malley, Chamot, Stewner-Manzanares, Russo, & Küpper, 1985a, 1985b; Paris & Winograd, 1990; Zimmerman, 1990). Cognitive psychology is essentially concerned with the structure and nature of comparatively complex knowledge processes (such as discovering, recognizing, conceiving, judging, reasoning, and reflecting) and their influences on or relationships to actions (Elman et al., 1997; Gagné, 1985; Shuell, 1986).

Cognitive Approach: History and Evolution

The history and evolution of the cognitive approach is integrally connected to that of cognitive psychology and the acceptance of trends in that discipline among educational psychologists (see Table 6.2). In particular, we are concerned with the evolution of the cognitive model of learning and perspectives on learning. Mayer (1998) summarized the evolution of these learning perspectives according to three general metaphors:

- *Learning as response acquisition* dominated psychological theory and educational practice (Mayer, 1998) during the first half of the twentieth century. Grounded in a history of research on animals, learning was perceived as a mechanical process wherein successful responses were more or less automatically strengthened and those that were unsuccessful were summarily weakened. This behaviorist metaphor tended to perceive the learner as a passive recipient of information whose repertoire of behaviors was determined by rewards and punishments encountered in the environment. Not surprisingly, drill and practice served as the epitome of instruction based on this learning perspective.
- *Learning as knowledge acquisition* was the product of the cognitive revolution of the 1950s and 1960s. According to this view, the learner was a processor of

information and the teacher a dispenser of information. In education, the curriculum thus became the focus of instruction. This curriculum-centered approach subdivided topics into studies, studies into lessons, and lessons into facts and formulas. Because the goal became the amount of knowledge the learner possessed, standardized testing became the assessment of choice.

- *Learning as knowledge construction* was the outcome of efforts to refine and enhance cognitive theory during the 1970s and 1980s. Research evolved to emphasize subject-area learning in realistic situations. The perception of the learner changed from one of recipient to a constructor of knowledge. Instructionally, the focus changed from curriculum-centered to child-centered. Assessment matured from its preoccupation with quantitative measurements to an acknowledgment of the merit of qualitative evaluation.

This child-centered perspective on learning has led to the long established 14 learner-centered principles that guide the ongoing research, theoretical, and practical efforts of the American Psychological Association (APA, 1997). Thematically, these principles are placed into four categories: cognitive/metacognitive factors, motivational/affective factors, development/social factors, and individual differences. Ultimately, these principles focus on the notion that learning can be a *meaningful* activity, which suggests a reconceptualization of learning as a process that is as much cognitive as it is biological, motivational, affective, cultural, social, and interactive—all while simultaneously based on individual experiences.

At the level of instruction for language acquisition, the cognitive approach traces the efforts of theorists, researchers, and practitioners to incorporate much of what has been learned from the evolution of cognitive learning theory. At the theoretical level, one example is the efforts of Ellen Bialystok to develop a model of second language acquisition. Her model, sometimes referred to as an *information-processing model* of second language acquisition, incorporates three components related to specific types of knowledge, including implicit and explicit linguistic knowledge (Bialystok, 1990). At the level of research and analysis, recent work on the cognitive side of language, language learning, and language instruction has contributed to the evolving foundations of the cognitive approach (Elman et al., 1997; Johnson, 1996; Kim & Hirsch, 1997). Finally, at the practical level, recent efforts to apply the cognitive model of learning to language instruction have resulted in the development of CALLA (Chamot & O'Malley, 1994; O'Malley & Chamot, 1990; O'Malley et al., 1985a, 1985b), which is the dominant contemporary method of language instruction grounded in the cognitive approach.

Cognitive Approach: Philosophical Foundations

Wittrock (1998) and Mayer (1998) argue that a renewed interest in **cognition** marks a fundamental shift in psychological research, especially that of educational psychology, from a behaviorist to a cognitive perspective on learning. Each of these analyses variously claim that the behavioral perspective on learning tended to (1) deny attention to the learner's active role in the learning process, (2) study learning in isolation from the school tasks it helped accomplish, and (3) inadequately account for the role of background knowledge in the learning process. Today, the cognitive perspective more directly ties to the challenges and processes confronted by the learner, as well as to the teaching and instructional protocols designed to address these issues. Among the emphases of the new cognitive perspective (Chamot, 2009; Chamot & O'Malley, 1994; Kroll, 1998; Mayer, 1998; Wittrock, 1998) are the following:

- The learner's background knowledge and socialization experiences in a particular culture, especially the ways in which these may facilitate connections to new learning
- The learner's strategies for knowledge acquisition, especially cognitive, metacognitive, and social/affective strategies
- The learner's metacognitive processes, especially her or his emergent capacities for introspection
- The learner's interaction with text relationships, such as cause and effect and sequence
- The learner's interaction with certain text structures, including enumeration, classification, and generalization
- The learner's perceptions of and interaction with discourse structure (e.g., expository and narrative) and certain genres of writing (e.g., indirect and linear)
- The learner's affective processes
- Means to research the learner's thought and affective processes
- Types of constructivist teaching procedures
- Ways to teach comprehension, analysis, critical thinking, and application

As these emphases demonstrate, the cognitive perspective affects a considerable variety of educational interests relevant to the CLD learner, including cultural and cross-cultural dynamics, learning in the content areas, critical thinking, literacy development, sociocultural and social affective effects on learning, constructivist learning environments and teaching, and the learner's application of acquired knowledge in different contexts.

Cognitive Model of Learning

Fundamentally, the cognitive approach is grounded in a cognitive model of learning. This perspective on learning is similar to that of Mezirow (1991) and views the learning process as active versus passive, dynamic versus static. This view holds that learning (at minimum) involves (1) information selection from the environment; (2) information categorization and organization; (3) the relation of new information to known concepts, categories, and premises; (4) the use of information in appropriate contexts; and (5) metacognition on the process (Chamot, 2009; Chamot & O'Malley, 1994; Gagné, 1985; Mezirow, 1991; Shuell, 1986).

Role of Memory in Learning. The cognitive perspective on learning is grounded in a differentiation among types of memory, including long-term memory, and **working memory**. Although the conceptual definition for long-term memory is comparatively self-evident, the study of working memory is a relatively new line of research (Awh & Jonides, 1998; Gilhooly et al., 1993; Johnson, 1996; Willingham, 2007). *Working memory* describes a system for temporarily holding and manipulating information for a brief period during the performance of an array of cognitive tasks

---

■ **Snapshot of Classroom Practice 6.1**   Learning Strategies

---

In this classroom, students are guided to use graphic organizers to support their understanding of the topic (a metacognitive learning strategy). The teacher uses technology to provide additional visuals and to promote student connections to and elaboration on their background knowledge (a cognitive strategy). Learners also have opportunities to work collaboratively within their small group to share ideas and information (a social/affective strategy).

(Courtesy of Jessica Barrand, Hillcrest Elementary, Lawrence, Kansas)

including, but not limited to, comprehension, learning, and reasoning (Baddeley, 1986; Just & Carpenter, 1992; Newell, 1990; Sousa, 2011). Working memory is characterized by limited storage capacity and rapid turnover, as differentiated from the larger capacity and archival system of long-term memory. When we engage in the literacy skill of listening, we tend to use the temporary storage capacity of working memory to hold segments of sentences online. We also use working memory like a mental blackboard to associate these sentence segments with verbs and objects in order to comprehend the messages and meanings of the sentences we hear.

Finally, the cognitive model of learning is also concerned with metacognitive knowledge. Livingston (1997) notes that a considerable degree of confusion exists about what constitutes **metacognition** and metacognitive knowledge. Livingston defines metacognition as "higher-order thinking that involves active control over the cognitive processes engaged in learning" (p. 1). She concludes that much of the confusion arises from the interchangeable use of a variety of terms (e.g., *executive control, self-regulation,* and *meta-memory*) with metacognition. Metacognition is most often associated with

Flavell (1979), who tended to be more precise in differentiating among terms applicable to metacognition. According to Flavell, metacognition consists of both metacognitive knowledge and metacognitive experiences or regulation. Therefore, Flavell has argued that *metacognitive knowledge* can be conceptualized as acquired knowledge about cognitive processes that may be used to control or regulate cognitive processes. *Metacognitive regulation,* on the other hand, can be conceptualized as the use of metacognitive strategies to control cognitive activities and to ensure that a cognitive goal (e.g., the understanding of a text written in L2) is attained.

Cognitive Approach: Methods

As illustrated in Table 6.1, although recent research and analysis (Cummins, 2001; Johnson, 1996) suggest ongoing efforts to connect cognitive theory and perspectives and premises for language instruction, to date only one compilation has been characterized as sufficiently robust to constitute a method of the cognitive approach. Indeed, through their development of the CALLA method, Chamot and O'Malley (Chamot, 2009; Chamot & O'Malley, 1994) have achieved a groundbreaking integration of cognitive theory with mostly communicative strategies for language instruction.

The CALLA Method. The CALLA method (Chamot, 2009; Chamot & O'Malley, 1994) is designed to enrich the language that CLD students can use for academic communication (see Table 6.1). At the same time, CALLA is designed to further the abilities of CLD students to comprehend the discourse of the various content areas and to enhance their capacities to be academically successful in those subject areas. The CALLA method originally was considered applicable to second language learners at intermediate and advanced levels of target language proficiency. However, research on its implementation has shown that the method is also effective with beginning students, as well as with native-English-speaking students, in developing higher-order thinking and literacy skills (Chamot, 1995; Montes, 2002). The method, which is detailed in Chapter 9, includes three primary components: topics from the major content areas, the development of academic language skills, and explicit instruction in learning strategies. Content topics are incrementally introduced and scaffolded with extensive contextual supports and reduced linguistic demands. The emphasis on the development of academic language skills targets all four literacy domains (listening, speaking, reading, and writing) in daily content lessons. Explicit instruction in learning strategies targets both content and language acquisition. Among learning strategies emphasized are cognitive, metacognitive, and social/affective strategies.

Cognitive Approach: Synopsis

It is important to remember that the cognitive approach also builds on what we already know about pedagogy that targets communication as the purpose of language and language acquisition. Accordingly, the cognitive approach as a foundation for CLD students (illustrated in Tables 6.1 and 6.2) variously emphasizes:

- Social interaction and communication in the environment for language acquisition
- Communication as the purpose of language and the motivation for language acquisition

theory *into practice* 6.4

Anderson (2002) provides a model of metacognition that guides students to incorporate the following five components into their learning processes: prepare and plan, select and use learning strategies, monitor use of strategies, orchestrate various strategies, and evaluate strategy use and learning. The first of the components, *prepare and plan,* emphasizes the need for learners to think about what they need to do in order to accomplish the goals set by the teacher or to accomplish their personal learning goals. Students then must *select and use learning strategies* pertinent to the task and apply them appropriately. For learners to successfully incorporate this second component of the metacognition model, teachers must instruct students on specific types of strategies—what they are, how to use them, and when to use them.

The third component of Anderson's model of metacognition involves the *monitoring of strategy use.* For students to be able to effectively use strategies, educators must teach learners to periodically stop what they are doing, reflect on the manner in which they are actually using a particular strategy, and determine if they need to realign their actions in order to employ the strategy more accurately. *Orchestrating various strategies,* the fourth critical component of Anderson's metacognition model, calls attention to the fact that some situations and tasks require the use of more than one strategy. Students must be able to evaluate their progress toward achieving the determined goals and realize when a strategy is not working for them. A new strategy or, as is often the case, a combination of strategies may be more effective for the situation (Anderson, 2002).

The fifth component of the metacognition model, *evaluate strategy use and learning,* guides learners to reflect on their progress in the learning process. Teachers help students develop the ability to ask self-directed questions similar to the following:

- What goals am I trying to accomplish?
- Which strategies am I currently using?

- How effectively am I using the strategies?
- What other strategies might work for this task?

In this way, the metacognitive model, which is graphically depicted in Figure 6.7, enables students to take control of their learning. While the teacher provides necessary instruction, modeling, and support, the students work to develop the metacognitive skills necessary for independent problem solving (Anderson, 2002).

■**figure 6.7**   Cognitive Growth

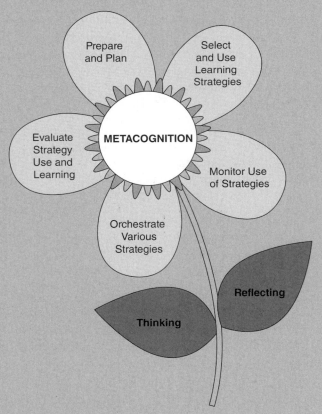

■ *In what ways might you teach CLD students to maximize this metacognitive model in their language and literacy development? What benefits might this model have for cross-disciplinary applications?*

- Attention to the affective motivators or inhibitors of language acquisition
- Elaboration of the student's prior knowledge of CALP in L1 and L2
- Collaboration with and maximization of parents or caregivers as valuable language resources and as partners in the reinforcement of classroom instruction
- Meaningful and relevant language instruction
- Scaffolded instruction for language acquisition
- Active, dynamic, learner-centered language instruction
- Content-area integration with language instruction
- Thematic instruction and cooperative learning
- Comprehensible input for language acquisition

According to Genesee (2000), the cognitive perspective on language acquisition and language instruction further enhances our recognition that provisions for learning and language learning must account for:

- Individual differences in learning styles by structuring alternative grouping arrangements, offering variation in the type and use of instructional materials, and modifying time frames for learning and response
- The second language learner's need for context-rich, meaningful learning environments

Thus, cognitivists argue that the ongoing developmental needs of students who are acquiring a second language are best addressed by attending to their primary patterns of prior socialization in a particular culture, especially the preferred learning styles they demonstrate as a result of that socialization. Students exhibit more or less favorable responses to certain types of learning environments, strategies, and so forth. Again, as with instruction designed to target multiple learning style preferences, variation is key to effectiveness. Ultimately, CLD students bring to the ESL/EFL classroom language acquisition needs that are best served through highly contextualized learning environments and constructivist, meaning-focused instruction that targets cognitive academic language proficiency.

Connect, Engage, Challenge

CONNECT
Review and Reflect on the Reading

1. In what ways would you define and differentiate among the terms *approach, method, strategy,* and *technique*?
2. What are the three dominant approaches to language instruction?
3. In what ways would you summarize the philosophical foundations of the grammatical approach?
4. In what ways would you summarize the philosophical foundations of the communicative approach?

5. In what ways would you compare and contrast a behaviorist and a constructivist perspective on learning?

6. In what ways would you summarize the philosophical foundations of the cognitive approach?

7. What are the noteworthy features of at least two methods of the grammatical approach?

8. In what ways would you compare and contrast early and contemporary communicative methods?

9. What are the noteworthy features of the integrated content-based (ICB) method of the communicative approach?

10. What are the noteworthy features of the sheltered instruction method of the communicative approach?

11. What three types of memory are explored by the cognitive perspective?

12. What are the noteworthy features of the CALLA method of the cognitive approach?

13. In what ways would you describe meaningful learning?

14. In what ways did Chomsky describe the role of the LAD in language acquisition?

15. What role does the zone of proximal development (ZPD) play in student learning?

16. What does it mean to ground language instruction in a philosophical approach?

ENGAGE
Share What You Learned

1. This chapter reviews the grammatical approach and associated methods for historical purposes. Discuss, in detail, at least two major reasons why the methods of the grammatical approach are problematic for CLD students.

2. The need to establish a common, consistent nomenclature to be used in instructional planning for CLD students is a benchmark of this chapter. Discuss the need for such consistency in terminology and the ways in which it enables communication and collaboration among policymakers, educators, and staff.

3. This chapter summarizes the philosophical foundations of the grammatical, communicative, and cognitive approaches to language instruction, as well as methods, strategies, and techniques associated with each approach. Discuss the unfavorable effects that can be anticipated when classroom instruction for CLD students mixes philosophical approaches or uses methods that are not consistent with a selected philosophical approach to language instruction.

CHALLENGE
It's Not Real until You Practice

The Umbrella Approach

To reinforce your own learning of the approaches, methods, strategies, and techniques, while also reviewing how they have been reflected in ESL texts and resource books written in the past, analyze authentic materials from the field, such as the following:

· Buhrow, B., & Garcia, A. U. (2006). *Lady bugs, tornadoes, swirling galaxies*. Portland, ME: Stenhouse.

• Lado, R. (1970). *Lado English series, book one*. New York: Simon & Schuster.

• Richards, J. C., & Hull, J. C. (1987). *As I was saying: Conversation tactics*. Reading, MA: Addison-Wesley.

Procedures for the Umbrella Approach

Step 1   Work in pairs or teams to skim and scan the book selected. Identify which of the three approaches the book is philosophically aligned with, based on what you learned from this chapter on approaches, methods, strategies, and techniques.

Step 2   As a team, create an umbrella chart for the text or resource book you analyzed (see pictures below). Be sure to align the approaches with their corresponding methods, strategies, and techniques (as modeled in Figure 6.1 and Table 6.1).

Step 3   Include both pros and cons of the text or resource book in the chart and share them with the class. While each team is presenting, the other class members can make notes on copies of the following table.

Approaches		
Grammatical	Communicative	Cognitive
Title:	Title:	Title:
Year:	Year:	Year:
Author(s):	Author(s):	Author(s):
	Methods	
	Strategies	
	Techniques	
	Pros and Cons	
Pros: Cons:	Pros: Cons:	Pros: Cons:

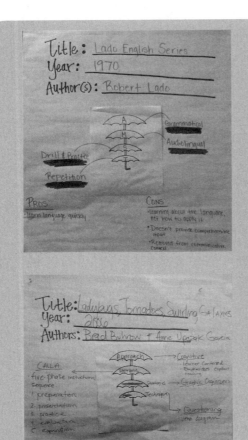

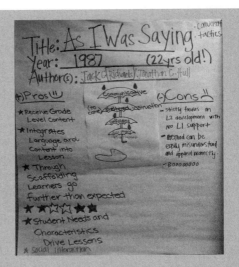

Source: Miki Loschky, Teacher
Trainer, Manhattan, KS

Preservice Teachers

1. After reading the following vignette, identify the instructional approach used. What are some of the characteristics of this approach? Identify the method(s) associated with the approach found in the vignette. What are some of the characteristics of the identified method(s)?

> The 20 students in Mr. Brown's sixth-grade class are engaged in writing a book report on ancient Egypt. The room is overflowing with posters, illustrations, hieroglyphics, books, and student work related to ancient Egypt. The class members have been studying ancient Egypt for two weeks, and their book reports are a culmination of their studies. Rather than having students turn in individual book reports, the teacher has required the students to work in collaborative groups of three or four students in which they will write, design, and present their report to the class.
>
> Half of the students in Mr. Brown's class are classified English learners (the other half are English-only), and several languages can be heard in the classroom. Students in all

parts of the classroom are talking excitedly while they are writing rough drafts, discussing their ideas with other students, and editing the work of their classmates. The teacher circulates from group to group in order to observe and provide assistance when necessary.

One of the student groups, led by Van, a Vietnamese English learner, is ready to present the group book report at the end of the day. Mr. Brown has the group go to the front of the room, where the group members begin to present their book report. Van begins by presenting a timeline on a large piece of chart paper. He describes the relevant events that took place during each of the dates his group has included using vocabulary he has learned over the course of the two-week unit. Margarita follows by presenting a visual representation of what homes were like in ancient Egypt. Ben then goes on to discuss the class system of ancient Egypt with a Venn diagram of the similarities and differences between the class system of ancient Egypt and the purportedly classless system of the United States.

In-Service Teachers

1. After reading the following vignette, identify the instructional approach used. What are some of the characteristics of this approach? Identify the method(s) associated with the approach found in the vignette. What are some of the characteristics of the identified method(s)?

In his science classroom, Mr. Babcock displays posters, several of which are written in Spanish and in English, of scientists and inventors from diverse cultures. His third-period physical science class is mostly made up of sophomores, with a few juniors and seniors who need the class to graduate. The students have a wide range of English language proficiencies. Mr. Babcock has carefully structured the lab groups to include both native English speakers and CLD students who demonstrate limited English proficiency. Students with a stronger command of English are placed in groups with CLD students to act as peer coaches.

The content and language objectives on the board cover the scientific method and related terminology. Each group is given a number of tools that students have used in previous work: a graduated cylinder partially filled with water, a ruler, a balance, a table of densities, and a piece of aluminum foil. Mr. Babcock has the students read the daily objectives aloud and gives the students the task of determining the thickness of the piece of aluminum foil. Students review on the board the steps they will take as scientists to design an experiment and predict the outcome. Each group has a leader, a recorder, a timekeeper, and a materials keeper.

The ensuing discussion is animated as the groups tackle the activity. The students within each group come to a consensus on the method of measurement, and the recorder writes down the plan. The leader calls on the materials keeper to begin the process. While the activity proceeds, the recorder keeps careful record of the steps taken, the questions, and the results. The timekeeper calls time. Then the leader from each group explains to the class his or her group's method of testing the thickness of the aluminum foil, the questions that the group members developed, and the results determined. As a class, the students review the content and language objectives on the board and explain to Mr. Babcock how they met the objectives or why they believe more practice is necessary to meet the objectives.

tips for practice

In elementary classrooms, consider:

- Assessing your CLD students by scaffolding assessment tasks in a contextualized manner. This can be done by incorporating easily accessible classroom materials (quotations, charts, graphics, cartoons, etc.), including questions for small-group discussion and individual writing, and enhancing the students' understanding of the assessment process by modeling the steps involved.

- Incorporating cloze exercises to help your students understand a lesson. For such an exercise, teachers write a summary or take an excerpt of a reading passage, lesson, or class activity and then delete every *nth* word. Students then "fill in the blank" with an exact word or related word.

- Having students keep daily reflective journals to help affirm their identity and culture. Topics can be provided to them or you may give them the freedom to write about their own thoughts and feelings in either their native language or English. When they write in English, do not correct grammatical errors. In this way, the students focus on personal expression rather than the conventions of writing.

In secondary classrooms, consider:

- Designing authentic assessment tasks such as exhibits, dramatic interpretations, interviews, observations, self-reflections, and a variety of writing samples that require different ways of demonstrating knowledge or skills.

- Helping your students acquire language in a contextualized manner by incorporating process writing in your classroom. Process writing provides opportunities for students to comprehend and acquire language in a meaningful and motivating manner, and targets all four language domains. Process writing can be accomplished through prewriting activities, such as viewing a film or sharing the reading of an article; reviewing key concepts and vocabulary to use in students' writing; and using word-processing programs, if they are easily accessible, to facilitate the drafting and editing processes.

- Creating personal timelines to help promote cultural awareness and understanding. By doing this, students can learn about how their own lives and the lives of their classmates are tied to various political, cultural, and historical events. Combine all timelines into a collective class timeline to better understand the relationship between everyone's lives and certain events.

- Planning lessons that will promote higher-order thinking skills among students, such as asking students to take a stance on a particular historical issue that has variable levels of cultural and political significance for different groups of people.

In EFL classrooms, consider:

- Reviewing curriculum to assess the adaptions that will need to be made in order to align with the approach and method that most influences your teaching.

- Making decisions about the strategies and techniques that you will use in practice based on your content and language objectives.

- Using strategies that support students in scaffolding their own learning and that also provide you with information for decision making during the lesson.

- Making decisions about the techniques you will use during the lesson to set conditions for learning and to advance learning as the lesson unfolds.

- Identifying authentic texts and materials to create a language-rich learning environment.

assessment tips and strategies

The following assessment tips and strategies are drawn from the content of Chapters 4 through 6.

ASSESSMENT

Formal and informal assessments are crucial to the measurement of process and product gains in language, acculturation, and content-area learning among CLD students. Student assessments in the area of second language development must be carefully implemented and accurately interpreted in order to ensure that students are progressing and to gauge what additional support will be needed. Furthermore, alternative and authentic assessments require CLD students to demonstrate their knowledge or skills in a variety of ways. Effective teachers select assessments that are appropriate for the developmental levels and linguistic backgrounds of the students by connecting these assessments to national or state standards as well as district guidelines.

Assessment Tips

- An informal assessment of a CLD student's language biography should include the following factors:
  - Dominant language of first schooling in native country
  - Dominant language spoken at home
  - Extent of L2 schooling in the United States
  - Actual cognitive academic language proficiency (CALP) versus apparent basic interpersonal communication skills (BICS) development in L1 and L2
- A formal assessment of a CLD student's language biography can be accomplished by using tests such as the following (see Herrera, Cabral, and Murry, 2013, for a detailed discussion of formal assessments of language proficiency):
  - To determine L1 proficiency, use the translated Language Assessment Scale (LAS) (Duncan & DeAvila, 1990), the Bilingual Verbal Ability Tests Normative Update (BVAT-NU) (Muñoz-Sandoval, Cummins, Alvaredo, Ruef, & Schrank, 2005), and so on.
  - To determine L2 proficiency, use the IDEA Proficiency Test (IPT) (Ballard & Tighe, 2004), LAS, and so on.

- An informal assessment of a CLD student's level of acculturation should include the following factors:
  - Circumstances and culture in home country prior to immigration
  - Recency of immigration
  - Current home dynamics
  - Parents' work obligations
  - Acculturation stressors
  - Coping strategies
  - The student's involvement in language brokering dynamics
  - Proximity to school and issues of transportation (check with parent, school records, social worker, etc.)
- A formal assessment of a CLD student's level of acculturation can be done through the Acculturation Quick Screen (AQS) (Collier, 1987).
- When teaching key concepts, teachers should assess student understanding by:
  - Asking open-ended questions that invite comparison and contrast.
  - Prompting students to integrate what they have observed and learned in their native countries.
- Informal content-area assessments should encompass measures such as rubrics, self-assessments, and portfolios.
- Formal (formative) content-area assessments should be incremental and criterion-referenced.
- Alternative assessments in L1 should include journals and one-on-one discussions.
- Assessment tasks should be scaffolded in a contextualized manner in order to accurately assess CLD students.
- A formal assessment of a CLD student's content-area knowledge and capacities should be done through modified district tools or pretests.

Assessment Strategies

- Informal assessment of the level of acculturation is primarily done through teacher–student (T–S) and teacher–parent (or family) (T–P) conversations.

- Scaffold assessments by incorporating easily accessible classroom materials such as brief quotations, charts, graphics, cartoons, and works of art.
- Scaffold assessments by including questions for small-group discussion and individual writing.
- Scaffold assessments by modeling the steps involved.
- Use alternative assessments that require CLD students to demonstrate their knowledge and skills in different ways, such as:
  - Exhibits
  - Dramatic interpretations
  - Interviews
  - Observations
  - Self-reflections
  - Writing samples
- Meet and collaborate regularly with the other teachers in your building to develop multiple formal and informal assessment measures for CLD students, such as:
  - Interview protocols
  - Questionnaires
  - Observation checklists
  - Rating scales and criteria
  - Holistic scoring

CHAPTER 7

The Integrated Content-Based Method of Instruction

our mission

Our mission for this chapter will be to:

- Explore key characteristics of the integrated content-based (ICB) method of instruction for CLD students.

We will accomplish this mission by helping you to meet the following learning outcomes:

- Discuss the evolution of content-based instruction.
- Summarize the benefits of ICB instruction in diverse classrooms.
- Explain the process of ICB lesson planning, instruction, and assessment.

Socorro Herrera

key theories and concepts

authentic activities

content-based instruction

content language

content objectives

English for specific purposes (ESP)

immersion instruction

integrated content-based (ICB) method of instruction

language across the curriculum

language for specific purposes (LSP)

language objectives

learning centers

thematic units

theme

topics

Much debate has surrounded the question of whether students can learn academic content if they do not yet have a high level of proficiency in the English language. The previous chapters of this book presented the theory and research-based rationales for the use of **content-based instruction** to promote both the linguistic and academic development of culturally and linguistically diverse (CLD) students. This chapter explores why the **integrated content-based (ICB) method of instruction** provides an excellent venue for language learning. Although the types of strategies and techniques associated with this method may prove beneficial with native-English-speaking students, they are crucial to the academic success of CLD students.

For second language learners, language proficiency involves more than basic interpersonal communication skills (BICS). Because language learners must develop the cognitive academic language proficiency (CALP) to succeed in grade-level academic classes in English, content classes such as biology, physics, calculus, economics, world literature, and U.S. history become their communicative environment (Mohan, 1986). The assumption that students must speak English before they can learn academic content is a serious threat to their academic success. For example, as discussed in Chapter 3, English learners often need five to ten years or more to acquire fully L2 cognitive academic language proficiency (Collier & Thomas, 2009; Thomas & Collier, 1997, 2012). If a school waits until CLD students have acquired CALP to begin content instruction, then students are at least five years academically behind their age-appropriate grade level. Even if a school waits until CLD students have acquired a BICS level of proficiency, these students are still two to three years academically behind their peers (Cummins, 1981; Thomas & Collier, 1997).

One way that educators can minimize the gap between monolingual English-speaking students and their CLD peers is to link language development with academic content (Short, 1993b). This practice of integrating grade-level language and content objectives presents a positive solution to the dilemma of how to prepare students who are not proficient in English while still using grade-level curricula. Research indicates that language learning and content-matter learning are interrelated and must be taught simultaneously if CLD students are to achieve both academic success and high levels of second language proficiency (Collier & Thomas, 2009; Cummins, 2000; Cummins, 2001; Freeman & Freeman, 1998; Freeman, Freeman, & Mercuri, 2002; Thomas & Collier, 1999, 2007, 2012). When CLD students learn English through content-based instruction, they attain a higher level of second language proficiency faster than when they study English as the focus of instruction (Collier & Thomas, 2009; Dulay, Burt, & Krashen, 1982; Thomas & Collier, 2012). In a synthesis of the findings of a longitudinal study on second language acquisition program effectiveness, Collier (1995) observed,

Global Connections 7.1
In an era of internationalizing U.S. universities, there is a higher level of connectivity that has occurred due to technological advances, making it easier for students and faculty to network on a global scale. English teachers throughout the world are beginning to reevaluate the end goal of their English classes. Will the goal be to prepare students to perform well in a social setting or to compete in a global context? As a method, ICB can support authentic teaching that moves EFL teachers from teaching for social performance toward an academic emphasis that prepares all students to compete and participate as global citizens.

> Students do less well in programs that focus on discrete units of language taught in a structured, sequenced curriculum with the learner treated as a passive recipient of knowledge; students achieve significantly better in programs that teach language through cognitively complex academic content in math, science, social studies, and literature, taught through problem solving and discovery learning in highly interactive classroom activities. (p. 2)

Culturally and linguistically diverse students learn their second language most effectively when academic content rather than the structure of the language itself is the context of language instruction.

The ICB method is a means of providing content-based second language instruction using academic **thematic units**. The **theme** of the unit provides a context for academic and language development (Brinton, Snow, & Wesche, 1989). A thematic unit can be defined as an array of learning activities that effectively support teachers to instruct in multiple content areas that are designed and organized around a central idea. The classroom, the environment, and the target culture are sources that can provide ideas for the unit's focus. Activities that integrate the teaching of content and language concepts are then incorporated into instruction, which is structured around the unit's theme (Curtain & Haas, 1995). As Haas (2000) notes, units planned in this manner facilitate the incorporation of a variety of language concepts into a thematic area that is interesting and worthy of study, thereby giving meaning to the language that students are learning. Thematic units specifically benefit CLD students because learning language through specialized content-based instruction allows the students to acquire CALP in a natural way and in a communicative environment. In the content-based ESL/EFL classroom, students receive comprehensible input to facilitate the mastery of key content concepts while learning the language necessary for academic success (Mohan, 1986).

■ Snapshot of Classroom Practice 7.1   Gingerbread Thematic Unit

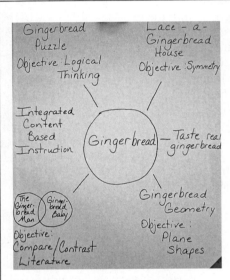

In organizing her ICB instruction for CLD and other students, one teacher selected the theme of gingerbread. This concept map for a unit based on the books *The Gingerbread Man* (Aylesworth, 1998) and *Gingerbread Baby* (Brett, 1999) illustrates how she uses the theme to incorporate language arts as well as math activities into her lessons.

Thematic instruction promotes students' development of cognitive and linguistic abilities and strategies that have applications across a number of subject areas. Such capacities are especially valuable to CLD students, who are often struggling to acquire a second language at the same time that they are learning new concepts in the content areas.

(Courtesy of Suzanne Heinen, elementary teacher, Leavenworth, Kansas)

Integrated content-based instruction is grounded in the communicative approach, which was introduced in Chapter 4 and discussed in Chapter 6. The primary ways in which ICB instruction reflects the communicative approach include an emphasis on communication, the authentic use of literacy in context, and the cultivation of all language domains (listening, speaking, reading, and writing). This chapter explores the evolution of the ICB method and its emphasis on second language acquisition, as interrelated with academic development. We describe and provide examples in this chapter of how this method works in practice in elementary and secondary settings. Discussion and chapter features explore the implementation of this method in both ESL and EFL classroom settings.

Evolution of Content-Based Instruction

The research base for ICB instruction can be traced to a movement known as **language across the curriculum**. This movement espouses a reciprocal relationship between language and content learning (Brinton et al., 1989). The language-across-the-curriculum movement found that directing the attention of learners to **content language** more specifically addressed the language acquisition needs of CLD students in the academic context. This integration of content and language instruction occurred through the teaching of specific content with language teaching aims (Brinton et al., 1989). By proposing the integration of content and language instruction, the language-across-the-curriculum movement provided a methodological foundation for teachers of English learners to provide content-based language instruction. This new method of second language instruction provided comprehensible content-based instruction to CLD students with varying levels of second language proficiency so that they could successfully acquire academic content.

For decades, foreign language departments, adult education programs, and military programs have been teaching content classes for language learning purposes. Because industries have globalized, many countries have provided specific programming that allows employees to learn English, either in those home countries or in the United States, in order to be successful in the global market. These programs, often referred to as **English for specific purposes (ESP)** or **language for specific purposes (LSP)**, seek to prepare students to learn language for different environments, including the fields of medicine, engineering, computer science, and others. Both ESP and LSP instruction use specially designed content-based texts and lectures to assist adult students in developing speaking, listening, reading, and writing skills in English. Using content curricula allows educators to provide language instruction that focuses on the language-learning needs of adult students who are preparing to enter professional studies or the workforce or who are developing additional work-related skills. Through multiple strategies and techniques, ESP and LSP instruction introduce students to vocabulary, syntax, and discourse styles of the target area. Materials and activities that reflect the target area and represent the key concepts are used in instruction.

Similarly, content-based instruction in foreign language programs, often referred to as **immersion instruction**, has focused on teaching students a new language through the medium of academic content areas. Immersion instruction uses strategies and techniques to increase the likelihood that the academic content language of instruction is comprehensible to the learner. With immersion instruction, however, success is almost exclusively linked to language majority students—those whose native language is that of the majority group—thereby making this model most successful in foreign language teaching (Brinton et al., 1989). Culturally and linguistically diverse students whose native language is not that of the dominant group receive inadequate native language support and insufficient comprehensible input through this model to be academically successful (see Chapter 4 for a more detailed discussion of second or foreign language immersion).

Content-Centered Methods of Instruction

More recently the U.S. education field witnessed a search for alternative programs to serve CLD students. Programs with a focus that goes beyond language in isolation, life skills vocabulary, or redundant content already known in the students' first language resulted. Many language teaching programs focus on the integration of language and content as the vehicle for reaching the academic potential of students in ESL/EFL classrooms. The method that is the focus of this chapter is the integrated content-based method of instruction with a thematic focus. In recent years there has been a move away from ICB in the United States. However, research on the ICB method has provided a solid theoretical framework for effective instruction in the following learning environments:

- Classrooms in which a language teacher and a grade-level teacher are collaborating to meet the needs of all students
- Pull-out programs in which the CLD specialist closely aligns instruction with local and state academic content standards
- Schools in which the curriculum for all grade levels is based on themes aligned with local and state academic content standards
- Middle school and high school classrooms in which content-area teachers team to collaborate and integrate themes and topics from different subject areas
- English as a foreign language classrooms that have moved beyond teaching language in isolation and toward literacy development, in preparation for learning academic content in the target language

The ICB method of instruction is ideal for EFL settings in which educators and administrators are transitioning from grammar-based instruction to language instruction that integrates linguistic modifications, meaning-making through conceptualization, and real-life applications of content.

▇ Integrated Content-Based Instruction

In ICB instruction, language acquisition and content learning are not separate acts of teaching. Rather, language serves as a medium of instruction and learning. Context functions as the central component of interactions between the teacher and the student. The integration of language and content instruction provides students with contextualized learning experiences that facilitate simultaneous development of L2 proficiency and academic knowledge and skills.

The ICB method challenges the myth that academic instruction needs to be delayed until CLD students have developed a high level of English language proficiency. With ICB instruction, the student immediately receives instruction rooted in the academic content of the lesson. As Short (1991) notes, by providing students with the opportunity to use language in meaningful contexts while studying the academic subject matter, teachers create an ideal learning environment for facilitating language development. The more the student learns and comprehends language related to a specific content area, the more likely he or she is to comprehend future instruction in that content area.

Integrated content-based instruction engages students in **authentic activities** linked to specific subject matter that is incorporated within a theme. Teachers integrate language and concept development by providing English learners with real-world experiences through hands-on activities. In this way, the ICB method reflects a whole-language approach. It also encourages students to use targeted academic language for relevant, cognitively demanding purposes.

Benefits of ICB Instruction for CLD Students

Research by Pessoa, Hendry, Donato, Tucker, and Lee (2007) suggests that language-learning students, specifically those in EFL classrooms, greatly benefit from content-based instruction because classroom activities provide a meaningful context for language development and use. Additionally, ICB tasks have greater cognitive demands and emphasize the school curriculum. Caine and Caine (1991) explain that learning facts and skills within a meaningful context, rather than in isolation, enables the individual to store the material in memory with less time required for practicing and rehearsing the information. This is particularly true for English learners who are simultaneously acquiring academic content and language. Therefore, when teachers present lessons that integrate academic content and language development across the curriculum, the student enjoys an enhanced opportunity to internalize and process new learning and language. Table 7.1 provides a brief summary of the similarities and differences between segregated and integrated skills instruction.

Using the ICB method, the integration of language and content instruction is done by incorporating subject-area content into language programs (Curtain & Haas, 1995). Curtain and Haas suggest that language and content instruction are also integrated by putting language into a larger, more meaningful context and by providing situations that require authentic language use. With ICB instruction, the language emphasized in the curriculum is based directly on the academic needs of the students. For example, the sequence of skills and language introduced is structured to reflect the needs of the student by bridging gaps and making concrete connections to background knowledge. Through repeated exposure to academic language, students begin to transfer second language skills to other academic subject areas.

Vygotsky (1978) proposed that increased social interaction and scaffolding of instruction enable students to better contextualize and comprehend new material.

■ **table 7.1**   Segregated versus Integrated Skills Instruction: Comparisons and Contrasts

Criterion	Integrated Skills Instruction		Segregated Skills Instruction
	ICB	**SI**	
An ESL-certified/endorsed teacher typically delivers classroom instruction.	+		
Emphasis is on all literacy skills of language.	+	+	
L2 development is a goal.	+	+	
Content knowledge/skills and L2 development are goals.	+	+	
Focus is on requisite terminology for content.	+	+	
Focus is on core, grade-level curriculum.	+	+	
Content and ESL standards guide instruction.	+	+	
Classroom instruction typically follows the scope and sequence of a grade-level class.	+	+	
A subject-area certified teacher, with professional development for CLD student needs, typically delivers classroom instruction.		+	
Focus is on isolated/discrete language skills.			x
Language and content learning are separated.			x
Basic skills orientation of instruction.			x
A subject-area certified teacher with no professional development for CLD students may lead instruction.			x

ICB = Integrated content-based method
SI = Sheltered instruction method
x = Not appropriate for CLD students
+ = Appropriate for CLD students

The ICB method not only provides students with the opportunity for increased social interaction with their peers but also scaffolds learning by providing repeated exposure to content and language that is meaningfully contextualized. Thus, the ICB method eliminates any artificial separation between language instruction and subject-area instruction.

Attention to each of the four dimensions of the CLD student biography— sociocultural, cognitive, academic, and linguistic—increases student achievement in all classrooms. Genesee (1994) suggests that language instruction is often an isolated part of the student's day when conventional language instruction methods are used. The student's learning of language concepts and skills is commonly segregated from her or his development of social, cognitive, and academic skills and

dilemmas *of Practice* 7.1

Ms. Reyes is a sixth-grade English teacher at an urban middle school. Many students at this school do not yet exhibit high levels of English proficiency. On a weekly basis, Ms. Reyes reads a list of vocabulary words and their definitions to the students but does not provide any opportunities for student discussion or dialogue about them. Rather, she asks students to write down the definitions and then write sentences using each word appropriately. She is disappointed with her CLD students who are having difficulty completing the sentence-writing homework and are not prepared for the weekly vocabulary tests. What can Ms. Reyes do to create a more successful language acquisition process for her struggling English learners?

■ *The way that Ms. Reyes has designed her vocabulary instruction does not include strategies to present these words in a meaningful and relevant way for CLD students. Without being able to form a connection between the new vocabulary terms and their existing background*

knowledge, Ms. Reyes's students are likely to feel overwhelmed by this information that has little meaning for them. It's important for Ms. Reyes to understand that vocabulary development is best accomplished through activities that promote listening, speaking, reading, and writing in meaningful contexts. Such activities might include use of graphic organizers that promote connections to prior knowledge and experiences, collaborative group work, think-pair-share activities, jigsaw reading (activity in which each student reads a different portion of the same passage and shares learning with peers), student presentations, and more.
Ms. Reyes also could plan with other content-area teachers who teach the same students. These collaborating educators could decide which themes would target the necessary vocabulary to be acquired in each subject area to ensure students' academic success. Meaningful connections could then be established across content courses.

understandings. In contrast, the ICB method integrates these four aspects of the CLD student biography, which facilitates students' language acquisition as well as cognitive development (Curtain & Haas, 1995). Integrated content-based instruction motivates learners because language becomes the medium through which all learners have access to meaningful and developmentally appropriate content material (Genesee, 1998; Grabe & Stoller, 1997; Met, 1991). The ICB method decreases perceptions of marginalization among students (Short, 1993a) and enables teachers to capitalize on the content knowledge, expertise, and background knowledge that CLD students bring to a lesson.

Integrated content-based instruction promotes students' negotiation of meaning in context (Grabe & Stoller, 1997). When meaning is negotiated, the language learner and the teacher (or other students) work together to ensure the student's comprehension of the language or content material. The teacher tries to present the information in multiple meaningful ways, and the student tries to construct meaning from the multiple interactions. Such meaning negotiation is known to enhance language acquisition as

Global Connections 7.2
For grammar-based programs, often the norm in EFL classrooms, ICB may be adapted to include more authentic language use that integrates the lived experiences of the learner and academic content the student may already be familiar with from previous experiences. Integrated content-based instruction, regardless of English learning context, is a method that utilizes the language and knowledge of the learner to accelerate language and content learning.

the CLD student learns how to engage in communication, focusing on both form and content (Grabe & Stoller, 1997). This negotiated meaning provides a forum for teaching more complex language in authentic contexts.

Finally, incorporating opportunities for higher-order thinking using the ICB method develops a wider range of discourse skills among CLD students than does traditional segregated skills language instruction (Crandall, Spanos, Christian, Simich-Dudgeon, & Willetts, 1987). As suggested by the Center for Advanced Research on Language Acquisition (CARLA, n.d.), the ICB method provides teachers with opportunities to integrate the following cognitive skills, each of which enhances language development (Curtain, 1995; Met, 1991):

- *Information-gathering skills*—absorbing, questioning
- *Organizing skills*—categorizing, comparing, representing
- *Analyzing skills*—identifying main ideas, identifying attributes and components, identifying relationships and patterns
- *Generating skills*—inferring, predicting, estimating

Delivering Integrated Content-Based Instruction

The ICB method emphasizes three key factors that are each applicable to both language and content teachers: (1) the use of a variety of media, (2) the development of students' thinking skills, and (3) the use of student-centered instruction (Bauer, Cook, & Mayak, 2010; Chien, 2012; Huang, 2011; Wu, Marek, & Chen, 2013). By using multiple media, the content-area teacher is able to increase students' comprehension of key content through the presentation of information in a variety of ways (Wu et al., 2013). A targeted focus on thinking skills in ICB instruction also increases CLD students' comprehension of content. Finally, the student-centered organization of the ICB method builds on the existing background knowledge that CLD students bring to the classroom.

Implementation of the ICB method requires teachers to select rich content that drives language instruction and contextualizes learning. This type of instruction also necessitates a commitment on the teacher's part to adapt and modify curriculum materials so that student needs guide curriculum development. To maximize the effectiveness of implementation, language teachers and content-area teachers often work collaboratively to ensure learner success.

Integrated content-based teachers understand that the CLD student is an active constructor of meaning. Language learning is most likely to occur when the student actively participates in meaningful, content-based contexts. Thus, delivering ICB instruction requires the teacher to create an environment for learning that not only reflects the goals and objectives of instruction but also promotes the integration of language, content, and the culture of the student. When planning, instructing, and assessing an ICB lesson, teachers consider several components. (See Figure 7.1 for an outline of the components of the ICB method.) The following sections explore each of these components and their related subcomponents in greater detail.

■**figure 7.1**

The Process of Creating
and Implementing an ICB
Lesson

I. **Planning**
   A. Select the theme.
   B. Choose topics relevant to the theme.
   C. Create language and content objectives.
   D. Gather appropriate instructional materials.
   E. Arrange the classroom environment.
II. **Instruction**
   A. Preteach key content vocabulary.
   B. Build background.
   C. Facilitate collaborative learning.
   D. Use authentic activities for integrating literacy.
   E. Engage CLD students cognitively.
   F. Provide visual support and graphic organizers.
   G. Develop learning centers.
III. **Assessment**
   A. Provide formative assessment.
   B. Provide summative assessment.

Planning an ICB Lesson

Planning an ICB lesson for students in ESL/EFL classrooms requires special attention to the students' linguistic and academic needs. Teachers begin ICB lesson planning by choosing an overarching theme. Other elements of the planning phase include choosing topics related to the theme, creating language and content objectives, designing meaningful student-centered activities, gathering appropriate materials, and arranging the classroom environment. These elements of the planning phase should all support the development of students' deep conceptual understandings of the theme and their capacities to communicate these understandings.

Selecting a Theme

A theme in ICB instruction provides the framework on which the teacher can map the identified needs of the students in the classroom. The theme is the overarching idea that shapes the unit, topics, and lessons that constitute the ICB method. Although themes require time, in terms of curriculum development and adaptation as well as in the coordination of materials, the impact on student motivation and academic achievement is well worth the effort.

    In ICB instruction, selecting a theme often requires a new way of thinking about instructional delivery and student learning. This selection process acknowledges the interrelationships of various bodies of knowledge and demonstrates the relationship between principles and processes. Selection of the theme is important in setting the vision for the unit. For the teacher, the theme becomes the framework within which to begin reflecting on instruction. For the student, the theme is a frame of reference from which connections are made to prior knowledge, personal interests, and academic content.

    Themes selected are based on deep conceptual issues inherent in content-area curricula as well as on the linguistic and academic needs of the CLD students being served. Teachers consider what the students already know and what is of interest to them. They also consider the cultural relevancy of the theme to students and their own knowledge base and interest in the theme and possible associated **topics**. Pesola (1995) suggests that as teachers begin to consider choosing a theme, they think about questions similar to the following:

- What learner characteristics, such as developmental level, learning style, experiential background, and culture, describe the students as individuals?
- Does the classroom environment support the proposed theme?
- What understandings about the culture and the subject matter will the students develop?
- Are materials available to support a given range of activities related to the theme and associated topics?

Selecting a Theme: In Practice. For the purpose of illustrating how to design an ICB lesson, this chapter presents a practical scenario highlighting the essential points of the ICB method. In this example, Ms. Gallardo is a high school teacher who teaches a government class the first period of every day. Of the 20 students in her classroom, 13 are culturally and linguistically diverse and the remaining 7 are native English speakers.

As Ms. Gallardo plans her instruction for the two weeks to follow, she considers the population she is serving and the content area she teaches. It has been her experience with this particular class that her students learn best when exposed to concepts that can be related easily to prior knowledge. This tends to be true for any learner, even though the high school–level instruction generally is more context-reduced, or abstract. Because many of the students in her class are neither completely proficient in English nor familiar with many of the cultural norms of the United States, Ms. Gallardo decides to teach rights, privileges, and responsibilities in the weeks to follow. This theme allows for many enriching activities that foster the transfer of concepts from one culture to another. There will also be plenty of opportunities for expression through dialogue and other forms of communication and exploration with language. Ms. Gallardo chooses to teach the theme of rights, privileges, and responsibilities also because this theme directly correlates with the standards she must address during the first quarter of her government class. By aligning instruction with grade-level standards, Ms. Gallardo increases CLD student engagement and motivation by providing the students with challenging academic and linguistic content.

Choosing Topics Relevant to the Theme

The selection of a theme sets the stage for topic development and decisions regarding the linguistic and academic objectives that will allow for optimal language development and content learning. When beginning the task of choosing topics, teachers consider the following question: Which topics related to the theme will maximize learning, capture student interest, and motivate student involvement? Topics are critical to planning lessons that reflect the integration of language and content at multiple levels. Topics become the backbone of the theme selected and influence all future decisions about the most appropriate instruction for the learner.

Topics align with the selected theme and are revisited as the theme progresses over time. The scope and sequence of the grade-level or content curriculum should be analyzed when selecting topics within a theme. Topics dictate the language and academic syllabus and provide a map for the delivery of instruction. They also determine how grade-level and content-area texts, authentic literature, and materials will be used to achieve the content and language objectives. After the teacher decides on the number of topics to use and selects those that are most appropriate, he or she begins thinking about a timeline for delivery. Additionally, the teacher considers specific ways in which each topic will address local, state, and national standards.

Making decisions regarding the most appropriate topics that align with the overarching theme involves multiple considerations. The following suggestions may assist educators in the selection of topics that effectively guide the successful delivery of an ICB lesson for CLD students:

- The topic must reflect the identified theme.
- The topic must be selected for its linguistic, cultural, cognitive, and academic merits, as well as its timeliness, student appeal, and potential for enhancing the future academic success of CLD students.
- The topic needs to engage the students academically as well as linguistically.
- The topic selected should provide coherence and continuity across skill areas and encourage progress in higher-level language skills.
- A variety of topic-related materials that match the students' proficiency levels should be available.

Choosing Topics Relevant to the Theme: In Practice. Now that Ms. Gallardo has decided on the theme of instruction for the weeks to follow, she must reflect on the topics related to the theme. Ms. Gallardo's class begins first thing in the morning, and she wants to choose topics that are interesting and relevant to her students' lives. She considers the fact that many of the students are new to the United States. She also considers how various topics that deal with rights, privileges, and responsibilities relate to the national and state standards that her government class must address. The topics Ms. Gallardo chooses to focus on include the nature of human rights; the U.S. Constitution, with an emphasis on the Bill of Rights; and the evolution of civil and human rights in the United States and other selected countries. Ms. Gallardo purposely selects topics that are likely to promote meaningful language experiences in context.

The first topic to be covered in Ms. Gallardo's class is the nature of human rights. She plans to use each topic as a building block for the subsequent topic while reintroducing each topic strand throughout the instruction of the entire theme. Common language that is used and revisited throughout the unit will be valuable to the students in her classroom and will help reinforce new concepts taught. In this way, Ms. Gallardo will facilitate for all students the construction of new knowledge on the foundation of prior knowledge.

Given the topics that Ms. Gallardo will deliver throughout the timeline of the theme at hand, she decides to seek out literature that encourages meaningful connections to students' prior experiences. Some of the literature she chooses includes information regarding human rights in the home countries of her CLD students. Ms. Gallardo plans to use the information from these readings to maximize higher-level questioning with her students. Such questioning is designed to prompt her students to think about the topics presented and extend their learning as they question and investigate the nature of human rights.

Using the ICB method, Ms. Gallardo has decided to allow ample time for the coverage of each topic so that her students form a solid grasp of content vocabulary and concepts. She will gauge her students' progress with each topic and ensure that her students are reaching at least 80 percent mastery of content concepts before she moves on to a new topic. As Ms. Gallardo considers the topics chosen, the developed timeline, the level of student interest, the language enrichment needs, and the cognitive challenges for her students, she places herself in a much better position to begin planning smaller elements of instruction.

Creating Language and Content Objectives

Once the theme has been chosen and the topics have been selected, teachers who use the ICB method begin the decision-making process regarding both **language objectives** and **content objectives** designed to maximize language acquisition and academic development. When selecting language and content objectives, attention should be given to their specific connections to the topic. Additionally, a comprehensive examination of students' linguistic, academic, cognitive, and sociocultural needs provides guidance in developing appropriate objectives. In this way, language and content objectives are compatible with the curriculum selected and reflect the needs of the students. When developing content and language objectives for a lesson, Table 7.2 may be a useful tool in ensuring that lessons include objectives that reflect a variety of activities and levels of cognitive complexity.

Illustrated Concept 7.1

Clearly identify the content and language objectives for each lesson and continually reinforce them throughout the lesson to give CLD students a clear understanding of expectations and focus for learning. For instance, at the beginning of a lesson, write objectives on the board and ask a student to read them aloud. Throughout the lesson, direct questions back to the objectives. At the end of the lesson, ask students questions directly related to the objectives.

Language Objective Development. The design of ICB instruction begins with student needs and culminates with an understanding of the unique linguistic challenges English learners face within the target subject. Mathematics, science, language arts, and social studies all have specific vocabulary, syntax, semantics, and discourse features that are particular to the subject area. Morris (1975) explains that teaching, or learning, in a second language is challenging, especially when mathematics is the subject. Morris recognizes that due to the abstract nature of the subject, students who are acquiring English can find the learning process difficult, and due to these challenges, the student must be provided with the basic linguistic concepts and structures in order to become proficient in math. Although Morris has argued the need for students to understand the

■ **t a b l e 7 . 2**   Lesson Plan Word List

Content Objectives	Language Objectives
Contrast	Listen to
Reflect	Write
Justify	Describe
Select	Clearly articulate
Reflect on	Define
Generate	List
Rationalize	Inform
Apply	Summarize
Analyze	Discuss
Identify	Rewrite
Compare	Recommend
Demonstrate	Convince
Examine	Explain
Cooperate	Clarify
Judge	Support
Use reference materials to	Differentiate
Distinguish	Monitor
Demonstrate	Paraphrase
Modify	Defend
Relate	Debate
Classify	Argue
Integrate	Propose
Create	Comprehend
Design	
Invent	
Formulate	
Prepare	
Decide	
Differentiate	
Plan	
Predict	
Organize	
Self-assess	
Make connections between	
Use a rule to	
Make a rule about	
Visualize	
Infer	

linguistic concepts and structures of mathematics lessons, his concerns could apply to any content area. Given these implications, designing clear language objectives is critical in the planning of ICB instruction. Understanding the interrelationship between student needs and the linguistic challenges students face in academic contexts prepares the teacher to design clear language objectives for specific content-area lessons.

The process of determining appropriate language objectives is typically initiated through the teacher's reflections on the proficiencies of students in each of the literacy domains of listening, speaking, reading, and writing. Understanding the implications of each of the different levels of language proficiency in these areas for student engagement and academic performance makes it much easier for the teacher to make decisions regarding appropriate language objectives. Teachers of the ICB method also coordinate both language and content objectives in planning for the implementation of daily lessons. This coordination facilitates planning activities that support and complement both linguistic and academic processes. Consequently, teachers preparing to write language objectives reflect on (1) the language proficiency of their CLD students, (2) district, state, and national language standards, and (3) the language of the targeted content or grade-level curriculum.

In designing instruction using the ICB method, teachers differentiate instruction for students who are at different levels of second language proficiency. For example, language objectives are designed to address the needs of CLD students at the speech-emergent stage as well as at the preproduction stage of second language acquisition. Additionally, teachers plan language objectives to support students in developing the cognitive academic language proficiency necessary to succeed in content-area classes. Language objectives are carefully designed to stretch CLD students a step beyond their current level of language proficiency. The teacher supports learners in reaching language objectives by providing them with comprehensible input, as discussed in Chapter 6. This teacher-supported challenging of CLD students' linguistic abilities scaffolds and accelerates the students' development of language skills necessary for academic success.

Of the linguistic factors affecting academic achievement in the content areas, Saville-Troike (1984) has written that knowledge of vocabulary is the most critical to the academic success of English learners. Knowledge of specific content vocabulary is far more important to comprehension than morphology and knowledge of syntactic structures. Therefore, targeting in every lesson language objectives that focus on vocabulary development is a prerequisite to the integration of language and content. For example, when writing language objectives in social studies, the teacher considers the fact that CLD students may be unfamiliar with specialized vocabulary related to social studies content as it pertains to events in the United States.

Reflecting on the following questions will facilitate the decision-making process involved in writing language objectives that will guide successful lesson delivery:

- What are your students' proficiency levels in listening, speaking, reading, and writing?

- In what ways can listening, speaking, reading, and writing in English be developed?
- What language knowledge is necessary for CLD students to understand the language structures of the content area(s) you are teaching?
- What vocabulary is necessary for language learners to express themselves in the target content area(s)?
- How does the structure of the text influence reading comprehension in the content area(s)?
- Do the symbols or language of the content area(s) have different meanings in other countries?
- How might inferences drawn from the readings differ based on cultural background?
- How can the linguistic load be scaffolded to support CLD student learning?

Language Objective Development: In Practice. The language objectives of Ms. Gallardo's ICB instruction are determined based on a number of factors. She ensures that all language domains are addressed as she plans to deliver the topics that fall under the theme of rights, privileges, and responsibilities. All the students in her room, particularly those who are CLD students, must be meaningfully engaged in the listening, speaking, reading, and writing aspects of the instruction she provides.

During the planning stages of instruction, Ms. Gallardo uses her knowledge of the students' academic backgrounds. Students' prior educational experiences are crucial to helping her plan the direction of her lessons so that all her students are receiving instruction that is appropriate for their level as well as adequately challenging. Although she will be making some modifications to text when it is too structurally or linguistically complex for her CLD students, she is committed to ensuring that all her students receive the full benefits of the lesson. Therefore, when she writes language objectives, she is careful not to reduce the academic or cognitive challenge of the curriculum.

Ms. Gallardo understands that her content area offers CLD students the perfect opportunity to learn government concepts as well as to work with language in ways that enable them to manipulate language concepts and extend their linguistic understandings. Using the ICB method, Ms. Gallardo does not have to focus specifically on separating the language objectives from the content-area material because they naturally serve each other. Her students will become interested and engaged in the lessons as they increase their understanding of social studies concepts using the second language.

Keeping the previously mentioned factors in mind, Ms. Gallardo decides on the following language objectives for her ICB instruction. Each student will be able to:

- Read and comprehend an article about the rights that people in different countries enjoy.
- Define *rights* in her or his own words.

- Write an essay about a fundamental human right in which the student provides three reasons why all people should be afforded that right (adaptations include prewriting graphic organizers and paragraph frames).

Illustrated Concept 7.2

To enhance CLD student comprehension across the content areas, frequently summarize the most important ideas of a lesson by using visuals and graphic organizers, paraphrasing key ideas, or having students individually provide brief oral summaries.

Content Objective Development. Teachers often struggle with the development of content objectives that target the needs of CLD students in their classrooms and that are also rigorous. Thinking about and writing content objectives for a new population requires a shift in one's conceptualization of what is relevant within a content-area curriculum. Teachers must decide on the essential academic content to include in a lesson.

When planning ICB instruction, teachers ask questions about the most critical concepts necessary for English learners' full access to and conceptualization of the grade-level academic content. These concepts are then negotiated with students to connect what is taught to their prior knowledge and cultures. Teachers also show how previously studied academic material aligns with the new topic so that CLD students develop an understanding of the relationships among concepts within a content area.

For certain content areas, teachers may also find it necessary to think about content objectives in relation to the sequence of the curriculum. For example, in the mathematics curriculum, making decisions about content objectives is easier when the teacher refers to the district, state, and national content standards for guidance. Then, after compiling a list of possible content objectives, the teacher can collaborate with other professionals in the content area to determine which objectives would best address the mathematics concepts that are essential for the academic success of all students in the classroom.

When writing content objectives, teachers who use the ICB method consider the multiple cognitive and academic needs of their language learners. Knowledge of students' backgrounds in the targeted content area is crucial because their previous schooling experiences and knowledge bases determine what academic content to target and for what purposes. For example, in science education, some terminology and symbol systems are recognized internationally. Therefore, knowing if CLD students have strong backgrounds in specific science concepts will help guide the teacher in making decisions for the lesson.

Equally important is the teacher's understanding of how the content of the subject area is taught in a student's country of origin. This consideration is necessary because pedagogy differs from country to country and can influence motivation and engagement in the classroom setting. Giving thought to the impact that a student's academic background and educational experiences may have on her or his learning will help the teacher write content objectives. When such aspects of the student biography are taken into consideration, the teacher can create content objectives that will enable students to build on their existing strengths in the specific content area.

Reflecting on the following questions will facilitate the decision-making process involved in writing content objectives that guide successful lesson delivery for CLD students:

- What is the academic knowledge base of my language learners in this content area?
- How is this content area taught in my students' countries of origin?
- What are the critical concepts necessary for the future success of my CLD students in this content area?
- What are the critical concepts that my students need to know before learning the new content material?

Content Objective Development: In Practice. In teaching according to the ICB method, Ms. Gallardo targets specific content objectives that she will use to assess her students. She has consulted both national and state standards as a starting point for developing the objectives. She also focuses carefully on what her students bring with them to the academic setting. Ms. Gallardo asks herself about her students' prior knowledge that can relate to the content instruction she is planning. This type of knowledge helps her decide on appropriate content objectives that are suitable for her students.

Given the standards that Ms. Gallardo must address throughout the thematic unit, she carefully examines the course materials. She finds that the literature easily relates to her students' previous lives and educational experiences in their respective countries of origin. Ms. Gallardo ties the critical concepts her students have learned in their home countries to those that will be presented in the following weeks. Her CLD students will learn how to make connections between their prior knowledge and the new understandings they are constructing, and they will become more proficient at identifying how they can make such connections when new themes and topics are presented. After giving the matter considerable thought, Ms. Gallardo chooses the following content objectives:

- Each student will choose one right that he or she believes should be a fundamental human right and justify why that right should apply to all people.
- Each student will compare and contrast the rights and privileges afforded residents of the United States and those of at least one other country.
- Each student will identify how particular types of government can affect the rights that citizens within the country experience.

Gathering Appropriate Instructional Materials

When gathering materials to support the selected topic of instruction, the teacher considers the overall goal and objectives of the lesson. Each of the materials the teacher selects needs to reflect the critical concepts in the lesson as well as support CLD students' comprehension of and engagement in the lesson. Therefore, when selecting materials, teachers consider the following questions:

- In what ways does the material support and enhance the content of the lesson?
- How might technology be used to reinforce student learning?
- In what ways can visuals, realia, and discovery learning be used to reinforce the content of the lesson?
- How might native language resources be identified and incorporated into the lesson to support and facilitate CLD students' comprehension?

By considering each of these factors, the teacher is able to better plan instruction that will build student capacity toward higher-level thinking and language processing.

Because the texts used in the classroom often guide activity development as well as class discussions, teachers carefully choose appropriate texts for ICB instruction. Brinton and colleagues (1989) suggest that teachers consider the following factors in the selection of texts:

- Student interest level
- Difficulty level of the text
- Accessibility of the text in terms of student comprehension
- Availability of the text
- Flexibility of the text (i.e., Does the text allow for the integration of multiple skills and activities?)

When appropriate texts are selected, the opportunities for student learning are enhanced. The teacher is able to provide content material that is not only comprehensible for students but also sufficiently challenging to interest and motivate them to participate in the learning process.

Gathering Appropriate Instructional Materials: In Practice. In planning materials for the ICB lesson that she will teach her students as an introduction to the theme of rights, privileges, and responsibilities, Ms. Gallardo considers all the language and content objectives she has already outlined. For the introductory lesson to the theme, she chooses to touch on the rights of Americans that are outlined in the Bill of Rights. In considering how to make the concepts comprehensible to her CLD students, Ms. Gallardo decides to highlight important aspects of the document by using portions of it as realia. She will also use translations of the Bill of Rights she found on the Internet in the students' native languages. She accommodates her CLD students by modifying the language of the Bill of Rights in English so that those students are able to comprehend the document in the second language after having read it in their native languages.

During this lesson, the students will have the opportunity to explore how the Bill of Rights compares to a document that describes the rights of citizens in their home countries. In this way, Ms. Gallardo will guide her students to elaborate on their background knowledge as they make meaningful connections to new information. She decides she will also use a film about the Bill of Rights that the students will view during the introductory lesson. This film will give the CLD students a visual representation of the events that surrounded the Bill of Rights in

theory *into* Practice 7.1

Preview, view, and review is an effective instructional strategy in which content is previewed in one language, presented (viewed) in the other, and reviewed in the first (Freeman & Freeman, 1998; Lessow-Hurley, 2012). The following vignette illustrates an appropriate use of this strategy in practice.

Preview, View, and Review in Action in a Science Classroom

Mrs. Rodriguez is introducing Newton's Three Laws of Motion, a very abstract and complex lesson for all students. She uses preview, view, and review to help her CLD students with comprehension of the lesson.

- *Preview:* Students are provided the text of the lesson in their native language the night before the lesson is implemented. The text has been summarized to highlight key concepts and key vocabulary.

- *View:* Mrs. Rodriguez presents the lesson in English and encourages her CLD students to use their native language as a guide.
- *Review:* At the end of the week, Mrs. Rodriguez reviews for the test on Friday. This review is conducted in the native language of the CLD students—in this case, Spanish. She groups her students heterogeneously by second language proficiency and ability level. The groups then discuss and record their responses to the review questions on chart paper. This collaborative review allows the students to clarify content and vocabulary with one another. Groups are also encouraged to include visuals such as graphic organizers and illustrations to represent their learning.

■ *How might a teacher who does not speak a language other than English use preview, view, and review? How could you evaluate the effectiveness of preview, view, and review with CLD students?*

the 1700s and help the students understand the significance the document holds for Americans today.

Arranging the Classroom Environment

The classroom environment plays a pivotal role in the success of any ICB lesson because the classroom environment sets the stage for the lesson. When planning a lesson according to the ICB method, teachers consider various ways in which the classroom environment might affect student dynamics and engagement. For example, the environment of the classroom should accommodate multiple types of student groupings (e.g., one on one, small group, and whole group). Each type of student grouping needs to reflect the goals and objectives of the lesson. Items such as bulletin boards that support student learning and are strategically placed can be valuable additions to the classroom environment.

Teachers also seek to create a learning environment in which respect and rapport are evident. Such an environment is characterized by the following traits:

- The learning culture reflects the importance of the content as well as the learning needs of CLD students.
- The classroom is a safe environment in which the opinions and insights of every student are valued and respected.
- Teacher–student interactions reflect the willingness of each to learn from the other.

To learn more about the importance of the classroom setting, specifically for language learners, watch the following video.

Arranging the Classroom Environment: In Practice. The environment of the classroom plays a significant role in the instructional process for Ms. Gallardo. Maximizing the ICB method, she first thinks about how she can best promote learning for the students in her class as they work with the theme at hand. Ms. Gallardo then lists ways she will specifically give attention to the details of the environment in her classroom.

The physical arrangement of the desks and chairs in her classroom is one of the ways in which the environment reflects the language and content objectives Ms. Gallardo has outlined. The desks in her classroom are arranged so that she has easy access to all her students and her students can easily dialogue and interact with one another. Grouping desks in numbers of no more than five helps her accomplish this goal. Ms. Gallardo's grouping allows CLD students of varied levels of proficiency in English to help one another, and it maximizes the input and helpfulness of more capable peers. At the same time, native English speakers serve as language models who support the acquisition of English for the language learners. The environment Ms. Gallardo creates is designed to lower the affective filters of the CLD students and provide a positive environment in which to learn.

On the walls of the classroom, Ms. Gallardo places visual representations that relate to the theme. For example, representations of the Bill of Rights are posted on the walls and accompanied by rich descriptions. In one area of the room, Ms. Gallardo has created and made available an interactive bulletin board for her students. This bulletin board will serve as a questioning and evaluation tool for her students. The interactive bulletin board includes questions that correspond to the language and content objectives that she will target throughout the lesson. Each of the questions has a visual aid next to it that signifies its meaning. The students will reach into a pocket that contains the answers to the questions and must post the answers alongside the questions to which they correspond. Ms. Gallardo will change the questions and answers when she observes that all students have had an opportunity to use the interactive bulletin board.

Copies of texts and other literature that support the theme are placed around the room. Ms. Gallardo also intends to provide opportunities, such as small-group activities, for students to interact as much as possible within the context of what she is teaching. In addition, she posts websites at each of the four computers in the room so that students have the opportunity to use technology as a resource to access information.

Instruction

As discussed in Chapter 1, curricula in U.S. schools tend to assume that students are fluent in English, and they reflect a middle-class, Eurocentric point of view. Consequently, for White, middle-class, native-English-speaking students, these curricula often reflect their prior knowledge and experiences, culture, and levels of English language proficiency. However, language learners bring other prior school and life experiences, cultures, and languages to U.S. classrooms. Therefore, Euro-centric, English-based curricula do not always coincide, and sometimes conflict, with the wealth of knowledge and experiences of CLD students. This difference in knowledge and experience requires teachers to devote special consideration to their CLD students' prior knowledge and experiences, cultures, and levels of native and English language proficiency. When delivering an ICB lesson in ESL/EFL class-rooms, teachers do the following:

- Preteach key content vocabulary.
- Build on the background knowledge of students.
- Facilitate collaborative learning to promote linguistic and conceptual development.
- Integrate the four literacy domains.
- Ensure all students' cognitive engagement.
- Provide visual aids and graphic organizers to support student comprehension.
- Develop centers that encourage active student learning.

Preteaching Key Content Vocabulary

In an ICB lesson, the use of content language that targets both academic and linguistic development is critical. To enhance CLD students' comprehension of the content material, teachers select and preteach key vocabulary terms from the lesson. This preteaching of key vocabulary helps language learners prepare for the lesson as well as make connections to their background knowledge. Strategies for preteaching vocabulary include:

- Use graphic organizers, such as semantic webbing or vocabulary maps, to graphically illustrate for CLD students how they might associate new vocabu-lary words with background knowledge.
- Select high-frequency words to add to a word wall (using separate English and L1 word walls).
- Associate vocabulary words with concrete objects.
- Have students act out or role-play vocabulary words.
- Use visual cues to assist students as they make connections to and develop an understanding of key vocabulary.

Once the key vocabulary words have been selected and taught, the teacher reiter-ates and incorporates these key terms throughout the lesson. This repetition of vocabulary reinforces language acquisition and the comprehension of academic content among CLD students.

Preteaching Key Content Vocabulary: In Practice. Ms. Gallardo wants to ensure that her students are using a common language as they study the theme of rights, privileges, and responsibilities. Using a common language enables students to communicate more effectively with one another as they share their thoughts on thematic topics. Consistency in language also facilitates future learning in subse-quent themes by providing students with a knowledge foundation they will be able to use to understand new ideas and concepts they encounter. Ms. Gallardo uses graphic organizers and the vocabulary posted throughout the room as consistent references during her lessons. She also uses the texts in the room and the bulletin boards to reinforce key vocabulary terms that may be abstract for language learners. The visuals around the room further support the key concepts and vocabulary of the lesson.

Ms. Gallardo's students become more familiar with the vocabulary words and learn to use them in various contexts. After the students dialogue in groups and as a whole class, Ms. Gallardo asks them to role-play the creation of the Bill of Rights. As they dramatize this activity, the students interact using the common language that they will continue to share throughout the thematic unit.

Building Background

When presenting an ICB lesson, teachers guide students to make connections between the content-area curriculum and their past experiences and knowledge. Making such connections to prior knowledge and experiences can be beneficial to language learners for both academic and affective reasons. First, these connections cognitively engage students in the learning process by creating a meaningful context from which they can understand the lesson. Additionally, the attention given to students' past experiences and knowledge validates their background and culture as worthy of attention and study.

Strategies to incorporate and build on students' background knowledge include, but are not limited to:

- Posing questions to CLD students about their past experiences
- Asking language learners what they already know about the key concepts
- Having students freewrite about the topic so that the teacher can assess their knowledge and understanding of the lesson material before teaching
- Providing visual cues and examples to promote meaningful connections between the content and CLD students' background knowledge
- Inviting family or community members to share information about the topic with the class

Building Background: In Practice. One of the most important elements Ms. Gallardo emphasizes in her ICB lesson is that of connecting new information or concepts to the prior knowledge her students possess. This helps her develop a deeper understanding of what her students know and makes her better able to determine the best way to approach instruction. She also validates her students by inviting them to share their expertise.

Ms. Gallardo begins by asking her students about the rights they have in their lives. These rights might pertain to the contexts of home, school, or other organizations and activities in which they may be involved. Ms. Gallardo encourages her students to discuss what they know about the rights of citizens in their native countries and what they know about the rights of U.S. citizens. The discussion also centers on the idea of the necessity of delineating rights for a country's citizens and the idea that these rights are crucial to the success and continuous development of any country. Ms. Gallardo asks students to write a paragraph describing what having rights means for a citizen of a country. She also asks the students to explain why those rights may be the same or different across countries.

Facilitating Collaborative Learning

When presenting an ICB lesson, the structuring of a variety of collaborative learning groupings facilitates content and language development among all students. Vygotsky (1978) proposed that individuals learn as a result of social interaction. Cooperative learning allows students to interact with one another using language that pushes them beyond basic interpersonal communication to develop their cognitive academic language proficiency (CALP). Cooperative learning groups also encourage the active engagement of English learners in content instruction. Students in heterogeneous language and content proficiency groups are prompted to negotiate the meaning of language and content using the target language. A language learner's peers can enhance his or her comprehension by clarifying information, providing academic dialogue to deepen conceptual understandings, and enabling transfer from L1 to L2.

> **Illustrated Concept 7.3**
>
> Provide students with ample opportunities to communicate about the concepts being covered by allowing them more time to speak (when they feel comfortable doing so), encouraging small-group discussions, and asking open-ended questions.

Using multiple types of grouping allows students to experience a variety of linguistic and cognitive supports and challenges. In comparison to whole-group activities, smaller groups provide language learners with more opportunities to communicate, as well as a less intimidating context in which to use the target language as a tool for negotiation and learning. The primary considerations for educators when creating cooperative learning groups include the following:

- Make sure group work is developmentally appropriate.
- Provide opportunities for students to discuss the material.
- Use a variety of grouping configurations (independent, pairs, small groups, whole group).
- Foster interdependence among students by structuring groups so that no one individual can complete the task alone.
- Motivate groups to work together by making sure that each member of the group is held accountable for his or her tasks.
- Create a group setting in which communication in any language is accepted and respected. Use more capable peers to scaffold English language use and development.
- Work with groups to ensure that students are being supportive of one another.
- Provide feedback that acknowledges the efforts of the entire group.

Facilitating Collaborative Learning: In Practice. At the beginning of the ICB lesson, Ms. Gallardo addresses the whole class when eliciting prior knowledge. She makes sure that everyone understands what the topic is and what the collaborative group activity will entail. After the class discusses the nature of rights and the students share what they know about individuals' rights, Ms. Gallardo asks the students to work in their groups. She structures each group with the goal of ensuring that all students feel comfortable taking risks as they engage in learning concepts and language simultaneously. To this end, Ms. Gallardo considers several factors, including the linguistic abilities of her English learners. Grouping a CLD student who has less proficiency in English with a language learner who is more proficient reduces the anxiety levels of students who are new to the English language and enhances the potential of language transfer. Ms. Gallardo also places native English speakers in these groups; they model the English language in a nonthreatening manner for language learners and benefit from the perspectives and content insights of the CLD students. Other factors she considers when grouping students include gender, maturity, ability, and the likelihood for positive student interaction.

Using Authentic Activities for Integrating Literacy

Activities in an ICB lesson allow the teacher to create authentic experiences that involve speaking, listening, reading, and writing throughout the lesson. These activities reflect the interests, developmental levels, experiences, and various learning styles of students. In addition, authentic activities provide language learners with many opportunities for hands-on involvement through discovery learning. When creating activities to engage CLD students, teachers might consider the following recommendations of Curtain and Haas (1995):

- Engage students by tapping into their prior knowledge and experiences.
- Provide holistic learning opportunities that integrate listening, speaking, reading, and writing in ways that naturally connect language and content.
- Challenge students to engage with content through higher-order/critical thinking.
- Incorporate activities that reflect a variety of different learning styles.

By following these guidelines, teachers are better able to provide all students with opportunities to engage in authentic, content-specific activities that challenge them not only academically but also linguistically.

Using Authentic Activities for Integrating Literacy: In Practice. For the introductory lesson and for subsequent lessons, Ms. Gallardo includes a variety of activities to engage her students in learning content concepts and language. Maximizing the ICB method, she uses whole-group instruction to access prior knowledge through discussion and visuals. She also uses small groups for writing and role-plays, and allows time for individual reading of text. As they participate in activities that require them to recall, evaluate, synthesize, and apply new information, students develop sophisticated understandings of human rights. They compare what they know about this theme in their home countries to what they are learning about this theme in the United States. After analyzing this comparison, students practice articulating the concept of human rights. Finally, each student chooses one right that she or he believes is fundamental to human existence and writes an essay to justify why all people should be afforded that basic human right.

■ Voices from the Field 7.1

"[I]t was determined that our high school would create a team of teachers to teach a randomly selected group of students over a two-year period, integrating the subjects of math, English, and science. For this team, four teachers were selected. Three content-area teachers and one special education resource teacher comprised the team. When assigned this endeavor, we were both anxious and nervous about trying this instructional method at our high school for the first time.

Our first objective as a team was to find a way to integrate the different content areas. Since earth science and algebra must follow a logical sequence, it was decided that the teachers of those two classes would provide for me an outline of their projected monthly lessons. Using their outlines as a guide, I developed my English lessons. While it was fairly easy to find literary selections to coincide with earth science (*The Perfect Storm* during the weather unit), algebra proved to be a little harder to integrate into English. I eventually did discover that some of the stories lent themselves to the creation of graphs and charts: If 8 percent of the population of London died from the plague during Shakespeare's time, how many people from our community or school would that be? History was also fairly easy. The Montagues and the Capulets from *Romeo and Juliet* can easily be equated with the Israelis and the Palestinians, or the Puritan thought from *The Crucible* can be compared with the beliefs of the Taliban.

Literature was not the only way we integrated the subjects, though. A required research paper for earth science was written in the English classroom with students receiving both English and science credit. The science teacher graded for content, while I graded for the composition traits. Another paper required that data taken from sources be put into a graph. Another paper required that the students use a modified version of the inquiry method of research, a method they had previously used in science. Although American history was not a class included on the team, we did request and receive a course syllabus from a teacher of that subject which I tried to follow with American literature during the sophomore year. The special education teacher's degree in social science came in very handy when integrating history into the English curriculum.

Everyone in the team had skills, expertise, and knowledge in various areas that contributed to a successful year. I never felt like I was alone. I had three other colleagues by my side in this endeavor. Students really enjoyed the class discussions and made connections with concepts previously discussed in other classes. I've had a renewed interest in teaching high school English because I'm covering new topics in creative and exciting ways."

■ *Reprinted by permission from Karen Myers. Copyright © by Karen Myers, high School English teacher, Emporia, KS.*

Engaging CLD Students Cognitively

In addition to creating activities that are content-specific and academically challenging, teachers implementing the ICB method find ways to cognitively engage their students during lessons. One of the primary ways to create more cognitively engaging and intrinsically motivating lessons is to relate academic content and language tasks in ways that guide students to use higher-order thinking skills. For example, students initially strive to understand the literal meaning of the lesson's grade-level content. The teacher may then ask students to relate what they are learning explicitly to their previous experiences and share their insights with the class. Culturally and linguistically diverse students are validated and motivated when they know that their input is as important and relevant to the academic content as that of their native-English-speaking peers. Finally, the teacher may prompt the students to use higher-order thinking skills by asking them to evaluate the information provided in the lesson. For example, students might be prompted to engage in a debate that centers on the following questions:

- Is the information true in every situation?
- Which situational factors influence the applicability of this information?
- From whose point of view is this information presented?
- Might others have different opinions?

Specific considerations for providing cognitively engaging and intrinsically motivating lessons for CLD students according to the ICB method include:

- Foster opportunities for students to engage in extended discourse.
- Increase percentage of questions asked of CLD students that require the use of inferential and higher-order thinking skills.
- Develop activities that engage students in cognitively challenging academic tasks, such as doing research projects; problem posing and solving that pertains to student-relevant issues; and writing essays, plays, and poetry.

Engaging CLD Students Cognitively: In Practice. As Ms. Gallardo thinks about the ways in which her students process new concepts, she reviews the topics, objectives, literature, activities, and groupings she selected for teaching the theme. She knows that her ICB content objectives hold CLD students to the same grade-level expectations as their native-English-speaking peers. Because Ms. Gallardo ensures that the authentic activities address the language and content objectives, she is also confident that her students are sufficiently challenged to question, apply, analyze, and reflect on what they are learning. Ms. Gallardo wants her students to interact with new vocabulary and concepts in a rigorous yet nonthreatening way.

As she thinks about future lessons using the ICB method, she decides that she will incorporate an activity that will require the students to work together as a class to develop a set of student rights. These rights will specifically address the following: (1) characteristics of interpersonal relationships among faculty, staff, and students; (2) school and classroom environments; and (3) services and resources provided by schools that enable students to learn most effectively. First, Ms. Gallardo plans to ask the students to individually reflect on their academic progress thus far and write a one-page journal entry in which they discuss aspects of their education that have negatively or positively affected their success. Next, she will encourage students to share their thoughts in small groups and then with the class as a whole. Finally, she will guide the whole class to a consensus on the specific rights that should be included in their set of student rights.

Providing Visual Support and Graphic Organizers

Visual aids and graphic organizers play a vital role in an ICB lesson because they help provide contextual cues that CLD students can use to make meaningful connections to the content. Therefore, when teaching an ICB lesson, teachers plan for an increased use of visual support and realia throughout the lesson. Visual support can include items such as illustrations, maps, photos, and videos. Realia can include authentic objects that accurately represent the key content and concepts of the lesson (e.g., three-dimensional models, food, animals, clothing). Graphic organizers used in a lesson may include, but are not limited to:

- Semantic webs
- KWL charts
- T-charts
- Venn diagrams
- Categorization or classification charts

These instructional aids help students focus their thoughts on the lesson material and make connections regarding relationships among pieces of information. Such tools also help students organize the topic-related understandings and ideas they bring from their prior experiences and background knowledge.

Providing Visual Support and Graphic Organizers: In Practice. Ms. Gallardo selects numerous visuals and graphic organizers that match the objectives and standards she is targeting during her coverage of the theme of rights, privileges, and responsibilities. Through the classroom environment, she immerses CLD students in the context of the concepts they are learning. Bulletin boards (both visual and interactive), maps, and documents (such as the Bill of Rights and those documents that highlight the functions of government in the United States) are posted around the room. Word walls that contain vocabulary terms for each topic are also displayed in three different areas of the room.

Ms. Gallardo used a KWL chart as one part of the introductory lesson to record what the students shared in various activities about their background knowledge related to the upcoming topics. T-charts are used to compare the differences between governments of various countries, and Venn diagrams support students in comparing, contrasting, and analyzing information. Ms. Gallardo clarifies the purpose of the visuals and graphic organizers for her students so they understand how to use the tools to increase their knowledge of concepts and better understand their own ways of learning.

Developing Learning Centers

Learning centers offer CLD students the opportunity for extended explorations of theme-based content and language according to the ICB method. Using centers involves the formation of several small areas around a classroom that provide activities to promote active student engagement. A class breaks into small groups and, while the teacher provides individualized instruction at one center with one

Illustrated Concept 7.4

Provide contextual cues for students by using multiple media in the ESL/EFL classroom such as compact discs, the Internet, videos, apps on tablets, and more. This allows you to highlight content information in concrete contexts that facilitate language acquisition.

group, other groups work at different centers. Centers assist students as they make concrete connections to target concepts and language, and centers provide students with opportunities to practice and apply new concepts in a variety of settings and through a variety of media.

For example, centers allow English learners to work individually, in pairs, or even in small groups to practice and apply learning through hands-on activities. These hands-on activities require that students use their reading, writing, listening, and speaking skills. Additionally, through the use of technology resources (computers, tape recorders, video), visuals (magazines, photos, pictures), realia (food, clothing, books), and manipulatives (cubes, counting bears, sentence strips, white boards), students develop thorough understandings of the lesson's concepts.

When planning centers, educators consider a variety of linguistic, academic, and cognitive factors. Among such factors are the following:

- The ways in which the centers intentionally reflect the language and content objectives of the lesson
- Student interactions (e.g., how large or small and how collaborative do you want to make the centers to maximize the equipment needed for each center, including computers?)
- Familiarity of CLD students with the media of the centers
- Levels of support that students may need to successfully complete center activities
- Length of time necessary to complete center activities (keep in mind the developmental levels and the attention spans of students)
- Length of time needed for the setup and cleanup of the centers

Developing Learning Centers: In Practice. After working with the students as a class to connect students' prior knowledge to new concepts, Ms. Gallardo uses centers to help her students develop their understandings of the content material. She explains what the students will do when she breaks the class into smaller groups for center work. She discusses the activities to be done in each center, and she makes sure that all her students are familiar with the texts they are to read, the way in which the role-plays are to be structured, and the expectations she has for the piece of writing they are to produce. At the teacher-facilitated center, Ms. Gallardo works with students on the history of the Bill of Rights. In this center, Ms. Gallardo's students work daily on their culminating project, which is an essay on a universal human right. She provides additional support to her CLD students as their essays evolve and as they maximize their learning from the centers.

At the interactive center, a group of students uses text, reference materials, visuals, and their own prior knowledge to create a role-play that demonstrates the importance of individual rights within a given country. Students at the listening and reading center listen to a portion of a book on tape about the Bill of Rights. Ms. Gallardo has chosen an audiobook that contains vocabulary that is part of the common language her class is sharing. In this way, the information is made more comprehensible for her language learners. In the current events center, students choose three (of several) newspaper or magazine articles on national or international human rights issues to read, and then they create a graphic organizer summary for each. These articles reflect a wide range of reading levels and several languages. (Ms. Gallardo collected the multiple language articles from her students.) At the writing center, students use text and varied literature around the room to write about the comparison of individuals' rights in their respective home countries (or a country of their choice) with those ensured to citizens of the United States.

Ms. Gallardo's school uses block scheduling, so she has a 120-minute span of time with her students every other day. Because there are five centers operating at the same time and all students are to receive the benefit of each, Ms. Gallardo spends 20 minutes in whole-group instruction at the beginning of each day, and the rest of the time is devoted to the centers. Students rotate from center to center and begin their tasks immediately to make the most of the time they have to work with the content. Ms. Gallardo leaves the centers a few minutes before the end of each class period to bring closure to the lesson. When using the ICB method, such closure is crucial for students because it clarifies the key information they should have gleaned from the lesson's events, and it informs students of ways the subsequent lesson will connect to what they learned.

Assessment

Assessment is an integral aspect of every lesson. On the one hand, assessment provides teachers with valuable information regarding lesson effectiveness. On the other hand, assessment is a valuable source of information about the development of conceptual understandings among all students and language acquisition among English learners. Ongoing, or *formative,* assessment enables the teacher to provide timely feedback to clarify misconceptions, affirm new understandings, and challenge students to think more deeply about key content concepts. Students' work on learning logs, projects, and in-class writing assignments provide opportunities for formative assessment. Formative assessment enables teachers to dispel misconceptions before they become too entrenched in students' conceptualizations. Students then can revise their understandings as they are learning. Culminating, or *summative,* assessment occurs at the end of lessons. Teachers collect evidence from sources such as finished projects and essays to determine the degree to which students attained the lesson objectives.

Providing Formative Assessment

Throughout the delivery of an ICB lesson, teachers conduct ongoing and regular evaluation of CLD student performance. This type of ongoing assessment allows the teacher to evaluate the effectiveness of the lesson and ensure student compre-hension. A primary way for the teacher to promote student comprehension is to adjust and modify instruction as needed. Modifications to the lesson occur when the teacher observes student behavior or responses that are indicative of confusion or misunderstanding. The immediate modification of a lesson requires the teacher to be flexible and responsive to the needs of all learners.

Continuous feedback to the student is another way in which ongoing or in-process assessment can be conducted. Feedback should be specific, constructive, and thorough. This helps the CLD student obtain a clear picture of teacher expec-tations and meet the lesson objectives. Ways in which the teacher can provide continuous feedback through the ICB method include, but are not limited to, the following:

- Offer feedback that focuses on one aspect or area of the lesson to avoid over-whelming the language learner.
- Engage the CLD student in a brief discussion about the lesson to determine her or his comprehension of key concepts. Follow this discussion with specific recommendations or tips that the student can use immediately to increase his or her understanding of the lesson.
- Pose constructive questions to help the student assess her or his own compre-hension of the lesson.
- Provide feedback that is comprehensive and comprehensible to the learner.

Finally, ongoing evaluation requires the teacher to make certain that the lesson itself aligns with the overall instructional goals and objectives of the lesson, as guided by the unit topic and theme. By continually checking instruction against these objectives, the teacher is able to ensure alignment of the lesson with instruc-tional goals.

Providing Formative Assessment: In Practice. The only way for Ms. Gallardo to make certain that her CLD students are achieving mastery of the language and content objectives that she set for the lesson is to consistently monitor the stu-dents' ongoing progress. Ms. Gallardo carefully observes her students' responses, especially their responses to higher-order thinking questions, to ensure that they comprehend the language and concepts. She notes body language and facial expressions to detect feelings of frustration or success. She also watches student dynamics during group work to gauge the effectiveness of the activities.

Ms. Gallardo facilitates the learning that occurs in her classroom by providing consistent and continuous feedback to her CLD students. In this way, her students become aware of her expectations, and this awareness fosters greater student prog-ress toward mastering lesson objectives. All the feedback Ms. Gallardo gives her students is positive and constructive. She also uses her feedback to model appro-priate use of the common language students in the class share regarding the theme of rights, privileges, and responsibilities.

Providing Summative Assessment

Summative assessment typically occurs at the end of a project or lesson. During summative assessment, teachers and students examine revised and completed student work to collect evidence of language and content development. Summative assessment describes and documents students' proficiency levels in meeting lesson objectives. For CLD students, a teacher defines levels of acceptable language production based on the expected characteristics of the students' levels of second language proficiency. For example, language production from a student who is at an intermediate-fluency level of second language acquisition (SLA) will contain fewer errors, more complex sentence structures, and more descriptive vocabulary than that of a student at a speech-emergent level of SLA. Teachers of the ICB method are careful to avoid confusing limited language proficiency with difficulty in expressing oneself due to a lack of conceptual understanding.

Rubrics can be useful tools in summative assessment. When students help develop rubrics, they gain insight into the characteristics of high-quality products. To guide students in the creation of rubrics, a teacher may distribute work samples (without names or other identifiers, preferably from a different year or school) that reflect varying degrees of language and content proficiency. Groups of students review the samples and rank them according to levels of proficiency. As a class, the groups discuss how and why they ranked the samples. The teacher then guides the students to consensus regarding the ranking that most appropriately corresponds to each particular sample.

Next, students discuss in groups the defining characteristics of each level of ranking. The groups share their defining characteristics with the entire class and the class comes to consensus about the characteristics of each level of proficiency. The first several times the class creates a rubric in this manner, the teacher provides extensive modeling and support to help students define high-quality work. As the students continue to create and use such rubrics to assess their own work, the class creates a common expectation for academic work. Students can use these rubrics to reflect on their strengths and areas of inexperience in order to create goals for their own language and academic development.

Providing Summative Assessment: In Practice. Ms. Gallardo looks forward to having her CLD students write their essays as the culminating project for their unit on rights, privileges, and responsibilities. Before they begin their essays, the students create a rubric by which their essays will be evaluated. In creating this rubric, students examine exemplary, proficient, and basic sample essays to identify the key characteristics of each level of writing and the extent to which each level of content proficiency addresses the content-area concepts of the unit. These students have experience with creating assessment rubrics, so they are able to tackle the challenge of creating rubrics for both content and language proficiency.

When the time arrives to assess the students' essays, the students and Ms. Gallardo will collect evidence of language and content development from the essays to provide a basis for assessment. Ms. Gallardo will meet with each student to discuss the evidence and arrive at meaningful conclusions regarding the student's progress in language and content development. They will also explore areas in which the student needs to grow. This type of summative assessment encourages Ms. Gallardo's students to think about their own learning and the strategies they use to gain new understandings.

■ **Snapshot of Classroom Practice 7.2**   Authentic Summative Assessment

In this fifth-grade classroom, the teacher used a Tri-Fold at the end of the Bones unit. To show cumulative learning, students drew and labeled the skeletal system first, and then drew and labeled a detailed diagram of a bone. On the last part of the Tri-Fold, the students wrote a summary sharing one part of the skeletal system in detail. When the Tri-Folds were completed, they were hung on the walls. Then the students shared an oral presentation, using their Tri-Fold as the only resource to demonstrate their end-of-unit understandings.

(Courtesy of Denise Johnson, elementary teacher, Lawrence, Kansas.)

■ Concluding Thoughts

Effectively implementing instruction according to the ICB method takes time, practice, and critical self-reflection. We have included an example of an ICB lesson plan to support your development of lesson plans that meet your site-specific needs (see Figure 7.2). Although this plan does not strictly follow the narrative throughout this chapter, it does provide some basics for creating your own ICB lessons.

It is important to remember that planning for, instructing, and assessing students with accommodation in mind requires special attention to their language development needs. For many ICB teachers, modifying the language of instruction without simplifying the grade-level content can be a difficult skill to master. Yet if educators do not provide English learners with the support they need to reach the same high standards as their native-English-speaking peers, the achievement gap will continue to widen. By soliciting the help of teachers experienced in this method or by forming learning communities with other teachers to implement ICB instruction, educators can find the support needed to change teaching practice.

■**figure 7.2**   ICB Lesson Plan: Grade Level 1

I. PLANNING

1. The theme of the lesson will be *Bugs!*
2. Topics relevant to the theme of *Bugs!* include types of bugs and characteristics of bugs (color, shape, size, special features, etc.).
3. Content Objective:
   - We will be able to distinguish between different types of bugs and identify their unique characteristics.

   Language Objectives:
   - We will listen to a story about bugs as it is read aloud.
   - We will compose and illustrate our own individual bug story.
   - We will share our bug story by presenting it to the class.
   - We will comprehend information about bugs as we read books of interest related to the theme.
4. The necessary materials for this lesson include: *Bugs!* by David T. Greenberg; word wall; plastic bugs (10 each in plastic bags, and enough bags for each student at the learning center); bug pictures and/or realia; bug worksheet; paper egg carton sections; pipe cleaners cut into small pieces; books, magazines, catalogs, etc. on the subject of bugs (these materials should be in both Spanish and English); blank paper; markers/crayons.
5. The classroom environment will be arranged for students to sit as a whole class while they take part in a shared reading of the book *Bugs!* Following this activity, students will engage in content learning centers (math, writing, science, creative expression). Each of the four centers will be placed in the various corners of the room. For the final two activities, the familiar reading and modeled writing, students will return to their desks within their learning groups.

II. INSTRUCTION

1. Key content vocabulary will be pretaught before the book *Bugs!* by David T. Greenberg is read aloud. The teacher will introduce the new vocabulary words in both Spanish and English and students later will fill in the words as the book is read.
2. Building background will occur before the reading of the book *Bugs!* as well. The teacher will review past vocabulary with students using a class word wall. This will help the teacher to gauge comprehension and to prepare a foundation for the connections between prior knowledge and new knowledge. This lesson serves as one in the middle of a unit. Students will already be familiar with several key concepts as they are discussed further, and the teacher will continue to relate the theme to the students' life experiences.
3. Collaborative learning will be facilitated throughout the lesson. During the shared reading activity, the teacher will pause to discuss the story with the entire class by asking questions. Students also will take part in collaborative learning during the learning center activities, as they will work in pairs to complete the tasks in the math and the science centers. Students also will be encouraged to read or tell stories to a partner during the familiar reading activity, and they will share their stories with the entire class after they have completed the modeled writing activity.
4. Authentic activities for integrating literacy will occur throughout the lesson. Opportunities for reading, writing, speaking, and listening will play an integral

role in the various activities for meaningful connections between the content and the language. Not only will the students take part in a shared reading, but they will also engage in hands-on activities in the learning centers. Some examples include using realia (plastic bugs) to count the number of bugs in the illustrations as they re-read the story *Bugs!*, writing a letter to a friend about their favorite bug, using realia and scientific photographs to describe the characteristics of many different spiders (arachnids, not bugs) and insects, and using egg cartons to create different types of bugs. Students also will take part in a familiar reading where they choose books about bugs that interest them. This will be followed by a modeled writing activity where students write and illustrate their own story about bugs and then share it.

5. Culturally and linguistically diverse students will be engaged cognitively as they participate in discussion and discourse, both as an entire class and in pairs. Likewise, the experiences that students will have in the learning centers and with the modeled writing activity will provide them with challenging academic tasks that require problem-solving and higher-order thinking skills. The teacher also will be sure to ask a number of different questions throughout the lesson that will help engage the students cognitively. During the shared reading, for example, questions such as "What is your favorite bug, and why?" "Where is your favorite bug?" "What color is your favorite bug?" and "How many legs does it have?" will be asked.

6. Although graphic organizers will not be used in this lesson, the use of visual support will be achieved by using a word wall; realia and several photographs/pictures of bugs; and the illustrations in books, magazines, catalogs, etc. for students to observe and utilize as they enhance their knowledge of the content and English.

III. ASSESSMENT

1. Formative assessment will take place during the discussion the teacher conducts with the students during the shared reading activity. By asking the students specific questions, the teacher will be able to determine how well the students understand the content, and will then be able to provide appropriate feedback that is valuable and comprehensible. The teacher will also be able to monitor student work as students complete various tasks in the math, writing, science, and creative expression learning centers.

2. Summative assessment for the lesson will be the students' final product from the modeled writing activity. After the students share their bug stories with the entire class, the teacher will collect the students' work and evaluate the stories using a rubric. One of the key requirements will be that the stories follow the same pattern as a story read in a previous lesson.

Source: From Center for Intercultural and Multilingual Advocacy (CIMA). *ICB lesson plan: Bugs!* Lesson plan created at Kansas State University, Manhattan, KS. Copyright © 2013 by Socorro G. Herrera. Reprinted with permission from Socorro G. Herrera.

Connect, Engage, Challenge

CONNECT
Review and Reflect on the Reading

1. What is content-based instruction?
2. What are the benefits of content-based instruction for CLD students?
3. What are the primary differences among language across the curriculum, English for specific purposes/language for specific purposes, and immersion instruction? How did each of these contribute to the development of integrated content-based instruction?
4. What are thematic units? Why is it important to have a theme when planning ICB instruction?
5. How should you select a theme? What considerations should be given to the academic and experiential backgrounds of CLD students when selecting a theme?
6. What is a topic? How should a topic be selected for inclusion in an ICB thematic unit?
7. What is the difference between a language objective and a content objective? What role does each play in the development of an ICB lesson?
8. Why and how are materials and content interrelated in ICB instruction? What are the benefits of this for CLD students? What considerations must the teacher make to interrelate materials and content?
9. What considerations should be given to student dynamics when planning and implementing an ICB lesson?
10. Why is it essential to include authentic activities in ICB lessons?
11. Why is it important to include higher-order thinking skills in ICB instruction? How can higher-order thinking skills be incorporated into instructional delivery?
12. What key factors should be considered when developing learning centers?
13. How is formative assessment different from summative assessment? What are the benefits of each type of assessment for CLD students?
14. What approach does the ICB method reflect, and what are the implications of this philosophical orientation for how teachers approach ICB instruction with CLD students?

ENGAGE
Share What You Learned

1. Discuss the challenges in selecting a theme in your content area. What considerations would you make to ensure students' cognitive engagement and interest in the selected theme?
2. Discuss how language and content are integrated in ICB instruction to maximize learning for CLD students.
3. Discuss the process of decision making when planning an ICB lesson.
4. Discuss possible challenges in implementing ICB instruction at the elementary, middle, and secondary levels.
5. Discuss how the ICB method of instruction complements or challenges your current instructional practice.

CHALLENGE

It's Not Real until You Practice

Preservice Teachers

1. When planning a content-based unit on a particular topic, it can be helpful to create visuals. Visuals can suggest ways to integrate the topic across different content areas more effectively. Use Figure 7.3 to create an outline for a content-based unit. Target a specific theme and grade level and note these at the bottom of the template. Identify and briefly describe at least two activities per box on your template.

figure 7.3   Theme-Based Planning

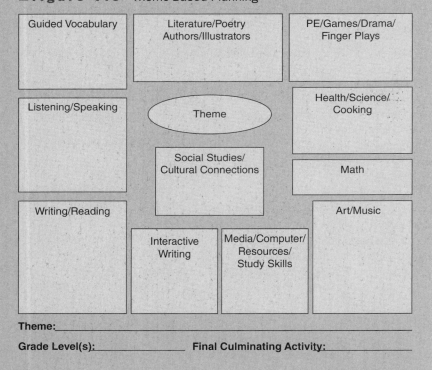

Theme:_____

Grade Level(s):_____   Final Culminating Activity:_____

2. Observe the classroom practice of an educator of CLD students. List at least five ways in which he or she successfully integrates content and language so that the key content is covered in ways that are meaningful to English learners. Then identify ways in which you would target listening, speaking, reading, and writing if you were teaching the lesson.

3. With other preservice teachers of various content areas, identify and list ways in which a theme could be integrated in all of the represented content areas. Generate at least three activities that infuse language development (listening, speaking, reading, and writing) across these content areas.

In-Service Teachers

1. Set up a mini-conference with at least two other teachers in your school who share the same CLD students you teach. Collaborate with these teachers to decide on a specific theme that can be integrated across all of your content areas. Next, decide on a topic related to the theme that each of you could address. Discuss and share ideas on how and when you could integrate this topic in all the content areas. Also share ideas about ways to integrate language skills into your lessons. What materials will you use? What key vocabulary will you emphasize? For example, the overriding theme of your lessons may be "Agriculture—Important Food Crops." The topic of your lessons might be "corn." For American history, you might incorporate this topic while discussing Native Americans, Pilgrims, or agricultural resources. For world social studies, you could discuss any corn-producing country's agricultural system, differences between agricultural and industrial economies, or current events regarding international trade. Focusing on the math curriculum, students could estimate the number of kernels or the weight of corn. They might also create word problems incorporating the topic-related vocabulary. For health and science, incorporate discussions on the food group to which corn belongs and the nutrients it contains, as well as similar discussions on corn-based products.

2. Authentic text can be used effectively for integrating language development with content lessons. Select one of the following ideas to implement in your classroom practice. Provide a brief description of the activity you designed. What types of accommodations did you need to make for the various stages of second language acquisition of your CLD students? What were the activity's highlights and challenges for English learners? How will you address these challenges in the future?

   • Plan a lesson in which you will use newspapers and magazines in your classroom for language and content development. For instance, if you are a political science teacher, you might have students find an article related to the current content they are studying. Students might write a paragraph summarizing this article, circle new words in the article and define them, or have a class debate on a controversial issue addressed in the article.

   • Classified ads can be used in many ways to promote real-world connections for CLD students. For example, students can circle new words and define them, find abbreviations and define them, or write a business letter to apply for a job that has been advertised and practice interviewing for the job.

3. Develop an ICB lesson that links a variety of content areas and literacy skills. Consider and list ways in which this lesson addresses the following to enhance CLD student success:

   • Content objectives
   • Language objectives
   • Cognitive dimensions of learning
   • Sociocultural dimensions of learning

tips for practice

In elementary classrooms, consider:

- Teaching students the strategy of going from the general to the specific when studying a concept in content-area textbooks. Demonstrate how to identify global concepts by using the table of contents, headings, subheadings, and illustrations in content-area chapters.

- Using poetry, chants, music, demonstrations, and discussions of pictures and real objects to build language related to content concepts.

- Using visuals such as pictures, diagrams, or realia for the development of language through literature. Talk through a story or a particular chapter of a book to help CLD students grasp the story line first. Reread the story or chapter to build vocabulary and foster comprehension.

In secondary classrooms, consider:

- Making content and language acquisition meaningful by collaborating with other teachers and selecting a theme that can be infused across content areas.

- Adapting or incorporating materials such as alternate versions of textbooks, newspaper articles, outlines, or magazine articles that enhance understanding and connect language learning to the real world.

- Designing a discovery learning lesson that allows students to research or solve a problem on their own. Students identify a problem, generate a hypothesis, design procedures or experiments to test the hypothesis, and conduct research to solve the problem.

- Including information gap activities such as jigsawing, in which each student reads a different portion of a passage, problem solving, and simulations while working on difficult content concepts. Set up these activities so that each student in a group has one or two pieces of information needed to complete the activity but not all the necessary information. This will help to promote collaboration, use of language skills, and critical thinking skills.

In EFL classrooms, consider:

- Using technology, if available, to have students interact with authentic texts (e.g., menus, recorded stories, social media) to enhance reading, writing, listening, and speaking skills. Use poetry, chants, music, demonstrations, and discussions of pictures and real objects to build language related to content concepts.

- Providing students opportunities to interact with native English speakers through videoconferencing.

- Contacting local tourism agencies, if technology is unavailable, to acquire brochures that will most likely be available in English. Students can use these brochures not only to learn about the United States and other countries but also as a model to create their own tourism brochure in English that highlights their own towns, cities, and culture.

assessment tips and strategies

The following assessment tips and strategies are drawn from the content of Chapter 7.

ASSESSMENT

Formative assessments are a type of ongoing or in-process evaluation that allows the teacher to evaluate the effectiveness of the lesson to ensure student comprehension. Summative assessments, on the other hand, refer to the culminating assessments that occur at the end of lessons. When conducting summative assessments, teachers might work with students to examine revised and completed student work or to collect evidence of students' language and content knowledge development. This latter type of assessment documents and describes students' proficiency levels in meeting lesson objectives.

Assessment Tips

- Formative assessments are used in order to:
  - Clarify misconceptions.
  - Affirm new understandings.
  - Challenge the student to think more deeply about key concepts.
- Formative assessments rely on the teacher's feedback, which should be specific, constructive, and thorough.
- When modifying instruction according to assessment feedback, teachers must observe CLD students and look for student behavior or responses, including body language and facial expressions, that are indicative of confusion or misunderstanding.
- Effective ESL/EFL teachers are flexible and responsive to the needs of English learners, as indicated by assessment feedback, and incorporate needed modifications immediately into a lesson.

- Reflective teachers use the evaluation from summative assessments to check the degree to which the lesson aligned itself with its overall instructional goals and objectives.

Assessment Strategies

- Examples of formative assessments include learning logs, projects, and writing tasks.
- Rubrics can be useful tools in summative assessments:
  - Rubrics grant the student insight into the characteristics of high-quality products.
  - Teachers distribute sample work at varying degrees of language and content proficiency.
  - Groups of students review samples and rank them according to levels of proficiency.
  - Teachers guide students to consensus.
  - The class creates a common expectation regarding the quality of academic work at each level of proficiency.
  - Students learn how to assess their own work.
  - Students can reflect on their strengths and inexperience to create personal learning goals.

CHAPTER 8

The Sheltered Method of Instruction

our mission

Our mission for this chapter will be to:

- Discover how teachers use the sheltered method of instruction to enhance their effectiveness with CLD students.

We will accomplish this mission by helping you to meet the following learning outcomes:

- Identify and distinguish between the many variations of sheltered instruction with attention to common themes.
- Summarize myths and misconceptions associated with the sheltered instruction.
- Outline key elements of sheltered instruction according to SDAIE.
- Identify essential elements of instruction according to the SIOP model.

Jessica Barrand

key theories and concepts

adaptation of content
appropriate content concepts
building background
cloze sentences
cognates
content objectives
cooperative learning
guarded vocabulary
hands-on activities
language objectives

level playing field
scaffolding
SDAIE
sheltered instruction
SIOP indicators
SIOP model
supplementary materials
visuals
zone of proximal development (ZPD)

The traditional school curriculum and most classroom instructional practices are grounded in the notion of a level playing field (Escamilla, 1994, 1999; Walqui, 2000). Yet, Chapter 1 discussed the fact that culturally and linguistically diverse (CLD) students do not participate on a **level playing field** when they attend public school in the United States. At the same time that they and their caregivers must often adapt to a new country, transition to a new culture, and rapidly learn a new language, these students are asked to perform, often at grade level, in the content areas. Therefore, unlike their grade-level peers, CLD students face singular challenges and processes that pose formidable obstacles to their success in school, as discussed in Chapters 1, 2, and 3. This is not to say that CLD students do not bring assets to the school. In fact, we can utilize these assets in ways that support the students as they compete with their grade-level peers. Yet, the challenges and obstacles that contribute to the creation of an uneven playing field are among just a few of the reasons why we recognize that CLD students arrive at school with diverse learning and transition needs, which must be accommodated if these students are to reach their full academic and career potentials.

Sheltered instruction methods are specifically designed to target these potentials and to recognize these varied learning and transition needs. Sheltered methods promote student potentials such as the following:

- There is potential for communicative, interactive, and literacy-focused language acquisition toward development of cognitive academic language proficiency (CALP) in the second language (L2).
- There is potential for academic achievement in the content areas based on elaborated background knowledge, exposure to the full scope and sequence of the curriculum, and alternative and equitable process and product assessment practices.
- There is potential for *all* students to receive an equitable, high-quality education—the foundation on which any individual can aspire to success.

Sheltered methods protect English learners from anxiety, ambiguity, confusion, frustration, and many other factors reflected in the affective filter hypothesis (Krashen, 1982)—factors that we know inhibit learning and language acquisition.

In EFL and other contexts, the scope of teaching and curriculum has long focused on teaching English through grammatical approaches, using strategies and techniques that lead to language learning in which students are passive recipients of isolated vocabulary and English rules. Sheltered instruction, however, provides an alternative for moving students to a more dynamic, communicative learning environment that targets language development, literacy, and academic learning. The goal for teaching English is no longer that the learner will be able to say, "Hello, my name is Thao." Rather, teaching is best when the goal is to prepare students, regardless of context, socioeconomic level, or grade level, to have access to the English-speaking world by holding them to high expectations. Sheltered instruction provides the teacher with the knowledge, skills, and tools to "level the playing field" for CLD students in any classroom or program.

In this chapter, we first explore the realities of and variations on sheltered instruction. Second, various myths and misconceptions associated with the instructional method are discussed. Next, alternate forms of sheltered instruction are compared and contrasted. Finally, the chapter details the sheltered instruction observation protocol (SIOP) model of sheltered instruction as a thoroughly comprehensive variation of sheltered instruction, specifically designed for the differential learning and transition needs of CLD students.

■ Realities of Sheltered Instruction

Sheltered instruction is a method for combining philosophies, strategies, and techniques that appropriately recognize the many challenges that CLD students confront. At the same time, the method provides English learners with instruction that is comprehensible, relevant, and motivating. It is more than content-based English as a second language (ESL) because it explicitly emphasizes language and content

■ **t a b l e   8.1**   Comparison of Segregated and Integrated Skills Instruction

Criterion	Segregated Skills Instruction	Integrated Skills Instruction	
		ICB	SI
The focus is on isolated or discrete language skill development.	x		
Language and content learning are separated.	x		
Instruction reflects a basic-skills orientation.	x		
A subject-area certified teacher, with no professional development relating to CLD students, may lead instruction.	x		
An ESL certified or endorsed teacher typically delivers classroom instruction.		+	
There is an emphasis on integrated skill development in all language domains (listening, speaking, reading, and writing).		+	+
Development of cognitive academic language proficiency in L2 is a goal.		+	+
Concurrent development of L2 and content knowledge and skills is a goal.		+	+
The focus is on requisite terminology for content-area learning.		+	+
The focus is on the core, grade-level curriculum.		+	+
Content and ESL/EFL language standards guide instruction.		+	+
Classroom instruction typically follows the full scope and sequence of a grade-level class.			+
A subject-area certified teacher, with professional development relating to CLD student needs, typically delivers classroom instruction.			+

Legend:
ICB = Integrated content-based method
SI = Sheltered instruction method
x = Not appropriate for CLD students
+ = Appropriate for CLD students

objectives. In some ways, sheltered instruction is viewed as integrated skills instruction because it does not emphasize a basic skills curriculum or focus on the development of discrete language skills in isolation, as does segregated skill instruction. But, as illustrated in Table 8.1, sheltered instruction is also more than integrated skills instruction (e.g., integrated content-based instruction, detailed in Chapter 7 of this text) because the full scope and sequence of curriculum is used to target development of students' academic language proficiency and a deeper conceptual understanding of the content material.

Variations on Sheltered Instruction

Although Echevarria and Graves (2010) argue that sheltered instruction was first introduced by Stephen Krashen in the early 1980s, this method has evolved through a variety of forms and has been identified by a number of labels. In fact, this type of support for CLD students has been variously labeled *sheltered, sheltered instruction, sheltered English, integrated skills instruction, content-based English language teaching (CELT), scaffolding, specially designed academic instruction in English (SDAIE),* and the *sheltered instruction observation protocol (SIOP).* After first examining commonalities among variations of sheltered instruction, we briefly explore the SDAIE model of sheltered instruction, owing to its popularity in practice, specifically in the state of California (California Commission on Teacher Credentialing, 2014). However, we consider the SIOP model to be the most developed, explicated, and researched; therefore, we emphasize this variation in subsequent sections of this chapter.

Common Themes in Sheltered Instruction

Among the many variations of sheltered instruction that have evolved over time, most tend to share certain commonalities or themes in addressing the differential learning and transition needs of CLD students. At least four of these themes are relatively common across almost all variations associated with the method. These four common themes are illustrated in Figure 8.1 and include hands-on activities, cooperative learning, guarded vocabulary, and visuals. This particular figure is, for the purpose of illustration, grounded in the use of the sheltered method with secondary-level English learners.

■ **Snapshot of Classroom Practice 8.1**   Use of Visuals

Students prepare for an activity that incorporates visuals, one of the common themes in the sheltered instruction method.

(Courtesy of Chelsea Hiltibrandt, elementary teacher, Fort Riley, Kansas)

■ figure 8.1   Overview of Common Themes among Variations of the Sheltered Method

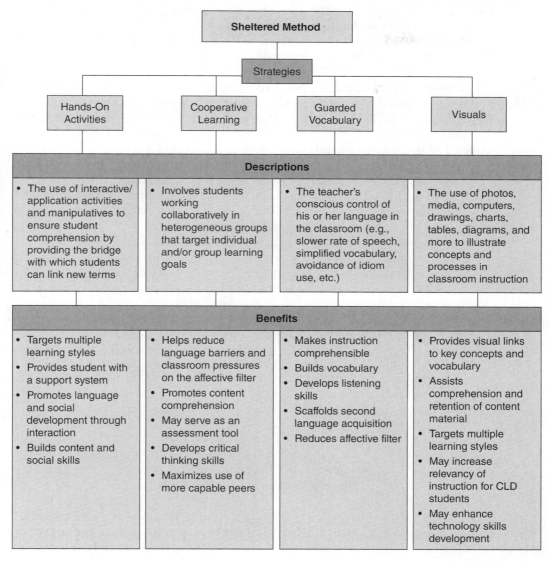

Hands-On Activities. The **hands-on activities** theme of sheltered instruction is also consistent with an emphasis on interaction, which is highlighted as a component of some sheltered variations. Such interaction, especially hands-on learning situations, is considered essential for CLD students as a means by which they can practice their emergent L2 skills. For example, a sheltered lesson on corn, delivered as part of a thematic unit on agriculture, might involve an interactive, hands-on activity in which CLD students (in groups) weigh ears of corn. They might then compare the weight of an ear with and without kernels to gauge yield. Activities that enable communicative, student-centered, student-to-teacher, and peer-to-peer interaction at appropriate language and content levels are crucial. These interactions may stress either homogeneous or heterogeneous student groupings, the latter of which allows students to benefit from the capacities of a more capable peer. Hands-on interaction also provides students with new ways to clarify concepts and to demonstrate what they have learned.

Cooperative Learning. The **cooperative learning** theme of sheltered instruction builds on research that highlights the many benefits of such learning (Cohen, 1986; Gillies & Ashman, 2013; Kagan, 1986; Slavin, 1983), especially for students who are acquiring English (DelliCarpini, 2009; Hertz-Lazarowitz & Calderón, 1993; Slavin, 1995). Cooperative learning is often understood as a descriptor of the many ways in which students may be placed into small, primarily heterogeneous collaborative groups in ways that maximize interdependence and target either individual or group goals for learning. Positive interdependence is one valuable outcome of collaboration toward a common goal. It fosters the perspective that each student should care about another's learning. Research on cooperative learning has suggested a number of benefits for bilingual students that may be associated with this theme or strategy of sheltered instruction. Specifically, research (Calderón, Tinajero, & Hertz-Lazarowitz, 1992; McGroarty, 1989; Slavin, 1995; Tinajero, Calderón, & Hertz-Lazarowitz, 1993) indicates that, for CLD students, cooperative learning:

- Enables students to act as mutual resources in active learning
- Fosters opportunities to integrate language with content learning
- Encourages the incorporation of a variety of curricular materials that enhance content learning and language production
- Increases both the variety and frequency of L2 practice through a multiplicity of interaction opportunities
- Enhances both L1 and cognitive development through social interaction

Consequently, cooperative learning becomes an essential theme of sheltered instruction that promotes the integration of language and content, the ongoing support of CALP development in L1, and active constructivist learning that is relevant to students' interests.

Global Connections 8.1
Cooperative learning in EFL classrooms is key to promoting student expression. Even within single-level classrooms, learners possess different degrees of fluency, understanding of the linguistic nuances, and confidence in producing language. Small groups that are intentionally configured to include students with complementary strengths provide built-in scaffolding for language development and engagement in learning tasks.

Guarded Vocabulary. As further illustrated in Figure 8.1, **guarded vocabulary** is another common theme among variations of sheltered instruction. Also sometimes referred to as reducing the linguistic load of instruction, this strategy involves linguistic choices on the part of the teacher that increase the comprehensibility of instruction for English learners. It does not involve actions such as unnatural speech or raising the volume of instruction. Rather, teacher actions include linguistic controls on instructional delivery such as:

- Slowing the rate of speech
- Emphasizing word enunciation

■ Voices from the Field 8.1

The cooperative learning strategy has great potential for application in Ecuador because of the large number of students in each classroom. Traditional teaching strategies engage just some students in the class, and teacher talk time greatly outweighs student talk time. Cooperative learning actively engages every student. Students are active learners in the process of teaching and learning because they have plenty of opportunities to share their ideas and thoughts with the members of their groups. They are able to share their background knowledge and experience with their partners; additionally, they gain knowledge from their peers. When students discuss information with their group, they feel more comfortable and do not hide to avoid their participation. They are able to develop their capacity to solve problems and increase their communicative skills through interaction. At the same time, students practice leadership and organizational skills, too. Working collaboratively in groups, students are no longer isolated or competing against each other. They celebrate each other's success.

■ *Elba Gabriela Aguilar Sanchez, EFL teacher, Quito, Ecuador*

- Simplifying the vocabulary used
- Inserting more pauses between phrases

Accordingly, guarded vocabulary extensively emphasizes the linguistic dimension of CLD student learning and language acquisition.

Visuals. A fourth theme common among variations of the sheltered instruction method is **visuals** (see Figure 8.1). Basically, this theme is inclusive of what Echevarria, Vogt, and Short (2000, 2013) refer to as **supplementary materials,** and it encompasses instructional supports such as commercial illustrations, big books, realia, multimedia presentations, demonstrations, graphics, bulletin boards, maps, and more. These visuals not only contextualize curriculum and instruction but they also provide powerful visual links between language and content. Echevarria and Graves (2010) report that the graphic depiction of text, through visuals such as charts, diagrams, and webs, enables CLD students to modify difficult texts, organize thoughts in a meaningful way, and recap a topic or theme. For example, a story map reduces text to the most important points and also teaches students to expect certain recurring patterns in stories and books. Likewise, concept maps enable students to visualize the relationships between or among the components of a process.

> **Illustrated Concept 8.1**
>
> Effectively guarding vocabulary takes practice and purposeful observation of students' responses to instruction. Record yourself teaching a lesson, or ask a colleague to observe you teaching. Reflect on observations made about ways you might increase students' comprehension through guarded vocabulary techniques.

Scaffolding in Sheltered Instruction

Certain models of sheltered instruction also emphasize the notion of **scaffolding.** As discussed in Chapter 6, Vygotsky (1962) has argued that through social interaction and the assistance of an adult or a more capable peer, the learner may surpass his or her level of actual or predictable development to attain a new or potential level of development. The sort of support and assistance from adults or more capable peers that students might need to target the **zone of proximal development (ZPD)** is referred to as scaffolding. Such scaffolding enables the student to be challenged to the next level of performance or development.

Vogotsky's ZPD theory is often misunderstood by teachers in classroom practice. Oftentimes, scaffolding is defined by the English teacher as something one does with the curriculum to make it accessible to the learner rather than an action and reaction that occur as the lesson unfolds. Scaffolds, such as student leaning strategies, using more capable peers, and questioning the learner to support understanding, are essential to promoting students' academic learning. What is often viewed as scaffolding can actually become a crutch for the English learner. Both ESL and EFL teachers must be aware of the individual learner's needs throughout the lesson to provide scaffolds "in the moment" as students struggle to make sense and meaning of what is being learned.

The notion of scaffolding is consistent with a constructivist perspective on learning (see Chapter 2) and the argument that students learn by constructing meaning from their experiences and interactions. Similar to scaffolding that surrounds a building that is under construction, this type of scaffolding promotes effective application for students going through the second language acquisition (SLA) process. In the latter case, scaffolding refers to certain structures that are put into place so that the student grows academically. Gradually, as the CLD student becomes more confident and her or his linguistic abilities increase, the scaffolds are removed. The scaffolding strategy provides the support, structure, and assistance that CLD students often require to construct meaning from the complex academic language of textbooks and that of instruction delivered in L2. For example, in sheltered instruction, new vocabulary is sometimes previewed in the native language, contextualized in English, and reviewed again in the native language (Herrera, 2001; Kole, 2003; Perez, 2002).

■ Misconceptions and Realities Associated with Sheltered Instruction

A variety of misconceptions tend to be associated with the sheltered method of instruction. Similarly, the origins of these misconceptions can be attributed to a variety of reasons, including:

- The broad range of evolving variations of the sheltered method that are discussed in the literature
- Occasional misinterpretations and misapplications of the method in practice
- Confusion among practitioners about this method and other methods of the communicative approach (see Chapter 6) in reference to English language development among CLD students

Many of the strategies and materials associated with the sheltered method have long been used in isolation with both CLD and grade-level students, but they have not always been integrated into a holistic method for second language learners.

dilemmas *of Practice* 8.1

Mr. Cottonware has been teaching biology in a rural high school for three years. During this time, he has become increasingly frustrated with the low performance of his fluent English-speaking CLD students. He does not understand why the students are performing so poorly on laboratory assignments because language does not seem to be a problem. The class works in the laboratory at least twice a week, which Mr. Cottonware schedules for every Tuesday and Thursday. Mr. Cottonware orally explains the experimental setup the day before everyone is to perform the experiment and then again right before breaking the students into work-groups the day of the experiment. He feels that the fluent English-speaking CLD students frequently prevent everyone else from working productively because they walk around talking extensively to others and continually ask peers for directions.

■ *What should Mr. Cottonware do? Mr. Cottonware first should consider the differences between BICS and CALP; the "fluent" English-speaking CLD students likely need additional language support to be successful in the science course. He should heterogeneously group students according to proficiency level in both the English language and content-area understanding. It is evident that the CLD students are having a hard time understanding the procedures of experiments, which is causing them*

to constantly look to their peers for directions. Heterogeneous grouping can help minimize disruptions in the classroom by allowing students to dialogue with one another without having to walk around or try to converse with a peer across the room. This type of grouping will give CLD students an opportunity to articulate their knowledge and understanding of the content without getting off task and distracting others. More capable peers who have a better grasp of the language and content then can aid struggling students by providing them with needed clarification. This will not only minimize disruptions but also enhance learning for all students.

■ *The CLD students need frequent opportunities for visual support related to the lesson's language and content. A demonstration of the experiment beforehand can help the students by providing them with step-by-step procedures to follow. Mr. Cottonware should also display or otherwise have available written instructions and the steps of the experiment procedures in simplified language. This will allow students to follow along and refer back to the steps when necessary. Incorporating these supports will enhance vocabulary and content learning for the CLD students, who likely will be more interested and engaged in the procedure and more likely to do well on related assignments.*

Among misconceptions concerning the sheltered instruction method, some relate to the type of student for which the method is applicable. Others relate to the languages spoken by, or the language proficiencies of, the students to be taught. And still others relate to connections between the method and standards for best practice with CLD students. It is our hope that in the following sections, some of the misconceptions of sheltered instruction are clarified and the realities become clearer.

Types of Students

One misconception regarding the sheltered method asserts that sheltered instruction is designed only for self-contained classes of English learners. In reality, the sheltered method uses strategies and techniques that are applicable to both CLD and grade-level students and therefore may be used in the grade-level classroom (Echevarria, Vogt, & Short, 2000, 2013; Sheppard, 1995). Necessarily, the teacher will need targeted professional development in methods, strategies, and techniques for instructing CLD students, but the sheltered method is regularly used in grade-level classrooms. For example, in secondary schools the sheltered method allows subject-area teachers who are trained in addressing the diverse needs of language learners to deliver courses that allow students to participate in the regular content of the curriculum rather than in elective or pull-out courses for graduation. The method can also be used for self-contained classes of CLD students, where its various strategies and techniques of instruction and assessment are equally effective. Refer to Table 8.2 for a comparison of sheltered instruction versus traditional ESL pull-out instruction. For the grade-level student, the sheltered method shares many of the same characteristics of instruction that are considered effective for all students (Echevarria & Graves, 2010). Such characteristics include the following:

- A variety of grouping strategies
- An emphasis on higher-order thinking skills
- Clear explanations of learning tasks
- Links to prior learning
- Use of supplementary materials
- Consistent feedback on performance
- Student engagement

As Echevarria and Graves (2010) have noted, sheltered instruction shares many of the characteristics of what we know about effective instruction, but sheltered instruction goes beyond good teaching; it offers much more. Whereas sheltered instruction methods, strategies, and techniques are beneficial to all students, these types of accommodations are *essential* to the academic success of CLD students.

Language Proficiency of CLD Students

Some educators also believe that the sheltered method is designed solely for students with intermediate or advanced language proficiency. In some cases, this misconception arises from the fact that the specially designed academic instruction in English (SDAIE) model of sheltered instruction (one variation among many) is limited to CLD students with these levels of L2 proficiency (Russell, 2002). In other cases, this misconception arises from the reality that the sheltered instruction method generally targets not just second language acquisition but also rigorous grade-level content-area learning. In fact, high-quality sheltered instruction is characterized by professional attention to the particular language development needs of CLD students, as well as the incorporation of both language and content objectives into curriculum and lesson preparation and instructional delivery.

■ **t a b l e 8 . 2**   Comparison of Sheltered Instruction versus ESL Pull-Out Instruction

Sheltered Instruction	ESL Pull-Out Instruction
Students remain in grade-level content-area classroom.	Students lose access to content while in ESL class and are therefore often confused after returning to the classroom.
Students remain with peers (nonstigmatizing).	Students feel stigmatized; instruction is perceived as remedial, or as review year after year.
Language instruction is integrated with content instruction.	English learning is isolated (many times with grammatically based exercises that are not often effective).
Teacher is trained with best practices for CLD students.	No training is provided for the grade-level content teacher.
Lessons are modified within the content area to meet students' linguistic and academic needs.	Students limited to this type of programming take longer to develop language skills because there is no meaningful connection to content.
Students achieve academically and linguistically while progressing in their grade level.	Students find it increasingly difficult to catch up with or keep pace, academically or linguistically, with their native-English-speaking peers.
Native language support is easily incorporated through more proficient bilingual peers and through supplemental material provided by the grade-level content teacher.	There is minimal (or no) native language use.
All students benefit by reaching their potential through cooperative learning and by becoming more appreciative of cultural and linguistic differences.	Relationships among immigrants from various linguistic and cultural backgrounds are fostered; however, students lack significant interaction with native-English-speaking peers.
This is the most effective program model for L2 development in classrooms with learners from many different L1 backgrounds.	This is the least effective program model for L2 development.
This is the least expensive program model, with the ESL teacher in the classroom as an additional resource teacher.	This is the most expensive program model; an extra resource specialist (the ESL teacher) must be hired.

According to Echevarria, Vogt, and Short (2000, 2013), in sheltered instruction courses, language and content objectives are embedded into the curriculum. The classroom teacher provides the grade-level content to the students through modified instruction in English; however, some additional curricula might be created for students who have lower literacy levels or major inconsistencies in their educational backgrounds. It is important for teachers to consistently develop the student's academic language proficiency as part of the daily lesson plan delivery.

For students whose L2 proficiency is not advanced, the teacher's English use in classroom instruction is guarded to increase comprehensibility and lower students' affective filter. High-quality sheltered instruction for students empha-sizes the explicit instruction of academic language skills, such as asking for clari-fication, confirming information, and persuading through language. Therefore, although accommodations must be implemented to enhance the comprehensibil-ity of content material for students who possess beginning levels of English profi-ciency, the sheltered instruction method can be used effectively for the instruction of *all* CLD students.

Sheltered instruction is not limited to classrooms in the United States. Coun-tries around the world that are seeking to move away from teaching the English language in isolation have adopted the sheltered method, strategies, and techniques to advance English learning and prepare students for opportunities to participate in English contexts for more than social purposes.

Similarly, some teachers believe that sheltered instruction is specifically designed for CLD students who are homogeneously grouped according to the level of L2 (English) proficiency. Instead, sheltered instruction enables successful practice with either homogeneously or heterogeneously grouped CLD students. In some schools where students are homogeneously grouped according to L1 or L2 proficiency, bilingual instructors are used. In other schools where students are heterogeneously grouped, even in the grade-level classroom, ESL/EFL or trained content-area teachers provide instruction.

■ **Snapshot of Classroom Practice 8.2**   Use of Cooperative Learning

---

Students interact in a cooperative learning activity that promotes the engagement of all learners in the grade-level classroom.

(Courtesy of Shabina Kavimandan, teacher trainer, Manhattan, Kansas)

Standards of Best Practice

A final misconception about sheltered instruction concerns the belief that such instruction is not grounded in standards of best practice with CLD students. Echevarria, Vogt, and Short (2013) explain that, in reality, high-quality sheltered instruction has a critical emphasis on teaching academic language, which is reflected in TESOL's Pre-K–12 English Language Proficiency Standards and WIDA's standards (see Chapters 1 and 5 for more information on WIDA standards). According to Echevarria, Vogt, and Short (2013), accommodative sheltered instruction is founded in second language development principles such as the following:

- The process of L2 acquisition is influenced by multiple complex variables (e.g., L1 literacy, L2 oral proficiency, socioeconomic status).
- Some L1 skills transfer to English literacy.
- Literacy and oral proficiency develop simultaneously.
- Academic language proficiency in L1 aids the development of English academic literacy.

The National Literacy Panel (NLP) and the Center for Research on Education, Diversity & Excellence (CREDE) concur with these principles, based on two separate reviews of academic literacy research in relation to English learners' educational needs.

Specially Designed Academic Instruction in English (SDAIE)

A particularly popular variation of sheltered instruction in certain regions of the United States is known as *specially designed academic instruction in English*, or **SDAIE** (California State Department of Education, 2013). For students who have attained an intermediate or advanced level of proficiency in English, SDAIE emphasizes cognitively demanding, grade-level–appropriate core curricula. Among the objectives of SDAIE that are applicable to CLD students are:

- Opportunities for social interaction as a means to cognitive and language development
- Access to the core curriculum
- Ongoing English (L2) language development

Similar to other sheltered variations, SDAIE stresses comprehensible input, guarded vocabulary, hands-on interaction, and the use of supplementary materials, especially visuals. The following elements of the SDAIE variation of the sheltered instruction method are also generally incorporated:

- Goals and objectives that focus on language, content, and social affective strategies
- Cooperative learning that focuses on small homogeneous or heterogeneous groups, targeting collaborative learning

- Modified instruction that incorporates thematic units taught through scaffolding strategies and language-level–appropriate lesson adaptations
- Multifaceted assessment that includes both formal and informal assessments that evaluate process and product, with a process emphasis on portfolios, running records, and anecdotal records

The primary goal of SDAIE is to teach content as language learners continue to improve their capacities for speaking, reading, and writing in L2 (Rohac, 2000; Russell, 2002). Nonetheless, students who learn this content through SDAIE will continue to need support when acquiring academic English, which can be provided by intermediate and advanced English language development (ELD) classes (Russell, 2002). Therefore, Russell reports that SDAIE, despite the many ways in which it has been applied in field practice, was never intended for use with remedial students or with students who are at the beginning stages of second language acquisition.

■ The Sheltered Instruction Observation Protocol (SIOP)

As distinct from the SDAIE variation, we consider the **SIOP model** of sheltered instruction to be the most researched, developed, and explicated of the sheltered instruction variations. Consequently, we devote the remainder of the chapter to a brief history of the model's development and a detailed exploration of the model and its application in practice.

After five years of collaboration with practicing teachers, CREDE researchers Jana Echevarria, MaryEllen Vogt, and Deborah Short developed a high-quality model of sheltered instruction known as the *sheltered instruction observation protocol (SIOP)*. They specifically designed this variation of sheltered instruction to provide an explicit and consistent framework that is grounded in research and field-tested by teachers to identify effective practices for sheltered instruction. The SIOP model is a professional development instrument for teachers in culturally and linguistically diverse school settings (Echevarria, Vogt, & Short, 2000, 2013). It is the most comprehensive form of sheltered instruction because it goes beyond strategies and techniques to include the major indicators of well-developed lessons for CLD students. Such indicators include language and content objectives, supplementary materials, connections between content and the prior knowledge and experiences of students, vocabulary development, appropriate speech, learning strategies, interaction with teachers and other students, activities that require students to apply knowledge of content and language, and a cycle of review, feedback, and assessment (Echevarria, Vogt, & Short, 2000, 2013).

Many devoted teachers have tried to find ways to make their instruction more comprehensible for English learners. For all their efforts and best intentions, however, these teachers are often unable to find resources that demonstrate exactly *how* they can modify curriculum and instruction to meet the needs of their students. In providing a rationale for their development of the sheltered instruction observation protocol, Echevarria, Vogt, and Short (2013) explain,

Traditionally, to meet the needs of students who struggled with grade-level reading materials, texts have been rewritten according to readability formulae or Lexile levels (Gray & Leary, 1935; Stenner & Burdick, 1997). The adapted texts included controlled vocabulary and a limited number of concepts, resulting in the omission of critical pieces of information. We have learned that if students' exposure to content concepts is limited by vocabulary-controlled materials, the amount of information they learn over time is considerably less than that of their peers who use grade-level texts. The result is that the "rich get richer and the poor get poorer" (Stanovich, 1986). (pp. 25–26)

For these authors, oversimplifying curricular materials leads to the widening of the gap between native English speakers and second language learners. This, in turn, can eventually contribute to the high dropout rates among CLD students. Therefore, effective teachers plan lessons that are accommodative but also challenging for students who are acquiring English. Appropriately adapted lessons include and do not omit age-appropriate content and materials. The SIOP model of the sheltered instruction method provides teachers with a research-based tool for putting these appropriate accommodations into place and for making grade-level content comprehensible for all students.

> **Illustrated Concept 8.2**
>
> According to Echevarria, Vogt, and Short (2013), field testing accomplished with CREDE concluded that English learners who had teachers who were trained in SIOP and who implemented the model in the classroom performed significantly better on academic writing assessments than students whose teachers had no background in the SIOP model.

In the design and implementation of appropriate content-based lessons for students, the SIOP model considers the following three critical aspects of the teaching process: preparation, instruction, and review and assessment. The sheltered instruction observation protocol explores the spectrum of teaching practices through the examination of 30 essential indicators, each of which pertains to one of the three aspects of the teaching process illustrated in Figure 8.2. For additional clarification in the many ways teachers can effectively implement the various indicators of the SIOP model of sheltered instruction, see Figure 8.3, a basic SIOP lesson plan.

Preparation

Of the three critical aspects of the SIOP model, perhaps the most fundamental is preparation. Effective teachers in schools with culturally and linguistically diverse populations consider many different factors when creating lesson plans. In an SIOP lesson, student needs and characteristics drive the ways in which teachers design their content-area lessons. Therefore, six **SIOP indicators** guide teachers to do the following:

- Write content objectives for the lesson.
- Write language objectives for the lesson.
- Select content-area concepts appropriate for the grade level and educational background of the students.
- Gather supplementary materials that provide students with comprehensible input by contextualizing information.

■ **figure 8.2** Critical Aspects and Indicators of the SIOP Model

Aspect of Preparation
- Content objectives
- Language objectives
- Appropriate content concepts
- Supplementary materials
- Adaptation of content
- Meaningful activities

Aspect of Instruction

Building Background *(category of instruction)*
- Students' life experiences
- Students' prior learning experiences
- Key vocabulary

Comprehensible Input *(category of instruction)*
- Appropriate speech
- Techniques to clarify content concepts
- Clear explanations of academic tasks

Strategies *(category of instruction)*
- Opportunities for students to use strategies
- Use of a variety of question types
- Scaffolding techniques

Interaction *(category of instruction)*
- Discussion and in-depth responses about concepts

- Sufficient response wait time
- Appropriate grouping configurations
- Clarification of lesson material in L1

Practice and Application *(category of instruction)*
- Hands-on materials and manipulatives
- Activities requiring students to apply knowledge of content and language
- Activities that use all language domains

Lesson Delivery *(category of instruction)*
- Support of content objectives
- Support of language objectives
- Appropriate engagement of students
- Appropriate pacing

Aspect of Review and Assessment
- Review of key vocabulary
- Review of content concepts
- Ongoing feedback to students regarding language production and the application of new content concepts
- Formal and informal assessment of student progress toward attaining content and language objectives

- Develop ways to adapt content to the language proficiency levels of all students.
- Create meaningful activities that allow students to practice and apply content knowledge using all four language domains (listening, speaking, reading, and writing).

Integrating Content and Language Objectives

The first two indicators of quality preparation are integrating **content objectives** and **language objectives**. For several decades, researchers in the field of second language acquisition have recognized the need for educators of language learners to integrate content and language objectives into their lessons (Cantoni-Harvey, 1987; Chamot, 1985; Cummins, 2001a; Enright & McCloskey, 1988; Mohan, 1986; Thomas & Collier, 1997). Content objectives clarify the essential information and understandings that students should glean from the lesson. With the overarching goals of the lesson in mind, students have a framework within which to organize specific details of the lesson. Language objectives help students focus

■ **figure 8.3**   SIOP Lesson Plan

Grade Level: 4 Subject: Health/Science

Preparation
Content Objectives:

- We will be able to identify parts and functions of the circulatory system.
- In groups, we will be able to create an illustration of the circulatory system that demonstrates how it works, using the appropriate vocabulary.

Language Objectives:

- We will listen to a shared reading and class discussion of the text, and then reread the text in groups.
- We will discuss our knowledge about the circulatory system.
- We will conduct a shared reading with a partner.
- In groups, we will draw and write on a poster using the proper vocabulary and then orally explain our poster to the other groups.

Materials:

Books on the circulatory system, vocabulary cards with pictures, sample poster of the circulatory system, large pieces of chart paper, markers

Instruction
Building Background:

Students have already learned about the hierarchy of cells, organs, tissues, and systems, and have studied the skeletal and respiratory systems.

Students will be arranged in groups of four, and CLD students are to be placed evenly in each group for the Numbered Heads Together activity. The students will brainstorm with their group about what they know about blood, why they have blood, and how blood is transported in their bodies. **During the sharing, the students should be able to use gestures, pointing, pictures, sketches, and brief oral responses to share their individual ideas.** The students will discuss the ideas presented by the class and which explanations make the most sense.

> *Key Vocabulary:*
> circulatory system, blood, arteries, capillaries, veins, heart, red blood cells, white blood cells

Comprehensible Input:

Visuals, realia and other items, and hands-on activities will be incorporated to promote meaning through the lesson. The teacher will focus on making meaning of new vocabulary in context. The teacher starts with the concrete and moves to the abstract information in the lesson.

Strategies:

- Numbered Heads Together
- Hands-on activity
- Gallery Walk

(continued)

■ **figure 8.3**   Continued

Interaction:
- All opportunities will help to foster student–student interaction.
- Grouping configurations: partners, small groups, large groups/whole class.
- Appropriate wait time will be given in order to receive student responses.
- Clarification of material in L1 will be given in groups and in whole class discussion through vocabulary cards and peer talk.

Practice and Application:
The students will work in pairs during a shared reading activity, where they are able to choose from several different books about the circulatory system in the room. The teacher will pause often to rephrase what is being discussed, and to answer questions as they arise. In groups, the students will reread the text and discuss the information until they come to a shared understanding of it. **Students who are less proficient in English should be paired with fluent students, and of the same language background, if possible. These "peer buddies" will work together throughout the activity. Students of lower English proficiency should be encouraged to observe how the fluent students engage in the conversation about the content. They should also try to echo read while the fluent student reads the text.**

Groups will then use the chart paper and markers to create their own poster that they will use to teach the class about the circulatory system. The teacher should remind students to be creative and to use all the vocabulary words correctly. Students may not copy the poster from the board or the book. Each poster will be hung so that the students can participate in a Gallery Walk.

Lesson Delivery:
The teacher will inform the students that there is a name for blood moving through one's body and the things that help it do so; it is called the *circulatory system*. The teacher will point to the circulatory system poster and explain that blood is pumped from the heart to the entire body using arteries, capillaries, and veins, ultimately returning to the heart again. Utilizing vocabulary cards to illustrate this process and allowing use of the L1 to clarify information at this time will be beneficial to CLD students.

The teacher will then write on the board to further explain how the blood circulates through the body as it leaves the heart. She or he will use a red marker to represent the arteries and a blue marker to represent the veins. *Note:* The teacher will write all applicable words in a circular graph to represent that the process doesn't have an ending; rather, it just keeps repeating itself. The teacher will also refer back to the poster to emphasize how blood circulates, repeating key vocabulary. **The CLD students will benefit greatly from repetition, and further explanation will help in clarification and retention of information.** Students should be encouraged to read the words aloud after they are introduced. **The CLD students who do not often speak may feel more comfortable saying the words in unison with the class.**

Review and Assessment
Throughout the lesson, the teacher will circulate among the students to ensure that they are participating and using the vocabulary correctly. The teacher will evaluate the effectiveness of each group's poster and presentation using a rubric.

Source: From Center for Intercultural and Multilingual Advocacy (CIMA). (2013). *SIOP lesson plan: Circulatory system.* Lesson plan created at Kansas State University, Manhattan, KS. Copyright © 2013 Socorro G. Herrera. Reprinted with permission from Socorro G. Herrera.

on acquiring the academic language they need in order to develop the vocabulary, language structures, and cognitive language necessary to accomplish the goals of the lesson and perform well in school.

When developing content and language objectives, an effective teacher selects appropriate objectives derived from district, state, and national grade-level content and language standards. Throughout lessons, the teacher shares the objectives with his or her students by posting the objectives in a visible place in the classroom and explicitly relating lesson content and activities to the posted objectives. The teacher encourages students to self-assess their progress toward meeting the lesson objectives as they proceed through each lesson.

Integrating Content and Language Objectives: In Practice. To get a better sense of what content and language objectives might actually look like, let us examine the efforts of Ms. Nygaard, our hypothetical science teacher at Konza Middle School. Ms. Nygaard is confident that her content objectives are appropriate for the grade level of her students. She has 10 years of teaching experience with eighth-grade science, and she wrote her objectives using her school district's curriculum frameworks for eighth-grade science and middle school English as a second language. She also talked to the school's ESL teacher about the language objectives. She wrote three content objectives and two language objectives.

Content Objectives for Students
- List the names of the planets in the order that they orbit the sun.
- Describe three ways in which the inner and outer planets are different from each other.
- Explain the unique characteristics of Earth that allow the development and sustenance of life.

Language Objectives for Students
- Using ordinal numbers, list the planets in the order that they orbit the sun.
- Compare and contrast the inner and outer planets using comparative and superlative adjectives.

Although her class includes students at varying levels of proficiency in English, Ms. Nygaard knows that most of the CLD students will be able to list the planets in their order from the sun using ordinal numbers. However, because some of the newer students who are acquiring English may experience difficulty using comparative and superlative adjectives, she will have them focus more on using descriptive adjectives. All of the materials, concepts, adaptations, and activities used in the SIOP lesson will support the language-learning students in attaining the lesson objectives.

Appropriate Content Concepts

When preparing an SIOP lesson, a third indicator of high-quality preparation addressed by effective teachers is the choice of **appropriate content concepts**.

Accommodative teachers use the lesson objectives to develop content concepts that are central to the theme of the unit or text chapter and are appropriate for the grade level and educational backgrounds of the students (Echevarria, Vogt, & Short, 2000, 2013). Some teachers mistakenly underestimate the cognitive and academic abilities of language learning students because some students do not speak much English. However, limiting CLD students to a remedial curriculum based on assumptions negatively affects their academic achievement (Thomas & Collier, 2002). It is essential to keep the quality of the content intact.

For students to comprehend grade-level content concepts, they must have the prerequisite knowledge base essential for the concepts covered. This means that when planning a lesson, the effective teacher examines the basic understandings, theories, and premises on which the specific content concepts are based. If students lack such background knowledge, the teacher incorporates the necessary explication before covering the actual concepts of the lesson (Echevarria, Vogt, & Short, 2000, 2013).

Appropriate Content Concepts: In Practice. After analyzing the content objectives she has written, Ms. Nygaard determines that the lesson will focus on the following two grade-appropriate content concepts:

* Each planet in the solar system has a unique set of characteristics.
* The Earth has characteristics that make the development and sustenance of life possible.

Ms. Nygaard then reflects on the background information that is necessary for her students' understanding of the concepts.

Although she knows that all her students have the capacity to understand the concepts of the lesson, Ms. Nygaard is aware that some of her CLD students have no background knowledge of the basic components of an atmosphere. Many of her students are also unaware of how an atmosphere influences a planet's environment. Therefore, to ensure that all students will be able to fully understand the lesson's content concepts, Ms. Nygaard develops a short introductory lesson that explains key information relevant to an atmosphere.

Supplementary Materials

A fourth indicator of high-quality preparation according to the SIOP model of sheltered instruction involves the use of supplementary materials. Culturally and linguistically diverse students need opportunities to use supplementary materials, including many hands-on, visual, and kinesthetic materials, in order to practice and more fully understand key grade-level content concepts (Echevarria, Vogt, & Short, 2000, 2013). Supplementary materials also provide students with the chance to practice new vocabulary and language structures. Not surprisingly, in a long-term longitudinal research project, Thomas and Collier (2002) found that lessons using multiple media, a natural learning environment, real-world problem-solving applications of content concepts, and unifying themes facilitated the second language acquisition and academic achievement of students.

Supplementary Materials: In Practice. For visual support, Ms. Nygaard turns her classroom into a representation of our solar system. Using supplementary materials to enhance her instruction, she hangs representations of the sun and planets across the back of her classroom. Each planet has note cards hanging from it on a string. The top note card for each planet has its ordinal number describing its position from the sun. Each of the other note cards states a key fact about the planet. She also displays a pictorial word wall with the key content vocabulary as well as descriptive adjectives related to the planets.

To supplement her course materials and support her content and language objectives, Ms. Nygaard chooses several alternative texts and hands-on materials. The textbook set for eighth-grade science came with a Spanish text and recording of the chapter that her Spanish-speaking students can use, but not all her students speak Spanish. So she instructs her CLD students who do not speak Spanish to find readings on the Internet at the technology center in the classroom. She encourages her students to read their first language texts at home or in groups during their resource period before they read and discuss the text in English during class.

When students have finished their work and during designated reading times, students can choose reading materials from the classroom's solar system library. Ms. Nygaard and the school media specialist collaborated to assemble a space-related collection of fiction and nonfiction books, comic books, and magazines at different reading levels and in different languages.

Adaptation of Content

The **adaptation of content** is a fifth indicator of high-quality preparation using the SIOP model of sheltered instruction. Grade-level texts and lectures are often difficult for CLD students to understand. However, using texts from lower grade levels and more simplified lectures does not provide English learners with age- and grade-appropriate concepts and vocabulary. Therefore, to make grade-level texts and materials accessible to students, teachers need to scaffold the content before, during, and after reading.

Adaptation of Content: In Practice. Ms. Nygaard understands the importance of using grade-level text with her CLD students. However, she knows that the CLD students, as well as many native-English-speaking students, experience difficulty when trying to fully comprehend the grade-level texts. Therefore, Ms. Nygaard provides students with activities before, during, and after reading a text to help all her students better understand the key concepts. The following paragraphs highlight some of these adaptations, and other accommodations appear in subsequent sections.

Ms. Nygaard knows that her students can understand grade-level text better if she contextualizes information, so she decides to show a video about the planets in the solar system before the students read the grade-level text. Throughout the video, she frequently pauses the DVD player and asks the students to describe the main ideas. Then she clarifies any misunderstandings and explains any unmentioned but important key concepts. In their learning logs, the students record what they are learning using the language they know best.

In the days after the video showing, the students read the text. They preview the text by looking at all the pictures and headings. Ms. Ramirez, a Spanish-speaking paraprofessional, also takes a few moments to preview the material in Spanish, the language spoken by the majority of the CLD students. As the class is previewing, the students share what they know about the topics and predict what the chapter will say. While the class then reads and discusses the English text, Ms. Nygaard and the students create a table that summarizes the characteristics of each planet. Ms. Nygaard consistently refers students to pictures, tables, and figures as well as the text while they are gathering information and discerning main ideas. The students add the Planets of Our Solar System table (see Table 8.3) and their own additional insights to their learning logs.

■ **t a b l e 8 . 3**   Planets of Our Solar System

Planet	Position Relative to the Sun	Diameter	Composition	Distinguishing Features	Temperature	Atmosphere
Mercury	Inner planet	4,880.0 km	Terrestrial	Craters and plains	90–700 K	Thin atmosphere; planet atoms
Venus	Inner planet	12,103.6 km	Terrestrial	Rolling plains	740 K	Dense atmosphere; carbon dioxide and sulfuric acid
Earth	Inner planet	12,756.3 km	Terrestrial	71% water	288–293 K	77% nitrogen and 21% oxygen
Mars	Inner planet	6,794.0 km	Terrestrial	Mountains, bulges, canyons, and craters	186–268 K	Thin atmosphere; carbon dioxide
Jupiter	Outer planet	142,984.0 km	Gas	Great Red Spot and small, faint rings	288–293 K	Hydrogen and helium
Saturn	Outer planet	120,536.0 km	Gas	2 distinct rings, 1 faint ring	134 K	Hydrogen and helium
Uranus	Outer planet	51,118.0 km	Gas	11 faint rings	76 K	Hydrogen and helium
Neptune	Outer planet	49,532.0 km	Gas	4 faint rings	73 K	Hydrogen and helium

Meaningful Activities

A sixth indicator of high-quality preparation involves incorporating meaningful activities. Meaningful activities that provide CLD students opportunities to read, write, listen, and speak promote their cognitive, linguistic, and academic development. Saunders, O'Brien, Lennon, and McLean (1999) found that when CLD students have many opportunities to use writing, speaking, and listening to help them work with information from text, they have a much greater understanding of the content than if they had merely read the material. Proactive teachers incorporate all the language domains when creating lesson plans to enhance the linguistic capacities of students who are acquiring English as a second language. This allows students to communicate for authentic social and academic purposes.

Teachers can make activities meaningful for all students by first considering the levels of English proficiency represented in their classroom and then adapting assignments accordingly. For example, when creating writing assignments in which students practice writing persuasive, descriptive, chronological event, or compare–contrast paragraphs, effective teachers differentiate between the expectations they have for newcomer students and those they have for students with greater proficiency in English. Although the content remains the same, extra scaffolding, such as that illustrated in Figure 8.4, is provided to accommodate the needs of students who are still in the early stages of acquiring English.

> **Global Connections 8.2**
> Sentence starters and sentence frames can provide learners with tools for initial practice with new vocabulary and grammar structures. However, students in EFL classrooms develop enhanced levels of English proficiency when they are challenged to produce language that reflects original thought. Planning systematic opportunities for learners to use creative and critical thinking as the basis for their writing encourages more native-like language use and increases motivation.

Meaningful Activities: In Practice. Ms. Nygaard structures the activities in her classes to create authentic opportunities for all students to use oral and written language to communicate for both social and academic purposes. A few examples include learning logs, a postcard activity that deals with the planets' characteristics, and a planet colony project. The learning logs give students a place to record their ideas, understandings, new vocabulary, and language structures. Such logs enhance students' capacities for metacognitive learning and encourage students to put their thoughts into words and use their languages for their own purposes and in their own ways. As the students learn about the planets, they are also encouraged to be creative and apply their new knowledge through the planet postcard activity. For this activity, the students create a postcard that describes what they see and their experiences as they "visit" each planet. Such postcards emphasize personal relevancy and provide opportunities for experiential and constructivist learning. As a final project, students work together in small groups to develop a colony on a planet of their choice. The only requirement is that their colony designs must provide the necessary accommodations to sustain human life.

Instruction

When a teacher has completed preparation by deciding on content objectives, language objectives, appropriate content concepts, supplementary materials, content

■ **figure 8.4**   Adapting Writing Assignments

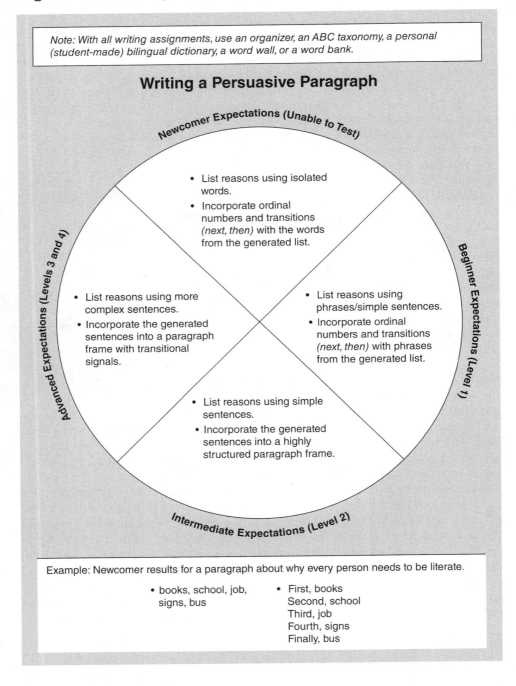

Note: With all writing assignments, use an organizer, an ABC taxonomy, a personal (student-made) bilingual dictionary, a word wall, or a word bank.

Writing a Persuasive Paragraph

Newcomer Expectations (Unable to Test)

- List reasons using isolated words.
- Incorporate ordinal numbers and transitions *(next, then)* with the words from the generated list.

Beginner Expectations (Level 1)

- List reasons using phrases/simple sentences.
- Incorporate ordinal numbers and transitions *(next, then)* with phrases from the generated list.

Advanced Expectations (Levels 3 and 4)

- List reasons using more complex sentences.
- Incorporate the generated sentences into a paragraph frame with transitional signals.

Intermediate Expectations (Level 2)

- List reasons using simple sentences.
- Incorporate the generated sentences into a highly structured paragraph frame.

Example: Newcomer results for a paragraph about why every person needs to be literate.

- books, school, job, signs, bus

- First, books
  Second, school
  Third, job
  Fourth, signs
  Finally, bus

Writing a Descriptive Paragraph

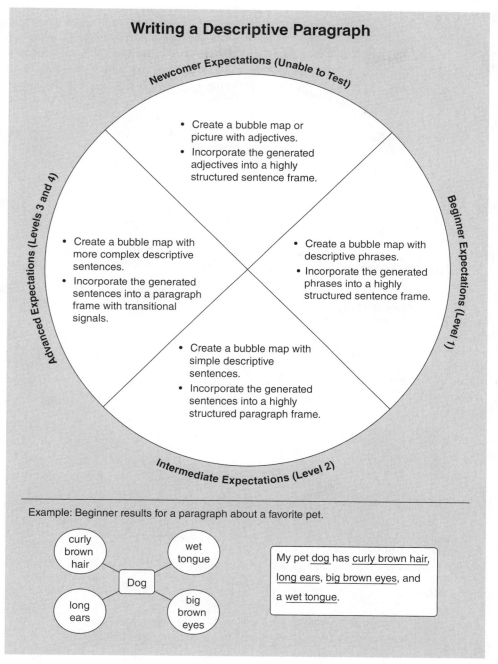

Newcomer Expectations (Unable to Test)

- Create a bubble map or picture with adjectives.
- Incorporate the generated adjectives into a highly structured sentence frame.

Beginner Expectations (Level 1)

- Create a bubble map with descriptive phrases.
- Incorporate the generated phrases into a highly structured sentence frame.

Advanced Expectations (Levels 3 and 4)

- Create a bubble map with more complex descriptive sentences.
- Incorporate the generated sentences into a paragraph frame with transitional signals.

Intermediate Expectations (Level 2)

- Create a bubble map with simple descriptive sentences.
- Incorporate the generated sentences into a highly structured paragraph frame.

Example: Beginner results for a paragraph about a favorite pet.

curly brown hair

wet tongue

Dog

long ears

big brown eyes

My pet <u>dog</u> has <u>curly brown hair</u>, <u>long ears</u>, <u>big brown eyes</u>, and a <u>wet tongue</u>.

(continued)

■ **f i g u r e 8 . 4**   Continued

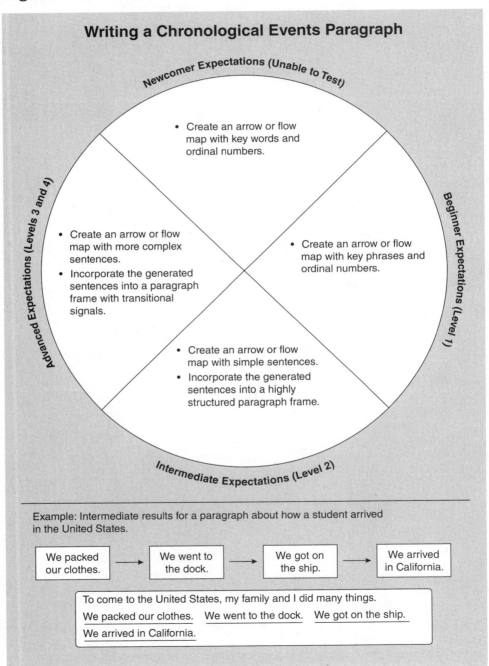

Writing a Chronological Events Paragraph

Newcomer Expectations (Unable to Test)

- Create an arrow or flow map with key words and ordinal numbers.

Advanced Expectations (Levels 3 and 4)

- Create an arrow or flow map with more complex sentences.
- Incorporate the generated sentences into a paragraph frame with transitional signals.

Beginner Expectations (Level 1)

- Create an arrow or flow map with key phrases and ordinal numbers.

- Create an arrow or flow map with simple sentences.
- Incorporate the generated sentences into a highly structured paragraph frame.

Intermediate Expectations (Level 2)

Example: Intermediate results for a paragraph about how a student arrived in the United States.

We packed our clothes. → We went to the dock. → We got on the ship. → We arrived in California.

To come to the United States, my family and I did many things. We packed our clothes. We went to the dock. We got on the ship. We arrived in California.

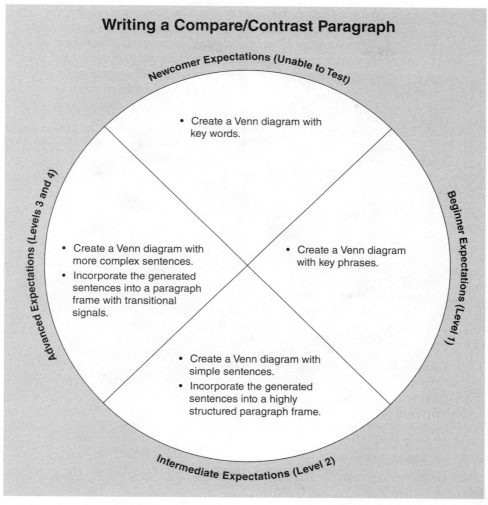

Writing a Compare/Contrast Paragraph

Newcomer Expectations (Unable to Test)

Beginner Expectations (Level 1)

Intermediate Expectations (Level 2)

Advanced Expectations (Levels 3 and 4)

- Create a Venn diagram with key words.

- Create a Venn diagram with key phrases.

- Create a Venn diagram with more complex sentences.
- Incorporate the generated sentences into a paragraph frame with transitional signals.

- Create a Venn diagram with simple sentences.
- Incorporate the generated sentences into a highly structured paragraph frame.

(continued)

adaptations, and meaningful activities, she or he determines how to deliver instruction to help all students meet the language and content objectives. The manner in which a teacher delivers instruction, the second critical aspect of the SIOP model, is guided by indicators that are grouped into the following six categories: building background, comprehensible input, strategies, interaction, practice and application, and lesson delivery (refer to Figure 8.2). The SIOP lessons that include these categories of indicators provide the necessary support to promote academic success and language development for all students (Echevarria, Vogt, & Short, 2000, 2013). These categories do not occur in any specific order. Rather, they are interwoven throughout a lesson.

■ **figure 8.4**   Continued

Example: Advanced results for a paragraph about the processes of mitosis and meiosis.

Mitosis

- Mitosis is the process of cell division.
- Each of the four main phases occurs once.
- Mitosis takes place in various types of animal cells.
- The result is two daughter cells.

- The process involves division.
- The four main phases are prophase, anaphase, metaphase, and telephase.

Meiosis

- Meiosis is the process of nuclear division.
- Each of the main phases occurs twice.
- Meiosis takes place only in the sex cells of animals.
- The result is four daughter cells.

Mitosis and meiosis are each biological processes that <u>involve division</u> and <u>the four main phases of prophase, anaphase, metaphase, and telephase.</u> However, there are many differences that distinguish mitosis from meiosis. For example, mitosis <u>is the process of cell division. Each of the four main phases occurs once. Mitosis takes place in various types of animal cells. The result is two daughter cells.</u> In comparison, meiosis <u>is the process of nuclear division. Each of the four main phases occurs twice. Meiosis takes place only in the sex cells of animals. The result is four daughter cells.</u> Together, both processes enable species of animals to continue in existence.

Building Background

Effective instruction using the SIOP model of sheltered instruction accommodates both the differential learning needs of CLD students and the assets they bring to the classroom. One of the most overlooked of the six categories of accommodative instruction is **building background**. Building background is necessary for the instruction of English learners for several reasons. First, language learners' prior knowledge greatly affects their ability to understand new information. If students have already been exposed to the concepts discussed in the text, their comprehension is much greater than if the concepts are completely unfamiliar (García, 1991; Jimenez, 1997). In addition, instruction that helps CLD students connect new concepts to their prior life and learning experiences improves their language comprehension (Saunders et al., 1999).

The SIOP model encourages teachers to consider three indicators when building background: students' life experiences, students' prior learning experiences, and key vocabulary (Echevarria, Vogt, & Short, 2000, 2013). When building background during instruction, effective teachers always begin lessons by helping students evoke memories of personal or educational experiences relating to the key content concepts in the lesson. This points to the importance of the teacher's prior understanding of the students' experiential and academic backgrounds, which should be obtained through preassessment (see Chapter 5). By encouraging students to tap into their prior experiences, teachers help them make connections between what they already know and what they are going to learn. These connections create a constructivist context for understanding new concepts. In addition, knowledge of students' backgrounds enables teachers to build into instruction the scaffolding that students need to accomplish the lesson objectives (Echevarria, Vogt, & Short, 2000, 2013). Consequently, including culturally familiar perspectives, materials, and themes as an integral part of the grade-level curriculum not only shows respect for and validation of different cultures and points of view but also promotes academic achievement for all students in culturally rich classrooms. To learn more about the importance of incorporating students' background knowledge, watch this video.

Key vocabulary is another essential indicator of effectiveness in building background using the SIOP model. Emphasizing key content vocabulary helps students connect what they know to new words in the target language. Vocabulary knowledge is a crucial component of literacy development for CLD students (García, 1991; Perez, 2002). Vocabulary knowledge forms a major component of cognitive academic language proficiency (Cummins, 2001a). Yet the sort of vocabulary development encouraged by the SIOP model is not the traditional instruction that often focuses on dictionary skills and the memorization of definitions. Rather, Echevarria, Vogt, and Short (2000, 2013) advocate for a more meaning-based set of vocabulary development techniques.

Students acquire new words best when they encounter words several times in meaningful contexts (Stahl & Fairbanks, 1986). For example, although it is important for students to see the specific words in the text as they appear, it is also helpful if they can hear the words in a paraphrased sentence or have the words explained to them through synonyms or antonyms. Concept definition maps, similar to the one depicted in Figure 8.5, and **cloze sentences**, like those shown in Figure 8.6, are examples of other tools teachers can use to provide students with additional contexts for constructing an understanding of key vocabulary terms.

Students also benefit from instruction that teaches them to consider **cognates** in discerning the meaning of unfamiliar words (Hancin-Bhatt & Nagy, 1994; Jimenez, 1997; Jimenez, García, & Pearson, 1996). Figure 8.7 provides examples of cognates related to cell biology. It should be noted, however, that asking students to find cognates between their L1 and English does not guarantee that students will then be able to understand the concept being taught. Additional efforts must be made by educators to determine whether students understand the terms in their L1.

Building Background: In Practice. Throughout her lessons, Ms. Nygaard incorporates the SIOP indicators that are pertinent to building background. She helps her students

■ **figure 8.5**
Civil War Concept
Definition Map

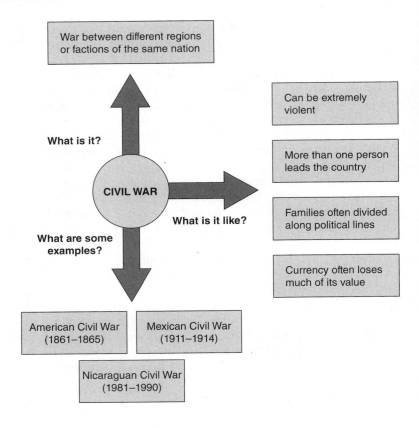

■ **figure 8.6**
Civil War Cloze
Sentences

During a _____, two or more individuals attempt to lead the people of a country. *(civil war)*

In times of civil war, the possession of natural resources such as gold and silver are extremely important because the _____ of a country often becomes worthless. *(currency)*

Those who are displeased with the actions of their government and decide to fight against the nation's leaders are often referred to as _____. *(rebels)*

connect what they are learning to their life experiences and what they already know. She also emphasizes key vocabulary. One activity she often uses with her students is a picture preview. When starting a unit or beginning to read a new text, she displays a picture that is related to the main content concepts that will be covered. For instance, in the solar system unit, she displays a diagram of the solar system.

When creating the pictures, Ms. Nygaard often copies and pastes pictures from the Internet into a word-processing document. Then she displays the picture

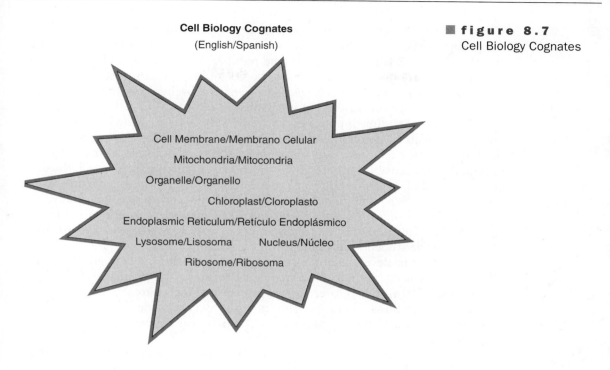

Cell Biology Cognates
(English/Spanish)

Cell Membrane/Membrano Celular

Mitochondria/Mitocondria

Organelle/Organello

Chloroplast/Cloroplasto

Endoplasmic Reticulum/Retículo Endoplásmico

Lysosome/Lisosoma   Nucleus/Núcleo

Ribosome/Ribosoma

■ **figure 8.7**
Cell Biology Cognates

using a projector. Each student writes about the picture in his or her most mean-ingful language. Ms. Nygaard encourages the students to write what they know about the topic, what the picture reminds them of, and a personal experience related to the picture. Then the students get into collaborative groups and label printed copies of the picture with English words they think might relate to the unit. Finally, the groups share their words with the class as Ms. Nygaard records them on the digital version of the picture. During the discussion, she stretches students to explain how the words they share relate to the topic. She emphasizes the key vocabulary words of the unit and elicits any critical vocabulary words the students do not mention.

Comprehensible Input

Comprehensible input is the second category of accommodative instruction using the SIOP model of sheltered instruction. Providing comprehensible input to learners is one of the many features that distinguishes SIOP instruction from instruction one would see in a nonsheltered lesson taught by a master teacher (Echevarria, Vogt, & Short, 2000, 2013). Comprehensible input, which is a critical component of second language instruction, occurs when the language environment makes the second language more meaningful, contextualized, and understandable to second language learners (Cummins, 2001b; Krashen, 1991). For example, a person who does not speak Spanish may not understand the phrase *En sus libros de ciencia, vayan a la pagina cuarenta y dos*. However, if the person speaking the phrase picks up a science book, turns to page 42, shows the class page 42 while pointing to the number on the page, and then praises students who are opening their science books and turning to page 42, the non-Spanish speaker may have received sufficient comprehensible input to understand what the person was saying in Spanish.

The comprehensible input category of the SIOP model consists of the following three indicators of accommodative instruction: appropriate speech, techniques to clarify content concepts, and clear explanations of academic tasks. Teachers provide comprehensible input to CLD students by modifying their speech through guarded vocabulary and supporting the meaning of what they are saying by using nonverbal cues. When modifying their speech, SIOP teachers speak naturally, but they enunciate their words, simplify sentence structure, speak a little more slowly, emphasize key information, and pause momentarily between sentences or main ideas to provide students with time to create meaning.

For language development to occur in an English language environment, CLD students need enough contextual cues to make the language meaningful (Cummins, 2001a). Therefore, as they are discussing content concepts, SIOP teachers use gestures, pictures, objects, role-playing, video clips, modeling, manipulatives, and demonstrations to help clarify content concepts (Echevarria, Vogt, & Short, 2000, 2013).

Effective teachers communicate to CLD students exactly what they need to do to accomplish academic tasks. This clear explanation of academic tasks to be accomplished might take the form of modeling procedures or posting checklists

theory *into* Practice 8.1

Sheltered instruction traces its origin to Stephen Krashen's (1982, 1985) input hypothesis ($i + 1$). Krashen argues that language is acquired in a developmental sequence when students receive abundant comprehensible input. When messages that contain new linguistic information are comprehensible, learners move a little beyond their current level of competence. In other words, they move from their actual development level (i) to their next level of development ($+1$). The input hypothesis is often called the $i + 1$ theory.

Academic content often tends to become more abstract and complex for CLD students in the higher grade levels. Therefore, it is even more crucial to provide adaptations such as:

- Previewing key content vocabulary in the first and second languages.
- Highlighting or outlining key concepts.
- Gesturing to emphasize key points.
- Providing time for clarification of key concepts in the first language with a peer or paraprofessional.
- Simplifying and modifying the language used during instruction, while maintaining an emphasis on key academic vocabulary.

◼ *What does this imply for educators who wish to create an effective classroom climate that bolsters the CLD student's capacity for i + 1? In what other ways can teachers enhance the comprehensibility of their instruction?*

in simple English or pictures. However, even when using techniques for providing comprehensible input, effective SIOP teachers frequently check for student understanding (Echevarria, Vogt, & Short, 2000, 2013).

Comprehensible Input: In Practice.   Ms. Nygaard uses many nonverbal cues to support language use in her classroom. As previously described, she uses pictorial word walls, pictures, displays, graphic organizers, and videos. In this lesson, she is also using realia and demonstrations to support the meaning of text as she reads the grade-level text with her students. For example, as the students talk about the dryness of Mars (dried lakebeds, dry hydrothermal spring), they can examine labeled boxes of dry and wet sand. The students also have a labeled box of rocks they can refer to as they talk about the rocky terrain of Mars. As they read through the text, Ms. Nygaard points out key features (such as craters), using the projector to display labeled pictures of Mars.

Then, after the students discuss the meanings of *rotation, orbit, day,* and *year,* the class goes out into the hallway and the students have a chance to "practice" the words with their bodies. In this role-play, one student is the sun and another student is a planet. The planet student orbits the sun when Ms. Nygaard says, "Orbit," and rotates when Ms. Nygaard says, "Rotate." Ms. Nygaard first asks for volunteers to model the role-play before having additional students participate. Students also act out the words *year* and *day* in the same manner.

■ Snapshot of Classroom Practice 8.3   Adapted Curricular Materials

In the SIOP model, both the lesson preparation and comprehensible input components emphasize the importance of providing CLD students with materials that are age- and grade-level appropriate. Under the lesson preparation component, educators are encouraged to adapt content-area curricular materials so that CLD students can access the same content as their native-English-speaking peers. The comprehensible input component focuses on the importance of adapting materials so that they are more accessible to CLD students through the use of visual scaffolds, language that is appropriate for the students' level of English language proficiency, and other supports. By referring to the CLD student's biography, the teacher can better understand how to modify grade-level content in order to reflect the student's current stage of second language acquisition (SLA).

The following is an example of an adapted fifth-grade earth science study guide and test on renewable and nonrenewable resources for students who are at the earlier stages of SLA, such as the early production and speech emergence stages of English language acquisition. One important feature of both the study guide and test is that they are designed to build CLD students' confidence in their ability to comprehend grade-level content concepts. Gradually, the simplified test format will become more and more complex and will include an increasing number of grade-level concepts.

Chapter 2, Lesson 1:
Earth Science

STUDY GUIDE FOR _____

* * * * * *Quiz on _____

Study RENEWABLE and NON-RENEWABLE RESOURCES pages 44, 45, 46, 47.

Renewable resources are things that can be replaced.

Non-renewable resources cannot be replaced.

Renewable resources	Non-renewable resources
1. trees	1. fossil fuel
2. fish	2. aluminum
3. tomatoes	3. coal

Name: _____

Date: _____

Chapter 2, Lesson 1 Test: The Earth's Resources

Write the name of the picture under renewable resources or non-renewable resources.

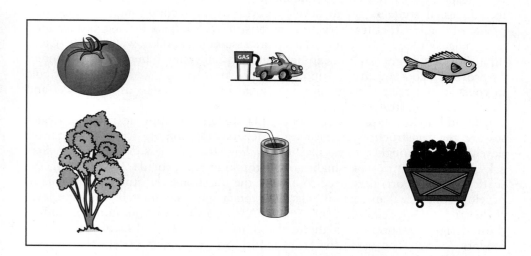

<u>Renewable resources</u>

1. _____

2. _____

3. _____

<u>Non-renewable resources</u>

1. _____

2. _____

3. _____

Write about renewable resources.

_____

_____

_____

Write about non-renewable resources.

_____

_____

_____

(Courtesy of Jory Samkoff, ESL resource teacher, Clifton, New Jersey)

Strategies

As depicted in Figure 8.2, strategies is the third category of accommodative instruction using the SIOP variation of sheltered instruction. Attention to the following indicators is necessary to achieve instruction that effectively incorporates this category: opportunities for students to use strategies, a variety of question types (especially those that promote higher-order thinking skills), and scaffolding techniques. If students are to develop CALP in the second language, the comprehensible input that teachers provide must move students beyond surface-level comprehension of words to form a deep understanding and knowledge base (Cummins, 2001a). While teachers can help students understand language and content by providing comprehensible input, students can learn to take a more active role in constructing their own meaning through opportunities to use, practice, and develop learning strategies.

In addition to explicitly teaching CLD students to apply learning strategies toward the construction of meaning, teachers can promote students' cognitive development through the ways in which they structure lessons. When teachers ask questions that provoke higher-order thinking and provide students with the scaffolding (support) they need to answer the questions, the students are able to develop conceptual understandings at a much more cognitively complex level (Echevarria, Vogt, & Short, 2000, 2013). Asking a variety of questions, including those designed to promote higher-order thinking, is a critical feature of accommodative instruction using the SIOP model. Some teachers believe that second language learners are incapable of higher-order thinking in English. Lessons that simply focus on learning basic English often deny CLD students the opportunity to obtain the cognitively rich curriculum they need (Echevarria, Vogt, & Short, 2000, 2013). Rather than focusing primarily on lower-level thinking skills, such as repeating memorized facts, students need to be able to practice comprehension, application, analysis, evaluation, and synthesis or creation of new information (Anderson and colleagues, 2001; Bloom, 1956).

Nonetheless, teachers cannot expect students to venture into higher-order thinking about new material unless the instruction regarding that content is appropriately scaffolded. The SIOP model uses both verbal and procedural scaffolding to support students as they engage in higher-order thinking. During verbal scaffolding, SIOP teachers orally guide students through the thought processes necessary to apply higher-order thinking to new concepts and information. A teacher first presents a problem to the students. Then she or he thinks aloud to demonstrate how to solve the problem. The teacher describes how she or he would approach the problem and verbalizes the internal dialogue running through her or his mind while solving the problem.

Procedural scaffolding involves organizing instruction so that lessons within a unit build on one another and become increasingly complex at the cognitive level. Effective teachers organize lessons to progress from presenting a new content concept to modeling its actual application. The next critical step is to provide students with guided practice in applying the new information. Finally, after students have received the instructional support they need to feel more confident about their understanding of new material and its practical application, effective SIOP teachers provide students with opportunities to apply the new concept independently (Echevarria, Vogt, & Short, 2000, 2013).

■**Snapshot of Classroom Practice 8.4**   Use of a Learning Strategy

---

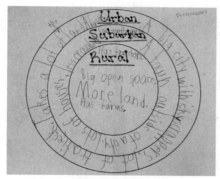

(Courtesy of Cara LeMoine, elementary teacher, Fort Riley, Kansas)

Students use a learning strategy to enhance their understanding of vocabulary words tied to content concepts.

(Courtesy of Cara LeMoine, elementary teacher, Fort Riley, Kansas)

Strategies: In Practice. Ms. Nygaard knows that proficient readers make predictions about content and meaning before and during reading (Clay, 1991; Fountas & Pinnell, 1996). Therefore, she explains to her class the importance of making predictions. She prompts the students to think of a mystery or suspense television show or movie they have watched. She instructs the students to discuss with a partner the story line and how they tried to guess what was going to happen next. Each pair then shares some examples with the class.

Ms. Nygaard continues by explaining to the students that good readers collect clues from what they are reading and what they know in order to make good predictions about the reading material. She displays a copy of the grade-level science text on the projector. Ms. Nygaard begins by pointing out some of the pictures and words in bold print. Guiding them to make connections between contextual clues and predictions, she asks the students what they think the topic might be. The students then list these clues in their learning logs. Ms. Nygaard further prompts the students to offer suggestions of other clues from the text that are found in diagrams, tables, and section headings. The students discuss and record these clues.

Next, using their clues as evidence, the students predict what the text might say. Ms. Nygaard explains to the students that good detectives add to or change their ideas when they collect new clues. Therefore, as they read along in their texts, students add new clues and revise their predictions. After this activity, Ms. Nygaard debriefs the students on how and why they used the strategy, and the students discuss what effect it had on their understanding. After practicing this prediction strategy several times as a class over several days, the students practice the strategy in small groups, and eventually they are able to use the strategy independently. (See the next section for an example of how Ms. Nygaard uses questioning with her students.)

Interaction

Accommodative, SIOP-based instruction for CLD students also involves the category of interaction. Teachers know that students cannot learn what they do not practice. Therefore, if students are going to develop CALP in a second language, they must have frequent opportunities to practice language use in academic settings (Thomas & Collier, 2002). Social interaction will help students develop social language, but this use of language does little to promote a student's language development for cognitive and academic purposes. In an SIOP lesson, instruction should minimize teacher-centered lecturing and maximize student interaction with the teacher and other students (Echevarria, Vogt, & Short, 2000, 2013). The interaction category of the SIOP model incorporates the following four indicators of effective instruction: discussion and in-depth responses about concepts, sufficient response wait time, appropriate grouping configurations, and clarification of lesson material in L1.

Sometimes when students are not proficient in English, they respond to discussions with brief answers. Teachers using the SIOP method become skilled at asking follow-up questions that require students to elaborate on their responses. These teachers use this opportunity to ask questions that push language learners to higher-order thinking. By using prompts similar to the following examples, teachers ask the students to explain their answers: *Tell me more about . . .* ; *Why do you think . . .* ; *What connections can you make between . . .* ; *How does X relate to what you know . . .* ; *How would you change . . .* ; *What if . . .* ; *What would you recommend . . .* ; and so on. Having students elaborate on their answers guides them to use more complex thought processes as well as complex language structures and vocabulary (Echevarria, Vogt, & Short, 2000, 2013). However, when teachers ask students to respond to questions, especially higher-order think-ing questions, it is imperative that they allow students sufficient time to process the question, think about the concept or issue, and develop a response.

When students work in collaborative groups, teachers have the perfect oppor-tunity to walk around the classroom, discuss projects or tasks with small groups of students, and challenge the students' understandings of the key content concepts. Small groups provide CLD students with a safe context in which to stretch a bit beyond their comfort level of content comprehension and language usage toward their potential level, which is characterized by a deep conceptual understanding of the material and more advanced language proficiency (Vygotsky, 1978). In arrang-ing collaborative groups for lessons, teachers need to consider the grouping con-figurations that will best match the content and language objectives of a lesson and the characteristics of the learners. For example, effective teachers consider the ability of students to work independently with the new content and language concepts. If the students are beginning a unit, they may need a lot of support, so whole-class or small-group instruction might be most appropriate. If the students have some proficiency with the content and language, they may need less support. In such situations, a teacher might consider having students work with a partner or independently (Echevarria, Vogt, & Short, 2000, 2013).

Grouping students by first language is another consideration. When begin-ning a unit, a teacher might consider putting students in same-language groups so that the CLD students can work in their first language when making connections between prior knowledge and key content concepts. Students need to be able to use the native language, even in school settings where English is the primary lan-guage of instruction. Students who have the opportunity to use their L1 to discuss second language text have greater second language reading comprehension than students who do not make use of their L1 to help create and clarify meaning (García, 1998; Graves, August, & Mancilla-Martinez, 2012; Jimenez, 1997; Jimenez et al., 1996; Saunders et al., 1999).

Language learners also need opportunities to use English in order to negotiate meaning and solve complex problems to develop their CALP in English (Cummins, 2001a). Therefore, as students progress through a unit and acquire new language structures, vocabulary, and critical content understandings, it is essential that they practice delving into more cognitively complex tasks using English. In this case, mixed-language groups encourage students to use English to solve problems together.

Teachers might also consider level of second language proficiency when grouping students. However, it is important to keep in mind that although group-ing students by second language proficiency can be useful for some lessons, stu-dents generally benefit more from participating in mixed language proficiency groups. When students are grouped, or tracked, by proficiency level for extended periods of time, teachers tend to hold students with less English language profi-ciency to lower expectations. As a result, these students are more likely to partici-pate in a cognitively, linguistically, and academically poor curriculum (Thomas & Collier, 2002). Heterogeneous grouping is beneficial to all students. More proficient students can serve as good linguistic models and give less proficient students the comprehensible input they need to understand difficult concepts. Questions posed by less proficient students can challenge more proficient students to clarify their understandings of content and language concepts.

Interaction: In Practice. Ms. Nygaard uses collaborative student groups throughout her lessons. The group work activities provide students with opportunities to interact in a constructivist environment and enable Ms. Nygaard to provide more individualized attention to her students. The students' cumulative project, in which they create a colony on a planet, is a good example of how she facilitates student interaction in her classroom. Ms. Nygaard arranges the groups so that language groups (English learners and native English speakers) are mixed. She wants students to use English to negotiate meaning, but within the collaborative groups she also pairs students together who speak the same native language (a less English-proficient student with a more English-proficient student) to encourage more project participation by students who are less English-proficient. The more English-proficient student then can clarify information and concepts for the less English-proficient peer in the L1, if necessary.

In these groups, students ask and answer questions, assemble key information, and bring together their different ideas to come to consensus. Through such interaction, the students' use of dialogue goes far beyond a basic interpersonal communications skills (BICS) level. While the students work together to design their colonies, Ms. Nygaard circulates from group to group. She challenges the students' thinking by questioning *why* and *what if*. She tries to guide students to revise their own understandings rather than simply telling them the "right" answer. She wants her students to think for themselves and develop their own solutions.

■ **Snapshot of Classroom Practice 8.5**   Use of Hands-On Materials

Students become active learners when they are allowed to practice and apply their growing understanding of concepts through hands-on activities.

(Courtesy of Tiffany Junghans, elementary teacher, Fort Riley, Kansas)

Practice and Application

As illustrated in Figure 8.2, the fifth category of accommodative instruction using the SIOP model of the sheltered instruction method is practice and application.

For CLD students to internalize new concepts and language with the deep understanding necessary for the development of CALP, instruction needs to incorporate the following three indicators of this category: hands-on materials and manipulatives, activities requiring students to apply knowledge of content and language, and activities that use all domains of language. It is essential that students be active participants in real uses of language and content concepts (Cummins, 2001a; Echevarria, Vogt, & Short, 2000, 2013).

As previously discussed, students' learning is enhanced if new information and concepts are relevant to them. Physical and mental manipulation of information using hands-on materials and manipulatives supports students to make the content material pertinent to their personal lives. Students who are passive learners (listening to a teacher or reading a text as a primary source of information) rather than active learners (manipulating information to create personal meaning) may not have sufficient opportunity to create deep personal meaning with new content and language concepts. Knowing about a subject such as polynomials or prejudice is not sufficient; students must come to think and communicate like mathematicians or social scientists if they are going to become proficient in a particular subject area such as math or science (Costa & Liebmann, 1997). Teachers can actively involve students in applying content and language knowledge by providing opportunities for them to conduct experiments, create models, role-play historical and literary events, take action on social issues, write bilingual books, and more.

Culturally and linguistically diverse students must also practice extensively the use of academic language (reading, writing, speaking, and listening) in academic contexts if they are to acquire the ability to use English as a tool for learning. The four language domains (listening, speaking, reading, and writing) are interdependent—development in one area facilitates development in another (Genesee, 1999). For example, students who have opportunities for in-depth discussion with teachers and peers concerning text they have read in English have greater reading comprehension skills than students who do not have as many opportunities to discuss readings (Saunders et al., 1999). Students who read extensively have much better writing and grammar usage skills than those students who do not (Alexander, 1986; Elly, 1991; Nagy, Herman, & Anderson, 1985; Polak & Krashen, 1988). Because academic language is more cognitively and structurally complex than social language, students will develop high levels of second language proficiency only if they engage in language use for academic purposes (Cummins, 1991, 2001b; Thomas & Collier, 2002).

■ **Snapshot of Classroom Practice 8.6**   Information Gap Activity

---

One way to promote language use for academic purposes between CLD and other students is to foster an *information gap*. For example, through communication and interaction with a partner, students in pairs (especially those paired according to different target language abilities) can complete the photosynthesis fact table shown here by writing down the missing information (without seeing each other's tables). The two different versions of the photosynthesis fact table (as illustrated) create a situation in which part of the information is known only by Student A, and part of the information is known only by Student B. To complete the task, each student needs to obtain the missing information from his or her partner.

This arrangement, or information gap, encourages the students to ask each other questions and to listen to each other's answers. Through such arrangements, CLD students may be exposed to both critical, content-area information and academic English. For example, Student A might ask a question such as "How do plants grow?" to which Student B has the answer. Similarly, Student B might ask Student A, "What makes plants green?" As a result of completing this task, students will have practiced at least four language skills (listening, speaking, reading, and writing) while learning about the content of the science lesson. In technology-based learning centers, student pairs might also maximize the skills of *viewing* (e.g., cloze sentences about chlorophyll or breathing) and *representing* (e.g., illustrative concept maps of the process of photosynthesis).

Student A:

Topic	Characteristics	Characteristics
Plants	Chlorophyll helps plants absorb sunlight.	Plants need water, light, and ___?___ to grow.
Animals	Animals breathe out ___?___, which plants use to perform photosynthesis.	Photosynthesis creates glucose, water, and oxygen, which people and other animals breathe.

Student B:

Topic	Characteristics	Characteristics
Plants	___?___ helps plants absorb sunlight.	Plants need water, light, and carbon dioxide (CO_2) to grow.
Animals	Animals breathe out carbon dioxide (CO_2), which plants use to perform photosynthesis.	Photosynthesis creates glucose, water, and ___?___, which people and other animals breathe.

(Courtesy of Miki Loschky, teacher trainer, Manhattan, Kansas)

Practice and Application: In Practice. Ms. Nygaard uses the cumulative project, in which the students design their own colonies, to help her students practice and apply the language and content concepts from the solar system unit. The students synthesize and analyze what they have learned about the characteristics of a planet and the unique characteristics of Earth that have allowed for the creation and sustenance of life. Then they apply that information to create an inhabitable colony on another planet. This activity affords students the opportunity to use skills in all four language domains and integrate their voices into the content. It also pushes them to understand the material and its implications on a much deeper level than that achieved when students are merely required to regurgitate information back to their teacher on a test.

Lesson Delivery

Lesson delivery is the sixth category of accommodative instruction grounded in the SIOP model of sheltered instruction. This category emphasizes that teachers incorporate the following four indicators into their lessons: support of content objectives, support of language objectives, appropriate engagement of students, and appropriate pacing. The lesson delivery category of the SIOP model is designed to help teachers examine whether they have actually met content and language objectives, evaluate the effectiveness of the lesson in actively engaging students, and determine if the pacing of the lesson matched the students' academic and language proficiency levels.

Effective SIOP teachers explicitly state and display a lesson's content and language objectives so that all students know the purpose of a lesson, the key ideas they need to learn, and the tasks they need to be able to accomplish with the information (Echevarria, Vogt, & Short, 2000, 2013). Explicit knowledge of lesson objectives helps both teachers and students assess how the students are progressing throughout the lesson toward meeting the objectives. Displayed objectives also serve as a tool with which students can refocus on the content concepts if their attention momentarily drifts away from the lesson.

To maximize the time students spend on task, proactive teachers deliver lessons in a manner that keeps students actively engaged. The SIOP lessons with well-developed opportunities for interaction and hands-on activities encourage students to be actively engaged in instruction. Teachers must be careful to ensure that student engagement is centered on activities that help students meet content and language objectives. Activities that do not align with lesson objectives but engage students simply because they are fun should not be part of an SIOP lesson (Echevarria, Vogt, & Short, 2000, 2013).

Finally, teachers should make sure that the pacing of a lesson accommodates students' prior knowledge bases and content or language proficiencies. Prior knowledge development activities can serve as a preassessment from which teachers can gather information about students' areas of strength and inexperience concerning a particular topic for study. Effective teachers use this information to develop appropriate pacing for lessons. Such teachers realize that students will be at various levels of preparedness to engage in a new topic. Therefore, these teachers use scaffolding to help bridge the gap between students who have more experience and students who have less experience with the lesson topic (Echevarria, Vogt, & Short, 2000, 2013). Teachers using the SIOP model frequently check for student understanding and revise the pace of their lessons accordingly. They use collaborative student learning time to provide individual students the support they need.

Lesson Delivery: In Practice. Ms. Nygaard knows that a good lesson plan means nothing if the actual implementation fails to respond to the needs of the students. Therefore, she begins every lesson by reading the content and language objectives, which she has written on poster board with brightly colored markers. Throughout the lessons and units, she continually reflects on whether the students are actively engaged in the learning process and in making progress toward attaining the objectives. Ms. Nygaard subsequently adjusts her instruction to go into more or less detail and to emphasize areas of concern. When the class finishes an activity, she prompts the students to share various ways in which they feel the activity has helped them create stronger understandings of the content concepts.

■ **Snapshot of Classroom Practice 8.7**   Informal Assessment

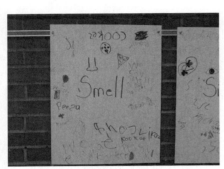

As students worked together to create mind maps such as the one pictured here, the teacher was able to gauge their understanding of the lesson's content and vocabulary related to the five senses.

(Courtesy of Ashton Hall, elementary teacher, Lawrence, Kansas)

Review and Assessment

Review and assessment is an aspect of professional practice that is essential to the effectiveness of any method used with CLD students, and accordingly it is the third critical aspect of the SIOP variation of the sheltered instruction method (see Figure 8.2). Echevarria, Vogt, and Short (2000, 2013) combine notions of review and assessment because they believe that teaching, reviewing, providing feedback to students, and assessing should be a cycle that runs throughout an SIOP lesson. In considering review and assessment, SIOP teachers make sure they incorporate the following four indicators in the lesson: review of key vocabulary, review of content concepts, ongoing feedback to students regarding language production and the application of new content concepts, and formal and informal assessment of student progress toward attaining content and language objectives. Then they use the information they gather from the review and assessment cycle to revise lesson plans to ensure that students meet content and language objectives.

Review and Assessment: In Practice

Ms. Nygaard provides her students with positive feedback throughout the lesson. She knows that her students desire her approval and want to succeed. Therefore, she tries to monitor the ways she reacts to her students' responses to review questions. In addition to clarifying concepts and explaining misunderstandings,

Ms. Nygaard emphasizes the correct aspects of answers. She also models correct language usage by rephrasing the students' responses as she incorporates them into her verbal feedback.

As mentioned earlier, Ms. Nygaard encourages her students to make extensive use of learning logs. In these logs, the students write for themselves. They record their ongoing development of understanding regarding key concepts and language. Students use these learning logs to reflect on and assess their own learning. They determine how they are progressing and what they still need to master. Ms. Nygaard also reviews her students' learning logs to gain a better understanding of where the students are in their language and concept development. Using the learning logs helps her make better instructional decisions when revising her lesson plans in response to her students' progress.

During the five minutes she specifically sets aside for review at the end of each lesson, Ms. Nygaard asks a few students to summarize what the class has learned about specific content concepts. She then encourages students to share any discoveries they made during the lesson that were particularly intriguing or surprising. She also prompts students to discuss any ways in which they will use what they learned in their daily lives.

■ **Snapshot of Classroom Practice 8.8**   Review of Key Vocabulary and Concepts

---

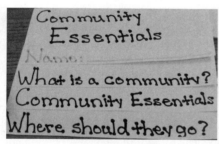

Students are able to document their learning and create a study tool through the use of a single strategy.

(Courtesy of Cara LeMoine, elementary teacher, Fort Riley, Kansas)

Closing Thoughts on the SIOP Model of Sheltered Instruction

Echevarria, Vogt, and Short (2002) developed SIOP indicators and modules for school educators. These modules emphasize implementation of SIOP as an eight-component model for sheltered instruction, involving the following components:

- Preparation
- Building background
- Comprehensible input

- Strategies
- Interaction
- Practice and application
- Lesson delivery
- Review and assessment

Regardless of whether teachers implement SIOP emphasizing its three critical aspects or its eight components, the model provides educators with a rigorous and field-tested framework for sheltered instruction that appropriately accommodates the differential learning needs of CLD students. Teachers can then evaluate the effectiveness of their implementation of SIOP using the 30 indicators of the model's protocol (Echevarria, Vogt, & Short, 2013). Each of the 30 indicators is specified as a bullet in Figure 8.2.

Through their use of the SIOP variation of the sheltered instruction method, effective teachers are able to enhance the success of students who are acquiring English. Such teachers use the indicators of the SIOP model to focus on the key elements of lesson preparation, instruction, and review and assessment that help students develop both their academic and language skills. Teachers using the SIOP model provide all students with an affirming environment in which they can share their individual talents and cultures and work together to create new knowledge.

Connect, Engage, Challenge

CONNECT
Review and Reflect on the Reading

1. What are the six indicators of preparation according to instruction that is delivered using the SIOP model?
2. In what ways are content and language objectives integrated into an SIOP lesson?
3. In what ways is the adaptation of content beneficial for CLD students who are taught according to an SIOP lesson?
4. What are the six categories of instruction when it is delivered according to the SIOP model of sheltered instruction?
5. List and discuss at least three ways teachers can build background among CLD students as part of an SIOP lesson. Why is building background important?
6. In what ways does the SIOP model target comprehensible input? (Be specific.)
7. List and discuss three ways teachers can target the strategies category of instruction in an SIOP lesson to support CLD students' academic learning.
8. What is the role of interaction in an SIOP lesson?
9. Differentiate lesson delivery in an SIOP lesson from traditional grade-level lesson delivery. In what ways is the former beneficial for CLD students?
10. In what ways do the 30 SIOP indicators enhance instruction delivered according to the SIOP model of the sheltered method?

ENGAGE
Share What You Learned

1. This chapter explores the academic and career potentials that are possible when CLD students receive the accommodative instruction they require to be successful in academic settings. Discuss the ways in which the perspective of a level playing field often denies students the appropriate instructional accommodations they require to address their differential learning and transition needs.

2. Despite the many variations of the sheltered instruction method that have evolved over time, themes are common to this accommodative instruction for CLD students. Discuss each of these themes of sheltered instruction and the ways in which each is beneficial for students who are acquiring English.

3. The SIOP model of the sheltered instruction method is defined by three aspects (or eight components). Discuss how a teacher might undertake the evaluation of his or her effectiveness in using the SIOP model with CLD students.

CHALLENGE
It's Not Real until You Practice

Preservice Teachers

1. Sonia, a 10-year-old student from Ecuador, arrived in the United States three months ago and has had no formal schooling in her home country. Choose two of the eight components of the SIOP model and elaborate on how you will meet her needs within the heterogeneous classroom by means of thorough implementation of these two components. For example, if you choose the comprehensible input component, through what techniques can you promote her understanding of the key concepts in a specific content area?

2. Observe a classroom teacher with CLD students. Choose one of the eight components from the SIOP method on which to focus for this observation. For example, you might observe lesson delivery and watch how the teacher implements and carries out the content and language objectives clearly, how much time students are engaged during the class period, and how the teacher paces the lesson to match the ability level of the students. Watch for innovative ways in which the teacher is accommodating the CLD student consistent with the component emphasized. In what ways is his or her teaching consistent with what you have learned about the SIOP model of sheltered instruction? What alternative strategies and techniques might the teacher have used to target the chosen component of the SIOP method?

3. Based on what you have learned from your previous observation of an educator serving English learners and your knowledge of the SIOP model, what are the implications for *your* future classroom?

In-Service Teachers

1. Review the eight components of the SIOP model of sheltered instruction and reflect on your classroom instruction.

   • In what two or more components of your instruction do you find your strengths in meeting the needs of your CLD students?

   • In what two or more components of your instruction do you find improvement needed to meet the needs of your language learners? How can these areas of improvement be addressed to meet the needs of students in your classroom more effectively?

2. Reflect on a concept in a content area that has been of particular difficulty to teach. Target that area through the following activity:

   • Implement the use of student learning logs for one week. Through such logs, students write and reflect on what they have learned. For instance, if the targeted area is word problems in math, a log might begin with: "Today I learned three ways to solve word problems." Subsequently, the students will write about the three ways while reflecting on the processes learned. Adapt these logs as needed for academic and language proficiency, noting that students may also include illustrations of a concept, diagrams with labeled parts, poems, outlines, graphic organizers, and more.

   • What gains have your students made in this content area after this first week of using learning logs?

   • Can your students articulate key concepts and content vocabulary more readily? Why or why not?

   • What frustrations are you encountering, and how can these be overcome?

   • Think about the population in your classroom. List two areas of need specific to each CLD student that can be addressed effectively using the SIOP model. For example, if you have a non-English–proficient student schooled in his first language, you can provide material in his native language or ask a proficient bilingual peer to preview the lesson and then review for a few minutes after a lesson for clarification of content (comprehensible input).

tips for practice

Note: The following tips for practice are provided according to each of the eight components of the SIOP model. Although setting-specific adaptations may be needed, these tips are applicable to learners in ESL and EFL classrooms.

Preparation

1. When introducing the content and language objectives of a lesson:
   • Ensure that the content and language objectives are written or posted in a location easily visible to students. Ask students to volunteer to read the objectives aloud.
   • Use language that clarifies and simplifies the objectives that may be difficult for students to understand.

2. Select content-area concepts that are at the appropriate academic grade level for students. It is important to continually challenge CLD students with grade-level content material. Content can be adapted to meet the varying student levels of language proficiency in the following ways:

   • Before presenting a concept or lesson from the textbook, highlight the key vocabulary, concepts, and summary statements.

   • Audio-record key portions or entire texts for students to follow along with as they read. This is ideal for use at learning centers at any grade level.

   • Rewrite difficult text by looking for passages that are the most powerful in conveying the main ideas. That is, summarize the text, making sure to include important concepts and content-specific vocabulary in shorter, linguistically simpler sentences that will be easier for CLD students to comprehend. The exact number of sentences used is not important; however, it is essential that key information is retained and content is not watered down.

- Create study guides that are modified for the language proficiencies of students. These study guides might include questions, important statements, and summaries of the text. Also, adapt exercises and activities related to the lesson according to the varying language proficiencies among students.

3. Provide supplementary materials and meaningful activities to help students better comprehend new concepts, make clearer connections with the content, and learn new vocabulary related to a lesson. Educators may find the following tools effective:

- *Graphic Organizers:* Before reading content text, prepare a graphic organizer for CLD students (e.g., T-charts, Venn diagrams, timelines).
- *Hands-On Manipulatives and Realia:* Select real-life objects that will help students make connections from content concepts to their own experiences.
- *Word Walls:* Create word walls with key content vocabulary in both English and the native language of the majority of CLD students (additional languages as feasible). Include pictures and symbols on the word wall for clarification. Word walls in both the native and second language should be placed in separate locations of the classroom (e.g., the English word wall on one side of the chalkboard and the native language word wall on the other side of the chalkboard), especially if the CLD students are predominantly non-English–proficient students.

Building Background

1. Create meaningful connections between the existing knowledge and personal experiences of CLD students and the content concepts to be taught. Foster the relevant connections through:

- *Picture Walks:* Before reading a content-specific text, "walk" the students through the reading selection by skimming through the text and looking at the visuals provided. The visuals highlighted might include timelines, pictures, graphs, and more. Encourage students to take note of boldface vocabulary words found along this "walk" in order to familiarize and introduce them to content-specific vocabulary.
- *Picture Prompts:* Use picture prompts to help students connect prior knowledge to what they are studying. For example, when teaching the concept of a democracy, you might begin a lesson by showing a picture of the Statue of Liberty as well as international icons representing freedom that are relevant to your students' cultural backgrounds. Examples from other countries include the India Gate/Red Fort in India and the Dove in Mexico. Give students five minutes to write what they know about the pictures or what thoughts the pictures prompt. More linguistically proficient students can write sentences or even a paragraph. Those newer to English can write words related to the picture that they know in English or the native language. Have a class discussion about what the students wrote. Ask students to share ideas with a partner before calling on volunteers to share with the class. This affords all students an opportunity to share and allows those who are less proficient in English to share first in a less anxiety-provoking way.
- *ABC Taxonomy:* This provides vocabulary development in the first and second languages and is also a tool that can be used for assessing the prior knowledge that CLD students bring to the classroom. Supply students with a piece of paper that has the alphabet listed letter by letter down the left-hand column. In collaborative groups, round-robin style, students brainstorm words related to the current topic using each letter of the alphabet. Encourage students to generate at least one word for each letter of the alphabet. For example, when studying the theme of transportation, students might begin their lists with A = airplane, automobile, *autobús*; B = boat, bus, *barco*; C = car, carriage, *carro, coche*; etc. As an ongoing process, students can continually add words, such as new key vocabulary words, to the master group or class list.

• Ask students to list five things they know about the theme or concept of focus. English learners may write in the native language or draw pictures related to the topic (use paraprofessionals or parent volunteers as translators as needed).

Comprehensible Input

1. Modify speech patterns and language use to accommodate the proficiency levels of students and provide clarity of content through the following:
   • Speak clearly and slowly, and use plenty of gestures. Avoid unnecessary jargon or idioms that may cause confusion.
   • Paraphrase and repeat key concepts.
   • Use cognates to help students make connections between their native language and English. This is most effective when used for the Romance languages such as Spanish, French, Italian, and Portuguese.

2. Use a variety of techniques for clarifying concepts. For example:
   • Rather than correcting student errors as the student speaks, model the correct way to say something by paraphrasing what the student has said. For example, when Gina says, "Spider, ants, and flies is all insects," reply with, "Yes, you're right. Spiders, ants, and flies are all insects."
   • During explanation or reading, restate, emphasize, or explain terms that may be unfamiliar or difficult for CLD students (e.g., "After these three difficult days, the family was famished—extremely hungry or starving—and knew they could not carry on like this much longer.").

3. Academic tasks can be further clarified for CLD students when the following techniques are used:
   • Present and model instructions in a clear, step-by-step manner using a visual to guide students through the process.
   • Ask a student volunteer to summarize instructions in his or her own words and perhaps in the native language of your students.
   • Encourage more-English-proficient CLD speakers to clarify directions for those students

who are not as proficient in the second language.

Strategies

1. Provide general guidance in the use of learning strategies to help students understand, study, and retain information. These strategies become the tools that students can continually use to become independent, active learners. The following suggestions may help CLD students attain this goal:
   • *Think-Alouds:* Model think-alouds to help students understand the processes you use to better understand content concepts. Encourage students to exercise the same think-alouds as they practice different learning strategies.
   • *Questioning:* Provide questions that target higher levels of thinking while still simplifying language. For example, instead of asking, "Do we depend on rain forests for our survival?" ask a higher-level question such as, "Why are we dependent on the rain forest for survival on Earth?"
   • *Word Sorts:* Have students categorize words according to meaning, structure, word endings, or sounds. For example, students can make a list of all words from a unit ending in *-ion* (e.g., *revolution, taxation, solution*) or *-sion* (e.g., *tension, mission, vision*).
   • *Directed Reading–Thinking Activities:* Before CLD students read a text, ask them to predict what will happen. Stop periodically to ask for confirmation, revisions, or additional predictions as the students read the text orally or silently in pairs or as a group.

Interaction

1. Keep in mind the following when pairing CLD students or forming groups for successful collaborative interaction:
   • The linguistic and academic abilities of each student within each group
   • The content and language objectives of the current lesson
   • Particular personality conflicts that may arise
   • The advantages to be gained by maximizing more academically and linguistically capable peers

2. The following tips may be helpful for beneficial interaction among CLD students:

   - If possible, occasionally group students with the same native languages. A group peer can clarify new concepts as well as relate prior knowledge in the first language to the current topic introduced in the second language.
   - Frequently, group students of mixed language proficiencies. Structure activities to encourage more proficient peers to help peers newer to the second language understand concepts and learn key vocabulary.
   - Use a variety of strategies to group students. Consider the purpose of each type of group to make decisions about the duration of the groups (e.g., daily, weekly, bimonthly, by semester, by thematic unit).
   - Regulate and vary wait time as needed for students to process questions and formulate answers according to their levels of second language proficiency.

Practice and Application

1. Culturally and linguistically diverse students need to consistently practice and apply the interdependent language domains of listening, speaking, reading, and writing throughout the lesson. In this way, they will become more independent thinkers and learners, and the acquisition of knowledge and language will occur more successfully. Implement the following to effectively encourage practice and application for the acquisition of content knowledge and language:

   - Provide CLD students with a fill-in-the-blank note outline that is partially completed. This is a cloze activity in which vocabulary is taught in context by leaving out the key term of a sentence and having students fill it in. This will help students take notes as a lesson progresses.
   - Structure writing activities that focus on organization by creating passages like the following:
     I believe that a good friend must have three important qualities. First, _____.
     Second, _____.
     Finally, _____. If a person does not have these three qualities, he or she may not be a good friend.

   - Read aloud to your students or have your students read aloud in pairs. Then have them write or answer questions about what they heard. Post the questions to be asked on the board or a projector so that all students can refer to them as they read. The questions should include those that promote higher-order thinking skills as well as basic knowledge. Students may also be tape-recorded as they read so they can listen to it later. Be aware of the language proficiencies of students in their ability to understand what is being read orally, as well as of those asked to read; be careful not to force non-English–proficient students into producing language before they are ready. Find more comfortable ways for them to express the information requested.
   - Have students design and create their own trade books in order to demonstrate mastery of key concepts and content vocabulary. They can share their books aloud in pairs, in groups, or with the entire class.
   - Ask CLD students to explain a process to a peer in their cooperative learning group using newly learned vocabulary. Keep in mind the language proficiencies represented. Students who are not yet highly proficient in L2 (English) may need to explain concepts in the native language.

Lesson Delivery

1. To support attainment of content and language objectives, adapt the pace of the lesson according to the ability levels of the CLD students, and engage students for the majority of the time (90 to 100 percent):

   - Use a variety of activities such as games, discovery learning, and inquiry tasks.
   - Consistently use and practice the academic vocabulary throughout the lesson or school day, dependent on your setting. This will help link content language to students' real-life experiences and also help them become familiar with and comfortable using the vocabulary.
   - Create engaging and meaningful activities for students that are directly related to the language and content objectives of the lesson.

- Observe the progress of students throughout a lesson and take anecdotal notes. Make modifications through pacing, reteaching, and enriching the content and language according to the needs of students.
- Lead students in reading a paragraph from a selection. First, read the paragraph aloud by individual words, phrases, or sentences to concentrate on key vocabulary and main points. Then have students repeat what is read orally (echo) as a choral group. This activity will help your students remember key points and vocabulary and improve their sight vocabulary.

Review and Assessment

1. Review and assessment throughout the instructional process provides opportunities for supportive, constructive feedback and helps identify those CLD students who need additional instruction as well as those who are ready to move on. To be assured of student understanding and retention of content concepts and key vocabulary:
   - Use a variety of methods for eliciting group responses that are sensitive to student needs and aid in the determination of student comprehension levels. A few may include "pencils up" to agree, "pencils down" to disagree; number cards numbered 0 to 5 to indicate answers to questions or statements with multiple-choice responses; or dry-erase response pads for written responses.

- Introduce and model academic tasks throughout the lessons and units so that CLD students are less anxious about "school talk." For example, English learners who will be involved in literary discussions may need to review what the word *discussion* means as well as what it means to "share ideas." This will also provide a format for understanding the process of asking and answering questions.
- Plan a consistent time at the end of every class period to informally evaluate the extent to which students have understood key concepts and key vocabulary terms. Attaching sticky notes to a clipboard and making anecdotal notes on students throughout the class period can support this process.
- As needed, modify and simplify the language of the assessment tool used for the various levels of English language proficiencies represented. For instance, when creating an assessment for a heterogeneously language-proficient class, think about having:
  - Students less proficient in English draw the known information with an accompanying description in the native language, or use the known English vocabulary to describe the drawing.
  - Students with more advanced English proficiency draw the known information with a written paragraph in English describing the drawing.

assessment tips and strategies

The following assessment tips and strategies are drawn from the content of Chapter 8.

ASSESSMENT

Review and assessment is the third critical aspect of the SIOP model. The information gathered from the review and assessment cycle is used to revise lesson plans and to ensure that students are meeting content and language objectives. Multifaceted assessments, which can be formal or informal, can be used to evaluate process and product, with a process emphasis on portfolios, running records, and anecdotal records.

Assessment Tips

- The review and assessment aspect of the SIOP model includes the following four indicators:
  - Review of key vocabulary

○ Review of content concepts

○ Ongoing feedback to students regarding language production and the application of new content concepts

○ Formal and informal assessment of student progress toward attaining content and language objectives

- Learning logs enhance students' metacognitive learning and encourage students to put their thoughts into words and to use their L1 and L2 for their own purposes in their own ways.

- Informal multifaceted assessments are used to determine the general level of understanding in the class; examples include purposeful observations and verbal questioning.

- Formal multifaceted assessments, such as tests, quizzes, and projects, help educators plan lessons to enhance the students' levels of understanding.

Assessment Strategies

- Use learning logs as a type of multifaceted assessment in which students can:

  ○ Record their connections to prior learning and life experiences.

  ○ Write their new understandings.

  ○ Record their new vocabulary and language structures.

- Use a variety of methods to elicit group responses to assess comprehension levels:

  ○ "Pencils up" means agree; "pencils down" means disagree.

  ○ Use dry-erase boards for written responses.

  ○ Use numbered note cards for indicating multiple responses.

CHAPTER 9

The CALLA Method of Instruction

our mission

Our mission for this chapter will be to:

- Discuss the foundations and development of, as well as applications for, the CALLA method of instruction.

We will accomplish this mission by helping you to meet the following learning outcomes:

- Explain the benefits of cognitive methods and learning strategies for CLD students.
- Outline the five phases of CALLA instruction.
- Describe considerations for selecting and teaching learning strategies.

Denise Johnson

key theories and concepts

CALLA method

code-switching

cognitive approach

cognitive learning strategies

content objectives

cross-linguistic learning strategies

evaluation phase of CALLA

expansion phase of CALLA

higher-order thinking skills

language objectives

learning strategy objectives

manageable task

metacognitive learning strategies

practice phase of CALLA

preparation phase of CALLA

presentation phase of CALLA

self-talk

social/affective learning strategies

Cognitive methods share many of the same characteristics as the communicative methods, but they take instruction a step further to include components that stem from recent research on second language acquisition and cognitive development. Specifically, cognitive methods place a greater emphasis on the explicit teaching of **higher-order thinking skills**, the social/affective dynamics of learning, and the development of students' metacognitive awareness. Although some educators may believe that young children are not developmentally ready for complex thought processes, even first-graders can develop metacognitive awareness (Chamot & El-Dinary, 2000). The cognitive–developmental view argues that children are active thinkers and hypothesizers, and it concludes that higher-order thinking activities are necessary to stimulate their active and higher-level thinking skills (Piaget & Inhelder, 1969). Thus, to promote the best avenue for the acquisition of knowledge and language with the English learner, activities need to encourage higher-order thinking in ways that challenge and are relevant to the student.

Extensive, explicit instruction in applying learning strategies to facilitate the student's cognitive development also differentiates the **cognitive approach** from other approaches. As a foundation for understanding methods that are grounded in the cognitive approach, we share in this chapter some of the findings of research on second language acquisition and the explicit instruction of learning strategies. We also present related teaching strategies and techniques that educators have used to translate these findings into practice.

■ Cognitive Methods and Learning Strategies

Cognitive methods, strategies, and techniques are often absent from classrooms, given the prescriptive nature of current curriculum. Oftentimes, educators struggle to differentiate a teacher activity from a student learning strategy. Moreover, many teachers believe that students who are at lower levels of English proficiency may find higher-order thinking strategies inaccessible. In reality, *all* students need encouragement, guidance, and practice to build their capacities to apply learning strategies. Teachers must model learning strategies and provide structured opportunities for practice before releasing the strategies to students in order to guide their own learning. Teacher-provided tools that the students use to document their learning allow them to be independently responsible for demonstrating new knowledge and skills gained.

Many native-English-speaking students also struggle with reading, writing, and using higher-order thinking skills. As research shows, explicit instruction in applying learning strategies benefits not only English learners but also native-English-speaking learners (Clay, 1991; Rosenshine, Meister, & Chapman, 1996; Stevens, Slavin, & Farnish, 1991). Certainly, all students benefit from this type of differentiated instruction, but CLD students are not likely to succeed academically without it. For more information on differentiated instruction, watch this video.

Effective teachers integrate strategy instruction with content-area instruction rather than using drill-oriented worksheets on thinking skills as a separate component of the curriculum. As research indicates, students require extensive practice over extended periods to learn to apply learning strategies effectively (Nist & Simpson, 1990; Pressley, 1995). If teachers spend a large amount of instructional time focusing on drills related to thinking skills, they neglect the content curriculum. If strategy instruction is a key aspect of content instruction, however, teachers can use course materials as the context of strategy instruction, which results in a much more efficient use of instructional time.

Cognitive methods emphasize three main categories of learning strategies: cognitive, metacognitive, and social/affective strategies. However, recent research on learning strategies used by CLD students demonstrates that these students also use some unique strategies that fall under a fourth category—cross-linguistic strategies (García, 1998; Jimenez, García, & Pearson, 1996). **Cognitive learning strategies** involve the mental or physical manipulation of information. These strategies include classification, linking new information to prior knowledge, and summarizing (Chamot, 2009; Chamot & O'Malley, 1994).

Metacognitive learning strategies incorporate three domains: awareness of one's own cognitive abilities, the ability to discern the difficulty of a task, and knowing how and when to use specific strategies (Flavell & Wellman, 1977). This awareness of the learning process involves (1) deciding how to approach a task;

> **Illustrated Concept 9.1**
>
> Cognitive learning strategies focus on providing the students with space to form predictions and make inferences. If conducting scientific experiments in the classroom, provide a brief introduction to each experiment. Then allow time for students to predict what they think will happen by using context from the introduction and their prior knowledge and experiences.

■ **Snapshot of Classroom Practice 9.1**   Graphic Organizers

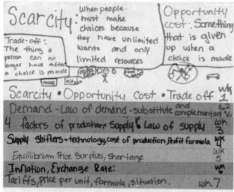

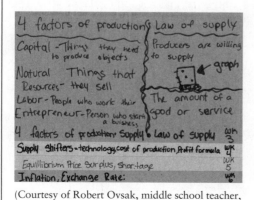

The capacity to create and maximize *graphic organizers* is a learning strategy with applications in a variety of subject areas. Through the hands-on activities of this strategy, CLD students gain multiple and authentic opportunities to demonstrate what they know (declarative knowledge) and what they know how to do (procedural knowledge). In the middle school example here, the social studies teacher has taught students graphic organization through the use of a "foldable." As students use this strategy to support their understanding of economics lessons throughout a unit, they are able to organize their learning and use the tool to develop their metacognitive skills.

At the beginning of each week throughout the unit, the students were asked to reread, rephrase, and record the content and language (e.g., vocabulary) they had learned the previous week. Students were encouraged to write using both the L1 and L2 and include illustrations that supported their learning and retention of the information. Then they shared their ideas and learning with the rest of the class.

(Courtesy of Robert Ovsak, middle school teacher, Emporia, Kansas)

Global Connections 9.1
Student learning strategies help build students' cognitive belief systems about their potential to learn a new language and their ability to be academically successful. Students who identify the most useful strategies to scaffold their own learning often have greater success in the classroom. Students learning in EFL, ESL, or bilingual contexts will all benefit from using learning strategies to access new language and concepts, monitor their comprehension, and become self-evaluators of their own knowledge-acquiring processes.

(2) self-monitoring of understanding and producing language; and (3) self-assessment of how well one is attaining cognitive, academic, and linguistic objectives. Specific metacognitive strategies include skimming for information, monitoring comprehension and production, and reflecting on what one has learned (Chamot, 2009; Chamot & O'Malley, 1994).

Social/affective learning strategies involve the use of socially mediated learning and efforts to lower one's own affective filter. In socially mediated learning, students interact with one another in order to better understand content and to develop language skills naturally. In classrooms that focus on socially mediated learning, students work collaboratively to solve problems. This student-centered time allows students to negotiate meaning with their teachers and with other students by asking for more information and clarifying misconceptions. Using affective strategies such as positive **self-talk** encourages students to lower their affective filters. Instead of telling themselves *I can't do this,* or *I'll never understand anything,* students use self-talk to tell themselves they can succeed—*I can do this if I break it down into smaller steps,* or *I will understand more in a few months. Language learning takes time* (Chamot, 2009; Chamot & O'Malley, 1994).

Cross-Linguistic Strategies

Cross-linguistic learning strategies constitute the most recently researched area of CLD student strategy use. Because the use of learning strategies with students

theory *into* Practice 9.1

According to Chamot (2009), classification schemes that organize learning strategies into categories are primarily developed to support educational research. Depending on learner and instructional goals, different classification systems can coexist. In language learning classrooms, students must develop the metacognitive skills needed for selecting and using effectively the strategies that will best support them in meeting their learning needs and accomplishing specific language learning tasks. The organization of language learning strategies into the broad categories delineated in this text—cognitive strategies, metacognitive strategies, and social/affective strategies—reflects research in first and second language contexts as well as the first edition of *The CALLA Handbook* (Chamot & O'Malley, 1994).

For instructional purposes, Chamot (2009) provided a simplified classification scheme that organizes language learning strategies into two categories: metacognitive strategies and task-based strategies. Metacognitive strategies encourage students to plan, monitor, evaluate, and manage their learning. Task-based strategies ask learners to (1) use what they know—*cognitive strategies*; (2) use their senses—*sensory strategies*; (3) use their organizational skills—*memory strategies*; and (4) use a variety of resources—includes *social and affective strategies*.

■ *With which types of strategies are you most familiar? How might you support students' development of metacognitive and task-based strategies within your current or future teaching context?*

evolved from research on learning strategy use by monolingual students, research on cross-linguistic strategies had (until recently) been neglected. This lack of focus on cross-linguistic strategies for second language learners has, in a way, denied the power and legitimacy of a child's first language as well as a critical part of the child's identity. Students who have learned two or more languages have unique resources for negotiating meaning. For example, bilingual students are often able to code-switch, which means that they sometimes use both languages in the same conversation to express themselves. **Code-switching**, however, is not only about creating communicative meaning through using multiple languages in one conversation but also about the social meaning that depends on the context (Auer, 1999).

Bilingual students also frequently use a second strategy, *translation,* but the effectiveness of the strategy depends on its use. García (1998) found that when successful bilingual students translated text, they paraphrased meaning, whereas less successful language learners tended to translate text word for word. García, as well as other researchers, has also found that bilingual students benefit from recognizing cognates and using them to construct meaning in the second language (García, 1998; Jimenez, 1997; Jimenez et al., 1996). However, bilingual students may gain an advantage from explicit instruction in using cognates as a reading comprehension strategy (García, 1998).

Finally, bilingual students who understand that reading in all languages is a similar process and that the strategies they use to negotiate meaning in one language can be applied to negotiating meaning in the second language tend to be more successful language learners (Jimenez, 1997; Jimenez et al., 1996). Figure 9.1 compares the strategy use of more successful language learners with that of less successful language learners, as evidenced in the literature (Chamot & El-Dinary, 2000; Jimenez et al., 1996). For a more comprehensive description of learning strategies and the cognitive approach, see Chapters 2 and 6.

Students at the secondary level, as well as adult learners, in EFL and ESL programs benefit from explicit guidance on how to use their native language as a natural scaffold while they transition into another language. Too often these older students acquiring English are placed in classrooms where the language and content are oversimplified, thus having little to no appeal to the learner. Finding authentic texts and academic content that is already familiar to the learner, while explicitly teaching cross-linguistic strategies, sets the stage for the acceleration of English language development. Currently, EFL programs around the world are transitioning from a grammar-based approach to a more communicative and cognitive focus in teaching English.

Cognitive Teaching Methods for Instructing CLD Students

Research on second language acquisition and cognitive development in the 1980s and 1990s led to the specification of a cognitive approach to teaching language learners. The most well-known method arising from this research is the cognitive

■ **f i g u r e   9.1**   CLD Students and Learning Strategies

More successful language learners

1. Are more likely to rely on background knowledge (inferences, predictions, elaborations).
2. Tend to focus more on metacognitive strategies.
3. Are more flexible at adapting strategy use to fit with a particular task; are more flexible in strategy use.
4. Tend to use multiple strategies to resolve situations.
5. Tend to view comprehension holistically; an unknown word does not hinder comprehension.
6. Often use more complex strategies more appropriately.
7. Usually focus on meaning.

All students benefit from explicit strategy instruction.

Less successful language learners

1. Are more likely to use phonetic decoding.
2. Tend to focus on cognitive strategies when they use strategies.
3. Are more likely to use strategies that are ineffective for a task; are less flexible in strategy use.
4. Tend to use only one strategy to resolve a situation.
5. Use fewer strategies than more successful language learners.
6. View comprehension discretely; get stuck on a word; comprehension is lost in the details.
7. Tend to focus more on form or structure.

academic language learning approach (CALLA), a teaching method developed by Anna Uhl Chamot and Michael O'Malley (1994). Extensive field-testing has created a body of research supporting the effectiveness of the CALLA method (Chamot, 1995, 2007; Chamot & El-Dinary, 1999, 2000; Chamot & O'Malley, 1996). The following section provides an overview of the CALLA instructional method.

The CALLA Method

The **CALLA method** was developed from the research on learning strategy use among language learning students (O'Malley & Chamot, 1990; O'Malley, Chamot, Stewner-Manzanares, Russo, & Küpper, 1985a, 1985b; Paris & Winograd, 1990; Wenden & Rubin, 1987). During the 1980s, researchers became interested in and began examining learning strategy use by students who were acquiring English. Many of the researchers interviewed students who were identified by their teachers as successful learners to determine which strategies the students used to comprehend and acquire the second language. They found that the students identified as more successful learners were aware of the strategies they employed to learn the new language. The researchers used the information gathered to create an inventory of language strategies and their applications as used by more successful language learners (O'Malley et al., 1985a).

Later, researchers created studies to discover if the strategies applied by more successful language learners could be explicitly taught to less successful language learners. They found that these strategies could, in fact, be explicitly taught and that less successful language learners who learned to use the new strategies became better language learners (O'Malley et al., 1985b). In subsequent studies, researchers found that more successful language learners used a greater number of strategies and selected more appropriate strategies for a given task than less successful language learners (O'Malley, Chamot, & Küpper, 1989). These studies, in addition to the work of other researchers such as Cummins, Collier, and Thomas, compelled Chamot and O'Malley to create the CALLA method in order to provide educators with a framework from which to operate when helping students to enhance their cognitive academic language proficiency (CALP) (Chamot & O'Malley, 1994).

Chamot and O'Malley designed the CALLA method to provide intermediate CLD students with (1) grade-level–appropriate cognitive and academic instruction; (2) instruction that promotes second language development (reading, writing, speaking, and listening) in content areas; and (3) instruction that focuses on explicit instruction in using learning strategies (Chamot, 1995). Consequently, CALLA lessons include content, language, and learning strategy objectives. Although Chamot and O'Malley (1994) originally recommended CALLA for intermediate students, research on its implementation has shown that the method is also effective with beginning students, as well as with native-English-speaking students, in developing higher-order thinking and literacy skills (Chamot, 1995; Montes, 2002). Use of CALLA has also expanded to implementation in bilingual programs in which the students' native language is used to provide CALLA instruction (Chamot, 2009).

CALLA and Learning Strategy Instruction

The CALLA method focuses on explicitly teaching language learners to understand and tactically apply metacognitive, cognitive, and social/affective strategies (Chamot, 2009; Chamot & O'Malley, 1994). Table 9.1 offers a synopsis of sample descriptions, potential benefits, and research foundations for the three types of learning strategies emphasized by the CALLA method. Four foundational beliefs, summarized here, form the basis of explicit learning strategy instruction according to the CALLA method (Chamot, 2009; Chamot & O'Malley, 1994).

- *Students can learn more effectively when they are mentally active and strategic.* Students who are mentally engaged in learning and who, for example, relate new information to existing language and content knowledge and who monitor their comprehension and language production are better learners.
- *Students can learn strategies.* Students who are unfamiliar with learning strategies can be taught to use such strategies appropriately and with increased frequency, if provided with proper instruction, modeling, and support.
- *Students can use learning strategies to increase their achievement on language and content tasks.* Students who use learning strategies effectively are better able to manage their efforts toward task completion by utilizing available assets and resources.

■ **t a b l e 9 . 1**   Selected Learning Strategies Emphasized by the Methods of the Cognitive Approach: Descriptions, Benefits, and Research Foundations

METACOGNITIVE			
Strategy	**Strategy Description**	**Benefits of Strategy for CLD Students**	**Research Base**
Graphic organizers (e.g., KWL charts and other organizational planning tools)	K—Ask the student what she or he knows about the topic. W—Ask the student what she or he wants to know about the topic. L—At the end of the lesson, ask the student what she or he learned from the lesson.	By asking the student what he or she knows about the topic, the teacher is engaging the CLD student's background knowledge and is preassessing. By asking what the student wants to know, the teacher is actively engaging the CLD student in setting goals for learning. Finally, when the teacher asks the student what he or she has learned, comprehension is being assessed and reinforced.	Armbruster, Anderson, & Meyer, 1991; Gordon & Rennie, 1987
Self-monitoring	The language learner monitors his or her use of strategies.	By engaging in the active monitoring of the use of strategies in learning, the CLD student is able to assess and refine strategies in practice that will enhance comprehension and capacity building across subject areas.	Anderson, 2002; Bialystok, 1981; Miller, Giovenco, & Rentiers, 1987; Payne & Manning, 1992

COGNITIVE			
Strategy	**Strategy Description**	**Benefits of Strategy for CLD Students**	**Research Base**
Elaboration of background knowledge	The English learner draws on background knowledge and prior experiences to make meaningful connections to the lesson.	By building on her or his prior knowledge as a basis for constructivist connections to new learning, the student increases the likelihood of retaining new language and concepts.	Au, 1980; Spires, Gallini, & Riggsbee, 1992
Predicting/making inferences	The CLD student anticipates what is coming in the text or lesson by making predictions based on contextual cues.	Predicting and making inferences encourages CLD students to use context to construct meaning.	Carr, Dewitz, & Patberg, 1983; Jimenez, 1997

■ **t a b l e   9 . 1**   Continued

SOCIAL/AFFECTIVE			
Strategy	**Strategy Description**	**Benefits of Strategy for CLD Students**	**Research Base**
Questioning for clarification	The student asks questions to elaborate on material or verify comprehension, thereby reducing anxiety.	Ongoing questioning and reflection on content enables the student to continually evaluate his or her comprehension of new concepts/content and recognize the progress that he or she is making.	Jimenez, 1997; Muñiz-Swicegood, 1994
Cooperative learning	The CLD student works with peers to complete activities and share information, thereby maximizing social and communicative interaction in the learning process.	Vygotsky (1978) has argued that comprehension is enhanced when the student is able to work cooperatively with her or his peers to build and foster a deeper level of understanding, especially when she or he learns from a more capable peer.	Vygotsky, 1978; Moll, 1990

- *Students can apply learning strategies to new tasks and content areas.* Students who are supported in developing metacognitive awareness of how strategies work, when they should be implemented, and which strategies work best for them as learners can apply such strategies to future learning endeavors.

These foundations suggest that it is possible to improve student achievement and language acquisition through a variety of instructional actions explicitly designed to focus learning. Specifically, such actions focus learning on active participation, strategy development and use, and capacity building for the transfer of strategies learned across subject areas.

The Five Phases of the CALLA Instructional Method

Lessons designed from the perspective of the CALLA method follow a specific five-phase instructional sequence: preparation, presentation, practice, evaluation, and expansion. This sequence provides scaffolding for students as they progress through the phases by gradually shifting from student dependence on the teacher to employ strategies and content concepts to the student's independent ability to apply the declarative and procedural knowledge he or she has learned (Chamot, 2009; Chamot & O'Malley, 1994). The following sections of this chapter describe how to teach content and strategies in each phase of the CALLA instructional sequence.

Illustrated Concept 9.2

Metacognitive learning strategies highlight students' ability to think about their own thinking. To promote this type of strategy use, allow students to choose which techniques will be the most effective for their success. For example, when introducing a writing assignment, encourage students to use the brainstorming technique that works best for them: freewriting, lists, mapping/webbing, six journalist questions (who, what, when, where, why, how), small group discussion, or role-play.

For the purposes of illustration, an example from the hypothetical Mrs. Reddy's first-grade mathematics lessons accompanies each phase of CALLA instruction. Her first-grade class is located in a rural community. The class includes non-native and native-English-speaking students. The students' stages of second language acquisition range from the preproduction to the intermediate fluency stages of English language proficiency. (See Chapter 3 for a description of the stages of second language acquisition [SLA].) The languages of the class include Bosnian, Spanish, and English. Mrs. Reddy has chosen to use the CALLA method in her class because she knows that, although all her students benefit from explicit instruction in and modeling of learning strategies, without this kind of differentiated instruction, her language learners are not likely to succeed academically.

The Preparation Phase. The **preparation phase of CALLA** primarily emphasizes students' prior knowledge and experiences (Chamot, 2009; Chamot & O'Malley, 1994). This phase is the cornerstone of the entire learning experience because the relevance of new concepts and language to a student's prior knowledge and experiences is a crucial factor in long-term memory retention (Jensen, 2008). In other words, students will only understand and remember new concepts and language if they can relate new information to what they already know. Unfortunately, students do not always make these critical connections independently. Accordingly, effective CALLA teachers start new learning experiences by helping their students establish connections between prior knowledge and key content concepts, language, and strategy applications.

The preparation phase of the CALLA method emphasizes the concepts, language, and thought processes that will allow students to attain the lesson's **content objectives, language objectives,** and **learning strategy objectives.** Consequently, when planning the lesson's objectives, it is important that the language of the objectives reflects the higher-order thinking that is a targeted outcome of the lesson. The verbs depicted in Figure 9.2 are categorized according to the original levels of Bloom's taxonomy of educational objectives (Bloom, 1956) and can help educators develop objectives that guide students to the appropriate levels of cognitive engagement. The cognitive levels of Bloom's taxonomy, listed in order of increasing complexity, are as follows: knowledge, comprehension, application, analysis, synthesis, and evaluation.

Within the preparation phase of the CALLA instructional sequence, the teacher provides the students with an overview of the lesson's theme and objectives in order to give them a general idea of what they will learn and why the concepts and skills are important. Next, the teacher guides the students through hands-on and visual activities that promote reflection on how the students' personal and educational experiences relate to these new concepts, strategies, and skills. This reflection also assists the teacher and students in identifying areas of student inexperience and misunderstanding. The teacher can then use his or her knowledge of student inexperience, as well as knowledge of students' strengths and assets, to sculpt the lesson to the specific cognitive, academic, and linguistic

■ **f i g u r e 9 . 2** Action Verbs Describing Each Level of Bloom's Taxonomy

Evaluation

A focus on judging the personal value or usefulness of given information/topics

Evaluate, judge, assess, reflect, appraise

Synthesis

A focus on integrating prior knowledge and experiences with new information to create a new conceptual understanding

Hypothesize, synthesize, integrate, design a new . . . , formulate

Analysis

A focus on understanding the relationship between facts/concepts and how the facts/concepts are organized within the topic

Categorize, relate, distinguish relevant from irrelevant information, conclude, identify assumptions, support conclusions with evidence

Application

A focus on making generalizations using information related to the topic

Apply, predict, relate, demonstrate, solve

Comprehension

A focus on understanding the information related to the topic

Translate, interpret, infer, generalize, summarize, estimate

Knowledge

A focus on factual recall regarding the topic

Recall, define, recite, recognize, describe, tell

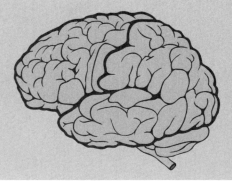

■ **t a b l e   9 . 2**   Challenges and Accommodations for CLD Students in the Classroom

Content Area	Vocabulary/Structures	Cognition	Culturally Unfamiliar Topics
Language arts	Colloquial language Dialects Archaic language English character names Academic syntax Metaphors Idioms Introductory prepositional phrases Personification	Reading/writing strategies Irony Symbols Sequence of events Foreshadowing and flashback Character analysis Motive Mood Tone Theme	Settings Story patterns/frameworks Cultural values Belief systems Discourse patterns (circular versus linear) Point of view Allusions specific to a particular culture
Recommendations for Promoting CLD Student Success	Select literature that reflects the identity of your CLD students. Use folktales and myths that have their origin in the cultures of your students. Select literature written by authors from underrepresented groups. Use graphic organizers (e.g., semantic maps and webs, storyboards, clusters, matrices, Venn diagrams). Use student journals. Encourage predictions about the content or conclusions of a work. Uncover background knowledge through prereading activities (e.g., agree/disagree statements). Encourage multiple viewpoints and interpretations. Offer a writing program that emphasizes a balance of fluency, clarity, and correctness. Have students/teacher read parts of the texts out loud to enhance the speaking (inflection, pronunciation, and more) and listening skills of the students. Incorporate activities that challenge students to clarify their thoughts and think critically about the material (e.g., compare different versions of the Cinderella tale).		

■ **t a b l e   9 . 2**   Continued

Content Area	Vocabulary/Structures	Cognition	Culturally Unfamiliar Topics
Mathematics	Homophones (e.g., *sum/some*) Technical terms (e.g., *exponent, quotient*) Common terms used in new ways (e.g., *mean, product*) Symbols Multiple words or phrases indicate the same mathematical operation Passive voice for questions and statements Typical syntax often reversed Comparatives Superlatives	"If . . . then . . ." statements Abstract concepts and representational nature of math	New information that clashes with previously acquired methods of notation and problem solving Culture-specific symbols Word problems drawn from unfamiliar situations
Recommendations for Promoting CLD Student Success	Use practical application problems to help beginning CLD students acquire computation skills. Incorporate explicit teaching of metacognitive strategies (e.g., planning how to solve various types of problems, self-monitoring, self-evaluation). Instruct students on the sequence of steps that should be used to solve problems. Use authentic problems and real-life situations (avoid those that accentuate class distinctions). Incorporate explicit instruction of the mathematical language related to the concepts you cover. Have students use journals to clarify ideas, justify rationales, summarize ideas, connect concepts, review material, and express frustrations, accomplishments, and discoveries. Engage students in a variety of ways, such as through cooperative learning, direct instruction, computer-assisted learning, and guided discovery. Connect concepts to the background knowledge of your students by asking them to write their own word problems. Find out how your students mentally manipulate and organize content information by encouraging them to explain their problem-solving process.		

(continued)

■ **table 9.2** Continued

Content Area	Vocabulary/Structures	Cognition	Culturally Unfamiliar Topics
Science	Technical terms (e.g., *catalyst*) Common terms with new meanings (e.g., *table, mass, solid*) Homophones (e.g., *cell/sell*) Connecting words for argumentation Passive voice Clauses	Abstract thought Reading for specific, detailed information Making inferences Forming hypotheses Cause and effect relationships Creating and defending an argument Classification	Topics tied to geographical locations and resources (e.g., boreal forest, water purification)

Recommendations for Promoting CLD Student Success	Develop instruction that emphasizes a focused, in-depth study of the major principles and unanswered questions related to a concept rather than a broad overview of general information. Use inquiry-based instruction; formulate questions to guide students and model the process. Discuss misconceptions and confusion that students may initially have about science concepts. Contextualize new terms using hands-on activities. Use a word wall for key terms (use separate word walls for different languages). Repeat or paraphrase difficult processes and concepts. Allow students to use bilingual learning logs for brainstorming, recording questions, and describing observations. Incorporate field trips to local science-related businesses. Ask students to collaboratively collect data through investigations, research, or interviews and then report to the rest of the class. Have students work in pairs or teams (maximize use of more capable peers). Allow students to choose from a list of projects to complete. Focus on the correct aspects of student responses rather than on the errors. Adapt materials by adding flowcharts, pictures, more background information, and sequence words such as *first* and *next*. Provide students with a unit organizer.

■ **table 9.2**   Continued

Content Area	Vocabulary/Structures	Cognition	Culturally Unfamiliar Topics
Social studies	Abstract terms (e.g., *liberty*) Culturally connotative meanings (e.g., justice) Complex sentence structure and use of past-tense verbs Prevalence of referent terms (e.g., *it, them*) Conjunctions and words that imply causation (e.g., *as a result, so*) Historical present tense	Cause and effect relationships Comparison and contrast Generalization and example Chronology Reading for specific details Historical narratives Multiple points of view Analysis and interpretation of historical events and patterns Reading maps, timelines, and globes Making inferences	Topics tied to democracy (e.g., voting) Famous people from American history (e.g., Abraham Lincoln) Geographical places of import (e.g., Plymouth, Massachusetts)
Recommendations for Promoting CLD Student Success	Promote a thorough, in-depth understanding of topics by using units and periodically revisiting and embellishing on previously studied material. Use prereading and prewriting activities to uncover the background knowledge of your students. Incorporate community and parental involvement. Invite guest speakers (especially those from the community). Have students conduct and share the results of interviews. Encourage students to share past experiences that relate to the topics being covered. Motivate students by having them role-play important historical figures. Use historical artifacts and encourage students to bring items from home. Use graphic organizers (e.g., semantic maps and webs, storyboards, clusters, matrices, Venn diagrams).		

needs of the students in the class. Table 9.2 provides a brief summary of research ideas from the literature (Amaral, Garrison, & Klentschy, 2002; Anstrom, 1998a, 1998b, 1999a, 1999b; Chamot, 2009; Chamot, Dale, O'Malley, & Spanos, 1992; Chamot & O'Malley, 1994; García, 1998; Kober, n.d.; Short, 1993) as well as from the authors regarding many ways in which teachers can help students overcome the challenges they often face when building knowledge in the content areas.

The essence of the preparation phase is to help students discover what they already know. The *what* in CALLA lessons includes facts, concepts, language, skills, and learning strategies. An effective CALLA teacher escorts students through a process of self-examination and brainstorming designed to uncover prior knowledge and experiences related to the topic at hand. Students can make these connections together as a class, in small groups, or with a partner. When educators fail to help students make these connections, the presentation of new information to students will be less effective because students are less likely to know how the new information relates to their existing knowledge base.

■ **Snapshot of Classroom Practice 9.2**   The Preparation Phase

A teacher uses vocabulary previews to assist her in examining her students' prior knowledge of key vocabulary terms. Students indicate if they already know a word, have seen the word before, or are unfamiliar with the word. As they read the literature, learners record the page on which they found the word. The preview provides context for vocabulary-related discussions and activities throughout the lesson.

(Courtesy of Emily Seaman, elementary teacher, Lawrence, Kansas)

The Preparation Phase: In Practice. Mrs. Reddy prepares her students for a lesson on measurement conversion by previewing the following content, language, and learning strategy objectives:

1. Content objectives
   a. Students will identify fractions as part of a whole.
   b. Students will illustrate halves and fourths.
2. Language objectives
   a. Students will say the names of their favorite foods in English.
   b. Students will write the names of their favorite foods in English.

■ Voices from the Field 9.1

Graphic Organizers for Secondary Classrooms

"Graphic organizers are important for students to organize concepts. ELL [CLD] adolescents especially need to see what they have learned and how to gather information. One of the biggest differences between adolescents and elementary students is the attitude of approach. For example, it usually works to ask elementary students, 'What do you want to learn?' in a KWL chart, whereas adolescents need to be asked, 'What does your teacher expect you to learn?' Graphic organizers are especially effective when students have the opportunity to work on them in pairs or groups. This is so critical for ELL students when considering that most high school English books lack visuals.

Another motivational aspect for adolescents is to see growth from one graphic organizer to the next. In my English IV class, ELL students track their growth in vocabulary as words move into categories of increasing familiarity and usage. Without this activity, students are often unaware of successful growth. I can also use this information for alternative planning for each unit. As the usage becomes more familiar, I can increase the complexity and change the settings of the usage, so that students can make new connections and apply prior learning to new situations. When ELL students become excited about making connections to things they already know, discipline problems usually disappear and teaching and learning is a joyful experience for everyone."

- ■ *Reprinted by permission from Thom Ressler. Copyright ©*
  by Thom Ressler, high school ESOL instructor, Kansas
  City, MO

   c. Students will listen and respond to members of their collaborative groups.
   d. Students will read or identify the initial sounds of the written words for their favorite foods.
3. Learning strategy objectives
   a. Students will relate new information to their prior knowledge and experiences.
   b. Students will work collaboratively with other students to solve problems.
   c. Students will assess the quality and accuracy of their own work.

Mrs. Reddy first chose content objectives from her school district's first-grade mathematics curriculum framework. (For more information regarding using content standards as a guide to planning instruction, refer to Chapter 6.) Then she determined three learning strategy objectives that students would need to accomplish the content objectives. She made sure to include a cognitive, a social/affective, and a metacognitive strategy. Mrs. Reddy knows that she should focus on only one new strategy at a time. Therefore, she chose the collaborative learning and prior knowledge elaboration for two of the strategies because her students already have extensive experience in applying those strategies in multiple contexts. Self-assessment was the new focus strategy. Finally, Mrs. Reddy examined the lesson's content and learning strategy objectives for natural ways to emphasize language use. Then she incorporated reading, writing, speaking, and listening objectives into her lesson plans.

Mrs. Reddy uses a wall chart checklist with the objectives listed in simplified language as a reference. For example, instead of saying, "Students will illustrate halves and fourths," the checklist says, "I can draw one-half" and "I can draw one-fourth." This wall chart becomes an important part of student learning as the students begin to develop the art of self-assessment. Each student gets a personal copy of the wall chart on a piece of paper.

As Mrs. Reddy begins the lesson, she emphasizes to the students that they will be using their prior knowledge of sharing food with others as a way of understanding fractions. In collaborative groups of four students, the students discuss with one another the foods they like to eat. Then, on a piece of chart paper, they draw pictures of their favorite foods. After making their drawings, the students write the names of the foods to the best of their abilities. (They should at least write the initial sounds for most of the food words.) Many groups also include some ending sounds as well. Mrs. Reddy circulates around the room, providing assistance to students as necessary, giving students feedback on their work, and informally assessing their progress.

As the students finish writing the food words to the best of their abilities, Mrs. Reddy points to the lesson objectives wall chart. She asks students, "Did you write the first sound for each food word? If you say *yes,* draw a smiley face next to this sentence on your paper," as she points to the sentence on the wall chart and holds up a self-assessment paper. Then she reads and draws a smile next to the sentence that says, "I can write the first sound of my food words." She walks around the room, assessing whether the students understand the self-assessment checklist.

The students share their responses as Mrs. Reddy writes the words and projects them for the class to see. She saves this list to make a pictorial word wall for all the food words. She gives the list to Bosnian- and Spanish-speaking parent volunteers so that they can make word wall cards in Bosnian and Spanish. She goes through the same self-assessment procedure using the lesson objectives wall chart, only this time the students indicate whether they have said the names of their favorite foods in English.

Next, Mrs. Reddy asks each student to choose a partner. Each pair of students gets one candy bar. Mrs. Reddy tells them to unwrap the candy bar as she unwraps hers. She tells the students not to eat the candy bar until she tells them it is okay. Then she puts her hand over her mouth and shakes her head *no* to ensure that everyone understands not to eat the candy bar. She tells them to break the candy bar into two pieces so that they can share it with each other. Subsequently, the class discusses whether the students divided each candy bar into two pieces of the same size or of different sizes. Most of the pairs divided the candy bar into two equal parts because they thought that having equal parts was the fairest way to divide. Mrs. Reddy explains that fractions are dividing something into pieces that are all the same size. She guides the students through the self-assessment procedure using the lesson objectives wall chart. This time the students indicate if they met one of the language objectives by speaking with and listening to their partners.

The Presentation Phase. In the **presentation phase of CALLA**, the teacher usually begins by presenting information, supporting what she or he says using visual or hands-on materials and uncomplicated language (guarded vocabulary). During this presentation, the teacher frequently checks for student understanding of key concepts and clarifies any misunderstandings. After the students demonstrate at least a basic understanding of key concepts, the teacher introduces and guides students through the written text for the lesson as the students practice asking questions to clarify any confusion (Chamot, 2009; Chamot & O'Malley, 1994).

The foundation for a well-planned presentation phase is making new information meaningful to students. Throughout this phase, the teacher should frequently demonstrate how the new information relates to and builds on students' prior knowledge and experiences. Because students who are learning English may not understand new concepts when they are presented orally, an effective teacher in a culturally rich classroom surrounds students with pictures, objects, demonstrations, and so forth, to support the meaning of what he or she is explaining. An effective CALLA teacher demonstrates the skills and strategies that he or she expects the students to know and apply as a result of the lesson. In bringing closure to this phase of the CALLA instruction, the teacher discusses how, why, and when to use the skills and apply the strategies.

■ **Snapshot of Classroom Practice 9.3**   The Presentation Phase

---

A teacher uses an interactive whiteboard in her classroom to reinforce new vocabulary terms presented to her students at the beginning of a unit.

(Courtesy of Deena Clark, Elementary teacher, Fort Riley, Kansas)

The Presentation Phase: In Practice. Mrs. Reddy and the class discuss the drawings the students made the previous day. Each group of students takes turns holding up their illustrations. Mrs. Reddy asks them to point out some of the foods that lend themselves to illustrating one whole (e.g., pizza, candy bars, pies). Then the students illustrate some of these foods on the chalkboard. Mrs. Reddy shows them how to divide the whole food into two equal parts, emphasizing that they are halves, and then into four equal parts, emphasizing that they are fourths.

Mrs. Reddy shows the students a large laminated picture of a pizza. Then she asks the students if they have ever eaten pizza before. All of the students have eaten pizza during lunch in the school cafeteria. She asks them if they eat the whole pizza all by themselves (as she holds up the picture of the whole pizza in one hand), or if they eat one piece at a time, and she holds up a picture of a slice of pizza that is one-fourth of a whole pizza. The students all indicate that they eat the piece of pizza. Mrs. Reddy passes out to each student one cutout picture of a piece of pizza that is one-fourth of a whole. The students get into groups of four. Then Mrs. Reddy guides the discussion toward what a "whole" pizza looks like and verbally compares it to what "part" of a pizza looks like.

Each group also gets a picture of a whole pizza that is the same size as four of the pictures of pizza pieces. The students practice making whole pizzas out of their pieces and dividing their whole pizza into four parts. She explains to students that today they are learning about *fractions*. A fraction is part of a whole. For example, a pizza that does not have any pieces missing is one whole pizza. A pizza that has some pieces missing has only a fraction or a part of the pizza left for people to eat. Mrs. Reddy explains to the students that fractions help people show how to break up whole candy bars, pizzas, or pies into equal pieces to share with friends. Mrs. Reddy and the students discuss and the students self-assess, using the self-assessment checklist, their ability to make fractions from wholes and to put fractions together to make wholes.

The Practice Phase. The **practice phase of CALLA** is much more student-centered than previous phases. In this stage, students collaborate in hands-on activities to practice applying new concepts, language, and strategies. Each activity is designed to provide students with the practice they need to attain content, language, and learning strategy objectives. Through scaffolding, the teacher provides more support in the beginning and less support as students become more adept at applying what they are learning.

All CLD students need a supportive environment in which to experiment during the practice phase. They will be working with new information, language, and strategies, so they will make mistakes. During this phase, teacher support is critical. The students do not have enough practice and skill to apply new understandings independently, and their understandings may be naive at this point. Consequently, an effective CALLA teacher will use this time to work with collaborative groups to provide additional modeling when necessary, use questioning to guide students into deeper understandings, and clarify misunderstandings. Teachers can use this time to tailor small-group instruction to the individual needs of the students.

The Practice Phase: In Practice. Mrs. Reddy tells the students to form groups once again. She gives each of them a fresh piece of chart paper, and each student draws a line down the middle of the paper. On one side of the chart paper, the students draw some of the foods from their original drawings. On the other side of the line, they illustrate what the foods look like when half of the portion originally drawn is missing. Then Mrs. Reddy asks her students to examine the illustrations on each

■ **Snapshot of Classroom Practice 9.4**   The Practice Phase

In this photograph, students match vocabulary terms and pictures. For example, the students have grouped the terms *rural, country,* and *very few people* with the pictures *tractor, farm,* and *wheat field.*

(Courtesy of Cara LeMoine, elementary teacher, Fort Riley, Kansas)

side of their paper and discuss the difference between the parts and the wholes. The students conclude that the items on one side show foods that are whole and the items on the other side show foods that are a fraction or part of a whole.

Mrs. Reddy models the fraction one-half by drawing a circle or pizza on the chalkboard and dividing it into two equal parts. Then she shades in one of the two parts. Next, she does the same with a rectangle or a candy bar. Under each illustration, she writes "/." She asks the students how many pieces are in the whole pizza or candy bar. They respond, "Two." She explains that when writing a fraction, they should put the whole number on the bottom of the horizontal line. Then she erases half of both the candy bar and the pizza. She asks the students how many pieces are left. The students reply, "One." Mrs. Reddy explains that when writing a fraction, they should put the number of pieces on top of the line.

Next, Mrs. Reddy models the fraction one-fourth by drawing a circle and dividing it into four equal parts. She explains to the students that the size and shape of the pizza or candy bar does not change, but the number of pieces you cut them into can change. In this case, they would cut their pizza and candy bar into four equal pieces. If the students have three friends instead of one, they would make four pieces because two pieces would not be enough for four friends. She tells the students that the pieces are called fourths because there are four pieces. Mrs. Reddy shades in one out of the four parts. Then she does the same with a rectangle and she writes "/" next to each illustration.

The students form collaborative groups. Mrs. Reddy tells them to make their own halves and fourths on the other side of their chart paper. Each group presents its fractions to the other groups. Mrs. Reddy leads the students through the process of self-assessment using the lesson objectives wall chart.

Working in small groups throughout the lesson helps the English learners feel more comfortable with the concept of fractions. A common language of terms such as *fractions, halves,* and *fourths* should become easier for students to engage

Social/affective learning strategies promote a low-risk classroom environment for all students. When working with new material, provide numerous opportunities for students to ask you and their peers clarifying questions. Encourage students to talk to themselves about the content as they move through the steps of an assignment. In both cases, remember to provide positive, reassuring feedback to keep students' affective filters lowered.

in as they progress through the lesson. Using the technique of cutting commonly known foods into equal pieces and actually sharing candy bars allows students to relate the content knowledge to what they already know and to engage in hands-on learning at the same time.

The Evaluation Phase. In the **evaluation phase of CALLA,** the students are given the opportunity to reflect on their own learning. In many models of teaching and learning, teachers tend to be the primary assessors. In the CALLA method, however, students become important assessors of their own work. Developing higher-order thinking skills is a major focus of CALLA, and self-assessment is a critical metacognitive strategy (Chamot, 2009; Chamot & O'Malley, 1994). If students are to understand themselves as learners and take responsibility for their own learning, then they must learn to examine the quality of their own work and determine whether they are achieving lesson objectives. This process of self-assessment is critical to becoming a lifelong, self-directed learner (Murry, 1996; Murry & Herrera, 1999).

For language learners who are not accustomed to evaluating themselves, this phase can be particularly difficult. Students need to see others evaluating themselves. They benefit from discussion of the essentials of a high-quality project or assignment. They also need practice evaluating work together. Examples of exemplary work and collaborative, student-created rubrics help students develop the discernment needed to effectively evaluate their own thinking and performance. Eventually, after much modeling and practice, students are able to evaluate their understanding of lesson objectives, as well as the quality of their classroom products.

The Evaluation Phase: In Practice. Mrs. Reddy uses both group and self-assessment in the evaluation phase of CALLA. The lesson on fractions ends with the students commenting on one another's fraction charts with illustrations, a form of peer evaluation. Then Mrs. Reddy leads the students through a review of the entire self-assessment checklist as the students discuss the objectives they thought were easy for them and the ones they thought were difficult. Mrs. Reddy explains to the students that knowing what they can do well and what is difficult for them is important because it will help them decide what they should practice. Mrs. Reddy reteaches the objectives that the students said were still difficult.

The Expansion Phase. In the **expansion phase of CALLA,** students integrate the new knowledge they are gaining with their existing knowledge base. Students reflect on the relevance of information to what they have experienced and learned in the past and how they can apply it to tasks or to their own lives (Chamot, 2009; Chamot & O'Malley, 1994). This phase stimulates students to take possession of the new knowledge as their own. To successfully take possession of this new knowledge, students may need to reflect on the ways in which their previous understandings need to be revised in order to incorporate them into what they are learning (Chamot, 2009; Chamot & O'Malley, 1994).

In this phase, the teacher leads students to reflect on how the new knowledge they have learned can be applied in various situations in their lives or in the world in general. Then the students choose (or are assigned) an activity that will allow them to apply the new knowledge for personal meaning (Chamot, 2009; Chamot & O'Malley, 1994). Encouraging students to apply new knowledge to meaningful activities facilitates the process of integrating the new knowledge into students' existing conceptual understandings.

The Expansion Phase: In Practice. For homework the students are asked to illustrate and write two fractions that represent two ways they use fractions at home. For example, if a student shares a twin popsicle with a sibling, the student can represent his or her portion with a fraction. Another example might involve family members. Perhaps a student has four family members living at home. In this case, the student could represent the fraction of the family present in the house when his or her mother is home alone. When the students return with their home fractions, they show their fractions to the class and explain how they see fractions in their lives.

For an example of a CALLA lesson plan in social studies for students in sixth grade, see Figure 9.3.

Choosing Learning Strategies with CALLA: Suggestions

Chamot and O'Malley (Chamot, 2009; Chamot & O'Malley, 1994) offer several suggestions for choosing and teaching learning strategies:

- Align strategies with content and language objectives or essential questions.
- Teach one or two related strategies at a time.
- Teach strategies using manageable tasks.
- Select research-supported strategies (beginning with easily demonstrated strategies, and including both observable strategies and mental strategies).
- Focus on strategies that students can use in many different subjects or content areas.

These suggestions for choosing learning strategies will promote effective strategy instruction because they make the strategies more relevant and accessible to students and can lower their affective filters. Each of these suggestions for choosing and teaching learning strategies is explored more comprehensively in the following sections.

Aligning Learning Strategies. First, Chamot and O'Malley (Chamot, 2009; Chamot & O'Malley, 1994) recommend that the strategies taught align with content and language objectives relevant to the lesson or unit theme. A teacher should choose strategies that help students develop the communication and thinking skills necessary to successfully comprehend a situation and complete a task independently. Ideally,

■ **figure 9.3** Example of a CALLA Lesson Plan: Grade 6

Lesson Title: Buddha's Visions vs. Hindu Reincarnation

Strategy: advanced organizer (Venn diagram) – cognitive

Content Objectives:
- We will be able to define the word *Nirvana*.
- We will be able to compare the Hindu belief of reincarnation with Buddha's visions of his past lives, which led him to Nirvana.

Language Objectives:
- We will discuss the similarities and differences between the Hindu belief of reincarnation and Nirvana in partners and as a whole group.
- We will listen to and comprehend group members' ideas as we finish reading the story of Prince Siddhartha (Buddha).
- We will interpret and report the information from the story of Prince Siddhartha in a Venn diagram.
- We will write a paragraph about information contained in a Venn diagram.

Learning Strategy Objectives:
- We will make connections between our prior knowledge and new information.
- We will use a Venn diagram as an advanced organizer to support our learning.
- We will collaborate with peers to complete the Venn diagram.

Materials:
chart paper (five pieces), markers, SmartBoard, *Prince Siddhartha: The Story of Buddha* by Jonathan Landaw

PROCEDURES

Preparation Activity:

The teacher will begin by reviewing material from the previous lesson, including what the students have learned up to this point in reading *Prince Siddhartha: The Story of Buddha* by Jonathan Landaw. This will be done by asking students various questions as an entire class. The teacher will record students' responses on the front board.

To review further, the teacher will ask students to get into their reading groups (previously selected by the teacher, based on student abilities and language proficiency levels). Each of the five reading groups will be given a piece of chart paper and a marker for each of its members. The teacher will ask that all students in each group write an idea (in either L1 or L2) of what they remember about the Hindu belief of reincarnation. After five minutes have passed, the teacher will ask each group to share the responses on their paper with the rest of the class.

The students will then get back together with their groups to finish reading *Prince Siddhartha: The Story of Buddha*. The teacher will ask students to locate the key word *Nirvana* as they continue reading, and to individually document what they believe the definition to be. Students will also be asked to note ideas that they think are similar to or different from the

■ **figure 9.3**   Continued

ideas written on their chart paper about reincarnation. When the groups are finished reading, the members will share their ideas about Nirvana and reincarnation, and engage in a discussion. Individually, students will then write their own sentence about the meaning of Nirvana and include an illustration as a visual representation.

Presentation Activity:

The teacher will ask for volunteers to share their definition and illustration of Nirvana with the rest of the class. The teacher will also take this opportunity to engage the students in further discussion by asking questions, and will also help resolve any misconceptions.

With students back at their desks, the teacher will introduce the concept of a Venn diagram. Using the SmartBoard, the teacher will display a Venn diagram comparing and contrasting cats and dogs, as an example. The teacher will explain that the two circles represent ideas/characteristics that are different about the two subjects, but that the middle part, where the two circles overlap, expresses the subjects' similarities. The students will be called on individually to come up to the SmartBoard and move different statements (i.e., "I have four legs," "I bark," etc.) and pictures (which will be helpful for students who are less proficient in English) into the correct parts of the Venn diagram. The teacher will then ask students why they think a Venn diagram is considered an advanced organizer and how it can be useful in their learning.

Practice Activity:

In partners (the person to the right/left in the students' learning group), students will use knowledge gleaned from *Prince Siddhartha: The Story of Buddha,* information on reincarnation from the groups' chart paper, and previous readings and discussions to create a Venn diagram comparing the Hindu belief of reincarnation and Buddha's visions of his past life that led him to Nirvana. Although the students will be collaborating together, each student will create his or her own diagram. The teacher will encourage students to use illustrations in their Venn diagram as well. For students with a lower level of English proficiency, only three ideas in each section will be required, while students with a higher proficiency will need at least four.

The teacher will monitor sets of partners and provide feedback as observations are made. When students have completed this task, the teacher will ask for volunteers to share their Venn diagram with the rest of the class. As students present, the rest of the students will refer to their own Venn diagram and add any new ideas, indicating that they borrowed it by placing a star next to the sentence or image.

Self-Evaluation Activity:

The teacher will ask the entire class to verbally reflect on how the Venn diagram helped them to identify the similarities and differences between the two topics, and to indicate what those similarities and differences are. The teacher will also ask students to verbally answer if they would use this type of organizer in the future (and why or why not), and in what situations they would consider using it again to enrich their learning.

(continued)

■ **figure 9.3**   Continued

Expansion Activity:

For homework, students will write a paragraph about the information contained in their Venn diagram, explaining the differences and similarities that they found. In addition, students will include an opinion statement on which belief they agree with the most, or why they do not agree with either of the beliefs. For students with a lower level of English proficiency, a full paragraph with this information is not necessary. Rather, they may write a sentence with an accompanying illustration. Alternatively, a spoken statement may be given the next day in class.

Source: From Center for Intercultural and Multilingual Advocacy (CIMA). (2013). *CALLA lesson plan: Buddha's visions vs. Hindu reincarnation.* Lesson plan created at Kansas State University, Manhattan, KS. Copyright © 2013 Socorro G. Herrera. Reprinted with permission from Socorro G. Herrera.

content, language, and learning strategy objectives describe content-specific declarative and procedural knowledge that students need to think and communicate like a person proficient in the field. For example, a mathematics student needs to learn to understand, apply, and communicate information like a mathematician. Therefore, learning strategies that support the student in understanding, applying, and communicating knowledge related to the learning objectives should be the natural choice in selecting strategies to be taught explicitly during a particular lesson or unit.

Aligning Learning Strategies: In Practice. Effective teachers of the CALLA method choose learning strategies that students will need in order to independently demonstrate proficiency in both language and content objectives. For example, Mrs. Huang, a ninth-grade biology teacher, decides to focus on classification as a strategy for a unit covering the biological classification system (i.e., kingdom, phylum, class, order, family, genus, and species). She wants her students to understand how particular sets of characteristics can distinguish one group of organisms from another. In another example, Mr. Mambo, an eighth-grade social studies teacher, chooses the monitoring of listening and reading comprehension as a natural strategy for a reading- and video-based lesson on how the writings of Gandhi influenced the views of Dr. Martin Luther King Jr. regarding nonviolent resistance. He knows that his students will become more independent learners in his class if they learn to recognize when they do not comprehend oral or written language and learn to take corrective steps in order to create meaning. Both Mrs. Huang and Mr. Mambo choose strategies that students will need to use in order to think and communicate in English like experts in their content areas.

Beginning with a Limited Number of Learning Strategies. In teaching, according to the guidelines of the CALLA method, educators should begin explicit strategy instruction with one strategy or two closely related strategies. Students need to concentrate intensively on understanding and applying one or two strategies in multiple ways in various situations. They need to become adept at using current strategies before learning to use additional strategies. Learning a few strategies at a time helps students gain confidence in their abilities to learn and apply strategies

(Chamot, 2009; Chamot & O'Malley, 1994). Many teachers underestimate the amount of time and effort needed for students to acquire new understandings and skills. Sometimes adults do not understand that concepts that often seem obvious to them are more difficult for students who have not yet learned the material. For those students who have not had the modeling and practice necessary to learn a new concept or skill, the *obvious* may not be so obvious.

Beginning with a Limited Number of Learning Strategies: In Practice. Miss Chen, a high school literature teacher, knows that if she chooses several strategies on which to focus, her students may feel overwhelmed and not learn any of the strategies thoroughly because their attention is divided. If she chooses one or two strategies, however, students can concentrate on learning to apply the strategies in many different ways and in many different situations. Miss Chen also realizes that literature can be a difficult class for many of her CLD students because the meaning of writing reflects an author's culture. Keeping the culture-specific nature of literature in mind, Miss Chen chooses literature for her class that was written by authors from many different cultures. Consequently, students, and sometimes even Miss Chen, may not have the necessary experiential background to understand the true meaning of the literature.

Miss Chen chooses to teach her students to use their prior knowledge as a strategy for creating meaning as one of her first strategies of the school year. Because she has such a culturally rich classroom, her students can serve as cultural informants for one another. For example, the Dominican students in Miss Chen's class help the other students in their collaborative groups to understand their cultural insights regarding the Dominican Republic before, during, and after reading *How the García Girls Lost Their Accents* (Alvarez, 1991), a collection of vignettes about sisters who emigrate from the Dominican Republic to the United States. As the Dominican students serve as cultural informants, the other students share how their own experiences relate to the issues presented in the story.

Maximizing Manageable Tasks. Another suggestion for the initial teaching of learning strategies according to the CALLA method involves choosing a **manageable task**. For instruction involving a new strategy, teachers should choose material that has familiar information and language (Chamot, 2009; Chamot & O'Malley, 1994). If the material is too difficult, the students will not be able to concentrate as much on understanding and applying the strategy because they will also have to struggle with unfamiliar content and language. As students become more skillful at applying the new strategy, the teacher can support them as they use the strategy with less familiar topics or with tasks using more unfamiliar language. Therefore, effective teachers who use the CALLA method teach learning strategies by maximizing manageable tasks.

Maximizing Manageable Tasks: In Practice. Ms. Nguyen, a fourth-grade teacher, wants to teach her students to monitor their reading comprehension, so she chooses a manageable task to introduce the new strategy. She knows that encountering a large amount of new information while learning a new strategy might overwhelm her students. So, Ms. Nguyen decides to teach the students to monitor

dilemmas of Practice 9.1

Mr. Maxwell has been teaching U.S. and world history in high school for the past 10 years. In recent years, he has experienced a dramatic increase in the number of students who speak languages other than English at home. Mr. Maxwell is well aware that there is little support for the first languages represented by his CLD students. His English learners are failing with strategies and techniques that he feels are successful with other grade-level students, such as answering questions at the end of the chapter, reading, and completing worksheets. With the variety of English proficiencies represented in his classroom, he is frustrated trying to meet the content standards set for his courses.

■ *What should Mr. Maxwell do? Conceptual development in social studies classes calls for the thoughtful and active participation of all students. Mr. Maxwell should implement activities involving learning strategies that stress the necessary academic language. It is important that Mr. Maxwell first preassess the background knowledge of his CLD students and then focus his strategies on making connections to this background knowledge.*

■ *One way to do this might be the use of interviews, conducted by the CLD students,* *designed to ascertain family history information. The histories can then be placed on preconstructed timelines containing relevant information from the chapter being studied. The use of realia and visuals such as maps, timelines, globes, photos, documentation, and so on, is essential in Mr. Maxwell's class. He can also provide a video that the students can discuss and then freewrite about any personal associations they made. He may also want to try role-playing or reenactments to assess the students' comprehension levels, focusing on particular concepts in the lesson.*

■ *Mr. Maxwell needs to consistently implement activities that are specific to the academic language of history because the students will later be asked to listen, read, discuss, write, and make presentations regarding the information. Mr. Maxwell needs to provide opportunities for his students to engage in higher-order thinking activities in which they can demonstrate and apply what they have learned. Such opportunities are especially valuable in allowing students to relate the lesson to their cultural experiences and their personal lives.*

their reading comprehension using text that concerns a familiar topic and that contains many words her students already know. She chooses *Cam Jansen and the Mystery of the Dinosaur Bones* (Adler, 1997) because the book is written just below the fourth-grade level, the class has just finished a unit on dinosaurs, and the students have listened to other Cam Jansen mysteries as read-aloud books in the third grade. Choosing such a text will allow her students to concentrate on learning the strategy because they will not have too many aspects of reading on which to focus. As the students become more skilled in using the new strategy, Ms. Nguyen will lead them through learning to monitor their reading comprehension on less familiar topics and with more difficult text.

Maximizing Research. In selecting strategies to teach students, a teacher should look for strategies supported by either content-specific strategy research (e.g., mathematical strategies, reading strategies) or the growing body of strategy research with CLD students (Chamot, 2009; Chamot & O'Malley, 1994). Because learning strategy instruction has become a popular topic in education, many different print and electronic sources recommend teaching students various learning strategies. In choosing a strategy, however, teachers should make certain that the strategy facilitates academic, cognitive, and linguistic development among language learners. Many such research-based strategies are listed in Table 9.1.

Maximizing Research: In Practice. In his search to find appropriate, research-supported learning strategies, Mr. Diomande, a fifth-grade teacher, has read journal articles about how more successful English learners paraphrase rather than directly translate text for understanding. He decides he is going to explicitly teach the paraphrasing strategy to his students. He begins by explaining that readers who paraphrase, rather than directly translate, tend to understand text better. Next he displays a story for the class with a projector. The class reads a small part of the story together. Then Mr. Diomande covers the text and models paraphrasing by retelling the story in his own words. He asks the students to write in their first languages what the story said. The students share their responses. The process is repeated, except this time the students provide a paraphrase as a class. After practicing as a whole class, students practice other portions of the story in groups, then in pairs, and finally independently.

Focusing on Contexts. Effective CALLA teachers prioritize the teaching of learning strategies by focusing on strategies that students can use in many different contexts (Chamot, 2009; Chamot & O'Malley, 1994). If students can apply a strategy in many different classes, they are more likely to employ the strategy and reap its benefits. Consequently, teaching students in ESL/EFL classrooms highly applicable strategies rather than context-specific strategies is more likely to affect their overall academic achievement. For example, students would benefit from learning to monitor their comprehension because they could apply the strategy in all content areas. When students monitor their reading comprehension in a science class, they ensure that they are discerning and comprehending the key facts and understanding the important concepts. In a literature class, the same students monitor their reading comprehension by attending to various points of view, character development, plot analysis, themes, and symbolism. Teachers must keep in mind, however, that teaching students to employ a strategy in one circumstance does not mean that the students will recognize the strategy application in other contexts. In developing the procedural and conditional knowledge of applying learning strategies, students benefit from practice in applying the strategies in different contexts (Mayer, 1996; Pressley, 1995). Therefore, teachers who effectively use the CALLA method provide students with modeling of and opportunities to practice the same strategy in multiple contexts (Chamot, 2009; Chamot & O'Malley, 1994).

Focusing on Contexts: In Practice. Mr. Ibarra, a seventh-grade health teacher, wants to teach his English learners strategies they can use not only in his class but also in other classes. He collaborates with the seventh-grade team of teachers to choose a strategy that all the seventh-grade teachers will emphasize over the next couple weeks. The team decides to focus on the metacognitive strategy of questioning for clarification. Through the health lessons, Mr. Ibarra models asking questions for clarification by thinking aloud as if he were a student. Then he asks students to ask their own questions. On an index card, the students write interesting pieces of information they learned and a question they still have at the end of each lesson. Mr. Ibarra uses selected questions as an introduction to the next day's lesson.

New Directions

Through the preparation, presentation, practice, evaluation, and expansion phases of the CALLA instructional sequence, effective educators enable students to develop their understandings of learning strategies, content, and language. CALLA's particular emphasis on the explicit instruction of learning strategies assists educators as they guide students to improve their capacities for critical thinking and independent learning. The CALLA method was developed from a strong research base in second language acquisition and cognitive development. Nearly a decade of research on implementation of the method has demonstrated its effectiveness in helping students acquire second languages (Chamot, 1995; Chamot & El-Dinary, 2000; Montes, 2002). As a result of its robust research base and nationwide implementation, the CALLA method is perhaps the most well-known method of the cognitive approach to appropriate accommodative instruction for CLD students.

Despite the noted benefits of the CALLA method, teachers in many educational settings view it as having too much complexity and not enough ready-made materials to serve as a viable method for planning or instruction. An emerging method of the cognitive approach that addresses these types of concerns and promotes the linguistic and academic success of CLD students is biography-driven instruction (Herrera, 2010). This method has resulted from the authors' more than 15 years of work and research on effective instructional practices for CLD learners of all ages. Biography-driven instruction (BDI) emphasizes building on what students already know as they acquire new language and concepts.

A BDI lesson is conceptualized as having three phases: activation, connection, and affirmation. Teachers use one of a number of BDI strategies to provide a through-line for the activities, student interactions, and discussions that take place throughout the lesson (Herrera, Kavimandan, & Holmes, 2011; Herrera, Perez, Kavimandan, & Wessels, 2013). The strategies offer tools that scaffold the learning processes for students. Like CALLA, BDI also incorporates the use of learning objectives, such as content and language objectives, to provide transparency for students about the intended outcomes of the lesson.

During the *activation* phase, the teacher introduces the topic and the lesson's learning objectives. Students then document their existing knowledge or experiences from home, community, and school that relate to the key vocabulary and concepts. Participation of all students, regardless of level of English language proficiency, is ensured when educators allow students to record their initial associations using their native language, English, and/or drawings. The teacher purposefully observes students as they work during this phase and documents insights for later use in the lesson.

Throughout the *connection* phase, educators guide students to make connections between their background knowledge (which they documented in the activation phase) and the new material. For the rest of the class, teachers highlight how individual students' existing knowledge is relevant to, or provides a foundation for, the day's learning. As they explain and discuss target vocabulary and concepts in the context of the larger lesson, teachers make explicit connections to students' words and images. Student interaction is pivotal throughout a BDI lesson, but it is especially crucial during this phase, as students work together to make sense of the new information. Learners also are challenged to revisit their initial associations to vocabulary words and concepts in order to confirm or disconfirm their previous understandings. Educators embed social/affective, cognitive, and metacognitive learning strategies to support students' attainment of the lesson goals.

In the *affirmation* phase, educators allow students to document their linguistic and academic learning. Students use the strategy tool(s), with which they have interacted and added to throughout the lesson, to scaffold their writing, complete end-of-lesson tasks, or produce other work products that enable the teacher to assess both individual and collective learning. Students have opportunities to consider how their overall understandings of the topic were reinforced or changed, as needed, throughout the learning process. Teachers again revisit the lesson's learning objectives to affirm learning and bring closure to the lesson.

Through the three phases of a BDI lesson, educators situate students' learning in their biographies/background knowledge. As insights into student cognition discussed in Chapter 2 indicate, learning is only successful when students are able to make sense of information and find it relevant to their own lives. When teachers create a safe space for students to share past experiences, they enable students to share the wealth of knowledge that can then be used to make the lesson meaningful. This mutually beneficial relationship between teachers and students allows all learners to reach high standards while simultaneously resulting in ESL and EFL classrooms where every member of the learning community is engaged.

Connect, Engage, Challenge

CONNECT
Review and Reflect on the Reading

1. In what ways can a capacity for metacognition enhance the academic performance of CLD students?
2. In what ways would you describe the cross-linguistic strategy of code-switching?
3. Why is language learning more effective with explicit strategy instruction?
4. What are the five phases of instruction using the CALLA method?
5. What are cognitive learning strategies? Define and provide and least three examples.
6. Among the five phases of the CALLA instructional sequence, which phases are not student-centered? Why?

7. In what ways can teachers conduct frequent checks for understanding as part of the presentation phase of CALLA instruction?

8. What types of activities for language learners are appropriate in the practice phase of CALLA instruction? Why?

9. In what ways might teachers support the CLD student's ability to self-assess in the evaluation phase of CALLA instruction?

10. What is the key purpose of the expansion phase of the CALLA instructional sequence? What benefits does this phase provide for CLD students?

11. What are at least three guidelines for choosing among learning strategies, according to the CALLA method?

12. In what ways can a teacher maximize manageable tasks in selecting learning strategies?

13. In what ways can a teacher increase the likelihood that students will be able to transfer learning strategies to different contexts?

14. What specific outcomes do CLD students typically gain from learning social/affective strategies?

ENGAGE
Share What You Learned

1. This chapter explores the grounding of the CALLA method in the cognitive approach. Discuss some of the foundations and tenets of the cognitive approach. In what ways is the cognitive approach applicable to the differential learning and adjustment needs of English learners?

2. This chapter discusses research on cross-linguistic strategies used by CLD students. Some of these strategies, such as code-switching, are considered by some educators to be indicators of a lack of language acquisition in either L1 or L2. Discuss why such assumptions arise and the ways in which they should be addressed by effective professional educators of CLD students.

3. For CLD students, learning strategies should be aligned with content and language objectives. Discuss why this is so and why content, language, and learning strategy objectives should be targeted simultaneously with English learners.

CHALLENGE
It's Not Real until You Practice

Preservice Teachers

1. Observe a grade-level elementary or secondary classroom in which English learners are instructed. Identify which (if any) learning strategies discussed in this chapter are evident in the teacher's method of classroom instruction.
   - Metacognitive
   - Cognitive
   - Social/affective

   For each strategy observed, discuss the way it aided comprehension or critical thinking for CLD students in the classroom. If no strategies were observed, discuss ways in which each type of strategy could have aided comprehensibility for students acquiring English.

2. Imagine that you are an educator for an agriculture education class, a heterogeneous class with several language learners of varying proficiency levels. What strategies are well suited to meet the needs of *all* the students? Justify your answers with examples and reasons for effectiveness.

3. Select a lesson in a teacher's edition of a content-area textbook. Modify this lesson (using the strategies found in this chapter as a framework) so that the lesson content more appropriately encourages higher-order thinking for CLD students and is more comprehensible.

In-Service Teachers

1. Adapt a content-area lesson that may prove challenging for students who are acquiring English by:
   - Providing an outline to be completed as the lesson is presented
   - Asking students to write one-sentence summaries for each of the top five key concepts
   - Prompting students to draw key concepts beside each key concept summary
   - Providing an opportunity for students to work in heterogeneous groups and explain the key concepts to one another
   - Reflecting after the lesson on the following: What worked? What was a challenge? How will you address this challenge in the future?

2. To review key concepts in a content area, encourage students to state or write outcome sentences in a learning log, such as "I learned . . . ," "I was surprised . . . ," "I think . . . ," and then share with their group or with the class. Observe and document the specific ways in which outcome sentences about content concepts aid students' learning, retention, and higher-order thinking.

tips for practice

Note: Tips for practice are listed according to each of the three main categories of learning strategies essential for CLD student success and independent learning. These tips are applicable to learners in ESL and EFL educational contexts.

Tips for Implementing Cognitive Strategies

1. Allow time for the use of reference materials. The use of resources such as textbooks, dictionaries, and encyclopedias will help students make cognitive connections with the information you are providing. The Internet can also be used to help students make real-world connections to the topics being discussed.

2. Provide students with an outline of the content concepts to be discussed in the lesson. Also, provide the students time and opportunities to follow along and make notes on the outline. This will give them an idea of the important information relating to the concepts they should note and learn.

3. Read aloud information regarding the new concept to be learned. Have students discuss the information heard in small groups and then recap as a whole class. Have students work with a partner or individually to record a summary of the information in written form.

4. Use imagery to illustrate a concept or strategy. Have the students close their eyes and visualize the concept at hand. Then ask them to draw a picture of the concept being studied. Finally, ask student volunteers to explain the concept using their pictures.

5. Use the list-group-label strategy to present vocabulary and concepts before reading in order to activate prior knowledge, stimulate thinking, and set purposes for learning. With this strategy, CLD students typically work in heterogeneous groups to categorize a set of words related to the content being studied. This provides a foundation for use later when the students encounter the words in the lesson. You can provide a list of words related to the topic or provide the topic and have the students brainstorm words they associate with the topic.

6. Provide a story map that includes the setting, characters, problems, and key events leading to the solution and conclusion of the problem. Students will use the story map as a graphic representation of the story's narrative structure. Such types of maps can also be used to illustrate hierarchical and sequential relationships (see Figure 9.4 for an example of a story map).

7. Encourage students to use brainstorming during the first phase of a new lesson, when you are introducing a new content concept. Brainstorming can engage, prepare, and direct student understanding of the new concepts. This strategy also allows for creativity and idea development without immediate evaluation or critique by you or the student's peers. Each student will first list words he or she associates with the information you provide. All ideas are recorded so that everyone can view them. This strategy can be completed as a class, as a small group, in pairs, or by an individual.

8. Use mnemonics such as rhyming or acronyms to facilitate students' learning of new concept terms. For example, "King Phillip Crossed Over From Germany to Spain" is a tool for learning the biological classification system (kingdom, phylum, class, order, family, genus, and species).

Tips for Implementing Social/Affective Strategies

1. Provide extra time and opportunities for CLD students to ask clarifying questions when new concepts are introduced. Rephrase or adjust language use to suit proficiency levels for each

■ **figure 9.4**

Story Map: *Because of Winn-Dixie*

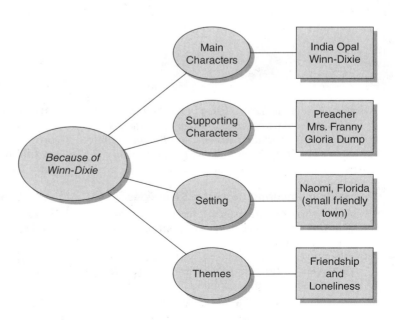

student. Questioning for clarification will help promote students' understanding of the concepts as well as encourage English learners' participation. The students will be more willing to contribute to classroom discussion if they feel comfortable with and confident about the new concepts.

2. Model self-questioning techniques to check for understanding while reading aloud. Ask questions such as, "Is this making sense to me?" or "Do I understand this?" Self-questioning will help students comprehend new content and language concepts. At the same time, the CLD students will be able to draw on prior knowledge in order to clarify the information. When the student is able to personally clarify information, his or her anxiety level goes down, and he or she is more comfortable to answer questions posed by peers or the teacher.

3. Encourage students to talk themselves through new material or challenging tasks. Self-talk is a strategy in which the language learner uses positive statements to reassure herself or himself that she or he will understand and will be able to complete each assignment. This strategy will aid students by reducing the anxiety level felt when discussing new concepts or approaching learning tasks.

4. Provide opportunities for CLD students to work in heterogeneous cooperative groups to complete an activity. Small groups allow English learners to feel more comfortable about using the second language while still being challenged to learn and comprehend the lesson. Cooperative groups allow all students to pool information to enhance understanding, solve problems, and get feedback for clarification.

Tips for Implementing Metacognitive Strategies

1. Prepare an anticipation guide that will engage students in discussion of the new concept to be learned by posting declarative statements such as, "Isaac Newton developed the theory of gravity" or "The Pythagorean theorem states that $a^2 + b^2 = c^2$." Discussion can be conducted in groups or as a whole class. The statements are to be revisited after reading about the topic to ensure the development and accuracy of student interpretation.

2. Talk aloud during the introduction of new concepts to illustrate the strategy of talking about one's thinking. This strategy, if first introduced by you, also builds vocabulary and demonstrates the sort of thinking processes that students will need as the discussion of the topic continues. To implement this strategy, first read aloud as an introduction to the topic. Pause in order to clarify meaning, connect to your prior knowledge, compare and contrast, and discuss areas that might cause confusion. Have students practice the strategy in pairs with a short additional reading passage about the topic. After one partner has an opportunity to read and talk aloud, have the next partner try it.

3. Encourage students to keep a learning log or journal throughout the academic year. The log allows for reflection on what has been learned. As illustrated in Figure 9.5, the log needs to include information the student has acquired as well as misconceptions, inaccuracies, or problems he or she experienced concerning concepts covered.

4. Use an organizational planner to introduce and guide discussions of content concepts. An outline of the material to be learned, along with a list of priorities explaining estimated time requirements, organization of materials, and schedule procedures, helps students focus on the objectives of the lesson. Developing a plan before beginning any task helps reduce CLD student anxiety and ensure task completion.

5. Provide time in the discussion of new concepts to check for understanding. This can be accomplished by grouping or pairing students. If students work in pairs, one student talks through a problem, describing her or his thinking processes. The partner listens and asks questions to help clarify thinking. Partners then switch roles.

■ **figure 9.5**   Example of a Student Learning Log Entry

	Gabriel Coronado 8th Grade Science
	Learning Strategies:
28 Aug 2014	
	1. Brainstorming—the teacher told us to make a list of words that go with the topic she gave us. We are studying the planets. My group will find words about the planet Saturn. I liked my group, because they helped me understand where the rings come from.
17 Sept 2014	
	2. Mnemonics—are words we can make up out of other words about the lesson we are learning to help us remember. Like ROY G BIV to help us remember the order of colors in the light spectrum. R means Red, O means Orange, Y means Yellow, G means Green, B means Blue, I means Indigo, and V means Violet. I always thought that light was white. I learned why the sky is blue and grass is green.
7 Oct 2014	
	3. Prediction—is when we guess what is going to happen when we do an experiment in class. Mrs. Smith asked me what I thought would happen with the air pressure experiment. I told her that nothing would happen to the can because it's metal. She put some water in an empty soft drink can and heated the can till the water boiled. Then she turned the can over in a tub with cold water. The soft drink can was crushed like someone stepped on it!! I was wrong about nothing happening to the can. I like to do experiments.

assessment tips and strategies

ASSESSMENT

The CALLA method emphasizes various types of assessment in the preparation, presentation, and evaluation phases of instruction. The findings from these assessments are used to plan instruction that builds on the knowledge and experiences that CLD students bring to the classroom. Such assessments also enable teachers to clarify any misunderstandings the students might have regarding lesson concepts, as well as determine which aspects of the lesson need to be repeated to ensure student understanding.

Assessment Tips

- Preassess the background knowledge of CLD students and then focus strategies on making connections to this background knowledge.
- Provide time in the discussion of new concepts to check for understanding.
- Question the students for clarification to ensure comprehension and encourage student participation.

- Encourage students to use self-questioning techniques to assess their own understanding as they read.
- Use both group and self-assessment of student work.

Assessment Strategies

- To check for understanding, observe students as they discuss content concepts in groups or pairs.
- When asking CLD students clarifying questions and responding to their questions, rephrase or adjust your language to suit the proficiency level of each student.
- While reading aloud, model for students the self-questioning techniques that are helpful for assessing one's comprehension of written material.
- When using group assessment, ask students to give one another feedback on individual work.
- Prompt students to self-assess their understanding of the lesson material by reviewing the content, language, and learning strategy objectives.

CHAPTER 10

Achieving Standards-Driven Professional Practice

our mission

Our mission for this chapter will be to:

· Explore the potential benefits of reflective, standards-driven practices in culturally and linguistically diverse classrooms.

We will accomplish this mission by helping you to meet the following learning outcomes:

· Summarize nationally recognized standards for professional practice in teaching.

· Describe benchmarks of standards-driven, effective practice with CLD students.

· Describe essential facets of a platform for best practice with CLD students.

· Explain the importance and process of ongoing goal setting and targeting in professional development for effectiveness in diverse schools and classrooms.

(Courtesy of Jessica Barrand, Hillcrest Elementary, Lawrence, Kansas)

key theories and concepts

advocacy

benchmarks of effective practice

CREDE standards

critical reflection

evidence

NBPTS standards

TESOL/NCATE standards

The first nine chapters of this text provide both theoretical and practical information on the appropriate instructional accommodation of culturally and linguistically diverse (CLD) students. By design, the content of each of these chapters is aligned with the most up-to-date research and nationally recognized teaching standards that guide educators toward effective practice for CLD students. In this chapter, we explore ways that educators can maximize nationally recognized standards of best practice to enhance the effectiveness of their efforts to appropriately accommodate the CLD students in their curriculum and to advocate for CLD students and families.

Given the minimal preparation most educators receive in preservice and in-service training for accommodating the needs of CLD students, teachers rarely begin their career already effective at working with diverse student populations. Fundamentally, the process of developing effective practice begins with an awareness of the following:

- The needs and assets of CLD students
- Research- and theory-based best practices
- Challenges to implementing accommodative practices with CLD students
- Critical reflection on effective practice

Often, educators fail to notice and investigate critical issues because they are unaware that the issues are relevant. Throughout this text, we attempt to increase awareness regarding issues that affect the education of CLD students.

A review of national teaching standards can also build awareness by providing educators with knowledge of what students should be able to do and by outlining research-based instructional practice for helping students meet language and content standards. After reviewing several national teaching standards relating to the education of students acquiring a second language, this chapter promotes teacher self-awareness by discussing ways in which educators can appropriately engage in the self-evaluation of instructional planning and implementation. These evaluation processes use national teaching standards as touchstones of comparison.

■ Standards for Effective Practice

High-quality standards for professional practice reflect the research on effective teaching practices for CLD students. Such standards translate theory and research into what accommodative and reflective practice looks like from a practitioner's point of view. Professional standards provide consistency in teacher education and offer teachers a framework for effective practice. These standards can provide teachers with the impetus and understanding to go beyond good teaching to encourage both personal and professional growth toward excellence. Educators can use these standards as a means of articulating valuable practice strategies and defending their own effective practice against the critiques of colleagues, administrators, and policy makers who may not understand the process of second language acquisition and the realities of teaching CLD students.

Global Connections 10.1
Standards provide the path in EFL settings for increasing the rigor in classroom practice. When EFL teachers plan instruction aligned with standards and have a clear understanding of the needs and assets of their students, it sets the stage for high-quality accommodative instruction to occur. Standards ultimately serve as the guide to make successful language and academic learning happen.

Over the years, educators have noted the development of a variety of professional standards. Professional consensus provides the foundation for some sets of standards, whereas others are built on educational theory and research. A combination of educational theory, research, and professional consensus grounds only a limited group of comprehensive standards. Most recently, a few nationally recognized entities have developed professional standards for practice to accommodate the unique and multidimensional needs of CLD students.

We have conducted an analysis of national teaching standards for professional practice with CLD students and found that the conception of effective teaching practice for such students is comparatively consistent across the various sets of standards, whether the standards are research-based, professional consensus–based, or a combination of both. The following organizations have developed professional standards of appropriate practice for educators who serve the needs of CLD student populations:

- The National Board for Professional Teaching Standards (NBPTS)
- The Center for Research on Education, Diversity & Excellence (CREDE)
- Teachers of English to Speakers of Other Languages (TESOL)

For highlights of each of these sets of standards, see Table 10.1.

■ **t a b l e   1 0 . 1**   A Closer Look at Professional Standards for Culturally and Linguistically Diverse Students

Professional Standards	Summaries/Highlights
NBPTS National Board for Professional Teaching Standards	This project was funded in part with grants from the U.S. Department of Education and the National Science Foundation. The standards lay the foundation for the English as a New Language certificate. They represent a professional consensus on the critical aspects of practice that distinguish accomplished teachers. The standards incorporate essential knowledge, skills, dispositions, and commitments that allow teachers to practice at a high level: • *Knowledge of students* • *Knowledge of language and language development* • *Knowledge of culture and diversity* • *Knowledge of subject matter* • *Meaningful learning* • *Multiple paths to knowledge* • *Instructional resources* • *Learning environment* • *Assessment* • *Reflective practice* • *Linkages with families* • *Professional leadership*
Unique Features:	Grounded in theory and has a fundamental philosophical foundation Professional consensus
CREDE Center for Research on Education, Diversity & Excellence, University of Hawaii at Manoa	This center was funded by the U.S. Department of Education to create the Standards for Effective Pedagogy and Learning through CREDE research and through an extensive analysis of the research and development literature on education and diversity. The standards represent recommendations on which the literature is in agreement, across all cultural, racial, and linguistic groups in the United States (with recent additional attention to international contexts); all age levels; and all subject matters. Thus, they express the principles of effective pedagogy for all students. CREDE's research and development is based on a sociocultural framework that is sensitive to diverse cultures and languages but powerful enough to identify the great commonalities that unite people. The research consensus can be expressed as five standards: • *Joint Productive Activity—Teacher and Students Producing Together* • *Language Development—Developing Language and Literacy Across the Curriculum* • *Contextualization—Making Meaning: Connecting School to Students' Lives* • *Challenging Activities—Teaching Complex Thinking* • *Instructional Conversation—Teaching through Conversation*
Unique Features:	Grounded on a sociocultural framework Based on over 30 research projects under 6 programmatic strands (experimental, quasi-experimental, qualitative, and consensus-based)

(continued)

■ **table 10.1**   Continued

Professional Standards	Summaries/Highlights
TESOL Teachers of English to Speakers of Other Languages (TESOL Board of Educators & the National Council for the Accreditation of Teacher Education)	A project that was completed and approved by the TESOL board of directors and the National Council for the Accreditation of Teacher Education (NCATE) in 2010 for use in accrediting ESL teacher preparation programs in the United States. The standards are expressed as five domains: • *Language—describing language, language acquisition and development* • *Culture—nature and role of culture, cultural groups and identity* • *Planning, Implementing, and Managing Instruction—planning for standards-based ESL and content instruction, managing and implementing standards-based ESL and content instruction, using resources effectively in ESL and content instruction* • *Assessment—issues of assessment for ESL, language proficiency assessment, classroom-based assessment for ESL* • *Professionalism—ESL research and history, partnerships and advocacy, professional development and collaboration*
Unique Features:	Professional consensus Includes performance indicators Includes rubrics for meeting the standards (self-evaluation)

dilemmas of Practice 10.1

Mrs. Espinoza is a first-year language arts teacher at an urban junior high school. The school district has a diverse student population, including students recently arrived from Mexico, Indonesia, and Vietnam, as well as native-English-speaking students. She has had numerous courses in professional practice and methods of classroom teaching and instruction. However, the administration asked Mrs. Espinoza to make accommodations for the diverse language needs of the students in her classroom by aligning her professional practice with nationally recognized standards of best practice with English learners, such as the TESOL/NCATE standards (TESOL, 2010). Panic has struck because she does not know how to begin aligning her practice with best practice standards for CLD students while still targeting the language arts standards in her state.

■ *What should Mrs. Espinoza do? The process of accommodation necessarily involves understanding high-quality standards for effective practice in diverse educational environments. Therefore, a review of the TESOL/NCATE standards for effective practice will open the door for Mrs. Espinoza to modify her practice with the CLD students in her classroom. She should seek research-based ways to adapt her classroom practice to ensure the academic success of CLD students. She should also seek the support and advice of colleagues who have additional experience in using both content and language learning standards to guide their effective professional practice with CLD students.*

NBPTS Standards

The National Board for Professional Teaching Standards (NBPTS), a project funded by the U.S. Department of Education and the National Science Foundation, used findings from educational research to create rigorous professional teaching standards. The goal of NBPTS is to enhance the content-area achievement of all students. As a result of the increasing numbers of CLD students in public school classrooms, NBPTS established English as a New Language standards to define high-quality practice in 12 areas of professional practice that address CLD student learning (NBPTS, 1998). These **NBPTS standards** emphasize teacher awareness of students' languages and cultures, meaningful learning environments, authentic assessments, strong home–school collaboration, and content-appropriate pedagogy.

CREDE Standards

The Center for Research on Education, Diversity & Excellence (CREDE) housed in the University of Hawaii at Manoa, as funded by the U.S. Department of Education, has created the Standards for Effective Pedagogy and Learning through extensive analysis of the research and development literature in education and diversity. The five broad standards encompass the commonalities among research on effective instruction, content-area instruction, and multicultural education across all age, cultural, ethnic, and linguistic groups in the United States (Dalton, 1998; Tharp, 2008). These five **CREDE standards** express the principles of effective pedagogy for all students, including CLD students. These standards are not prescriptive; instead, they serve as philosophical statements that suggest standards toward which teachers can align their practices.

TESOL/NCATE Standards

The National Council for the Accreditation of Teacher Education (NCATE) and the board of directors of the National Teachers of English to Speakers of Other Languages (TESOL) organization collaboratively developed their P–12 English as a second language (ESL) teacher standards (TESOL, 2010). These standards encompass five domains: (1) language; (2) culture; (3) planning, implementing, and managing instruction; (4) assessment; and (5) professionalism. The **TESOL/NCATE standards** aspire to provide consistency in teacher education programs across the United States by describing and specifying the competencies that ESL teachers need to demonstrate in professional practice. Various best practice indicators also specify different levels of attainment for each competency. The ESL teacher standards differ from content teacher standards in that the former acknowledge the central role of language in the academic achievement of CLD students and highlight the multidimensional learning styles, instructional needs, and assessment issues of English learners.

■ Standards-Driven Reflection on Professional Practice

After a review and analysis of all the previously mentioned sets of standards, we chose the TESOL/NCATE teacher standards (TESOL, 2010) to guide the content of this text. We selected these standards for several reasons: TESOL is the national professional organization for ESL educators, and NCATE is a national accreditation agency for teacher education programs. The TESOL/NCATE standards developed for P–12 ESL teachers reflect professional consensus on standards for the quality teaching of CLD students. The TESOL/NCATE standards also are consistent with the other national professional teaching standards and include performance indicators and rubrics that help educators effectively target the standards in practice. Due to our increasingly globalized society, TESOL has acknowledged that EFL standards need to be developed and will be forthcoming. For more information on this new development, please see the TESOL website at www.tesol.org.

Whether you are a content-area specialist or a second language acquisition specialist, the likelihood that you will encounter cultural and linguistic diversity within your professional practice increases almost daily. Therefore, this chapter is designed to assist you in building connections between what you have learned about appropriate programming and instruction for CLD students and the recommendations of nationally recognized teaching standards. To simplify the process, only the TESOL/NCATE P–12 teaching standards are used to illustrate ways in which practice can be effectively tied to standards. For more information on the importance of aligning curriculum to standards, watch this video.

Benchmarks of Effective Practice

Effective practice is not characterized by a one-size-fits-all formula. Methods and strategies that are successfully used with some school populations do not work well with others. The site-specific dynamics of a particular school or classroom are constantly changing from one year to the next. Therefore, it is unrealistic to think that teachers' efforts that constitute effective practice for a given population at a given point in time will be equally effective in situations in which one or both of these variables differ. A more practical way to ensure that students are receiving high-quality education is to incorporate the three **benchmarks of effective practice**: self-assessment, **critical reflection**, and refinement of practice.

Despite the learning nature of the teaching profession, teacher evaluation tends to flow from an administrator to a teacher, a situation that places the teacher in a passive role in the assessment process. This model of assessment does little to effect change in teaching practice (Danielson & McGreal, 2000). Accordingly, we place a high priority on the active participation of the educator in the learning process that is required for a teacher to be a reflective practitioner in educational settings with diverse student populations. Self-assessment is an empowering benchmark in becoming a constructivist learner–teacher.

However, simply determining the strengths and weaknesses of one's practice is not enough. After self-assessing current practices, effective educators critically reflect on the changes in ideology, perspectives, and attitudes that typically emerge before changes in instructional practice can be realized. One goal of this text is to foster an understanding of the research on the process of change in transforming one's own educational practice in ways that enhance the academic achievement and transitional successes of CLD students. After critically reflecting on the discrepancies between what they are currently doing and what they predict will be more effective with their students, proactive teachers make plans to take action.

When a teacher believes there are areas for growth in his or her professional practice, then she or he must make efforts to refine classroom practice if students are to reach higher levels of achievement. Effective teachers also realize the necessity of collaborating with colleagues and staying informed about current research. Research-based methods, strategies, and techniques that colleagues are successfully using may provide valuable insight concerning ways instruction can be modified to better meet the needs of CLD students.

Effective teachers also know that the benchmarks of effective practice—self-assessment, critical reflection, and practice refinement—do not occur just once

theory *into* Practice 10.1

Mezirow (1991) described the self-reflective process a learner must go through to transform his or her own perspectives. Explained in terms of teaching CLD students, these steps include the following:

1. Acknowledging that at least some CLD students are not faring well in your classroom.
2. Identifying the similarities and differences between your current teaching practice and what research says is effective teaching practice for CLD students.
3. Challenging your beliefs about the potential of discrepancies between your own practice and current theory- and research-based practice.
4. Recognizing that other educators face similar dilemmas of practice.
5. Seeking out new research-based teaching methods from the professional literature and knowledgeable colleagues.
6. Gathering as much information about the new theory- and research-based teaching methods as possible.
7. Understanding how and why certain methods are more effective with CLD students than others.
8. Creating an implementation plan for using a new method.
9. Experimenting with and refining the implementation of the new method.
10. Implementing the new research-based method as the foundation of your professional practice.
11. Evaluating the outcomes of implementation and refining professional practice based on the feedback gained.

To this end, Mezirow (1985, 1991) concluded that effective professional development must begin and end with an acknowledgement of the importance of critically reflective dialogue and discourse.

■ *In what ways can educators incorporate reflection and critical reflection in their professional practice? How might educators use technology to gather information and resources concerning research- and theory-based practices for CLD students? In what ways might collaboration with colleagues enhance the process of appropriately accommodating the differential learning and transition needs of CLD students?*

or twice each year. Rather, evidence of these benchmarks is apparent throughout the educator's professional practice. Effective teachers are continually self-assessing their practice as it relates to standards of best practice, critically reflecting on ways their practice could better reflect the existing research and educational theory, and refining their practice to provide students with the best education possible.

Fundamentals of a Platform for Best Practice

To assist the educator with the process of self-assessment, the subsequent sections of this chapter focus on the following key facets of a platform for best practice with CLD students (Herrera & Murry, 2009):

1. Language development and learning dynamics
2. Sociopolitical and sociocultural realities
3. Planning, implementing, and managing instruction
4. Professionalism, reflection, and evaluation of practice

Because this text emphasizes methodological issues related to the education of CLD students, each of these facets, and discussions of each, focus on the ways in which standards relate to methodological issues rather than issues of assessment. Although standards of best practice with students typically address other related issues, such additional challenges are beyond the scope of this text.

As you proceed through each of the self-assessment sections, answer the reflection questions as a source of evidence for the evaluation of your teaching practice. Remember, **evidence** is factual information, not opinion. You want to collect evidence that includes but is not limited to (1) factual descriptions of your actions, (2) factual descriptions of your students' actions, (3) quotations from lesson plans, (4) CLD student classroom documentation and samples of student work, (5) parent contact logs, and (6) professional development logs. Once you have gathered your evidence, determine which levels of professional performance best describe your current teaching practice under each rubric topic. Allow considerable time for the review in the following sections, for thinking about the self-reflection questions, and for then self-assessing your practice using the rubrics provided.

Facet 1: Language Development and Learning Dynamics

Language is a critical aspect of instruction. It is the primary means for communicating information, and it is the foundation of a person's thought processes (Vygotsky, 1962). Language and a teacher's beliefs about second language acquisition become critical issues of instruction when teaching students in ESL/EFL classrooms. For example, if a teacher believes that second language learners are incapable of benefiting from content-area instruction because of limited English proficiency, then that teacher will not provide CLD students with the content-based language instruction they need to develop high levels of academic language proficiency. Consequently, English learners may be unfairly excluded from educational opportunities that are available to other students and may not experience academic success to their full potential.

Effective teachers of CLD students know how to negotiate meaning using as many supports as possible in order to provide English learners with a wide range of content-based material from which to construct meaning. Such teachers understand the levels of language proficiencies that their students bring to educational experiences and adapt language and instruction accordingly. Finally, effective teachers of CLD students are adept at using various instructional materials and groupings of students to promote first and second language acquisition as well as content-related conceptual development.

■ **Snapshot of Classroom Practice 10.1**   Small Groups and Learning Centers

Students in this classroom build language and literacy skills by reading for meaning in small groups. Using learning centers allows the teacher to provide more individualized support and scaffolding to ensure all students attain the lesson's objectives.

(Courtesy of Jessica Barrand, Hillcrest Elementary, Lawrence, Kansas)

Consider the following TESOL/NCATE standard when reflecting on your knowledge base concerning learning and language learning, as well as the potential impact on instruction:

> Candidates understand and apply theories and research in language acquisition and development to support their ELLs' [CLD students'] English language and literacy learning and content-area achievement. (TESOL, 2010, p. 32)

Step 1: If you are unsure of the ways in which your knowledge of, or perspectives on, second language acquisition will affect your instruction of language learners, you are encouraged to refer to the chapters in this text that most significantly address language issues. Chapters 1 through 3 address the dynamic interaction between a CLD student's sociocultural realities and his or her cognitive, academic, and linguistic growth. Chapter 3 stresses the linguistic dimension of the CLD student biography. Chapters 7 through 9 provide a menu of contemporary teaching methods designed for English learners. These methods are designed to develop both language proficiency and content-area knowledge among CLD students. Some key questions to ask yourself include the following:

- How do I define learning and language learning?
- In what ways does my knowledge of first and second language acquisition influence my classroom instruction?

- In what ways does my knowledge of CLD students' levels of second language proficiency influence my instructional planning?
- How does my knowledge of the BICS–CALP distinction influence the programmatic decisions and recommendations I make for CLD students?
- How do I plan for CALP development in a student's first and second languages?
- In what ways does my classroom environment foster first and second language acquisition?
- What role does a student's first language play in my classroom?
- In what ways do I support a student's first and second language literacy development?
- How do I provide comprehensible input to CLD students?
- In what ways does the curriculum I am using need to be adapted to meet the language and learning needs of my CLD students?

Step 2: Your answers to the previous questions provide evidence for assessing your teaching practice. Using Figure 10.1 as a guide, write down your responses to the reflection questions on the right-hand side of the T-chart.

Step 3: Refer to Chapters 3, 7, 8, and 9 to collect evidence about what educational researchers have described as research-based teaching practice.

■ **figure 10.1** Language Development and Learning Dynamics Chart

Research-Based Teaching Practice	**My Teaching Practice**
Example:	*Example:*
• Jimenez, García, and Pearson (1996) found that CLD students benefit from explicit instruction in recognizing and applying learning strategies. • Jimenez, García, and Pearson (1996) found that CLD students benefit from using cross-linguistic transfer strategies (bilingual strategies).	• I often teach reading strategy recognition and use the directed reading–thinking activity (DR–TA), which involves using predictions to guide reading. • I do not promote student use of the native language when I teach reading strategies.

For any differences between what research indicates is good teaching practice and what you are currently doing, explain why you are choosing your alternative teaching practices.

Step 4: Write the evidence you collect regarding research-based teaching practice on the left-hand side of the T-chart.

Step 5: Compare how you currently address language development in your professional practice with what the research indicates is effective teaching practice. If you locate any discrepancy or difference between what research defines as good teaching practice and the ways in which you currently practice, explain what has led you to choose your current teaching practices.

Step 6: Finally, use the evidence you have gathered from the teaching practice T-chart to rate yourself using the rubric of Table 10.2.

Facet 2: Sociopolitical and Sociocultural Realities

As Haim Ginott (1993) once said, "To reach a child's mind a teacher must first capture his heart. Only if a child feels right can he think right" (p. 57). Culture is the heart of student perspectives, expectations, motivations, and evaluations. Indeed, culture lies at the center of the CLD student biography. Integral to engaging and motivating the CLD student is the consideration of his or her sociopolitical and sociocultural realities. Failure to consider these realities can deny the child equitable access to educational opportunities. Instruction that does not build on the student's culture-based socialization and does not address the sociocultural realities particular to the learner can negatively affect that student's cognitive, academic, and linguistic development.

Previous chapters emphasized the importance of comprehensible input in the learning processes of CLD students. Providing English learners with comprehensible input goes beyond merely helping them understand the literal meaning of information to making the information relevant to their lives (Cummins, 2000, 2001). Cognitive research supports the importance of making students' cultures an integral part of instruction. In fact, the relevancy of information to a student is a prerequisite to the storage of that information in long-term memory (Jensen, 2008; Sousa, 2011). Consequently, instruction that does not maximize the socialization experiences of a CLD student in a particular culture will do little to promote her or his learning and academic excellence.

A caring connection between students and teachers is also crucial to both content and language learning. Content and language learning are shared experiences between students and the teacher. As the CLD student learns about the language and culture of the teacher, the teacher learns about the language and culture of the student, even if the teacher is not proficient in the student's native language. A teacher conveys the importance of native language development by promoting the use of the native language in collaborative learning groups, encouraging students to write in their native languages, and providing native language materials whenever feasible.

Language use and curricular content both convey the educator's explicit and underlying perspectives on students' languages and cultures. In a classroom in which language and content learning is transmitted only from teacher to student, students have few opportunities to explore their prior knowledge and experiences in relation to content-area concepts. Such teacher-centered environments

■ **table 10.2** Language Development and Learning Dynamics Rubric

Element	LEVEL OF PERFORMANCE			
	Unsatisfactory	**Basic**	**Proficient**	**Distinguished**
I understand the critical concepts specific to the curriculum I teach and the implications of pedagogy on language acquisition and learning for students acquiring English.	I do not understand the critical concepts specific to the curriculum I teach as they relate to implications of pedagogy on language acquisition and learning for students acquiring English.	I have a basic understanding of the critical concepts specific to the curriculum I teach and the implications of pedagogy on language acquisition and learning for students acquiring English.	I have a solid understanding of the critical concepts specific to the curriculum I teach and the implications of pedagogy on language acquisition and learning for students acquiring English.	I have an extensive understanding of the critical concepts specific to the curriculum and the implications of pedagogy on language acquisition and learning for students acquiring English.
I design instruction based on my understanding of students' linguistic, cultural, and learning needs.	I design instruction that does not take into account an understanding of students' linguistic, cultural, and learning needs.	I design instruction based on basic knowledge of students' linguistic, cultural, and learning needs.	I design instruction based on solid knowledge of students' linguistic, cultural, and learning needs.	I design instruction based on extensive and thorough knowledge of students' linguistic, cultural, and learning needs.
I select instructional goals and objectives consistent with the linguistic abilities and learning processes of my CLD students.	My instructional goals and objectives are not consistent with the linguistic abilities and learning processes of my CLD students.	My instructional goals and objectives are somewhat consistent with the linguistic abilities and learning processes of my CLD students.	My instructional goals and objectives are consistent with the linguistic abilities and learning processes of my CLD students.	My instructional goals and objectives are highly consistent and aligned with the linguistic abilities and learning processes of my CLD students.
I select resources consistent with the content, linguistic characteristics, and instructional goals and objectives for my CLD students.	I do not select resources consistent with the content, linguistic characteristics, and instructional goals and objectives for my CLD students.	I seldom select resources consistent with the content, linguistic characteristics, and instructional goals and objectives for my CLD students.	I select resources that are generally consistent with the content, linguistic characteristics, and instructional goals and objectives for my CLD students.	I select resources that are highly consistent with the content, linguistic characteristics, and instructional goals and objectives for my CLD students.

Source: Adapted for use with CLD students from Danielson (2007).

■ Voices from the Field 10.1

"English language learners [CLD students] frequently need additional support beyond the traditional, grade-level classroom. They face many challenges when learning a new language, such as learning new phonemes not found in their first language, comprehending meanings between their first and second languages, and understanding how parts of speech work in English. In addition, ELLs are learning how to adapt to a new culture. They are making new friends, experiencing new food, and adapting to a new school environment. Some may even be considered refugees and could be dealing with a previous traumatic experience. Some ELLs face challenges of being illiterate in their native language. Other ELLs have big gaps in their former education. They might come to school with little or no math, reading, or writing skills. In order to meet all students' needs effectively, teachers need substantial training. They must understand that ELLs require additional kinds of support beyond those provided in the traditional classroom, and that one size doesn't fit all.

Oftentimes ELLs struggle in [unaccommodative] grade-level classrooms and are failing because the core teacher is not meeting their needs. Core teachers frequently lack proper training needed to work with ELLs. The traditional classroom is not designed for ELLs, yet they are expected to perform at the same level as a traditional English-speaking student. We might see a change in instructional practices if core teachers were required to take all the necessary course work to be licensed in ESOL, rather than just taking a test and adding it to their license.

ELLs are going through a lot developmentally. We as teachers must understand how the ELL brain works and be able to adapt to their needs. There is so much that we all still need to learn! We must advocate for our students and educate others on how to work with ELLs. We can collaborate with core teachers to share ideas and resources. We can suggest professional development that might support all educators in the school in better meeting the needs of this student population. It's our responsibility to fight for ELL students because if we don't, who else will?"

■ *Victor Rincon, high school ESOL teacher, Wichita, Kansas*

require students to abandon their cultures and languages in order to be accepted and succeed in the school environment (Cummins, 2000). Students in these situations enjoy few opportunities to explore their own identities and ways of personal expression. As a consequence, CLD students are less likely to develop a deep, personal understanding of the course content or the ability to express a profound understanding of key concepts in the target language. In other words, they fail to develop CALP (Cummins, 2001).

The following TESOL/NCATE standard of best practice demonstrates the expectation for the integration of cultural knowledge into professional teaching practice:

Candidates know, understand, and use major theories and research related to the nature and role of culture in their instruction. They demonstrate understanding of how cultural groups and individual cultural identities affect language learning and school achievement. (TESOL, 2010, p. 38)

Step 1: As you consider this teaching standard and the following reflection questions, you might want to refer to the chapters in this text that best emphasize sociocultural issues. Chapter 1 highlights the ways in which a CLD student's sociocultural realities affect her or his academic, cognitive, and linguistic development. The teaching methods presented in Chapters 7, 8, and 9 discuss culture in the form of prior knowledge connections. Consider the role of students' cultures in your professional practice as you reflect on the following questions:

- In what ways do I gather and use information regarding students' primary cultures, home environments, communities, and languages?
- For planning and instruction, how do I use the knowledge, skills, and experiences that CLD students bring to my classroom?
- In what ways does my instruction affect students' affective filter?
- In what ways do my instructional materials reflect the lives, experiences, cultures, and languages of all my students?
- In what ways do I use the prior knowledge, experiences, and native languages of students to enrich instruction for all students?
- How do I address the stages of acculturation that English learners tend to experience?
- In what ways does my instruction support my students' ethnic identities?
- In what ways do I facilitate or promote social and academic interaction between my English learners and my native-English-speaking students?

Step 2: Your answers to the previous questions provide evidence for assessing your teaching practice. Using Figure 10.2, write your responses to the reflection questions on the right-hand side of the T-chart.

Step 3: Refer to Chapters 1, 7, 8, and 9 to collect evidence regarding research-based teaching practice.

Step 4: Write the evidence you collect regarding research-based teaching practice on the left-hand side of the T-chart.

Step 5: Compare how you currently address culture in your professional practice with what the research indicates is accommodative teaching practice. For any difference that exists between your current teaching practices and those that research indicates are good teaching practices, explain what has prompted you to choose your current teaching practices.

Step 6: Finally, use the evidence you have gathered from the teaching practice T-chart to rate yourself using the rubric of Table 10.3.

Facet 3: Planning, Implementing, and Managing Instruction

Professional educators who are beginning the process of instructional planning for a culturally and linguistically rich setting first consider the sociocultural

■ **figure 10.2**   Sociopolitical and Sociocultural Realities Chart

Research-Based Teaching Practice	My Teaching Practice
Example: • C. Collier (1987) found that teachers' lack of understanding regarding the influences of the acculturation process was often responsible for the over-referral of CLD students to special education.	*Example:* • I have referred a much larger percentage of my CLD students than my native-English-speaking students for special education evaluation.

For any differences between what research indicates is good teaching practice and what you are currently doing, explain why you are choosing your alternative teaching practices.

realities of CLD students: their prior life experiences, their families, their communities, the school climate, and the school culture. They formally or informally preassess students' language proficiencies, educational backgrounds, preferred learning styles, levels of cognitive development, personal interests, areas of strength, and areas of inexperience. The characteristics of CLD students drive the teacher's responsive instructional planning process for these students.

Once the process of preinstructional student assessment has been thoughtfully addressed, knowledge gained from this process is combined with the professional educator's philosophies and perspectives concerning critical issues.

Illustrated Concept 10.1

Make sure to have open dialogue with your students. At the end of each unit, allow students to discuss (either verbally or in writing) what strategies worked for them. If students express frustration with a particular strategy, listen to their concerns. After receiving such feedback, evaluate and reassess how you might accommodate these concerns in your approach to future instruction.

■ **table 10.3**   Sociopolitical and Sociocultural Realities Rubric

| Element | LEVEL OF PERFORMANCE | | | |
	Unsatisfactory	Basic	Proficient	Distinguished
I consider my students' linguistic, cultural, academic, and cognitive needs when deciding instructional procedures in my classroom.	I do not consider my students' linguistic, cultural, academic, and cognitive needs when deciding instructional procedures in my classroom.	I partially consider my students' linguistic, cultural, academic, and cognitive needs when deciding instructional procedures in my classroom.	I frequently consider my students' linguistic, cultural, academic, and cognitive needs when deciding instructional procedures in my classroom.	I regularly consider my students' linguistic, cultural, academic, and cognitive needs when deciding instructional procedures in my classroom.
I establish a learning environment in which expectations for achievement are high regardless of linguistic abilities and academic backgrounds of students.	I do not establish a learning environment in which expectations for achievement are high regardless of linguistic abilities and academic backgrounds of students.	I generally establish a learning environment in which expectations for achievement are high regardless of linguistic abilities and academic backgrounds of students.	I always establish a learning environment in which expectations for achievement are high regardless of linguistic abilities and academic backgrounds of students.	I consistently and positively establish a learning environment in which expectations for achievement are high regardless of linguistic abilities and academic backgrounds of students.
I respect and acknowledge my students' cultures and native languages in supporting a risk-free environment.	I do not respect and acknowledge my students' cultures and native languages.	I often respect and acknowledge my students' cultures and native languages in supporting a risk-free environment.	I always respect and acknowledge my students' cultures and native languages in supporting a risk-free environment.	I positively and sensitively respect and acknowledge my students' cultures and native languages in supporting a risk-free environment.
I recognize and accept unique interaction styles, values, religions, and worldviews of different cultures represented in my classroom.	I do not recognize and accept unique interaction styles, values, religions, and worldviews of different cultures represented in my classroom.	I seldom recognize and accept unique interaction styles, values, religions, and worldviews of different cultures represented in my classroom.	I frequently recognize and accept unique interaction styles, values, religions, and worldviews of different cultures represented in my classroom.	I consistently and sensitively recognize and accept unique interaction styles, values, religions, and worldviews of different cultures represented in my classroom.

Source: Adapted from Danielson (2007).

For example, the educator should consider questions such as the following: What are my perspectives regarding the ways in which students learn most effectively? What is my view on the nature of best practice for second language acquisition? When discerning personal philosophies and perspectives, the professional educator relies on his or her knowledge of educational research regarding CLD students, as well as insight gained through reflection on his or her professional experience. An educator's understanding of and ongoing reflection on her or his perspectives as they relate to personal and instructional contexts contribute to the successful implementation of site-specific methods and strategies for the instruction of English learners.

When proactively planning instruction for students, professional educators turn to local, state, and national language and content standards. To receive an equitable education, English learners deserve to be held to the same standards as all other students. However, instructional approaches that appropriately account for the differential learning and transition needs of CLD students provide them with superior support in attaining these language and content standards. Backward mapping can guide standards-based instructional planning (Mitchell, Willis, & Chicago Teachers' Union Quest Center, 1995; Wiggins & McTighe, 2005). In backward mapping, educators identify learning goals and plan instruction to ensure that students can achieve the goals. Wiggins and McTighe (2005) delineate three stages in their backward design process:

1. Identify desired results.
2. Determine acceptable evidence.
3. Plan learning experiences and instruction.

The "desired results" of stage 1 of the process are national content and language learning standards (e.g., the TESOL standards [TESOL, 2010]. In choosing student standards, professional educators ask themselves, "Which knowledge bases and skills do my CLD students need in order to attain grade-level content and language proficiencies?"

In determining acceptable evidence, educators design assessments that measure levels of attainment of the targeted standards. These assessments can be both formal, such as tests, quizzes, and projects, and informal, such as observations and verbal questioning, to determine the general level of understanding in the class. During this stage of the planning process, professional educators ask themselves, "What formal and informal assessments can be used to measure English learners' understanding and incremental progress? In what purposeful ways can my CLD students express what they have learned?"

Finally, educators who use the backward design process plan learning experiences and instruction through which CLD students can gain the knowledge and skills needed to achieve the target standards. Key questions at this point in the process include: "Which learning experiences will give my CLD students the knowledge and skills they need to reach the goals of this lesson? What materials and resources can be developed or adapted to make learning more meaningful? In what ways can instruction be modified or differentiated to ensure that CLD students are able to match or exceed the target standards for this unit?"

The following domain descriptor from the TESOL/NCATE teacher standards applies to the planning, implementation, and management of instruction for CLD students:

> Candidates know, understand, and use evidence-based practices and strategies related to planning, implementing, and managing standards-based ESL and content instruction. Candidates are knowledgeable about program models and skilled in teaching strategies for developing and integrating language skills. They integrate technology as well as choose and adapt classroom resources appropriate for their ELLs [CLD students]. (TESOL, 2010, p. 43)

Step 1: In considering this standard and the following reflection questions, you may want to refer to the chapters in this text that best address the planning, implementation, and management of instruction for CLD students. Chapter 6 addresses approaches, methods, strategies, and techniques and provides the theoretical and research-based foundation for understanding the teaching methods discussed in Chapters 7 through 9. Chapter 7 introduces the integrated content-based method, Chapter 8 discusses the sheltered instruction method, and Chapter 9 provides an overview of the cognitive academic language learning approach (CALLA) method. Because all the contemporary methods presented in this text are grounded in a strong research base, educators can confidently choose from any one of the methods emphasized in Chapters 7 through 9 as a means of organizing and presenting instruction. The following questions should guide you as you reflect on your professional practice in terms of this key facet of a platform for best practice with CLD students:

- Do I know the national, state, and local teaching standards and benchmarks for my content area, as well as those that apply to the appropriate instruction of CLD students?
- In what ways do I use national, state, and local content and second language teaching standards and benchmarks as I plan instruction?
- Which instructional method do I use to teach my students? What is the research basis or rationale underlying my chosen method?
- How do I select the most appropriate strategies and techniques to differentiate instruction for students with varying levels of English and native language proficiency?
- In what ways does my instruction build on the preferred learning styles of my students?
- To what extent are my CLD students actively involved in classroom instruction?
- In what ways do I support my English learners in reaching grade-appropriate content standards?

- How and to what extent do I integrate language and content instruction?
- What kinds of opportunities and support do I provide for my students as they develop their speaking, listening, reading, and writing skills in my class?
- What kinds of supplementary materials do I use to support the cognitive, academic, and linguistic development of my English learners?
- In what specific ways do I ensure that my CLD students have access to the same challenging curriculum as other students?

Step 2: Your answers to the previous questions provide evidence for assessing your teaching practice. Using Figure 10.3, write your responses to the reflection questions on the right-hand side of the T-chart.

■**figure 10.3** Planning, Implementing, and Managing Instruction Chart

Research-Based Teaching Practice	My Teaching Practice
Example:	*Example:*
• Lessons that include both language and content objectives facilitate a CLD student's academic and linguistic development.	• My lessons always have both language and content objectives.

For any differences between what research indicates is good teaching practice and what you are currently doing, explain why you are choosing your alternative teaching practices.

Step 3: Collect evidence about what educational researchers have said regarding research-based teaching practice.

Step 4: Write the evidence you collect regarding research-based teaching practice on the left-hand side of the T-chart.

Step 5: Compare how you currently address planning, implementing, and managing instruction in your professional practice with what the research indicates is effective accommodative teaching practice. For any difference between what research indicates is good teaching practice and what you currently do in practice, explain what has led you to choose your current teaching practices.

Step 6: Finally, use the evidence you have gathered from the teaching practice T-chart to rate yourself using the rubric of Table 10.4.

Facet 4: Professionalism, Reflection, and Evaluation of Practice

Recently, signs of a new trend have emerged. This trend redefines and reconceptualizes the educator as an adult learner who is capable of ongoing, self-directed, and critically reflective practice. Educators are more frequently asking questions about the students they serve and are often successful in developing instructional plans that are better aligned with the needs of CLD students. Given the diversity of the languages and cultures represented in today's classrooms, as well as the individuality of the educators working in such classrooms, no one method or model can successfully address all challenges in all classrooms. Indeed, the educator's knowledge of theory, the history of second language instruction, current research, and site-specific practice dynamics, combined with the knowledge gained from preinstructional and postinstructional student assessments, should determine which approach, methods, and strategies will be implemented in a particular classroom or school setting.

> **Illustrated Concept 10.2**
>
> To become even more critically reflective regarding assumptions, beliefs, and classroom performance, stay apprised of second language acquisition scholarship. Consider forming a monthly study group with other educators to discuss new research in the field and ways to apply this new knowledge in your classroom, specifically with your English learners.

Self-directed, culturally conscious, profession-oriented educators are in the best position to undertake informed and authentic decision making that accommodates the complexity of practice settings and diverse student populations. Four key indicators characterize this profession-oriented approach to educational practice (Shanker, 1985). First, professional educators align their practice with national teaching standards. They read journals and practitioners' texts and participate in conferences to ground themselves in the constantly evolving professional knowledge base. Collaborative relationships with colleagues characterize the interactions of these educators. Finally, professionals act in the informed best interest of the learners in their classrooms and schools. They become true advocates for the needs of their students at the local, state, and even national levels.

■ **table 10.4**   Planning, Implementing, and Managing Instruction Rubric

| Element | LEVEL OF PERFORMANCE | | | |
	Unsatisfactory	Basic	Proficient	Distinguished
The content and instruction in my classroom is designed to maximize student engagement and learning.	The content and instruction in my classroom does not maximize student engagement and learning.	The content and instruction in my classroom is seldom designed to maximize student engagement and learning.	The content and instruction in my classroom is usually designed to maximize student engagement and learning.	The content and instruction in my classroom is always designed to maximize student engagement and learning.
I understand the academic and linguistic needs of my students and provide flexibility and responsiveness during lesson delivery.	I do not take into account the academic and linguistic needs of my students, and my instruction does not provide flexibility and responsiveness during lesson delivery.	I seldom take into account the academic and linguistic needs of my students and seldom provide flexibility and responsiveness during lesson delivery.	I frequently take into account the academic and linguistic needs of my students and often provide flexibility and responsiveness during lesson delivery.	I consistently and extensively take into account the academic and linguistic needs of my students and provide high levels of flexibility and responsiveness during lesson delivery.
I adjust questioning and discussion techniques to maximize student participation based on linguistic abilities.	I do not adjust questioning and discussion techniques according to students' linguistic abilities.	I seldom adjust questioning and discussion techniques to maximize student participation based on linguistic abilities.	I generally adjust questioning and discussion techniques to maximize student participation based on linguistic abilities.	I consistently and efficiently adjust questioning and discussion techniques to maximize student participation based on linguistic abilities.
I use multiple modes of communicating and facilitating feedback to ensure CLD students' understanding of expectations and lesson objectives.	I do not communicate and provide feedback to ensure CLD students' understanding of expectations and lesson objectives.	I often communicate and facilitate feedback in a way that ensures CLD students' understanding of expectations and lesson objectives.	I always use multiple modes of communicating and facilitating feedback to ensure CLD students' understanding of expectations and lesson objectives.	I efficiently and sensitively use multiple modes of communicating and facilitating feedback to ensure CLD students' understanding of expectations and lesson objectives.

Source: Adapted for use with CLD students from Danielson (2007).

TESOL/NCATE teaching standards define professionalism in the following manner:

> Candidates keep current with new instructional techniques, research results, advances in the ESL field, and education policy issues and demonstrate knowledge of the history of ESL teaching. They use such information to reflect on and improve their instruction and assessment practices. Candidates work collaboratively with school staff and the community to improve the learning environment, provide support, and advocate for ELLs [CLD students] and their families. (TESOL, 2010, p. 68)

Step 1: In considering this standard and the following reflection questions, you may want to refer to the chapters in this text that best address professional practice with CLD students and reflection on that practice. Chapter 4 discusses research regarding the effectiveness of various program models. Chapter 5 explores the following areas of educator readiness that are needed to deliver mutually accommodative instruction: critical reflection, CLD students and families, environment, curriculum, programming and instruction, and application and **advocacy**. As you reflect on your professional capacities, consider the following questions:

- Which journals, texts, and other materials have I read lately about teaching English learners?
- In what ways have I been involved in shaping local, state, or national guidelines, curriculum, or policy regarding CLD students?
- In what ways am I applying in practice what I have been learning about teaching CLD students?
- How do I involve the family members of my CLD students as well as community members in my classroom practice and in the school environment?
- In what ways do I share what I am learning about teaching CLD students with colleagues in my school, district, state, or country?
- To what extent and in what ways do I collaborate with my colleagues to provide CLD students with appropriate educational services?
- In what ways have I changed my professional practice as a result of getting to know my students, reading professional literature, collaborating with my colleagues, participating in workshops or graduate classes, and reflecting on my teaching practice?
- How do I become actively involved in advocating for the rights of CLD students and families?
- What role does social justice play in my professional practice and in my curriculum?

Step 2: Your answers to the previous questions provide evidence for assessing your teaching practice. Using Figure 10.4, write your responses to the reflection questions on the right-hand side of the T-chart.

Step 3: Refer to Chapters 4 and 5 to collect evidence concerning research-based teaching practice.

■**figure 10.4**   Professionalism, Reflection, and Evaluation of Practice Chart

Research-Based Teaching Practice	My Teaching Practice
Example:	*Example:*
• Adult or teacher reflection involves building a capacity for surfacing assumptions and testing the validity of those assumptions (Murry, 1996).	• As I read through this book, I actively compared what I am doing in my classroom to what the research indicates I should be doing, but I didn't try to identify my underlying assumptions regarding teaching CLD students.

For any differences between what research indicates is good teaching practice and what you are currently doing, explain why you are choosing your alternative teaching practices.

Step 4: Write the evidence you collect regarding research-based teaching practice on the left-hand side of the T-chart.

Step 5: Compare how you currently address professionalism in your professional practice with what research indicates is effective teaching practice. For any difference between what research indicates is good teaching practice and what you currently do, explain what has prompted you to choose your current teaching practices.

Step 6: Finally, use the evidence you have gathered from the teaching practice T-chart to rate yourself using the rubric of Table 10.5.

■ **table 10.5**   Professionalism, Reflection, and Evaluation of Practice Rubric

	LEVEL OF PERFORMANCE			
Element	**Unsatisfactory**	**Basic**	**Proficient**	**Distinguished**
I reflect on the multidimensional educational needs of my CLD students and take action to ensure academic success.	I do not reflect on the multidimensional educational needs of my CLD students and do not take action to ensure academic success.	I seldom reflect on the multidimensional educational needs of my CLD students and sometimes take action to ensure academic success.	I generally reflect on the multidimensional educational needs of my CLD students and often take action to ensure academic success.	I regularly reflect on the multidimensional educational needs of my CLD students and regularly take action to ensure academic success.
I communicate in a language the parents understand and pursue nontraditional ways of ensuring participation in their child's education.	I do not communicate in a language parents understand and pursue few ways of ensuring participation in their child's education.	I seldom communicate in a language the parents understand and pursue few nontraditional ways of ensuring participation in their child's education.	I regularly communicate in a language the parents understand and often pursue nontraditional ways of ensuring participation in their child's education.	I regularly and consistently communicate in a language the parents understand and sensitively pursue nontraditional ways of ensuring participation in their child's education.
I look for ways to share my knowledge of CLD students and their needs with colleagues and district administrators to ensure equity in access to high-quality education.	I do not share my knowledge of CLD students and their needs with colleagues and district administrators.	I sometimes share my knowledge of CLD students and their needs with colleagues and district administrators to ensure equity in access to high-quality education.	I frequently share my knowledge of CLD students and their needs with colleagues and district administrators to ensure equity in access to high-quality education.	I consistently and efficiently share my knowledge of CLD students and their needs with colleagues and district administrators to ensure equity in access to high-quality education.
I recognize the need to continue enhancing my professional knowledge and its role in advocacy and decision making.	I do not consider the need to enhance my professional knowledge and its role in advocacy and decision making.	I sometimes consider the importance of enhancing my professional knowledge and its role in advocacy and decision making.	I frequently recognize the need to continue enhancing my professional knowledge and its role in advocacy and decision making.	I consistently and regularly recognize the need to continue enhancing my professional knowledge and its role in advocacy and decision making.

Source: Adapted for use with CLD students from Danielson (2007).

■ Conclusion: Setting Goals for Professional Development

As you read this chapter, you should be assessing your professional practice in terms of current research and national teaching standards.

- How did you rate yourself?
- Were you honest with yourself?
- What surprised you?
- Did you confirm what you already knew about your professional practice?
- Was self-assessment uncomfortable? Why or why not?
- In what ways did you critically reflect on your self-assessments?
- In what ways will you refine your practice as a result of applying the benchmarks of self-assessment, critical reflection, and refinement of practice?

At this point in your self-assessment process, you should reexamine your responses to the reflection questions, the T-charts, and the rubrics to discern your areas of strength and your areas for growth. Then, using Table 10.6, choose two or three areas in which you have the most potential for growth. Use the table to write goals, list potential resources, decide on actions, and determine expected outcomes. In this manner, you can maximize Table 10.6 as a guide to your ongoing professional development.

Fullan (2007) has summarized the necessary conditions for change in a teacher's professional practice. Specifically, he discussed the importance of changing personal perspectives on teaching, using new instructional materials, and participating in professional development designed to support change in practice. However, all of these essential elements, as they relate to the education of English learners, may or may not be readily available in your teaching environment. If new instructional materials and professional development opportunities for educating students are not readily available, then you must rely on your own research and volition. Consider the ways in which you might (1) build your knowledge base through reading professional literature, (2) collaborate with other educators to advise and coach one another, (3) focus on your relative strengths to discuss with students how your teaching affects their learning, (4) make better use of or adapt available resources, and (5) gather new resources. This process of professional growth should not occur in isolation. Create a relationship of mutual support with other educators who are progressing through the same self-reflective process.

Now that you know what research-defined effective practice for CLD students entails, how will you share that information with students, parents, colleagues, administrators, and policy makers? What are you going to do to become a self-directed learner and make the necessary changes in your professional practice? In what ways are you going to address inappropriate teaching practices in your school? As Howard Zinn (2002) has so astutely observed, "You can't be neutral on a moving train" (p. i). We challenge you to move forward using what you have learned to initiate and sustain the change process in your own professional practice, encourage and support changes in the practice of other educators, and advocate for educational policies and practices that ensure equitable access to high-quality education for all CLD students.

■ **t a b l e 1 0 . 6**   Setting Goals for Professional Development

Perceived Area(s) of Growth	Related Goals	Potential Resources	Actions	Expected Outcomes
Example: Using CLD students' first languages as a resource	*Example:* CLD students in my classroom will use their native languages as a resource for understanding classroom instruction and texts.	*Example:* • Bilingual peers • Bilingual para-professionals • Parents • Siblings • Native language texts/materials • Teachers using the native languages of students for instruction • Professional books and journals	*Example:* 1. Read journal articles and talk to experienced teachers about providing students with native language support. 2. Encourage my students to use their native languages in more capable peer or collaborative group activities that emphasize literacy and connections to prior knowledge. 3. Teach my students to recognize and use cognates to enhance their understanding of content. 4. Use bilingual paraprofessionals or others to work on developing content understanding in the native language of the student, rather than translating homework. 5. Gather content-related texts in the languages represented in my classroom.	*Example:* 1. CLD students will increase their reading comprehension and content understanding as measured by a minimum of one letter grade higher average in my class. 2. CLD students' active involvement in classroom instruction will increase by 50 percent.

Connect, Engage, Challenge

CONNECT
Review and Reflect on the Reading

1. In what specific ways can an educator maximize standards of best practice with CLD students?
2. What are the origins and general purposes of at least two nationally recognized sets of standards for best practice with CLD students?
3. What are the benchmarks of effective practice with CLD students, as discussed in this chapter? In what ways do these benchmarks target standards-driven reflection on professional practice?
4. What role does a teacher's perspectives on content and language learning play in instructional planning?
5. In what specific ways is practice enhanced when it is well grounded in theory and research?
6. In what ways would you define evidence in the context of teaching?
7. In what ways can the use of backward mapping enhance instructional planning?
8. What is the role of a caring connection between the CLD student and his or her teacher in professional practice?

ENGAGE
Share What You Learned

1. This chapter demonstrates the ways in which ESL/EFL educators can achieve standards-driven professional practice with CLD students and families by maximizing self-assessment, critical reflection, and refinement of practice. Discuss the critical importance of standards-driven professional practice and at least three beneficial outcomes that are possible from targeting this level of practice.
2. This chapter serves as the evaluation component of Part Three of this text. Discuss the following: (1) the rationale behind the organization of this text in relation to professional practice with CLD students and (2) the role this chapter plays in that organization.

CHALLENGE
It's Not Real until You Practice

Preservice Teachers

1. Compare and contrast the four key facets of a platform for best practice with CLD students. Discuss the implications of each facet for providing CLD students with a high-quality education.
2. This chapter discusses the benefits of aligning classroom pedagogy with standards. When choosing standards that promote CLD student excellence, it is important to consider how you can address each of the four key facets identified in this chapter. Therefore, obtain a set of state or district standards and analyze the standards using the guiding questions below.

In the case of theory- and research-based support for best practices, consider the following:

- Are the standards based on cited sources of research and theory?
- How current are the sources cited?
- Are the sources derived from robust analyses of theory and rigorous research applicable to CLD students?
- How applicable is the supporting research to the differential learning and adjustment needs of CLD students in your region?

In the case of cross-cultural sensitivity, consider the following:

- Do the standards control for biases regarding culture and ethnicity?
- Do the standards consider important information related to culture and ethnicity?
- Do the standards demonstrate inclusive perspectives on culture and ethnicity?
- Do the standards promote diversity, multiculturalism, and cross-cultural affirmation in the school and in the classroom?
- Do the standards support student acculturation without assimilation?

In the case of the extent to which standards can be directly connected to classroom practice, consider the following:

- Can you make direct connections between the standards and your educational practice?
- Can you make a strong connection between the standards and the student populations represented in your school?
- Are specific indicators of best practice incorporated into the standards?
- Can language and content objectives be aligned with the standards?

In the case of advocacy and leadership, consider the following:

- Do the standards promote advocacy for appropriate programming, differentiated classroom instruction, and CLD student accommodation?
- Do the standards support and encourage ongoing CALP development in L1 for CLD students?
- Do the standards encourage teacher leadership in the school, district, state, and region?
- Do the standards support collaboration among educators in providing appropriate accommodations for CLD students and families?
- Do the standards endorse ongoing professional development, especially professional development that better prepares teachers, administrators, and staff members for the differential learning, language learning, and transitional needs of CLD students?

In-Service Teachers

1. In a collaborative group, discuss the four key facets of a platform for best practice with CLD students and the feasibility of implementing each of these key facets in your professional practice. Then, as a group, create a lesson plan that reflects elements of each key facet and implement it with CLD students. Assess the effectiveness of the lesson as a collaborative group.

2. As a collaborative group, select one of the four key facets and an element within that facet. Discuss what evidence you would collect as a group to demonstrate attainment of the highest level of performance.

3. In a collaborative group, discuss (1) current standards in your educational setting, (2) how standards influence selection of curriculum, and (3) ways you could redesign or adapt curriculum to address standards for best practice and student learning outcomes more effectively.

tips for practice

Note: Tips for practice are listed according to each of the four key facets of a platform for best practice with CLD students. These resources are variously applicable to teachers in ESL and EFL educational contexts.

If you would like more information on *language development and learning dynamics* as they relate to CLD students, the following books will further your professional development in this area:

1. Brown, H. D. (2006). *Principles of language learning and teaching* (5th ed.). Boston: Pearson.

   This book explores certain principles of language acquisition and teaching for that acquisition that is not always addressed by ESL texts.

2. De la Luz Reyes, M., & Halcón, J. (2001). *The best for our children: Critical perspectives on literacy for Latino students.* New York: Teachers College Press.

   This book provides tips for literacy instruction for CLD students, teaching CLD students who have learning disabilities, making literacy culturally relevant for CLD students, helping CLD students develop critical literacy, and involving parents in CLD students' literacy development.

3. Horwitz, E. (2012). *Becoming a language teacher: A practical guide to second language learning and teaching.* Boston: Allyn and Bacon.

   This book acknowledges that the development of academic literacy is the goal of many language teachers and is essential to the school success of English learners.

If you would like more information on the *sociopolitical and sociocultural realities* of practice as they relate to CLD students, the following books will further your professional development in this area:

1. Au, W., Bigelow, B., & Karp, S. (2007). *Rethinking our classrooms: Teaching for equity and justice,* Vol. 1. New York: Rethinking Schools Limited.

   This book explores the many connections between critical teaching and effective practice in socioculturally and sociolinguistically diverse schools.

2. Cummins, J. (2001). *Language, power, and pedagogy: Bilingual children caught in the crossfire.* Philadelphia: Multilingual Matters.

   This book explains how the sociopolitical realities of U.S. society affect the education of CLD students and provides a framework for addressing these realities through classroom instruction.

3. Darling-Hammond, L., French, J., & García-Lopez, S. (2002). *Learning to teach for social justice.* New York: Teachers College Press.

   This book describes ways in which teachers can lead students to identify and challenge cultural assumptions, restructure curriculum to examine topics from multiple points of view and challenge students to take action on social issues, promote respect and inclusion of all students within a classroom, encourage students to graduate from high school, and build community.

4. Diaz-Rico, L. T. (2014). *The crosscultural, language, and academic development handbook: A complete K–12 reference guide* (5th ed.). Boston: Allyn and Bacon.

This book connects culture and language in a comprehensive format and explores, in-depth, the educational challenges faced by classroom teachers.

5. Tse, L. (2001). *Why don't they learn English? Separating fact from fallacy in the U.S. language debate.* New York: Teachers College Press.

This book dispels misconceptions regarding language use and learning in the United States.

If you would like more information on *planning, implementing, and managing instruction* as they relate to CLD students, the following books will further your professional development in this area:

1. Brinton, D., Snow, M., & Wesche, M. (2003). *Content-based second language instruction: Michigan classics.* Ann Arbor: University of Michigan Press.

This book provides an in-depth description of integrated content-based instruction.

2. Chamot, A. (2009). *The CALLA handbook: Implementing the cognitive academic language learning approach* (2nd ed.). Reading, MA: Addison-Wesley.

This book provides an in-depth description of the CALLA method and its use in a variety of instructional settings.

3. Echevarria, J., Vogt, M., & Short, D. (2012). *Making content comprehensible for English language learners: The SIOP Model* (4th ed.). Boston: Allyn and Bacon.

This book offers teachers a framework for lesson planning and implementation that provides students with access to grade-level content as they acquire English.

If you would like more information on *professionalism, reflection, and evaluation of practice* as they relate to CLD students, the following books will further your professional development in this area:

1. Brown, H. D. (2007). *Teaching by principles: An interactive approach to language pedagogy* (3rd ed.). Boston: Pearson.

This book is a comprehensive survey of practical language teaching options, all firmly anchored in accepted principles of language learning and professionalism in teaching.

2. Danielson, C. (2007). *Enhancing professional practice: A framework for teaching* (2nd ed.). Alexandria, VA: Association for Supervision and Curriculum Development.

This book provides an extensive description of effective teaching practice as well as a teacher assessment tool that addresses effective teaching from multiple perspectives.

3. Fullan, M. (2007). *The new meaning of educational change* (4th ed.). New York: Teachers College Press.

This book provides an in-depth discussion of the educational change process and makes suggestions for initiating, implementing, and sustaining educational change.

4. Miramontes, O., Nadeau, A., & Commins, N. (2011). *Restructuring schools for linguistic diversity: Linking decision making to effective programs* (2nd ed). New York: Teachers College Press.

This book offers a decision-making framework for developing and implementing instructional programming for CLD students.

5. Vavrus, M. (2002). *Transforming the multicultural education of teachers: Theory, research, and practice.* New York: Teachers College Press.

This book gives recommendations for addressing the sociopolitical and multicultural realities of professional practice with diverse student populations. Vavrus goes beyond the celebration mentality of multicultural education to pose difficult but necessary questions to move teachers and teacher educators to a transformative view of multicultural education.

Critical Standards Guiding Chapter Content

TESOL/NCATE teacher standards reflect professional consensus on standards for the quality teaching of Pre-K–12 CLD students. To help educators understand how they might appropriately target and address national professional teaching standards in practice, we have designed the content of this book to reflect the following standards. All TESOL/NCATE standards are cited from TESOL (2010) and reprinted with permission.

■ Chapter 1
Multidimensional Foundations of Methods for Culturally and Linguistically Diverse Students

TESOL ESL Standards for P–12 Teacher Education Programs

TESOL ESL—Domain 1: Language. Candidates know, understand, and use the major theories and research related to the structure and acquisition of language to help English language learners (ELLs) [CLD students] develop language and literacy and achieve in the content areas. (p. 26)

- Standard 1.b. Language Acquisition and Development. Candidates understand and apply theories and research in language acquisition and development to support their ELLs' [CLD students'] English language and literacy learning and content-area achievement. (p. 32)

  1.b.4. Understand and apply knowledge of sociocultural, psychological, and political variables to facilitate the process of learning English. (p. 36)

  1.b.5. Understand and apply knowledge of the role of individual learner variables in the process of learning English. (p. 36)

TESOL ESL—Domain 2: Culture. Candidates know, understand, and use major concepts, principles, theories, and research related to the nature and role of culture and cultural groups to construct learning environments for ELLs [CLD students]. (p. 38)

- Standard 2. Culture as It Affects Student Learning. Candidates know, understand, and use major theories and research related to the nature and role of culture in their instruction. They demonstrate understanding of how cultural groups and individual cultural identities affect language learning and school achievement. (p. 38)

2.b. Understand and apply knowledge about the effects of racism, stereotyping, and discrimination to teaching and learning. (p. 40)

2.e. Understand and apply concepts about the interrelationship between language and culture. (p. 41)

Chapter 2
Cognitive and Academic Dimensions of Methods for Culturally and Linguistically Diverse Students

TESOL ESL Standards for P–12 Teacher Education Programs

TESOL ESL—Domain 1: Language. Candidates know, understand, and use the major theories and research related to the structure and acquisition of language to help English language learners (ELLs) [CLD students] develop language and literacy and achieve in the content areas. (p. 26)

- Standard 1.b. Language Acquisition and Development. Candidates understand and apply theories and research in language acquisition and development to support their ELLs' [CLD students'] English language and literacy learning and content-area achievement. (p. 32)

  1.b.5. Understand and apply knowledge of the role of individual learner variables in the process of learning English. (p. 36)

TESOL ESL—Domain 3: Planning, Implementing, and Managing Instruction. Candidates know, understand, and use evidence-based practices and strategies related to planning, implementing, and managing standards-based ESL and content instruction. Candidates are knowledgeable about program models and skilled in teaching strategies for developing and integrating language skills. They integrate technology as well as choose and adapt classroom resources appropriate for their ELLs [CLD students]. (p. 43)

- Standard 3.a. Planning for Standards-Based ESL and Content Instruction. Candidates know, understand, and apply concepts, research, and best practices to plan classroom instruction in a supportive learning environment for ELLs [CLD students]. They plan for multilevel classrooms with learners from diverse backgrounds using standards-based ESL and content curriculum. (p. 43)

  3.a.3. Plan differentiated learning experiences based on assessment of students' English and L1 language proficiency, learning styles, and prior formal educational experiences and knowledge. (pp. 44–45)

- Standard 3.c. Using Resources and Technology Effectively in ESL and Content Instruction. Candidates are familiar with a wide range of standards-based materials, resources, and technologies, and choose, adapt, and use them in effective ESL and content teaching. (p. 53)

  3.c.3. Employ a variety of materials for language learning, including books, visual aids, props, and realia. (p. 55)

■ Chapter 3
Linguistic Dimension of Methods for
Culturally and Linguistically Diverse Students

TESOL ESL Standards for P–12 Teacher Education Programs

TESOL ESL—Domain 1: Language. Candidates know, understand, and use the major theories and research related to the structure and acquisition of language to help English language learners (ELLs) [CLD students] develop language and literacy and achieve in the content areas. (p. 26)

- Standard 1.a. Language as a System. Candidates demonstrate understanding of language as a system, including phonology, morphology, syntax, pragmatics and semantics, and support ELLs [CLD students] as they acquire English language and literacy in order to achieve in the content areas. (p. 27)

    1.a.2. Apply knowledge of *phonology* (the sound system), *morphology* (the structure of words), *syntax* (phrase and sentence structure), *semantics* (word/sentence meaning), and *pragmatics* (the effect of context on language) to help ELLs [CLD students] develop oral, reading, and writing skills (including mechanics) in English. (pp. 28–29)

- Standard 1.b. Language Acquisition and Development. Candidates understand and apply theories and research in language acquisition and development to support their ELLs' [CLD students'] English language and literacy learning and content-area achievement. (p. 32)

    1.b.1. Demonstrate understanding of current and historical theories and research in language acquisition as applied to ELLs [CLD students]. (p. 34)

    1.b.2. Candidates understand theories and research that explain how L1 literacy development differs from L2 literacy development. (p. 34)

    1.b.3. Recognize the importance of ELLs' [CLD students'] L1s and language varieties and build on these skills as a foundation for learning English. (p. 35)

■ Chapter 4
Changing Perspectives in Platform Development for
Instructional Methods

TESOL ESL Standards for P–12 Teacher Education Programs

TESOL ESL—Domain 1: Language. Candidates know, understand, and use the major theories and research related to the structure and acquisition of language to help English language learners (ELLs) [CLD students] develop language and literacy and achieve in the content areas. (p. 26)

- Standard 1.b. Language Acquisition and Development. Candidates understand and apply theories and research in language acquisition and development to support their ELLs' [CLD students'] English language and literacy learning and content-area achievement. (p. 32)

  1.b.3. Recognize the importance of ELLs' [CLD students'] L1s and language varieties and build on these skills as a foundation for learning English. (p. 35)

TESOL ESL—Domain 5: Professionalism. Candidates keep current with new instructional techniques, research results, advances in the ESL field, and education policy issues and demonstrate knowledge of the history of ESL teaching. They use such information to reflect on and improve their instruction and assessment practices. Candidates work collaboratively with school staff and the community to improve the learning environment, provide support, and advocate for ELLs [CLD students] and their families. (p. 68)

- Standard 5.a. ESL Research and History. Candidates demonstrate knowledge of history, research, educational public policy, and current practice in the field of ESL teaching and apply this knowledge to inform teaching and learning. (p. 68)

  5.a.2. Demonstrate knowledge of the evolution of laws and policy in the ESL profession. (p. 69)

■ Chapter 5
A Framework of Accommodation Readiness

TESOL ESL Standards for P–12 Teacher Education Programs

TESOL ESL—Domain 2: Culture. Candidates know, understand, and use the major concepts, principles, theories, and research related to the nature and role of culture and cultural groups to construct learning environments for ELLs [CLD students]. (p. 38)

- Standard 2. Culture as It Affects Student Learning. Candidates know, understand, and use major theories and research related to the nature and role of culture in their instruction. They demonstrate understanding of how cultural groups and individual cultural identities affect language learning and school achievement. (p. 38)

  2.d. Understand and apply knowledge about communication between home and school to enhance ESL teaching and build partnerships with ESOL [CLD] families. (p. 41)

TESOL ESL—Domain 5: Professionalism. Candidates keep current with new instructional techniques, research results, advances in the ESL field, and education policy issues and demonstrate knowledge of the history of ESL teaching. They use such information to reflect on and improve their instruction and assessment practices. Candidates work collaboratively with school staff and the community to improve the learning environment, provide support, and advocate for ELLs [CLD students] and their families. (p. 68)

- Standard 5.b. Professional Development, Partnerships, and Advocacy. Candidates take advantage of professional growth opportunities and demonstrate the ability to build partnerships with colleagues and students' families, serve as community resources, and advocate for ELLs [CLD students]. (p. 71)

  5.b.1. Participate in professional growth opportunities. (p. 72)

  5.b.2. Establish professional goals. (p. 72)

  5.b.3. Work with other teachers and staff to provide comprehensive, challenging educational opportunities for ELLs [CLD students] in the school. (pp. 72–73)

Chapter 6
Planning and Grounding Instructional Methodology

TESOL ESL Standards for P–12 Teacher Education Programs

TESOL ESL—Domain 1: Language. Candidates know, understand, and use the major theories and research related to the structure and acquisition of language to help English language learners (ELLs) [CLD students] develop language and literacy and achieve in the content areas. (p. 26)

- Standard 1.b. Language Acquisition and Development. Candidates understand and apply theories and research in language acquisition and development to support their ELLs' [CLD students'] English language and literacy learning and content-area achievement. (p. 32)

  1.b.5. Understand and apply knowledge of the role of individual learner variables in the process of learning English. (p. 36)

TESOL ESL—Domain 5: Professionalism. Candidates keep current with new instructional techniques, research results, advances in the ESL field, and education policy issues and demonstrate knowledge of the history of ESL teaching. They use such information to reflect on and improve their instruction and assessment practices. Candidates work collaboratively with school staff and the community to improve the learning environment, provide support, and advocate for ELLs [CLD students] and their families. (p. 68)

- Standard 5.a. ESL Research and History. Candidates demonstrate knowledge of history, research, educational public policy, and current practice in the field of ESL teaching and apply this knowledge to inform teaching and learning. (p. 68)

  5.a.1. Demonstrate knowledge of language teaching methods in their historical contexts. (p. 69)

■ Chapter 7
The Integrated Content-Based
Method of Instruction

TESOL ESL Standards for P–12 Teacher Education Programs

TESOL ESL—Domain 1: Language. Candidates know, understand, and use the major theories and research related to the structure and acquisition of language to help English language learners (ELLs) [CLD students] develop language and literacy and achieve in the content areas. (p. 26)

- Standard 1.b. Language Acquisition and Development. Candidates understand and apply theories and research in language acquisition and development to support their ELLs' [CLD students'] English language and literacy learning and content-area achievement. (p. 32)

  1.b.1. Demonstrate understanding of current and historical theories and research in language acquisition as applied to ELLs [CLD students]. (p. 34)

  1.b.5. Understand and apply knowledge of the role of individual learner variables in the process of learning English. (p. 36)

TESOL ESL—Domain 3: Planning, Implementing, and Managing Instruction. Candidates know, understand, and use evidence-based practices and strategies related to planning, implementing, and managing standards-based ESL and content instruction. Candidates are knowledgeable about program models and skilled in teaching strategies for developing and integrating language skills. They integrate technology as well as choose and adapt classroom resources appropriate for their ELLs [CLD students]. (p. 43)

- Standard 3.b. Implementing and Managing Standards-Based ESL and Content Instruction. Candidates know, manage, and implement a variety of standards-based teaching strategies and techniques for developing and integrating English listening, speaking, reading, and writing. Candidates support ELLs' [CLD students'] access to the core curriculum by teaching language through academic content. (p. 47)

  3.b.3. Provide activities and materials that integrate listening, speaking, reading, and writing. (pp. 48–49)

TESOL ESL—Domain 4: Assessment. Candidates demonstrate understanding of issues and concepts of assessment and use standards-based procedures with ELLs [CLD students]. (p. 56)

- Standard 4.c. Classroom-Based Assessment for ESL. Candidates know and can use a variety of performance-based assessment tools and techniques to inform instruction for in [sic] the classroom. (p. 64)

  4.c.1. Use performance-based assessment tools and tasks that measure ELLs' [CLD students'] progress. (p. 65)

■ Chapter 8
The Sheltered Method of Instruction

TESOL ESL Standards for P–12 Teacher Education Programs

TESOL ESL—Domain 3: Planning, Implementing, and Managing Instruction. Candidates know, understand, and use evidence-based practices and strategies related to planning, implementing, and managing standards-based ESL and content instruction. Candidates are knowledgeable about program models and skilled in teaching strategies for developing and integrating language skills. They integrate technology as well as choose and adapt classroom resources appropriate for their ELLs [CLD students]. (p. 43)

- Standard 3.a. Planning for Standards-Based ESL and Content Instruction. Candidates know, understand, and apply concepts, research, and best practices to plan classroom instruction in a supportive learning environment for ELLs [CLD students]. They plan for multilevel classrooms with learners from diverse backgrounds using standards-based ESL and content curriculum. (p. 43)

  3.a.3. Plan differentiated learning experiences based on assessment of students' English and L1 language proficiency, learning styles, and prior formal educational experiences and knowledge. (pp. 44–45)

- Standard 3.c. Using Resources and Technology Effectively in ESL and Content Instruction. Candidates are familiar with a wide range of standards-based materials, resources, and technologies, and choose, adapt, and use them in effective ESL and content teaching. (p. 53)

  3.c.2. Select materials and other resources that are appropriate to students' developing language and content-area abilities, including appropriate use of L1. (p. 54)

  3.c.3. Employ a variety of materials for language learning, including books, visual aids, props, and realia. (p. 55)

TESOL ESL—Domain 4: Assessment. Candidates demonstrate understanding of issues and concepts of assessment and use standards-based procedures with ELLs [CLD students]. (p. 56)

- Standard 4.c. Classroom-Based Assessment for ESL. Candidates know and can use a variety of performance-based assessment tools and techniques to inform instruction for in [*sic*] the classroom. (p. 64)

  4.c.3. Use various instruments and techniques to assess content-area learning (e.g., math, science, social studies) for ELLs [CLD students] at varying levels of language and literacy development. (p. 66)

■ Chapter 9
The CALLA Method of Instruction

TESOL ESL Standards for P–12 Teacher Education Programs

TESOL ESL—Domain 1: Language. Candidates know, understand, and use the major theories and research related to the structure and acquisition of language to help English language learners (ELLs) [CLD students] develop language and literacy and achieve in the content areas. (p. 26)

- Standard 1.b. Language Acquisition and Development. Candidates understand and apply theories and research in language acquisition and development to support their ELLs' [CLD students'] English language and literacy learning and content-area achievement. (p. 32)

  1.b.3. Recognize the importance of ELLs' [CLD students'] L1s and language varieties and build on these skills as a foundation for learning English. (p. 35)

TESOL ESL—Domain 3: Planning, Implementing, and Managing Instruction. Candidates know, understand, and use evidence-based practices and strategies related to planning, implementing, and managing standards-based ESL and content instruction. Candidates are knowledgeable about program models and skilled in teaching strategies for developing and integrating language skills. They integrate technology as well as choose and adapt classroom resources appropriate for their ELLs [CLD students]. (p. 43)

- Standard 3.a. Planning for Standards-Based ESL and Content Instruction. Candidates know, understand, and apply concepts, research, and best practices to plan classroom instruction in a supportive learning environment for ELLs [CLD students]. They plan for multilevel classrooms with learners from diverse backgrounds using standards-based ESL and content curriculum. (p. 43)

  3.a.3. Plan differentiated learning experiences based on assessment of students' English and L1 language proficiency, learning styles, and prior formal educational experiences and knowledge. (pp. 44–45)

- Standard 3.c. Using Resources and Technology Effectively in ESL and Content Instruction. Candidates are familiar with a wide range of standards-based materials, resources, and technologies, and choose, adapt, and use them in effective ESL and content teaching. (p. 53)

  3.c.3. Employ a variety of materials for language learning, including books, visual aids, props, and realia. (p. 55)

TESOL ESL—Domain 4: Assessment. Candidates demonstrate understanding of issues and concepts of assessment and use standards-based procedures with ELLs [CLD students]. (p. 56)

- Standard 4.c. Classroom-Based Assessment for ESL. Candidates know and can use a variety of performance-based assessment tools and techniques to inform instruction for in [*sic*] the classroom. (p. 64)

    4.c.3. Use various instruments and techniques to assess content-area learning (e.g., math, science, social studies) for ELLs [CLD students] at varying levels of language and literacy development. (p. 66)

■ Chapter 10
Achieving Standards-Driven Professional Practice

TESOL ESL Standards for P–12 Teacher Education Programs

TESOL ESL—Domain 3: Planning, Implementing, and Managing Instruction. Candidates know, understand, and use evidence-based practices and strategies related to planning, implementing, and managing standards-based ESL and content instruction. Candidates are knowledgeable about program models and skilled in teaching strategies for developing and integrating language skills. They integrate technology as well as choose and adapt classroom resources appropriate for their ELLs [CLD students]. (p. 43)

- Standard 3.a. Planning for Standards-Based ESL and Content Instruction. Candidates know, understand, and apply concepts, research, and best practices to plan classroom instruction in a supportive learning environment for ELLs [CLD students]. They plan for multilevel classrooms with learners from diverse backgrounds using standards-based ESL and content curriculum. (p. 43)

    3.a.1. Plan standards-based ESL and content instruction. (p. 44)

- Standard 3.c. Using Resources and Technology Effectively in ESL and Content Instruction. Candidates are familiar with a wide range of standards-based materials, resources, and technologies, and choose, adapt, and use them in effective ESL and content teaching. (p. 53)

    3.c.1. Select, adapt, and use culturally responsive, age-appropriate, and linguistically accessible materials. (p. 54)

TESOL ESL—Domain 5: Professionalism. Candidates keep current with new instructional techniques, research results, advances in the ESL field, and education policy issues and demonstrate knowledge of the history of ESL teaching. They use such information to reflect on and improve their instruction and assessment practices. Candidates work collaboratively with school staff and the community to improve the learning environment, provide support, and advocate for ELLs [CLD students] and their families. (p. 68)

- Standard 5.b. Professional Development, Partnerships, and Advocacy. Candidates take advantage of professional growth opportunities and demonstrate the ability to build partnerships with colleagues and students' families, serve as community resources, and advocate for ELLs [CLD students]. (p. 71)

5.b.2. Establish professional goals. (p. 72)

5.b.5. Advocate for ELLs' [CLD students'] access to academic classes, resources, and instructional technology. (p. 73)

5.b.6. Support ELL [CLD] families. (p. 74)

5.b.7. Serve as professional resource personnel in their educational communities. (pp. 74–75)

Selected Examples of Activities Specific to Sociocultural, Academic, Cognitive, and Linguistic Growth among Mexican American Students

Because the overwhelming majority of CLD students in the United States are Spanish-dominant and because many of these students are Mexican American, this appendix provides examples of classroom activities that are specific to the background experiences and growth needs of these students. These activities are organized according to those applicable to elementary, middle, and high school. Within each of these categories, the activities are further subdivided according to those that apply to language arts, mathematics, and social studies.

■ Elementary School

1. **Mathematics:** Ask students to talk about their experiences at the *mercado* (market) in Mexico, in either Spanish or English (ask a paraprofessional, community volunteer, or more capable peer to translate as necessary). Have students draw their favorite items to buy at the *mercado* (especially items not typically available in your region of the United States). (*Note:* Students may be familiar with terms other than *mercado,* such as *colmado.*) Discuss with students a fair price to attach to their favorite items in U.S. currency based on their prior experiences. For example, if they have, in their prior experience, purchased a mango for 13 pesos and there are roughly 13 pesos to the dollar at this time, then the item would cost one U.S. dollar. Then ask students to select U.S. coins from a classroom box that will enable them to purchase two of their favorite items with the least amount of coins. Allow students to experiment in a meaningful and constructivist way with various coin combinations to arrive at the optimal mathematical solution.

2. **Mathematics:** Heterogeneously group students by language and mathematical capabilities. For any newcomer students, ensure that a more capable Spanish-speaking peer is also in that group (as feasible). Ask students to use the Internet to research the role of mariachi bands and music in Mexican culture. Have Mexican American students share their experiences with mariachi bands with the group in L1 or L2 (collaborate with paraprofessionals or more capable peers to translate as needed). Provide students with opportunities to listen to mariachi music that you have acquired through local sources or the Internet. Discuss the ways

in which many mariachi bands include as many as 12 members, each of whom may sing or play a different musical instrument. Have students locate pictures of mariachi bands on the Internet. Ask them to print these photographs (black-and-white or color) and cut pictures to form their own 12-member mariachi band. Have students collaborate to solve each of the following mathematical challenges involving fractions and their mariachi band: (a) If your mariachi band has been performing for several hours and ½ of the band decides to take a break of 10 minutes, what fraction of the band is left to perform and how many band members remain? (b) If ⅔ of your 12-member mariachi band perform in the restaurant and ⅓ performs on the patio, how many band members are on the patio? (c) If ⅙ of your complete mariachi band is featured in the performance of a particular song, how many band members are featured and what fraction of the band is not featured?

3. **Language arts:** Use modified preview-view-review (Kole, 2003) to explore a big book text available in both Spanish and English (e.g., *Cómo Nació el Arco Iris* [Ada, 1999]). First, use a paraprofessional, parent volunteer, or community liaison to *preview* the story in Spanish, using the big book for illustration. Discuss difficult vocabulary that may inhibit understanding in Spanish. Second, *view* or read the book to the students in English, again maximizing the big book illustrations to establish context. Third, *review* the book in Spanish to clarify any misunderstandings among students.

4. **Language arts:** Each week of the school year, encourage bilingual literacy development by conducting a Friday Free Day. During a designated time on this day, students are *free* to write about whatever they wish, in whatever language they are comfortable. Collaborate with paraprofessionals, parent volunteers, community members, or more capable peers to translate any passage written in Spanish by your Mexican American students. Encourage *freewriting* and *creative spelling*. Maximize the writing of your Mexican American students as informal preassessment and assessment of important information, including level of acculturation, literacy development in Spanish, prior schooling or academic experiences, interests and motivators, and so forth. Provide nonthreatening feedback on students' writing samples, especially feedback that is intentionally designed to encourage their future writing efforts in purposive directions. Periodically engage Mexican American students in encouraging dialogue about their writing and other academic interests based on the areas of curiosity they have demonstrated in their writing samples (collaborate with a translator as needed).

5. **Social studies:** As a means of reinforcing a lesson on direction in geography, provide cooperative groups of students with a blank map of Mexico. Ask the groups to identify north, south, east, and west on the blank map, as well as borders and coasts. Use student records or notes from prior preassessments to focus the activity on particular cities or geographic regions in Mexico (e.g., border cities, ports, mountainous regions) with which they are familiar. Ask groups of students to identify a northern border town, a western beach town, an eastern port, or a southern mountainous region with which they are familiar. Ask Mexican American

students to share their prior experiences with the group's selected town or region of Mexico. Then provide each group with a map of Mexico (e.g., from a travel atlas). Ask each group to discuss the direction they would proceed in traveling from their selected town or region to (a) Mexico City, (b) the United States, and (c) Guatemala.

6. Social studies: Schedule a Special Day once a month throughout the school year. On this day, allow students to present to or share with the class anything about the geography, lifestyles, culture, or history of their background. Encourage all students, especially the Mexican American students, to invite parents, extended family members, or community members to share with the class as part of the presentation. Permit students or guests to share in Spanish or English by collaborating with more capable peers, paraprofessionals, or community members to translate as needed. Encourage students also to share artifacts, documents, or maps, and copy them for the class as feasible. Use these presentations as points of focus for discussions about commonalities and differences across cultures, the value of bilingualism, the importance of parental involvement, and more. Each month of the school year, create a bulletin board on which highlights from students' presentations are posted for the class and guests to review and discuss.

■ Middle School

1. Mathematics: Heterogeneously group students by language and mathematical capabilities. For any newcomer students, ensure that a more capable Spanish-speaking peer is also in that group (as feasible). Ask students to plan a trip from Mexico City to at least two major sites of pyramids in Mexico (i.e., they will visit two sites in one trip from Mexico City). Allow students to maximize the Internet in locating pyramid sites (e.g., Tulum) and in selecting the locations to which they wish to travel. Provide the groups with a map of Mexico that appropriately simplifies distances to potential sites (according to the mathematical and geographical capabilities represented among students), but posts those distances in kilometers. Ask students to highlight their best route from Mexico City to the two sites and use L1 or L2 to rationalize their choice (collaborate with community volunteers, paraprofessionals, or more capable peers to translate as needed). Students should then calculate the distance from Mexico City to the final site, via the first pyramid site, using their selected routes. This distance should be calculated in kilometers. Then ask students to determine the total distance traveled on their trip, in miles, using the conversion 1 kilometer = 0.62 miles. Finally, have groups compare their routes and trips. During this process, students should determine who had the longest and shortest trips (in miles) and estimate the driving time for each of those routes.

2. Language arts: Ask students to form cooperative learning groups, the members of which have mixed second language abilities. Provide a miniature Mexican flag or a large illustration of the flag to each group. Have the group members discuss in L1 or L2 what each of the figures and colors of the flag symbolize. If group members are unsure of these connotations, ask them to discuss what the flag symbolizes for each of the members of the group. Based on these discussions, ask each student to individually write (or type) in L1 or L2 what the flag means to her or him. As necessary, ask more capable peers, parent volunteers, or paraprofessionals to translate passages written in Spanish.

3. **Social studies:** Ask students to individually identify with a particular state in Mexico in which they have lived or have an interest (e.g., Tamaulipas). Then cooperatively group students (to the extent feasible) by the state or region (which might encompass two or more neighboring states) with which they have identified. Tell students to collaboratively identify a state of common interest for discussion and group research. Ask them to discuss and focus on the following: (a) What is the main industry or source of employment in that state of Mexico? (b) What are the major population centers and their density in that state? (c) What aspects of culture (styles of living, foods, celebrations, etc.) are unique to that state? First, ask students to discuss and answer the questions from their own experiences. Next, ask them to fill the knowledge gaps they identify by using the classroom library, school library, or Internet. Finally, ask groups to develop a brief presentation that explores answers to each of the questions. Offer the students options for presentation format, such as a board meeting, drama, or PowerPoint.

4. **Social studies:** Discuss with the class the concept of a passport. Obtain a passport from a friend or use graphics from a book or the Internet to illustrate the concept. Discuss with the class what is typically included and not included in a passport. Explore what someone from a new country who wanted to be your friend might want to know about you and whether such information would be included in a typical passport. Create an assignment in which each student in the class develops a Learning Passport. In this passport, they will include a picture, their full name, their country of origin, the region of the country in which they were born, information about their family and extended family, information about their culture, information about their key learning interests, information about what they interpret to be their strengths and weaknesses as learners, and information about what occupation they hope to pursue as an adult. Students will also include in their passport one teacher section for each period of the typical school day. Students should develop their Learning Passports as a foldout brochure using word-processing software, and they should keep an electronic copy as well. Bilingual students should be encouraged to develop bilingual, two-part passports with the aid of a paraprofessional, community volunteer, or more capable peer. Once the format and student sections of the brochure are complete, students should meet in heterogeneous learning groups to share their passports and discuss what they learned from each other. Next, students should share their Learning Passports and associated electronic files with their various teachers each quarter. In the appropriate teacher section of the passports, teachers should update each student's file to include those methods, strategies, and techniques of instruction that are proving

effective for him or her. The teacher should then return the reprinted brochure and file to the student. Students can periodically update their own Learning Passports and share them with parents and extended family members. Teachers can learn from each student and other teachers in the building (a) what the student brings to the classroom that can be elaborated on in classroom instruction; (b) what interests or motivates the student; and (c) what methods, strategies, and techniques have proven effective with the student.

■ High School

1. **Mathematics:** Discuss with students ways in which to figure out the time required to travel between cities at a given rate of speed. Ask students to form cooperative learning groups, the members of which have mixed second language abilities. Provide the groups with maps of Mexico. Ask students to select three cities in Mexico that are at least 35 miles away from one another. Tell students that they will be taking a road trip from the first city to the second and then to the third, without stopping for gasoline. Ask them to determine the distances between their selected cities from the map. Then ask them to derive an average speed for the car based on their knowledge of the region, terrain, and traffic. Next, ask students to deliberate, collaborate, and determine the amount of time required to reach each of the two destinations (e.g., time from city 1 to 2, time from city 2 to 3, and total time from city 1 to 3). Ask each group to briefly present its findings (in L1 or L2) and the methods the students used to arrive at each solution (collaborate with paraprofessionals, parent volunteers, or more capable peers for translations). After these presentations, conduct a whole-class discussion of this exercise with an emphasis on applications to other types of mathematical challenges (allow newcomer students to respond in L1 as necessary). For algebra students, also ask them to construct a word problem from their exercise, with answers already calculated. Discuss the ways in which word problems in algebra can be reframed by students into more culturally and experientially meaningful problems.

2. **Language arts:** Teach the concept of Spanish–English cognates. Have heterogeneous groups of Spanish- and English-dominant students research (using the Internet or the library) which Spanish–English cognates are useful in the following subject areas: mathematics, science, and history. After the group members have developed their lists for each subject area, ask them to research, for each subject area, the hypothesis that increasingly technical terms are more likely to be cognates. Finally, ask each group to (a) present its cognate lists to the class, (b) discuss the findings of the group's research regarding the hypothesis, and (c) discuss potential implications for second language acquisition.

3. **Social studies:** Heterogeneously group students by language ability and academic ability in social studies or history. Have students use library and Internet resources to compare presidents. Ask them to identify one president from the history

of Mexico and one from the history of the United States who were similar in background, philosophy, management style, foreign policy, and so forth. Tell the students to develop one or more graphics that illustrate these similarities (e.g., T-chart, web, table). Discuss the notion of culture and the ways in which a person learns a particular culture. Ask the students to research and develop a bulleted summary of reasons why these two presidents are similar despite the fact that each was socialized in a different culture. Have each group present or discuss its graphic(s) and summary. Highlight discussions that explore the ways in which cultures are similar.

academic dimension one of the four dimensions of the CLD student biography that involves the apparent aspects of the curriculum and instruction that students receive from prekindergarten classrooms to high school graduation and beyond. Equally important to this dimension is an understanding of the often hidden aspects of access, engagement, and hope that help students overcome the differential academic challenges that they encounter in relation to curriculum, instruction, and academic policy.

academic language development building of vocabulary and language skills required for success in decontextualized, cognitively demanding communicative situations and language-learning tasks frequently found in educational settings.

accommodation readiness spiral an emergent framework for readiness that has been developed by the authors and is based on over 30 years of field experience and evolving research with CLD students and their educators, including six levels of readiness: Level 1—Readiness for Critical Reflection on Practice; Level 2—Readiness for CLD Students and Families; Level 3—Environmental Readiness; Level 4—Curricular Readiness; Level 5—Programming and Instructional Readiness; and Level 6—Readiness for Application and Advocacy.

acculturation the process of adjusting to a new or non-native culture.

acquisition or learning hypothesis Krashen argues that when language learners have opportunities to interact with native speakers for purposes of authentic communication in inductive language learning environments, they are able to develop functional proficiency in the target language, or truly *acquire* the language. In contrast, when students receive deductive instruction, they develop only knowledge about a language (e.g., linguistic rules), or *learn* about a language.

adaptation of content one of the indicators of high-quality preparation using the SIOP model of sheltered instruction. Sometimes, grade-level texts and materials are difficult for CLD students to understand. However, using texts from lower grade levels and more simplified lectures, for example, does not provide CLD students with age- and grade-appropriate concepts and vocabulary. Therefore, to make grade-level texts and materials accessible to CLD students, teachers need to scaffold the content before, during, and after reading.

additive bilingualism associated with positive cognitive effects that enable the CLD student to attain high levels of proficiency in both L1 and L2.

advocacy the support of a cause that prompts a person to take action in ways that promote equitable resolutions.

affective filter hypothesis Krashen argues that the amount of input reaching the CLD student is influenced by a number of affective variables, including anxiety, self-confidence, and motivation.

affective involvement a strong emotional response to what is being taught/learned that helps students remember what they learn.

approach the philosophical orientation to instruction that serves as a guide for choosing among methods that are considered to be consistent with the tenets of the theory and scientifically based research that ground the philosophy. Selecting an approach is the first step in developing a plan for accommodative and differentiated instruction.

appropriate content concepts the third indicator of high-quality preparation addressed by effective SIOP teachers, in which they use the lesson objectives to develop concepts that are central to the theme of the unit or text chapter and are appropriate for the grade level and educational backgrounds of the students.

asset perspective a mindset that adheres to locating and maximizing the cultural identity of CLD students and families and the associated assets that they offer, such as (but not limited to) cultural values and insights, familiarity with multiple cultures and ethnicities, and experience with other languages.

authentic activities activities in an integrated content-based lesson that allow the teacher to create hands-on learning opportunities and authentic experiences, which involve speaking, listening, reading, and writing throughout the lesson. These activities reflect the interests, developmental levels, experiences, and various learning styles of CLD students.

behaviorism   a developmental perspective on learning that views environmental stimuli as shaping an individual's behavior, such that rewarded behaviors increase in frequency and punished behaviors decrease in frequency.

behaviorist   reflects the theory that children are born without any linguistic knowledge, so all language learning is a result of the environment.

benchmarks of effective practice   standards of professional practice that ensure that students are receiving high-quality education by incorporating a continuous cycle of teacher self-assessment, critical reflection, and refinement of practice.

building background   one of the categories of instruction in the SIOP model of sheltered instruction. This hallmark of accommodative instruction acknowledges that CLD students' prior life experiences and prior learning experiences greatly affect their ability to understand new content and language. If CLD students have already been exposed to the concepts discussed in the text, their comprehension is much greater than if the concepts are completely unfamiliar. This category of instruction highlights the importance of selecting and emphasizing key vocabulary to support students in connecting what they know to the new concepts and language of the lesson, thereby improving their content and language comprehension.

CALLA method   an instructional method of the cognitive approach that focuses on explicitly teaching CLD students to understand and tactically apply metacognitive, cognitive, and social/affective strategies.

cloze sentences   a passage in which the learner must use his or her understanding of a language system and prior knowledge to fill in words that have been purposely deleted to gather information about students' progress in language acquisition and content-area learning.

code switching   the use of two or more languages in the same conversation to express oneself.

cognates   a word in one language—the form and definition of which resemble a word in a different language (e.g., *animals* [English] and *animales* [Spanish]).

cognition   the mental process of acquiring knowledge and understanding through thought, the senses, and lived experiences.

cognitive approach   an approach to second language instruction that is the product of efforts to examine and analyze the cognitive psychological side of learning, language learning, and instruction to promote language learning.

cognitive dimension   one of the four dimensions of the CLD student biography that involves the multiple ways in which teachers can capitalize on what students know, what/how students think about their learning process(es), and ways in which they apply their learning. Additionally, this dimension is concerned with students' background knowledge (i.e., funds of knowledge, prior knowledge, and academic knowledge), which highlights the interrelatedness of this dimension and the sociocultural dimension.

cognitive learning strategies   strategies that involve the mental or physical manipulation of information, including classification, linking new information to prior knowledge, and summarizing.

cognitively demanding   the level of cognitive engagement required of CLD students to deal with significant amounts of complex information that they are asked to process and assimilate.

cognitively undemanding   the level of cognitive engagement required of CLD students to deal with small amounts of relatively simple information that they are asked to process and assimilate.

common underlying proficiency (CUP)   the connections between the bilingual individual's two languages, in which prior knowledge and academic skills in one language are transferable to learning and performance in another.

communication as the purpose of language   the most common theme found among the methods derived from the communicative approach which emphasize (1) language as embedded in social contexts; (2) the multiplicity of language functions; (3) the need for student-centered, teacher-facilitated language instruction; and (4) the need to stress communication versus rules in language teaching.

communicative approach a more research- and theory-based approach to second language instruction, which derived from international concerns over the ineffectiveness of the grammar-based approaches in developing language learners who could actually use the target language in real-life situations.

communicative competence the level of language expertise that enables users to express and decipher messages and to interpersonally mediate meaning within particular contexts; includes four areas of language knowledge: grammatical competence, sociolinguistic competence, discourse competence, and strategic competence.

communicative language learning environment a classroom, for example, in which a teacher provides multiple opportunities for academic language interaction through fostering the construction of meaning from context and communication.

constructivism a developmental perspective on learning that views the human brain as having certain fundamental structures of understanding that enable it to draw meaning from experience; social constructivists believe that learning occurs as a result of interactions between the environment and the learner's mind.

constructivist learning environments classroom situations that emphasize students' construction of meaning through connections between their prior knowledge and the new language and concepts being taught. Such environments make possible cognitive–linguistic and cognitive–sociocultural connections at the contextual, intracultural, intercultural, and affective levels.

content-based instruction lessons that promote both the linguistic and academic development of CLD students. In foreign language programs, it is often referred to as *immersion instruction.*

content language key vocabulary terms from the lesson that the educator should preteach to CLD students. These efforts help students prepare for the lesson and allow connections to be made to their background knowledge.

content objectives statements that identify what students should know and be able to do in particular subject areas, which should also support attainment of state and district standards. These objectives should be presented orally and in writing at the beginning of a lesson in order to provide students with learning expectations and a focus for the lesson. Teachers revisit the objectives throughout the lesson to ensure alignment of the lesson to learning goals and to assess student progress.

context-embedded the presence of readily available paralingual cues, such as the context in which the discourse occurs, body language, and prior knowledge, to facilitate meaning construction.

context-reduced the presence of few, if any, paralinguistic cues to facilitate meaning construction. Therefore, meaning must come from the language itself.

contextualization teacher efforts to situate instruction in ways that promote meaning and relevance for students, given their individual student biographies. As such, contextualization requires teachers to know, document, and utilize—in instructional planning and lesson implementation—the assets that each student brings to the classroom from his or her background.

cooperative learning a common theme among variations of sheltered instruction. This is a descriptor of the many ways in which students may be placed into small, primarily heterogeneous collaborative groups in ways that maximize interdependence and target either individual or group goals for learning.

CREDE standards created by the Center for Research on Education, Diversity & Excellence (CREDE) housed in the University of Hawaii at Manoa, as funded by the U.S. Department of Education; the Standards for Effective Pedagogy and Learning reflect extensive analysis of the research and development literature in education and diversity and include Joint Productive Activity, Language and Literacy Development, Contextualization, Challenging Activities, and Instructional Conversation.

critical reflection a process that begins with the self, in which one analyzes and challenges the validity of his or her assumptions. In turn, one then assesses the influence of his or her socialization on assumptions made. Ultimately, this process allows one to assess level of knowledge and understanding given the current context.

cross-linguistic learning strategies strategies that allow the learner to use linguistic knowledge and competence in one language to support learning and acquisition of another.

culturally and linguistically diverse (CLD) student biography the incorporation of the sociocultural, linguistic, cognitive, and academic dimensions, with emphasis on related challenges and processes, which uses a holistic approach to help characterize and provide insight on students with diverse backgrounds.

culture of the school the practices and perceptions that positively or negatively influence CLD students' experiences within the school, including (dis)respect for non-English native languages, minority/majority cultures, emphasis on equality and meritocracy versus equity, as well as other challenges placed on CLD students.

curricular readiness the fourth level of readiness on the accommodation readiness spiral that requires teachers to have a basic understanding of curricular issues such as planning, scope, sequence, and consistency. Nonetheless, more recent curriculum trends have made it necessary to have a grasp of other, more complex dynamics such as the degree of alignment between the curriculum and selected standards for concept or context coverage and quality, the degree to which the curriculum encourages parental or caregiver involvement, how the curriculum addresses the unique needs of the student population being taught, and the cross-cultural sensitivity of the curriculum.

curriculum essentials fundamental beliefs about the core curriculum, standards of academic achievement, and student access to an appropriate curriculum that are reflected on critically in order to provide specific understandings and proactive actions to emphasize the differential learning and adjustment needs of CLD students. Ultimately, exploring and developing one's response to these beliefs help to formalize the educator's sense of curricular readiness.

deficit perspective a mindset in which CLD students are viewed as liabilities, or deficits, that characterize the hopelessness of appropriate educational accommodations for the students, instead of viewing the assets that the CLD students bring to the school and classroom.

developmental bilingual education also referred to as *maintenance bilingual education* or *one-way dual language education*; programming typically begins in kindergarten or first grade and offers content-area instruction both in students' first and second language (English) for at least five to six years. Full academic language proficiency in both languages is the goal of developmental bilingual programming.

discourse competence an ability to combine, recombine, and connect language utterances into a meaningful product that is promoted through interactive language instruction focusing on use of language for authentic communication.

elaboration the mental manipulation of new information. In this process, a CLD student compares new information with known information and draws analogies from his or her existing background knowledge; this process applies to all four literacy domains: listening, speaking, reading, and writing. By first assessing the prior experiences and knowledge that CLD students bring to the classroom and then guiding them to make curricular connections to those experiences and understandings, teachers encourage students to build on their prior knowledge.

enculturation the process in which an individual is gradually initiated into the home, native culture. This process is so gradual that one does not notice it, but the process allows one to develop a sense of group identity that informs values, guides beliefs and actions, and channels expectations.

English as a second language (ESL) programs language programs that serve students identified as having limited English proficiency by providing a certified teacher to help with language support, either within the classroom or in a pull-out situation.

English for specific purposes (ESP) content classes for very specific language learning purposes that seek to prepare students to learn language for different environments, including the fields of medicine, engineering, and computer science; such classes are common in foreign language departments, adult education programs, and military programs.

English-only movement a political movement that centers on laws being passed to enforce English as the sole language written and spoken in schools, voting venues, and government offices. Furthermore, government documents, including street signs and official websites, would be available only in English. Many English-only organizations advocate these changes in law in order to unite our pluralistic nation, rather than focus on languages that divide us. Many of these same organizations refuse to acknowledge research that proves the value of bilingual education.

environmental readiness the third level of readiness on the accommodation readiness spiral that demands an analysis of the external and internal environments that may affect professional effectiveness with CLD students and families.

equity vs. equality equality implies that no matter one's position, everyone would be given the same opportunities and resources, therefore assuming that everyone starts from the same place and that these opportunities and resources would be beneficial. This is not the case, especially when one's socioeconomic status, race, ethnicity, language, nationality, and ability are considered. Equity, on the other hand, suggests that everyone is provided opportunities and resources, based on individual need, in order to ensure that everyone achieves the same outcome. For example, providing everyone in the world with the same-size shirt would demonstrate equality. However, rather than offering a "one-size-fits-all" response, an equitable solution would provide shirts in the sizes that each person needs to ensure that everyone is clothed.

espoused readiness reflects what the educator says, and may believe, about her or his level of readiness for accommodation. Espoused readiness operates at the conscious level and can fluctuate or change rather easily in response to new information or ideas.

evaluation phase of CALLA the fourth phase of CALLA that provides students the opportunity to reflect on and take responsibility for their own learning.

evidence factual information, not opinion. In the context of the classroom, educators provide factual descriptions of their actions, students' actions, quotations from lesson plans, CLD student classroom documentation with samples of student work, parent contact logs, and accurate professional development logs.

expansion phase of CALLA the fifth phase of CALLA, in which students integrate the new knowledge they are gaining with their existing knowledge base.

first language acquisition the process through which children learn their first language; there are mul-

tiple theories that explain how the first language is acquired: the behaviorist theory, the innatist theory, and the interactionist theory.

grammatical approach a teacher-centered approach to second language instruction. The underlying philosophy of the approach assumes that learners acquire language most efficiently by memorizing language rules and sentence patterns in a methodical, sequenced curriculum.

grammatical competence an ability to recognize and produce the distinctive grammatical structures of a language and use them effectively in communication; this ability is developed through curriculum and instruction that prepares the CLD student to incorporate and apply the language code.

guarded vocabulary a common theme among variations of sheltered instruction. Also sometimes referred to as *reducing the linguistic load of instruction*, guarded vocabulary does not involve actions such as unnatural speech or raising the volume of instruction. Instead, the strategy involves linguistic actions on the part of the instructor that increase the comprehensibility of instruction (e.g., enunciating words, simplifying sentence structure, emphasizing key information).

hands-on activities a common theme among variations of sheltered instruction. Such interaction is considered essential for CLD students as a means by which they can practice their emergent L2 skills, clarify concepts, and demonstrate what they have learned.

higher-order thinking skills students' ability to analyze, evaluate, synthesize, and create new knowledge, which requires application of critical thinking and judgment skills.

iceberg metaphor Cummins's interdependence, or iceberg hypothesis, reveals the relationship of the first language to the learning of another language. This hypothesis, represented as a "dual-iceberg," states that every language contains surface features; however, underlying those surface manifestations of language are proficiencies that are common across languages.

immersion instruction content-based instruction in foreign language programs that focuses on teaching students a new language through the medium of academic content areas. Immersion instruction uses strategies and techniques to increase the likelihood that the academic content language of instruction is comprehensible to the learner. Use of this model is not suggested for CLD students whose native language is not that of the dominant group, as this model does not ensure adequate native language support or sufficient comprehensible input for such students to be academically successful.

innatist reflects the theory that learning is natural for human beings, meaning that babies enter the world with an inborn device to learn language.

input hypothesis according to Krashen, the CLD student is able to best incorporate new information (that is, progress in language acquisition) when the input the student receives is one step beyond his or her current stage of competence.

integrated content-based (ICB) method of instruction a method that integrates language and content instruction to provide students with contextualized learning experiences that facilitate simultaneous development of English proficiency and academic knowledge and skills. This method of instruction engages students in authentic activities linked to specific subject matter topics that are incorporated within a theme.

interactionist reflects the theory that language develops through interaction, and that language acquisition is similar to the acquisition of other skills and knowledge.

interference hypothesis the inference that ongoing development in the first language so interferes with second language learning that effort should not be wasted on either native language support or ongoing development in the first language.

Krashen's natural order hypothesis this hypothesis asserts that language is acquired in a more or less natural order—a predictable sequence of progression. Although individual variations will exist among students, certain grammatical features of the language tend to be acquired earlier, whereas others are acquired later in development.

language acquisition device (LAD) a theoretical construct proposed by Chomsky to describe an inherent mental system specifically devoted to language development and use. The LAD makes possible the idea that people are born with a genetically predetermined capacity to learn language

language across the curriculum a movement that adopts a reciprocal relationship between language

and content, in which directing the attention of learners to content language more specifically addresses the language acquisition needs of CLD students in the academic context.

language for specific purposes (LSP) see *English for specific purposes (ESP)*.

language objectives statements that identify how learners will use language to accomplish the content objectives. Such objectives reflect consideration of the language demands that are expected within the classroom. Like content objectives, these should be presented at the beginning of a class to share with students the expectations for learning and revisited throughout the lesson.

learning centers stations located around the classroom that offer all students the opportunity for extended explorations of theme-based instruction according to the ICB method; stations promote active student engagement either individually or in collaborative pair or small-group configurations.

learning strategy objectives statements that identify how learners will use learning strategies to accomplish the content and language objectives of the lesson. Such objectives reflect consideration of the metacognitive, cognitive, and social/affective learning strategies that will best support students' understanding of the lesson and completion of academic tasks. Like content and language objectives, these should be presented at the beginning of a class to share with students the expectations for learning and revisited throughout the lesson.

learning styles the ways in which students prefer to think, relate to others, and engage in classroom environments and experiences. Students' preferred learning styles are largely influenced by their socialization and cognitive development in the primary or home culture.

"less equals more" rationale the argument that CLD students will learn more English when they are first permitted to participate meaningfully in school activities that are provided in the language with which they are comfortable, the language that already equips them for oral and written communication.

level playing field a situation in which everyone has fair and equal opportunities for success.

linguistic dimension one of the four dimensions of the CLD student biography that emphasizes the CLD student's language proficiency in both the first language and the second language (as well as in any additional languages) within the scope of comprehension, communication, and expression.

manageable tasks   learning tasks that reflect material with familiar information and language; such tasks are used when teaching new learning strategies, so CLD students can concentrate on understanding and applying the strategy.

metacognition   the awareness and understanding of one's own thought and learning processes.

metacognitive learning strategies   strategies that incorporate three domains: awareness of one's own cognitive abilities, the ability to discern the difficulty of a task, and the knowledge of how and when to use specific strategies.

method   a body of philosophically grounded and purposively integrated strategies and techniques that constitutes one translation of an approach into professional practice.

monitor hypothesis   according to Krashen, language learners consciously apply the rules of the target language to self-correct or to self-repair during language production. These efforts are needed in the context of authentic communication in order to enhance the comprehensibility of the intended message for the receiver.

multilingualism   using, or having the ability to use, multiple languages, which is deemed as valuable in many cultures and countries.

mutual accommodation   the process in which neither the student nor the educator expects complete accommodation; instead, both collaborate to maximize the resources each brings to the educational process and to select from among the best strategies that fit each disposition.

NBPTS standards   created by the National Board for Professional Teaching Standards (NBPTS), a project funded by the U.S. Department of Education and the National Science Foundation to define high-quality practice in 12 areas of professional practice; these standards address CLD student learning and emphasize teacher awareness of students' languages and cultures, meaningful learning environments, authentic assessments, strong home–school collaboration, and content appropriate pedagogy.

one-way accommodation   the tendency among some educators to assume that unsuccessful students are either genetically or culturally inferior, which can negatively affect CLD learners and leads to educators questioning the students' intelligence and making assumptions about abilities and family members' capabilities.

practical readiness   reflects the educator's ingrained knowledge, beliefs, and assumptions (that frequently go unchecked), which shape and guide actions in practice. Unlike espoused readiness, an individual's level of practical readiness is formulated over years of socialization before and during professional practice. Therefore, one's level of practical readiness is not so easily recognized or changed.

practice phase of CALLA   the third phase of CALLA that is much more student-centered than previous phases, in which students collaborate in hands-on activities to practice applying new concepts, language, and strategies.

preparation phase of CALLA   the first phase of CALLA that primarily emphasizes students' prior knowledge and experiences in relation to new concepts and language.

presentation phase of CALLA   the second phase of CALLA, in which the teacher usually begins by presenting information, supporting what he or she says using visual or hands-on materials and uncomplicated language (guarded vocabulary).

prism model   four interrelated dimensions of the student—linguistic, academic, cognitive, and sociocultural—that must be addressed equally if the CLD student is to be successful.

programming and instructional readiness   the fifth level of readiness on the accommodation readiness spiral that encompasses (but is not limited to) an awareness of programming dynamics at the district and school levels; an understanding of the manner in which districts can frame or limit decisions about instructional approaches for CLD students; a grasp of which instructional methods would be effective with and realistic for CLD students; and an examination of opportunities for teacher-based, administrative, or collaborative advocacy to improve programming and classroom instruction for CLD students.

psychosocial processes   the development of a student's self-esteem, cultural identity, social identity, interpersonal relationships, and community building, which all profoundly influence her or his level of performance in the classroom.

readiness for application and advocacy the sixth level of readiness on the accommodation readiness spiral that requires theory-into-practice applications of what the teacher has learned about self, professional readiness, and best practices for CLD students in the school and/or classroom. In addition, teachers must implement certain accommodative practices in order to champion all students, not just in the current classroom context but also to safeguard their educational future.

readiness for CLD students and families the second level of readiness on the accommodation readiness spiral that requires teachers to actively seek out biography-based insights on CLD learners by holding conversations with students and their families. In addition, this level of readiness requires educators to critically reflect on the assumptions they may make as they interact with CLD students and their families.

readiness for critical reflection on practice the first level of readiness on the accommodation readiness spiral that is demonstrated by a capacity for the confronting/checking of assumptions in practice, validity testing on those assumptions (reflection), and reflection on the influence of prior socialization on the origin of any assumptions made.

reductionist curricula courses of study that inordinately focus on basic skills, redundant workbooks, drill-and-practice approaches to instruction, rote memorization of decontextualized facts and declarative knowledge, isolated practice of computations, and repetitive routines that target the retention of basic test-taking strategies.

relevance level of significance attached to information that arises from the learner's cultural lens, which filters incoming information according to schemata established by long-standing socialization in that culture.

scaffolding extensive instructional and contextual support in the early stages of learning, followed by a gradual withdrawal of such support as the student's performance suggests independence.

SDAIE specially designated academic instruction in English (SDAIE) is a variation of the sheltered instruction method that is used to teach academic courses to English learners. This design is for nonnative English speakers and focuses on increased comprehension of academic courses that are typically taught to native English speakers within the school.

self-talk a strategy in which the CLD student uses positive statements to reassure himself or herself that he or she will understand and will be able to complete each assignment; the strategy is intended to reduce the anxiety of the student when discussing new concepts or approaching learning tasks.

semi-structured conversations teacher–student or teacher–parent conversations that are only partially structured (i.e., they evolve as part of the conversation), in which the affective filter is kept low and the teacher remains free to further explore any information that surfaces as a means of enhancing teaching effectiveness with the CLD student.

separate underlying proficiency (SUP) a perspective that assumes two languages operate independently; therefore, no transfer occurs between them.

sheltered instruction an instructional method of the communicative approach that combines philosophies, strategies, and techniques that appropriately recognize the many challenges that CLD students confront. The method provides English learners with instruction that is comprehensible, relevant, and motivating.

silent period the first stage of the second language acquisition process, also known as the preproduction stage, in which the student may not communicate except in nonverbal ways. During this period, the CLD student is primarily listening to the new or target language and trying to understand its patterns and rules before attempting production in that language.

SIOP indicators 30 guidelines that support teachers to implement accommodative sheltered instruction according to the SIOP model. Indicators are organized according to the three critical aspects of preparation, instruction, and review and assessment.

SIOP model a research-based variation of the sheltered instruction method that is used to make grade-level content and academic language comprehensible for all students.

social/affective learning strategies strategies that capitalize on the interconnectedness of the cognitive and the sociocultural dimensions of the CLD student biography; they may involve the learner as an individual or the learner in interaction with another or others.

socialization the process by which humans (from infancy) acquire different behaviors, knowledge, biases, and assumptions based on family and cultural contexts and influences. These behaviors and assumptions are oftentimes so ingrained that we cannot always articulate why they exist.

sociocultural dimension one of the four dimensions of the CLD student biography that encompasses the complex social and cultural factors and variables that are critical to the transitional adjustments and the academic success of CLD students. This dimension often holds the key to a thorough understanding of the other three dimensions and thus is referred to as the "heart" of the CLD student biography.

sociocultural processes cultural and psychosocial processes that influence the performance, behaviors, and resiliency of CLD students inside and outside the classroom.

sociolinguistic competence an ability to interpret the social meaning of the choice of linguistic varieties and to use language with the appropriate social meaning. Within this scope, the goal of curriculum planning and language instruction becomes that of being intentionally focused on appropriate use of the target language in social and cultural contexts.

stages of second language acquisition the various linguistic stages that one encounters when acquiring a language, including preproduction, early production, speech emergence, intermediate fluency, and advanced fluency. These stages fall in line with Krashen's natural order hypothesis, meaning that language is essentially acquired in a natural order—a predictable sequence of progression.

strategic competence an ability to apply multiple strategies to keep the communication going and to enhance the effectiveness of the communication. Curriculum planning and instruction emphasize students' use of related vocabulary and language as well as paralinguistic cues, such as body language, to bolster the comprehensibility of communication.

strategy a collection of philosophically grounded and functionally related techniques that serves as an implementation component of an instructional method.

student-centered a focus on the holistic interests of the students, rather than those who are involved in the educational process, such as teachers and administrators.

subtractive (or limited) bilingualism associated with a student's first language being gradually replaced by the more dominant language. In the case of subtractive bilingualism, students may develop relatively low levels of academic proficiency in both languages.

supplementary materials instructional supports such as commercial illustrations, big books, realia, multimedia presentations, demonstrations, graphics, bulletin boards, maps, and more. These visuals not only contextualize curriculum and instruction but also provide powerful visual links between language and content.

technique specific actions or action sequences that have been designed to achieve a defined, strategic objective.

TESOL/NCATE standards created by the National Council for the Accreditation of Teacher Education (NCATE) and the board of directors of the National Teachers of English to Speakers of Other Languages (TESOL) organization to provide consistency in teacher education programs across the United States by describing and specifying the competencies that ESL teachers need to demonstrate in professional practice.

thematic units lessons that are focused on a particular theme or topic that can be taught across all core subject areas.

theme the overarching idea that shapes the unit, topics, and lessons that constitute the ICB method.

theory-into-practice applications the ways in which the teacher applies theory and research in the context of her or his own professional practice. No application of theory, no matter how robust the framework for effectiveness, will be successful with CLD students if that application is not cross-culturally and cross-linguistically sensitive.

topic a particular idea that is embedded within the theme of an ICB thematic unit. These thematic subcomponents determine how grade-level and content-area texts, authentic literature, and materials will be used in lessons to achieve the content and language objectives.

transfer hypothesis the argument that, although the two languages (L1 and L2) may seem separate on the surface, they are actually quite interdependent at the deeper level of cognitive functions. For example, it is a well-established finding that students who learn to read and write in their first language are able to readily transfer those abilities to learning a second language.

transitional bilingual education programs that provide students with instruction in their native language for all subject areas, as well as instruction in L2 (English) as a second language. Many of these programs, however, last only two to three years in the United States.

two-way immersion also known as *two-way dual language programs*; increasingly popularized programs, as a way to attract public support for multilingualism. The two-way model offers integrated language and academic instruction for both CLD students and native English speakers for at least five to six years. Among the objectives of two-way programming are first and second language proficiency, strong academic performance in the content areas, cross-cultural celebration, and cross-linguistic understandings.

U-curve hypothesis the hypothesis that there are four stages of the acculturation process that occur over time: the honeymoon phase, the hostility phase, the humor phase, and the home phase.

visuals a common theme among variations of sheltered instruction. This type of learning support includes pictures, graphics, charts, movies, video clips, or any other material with images that supplements the concepts being taught in the classroom.

working memory a system for temporarily holding and manipulating information for a brief period during the performance of an array of cognitive tasks including, but not limited to, comprehension, learning, and reasoning. Working memory is characterized by limited storage capacity and rapid turnover, as differentiated from the larger capacity and archival system of long-term memory.

zone of proximal development (ZPD) a theoretical construct developed by Vygotsky to describe the area between a learner's level of independent performance and the level of performance possible with assistance. Vygotsky argues that learning occurs when new information and skills fall within the zone, or the space between what the learner already knows and what he or she can do with the help of an expert. The ZPD shifts as the individual learns more complex concepts and skills and becomes capable of independently achieving the tasks that once required the assistance of another.

Chapter 1

Acton, W. R., & de Félix, J. W. (1986). Acculturation and mind. In J. M. Valdés (Ed.), *Culture bound* (pp. 20–32). New York: Cambridge University Press.

Alba, R., & Nee, V. (2005). *Remaking the American mainstream: Assimilation and contemporary immigration.* Cambridge, MA: Harvard University Press.

Bradford Smith, E. (2009, Spring). Approaches to multicultural education in preservice teacher education: Philosophical frameworks and models for teaching. *Multicultural Education, 16*(3), 45–50.

Brown, H. D. (1986). Learning a second culture. In J. M. Valdés (Ed.), *Culture bound* (pp. 33–48). New York: Cambridge University Press.

Brown, H. D. (1992). Sociocultural factors in teaching language minority students. In P. A. Richard-Amato & M. A. Snow (Eds.), *The multicultural classroom: Readings for content-area teachers* (pp. 73–92). White Plains, NY: Longman.

California Department of Education. (2013). Retrieved July 9, 2013, from http://www.myboe.org/portal/default/Content/Viewer/Content?action=2&scId=100051&sciId=1458

Carroll, D. M. (2006). Developing joint accountability in university-school teacher education partnerships. *Action in Teacher Education, 27*(4), 3–11.

Clayton, C., Barnhardt, R., & Brisk, M. E. (2008). Language, culture, and identity. In M. E. Brisk (Ed.), *Language, culture, and community in teacher education* (pp. 21–45). New York: Erlbaum.

Collier, C. (2010). *Separating difference from disability.* Thousand Oaks, CA: Sage.

Collier, V. P. (1987). The age and rate of acquisition of second language for academic purposes. *TESOL Quarterly, 21*, 617–641.

Collier, V. P. (1989). *Academic achievement, attitudes, and occupations among graduates of two-way bilingual classes.* Paper presented at the annual meeting of the American Educational Research Association, San Francisco, CA.

Collier, V. P. (1992). A synthesis of studies examining long-term language minority student data on academic achievement. *Bilingual Research Journal, 16*(1-2), 187–212.

Collier, V. P., & Thomas, W. P. (1989). How quickly can immigrants become proficient in school English? *Journal of Educational Issues of Language Minority Students, 5*, 26–38.

Collier, V. P., & Thomas, W. P. (2007). Predicting second language academic success in English using the Prism model. In J. Cummins & C. Davison (Eds.), *International handbook of English language teaching: Part one* (pp. 333–348). New York: Springer Science + Business Media.

Collier, V. P., & Thomas, W. P. (2009). *Educating English learners for a transformed world.* Albuquerque, NM: Dual Language Education of New Mexico Fuente Press.

Comber, B., & Kamler, B. (2004). Getting out of deficit: Pedagogies of reconnection. *Teaching Education, 15*(3), 293–310.

Council of Chief State School Officers (CCSSO). (1992). *Common core state standards for English language arts and literacy in history/social studies, science, and technical subjects.* Washington, DC: Author.

Crawford, J. (2000). *At war with diversity: U.S. language policy in an age of anxiety.* Clevedon, UK: Multilingual Matters.

Cushner, K., McClelland, A., & Safford, P. (2011). *Human diversity in education: An intercultural approach.* New York: McGraw-Hill.

Dulay, H., & Burt, M. (1977). Remarks on creativity in language acquisition. In M. Burt, H. Dulay, & M. Finocchiaro (Eds.), *Viewpoints on English as a second language* (pp. 95–126). New York: Regents.

Eggen, P., Kauchak, D. (2007). Group and individual differences. In J. W. Johnston & K. M. Davis (Eds.), *Educational psychology: Windows on classrooms* (7th ed., pp. 103–106). Upper Saddle River, NJ: Prentice Hall.

Félix-Ortiz, M., Newcomb, M. D., & Myers, H. (1994). A multidimensional measure of cultural identity for Latino and Latina adolescents. *Hispanic Journal of Behavioral Science, 16*(2), 99–115.

Florida, R., Cushing, R., & Gates, G. (2002). When social capital stifles innovation. *Harvard Business Review, 80*(8), 20.

Fránquiz, M. E. (2012). Key concepts in bilingual education: Identity texts, cultural citizenship, and humanizing pedagogy. *The NERA Journal, 48*(1), 33–40.

García-Castañón, J. (1994). Training Hmong refugee students. In G. D. Spindler & L. Spindler (Eds.), *Pathways to cultural awareness: Cultural therapy with teachers and students* (pp. 197–219). Thousand Oaks, CA: Corwin.

Gebeloff, R., Evans, T., & Scheinkman, A. (2013, July 9). Diversity in the classroom. *New York Times*.

Glassett, K., & Schrum, L. (2009). Teacher beliefs and student achievement in technology-rich classroom environments. *International Journal of Technology in Teaching and Learning, 5*(2), 138–153.

Goldenberg, C. (2008, Summer). Teaching English language learners: What the research does—and does not—say. *American Educator*, 8–44. Retrieved November 11, 2009, from http://aft .org/pubs-reports/american_eduator/issues/summer08/goldenberg.pdf

Gonzalez, R., Pagan, M., Wendell, L, & Love, C. (2011). *Supporting ELL/culturally and linguistically diverse students for academic achievement.* New York: International Center for Leadership in Education.

Haberman, M. (2013). Why school culture matters, and how to improve it. Retrieved July 10, 2013, from http://www.huffingtonpost.com/Michael-Haberman/why-school-culture-matter_b_3047318.html

Herrera, S. (2010). *Biography-driven instruction for culturally responsive teaching: An action model.* New York: Teachers College Press.

Herrera, S. G., Kavimandan, S. K., & Holmes, M. A. (2011). *Crossing the vocabulary bridge: Differentiated strategies for diverse secondary classrooms.* New York: Teachers College Press.

Herrera, S., Perez, D., Kavimandan, S., & Wessels, S. (2013). *Accelerating literacy for diverse learners: Strategies for the common core classroom, K-8.* New York: Teachers College Press.

Herrera, S., & Rodriguez Morales, A. (2009). Colorblind nonaccommodative denial: Implications for teachers' meaning perspectives toward their Mexican-American English learners. In R. Kubota & A. Lin (Eds.), *Race, culture, and identities in second language education: Exploring critically engaged practice* (pp. 197–214). New York: Routledge.

Kotkin, J. (2010). *The next hundred million: America in 2050.* London: Penguin.

Krashen, S. (1982). *Principles and practice in second language acquisition.* Oxford, UK: Pergamon.

Krashen, S. D. (1981). *Second language acquisition and second language learning.* London: Pergamon.

Krashen, S. D. (2002). Bilingual education and second language acquisition theory. In C. F. Leyba (Ed.), *Schooling and language minority students: A theoretical framework* (pp. 47–75). Los Angeles: Legal Books.

Lau v. Nichols, 414 U.S. 563 (1974).

Lewis, A. (2001, Winter). There is no "race" in an (almost) all-White school. *American Educational Research Journal, 38*(4), 781–811.

Li, G. (2013). Promoting teachers of culturally and linguistically diverse (CLD) students as change agents: A cultural approach to professional learning. *Theory Into Practice, 52*(2), 136–143.

Lim, J. (2013). School culture: Impact on teacher motivation. Retrieved July 9, 2013, from http://www.scholastic.com/teachers/classroom_solutions/2010/05/the-big-picture-impacting-school-culture

Lynch, M. (2012). *It's time for a change: School reform for the next decade.* Lanham, MD: Rowman & Littlefield.

Macneil, A., Prater, D., & Busch, S. (2009). The effects of school culture and climate on student achievement. *International Journal of Leadership In Education, 12*(1), 73–84.

Milner, H. R. (2003, Summer). Teacher reflection and race in cultural contexts: History, meanings, and methods in teaching. *Theory into Practice, 42*(3), 173–180.

Murry, K. (1996). Reflective-transformative professional development predicated upon critical reflection and enabled by a school–university partnership: A microethnographic case study. *Dissertation Abstracts International, 56*(12), 4643. [CD-ROM]. Abstract from: ProQuest File: Dissertations Abstracts Item: AAC 9610795.

National Governors Association Center for Best Practices & Council of Chief State School Officers (NGA & CCSSO). (2010). Common Core State Standards. Washington, DC: Authors.

Nieto, S., & Bode, P. (2012). *Affirming diversity: The sociopolitical context of multicultural education* (6th ed.). Boston: Pearson.

Olson, B. (2013). Rethinking our work with multilingual writers: The ethics and responsibility of language teaching in the writing center. Retrieved July 9, 2013, from http://projects.uwc.utexas.edu/index.php/praxis/article/view/103/html

Perez, D., Holmes, M., Miller, S., & Fanning, C. (2012). Biography-driven strategies as the great equalizer: Universal conditions that promote K-12 culturally responsive teaching. *Journal of Curriculum and Instruction, 6*(1), 25–42.

Samson, J., & Collins, B. (2012). *Preparing all teachers to meet the needs of English language learners.* Washington, DC: Center for American Progress.

Sewell, W. C. (2009). Entrenched pedagogy: A history of stasis in the English language arts curriculum in United States secondary schools. *Changing English, 15*(1), 87–100.

Sleeter, C. (2001). Preparing teachers for culturally diverse schools: Research and the overwhelming presence of whiteness. *Journal of Teacher Education, 52*(2), 94–106.

Suarez-Orozco, C., & Suarez-Orozco, M. M. (2001). *Children of immigration.* Cambridge: Harvard University Press.

Terrisse, S. (2001). Does your organization's gene pool need to make a bigger splash? Workplace diversity and its impact on creativity. *Public Relations Quarterly, 46*(1), 30.

Thomas, W. P., & Collier, V. P. (1997). *School effectiveness for language minority students* (NCBE Resource Collection Series No. 9). Washington, DC: National Clearinghouse for Bilingual Education. Retrieved October 7, 2002, from www.ncela.gwu.edu/ncbepubs/resource/effectiveness

Thomas, W. P., & Collier, V. P. (2002). *A national study of school effectiveness for language minority students' long-term academic achievement.* Santa Cruz, CA: Center for Research on Education, Diversity & Excellence.

Thomas, W. P., & Collier, V. P. (2012). Dual language education for a transformed world. Albuquerque, NM: Dual Language Education of New Mexico Fuente Press.

Thompson, G. (2009, March 14). Where education and assimilation collide. *New York Times.*

Trifonovitch, G. (1977). Culture learning—culture teaching. *Educational Perspectives, 16*(4), 18–22.

United Nations. (2013). World population prospects: The 2012 revision. Retrieved July 9, 2013, from http://esa.un.org/unpd/wpp/Documentation/publications.html

Chapter 2

Abedi, J., & Dietel, R. (2004, Winter). Challenges in the No Child Left Behind Act for English language learners. *CRESST Policy Brief, 7.* Retrieved November 2, 2009, from www.cse.ucla.edu/products/policy/cresst_policy7.pdf

Adams, M. J. (1990). *Beginning to read: Thinking and learning about print.* Cambridge, MA: MIT Press.

Anstrom, K. (1998). *Preparing secondary education teachers to work with English language learners: Science* (NCBE Resource Collection Series No. 11). Washington, DC: National Clearinghouse for Bilingual Education. Retrieved October 23, 2002, from www.ncela.gwu.edu/ncbepubs/resource/ells/science.htm

Appiah, K. A., & Gates, H. L. (1997). *The dictionary of global culture.* New York: Knopf.

Au, K. (2000). A multicultural perspective on policies for improving literacy achievement: Equity and excellence. In M. Kamil, P. Mosenthal, P. D. Pearson, & R. Barr (Eds.), *Handbook of reading research: Volume III* (pp. 835–851). Mahwah, NJ: Erlbaum.

Au, K. H., & Carroll, J. H. (1997). Improving literacy achievement through a constructivist approach: The KEEP Demonstration Classroom Project. *Elementary School Journal, 97,* 203–221.

August, D., Calderón, M., & Carlo, M. (2002). *Transfer of reading skills from Spanish to English: A study of young learners.* Report ED-98-CO-0071 to the Office of Bilingual Education and Minority Languages Affairs, U.S. Department of Education.

August, D., & Hakuta, K. (Eds.). (1997). *Improving schooling for language-minority children: A research agenda.* Washington, DC: National Academy Press.

Bastian, A., Fruchter, N., Gittell, M., Greer, C., & Hoskins, K. (1986). *Choosing equality.* Philadelphia: Temple University Press.

Bennett, C. I. (2010). *Comprehensive multicultural education: Theory and practice* (7th ed.). Boston: Allyn and Bacon.

Berlak, H. (1999). Standards and the control of knowledge [Electronic version]. *Rethinking Schools, 13*(3).

Burns, M. (1993). *Mathematics: Assessing understanding.* White Plains, NY: Cuisenaire Company of America.

Cahill, L., Prins, B., Weber, M., & McGaugh, J. (1994). Adrenergic activation and memory for emotional events. *Nature, 371,* 702–704.

Calderón, M. (2007). *Teaching reading to English language learners, grades 6-12: A framework for improving achievement in the content areas.* Thousand Oaks, CA: Corwin.

Chamberlain, S. P. (2005). Recognizing and responding to cultural differences in the education of culturally and linguistically diverse learners. *Intervention in School and Clinic, 40*(4), 195–211.

Chamot, A. (2007). Accelerating academic achievement of English language learners: A synthesis of five evaluations of the CALLA model. In J. Cummins & C. Davison (Eds.), *International handbook of English language teaching: Part one* (pp. 317–332). New York: Springer Science+Business Media.

Chamot, A. U. (2009). *The CALLA handbook: Implementing the cognitive academic language learning approach* (2nd ed.). Reading, MA: Addison-Wesley.

Chamot, A. U., Dale, M., O'Malley, J. M., & Spanos, G. (1992). Learning and problem solving strategies of ESL students. *Bilingual Research Journal, 16*(3–4), 1–33.

Chamot, A., & El-Dinary, P. (1999). Children's learning strategies in language immersion classrooms. *Modern Language Journal, 83,* 319–338. Retrieved October 24, 2002, from WilsonSelectPlus database.

Chamot, A. U., & O'Malley, J. M. (1994). *The CALLA handbook: Implementing the cognitive academic language learning approach*. Reading, MA: Addison-Wesley.

Chamot, A., & O'Malley, J. (1996). The cognitive academic language learning approach: A model for linguistically diverse classrooms. *Elementary School Journal, 96,* 259–273.

Chi, M. T. H., de Leeuw, N., Chiu, M. H., & LaVancher, C. (1994). Eliciting self-explanations improves conceptual understanding, *Cognitive Science, 18,* 439–477.

Cobb, C. (2004). *Improving adequate yearly progress for English language learners*. Naperville, IL: Learning Point.

Cobb, P. (1994). Where is the mind? Constructivist and sociocultural perspectives on mathematical development. *Educational Researcher, 23*(7), 13–20.

Cohen, A. D. (2011). *Strategies in learning and using a second language* (2nd ed.). New York: Longman.

Collier, V. P. (1995). *Acquiring a second language for school*. Washington, DC: National Clearinghouse for Bilingual Education.

Collier, V. P., & Thomas, W. P. (2007). Predicting second language academic success in English using the Prism model. In J. Cummins & C. Davison (Eds.), *International handbook of English language teaching: Part one* (pp. 333–348). New York: Springer Science+Business Media.

Collier, V. P., & Thomas, W. P. (2009). Educating English learners for a transformed world. Albuquerque, NM: Dual Language Education of New Mexico Fuente Press.

Common Core State Standards Initiative (CCSSI). (2012). In the states. Retrieved February 13, 2014, from http://www.corestandards.org/in-the-states

Coyne, M. D., Kameenui, E., & Carnine, D. (2010). *Effective teaching strategies that accommodate diverse learners* (4th ed.). Upper Saddle River, NJ: Prentice Hall.

Cummins, J. (1981). The role of primary language development in promoting educational success for language minority students. In C. F. Leyba (Ed.), *Schooling and language minority students: A theoretical framework* (pp. 3–49). Los Angeles: Evaluation, Dissemination and Assessment Center, CSULA.

Cummins, J. (1989). Language and affect: Bilingual students at home and at school. *Language Arts, 66,* 29–43.

Cummins, J. (1991). Interdependence of first- and second-language proficiency in bilingual children. In E. Bialystok (Ed.), *Language processing in bilingual children* (pp. 70–89). Cambridge, UK: Cambridge University Press.

Cummins, J. (1994). Primary language instruction and the education of language minority students. In C. F. Leyba (Ed.), *Schooling and language minority students: A theoretical framework* (2nd ed., pp. 3–46). Los Angeles: California State University, National Evaluation, Dissemination and Assessment Center.

Cummins, J. (2000). "This place nurtures my spirit": Creating contexts of empowerment in linguistically diverse schools. In R. Phillipson (Ed.), *Rights to language: Equity, power and education* (pp. 249–258). Mawah, NJ: Erlbaum.

Darling-Hammond, L. (1992, November). Reframing the school reform agenda: New paradigms must restore discourse with local educators. *The School Administrator, 19*(49), 22–27.

Darling-Hammond, L. (2007). Race, inequality and educational accountability: The irony of "No Child Left Behind." *Race Ethnicity and Education, 10*(3), 245–260.

Diaz-Rico, L. T. (2014). *The crosscultural, language, and academic development handbook: A complete K–12 reference guide* (5th ed.). Boston: Allyn and Bacon.

Earl, L., & LeMahieu, P. (1997). Rethinking assessment and accountability. In A. Hargreaves (Ed.), *Rethinking educational change with heart and mind* (pp. 149–168). The 1997 ASCD Yearbook. Alexandria, VA: Association for Supervision and Curriculum Development.

Escamilla, K. (2000). Teaching literacy in Spanish. In J. Tinajero & R. DeVillar (Eds.), *The power of two languages.* New York: Macmillan/McGraw-Hill.

Escamilla, K. (2004). *The psychological and emotional aspects of bilingualism: It's more than verbs.* Keynote address given at the Dual Language Pre-conference Institute, National Association for Bilingual Education, Albuquerque, NM.

Fitzgerald, J. (1995). English-as-a-second-language learners' cognitive reading processes: A review of research in the United States. *Review of Educational Research, 65,* 145–190.

Fox, B. J. (2003). *Word recognition activities: Patterns and strategies for developing fluency.* Upper Saddle River, NJ: Merrill Prentice-Hall.

Freeman, D. E., & Freeman, Y. (1998). *ESL/EFL teaching: Principles for success.* Portsmouth, NH: Heinemann.

Freeman, D. E., & Freeman, Y. S. (2011). *Between worlds: Access to second language acquisition* (3rd ed.). Portsmouth, NH: Heinemann.

Freeman, W. (1995). *Society of brains.* Hillsdale, NJ: Erlbaum.

Gagné, E. D. (1985). *The cognitive psychology of school learning.* Boston: Little, Brown.

Garbe, D. G. (1985). Mathematics vocabulary and the culturally different student. *Arithmetic Teacher, 33*(22), 29–42.

Garcia, E. (1996). Preparing instructional professionals for linguistically and culturally diverse students. In J. Sikula, T. Buttery, & E. Guyton (Eds.), *Handbook of research on teacher education* (2nd ed., pp. 802–813). New York: Macmillan.

García, G. E. (1998). Mexican-American bilingual students' metacognitive reading strategies: What's transferred, unique, problematic? *National Reading Conference Yearbook, 47,* 253–263.

García, G. E. (2000). Bilingual children's reading. In M. Kamil, P. Mosenthal, P. D. Pearson, & R. Barr (Eds.), *Handbook of reading research: Volume III* (pp. 813–834). Mahwah, NJ: Erlbaum.

Gay, G. (2000). *Culturally responsive teaching: Theory, research, & practice.* New York: Teachers College Press.

Gay, G. (2010). *Culturally responsive teaching: Theory, research, & practice* (2nd ed.). New York: Teachers College Press.

Genesee, F., Lindholm-Leary, K., Saunders, W., & Christian, D. (2006). *Educating English language learners.* New York: Cambridge University Press.

Gersten, R. (1996). Literacy instruction for language-minority students: The transition years. *Elementary School Journal, 96,* 227–244.

Goldenberg, C. (2008, Summer). Teaching English language learners: What the research does—and does not—say. *American Educator,* 8–44. Retrieved November 11, 2009, from http://aft.org/pubs-reports/american_educator/issues/summer08/goldenberg.pdf

Herrera, S. (2010). *Biography-driven instruction for culturally responsive teaching: An action model.* New York: Teachers College Press.

Herrera, S., Perez, D., & Escamilla, K. (2010). *Teaching reading to English language learners: Differentiated literacies.* Boston: Allyn and Bacon.

Hinkel, E., & Fotos, S. (Eds.). (2002). *From theory to practice: A teacher's view.* Mahwah, NJ: Erlbaum.

Jensen, E. (2008). *Brain-based learning: The new paradigm of teaching* (2nd ed.). Thousand Oaks, CA: Corwin.

Jimenez, R. (1997). The strategic reading abilities and potential of five low-literacy Latina/o readers in middle school. *Reading Research Quarterly, 32,* 224–243.

Jimenez, R., García, G. E., & Pearson, P. (1996). The reading strategies of bilingual Latina/o students who are successful English readers: Opportunities and obstacles. *Reading Research Quarterly, 31,* 90–112.

Jones, M. G., Jones, B., & Hargrove, T. (2003). *The unintended consequences of high-stakes testing.* Lanham, MD: Rowman & Littlefield.

Kersaint, G., Thompson, D. R., & Petkova, M. (2009). *Teaching mathematics to English language learners.* New York: Routledge.

Ketter, J., & Pool, J. (2001). Exploring the impact of a high-stakes direct writing assessment in two high school classrooms. *Research in the Teaching of English, 35,* 345–387.

Krashen, S. D. (1982). Principles and practice in second language acquisition. London: Pergamon.

Krashen, S. (2000). *Has whole language failed?* University of Southern California Rossier School of Education. Retrieved November 15, 2002, from www.usc.edu/dept/education/CMMR/text/Krashen_WholeLang.html

Krashen, S. D. (2002). Does transition really happen? Some case histories. *The Multilingual Educator, 3*(1), 50–54.

Lieberman, A., & Grolnick, M. (1997). Networks, reform and the professional development of teachers. In A. Hargreaves (Ed.), *Rethinking educational change with heart and mind* (pp. 192–215). The 1997 ASCD Yearbook. Alexandria, VA: Association for Supervision and Curriculum Development.

McCarthey, S. J. (2008). The impact of No Child Left Behind on teachers' writing instruction. *Written Communication, 25,* 462–505.

McLaren, P. (2007). *Life in schools: An introduction to critical pedagogy in the foundations of education* (5th ed.). Upper Saddle River, NJ: Prentice-Hall.

McNeil, L. (2000a). *Contradictions of school reform: Educational costs of standardized testing.* New York: Routledge.

McNeil, L. (2000b). The educational costs of standardization [Electronic version]. *Rethinking Schools, 14*(4). Retrieved April 14, 2003, from www.rethinkingschools.org/archive/14_04/tex144.shtml

Menken, K. (2009). Policy failures: No Child Left Behind and English language learners. In S. L. Groenke & J. A. Hatch (Eds.), *Critical pedagogy and teacher education in the neoliberal era* (pp. 49–62). New York: Springer.

Mohan, B. A. (1986). *Language and content.* Reading, MA: Addison-Wesley.

Moore, K. D. (2012). *Effective instructional strategies: From theory to practice* (3rd ed.). Thousand Oaks, CA: Sage.

Morrow, L. M., Pressley, M., Smith, J. K., & Smith, M. (1997). The effect of a literature-based program integrated into literacy and science instruction with children from diverse backgrounds. *Reading Research Quarterly, 32,* 54–76.

National Center for Education Statistics (NCES). (2002b). *U.S. Department of Education's survey of the states' limited English proficient students and available educational programs and service, 1989–90 through 1999–2000 summary reports.* Supplemented by state publications (1998–99 data) and enrollment totals from NCES. Retrieved August 7, 2003, from www.ncela.gwu.edu/ncbepubs/reports/state-data/2000/list.htm

Nieto, S. (1999). Critical multicultural education and students' perspectives. In S. May (Ed.), *Critical multiculturalism: Rethinking multicultural and antiracist education* (pp. 191–215). Philadelphia: Falmer.

No Child Left Behind Act of 2001, Pub. L. No. 107-110 (2002).

O'Malley, J. M., & Chamot, A. U. (1990). *Learning strategies in second language acquisition.* New York: Cambridge University Press.

Ovando, C. J., Combs, M. C., & Collier, V. P. (2011). *Bilingual & ESL classrooms: Teaching in multicultural contexts* (5th ed.). Boston: McGraw-Hill.

Pally, M. (1994). Lingua franca: Film and video in second language acquisition. *NABE News, 18*(3), 11–13, 17, 34.

Purcell-Gates, V. (1996). Process teaching with direct instruction and feedback in a university-based clinic. In E. McIntyre & M. Pressley (Eds.), *Balanced instruction: Strategies and skills in whole language* (pp. 107–127). Norwood, MA: Christopher-Gordon.

Putintseva, T. (2006, March). The importance of learning styles in ESL/EFL. *The Internet TESL Journal, 12*(3). Retrieved February 13, 2014, from http://iteslj.org/Articles/Putintseva-Learning Styles.html

Robinson, P., & Ellis, N. (Eds.). (2008). *Handbook of cognitive linguistics and second language acquisition.* New York: Routledge.

Rosebery, A. S., Warren, B., & Conant, F. R. (1992). Appropriate scientific discourse: Findings from language minority classrooms. *Journal of the Learning Sciences, 2*(1), 61–94.

Routman, R. (1996). *Literacy at the crossroads: Crucial talk about reading, writing, and other teaching dilemmas.* Portsmouth, NH: Heinemann.

Roxas, K. (2011). Creating communities: Working with refugee students in classrooms. *Democracy in Education, 19*(2). Available at http://democracyeducationjournal.org/home/

Sasser, L. (1992). Teaching literature to language minority students. In P. A. Richard-Amato & M. A. Snow (Eds.), *The multicultural classroom: Readings for content-area teachers* (pp. 300–315). White Plains, NY: Longman.

Saville-Troike, M. (1984). What really matters in second language learning for academic achievement? *TESOL Quarterly, 18*(2), 199–219.

Shepard, L. A. (1997). *Measuring achievement: What does it mean to test for robust understanding?* Princeton, NJ: Policy Information Center, Educational Testing Service.

Shuell, T. J. (1986). Cognitive conceptions of learning. *Review of Educational Research, 56,* 411–436.

Snow, C., Arlman-Rupp, A., Hassing, Y., Jobse, J., Joosten, J., & Yorster, J. (1976). Mothers' speech in three social classes. *Journal of Psycholinguistic Research, 5,* 1–20.

Sousa, D. A. (2011). *How the brain learns* (4th ed.). Thousand Oaks, CA: Corwin.

Thomas, W. P., & Collier, V. P. (1997). *School effectiveness for language minority students* (NCBE Resource Collection Series No. 9). Washington, DC: National Clearinghouse for Bilingual Education. Retrieved October 7, 2002, from www.ncela.gwu.edu/ncbepubs/resource/effectiveness

Thomas, W. P., & Collier, V. P. (2012). *Dual language education for a transformed world*. Albuquerque, NM: Dual Language Education of New Mexico Fuente Press.

Valdes, G. (1996). *Con respeto: Bridging the distance between culturally diverse families and schools: An ethnographic portrait*. New York: Teachers College Press.

Walqui, A. (2012). Instruction for diverse groups of English language learners. In K. Hakuta, & M. Santos (Eds.), *Understanding language: literacy, and learning in content areas* (pp. 94–103). Stanford, CA: Stanford University.

Walsh, E. (1989). *Mouse paint*. San Diego, CA: Voyager Books.

Wolfersberger, M. (2001). *The effects of second language proficiency on the transfer of first language composing processes to second language writing*. Thesis. Brigham Young University, Provo, Utah.

Young, K. M., & Leinhardt, G. (1996). *Writing from primary documents: A way of knowing in history* (Tech. Rep. No. CLIP-96-01). Pittsburgh, PA: University of Pittsburgh, Learning Research and Development Center.

Chapter 3

Akmajian, A., Demers, R. A., Farmer, A. K., & Harnish, R. M. (2010). *Linguistics: An introduction to language and communication* (6th ed.). Cambridge, MA: MIT Press.

Anderson, N. J. (1999). *Exploring second language reading: Issues and strategies*. Boston: Heinle & Heinle.

Bialystok, E. (1990). The dangers of dichotomy: A reply to Hulstijn. *Applied Linguistics, 11,* 46–52.

Brown, H. D. (2006). *Principles of language learning and teaching* (5th ed.). New York: Longman.

Calderón, M. (2007). *Teaching reading to English language learners, grades 6-12: A framework for improving achievement in the content areas*. Thousand Oaks, CA: Corwin.

Canale, M. (1983). From communicative competence to communicative language pedagogy. In J. Richards & R. Schmidt (Eds.), *Language and communication* (pp. 2–27). New York: Longman.

Clay, M. (1991). *Becoming literate: The construction of inner control*. Portsmouth, NH: Heinemann.

Collier, V. P. (1987). The age and rate of acquisition of second language for academic purposes. *TESOL Quarterly, 21,* 617–641.

Collier, V. P. (1989). How long? A synthesis of research on academic achievement in a second language. *TESOL Quarterly, 23, 509–531.*

Collier, V. P. (1992). A synthesis of studies examining long-term language minority student data on academic achievement. *Bilingual Research Journal, 16*(1–2), 187–212.

Collier, V. P., & Thomas, W. P. (1989). How quickly can immigrants become proficient in school English? *Journal of Educational Issues of Language Minority Students, 5, 26–38.*

Coyne, M. D., Kameenui, E., & Carnine, D. (2010). *Effective teaching strategies that accommodate diverse learners* (4th ed.). Upper Saddle River, NJ: Prentice-Hall.

Cummins, J. (1981). The role of primary language development in promoting educational success for language minority students. In C. F. Leyba (Ed.), *Schooling and language minority students: A theoretical framework* (pp. 3–49). Los Angeles: Evaluation, Dissemination and Assessment Center, CSULA.

Cummins, J. (1991). Interdependence of first- and second-language proficiency in bilingual children. In E. Bialystok (Ed.), *Language processing in bilingual children* (pp. 70–89). Cambridge, UK: Cambridge University Press.

Cummins, J. (1992). Bilingual education and English immersion: The Ramírez report in theoretical perspective. *Bilingual Research Journal, 16*(1–2), 91–104.

Cummins, J., & Swain, M. (1986). *Bilingualism in education*. New York: Longman.

Delgado-Gaitán, C. (1989). Classroom literacy activity for Spanish-speaking students. *Linguistics and Education, 1, 285–297.*

Dolson, D. P., & Mayer, J. (1992). Longitudinal study of three program models for language-minority students: A critical examination of reported findings. *Bilingual Research Journal, 16*(1–2), 105–157.

Dulay, H. C., & Burt, M. K. (1974). Errors and strategies in child second language acquisition. *TESOL Quarterly, 8*(2), 129–136.

Escamilla, K. (1987). *The relationship of native language reading achievement and oral English proficiency to future achievement in reading English as a second language* (Unpublished doctoral dissertation). University of California, Los Angeles.

Farstrup, A. E., & Samuels, S. J. (Eds.). (2008). *What research has to say about vocabulary instruction.* Newark, DE: International Reading Association.

Freeman, D. E., & Freeman, Y. S. (2004). *Essential linguistics: What you need to know to teach reading, ESL, spelling, phonics, and grammar.* Portsmouth, NH: Heinemann.

Genesee, F. (1987). *Learning through two languages: Studies of immersion and bilingual education.* Cambridge, MA: Newbury House.

Grabe, W. (2009). *Reading in a second language: Moving from theory to practice.* New York: Cambridge University Press.

Hakuta, K. (2011). Educating language minority students and affirming their equal rights: Research and practical perspectives. *Educational Researcher, 40*(4), 163–174.

Herrera, S. (2001). *Classroom strategies for the English language learner: A practical guide for accelerating language and literacy development.* Manhattan, KS: The MASTER Teacher.

Herrera, S. (2007). *By teachers, with teachers, for teachers: ESL Methods course module.* Manhattan, KS: KCAT/TLC.

Herrera, S., Perez, D., & Escamilla, K. (2010). *Teaching reading to English language learners: Differentiated literacies.* Boston: Allyn and Bacon.

Hudelson, S., & Serna, I. (1994). Beginning literacy in English in a whole-language bilingual program. In A. Flurkey & R. Meyer (Eds.), *Under the whole language umbrella: Many cultures, many voices* (pp. 278–294). Urbana, IL: National Council of Teachers of English.

Hymes, D. (1972). On communicative competence. In J. B. Pride & J. Holmes (Eds.), *Sociolinguistics* (pp. 269–293). Harmondsworth, UK: Penguin.

Jensen, E. (2008). *Brain-based learning: The new paradigm of teaching* (2nd ed.). Thousand Oaks, CA: Corwin.

Kole, N. (2003). *Native-language supported reading instruction: A VALID framework.* Unpublished doctoral dissertation, Kansas State University, Manhattan.

Krashen, S. (1982). *Principles and practice in second language acquisition.* Oxford, UK: Pergamon.

Krashen, S. D. (1987). *Principles and practices in second language acquisition.* New York: Prentice Hall.

Krashen, S. D., & Terrell, T. (1983). *The natural approach: Language acquisition in the classroom.* Oxford, UK: Pergamon.

Lesher-Madrid, D., & García, E. (1985). The effect of language transfer on bilingual proficiency. In E. García & R. Padilla (Eds). *Advances in bilingual education research* (pp. 53–70). Tucson: University of Arizona Press.

Lightbrown, P., & Spada, N. (2013). *How languages are learned* (4th ed.). Oxford, UK: Oxford University Press.

Marzano, R. J. (2004). *Building background knowledge for academic achievement: Research on what works in schools.* Alexandria, VA: Association for Supervision and Curriculum Development.

McLaughlin, B. (1990). Conscious versus unconscious learning. *TESOL Quarterly, 24,* 617–634.

Modiano, N. (1968). National or mother tongue in beginning reading: A comparative study. *Research in the Teaching of English, 2*(1), 32–43.

National Reading Panel. (2000). *Teaching children to read: An evidence-based assessment of the scientific research literature on reading and its implications for reading instruction.* National Institute of Child Health and Human Development. Retrieved April 14, 2003, from www.nichd.nih.gov/publications/nrp/smallbook.htm

Ninio, A., & Bruner, J. (1978). The achievement and antecedents of labeling. *Child Language, 5,* 1–15.

Ochs, E., & Schieffelin, G. G. (1984). Language acquisition and socialization: Three developmental stories and their implications. In R. Shweder & R. LeVine (Eds.), *Culture theory: Essays on mind, self, and emotion* (pp. 276–322). Cambridge, MA: Cambridge University Press.

Ovando, C. J., & Combs, M. C. (2011). *Bilingual & ESL classrooms: Teaching in multicultural contexts* (5th ed.). Boston: McGraw-Hill.

Perez, D. (2002). *Comprender: Comprehension: Orchestrating meaning and purpose for reading English among newly developing English language readers.* Unpublished doctoral dissertation, Kansas State University, Manhattan.

Ramírez, J. D. (1992). Executive summary. *Bilingual Research Journal, 16*(1–2), 1–62.

Reutzel, D. R., & Cooter, R. B. (2004). *Teaching children to read: Putting the pieces together and model lessons for literacy instruction.* Columbus, OH: Prentice-Hall.

Saville-Troike, M. (1984). What really matters in second language learning for academic achievement? *TESOL Quarterly, 18*(2), 199–219.

Schieffelin, B. B., & Eisenberg, A. (1984). Cultural variation in children's conversations. In R. L. Schiefelbusch & J. Pickar (Eds.), *The acquisition of communicative competence* (pp. 377–420). Baltimore, MD: University Park Press.

Skutnabb-Kangas, T. (1975, August). *Bilingualism, semilingualism and school achievement*. Paper presented at the Fourth International Congress of Applied Linguistics, Stuttgart, Germany.

Sousa, D. A. (2011). *How the brain learns* (4th ed.). Thousand Oaks, CA: Corwin.

Wong Fillmore, L. (1991). Second language learning in children: A model of language learning in social context. In E. Bialystok (Ed.), *Language processing in bilingual children* (pp. 49–69). Cambridge, MA: Cambridge University Press.

Wong Fillmore, L., & Valadez, C. (1986). Teaching bilingual learners. In M. C. Wittrock (Ed.), *Handbook of research on teaching* (3rd ed., pp. 648–685). New York: Longman.

Chapter 4

Anderson, N. J. (1999). *Exploring second language reading: Issues and strategies*. Boston: Heinle & Heinle.

Bialystok, E. (2001). *Bilingualism in development: Language, literacy, & cognition*. New York: Cambridge University Press.

Bley-Vroman, R. (1988). The fundamental character of foreign language learning. In W. Rutherford & M. Sharwood-Smith (Eds.), *Grammar and second language teaching: A book of readings* (pp. 19–30). New York: Newbury House/Harper & Row.

Boyson, B. A., & Short, D. J. (2003). *Secondary school newcomer programs in the United States*. Santa Cruz: Center for Research on Education, Diversity & Excellence, University of California.

Brisk, M. E. (1981). Language policies in American education. *Journal of Education, 163*(1), 3–15.

Brown, D. D. (1994). *Teaching by principles: An interactive approach to language pedagogy*. Upper Saddle River, NJ: Prentice Hall.

Carlson, S. M., & Meltzoff, A. M. (2008). Bilingual experience and executive functioning in young children. *Developmental Science, 11*, 282–298.

Chambers, J., & Parrish, T. (1992). *Meeting the challenge of diversity: An evaluation of programs for pupils with limited proficiency in English: Vol. 4. Cost of programs and services for LEP students*. Berkeley, CA: BW Associates.

Chamot, A. U. (2009). *The CALLA handbook: Implementing the cognitive academic language learning approach* (2nd ed.). Reading, MA: Addison-Wesley.

Chamot, A. U., & O'Malley, J. M. (1994). *The CALLA handbook: Implementing the cognitive academic language learning approach*. Reading, MA: Addison-Wesley.

Chomsky, N. (1966). Linguistic theory. In R. G. Mead, Jr. (Ed.), *Northeast conference on the teaching of foreign languages: Reports of the working committees* (pp. 43–49). New York: MLA Materials Center.

Christian, D. (1994). *Two-way bilingual education: Students learning through two languages* (Educational Practice Rep. No. 12). Washington, DC, and Santa Cruz, CA: National Center for Cultural Diversity and Second Language Learning.

Collier, V. P. (1987). The age and rate of acquisition of second language for academic purposes. *TESOL Quarterly, 21*, 617–641.

Collier, V. P. (1988, April). *The effect of age on acquisition of a second language for school*. Washington, DC: National Clearinghouse for Bilingual Education.

Collier, V. P. (1989a). *Academic achievement, attitudes, and occupations among graduates of two-way bilingual classes*. Paper presented at the annual meeting of the American Educational Research Association, San Francisco, CA.

Collier, V. P. (1989b). How long? A synthesis of research on academic achievement in a second language. *TESOL Quarterly, 23*, 509–531.

Collier, V. P. (1992). A synthesis of studies examining long-term language minority student data on academic achievement. *Bilingual Research Journal, 16*(1–2), 187–212.

Collier, V. P. (1995). *Promoting academic success for ESL students: Understanding second language acquisition for school*. Elizabeth, NJ: New Jersey Teachers of English to Speakers of Other Languages–Bilingual Educators.

Collier, V. P., & Thomas, W. P. (1988). *Acquisition of cognitive-academic second language proficiency: A six-year study*. Paper presented at the annual meeting of the American Educational Research Association, New Orleans, LA.

Collier, V. P., & Thomas, W. P. (1989). How quickly can immigrants become proficient in school English? *Journal of Educational Issues of Language Minority Students, 5*, 26–38.

Collier, V. P., & Thomas, W. P. (2004, Winter). The astounding effectiveness of dual language education for all. *NABE Journal of Research and Practice, 2*(1), 1–18.

Collier, V. P., & Thomas, W. P. (2009). *Educating English learners for a transformed world.* Albuquerque, NM: Dual Language Education of New Mexico Fuente Press.

Cooper, J. D. (1986). *Improving reading comprehension.* Boston: Houghton Mifflin.

Crawford, J. (1992). *Hold your tongue: Bilingualism and the politics of "English only."* Reading, MA: Addison-Wesley.

Crawford, J. (1997). *Best evidence: Research foundations of the Bilingual Education Act.* Washington, DC: National Clearinghouse for Bilingual Education. Online at www.ncbe.gwu.edu/ncbe-pubs/reports/bestevidence/

Crawford, J. (2000). *At war with diversity: U.S. language policy in an age of anxiety.* Clevedon, UK: Multilingual Matters.

Cummins, J. (1979). Linguistic interdependence and the educational development of bilingual children. *Review of Educational Research, 49*(2), 222–251.

Cummins, J. (1981). The role of primary language development in promoting educational success for language minority students. In C. F. Leyba (Ed.), *Schooling and language minority students: A theoretical framework* (pp. 3–49). Los Angeles: Evaluation, Dissemination and Assessment Center, CSULA.

Cummins, J. (1991). Interdependence of first- and second-language proficiency in bilingual children. In E. Bialystok (Ed.), *Language processing in bilingual children* (pp. 70–89). Cambridge, UK: Cambridge University Press.

Cummins, J. (1998). Language issues and educational change. In A. Hargreaves, A. Lieberman, M. Fullan, & D. Hopkins (Eds.), *International handbook of educational change* (pp. 440–459). Dordrecht, Netherlands: Kluwer Academic.

Cummins, J. (2001b). *Language, power, and pedagogy: Bilingual children in the crossfire.* Philadelphia: Multilingual Matters.

Cummins, J. (2001c). *Negotiating identities: Education for empowerment in a diverse society* (2nd ed.). Los Angeles: California Association for Bilingual Education.

Cunningham, P. M., Moore, S. A., Cunningham, J. W., & Moore, D. W. (2003). *Reading and writing in elementary classrooms: Strategies and observations* (5th ed). Upper Saddle River, NJ: Prentice-Hall.

de Lopez, M., & Montalvo-Cisneros, M. (1986). Developing community support for second language programs. *Foreign Language Annals, 19*(6), 529–531.

Donato, R. (1997). *The other struggle for equal schools: Mexican Americans during the civil rights era.* Albany: State University of New York Press.

Echevarria, J., & Graves, A. (2010). *Sheltered content instruction: Teaching English-language learners with diverse abilities* (4th ed.). Boston: Pearson.

Edelsky, C. (1982). Writing in a bilingual program: The relation of L1 and L2 texts. *TESOL Quarterly, 16,* 211–228.

Emmorey, K., Luk, G., Pyers, J. E., & Bialystok, E. (2008). Research report: The source of enhanced cognitive control in bilinguals: Evidence from bimodal bilinguals. *Psychological Science, 19*(12), 1201–1206.

Escamilla, K. (1999). The false dichotomy between ESL and transitional bilingual education programs: Issues that challenge all of us. *Educational Considerations, 26*(2), 1–6.

Faltis, C. (1986). Initial cross-lingual reading transfer in bilingual second grade classrooms. In E. García & B. Flores (Eds.), *Language and literacy research in bilingual education* (pp. 145–157). Tempe: Arizona State University Press.

Faltis, C. J., & Hudelson, S. J. (1998). *Bilingual education in elementary and secondary school communities: Toward understanding and caring.* Boston: Allyn and Bacon.

Feinberg, R. C. (2000). Newcomer schools: Salvation or segregated oblivion for immigrant students? *Theory into Practice, 39*(4), 220–227. Retrieved October 14, 2002, from WilsonSelectPlus database.

General Accounting Office (GAO). (1987). *Bilingual education: A new look at the research evidence* (Report No. PEMD-87-12BR). Washington, DC: U.S. General Accounting Office.

Genesee, F. (1983). Bilingual education for majority language children: The immersion experiments in review. *Applied Psycholinguistics, 4,* 1–46.

Genesee, F. (1987). *Learning through two languages: Studies of immersion and bilingual education.* Cambridge, MA: Newbury House.

Genesee, F. (1999). *Program alternatives for linguistically diverse students.* Washington, DC, and Santa Cruz, CA: Center for Research on Education, Diversity & Excellence.

Gleason, H. A. (1961). *An introduction to descriptive linguistics* (Rev. ed.). New York: Holt, Rinehart and Winston.

Glenn, C., & LaLyre, I. (1991). Integrated bilingual education in the USA. In K. Jaspaert & S. Kroon (Eds.), *Ethnic minority languages and education* (pp. 37–55). Amsterdam: Swets and Zeitlinger.

Gómez, L., Freeman, D., & Freeman, Y. (2005, Spring). Dual language education: A promising 50-50 model. *Bilingual Research Journal, 29*(1), 145–164.

Hakuta, K. (2011). Educating language minority students and affirming their equal rights: Research and practical perspectives. *Educational Researcher, 40*(4), 163–174.

Harris, P. (2009, January 22). City of Nashville rejects English-only law. *Reuters.* Retrieved from http://www.reuters.com/article/2009/01/23/us-usa-english-nashville-idUSTRE50M11420090123

Henderson, R., & Landesman, E. (1992). *Mathematics and middle school students of Mexican descent: The effects of thematically integrated instruction.* Santa Cruz, CA: The National Center for Research on Cultural Diversity and Language Learning.

Herrera, S., & Fanning, R. (1999). Preparing today's teachers for tomorrow's children. *Educational Considerations, 26*(2), 40–43.

Herrera, S. G., Cabral, R. M., & Murry, K. G. (2013). *Assessment accommodations for classroom teachers of culturally and linguistically diverse students* (2nd ed.). Boston, MA: Allyn & Bacon.

Herrera, S., Murry, K., & Perez, D. (2008). Classic: Transforming hearts and minds. In M. Brisk (Ed.), *Language, culture, and community in teacher education* (pp. 149–173). Mahwah, NJ: Erlbaum/Taylor & Francis Group for the American Association of Colleges of Teacher Education (AACTE).

Hudelson, S., & Serna, I. (1994). Beginning literacy in English in a whole-language bilingual program. In A. Flurkey & R. Meyer (Eds.), *Under the whole language umbrella: Many cultures, many voices* (pp. 278–294). Urbana, IL: National Council of Teachers of English.

Kang, H-W., Kuehn, P., & Herrell, A. (1996). The Hmong literacy project: Parents working to preserve the past and ensure the future. *The Journal of Educational Issues of Language Minority Students, 16.* Online at www.ncbe.gwu.edu/miscpubs/jeilms/vol16/jeilms1602.htm

Kloss, H. (1997). *The American bilingual tradition.* Rowley, MA: Newbury House.

Krashen, S. (1996). *Under attack: The case against bilingual education.* Culver City, CA: Language Education Associates.

Lanauze, M., & Snow, C. (1989). The relation between first and second language writing skills: Evidence from Puerto Rican elementary school children in bilingual programs. *Linguistics and Education, 1,* 323–339.

Lau v. Nichols, 414 U.S. 563 (1974).

Leibowitz, A. H. (1971). *Educational policy and political acceptance: The imposition of English as the language of instruction in American schools.* Washington, DC: Center for Applied Linguistics.

Lindholm, K. (1990). Bilingual immersion education: Criteria for program development. In A. M. Padilla, H. H. Fairchild, & C. M. Valdez (Eds.), *Bilingual education: Issues and strategies* (pp. 91–105). Newbury Park, CA: Sage.

Lindholm, K. (1992). Two-way bilingual/immersion education: Theory, conceptual issues, and pedagogical implications. In R. Padilla & A. Benavides (Eds.), *Critical perspectives in bilingual education research* (pp. 195–220). Tucson, AZ: Bilingual Review/Press.

Linquanti, R. (1999). *Fostering academic success for English language learners: What do we know?* Retrieved September 16, 2002, from www.wested.org/policy/pubs/fostering/adv_conc.htm

Medina, S. (1995). K–6 bilingual programs in the Los Angeles metropolitan area. *Bilingual Research Journal, 19*(3–4), 629–640.

Mezzacappa, E. (2004). Alerting, orienting, and executive attention: Developmental properties and sociodemographic correlates in an epidemiological sample of young, urban children. *Child Development, 75,* 1373–1386.

Minicucci, C. (1996). *Learning science and English: How school reform advances scientific learning for limited English proficient middle school students.* Santa Cruz, CA: National Center for Research on Cultural Diversity and Language Learning.

Moll, L. C., Amanti, D. N., & Gonzalez, N. (1992). Funds of knowledge for teaching: Using a qualitative approach to connect homes and classrooms. *Theory into Practice, 31,* 132–141.

Mora, J. K. (2009, April). From the ballot box to the classroom. *Educational Leadership, 66*(7), 14–19.

Nagy, W., García, G., Durgunoglu, A., & Hacin-Bhatt, B. (1993). Spanish–English bilingual children's use and recognition of cognates in English reading. *Journal of Reading Behavior, 25*(3), 241–259.

National Reading Panel. (2000). *Teaching children to read: An evidence-based assessment of the scientific research literature on reading and its implications for reading instruction.* National Institute of Child Health and Human Development. Retrieved April 14, 2003, from www.nichd.nih.gov/publications/nrp/smallbook.htm

Ney, J., & Pearson, B. A. (1990). Connectionism as a model of language learning: Parallels in foreign language teaching. *Modern Language Journal, 74,* 474–482.

Ovando, C. J., Combs, M. C., & Collier, V. P. (2011). *Bilingual & ESL classrooms: Teaching in multicultural contexts* (5th ed.). Boston: McGraw-Hill.

Padilla, A. M., & Gonzalez, R. (2001). Academic performance of immigrant and U.S.-born Mexican heritage students: Effects of schooling in Mexico and bilingual/English language instruction. *American Educational Research Journal, 38*(3), 727–742.

Pearson, P. D. (1984). *Twenty years of research in reading comprehension: The contents of school-based literacy.* New York: Random House.

Peregoy, S. F., & Boyle, O. F. (2012). *Reading, writing, and learning in ESL: A resource book for K–12 teachers* (6th ed.). Boston: Pearson.

Planas, R. (2013, October 23). Mexican American studies books un-banned in Arizona. *The Huffington Post.* Retrieved February 27, 2014, from http://www.huffingtonpost.com/2013/10/23/mexican-american-studies-book-ban_n_4149048.html

Porter, R. P. (1996). *Forked tongue: The politics of bilingual education.* New Brunswick, NJ: Transaction Publishers.

Ramírez, J. D. (1992). Executive summary. *Bilingual Research Journal, 16*(1–2), 1–62.

Ramírez, J. D., Yuen, S. D., Ramey, D. R., & Pasta, D. J. (1991). *Final report: Longitudinal study of structured English immersion strategy, early-exit and late-exit transitional bilingual education programs for language-minority children* (Vols. I and II). San Mateo, CA: Aguirre International.

Robbins, T. (2013, July 24). Tucson revives Mexican-American program. *National Public Radio.* Retrieved February 27, 2014, from http://www.npr.org/blogs/codeswitch/2013/07/24/205058168/Tucson-Revives-Mexican-American-Studies-Program

Saunders, W., & Goldenberg, C. (1999). *The effects of instructional conversations and literature logs on the story comprehension and thematic understanding of English proficient and limited English proficient students* (Research Rep. No. 6). Washington, DC, and Santa Cruz, CA: Center for Research on Education, Diversity & Excellence.

Seelye, K. Q., & Parker, A. (2012, March 15). For Santorum, trying to tamp down a firestorm over Puerto Rico remarks. *The New York Times.* Retrieved from http://www.nytimes.com/2012/03/16/us/politics/santorum-addresses-firestorm-over-puerto-rico-remarks.html?_r=2&

Short, D. J., Vogt, M. & Echevarria, J. (2008). *The SIOP model for administrators.* Boston: Allyn and Bacon.

Snow, C. E., Burns, M. S., & Griffin, P. (Eds.). (1998). *Preventing reading difficulties in young children.* Washington, DC: National Academy Press.

Stevens, C. (2002, October 28). Verdict still out on programs. *USA Today.* Retrieved November 4, 2002, from www.usatoday.com/news/opinion/editorials/2002-10-28-edit_x.htm

Swain, M., & Lapkin, S. (1982). *Evaluating bilingual education: A Canadian case study.* Clevedon, UK: Multilingual Matters.

Swain, M., & Lapkin, S. (1991). Additive bilingualism and French immersion education: The roles of language and proficiency and literacy. In A. Reynolds (Ed.), *Bilingualism, multiculturalism, and second language learning: The McGill conference in honour of Wallace E. Lambert* (pp. 203–216). Hillsdale, NJ: Erlbaum.

Thomas, W. P. (1992). An analysis of the research methodology of the Ramírez study. *Bilingual Research Journal, 16*(1–2), 213–245.

Thomas, W. P. (1994). *The Cognitive Academic Language Learning Approach project for mathematics.* Fairfax, VA: Center for Bilingual/Multicultural/ESL Education, George Mason University.

Thomas, W. P., & Collier, V. P. (1997). *School effectiveness for language minority students* (NCBE Resource Collection Series No. 9). Washington, DC: National Clearinghouse for Bilingual Education. Retrieved October 7, 2002, from www.ncela.gwu.edu/ncbepubs/resource/effectiveness

Thomas, W. P., & Collier, V. P. (2002). *A national study of school effectiveness for language minority students' long-term academic achievement.*

Santa Cruz, CA: Center for Research on Education, Diversity & Excellence.

Thomas, W. P., & Collier, V. P. (2012). Dual language education for a transformed world. Albuquerque, NM: Dual Language Education of New Mexico Fuente Press.

Trueba, H. T. (1994). Reflections on alternative visions of schooling. *Anthropology & Education Quarterly, 25*, 376–393.

U.S. English. (1990, May 21). The door to opportunity. *Roll Call.*

Valdes, G. (1997). The teaching of Spanish to bilingual Spanish-speaking students: Outstanding issues and unanswered questions. In M. C. Colombi & F. X. Alarcon (Eds.), *La ensenanza del espanol a hispanohablantes: Praxis y teoria* (pp. 93–101). Boston: Houghton Mifflin.

Valdez, L., & Steiner, S. (Eds.). (1972). *Aztlán: An anthology of Mexican American literature.* New York: Vintage Books.

Veeder, K., & Tramutt, J. (2000). Strengthening literacy in both languages in grades 2–5. In N. Cloud, F. Genesee, & E. Hamayan (Eds.), *Dual language instruction: A handbook for enriched education* (p. 91). Boston: Heinle and Heinle.

Vygotsky, L. S. (1978). *Mind in society: The development of higher psychological processes.* Cambridge, MA: Harvard University Press.

Whorf, B. (1956). Science and linguistics. In J. B. Carroll (Ed.), *Language, thought, and reality: Selected writings of Benjamin Lee Whorf* (pp. 207–219). Cambridge, MA: MIT Press.

Willig, A. C. (1981). The effectiveness of bilingual education: Review of a report. *National Association for Bilingual Education Journal, 6*(2–3), 1–20.

Willig, A. C. (1985). A meta-analysis of selected studies on the effectiveness of bilingual education. *Review of Educational Research, 55,* 269–317.

Chapter 5

August, D., & Shanahan, T. (Eds.). (2006). *Developing literacy in second language learners. Report of the National Literacy Panel on Minority-Language Children and Youth.* Mahwah, NJ: Erlbaum.

Bailey, A. (Ed.). (2007). *The language demands of school: Putting academic English to the test.* New Haven, CT: Yale University Press.

Baker, C., & Freebody, P. (1988). Talk around text: Construction of textual and teacher authority in classroom discourse. In S. de Castell, A. Like, & C. Luke (Eds.), *Language, authority, and criticism: Readings on the school textbook* (pp. 111–132). London: Falmer.

Banks, J., Cochran-Smith, M., Moll, L., Richert, A., Zeichner, K., LePage, P. et al. (2005). Teaching diverse learners. In L. Darling-Hammond & J. Bransford (Eds.), *Preparing teachers for a changing world: What teachers should learn and be able to do* (pp. 232–274). San Francisco: Jossey-Bass.

Brisk, M. E. (2005). Bilingual education. In E. Hinkel (Ed.), *Handbook of research in second language teaching and learning* (pp. 7–24). Mahwah, NJ: Erlbaum.

Capps, R., Fix, M., Murray, J., Ost, J., Passel, J. S., & Herwantoro, S. (2005). *The new demography of America's schools: Immigration and the No Child Left Behind Act.* Washington, DC: The Urban Institute.

Collier, V. P., & Thomas, W. P. (2009). *Educating English learners for a transformed world.* Albuquerque, NM: Dual Language Education of New Mexico Fuente Press.

Cummins, J. (2001). *Language, power, and pedagogy: Bilingual children in the crossfire.* Philadelphia: Multilingual Matters.

Díaz, S., Moll, L. C., & Mehan, H. (1986). Sociocultural resources in instruction: A context-specific approach. In Bilingual Education Office, California Department of Education (Ed.), *Beyond language: Social and cultural factors in schooling language minority students* (pp. 187–230). Los Angeles: Evaluation, Dissemination, and Assessment Center, California State University.

Diaz-Rico, L. T. (2014). *The crosscultural, language, and academic development handbook: A complete K–12 reference guide* (5th ed.). Boston: Allyn and Bacon.

Escamilla, K. (1994). The sociolinguistic environment of a bilingual school: A case study introduction. *Bilingual Research Journal, 18,* 21–48.

Genesee, F. (2004). What do we know about bilingual education for majority language students? In T. K. Bhatia & W. Ritchie (Eds.), *Handbook of bilingualism and multiculturalism* (pp. 547–576). Malden, MA: Blackwell.

Gibbons, P. (2003). Mediating language learning: Teacher interactions with ESL students in a content-based classroom. *TESOL Quarterly, 3,* 247–273.

Gonzalez, G. A. (2002, June). *A total integrated language approach.* Elementary strand session presented at the second annual CLD Education Institute, Wichita, KS.

Gonzalez, N., Moll, L. C., & Amanti, C. (2005). *Funds of knowledge: Theorizing practices in households, communities, and classrooms.* Mahwah, NJ: Erlbaum.

Grabe, W. (1991). Current developments in second language reading research. *TESOL Quarterly, 25*(3), 375–406.

Hamayan, E. (1994). Language development of low literacy students. In F. Genesee (Ed.), *Educating second language children* (pp. 166–199). Cambridge, UK: Cambridge University Press.

Hancock, D. R. (2002). The effects of native language books on the pre-literacy skill development of language minority kindergartners. *Journal of Research in Childhood Education, 17*(1), 62–68.

Hargreaves, A., & Fullan, M. (1998). *What's worth fighting for out there?* New York: Teachers College Press.

Herrera, S. (1996). The meaning perspectives teachers hold regarding their Mexican American students: An ethnographic case study. *Dissertation Abstracts International, 56*(12), 4643. [CD-ROM]. Abstract from: ProQuest File: Dissertations Abstracts Item: AAC 9610795.

Herrera, S. (2010). *Biography-driven instruction for culturally-responsive teaching: An action model.* New York: Teachers College Press.

Herrera, S., & Murry, K. G. (1999). In the aftermath of Unz. *Bilingual Research Journal, 23*(2–3), 113–132.

Hoffman-Kipp, P., Artiles, A. J., & López-Torres, L. (2003, Summer). Beyond reflection: Teacher learning as praxis. *Theory into Practice, 42*(3), 248–254.

Holmes, M. A., & Herrera, S. G. (2009). Enhancing advocacy skills of teacher candidates. *Teaching Education Journal, 20*(2), 203–213.

Howard, T. C. (2003). Culturally relevant pedagogy: Ingredients for critical teacher reflection. *Theory into Practice, 42*(3), 195–202.

Jacobs, J. (2006). Supervision for social justice: Supporting critical reflection. *Teacher Education Quarterly, 33*(4), 23–39.

Jiang, N. (2000). Lexical representation and development in a second language. *Applied Linguistics, 21*(1), 47–77.

Kaufman, D. (2004). Issues in constructivist pedagogy for L2 learning and teaching. *Annual Review of Applied Linguistics, 24*, 303–319.

Kowal, M. (2001). Knowledge building: Learning about Native issues outside in and inside out. In G. Wells (Ed.), *Action, talk and text: Learning and teaching through inquiry* (pp. 118–133). New York: Teachers College Press.

Ladson-Billings, G. (1995). Toward a theory of culturally relevant pedagogy. *American Educational Research Journal, 32*(3), 465–491.

Lucas, T., & Grinberg, J. (2008). Responding to the linguistic reality of mainstream classrooms: Preparing all teachers to teach English language learners. In M. Cochran-Smith, S. Feiman-Nemser, D. J. McIntyre, & K. E. Demers (Eds.), *Handbook of research on teacher education: Enduring questions in changing contexts* (3rd ed., pp. 606–649). New York: Routledge.

Lyster, R. (2007). *Learning and teaching languages through content: A counterbalanced approach.* Amsterdam: Benjamins.

Martinez, E. (2002). Fragmented community, fragmented schools: The implementation of educational policy for Latino immigrants. In S. Wortham, E. G. Murillo, Jr., & E. T. Hamann (Eds.), *Education in the new Lationo diaspora: Policy and the politics of identity* (pp. 143–168). Westport, CT: Ablex.

McCarthey, S. J. (2008). The impact of No Child Left Behind on teachers' writing instruction. *Written Communication, 25*, 462–505.

Mettetal, G., & Cowen, P. (2000). Assessing learning through classroom research: The Supporting Teachers as Researchers Project [Electronic version]. *Classroom Leadership, 3*(8). Retrieved February 22, 2003, from www.ascd.org/readingroom/classlead/0005/1may00.html

Mezirow, J. (1991). *Transformative dimensions of adult learning.* San Francisco: Jossey-Bass.

Milner, H. R. (2003, Summer). Teacher reflection and race in cultural contexts: History, meanings, and methods in teaching. *Theory into Practice, 42*(3), 173–180.

Murry, K. (1996). Reflective-transformative professional development predicated upon critical reflection and enabled by a school–university partnership: A microethnographic case study. *Dissertation Abstracts International, 56*(12), 4643. [CD-ROM]. Abstract from: ProQuest File: Dissertations Abstracts Item: AAC 9610795.

Murry, K. (1998). Diversity-driven program innovation in higher education: An incremental approach. *Continuing Higher Education Review, 62*, 119–126.

Murry, K., & Herrera, S. (1999). CLASSIC impacts: A qualitative study of ESL/BLED programming. *Educational Considerations, 26*(2), 11–18.

National Board for Professional Teaching Standards (NBPTS). (1998). *English as a new language standards.* Arlington, VA: Author.

Nieto, S. (1992). *Affirming diversity: The sociopolitical context of multicultural education.* New York: Longman.

Nieto, S., & Bode, P. (2012). *Affirming diversity: The sociopolitical context of multicultural education* (6th ed.). New York: Longman.

Norris, J., & Ortega, L. (2000). Effectiveness of L2 instruction: A research synthesis and quantitative meta-analysis. *Language Learning, 50,* 417–528.

Nunan, D. (2003). *Practical English language teaching.* New York: McGraw-Hill.

Perez, B., & Torres-Guzman, M. (2002). *Learning in two worlds: An integrated Spanish/English biliteracy approach* (3rd ed.). Boston: Allyn and Bacon.

Pompa, D., & Hakuta, K. (2012). *Opportunities for policy advancement for ELLs created by the new standards movement.* Paper presented at the 2012 Understanding Language Conference, Stanford, CA. Retrieved March 11, 2014, from http://ell.stanford.edu/papers/practice

Riches, C., & Genesee, F. (2006). Cross-linguistic and cross-modal aspects of literacy development. In F. Genesee, K. Lindholm-Leary, W. Saunders, & D. Christian (Eds.), *Educating English language learners: A synthesis of research evidence* (pp. 64–108). New York: Cambridge University Press.

Roberts, T. A. (2009). *No limits to literacy for preschool English learners.* Thousand Oaks, CA: Corwin.

Routman, R. (1996). *Literacy at the crossroads: Crucial talk about reading, writing, and other teaching dilemmas.* Portsmouth, NH: Heinemann.

Short, D., & Fitzsimmons, S. (2007). *Double the work: Challenges and solutions to acquiring language and academic literacy for adolescent English language learners. A report to the Carnegie Corporation of New York.* Washington, DC: Alliance for Excellent Education.

Teachers of English to Speakers of Other Languages (TESOL). (n.d.). *The ESL standards for pre-K–12 students, Appendix A: Access brochure—The TESOL standards: Ensuring access to quality educational experiences for language minority students.* Retrieved February 26, 2003, from www.tesol.org/assoc/k12 standards/it/11.html

Teachers of English to Speakers of Other Languages (TESOL). (2010). *TESOL/NCATE standards for the recognition of initial TESOL programs in P-12 ESL teacher education.* Alexandria, VA: Author.

Thomas, W. P., & Collier, V. P. (1997). *School effectiveness for language minority students* (NCBE Resource Collection Series No. 9). Washington, DC: National Clearinghouse for Bilingual Education. Retrieved October 7, 2002, from www.ncela.gwu.edu/ncbepubs/resource/effectiveness

Thomas, W. P., & Collier, V. P. (2002). *A national study of school effectiveness for language minority students' long-term academic achievement.* Santa Cruz, CA: Center for Research on Education, Diversity & Excellence.

Thomas, W. P., & Collier, V. P. (2012). Dual language education for a transformed world. Albuquerque, NM: Dual Language Education of New Mexico Fuente Press.

Tomlinson, C. A., & Edison, C. C. (2003). *Differentiation in practice, K-5: A resource guide for differentiating curriculum.* Topeka, KS: Topeka Bindery.

Tutwiler, S. W. (2005). *Teachers as collaborative partners: Working with diverse families and communities.* Mahwah, NJ: Erlbaum.

Valli, L., & Buese, D. (2007). The changing roles of teachers in an era of high-stakes accountability. *American Educational Research Journal, 44*(3), 519–558.

van Lier, L., & Walqui, A. (2012). *Language and the Common Core standards.* Paper presented at the 2012 Understanding Language Conference, Stanford, CA. Retrieved March 11, 2014, from http://ell.stanford.edu/papers/language

Vavrus, M. (2002). *Transforming the multicultural education of teachers: Theory, research, and practice.* New York: Teachers College Press.

Walqui, A., & Heritage, M. (2012). *Instruction for diverse groups of English language learners.* Paper presented at the 2012 Understanding Language Conference, Stanford, CA. Retrieved March 11, 2014, from http://ell.stanford.edu/papers/policy

World-Class Instructional Design and Assessment (WIDA) Consortium. (2007). *The WIDA English language proficiency standards, pre-kindergarten through grade 12.* Madison, WI: Author. Available online at www.wida.us/standards/elp.aspx

World-Class Instructional Design and Assessment (WIDA) Consortium. (2012). *2012 amplification of the English language development standards, kindergarten-grade 12.* Madison, WI: Author. Available online at http://wida.us/standards/eld.aspx

Chapter 6

Akmajian, A., Demers, R. A., Farmer, A. K., & Harnish, R. M. (2010). *Linguistics: An introduction to language and communication* (6th ed.). Cambridge, MA: MIT Press.

Al-Hashash, S. (2007). Bridging the gap between ESL and EFL: Using computer assisted language learning as a medium. *Indian Journal of Applied Linguistics, 33*(1), 5–38.

Anderson, N. J. (2002). *The role of metacognition in second language teaching and learning.* Washington, DC: ERIC Clearinghouse on Languages and Linguistics. (ERIC Digest No. EDO-FL-01-10.)

Anthony, E. M. (1963). Approach, method, and technique. *English Language Teaching, 17,* 63–67.

Anthony, E. M., & Norris, W. E. (1969). *Method in language teaching.* ERIC focus report on teaching of foreign languages No. 8. New York: Modern Language Association of America. (ERIC Document Reproduction Service No. ED031984.)

APA Work Group of the Board of Educational Affairs. (1997). *Learner-centered psychological principles: A framework for school reform and redesign.* Washington, DC: American Psychological Association.

Awh, E., & Jonides, J. (1998). Spatial selective attention and spatial working memory. In R. Parasuraman (Ed.), *The attentive brain* (pp. 353–380). Cambridge, MA: MIT Press.

Baddeley, A. D. (1986). *Working memory.* Oxford, UK: Clarendon Press.

Ballard & Tighe (2004). *IDEA Proficiency Test (IPT).* Brea, CA: Author.

Banich, M. T. (1997). *Neuropsychology: The neural bases of mental function.* Boston: Houghton-Mifflin.

Barani, G. (2011). The relationship between computer assisted language learning (CALL) and listening skill of Iranian EFL learners. *Procedia Social and Behavior Sciences, 15,* 4059–4063.

Bialystok, E. (1990). *Communication strategies.* Cambridge, MA: Basil Blackwell.

Blair, R. (Ed.). (1982). *Innovative approaches to language teaching.* Rowley, MA: Newbury House.

Brooks, N. (1960). *Language and language learning: Theory and practice.* New York: Harcourt, Brace & World.

Brown, H. D. (2007). *Teaching by principles: An interactive approach to language pedagogy* (3rd ed.). Upper Saddle River, NJ: Prentice-Hall.

Buhrow, B., & Garcia, A. U. (2006). *Lady bugs, tornadoes, swirling galaxies.* Portland, ME: Stenhouse.

Canale, M. (1983). From communicative competence to communicative language pedagogy. In J. Richards & R. Schmidt (Eds.), *Language and communication* (pp. 2–27). New York: Longman.

Chamot, A. U. (2009). *The CALLA handbook: Implementing the cognitive academic language learning approach.* Reading, MA: Addison-Wesley.

Chamot, A. U., & O'Malley, J. M. (1994). *The CALLA handbook: Implementing the cognitive academic language learning approach* (2nd ed.). Reading, MA: Addison-Wesley.

Chomsky, N. (1986). *Knowledge of language: Its nature, origin, and use.* New York: Praeger.

Collier, C. (1987). Comparison of acculturation and education characteristics of referred and non-referred culturally and linguistically different children. In L. M. Malare (Ed.), *NABE theory, research and application: Selected papers* (pp. 183–195). Buffalo: State University of New York.

Collier, V. P., & Thomas, W. P. (2009). *Educating English learners for a transformed world.* Albuquerque, NM: Dual Language Education of New Mexico Fuente Press.

Cummins, J. (2001). Instructional conditions for trilingual development. *International Journal of Bilingual Education and Bilingualism, 4*(1), 61–75.

Derry, S. J. (1999). A fish called peer learning: Searching for common themes. In M. O'Donnell & A. King (Eds.), *Cognitive perspectives on peer learning* (pp. 197–211). Mahwah, NJ: Erlbaum.

Diaz-Rico, L. T. (2014). *The crosscultural, language, and academic development handbook: A complete K–12 reference guide* (5th ed.). Boston: Allyn and Bacon.

Duncan, S. E., & DeAvila, E. A. (1990). *Language Assessment Scales.* Monterey, CA: CTB/McGraw-Hill.

Echevarria, J., Vogt, M., & Short, D. J. (2000). *Making content comprehensible for English language learners: The SIOP Model.* Boston: Allyn and Bacon.

Echevarria, J., Vogt, M., & Short, D. J. (2002, June). *SIOP training of trainers institute.* Symposium conducted at California State University, Long Beach, CA.

Echevarria, J., Vogt, M., & Short, D. J. (2013). *Making content comprehensible for English language learners: The SIOP Model* (4th ed.). Boston: Pearson.

Ehren, B. J., & Gildroy, P. G. (2000). Background knowledge (Module IV, Lesson 1). In B. J. Ehren (Ed.), *Building background knowledge for reading comprehension* [Online]. Lawrence: The University of Kansas, Center for Research on Learning. Retrieved March 7, 2003, from http://itc.gsu.edu/academymodules/a304/support/xpages/a304b0_20400.html

Elman, J., Bates, E. A., Johnson, M., Karmiloff-Smith, A., Parisi, D., & Plunkett, K. (1997). *Rethinking innateness.* Cambridge, MA: MIT Press.

Flavell, J. H. (1979). Metacognition and cognitive monitoring: A new area of cognitive-developmental inquiry. *American Psychologist, 34,* 906–911.

Gagné, E. D. (1985). *The cognitive psychology of school learning* (2nd ed.). Boston: Little, Brown.

Gattegno, C. (1982). Much language and little vocabulary. In R. Blair (Ed.), *Innovative approaches to language teaching* (pp. 273–292). Rowley, MA: Newbury House.

Genesee, F. (2000). *Brain research: Implications for second language learning.* Washington, DC: ERIC Clearinghouse on Languages and Linguistics. (ERIC Digest No. EDO-FL-00-12.) Retrieved March 6, 2003, from www.cal.org/ericcll/digest/0012brain.html

Gilhooly, K. J., Logie, R. H., Wetherick, N. E., & Wynn, V. (1993). Working memory and strategies in syllogistic-reasoning tasks. *Memory and Cognition, 21,* 115–124.

Hacking, I. (2000). *The social construction of what?* Cambridge, MA: Harvard University Press.

Herrera, S. (2007). *By teachers, with teachers, for teachers: ESL Methods course module.* Manhattan, KS: KCAT/TLC.

Herrera, S. G., Cabral, R. M., & Murry, K. G. (2013). *Assessment accommodations for classroom teachers of culturally and linguistically diverse (CLD) students* (2nd ed.). Boston: Pearson.

Howatt, A., & Widdowson, H. G. (1984). *A history of English language teaching* (2nd ed.). Oxford, UK: Oxford University Press.

Johnson, K. (1996). *Language teaching and skill learning.* Oxford, UK: Blackwell.

Just, M. A., & Carpenter, P. A. (1992). A capacity theory of comprehension: Individual differences in working memory. *Psychological Review, 99,* 122–149.

Kelly, L. (1976). *25 centuries of language teaching.* Rowley, MA: Newbury House.

Kim, K., & Hirsch, J. (1997). Distinct cortical areas associated with native and second languages. *Nature, 388,* 171.

Krashen, S. (1981). *Second language acquisition and second language learning.* London: Pergamon.

Krashen, S. (1982). *Principles and practice in second language acquisition.* Oxford, UK: Pergamon.

Krashen, S., & Terrell, T. (1983). *The natural approach: Language acquisition in the classroom.* Englewood Cliffs, NJ: Prentice Hall.

Krashen, S., & Terrell, T. (1983). *The natural approach: Language acquisition in the classroom.* Oxford, UK: Pergamon.

Kroll, L. R. (1998). Cognitive principles applied to the development of literacy. In N. M. Lambert & B. L. McCombs (Eds.), *How students learn: Reforming schools through learner-centered education* (pp. 113–142). Washington, DC: American Psychological Association.

Kukla, A. (2000). *Social constructivism and the philosophy of science.* London: Routledge.

Lantolf, J. P., & Appel, G. (Eds.). (1996). *Vygotskian approaches to second language research.* Norwood, NJ: Ablex.

Lado, R. (1970). Lado English series, Book one. New York: Simon and Schuster.

Livingston, J. A. (1997). *Metacognition: An overview.* Retrieved March 8, 2003, from www.gse.buffalo.edu/fas/shuell/cep564/Metacog.htm

Long, M. H., & Porter, P. A. (1985). Group work, interlanguage talk, and second language acquisition. *TESOL Quarterly, 19*(2), 207–228.

Lozanov, G. (1982). Suggestology and suggestopedia: Theory and practice. In R. Blair (Ed.), *Innovative approaches to language teaching* (pp. 146–159). Rowley, MA: Newbury House.

Mayer, R. E. (1998). Cognitive theory for education: What teachers need to know. In N. M. Lambert & B. L. McCombs (Eds.), *How students learn: Reforming schools through learner-centered education* (pp. 353–377). Washington, DC: American Psychological Association.

Mezirow, J. (1991). *Transformative dimensions of adult learning.* San Francisco: Jossey-Bass.

Moshman, D., Glover, J. A., & Bruning, R. H. (1987). *Developmental psychology.* Boston: Little, Brown.

Muñoz-Sandoval, A. F., Cummins, J., Alvaredo, C. G., Ruef, M., & Schrank, F. A. (2005). *Bilingual Verbal Ability Tests Normative Update (BVAT-NU).* Itasca, IL: Riverside.

Newell, A. (1990). *Unified theories of cognition.* Cambridge, MA: Harvard University Press.

Oller, J. W., Jr. (Ed.). (1993). *Methods that work: Ideas for literacy and language teachers* (2nd ed.). Boston: Heinle & Heinle.

O'Malley, J., & Chamot, A. (1990). *Learning strategies in second language acquisition.* New York: Cambridge University Press.

O'Malley, J., Chamot, A., Stewner-Manzanares, G., Russo, R., & Küpper, L. (1985a). Learning strategies used by beginning and intermediate ESL students. *Language Learning, 35,* 21–46.

O'Malley, J., Chamot, A., Stewner-Manzanares, G., Russo, R., & Küpper, L. (1985b). Learning strategy applications with students of English as a second language. *TESOL Quarterly, 19,* 285–296.

Ovando, C. J., Combs, M. C., & Collier, V. P. (2011). *Bilingual & ESL classrooms: Teaching in multicultural contexts* (5th ed.). Boston: McGraw-Hill.

Palmer, H. E., & Palmer, D. (1925). *English through actions.* London: Longman Green.

Paris, S. G., & Winograd, P. (1990). How metacognition can promote academic learning and instruction. In B. F. Jones & L. Idol (Eds.), *Dimensions of thinking and cognitive instruction* (pp. 15–51). Hillsdale, NJ: Erlbaum.

Richard-Amato, P. A. (1996). *Making it happen: Interaction in the second language classroom: From theory to practice* (2nd ed.). White Plains, NY: Longman.

Richards, J. C. (1983). Listening comprehension: Approach, design, procedure. *TESOL Quarterly, 17,* 219–240.

Richards, J. C., & Hull, J. C. (1987). *As I was saying: Conversation tactics.* Reading, MA: Addison-Wesley.

Richards, J. C., & Rogers, T. (1982). Method: Approach, design, procedure. *TESOL Quarterly, 16,* 153–168.

Richards, J. C., & Rogers, T. S. (2001). *Approaches and methods in language teaching: A description and analysis* (2nd ed.). Cambridge, UK: Cambridge University Press.

Searle, J. R. (1995). *The construction of social reality.* New York: Free Press.

Shuell, T. J. (1986). Cognitive conceptions of learning. *Review of Educational Research, 56,* 411–436.

Sousa, D. A. (2011). How the brain learns (4th ed.). Thousand Oaks, CA: Corwin.

Strain, J. (1986). Method: Design-procedure versus method-technique. *System, 14*(3), 287–294.

Strevens, P. (1980). *Teaching English as an international language.* Oxford, UK: Pergamon.

Terrell, T. (1991). The natural approach in bilingual education. In C. Leyba (Ed.), *Schooling and language minority students: A theoretical framework.* Los Angeles: Evaluation, Dissemination and Assessment Center.

Terrell, T., Egasse, J., & Voge, W. (1982). Techniques for a more natural approach to second language acquisition and learning. In R. Blair (Ed.), *Innovative approaches to language teaching* (pp. 174–175). Rowley, MA: Newbury House.

Thomas, W. P., & Collier, V. P. (2002). *A national study of school effectiveness for language minority students' long-term academic achievement.* Santa Cruz, CA: Center for Research on Education, Diversity & Excellence.

Thomas, W. P., & Collier, V. P. (2012). Dual language education for a transformed world. Albuquerque, NM: Dual Language Education of New Mexico Fuente Press.

Vygotsky, L. S. (1978). *Mind in society: The development of higher psychological processes.* Cambridge, MA: Harvard University Press.

Willingham, D. T. (2007). Cognition: The thinking animal (3rd ed.). Upper Saddle River, NJ: Pearson Prentice Hall.

Wittrock, M. C. (1998). Cognition and subject matter learning. In N. M. Lambert & B. L. McCombs (Eds.), *How students learn: Reforming schools through learner-centered education* (pp. 143–152). Washington, DC: American Psychological Association.

Wong Fillmore, L., & Valadez, C. (1986). Teaching bilingual learners. In M. C. Wittrock (Ed.), *Handbook of research on teaching* (3rd ed., pp. 648–685). New York: Longman.

Yule, G. (2010). *The study of language* (4th ed.). New York: Cambridge University Press.

Zimmerman, B. J. (1990). Self-regulated learning and academic achievement: An overview. *Educational Psychologist, 25*(1), 3–17.

Chapter 7

Aylesworth, J. (1998). *The gingerbread man.* New York: Scholastic.

Bauer, E. B., Cook, C., & Manyak, P. C. (2010). Supporting content learning for English learners. *The Reading Teacher, 63*(5), 430.

Brett, J. (1999). *Gingerbread baby.* New York: G.P. Putman's Sons.

Brinton, D. M., Snow, M. A., & Wesche, M. B. (1989). *Content-based second language instruction.* New York: Newbury House.

Caine, R. N., & Caine, G. (1991). *Making connections: Teaching and the human brain*. Alexandria, VA: Association of Supervision and Curriculum Development.

Center for Advanced Research on Language Acquisition (CARLA). (n.d.). *Why content-based instruction?* University of Minnesota. Retrieved September 16, 2002, from http://carla.acad.umn.edu/CBI.html

Chien, G. C. (2012). Integration of content-based instruction into elementary school EFL instruction. *Humanizing Language Teaching Magazine, 14*(4). Retrieved from http://www.hltmag.co.uk/aug12/sart05.htm

Collier, V. P. (1995). *Acquiring a second language for school*. Washington, DC: National Clearinghouse for Bilingual Education.

Collier, V. P., & Thomas, W. P. (2009). *Educating English learners for a transformed world*. Albuquerque, NM: Dual Language Education of New Mexico Fuente Press.

Crandall, J., Spanos, G., Christian, D., Simich-Dudgeon, C., & Willetts, K. (1987). Integrating language and content instruction for language minority students. *NCBE Teacher Resource Guide Series*. Retrieved March 5, 2003, from www.ncela.gwu.edu/ncbepubs/classics/trg/04integrating.htm

Cummins, J. (1981). The role of primary language development in promoting educational success for language minority students. In C. F. Leyba (Ed.), *Schooling and language minority students: A theoretical framework* (pp. 3–49). Los Angeles: Evaluation, Dissemination and Assessment Center, CSULA.

Cummins, J. (2000). "This place nurtures my spirit": Creating contexts of empowerment in linguistically diverse schools. In R. Phillipson (Ed.), *Rights to language: Equity, power and education* (pp. 249–258). Mawah, NJ: Erlbaum.

Cummins, J. (2001). *Negotiating identities: Education for empowerment in a diverse society* (2nd ed.). Los Angeles: California Association for Bilingual Education.

Curtain, H. (1995). *Helena Curtain: Integrating language and content instruction* [Video]. Manoa: University of Hawaii, NFLRC Second Language Teaching and Curriculum Center.

Curtain, H., & Haas, M. (1995). *Integrating foreign language and content instruction in grades K–8*. Washington, DC: ERIC Clearinghouse on Languages and Linguistics. (ERIC Digest No. EDO-FL-95–07.) Retrieved February 19, 2003, from www.cal.org/ericcll/digest/int-for-k8.html

Dulay, H., Burt, M., & Krashen, S. (1982). *Language two*. Oxford, UK: Oxford University Press.

Freeman, D. E., Freeman, Y. S., & Mercuri, S. (2002). *Closing the achievement gap*. Portsmouth, NH: Heinemann.

Freeman, Y. S., & Freeman, D. E. (1998). *ESL/EFL teaching: Principles for success*. Portsmouth, NH: Heinemann.

Genesee, F. (1994). *Integrating language and content: Lessons from immersion* (Educational Practice Report No. 11). Santa Cruz, CA, and Washington, DC: National Center for Research on Cultural Diversity and Second Language Learning. Retrieved March 5, 2003, from www.ncela.gwu.edu/miscpubs/ncrcdsll/epr11.htm

Genesee, F. (1998). Content-based language instruction (introduction to Chapter 5). In M. Met (Ed.), *Critical issues in early second language learning* (pp. 103–105). Reading, MA: Scott Foresman–Addison Wesley.

Grabe, W., & Stoller, F. L. (1997). Content-based instruction: Research foundations. In M. A. Snow & D. M. Brinton (Eds.), *The content-based classroom: Perspectives on integrating language and content* (pp. 5–21). White Plains, NY: Longman.

Haas, M. (2000). *Thematic, communicative language teaching in the K–8 classroom*. Washington, DC: ERIC Clearinghouse on Languages and Linguistics. (ERIC Digest No. EDO-FL-00-04.) Retrieved July 18, 2014, from http://www.usc.edu/dept/education/CMMR/FullText/Haas_CommunicativeLangTeachingK-8

Huang, K. (2011). Motivating lessons: A classroom-oriented investigation of the effects of content-based instruction on EFL young learners' motivated behaviours and classroom verbal interaction. ScienceDirect, System 39, 186–201.

Lessow-Hurley, J. (2012). *The foundations of dual language instruction* (6th ed.). White Plains, NY: Longman.

Met, M. (1991). Learning language through content: Learning content through language. *Foreign Language Annals, 24*(4), 281–295.

Mohan, B. A. (1986). *Language and content*. Reading, MA: Addison-Wesley.

Morris, R. W. (1975). Linguistic problems encountered by contemporary curriculum projects in mathematics. In E. Jacobsen (Ed.), *Interactions between linguistics and mathematical education: Final report of the symposium sponsored by*

UNESCO, CEDO and ICMI, Nairobi, Kenya, September 1–11, 1974 (UNESCO Report No. ED-74/CONF.808, pp. 25–52). Paris: United Nations Educational, Scientific and Cultural Organization.

Pesola, C. A. D. (1995). *Background, design, and evaluation of a conceptual framework for FLES curriculum.* Unpublished doctoral dissertation, University of Minnesota, Minneapolis.

Pessoa, S., Hendry, H., Donato, R., Tucker, G. R., & Lee, H. (2007). Content-based instruction in the foreign language classroom: A discourse perspective. *Foreign Language Annals, 40*(1), 102–121.

Saville-Troike, M. (1984). What really matters in second language learning for academic achievement? *TESOL Quarterly, 18*(2), 199–219.

Short, D. J. (1991). *Integrating language and content instruction: Strategies and techniques* (NCBE Program Information Guide Series No. 7). Washington, DC: National Clearinghouse for Bilingual Education. Retrieved March 13, 2003, from www.ncela.gwu.edu/ncbepubs/ pigs/pig7.htm

Short, D. J. (1993a). Assessing integrated language and content instruction. *TESOL Quarterly, 27*(4), 627–656.

Short, D. J. (1993b). *Integrating language and culture in middle school American history classes* (Educational Practice Report No. 8). National Center for Research on Cultural Diversity and Second Language Learning. Retrieved January 9, 2003, from www.ncela.gwu.edu/miscpubs/ncrcds11/epr8.htm

Thomas, W. P., & Collier, V. P. (1997). *School effectiveness for language minority students* (NCBE Resource Collection Series No. 9). Washington, DC: National Clearinghouse for Bilingual Education. Retrieved October 7, 2002, from www.ncela.gwu.edu/ncbepubs/resource/effectiveness

Thomas, W. P., & Collier, V. P. (1999). Accelerated schooling for English language learners. *Educational Leadership, 56*(7), 46–49.

Thomas, W. P., & Collier, V. P. (2012). Dual language education for a transformed world. Albuquerque, NM: Dual Language Education of New Mexico Fuente Press.

Tsai, Y., & Shang, H. (2010). The impact of content-based language instruction on EFL students' reading performance. *Asian Social Science, 6*(3), 77–85.

Vygotsky, L. S. (1978). *Mind in society: The development of higher psychological processes.* Cambridge, MA: Harvard University Press.

Wu, W. V., Marek, M., & Chen, N. (2013). Assessing cultural awareness and linguistic competency of EFL learners in a CMC-based active learning context. *ScienceDirect, System 41*, 515–528.

Chapter 8

Alexander, F. (1986). *California assessment program: Annual report.* Sacramento: California State Department of Education.

Anderson, L. W. (Ed.), Krathwohl, D. R. (Ed.), Airasian, P. W., Cruikshank, K. A., Mayer, R. E., Pintrich, P. R., et al. (2001). *A taxonomy for learning, teaching, and assessing: A revision of Bloom's Taxonomy of Educational Objectives* (Complete edition). New York: Longman.

Bloom, B. (1956). *Taxonomy of educational objectives: The classification of educational goals: Handbook I, cognitive domain.* New York: Longman.

Calderón, M., Tinajero, J., & Hertz-Lazarowitz, R. (1992). Adopting cooperative integrated reading and composition to meet the needs of bilingual students. *Journal of Educational Issues of Language Minority Students, 10*, 79–106.

California Commission on Teacher Credentialing. (2014). *English Learner Authorizations Advisory Panel.* Retrieved March 28, 2014, from www.ctc.ca.gov/educator-prep/ELA-panel.html

California State Department of Education. (2013). *Glossary of terms used in CBEDS and language census data reports.* Retrieved March 28, 2014, from www.cde.ca.gov/ds/sd/cb/glossary.asp

Cantoni-Harvey, G. (1987). *Content-area language instruction: Approaches and strategies.* Reading, MA: Addison-Wesley.

Chamot, A. U. (1985, December). Guidelines for implementing a content-based English language development program. *NCBE Forum, 8*(6), 2.

Clay, M. (1991). *Becoming literate: The construction of inner control.* Portsmouth, NH: Heinemann.

Cohen, E. G. (1986). *Designing groupwork: Strategies for the heterogeneous classroom.* New York: Teachers College Press.

Costa, A., & Liebmann, R. (1997). *Envisioning process as content: Towards a Renaissance community.* Thousand Oaks, CA: Corwin.

Cummins, J. (1991). Interdependence of first- and second-language proficiency in bilingual children. In E. Bialystok (Ed.), *Language processing in bilingual children* (pp. 70–89). Cambridge, UK: Cambridge University Press.

Cummins, J. (2001a). Instructional conditions for trilingual development. *International Journal of Bilingual Education and Bilingualism, 4*(1), 61–75.

Cummins, J. (2001b). *Language, power, and pedagogy: Bilingual children in the crossfire.* Philadelphia: Multilingual Matters.

DelliCarpini, M. (2009). Enhancing cooperative learning in TESOL teacher education. *ELT Journal, 63*(1), 42–50.

Diaz-Rico, L. T. (2014). *The cross-cultural, language, and academic development handbook: A complete K–12 reference guide* (5th ed.). Boston: Pearson.

Echevarria, J., & Graves, A. (2010). *Sheltered content instruction: Teaching English-language learners with diverse abilities* (4th ed.). Boston: Pearson.

Echevarria, J., Vogt, M., & Short, D. J. (2000). *Making content comprehensible for English language learners: The SIOP Model.* Boston: Allyn and Bacon.

Echevarria, J., Vogt, M., & Short, D. J. (2002, June). *SIOP training of trainers institute.* Symposium conducted at California State University, Long Beach, CA.

Echevarria, J., Vogt, M., & Short, D. J. (2013). *Making content comprehensible for English language learners: The SIOP Model* (4th ed.). Boston: Allyn and Bacon.

Elly, W. (1991). Acquiring literacy in a second language: The effect of book-based programs. *Language Learning, 41,* 375–411.

Enright, D., & McCloskey, M. (1988). *Integrating English: Developing English language and literacy in the multilingual classroom.* Reading, MA: Addison-Wesley.

Escamilla, K. (1994). The sociolinguistic environment of a bilingual school: A case study introduction. *Bilingual Research Journal, 18,* 21–48.

Escamilla, K. (1999). The false dichotomy between ESL and transitional bilingual education programs: Issues that challenge all of us. *Educational Considerations, 26*(2), 1–6.

Fountas, I., & Pinnell, G. (1996). *Guided reading: Good first teaching for all children.* Portsmouth, NH: Heinemann.

García, G. (1991). Factors influencing the English reading test performance of Spanish-speaking Hispanic children. *Reading Research Quarterly, 26*(4), 371–392.

García, G. E. (1998). Mexican-American bilingual students' metacognitive reading strategies: What's transferred, unique, problematic? *National Reading Conference Yearbook, 47,* 253–263.

Genesee, F. (1999). *Program alternatives for linguistically diverse students.* Washington, DC, and Santa Cruz, CA: Center for Research on Education, Diversity & Excellence.

Gillies, R. M., & Ashman, A. F. (2013). *Co-operative learning: The social and intellectual outcomes of learning in groups.* New York: Taylor & Francis.

Graves, M. F., August, D., & Mancilla-Martinez, J. (2012). *Teaching vocabulary to English language learners.* New York: Teachers College Press.

Gray, W. S., & Leary, B. E. (1935). *What makes a book readable?* Chicago: University of Chicago Press.

Hancin-Bhatt, B., & Nagy, W. (1994). Lexical transfer and second language morphological development. *Applied Psycholinguistics, 15,* 289–310.

Herrera, S. (2001). *Classroom strategies for the English language learner: A practical guide for accelerating language and literacy development.* Manhattan, KS: The MASTER Teacher.

Hertz-Lazarowitz, R., & Calderón, M. (1993). *Children's writing about learning in the Bilingual Cooperative Integrated Reading and Composition (BCIRC) project.* Baltimore, MD: Johns Hopkins University, Center for Research on Effective Schooling for Disadvantaged Students.

Jimenez, R. (1997). The strategic reading abilities and potential of five low-literacy Latina/o readers in middle school. *Reading Research Quarterly, 32,* 224–243.

Jimenez, R., García, G. E., & Pearson, P. (1996). The reading strategies of bilingual Latina/o students who are successful English readers: Opportunities and obstacles. *Reading Research Quarterly, 31,* 90–112.

Kagan, S. (1986). Cooperative learning and sociocultural factors in schooling. In *Beyond language: Social and cultural factors in schooling language minority students* (pp. 231–298). Los Angeles: Evaluation, Dissemination and Assessment Center, California State University.

Kole, N. (2003). *Native-language supported reading instruction: A VALID framework.* Unpublished doctoral dissertation, Kansas State University, Manhattan.

Krashen, S. (1982). *Principles and practice in second language acquisition.* Oxford, UK: Pergamon.

Krashen, S. (1985). *The input hypothesis: Issues and implications.* London: Longman.

Krashen, S. (1991). Bilingual education and second language acquisition theory. In C. F. Leyba (Ed.), *Schooling and language minority students: A theoretical framework* (pp. 51–79). Los Angeles, CA: Evaluation, Dissemination and Assessment Center, CSULA.

McGroarty, M. (1989). The benefits of cooperative learning arrangements in second language instruction. *NABE Journal, 13*(2), 127–143.

Mohan, B. A. (1986). *Language and content.* Reading, MA: Addison-Wesley.

Nagy, W., Herman, P., & Anderson, R. (1985). Learning words from context. *Reading Research Quarterly, 23,* 414–440.

Perez, D. (2002). *Comprender: Comprehension: Orchestrating meaning and purpose for reading English among newly developing English language readers.* Unpublished doctoral dissertation, Kansas State University, Manhattan.

Polak, J., & Krashen, S. (1988). Do we need to teach spelling? The relationship between spelling and vocabulary reading among community college ESL students. *TESOL Quarterly, 22,* 141–146.

Richard-Amato, P. A. (1996). *Making it happen: Interaction in the second language classroom: From theory to practice* (2nd ed.). White Plains, NY: Longman.

Rohac, R. (2000, May). S.D.A.I.E.—Specially Designed Academic Instruction in English. *ELT Newsletter.* Retrieved February 20, 2003, from www.eltnewsletter.com/back/May2000/art112000.shtml

Russell, S. (2002). *Specially designed academic instruction in English (SDAIE).* California State University, Dominguez Hills School of Education. Retrieved November 5, 2002, from www.pda.calstate.edu/arco/SDAIE.pdf

Saunders, W., O'Brien, G., Lennon, D., & McLean, J. (1999). *Successful transition into mainstream English: Effective strategies for studying literature.* Center for Research on Education, Diversity & Excellence. Retrieved December 9, 2002, from www.cal.org/crede/PUBS/edpractice/EPR2.pdf

Sheppard, K. (1995). *Content-ESL across the USA* (Volume I, Technical Report). Washington, DC: National Clearinghouse for Bilingual Education.

Slavin, R. (1983). When does cooperative learning increase student achievement? *Psychological Bulletin, 94*(3), 429–445.

Slavin, R. E. (1995). *Cooperative learning: Theory, research, and practice* (2nd ed.). Boston: Allyn and Bacon.

Stahl, S., & Fairbanks, M. (1986). The effects of vocabulary instruction: A model-based meta-analysis. *Review of Educational Research, 56,* 72–110.

Stanovich, K. E. (1986). Matthew effects in reading: Some consequences of individual differences in the acquisition of literacy. *Reading Research Quarterly, 21,* 360–406.

Stenner, A. J., & Burdick, X. (1997). *The objective measurement of reading comprehension.* Durham, NC: MetaMetrics.

Thomas, W. P., & Collier, V. P. (1997). *School effectiveness for language minority students* (NCBE Resource Collection Series No. 9). Washington, DC: National Clearinghouse for Bilingual Education. Retrieved October 7, 2002, from www.ncela.gwu.edu/ncbepubs/resource/effectiveness

Thomas, W. P., & Collier, V. P. (2002). *A national study of school effectiveness for language minority students' long-term academic achievement.* Santa Cruz, CA: Center for Research on Education, Diversity & Excellence.

Tinajero, J. V., Calderón, M. E., & Hertz-Lazarowitz, R. (1993). Cooperative learning strategies: Bilingual classroom applications. In J. V. Tinajero & A. F. Ada (Eds.), *The power of two languages: Literacy and biliteracy for Spanish-speaking students* (pp. 241–253). New York: Macmillan.

Vygotsky, L. S. (1962). *Thought and language.* Cambridge, MA: MIT Press.

Vygotsky, L. S. (1978). *Mind in society: The development of higher psychological processes.* Cambridge, MA: Harvard University Press.

Walqui, A. (2000). *Access and engagement: Program design and instructional approaches for immigrant students in secondary school.* Center for Applied Linguistics. McHenry, IL: Delta Systems.

Chapter 9

Adler, D. A. (1997). *Cam Jansen and the mystery of the dinosaur bones.* New York: Puffin Books.

Alvarez, J. (1991). *How the García girls lost their accents.* Chapel Hill, NC: Algonquin Books.

Amaral, O., Garrison, L., & Klentschy, M. (2002). Helping English learners increase achievement through inquiry-based science instruction. *Bilingual Research Journal, 26*(2), 213–239.

Anderson, N. J. (2002). *The role of metacognition in second language teaching and learning.* Washington, DC: ERIC Clearinghouse on Languages and Linguistics. (ERIC Digest No. EDO-FL-01-10)

Anstrom, K. (1998a). *Preparing secondary education teachers to work with English language learners: English language arts* (NCBE Resource Collection Series No. 10). Washington, DC: National Clearinghouse for Bilingual Education. Retrieved

January 13, 2003, from www.ncela.gwu.edu/ncbepubs/resource/ells/language.htm

Anstrom, K. (1998b). *Preparing secondary education teachers to work with English language learners: Science* (NCBE Resource Collection Series No. 11). Washington, DC: National Clearinghouse for Bilingual Education. Retrieved October 23, 2002, from www.ncela.gwu.edu/ncbepubs/resource/ells/science.htm

Anstrom, K. (1999a). *Preparing secondary education teachers to work with English language learners: Mathematics* (NCBE Resource Collection Series No. 14). Washington, DC: National Clearinghouse for Bilingual Education. Retrieved January 13, 2003, from www.ncela.gwu.edu/ncbepubs/resource/ells/math.htm

Anstrom, K. (1999b). *Preparing secondary education teachers to work with English language learners: Social studies* (NCBE Resource Collection Series No. 13). Washington, DC: National Clearinghouse for Bilingual Education. Retrieved January 13, 2003, from www.ncela.gwu.edu/ncbepubs/resource/ells/social.htm

Armbruster, B., Anderson, T., & Meyer, J. (1991). Improving content-area reading using instructional graphics. *Reading Research Quarterly, 26*(4), 393–416.

Au, K. (1980). Participation structures in a reading lesson with Hawaiian children. *Anthropology and Education Quarterly, 11,* 91–115.

Auer, P. (1999). *Code-switching in conversation: Language, interaction, and identity.* New York: Routledge.

Bialystok, E. (1981). The role of conscious strategies in second language proficiency. *Modern Language Journal, 65,* 24–35.

Bialystok, E. (2011). Reshaping the mind: The benefits of bilingualism. *Canadian Journal of Experimental Psychology, 65*(4), 229–235.

Bloom, B. (1956). *Taxonomy of educational objectives: The classification of educational goals: Handbook I, cognitive domain.* New York: Longman.

Carr, E., Dewitz, P., & Patberg, J. (1983). The effect of inference training on children's comprehension of expository text. *Journal of Reading Behavior, 15*(3), 1–18.

Chamot, A. U. (1995). Implementing the cognitive academic language learning approach: CALLA in Arlington, Virginia. *Bilingual Research Journal, 19*(3–4), 379–394.

Chamot, A. U. (2007). Accelerating academic achievement of English language learners: A synthesis of five evaluations of the CALLA Model. In J. Cummins & C. Davison (Eds.), *The international handbook of English language learning, part I* (pp. 317–331). Norwell, MA: Springer.

Chamot, A. U. (2009). *The CALLA handbook: Implementing the cognitive academic language learning approach* (2nd ed.). Reading, MA: Addison-Wesley.

Chamot, A. U., Dale, M., O'Malley, J. M., & Spanos, G. (1992). Learning and problem solving strategies of ESL students. *Bilingual Research Journal, 16*(3–4), 1–33.

Chamot, A., & El-Dinary, P. (1999). Children's learning strategies in language immersion classrooms. *Modern Language Journal, 83,* 319–338. Retrieved October 24, 2002, from WilsonSelectPlus database.

Chamot, A. U., & El-Dinary, P. B. (2000). *Children's learning strategies in language immersion classrooms.* Washington, DC: National Capital Language Resource Center. (ERIC Document Reproduction Service No. ED445518)

Chamot, A. U., & O'Malley, J. M. (1994). *The CALLA handbook: Implementing the cognitive academic language learning approach.* Reading, MA: Addison-Wesley.

Chamot, A. U., & O'Malley, J. (1996). The cognitive academic language learning approach: A model for linguistically diverse classrooms. *Elementary School Journal, 96,* 259–273.

Clay, M. (1991). *Becoming literate: The construction of inner control.* Portsmouth, NH: Heinemann.

Flavell, J., & Wellman, T. (1977). Metamemory. In R. Kail & J. Hagen (Eds.), *Perspectives on the development of memory and cognition* (pp. 3–33). Hillsdale, NJ: Erlbaum.

García, G. E. (1998). Mexican-American bilingual students' metacognitive reading strategies: What's transferred, unique, problematic? *National Reading Conference Yearbook, 47,* 253–263.

Gordon, C., & Rennie, B. (1987). Restructuring content schemata: An intervention study. *Reading Research and Instruction, 26*(3), 162–188.

Herrera, S. (2010). *Biography-driven culturally responsive teaching.* New York: Teachers College Press.

Herrera, S. G., Kavimandan, S. K., & Holmes, M. A. (2011). *Crossing the vocabulary bridge: Differentiated strategies for diverse secondary classrooms.* New York: Teachers College Press.

Herrera, S. G., Perez, D. R., Kavimandan, S. K., & Wessels, S. (2013). *Accelerating literacy for diverse learners: Strategies for the Common Core class-room K-8.* New York: Teachers College Press.

Jensen, E. (2008). *Brain-based learning: The new paradigm of teaching* (2nd ed.). Thousand Oaks, CA: Corwin.

Jimenez, R. (1997). The strategic reading abilities and potential of five low-literacy Latina/o readers in middle school. *Reading Research Quarterly, 32,* 224–243.

Jimenez, R., García, G. E., & Pearson, P. (1996). The reading strategies of bilingual Latina/o students who are successful English readers: Opportunities and obstacles. *Reading Research Quarterly, 31,* 90–112.

Kober, N. (n.d.). What special problems do LEP students face in science? What can teachers and schools do? [Electronic version]. *EDTALK: What we know about mathematics teaching and learning,* 32–33. Retrieved January 8, 2003, from http://enc.org/topics/equity/articles/document.shtm?input=ENC-111335-1335

Mayer, R. (1996). Learning strategies for making sense out of expository text: The SOI model for guiding three cognitive processes in knowledge construction. *Educational Psychology Review, 8,* 357–371.

Miller, G., Giovenco, A., & Rentiers, K. (1987). Fostering comprehension monitoring in below average readers through self-instruction training. *Journal of Reading Behavior, 19*(4), 379–394.

Moll, L. C. (Ed.). (1990). *Vygotsky and education: Instructional implications and applications of sociocultural psychology.* New York: Cambridge University Press.

Montes, F. (2002). Enhancing content areas through a cognitive academic language learning collaborative in South Texas. *Bilingual Research Journal, 26*(3), 697–716.

Muñiz-Swicegood, M. (1994). The effects of metacognitive reading strategy training on the reading performance and student reading analysis strategies of third grade bilingual students. *Bilingual Research Journal, 18,* 83–97.

Murry, K. (1996). Reflective-transformative professional development predicated upon critical reflection and enabled by a school–university partnership: A microethnographic case study. *Dissertation Abstracts International, 56*(12), 4643. [CD-ROM]. Abstract from: ProQuest File: Dissertations Abstracts Item: AAC 9610795.

Murry, K., & Herrera, S. (1999). CLASSIC impacts: A qualitative study of ESL/BLED programming. *Educational Considerations, 26*(2), 11–18.

Nist, S., & Simpson, M. (1990). The effect of PLAE upon students' test performance and metacognitive awareness. In J. Zutell & S. McCormick (Eds.), *Literacy, theory, and research: Analyses from multiple paradigms: Thirty-ninth yearbook of the National Reading Conference* (pp. 321–328). Chicago: National Reading Conference.

O'Malley, J., & Chamot, A. (1990). *Learning strategies in second language acquisition.* New York: Cambridge University Press.

O'Malley, J., Chamot, A., & Küpper, L. (1989). Listening comprehension strategies in second language acquisition. *Applied Linguistics, 10*(4), 418–437.

O'Malley, J., Chamot, A., Stewner-Manzanares, G., Russo, R., & Küpper, L. (1985a). Learning strategies used by beginning and intermediate ESL students. *Language Learning, 35,* 21–46.

O'Malley, J., Chamot, A., Stewner-Manzanares, G., Russo, R., & Küpper, L. (1985b). Learning strategy applications with students of English as a second language. *TESOL Quarterly, 19,* 285–296.

Paris, S. G., & Winograd, P. (1990). How metacognition can promote academic learning and instruction. In B. F. Jones & L. Idol (Eds.), *Dimensions of thinking and cognitive instruction* (pp. 15–51). Hillsdale, NJ: Erlbaum.

Payne, B., & Manning, B. (1992). Basal reader instruction: Effects of comprehension monitoring training on reading comprehension, strategy use and attitude. *Reading Research and Instruction, 32*(1), 29–38.

Piaget, J., & Inhelder, B. (1969). *The psychology of the child* (H. Weaver, Trans.). New York: Basic Books.

Pressley, M. (1995). More about the development of self-regulation: Complex, long-term, and thoroughly social. *Educational Psychologist, 4,* 1–32.

Rosenshine, B., Meister, C., & Chapman, S. (1996). Teaching students to generate questions: A review of the intervention studies. *Review of Educational Research, 66*(2), 181–221.

Short, D. J. (1993b). *Integrating language and culture in middle school American history classes* (Educational Practice Report No. 8). National Center for Research on Cultural Diversity and Second Language Learning. Retrieved January 9, 2003, from www.ncela.gwu.edu/miscpubs/ncrcds11/epr8.htm

Spires, H., Gallini, J., & Riggsbee, J. (1992). Effects of schema-based and text structure-based cues on expository prose comprehension in fourth graders. *Journal of Experimental Education, 60*(4), 307–320.

Stevens, R., Slavin, R., & Farnish, A. (1991). The effects of cooperative learning and direct instruction in reading comprehension strategies on main idea identification. *Journal of Educational Psychology, 83*(1), 8–16.

Vygotsky, L. S. (1978). *Mind in society: The development of higher psychological processes.* Cambridge, MA: Harvard University Press.

Wenden, A., & Rubin, J. (Eds.). (1987). *Learner strategies in language learning.* Englewood Cliffs, NJ: Prentice-Hall.

Chapter 10

Au, W., Bigelow, B., & Karp, S. (2007). *Rethinking our classrooms: Teaching for equity and justice,* Vol. 1. New York: Rethinking Schools Limited.

Brinton, D., Snow, M., & Wesche, M. (2003). *Content-based second language instruction: Michigan classics.* Ann Arbor: University of Michigan Press.

Brown, H. D. (2006). *Principles of language learning and teaching* (5th ed.). Boston: Pearson.

Brown, H. D. (2007). *Teaching by principles: An interactive approach to language pedagogy* (3rd ed.). Boston: Pearson.

Chamot, A. (2009). *The CALLA handbook: Implementing the cognitive academic language learning approach* (2nd ed.). Reading, MA: Addison-Wesley.

Chamot, A., & O'Malley, J. M. (1994). *The CALLA handbook: Implementing the cognitive academic language learning approach.* Boston: Longman.

Collier, C. (1987). Comparison of acculturation and education characteristics of referred and non-referred culturally and linguistically different children. In L. M. Malare (Ed.), *NABE theory, research and application: Selected papers* (pp. 183–195). Buffalo: State University of New York.

Cummins, J. (2000). "This place nurtures my spirit": Creating contexts of empowerment in linguistically diverse schools. In R. Phillipson (Ed.), *Rights to language: Equity, power and education* (pp. 249–258). Mawah, NJ: Erlbaum.

Cummins, J. (2001). *Language, power, and pedagogy: Bilingual children in the crossfire.* Philadelphia: Multilingual Matters.

Dalton, S. S. (1998). *Pedagogy matters: Standards for effective teaching practice* (Research Report No. 4). Santa Cruz: University of California, Center for Research on Education, Diversity & Excellence.

Danielson, C. (2007). *Enhancing professional practice: A framework for teaching* (2nd ed.). Alexandria, VA: Association for Supervision and Curriculum Development.

Danielson, C., & McGreal, T. L. (2000). *Teacher evaluation: To enhance professional practice.* Alexandria, VA: Association for Supervision and Curriculum Development.

Darling-Hammond, L., French, J., & García-Lopez, S. (2002). *Learning to teach for social justice.* New York: Teachers College Press.

De la Luz Reyes, M., & Halcón, J. (2001). *The best for our children: Critical perspectives on literacy for Latino students.* New York: Teachers College Press.

Diaz-Rico, L. T. (2014). *The crosscultural, language, and academic development handbook: A complete K–12 reference guide* (5th ed.). Boston: Allyn and Bacon.

Echevarria, J., Vogt, M., & Short, D. (2012). *Making content comprehensible for English language learners: The SIOP Model* (4th ed.). Boston: Allyn and Bacon.

Fullan, M. (2007). *The new meaning of educational change* (4th ed.). New York: Teachers College, Columbia University.

Ginott, H. (1993). *Teacher and child.* New York: Macmillan.

Herrera, S., & Murry, K. (2009). *Professional experience course module.* Manhattan, KS: CIMA.

Horwitz, E. (2012). *Becoming a language teacher: A practical guide to second language learning and teaching* (2nd ed.). Boston: Allyn and Bacon.

Jensen, E. (2008). *Brain-based learning: The new paradigm of teaching* (2nd ed.). Thousand Oaks, CA: Corwin.

Jimenez, R., García, G. E., & Pearson, P. (1996). The reading strategies of bilingual Latina/o students who are successful English readers: Opportunities and obstacles. *Reading Research Quarterly, 31,* 90–112.

Mezirow, J. (1985). A critical theory of self-directed learning. In S. Brookfield (Ed.), *Self-directed learning: From theory to practice* (pp. 17–30). New directions for continuing education No. 25. San Francisco: Jossey-Bass.

Mezirow, J. (1991). *Transformative dimensions of adult learning.* San Francisco: Jossey-Bass.

Miramontes, O., Nadeau, A., & Commins, N. (2011). *Restructuring schools for linguistic diversity: Linking decision making to effective programs* (2nd ed.). New York: Teachers College Press.

Mitchell, R., Willis, M., & Chicago Teachers' Union Quest Center. (1995). *Learning in overdrive.* Golden, CO: North American Press.

Murry, K. (1996). Reflective-transformative professional development predicated upon critical reflection and enabled by a school–university partnership: A microethnographic case study. *Dissertation Abstracts International, 56*(12), 4643. [CD-ROM]. Abstract from: ProQuest File: Dissertations Abstracts Item: AAC 9610795.

National Board for Professional Teaching Standards (NBPTS). (1998). *English as a new language standards.* Arlington, VA: Author.

Shanker, A. (1985). *Being a professional.* Presentation to the National Press Club, Washington, DC.

Sousa, D. A. (2011). *How the brain learns* (4th ed.). Thousand Oaks, CA: Corwin.

Teachers of English to Speakers of Other Languages (TESOL). (2006). *PreK–12 English language proficiency standards.* Alexandria, VA: Author.

Teachers of English to Speakers of Other Languages (TESOL). (2010). *Standards for the recognition of initial TESOL programs in P-12 ESL teacher education.* Retrieved from www.tesol.org

Tharp, R. G. (2008, January). *Effective teaching: How the standards come to be.* (Effective Teaching Document Series, No. 1). Retrieved December 9, 2009, from http://gse.berkeley.edu/research/crede/tharp_development.html

Tse, L. (2001). *Why don't they learn English? Separating fact from fallacy in the U.S. language debate.* New York: Teachers College Press.

Vavrus, M. (2002). *Transforming the multicultural education of teachers: Theory, research, and practice.* New York: Teachers College Press.

Vygotsky, L. S. (1962). *Thought and language.* Cambridge, MA: MIT Press.

Wiggins, G., & McTighe, J. (2005). *Understanding by design* (2nd ed.). Alexandria, VA: Association for Supervision and Curriculum Development.

Zinn, H. (2002). *You can't be neutral on a moving train: A personal history of our times.* Uckfield, East Sussex, UK: Beacon Press.

Appendix A

Teachers of English to Speakers of Other Languages (TESOL). (2010). *Standards for the recognition of initial TESOL programs in P-12 ESL teacher education.* Retrieved from www.tesol.org

Appendix B

Ada, A. F. (1999). *Cómo nació el arco iris* [How the rainbow was born]. Miami: Santillana USA.

Kole, N. (2003). *Native-language supported reading instruction: A VALID framework.* Unpublished doctoral dissertation, Kansas State University, Manhattan.